April 16–20, 2012
Beijing, China

**Association for
Computing Machinery**

Advancing Computing as a Science & Profession

IPSN'12

Proceedings of the 11th International Conference on

Information Processing in Sensor Networks

Sponsored by:
ACM SIGBED and IEEE SPS (Signal Processing Society)

Supported by:
Microsoft Research and University of Macau

Association for
Computing Machinery

Advancing Computing as a Science & Profession

The Association for Computing Machinery
2 Penn Plaza, Suite 701
New York, New York 10121-0701

Notice to Past Authors of ACM-Published Articles
ACM intends to create a complete electronic archive of all articles and/or other material previously published by ACM. If you have written a work that has been previously published by ACM in any journal or conference proceedings prior to 1978, or any SIG Newsletter at any time, and you do NOT want this work to appear in the ACM Digital Library, please inform permissions@acm.org, stating the title of the work, the author(s), and where and when published.

ISBN: 978-1-4503-1227-1

Additional copies may be ordered prepaid from:

ACM Order Department
PO Box 30777
New York, NY 10087-0777, USA

Phone: 1-800-342-6626 (USA and Canada)
+1-212-626-0500 (Global)
Fax: +1-212-944-1318
E-mail: acmhelp@acm.org
Hours of Operation: 8:30 am – 4:30 pm ET

ACM Order Number: 104125

Printed in the USA

Foreword

Welcome to IPSN 2012, the Eleventh ACM/IEEE Conference on Information Processing in Sensing Networks!

This year marks the first time IPSN is held in Asia, recognizing the region's growing interest and activities in the areas of sensor networks, Internet-of-Things (IoT), and Cyber-Physical Systems (CPS).

We hope that you will enjoy this diverse conference that is a leading venue for publications and idea exchange on sensor networks. IPSN is unique in its broad coverage of the field, ranging from foundations to system implementation and platforms. It is a meeting point of theory and practice, as embodied in its two tracks: Information Processing (IP) and Sensor Platforms, Tools and Design Methods (SPOTS).

In an effort to further unify the conference this year, we formed a joint technical program committee (TPC) and held a single TPC meeting. Authors could select the IP or the SPOTS track for their submissions and TPC members were able to provide their review preferences across all papers submitted to the conference. We believe that in this way, each paper received the most relevant and useful set of reviews.

The field of sensor networks has shown a continuing strength over the years as indicated by the number and the quality of submissions this year: 53 in the SPOTS track and 94 in the IP track, for a total of 147 submissions. These submissions underwent a two-stage review process during which each paper received at least three reviews and occasionally up to seven reviews. An online discussion followed the review process during which the set of papers that were discussed in the TPC meeting were selected. The set of accepted papers were decided during a face-to-face TPC meeting. 22 papers were selected for publication out of which 12 were in the IP track and 10 in the SPOTS track.

Assembling the program of IPSN 2012 has been a team effort. We would like to express our gratitude to the program committee members, external reviewers, and shepherds who worked very hard in reviewing papers and providing suggestions for their improvements. We would also like to thank the authors for providing exceptional contributions.

As in the past, the exciting demo and poster session provides an opportunity for attendees to examine and discuss the latest in sensing devices, systems and applications, following a special session with a rapid-fire series of short "pitch" talks from the authors of posters and demos. A new addition to the program this year is the PhD Forum where students working in the field present their dissertation ideas and get critical feedback from a panel of experts. The main conference is complemented by a number of workshops and tutorials in emerging or adjacent areas of sensor networks such as mobile, IoT, and smart objects.

The organizing committee has done an outstanding job in putting together the conference. We would like to thank the following for their effort: Thiemo Voigt for the workshops and tutorials, Xiaofan Jiang and Pei Zhang for the demos and posters, Li Cui and Luca Mottola for the PhD forum, Xenofon Koutsoukos for the finance and sponsorship, Jie Gao for the publications, Nic Lane for the web site, and Luca Mottola and Ying Zhang for the publicity.

We are grateful to the CPSWeek organizers, in particular, Wei Zhao, Chris Gill, Yunhao Liu, and Samson Cheong for all the support and logistical arrangements that made it possible to bring this program to the attendees.

We would like to thank ACM and IEEE for their sponsorship, and Microsoft Research Asia for providing support for student travels to the conference and the support from University of Macau.

Last but not least, we would like to thank the attendees for your patronage of the conference and for making it a successful meeting place for multiple communities and a catalyst for discussions and creative exchange.

We hope that you will find this program interesting and thought provoking and that the conference will provide you with a valuable opportunity to share ideas with other researchers and practitioners from institutions around the world.

General Chair
Feng Zhao
Microsoft Research Asia
China

Program Chair (IP)
Andreas Terzis
Johns Hopkins University
USA

Program Chair (SPOTS)
Kamin Whitehouse
University of Virginia
USA

Table of Contents

Demo Session

Session 4 — IP Track: Networking

Session 5 — SPOTS Track: Platforms

Session 6 — IP Track: Differentiating Knowledge from Noise

Session 7 — IP Track: Algorithms

Session 8 — SPOTS Track: Extreme Communications

IPSN 2012 Conference Organization

General Chair:	Feng Zhao *(Microsoft Research Asia, China)*
Program Co-Chairs:	Andreas Terzis *(Johns Hopkins University, USA)* Kamin Whitehouse *(University of Virginia, USA)*
Publications Chair:	Jie Gao *(Stony Brook University, USA)*
Demo Chair:	Xiaofan Jiang *(Microsoft Research Asia, China)*
Poster Chair:	Pei Zhang *(Carnegie Mellon University, USA)*
Workshop/Tutorial Chair:	Thiemo Voigt *(Swedish Institute of Computer Science, Sweden)*
Publicity Co-Chairs:	Luca Mottola *(Swedish Institute of Computer Science, Sweden)* Ying Zhang *(Palo Alto Research Center, USA)*
PhD Forum Co-Chairs:	Li Cui *(Institute of Computing Technology, Chinese Academy of Sciences, China)* Luca Mottola *(Swedish Institute of Computer Science, Sweden)*
Finance and Sponsorship Chair:	Xenofon Koutsoukos *(Vanderbilt University, USA)*
Web Chair:	Nic Lane *(Microsoft Research Asia, China)*
Steering Committee Chair:	Ravi Sandhu *(George Mason Institute and NSD Security, USA)*
Steering Committee:	Feng Zhao, Chair *(Microsoft Research Asia, China)* Tarek Abdelzaher *(UIUC, USA)* Deborah Estrin *(UCLA, USA)* Leo Guibas *(Stanford University, USA)* P.R. Kumar *(Texas A&M University, USA)* Sri Kumar *(SRI International, USA)* José Moura *(CMU, USA)* John Stankovic *(University of Virginia, USA)* Janos Sztipanovits *(Vanderbilt, USA)*

Program Committee (IP): Tarek Abdelzaher *(University of Illinois at Urbana-Champaign, USA)*

Jie Gao *(Stony Brook University, USA)*

Omprakash Gnawali *(University of Houston, USA)*

Polly Huang *(National Taiwan University, Taiwan)*

Karl Henrik Johansson *(KTH Royal Institute of Technology, Sweden)*

Andreas Krause *(California Institute of Technology, USA/ ETH – Zurich, Switzerland)*

Koen Langendoen *(Delft University of Technology, Netherlands)*

Jianzhong Li *(Harbin Institute of Technology, China)*

Chieh-Jan Mike Liang *(Microsoft Research Asia, China)*

Yunhao Liu *(Tsinghua University, China)*

Chenyang Lu *(Washington University in St. Louis, USA)*

Thomas Moscibroda *(Microsoft Research Asia, China)*

Luca Mottola *(Swedish Institute of Computer Science, Sweden)*

Gian Pietro Picco *(University of Trento, Italy)*

Utz Roedig *(Lancaster University, UK)*

Kay Roemer *(University of Luebeck, Germany)*

Antonio Ruzzelli *(University College Dublin, Ireland)*

Subhash Suri *(University of California - Santa Barbara, USA)*

Andreas Terzis *(Johns Hopkins University, USA)*

Thiemo Voigt *(Swedish Institute of Computer Science, Sweden)*

Tim Wark *(Commonwealth Scientific and Industrial Research Organization, Australia)*

Program Committee (SPOTS): Li Cui *(Institute of Computing Technology, Chinese Academy of Sciences, China)*

Adam Dunkels *(Swedish Institute of Computer Science, Sweden)*

Xiaofan Jiang *(Microsoft Research Asia, China)*

Dimitrios Lymberopoulos *(Microsoft Research, USA)*

Rahul Mangharam *(University of Pennsylvania, USA)*

Miklos Maroti *(University of Szeged, Hungary)*

Anthony Rowe *(Carnegie Mellon University, USA)*

Andreas Savvides *(Yale University, USA)*

Thomas Schmid *(University of Utah, USA)*

Mani Srivastava *(University of California - Los Angeles, USA)*

Kamin Whitehouse *(University of Virginia, USA)*

Additional reviewers:

Madhur Behl
Willy Bernal
Niels Brouwers
Doug Carlson
Marcus Chang
Haiming Chen
Yin Chen
Tsung-Yun Cheng
Hao-hua Chu
Simon Duquennoy
Philipp Glatz
Jayant Gupchup
Venkat Iyer
Zhihao Jiang
JeongGil Ko
Seng-Yong Lau
Dong Li
Po-Yen Lin

Po-Hung Lin
Yi-Hsien Lin
Andeas Loukas
Meng-Lin Lu
Miroslav Pajic
Andrei Pruteanu
Dinesh Ramasamy
Rik Sarkar
Anthony Schoofs
Vijay Srinivasan
Yang-Chun Su
Igor Talz
Tsung-Te Ted Lai
Nicolas Tsiftes
Zijian Wang
Yu-Ting Wang
Matthias Woehrle
Chiang Yi-Hsuan

Sponsors:

Supporters:

In-situ Soil Moisture Sensing: Measurement Scheduling and Estimation using Compressive Sensing

Xiaopei Wu
School of Computer Science and Engineering
Univ. of Electronic Science and Technology of China
Department of Electrical Engineering and Computer Science, Univ. of Michigan
wuxiaopei84@gmail.com

Mingyan Liu[*]
Department of Electrical Engineering and Computer Science
University of Michigan, Ann Arbor
mingyan@eecs.umich.edu

ABSTRACT

We consider the problem of monitoring soil moisture evolution using a wireless network of in-situ underground sensors. To reduce cost and prolong lifetime, it is highly desirable to rely on fewer measurements and estimate with higher accuracy the original signal (soil moisture temporal evolution). In this paper we explore results from the compressive sensing (CS) literature and examine their applicability to this problem. Our main challenge lies in the selection of two matrices, the measurement matrix and a representation basis. The physical constraints of our problem make it highly non-trivial to select these matrices, so that the latter can sufficient sparsify the underlying signal while at the same time be sufficiently incoherent with the former, two common pre-conditions for CS techniques to work well. We construct a representation basis by exploiting unique features of soil moisture evolution. We show that this basis attains very good tradeoff between its ability to sparsify the signal and its incoherence with measurement matrices that are consistent with our physical constraints. Extensive numerical evaluation is performed on both real, high-resolution soil moisture data and simulated data, and through comparison with a closed-loop scheduling approach. Our results demonstrate that our approach is extremely effective in reconstructing the soil moisture process with high accuracy and low sampling rate.

Categories and Subject Descriptors

I.6.m [**SIMULATION AND MODELING**]: Miscellaneous

---

[*]Corresponding Author

Keywords

Measurements Scheduling, Compressive Sensing, Soil Moisture Sensing

1. INTRODUCTION

This paper studies the efficient measurement scheduling and sensing of soil moisture. Soil moisture is a critical data type and measurement need in many scientific applications. For instance, it is used in all land surface models, water and energy balance models, weather prediction models, general circulation models, and ecosystem process simulation models [1]. It is also a key measurement need in precision farming and agricultural drought monitoring.

Soil moisture data has traditionally been collected using remote sensing techniques like radars and radiometers onboard satellites. Remote sensing covers large areas, but produces very coarse grained measurements, on the order of square kilometers. It was not until recently, with the advances in integrated wireless communication, sensing and processing technology, has in-situ sensing become a feasible option [2, 3]. In-situ moisture sensors can be densely deployed over a region of interest, at a resolution of one in every few square-feet, and thus can produce much finer grained measurements. To collect desired data at a single location, soil moisture sensor probes are typically placed vertically under the ground at different depths, up to 2 meters deep, with wires connecting them to a ground actuation and wireless transceiver module, see e.g., the SoilScape project [4][1]. This wireless node actuates the moisture probes to take measurements and transfers the collected data wirelessly to a remote central location or base station for processing; an example of such a network is described in more detail in [4].

To gather sufficient information on the temporal and spatial variations and characteristics of soil moisture, it is highly desirable to deploy moisture probes (and the associated wireless nodes) at sufficiently high density, and to take measurements at sufficiently high frequency. A competing objective is to have the network function in a unmanned fashion for as long as possible, since such networks are typically deployed in an open (sometimes remote) field without immediate access to power or human intervention. This requires us to

---

[1]Similar and alternative instrumentations have been used in other studies such as the Suelo project [3], which targets the monitoring of soil which includes but is not specifically designed for moisture data collection.

reduce the working times of the wireless nodes to conserve energy, even when renewable sources are used.

For a single wireless node, these competing interests imply that we need to make judicious decisions in measurement scheduling, i.e., when is the best time to take a measurement, so as to minimize the total amount of time the node needs to be active in actuating the moisture probes and in data transmission, while still satisfying the monitoring objective, i.e., achieving a desired level of accuracy in the estimated soil moisture evolution using the measurement data collected. In this paper we examine how compressive sensing and sparse sampling theory may be used to achieve these goals. Note that such measurement scheduling in general runs parallel to other energy efficient methods one may wish to adopt, including MAC and routing. It can also be jointly designed with a node's sleep schedules.

This problem belongs to the larger class of sensor scheduling problems. There are two general approaches. The first is a closed-loop approach that makes a measurement decision using past observations and decisions. This typically requires the knowledge of prior statistics of the underlying random process to be monitored, gained either through assumption or training, and is also sometimes referred to as the Bayesian approach; examples include [5, 6, 7, 8, 9, 10, 11, 12, 13, 14], with [10] focusing specifically on monitoring soil moisture.

The second is an open-loop approach whereby measurement decisions are made independent of past observations and decisions. Compressive sensing based measurement falls under this category. Recent advances in compressive sensing (CS) theory [15, 16, 17] allow one to represent compressible/sparse signals with significantly fewer samples than required by the Nyquist sampling theorem. It is therefore particularly attractive in a resource constrained setting like ours. This technique has been used in data compression [18], channel coding [19], analog signal sensing [20], routing [21] and data collection [22], with varying degrees of success. Applied to our context, the idea would be to sample the soil moisture in time in some fashion (typically randomly) and use compressive sensing techniques to reconstruct or recover the entire process.

There are two major challenges in applying CS techniques to our problem context. (1) It is not immediately clear how to find a good representation basis (Ψ) under which the soil moisture process may be sparsely represented. There is no systematic way of selecting such a matrix; it is usually done through trials and experience. (2) Under the CS framework the measurement scheduling is specified by a measurement matrix (Φ) (see e.g., the commonly used Gaussian matrix), which is often required to be dense, i.e., each measurement corresponds to a linear combination of multiple samples [18, 21, 22]. However, in our problem the physical nature of the monitoring device is such that each measurement corresponds to one and only one sample of the underlying physical process. This makes our measurement matrix extremely sparse, a feature that often does not bode well for its success, see e.g., [21]. An additional consequence of a sparse measurement matrix Φ is that it becomes hard to make it sufficiently incoherent from Ψ, a typical condition required for the success of CS techniques. We show in subsequent sections how these challenges can be addressed.

Our main results and contributions are summarized as follows. (1) We identify a representation basis Ψ, under which

the soil moisture process can be nearly sparsely represented. (2) This matrix is shown to work extremely well with a number of measurement matrices that are consistent with our application context, including those induced by random and uniform scheduling methods. (3) We further compare this approach to two non-CS based methods, a closed-loop approach and an interpolation based approach, to demonstrate its performance. In particular, the comparison with the closed-loop approach sheds light on the inherent limit of the latter. All our methods are tested using two sets of data: a real soil moisture data set collected from a botanical garden, and a simulated data set calibrated using data collected from a farm.

Even though our evaluation is based on two specific soil moisture data sets, the methodology presented in this paper is more generally applicable. Firstly, this method works well on soil moisture data from other soil types beyond the two data sets used in the study. This is because our method exploits the dynamics driven by rainfall events, which is common across all soil types. Secondly, the combination of representation basis we proposed and the recovery algorithm used can potentially work well with other signal types that are relatively smooth in nature as we note later in Section 4.2. This however must be borne out by further experiments which is out of the scope of the current paper but may be pursued in future studies. Finally, we believe the general methodology followed in this paper, i.e., the selection of a sampling method, a representation basis and a recovery algorithm, as well as verifying the sparsity and incoherence, is applicable to a broad range of similar studies that may wish to employ compressive sensing techniques. While the specific selections of these elements may vary from application to application, and is typically done through experience and trial-and-error, this study nevertheless represents as systematic as possible a scientific method that may be used by other studies.

The remainder of this paper is organized as follows. In Section 2 we describe the problem as well as the data sets we use for our study. Section 3 gives brief background information on related CS literature. In Section 4 we discuss the design of the two matrices in order to apply CS technique to our measurement scheduling problem. Numerical results are presented in Section 5, with comparison to two non-CS (closed-loop and interpolation) approaches discussed in Section 6. Section 7 concludes the paper.

2. THE SCHEDULING PROBLEM AND SOIL MOISTURE DATA

We will focus on the monitoring of soil moisture evolution at a single location, as the discussion and methodology equally applies to monitoring multiple locations. As mentioned in the introduction, typically multiple soil moisture probes are placed vertically, up to 2 meters deep underground, at a single lateral location [4]. While these probes can be activated separately, from an energy management point of view it is far more efficient to activate them all at the same time (i.e., to have them follow the same measurement schedule). This is because the processor (on the ground wireless node) needs to be on (in wake mode) in order to activate any probe, and once it is on it takes very little extra energy to activate an additional probe. For this reason we will treat a single location as having a single measurement schedule.

We will also assume that the underlying moisture process is discrete in time. This is obviously not true, but a sufficiently good representation of reality if the time unit is small enough with respect to the time scale of change in the soil moisture, which as we shall see is not very fast. More importantly, it should be noted that since the measurement device operates in discrete time no matter how high the frequency is, the best "ground truth" data is also inevitably discrete in time as a result. Therefore to adopt a discrete time model allows us to precisely quantify the performance of our method using the best ground truth we have available.

Denote by $\mathbf{x} = \{x_t, t = 0, 1, 2, \cdots, N\}$ an actual realization of the soil moisture process. A *measurement policy* π is given by a sequence of sampling times: $T^\pi = \{t_1, t_2, \cdots, t_n\} \in \{1, 2, \cdots, N\}$. Assuming perfect measurements (no error or noise), this policy induces the following *sampled sequence* $\mathbf{x}^\pi = \{x_{t_1}, x_{t_2}, \cdots, x_{t_n}\}$. An *estimation policy* λ then takes this sampled sequence and produces estimates of the original sequence $\hat{\mathbf{x}}^\lambda = \{\hat{x}_t, t = 1, 2, \cdots, N\}$, where $\hat{x}_t = x_t$ if $t \in T^\pi$, and $\hat{x}_t = \hat{x}_t^\lambda(\mathbf{x}^\pi)$ otherwise, for some estimation function $\hat{x}_t^\lambda()$.

The objective is to select the best measurement and estimation policies so as to minimize the estimation error subject to a requirement on the average sampling rate being no more than a certain desired level:

$$\min_{\pi, \lambda} \quad \text{Err}\left(\mathbf{x}, \hat{\mathbf{x}}^\lambda(\mathbf{x}^\pi)\right)$$

$$\text{s.t.} \quad n/N \leq \alpha \,,$$

where Err() is certain error measure, e.g., the mean-squared error, and α is the requirement on sampling or measurement rate.

We next discuss the moisture process $\mathbf{x}$ we use in our study. As mentioned, we will use two data sets. The first one, also referred to as the *garden data*, was collected at the Matthaei Botanical Garden at the University of Michigan, Ann Arbor ((latitude, longitude) approximately (42.300437, -83.663442)), over a 2-month period between August and October 2009. Three moisture probes were buried at depths 25mm, 67mm and 123mm, from the surface, respectively, and took measurements at the rate of once every 10 minutes. This is shown in Figure 1 in a progression of three figures, each with increasing resolution to show both a global as well as a zoomed-in view of the variation in the process.

A second data set, also referred to as the *farm data*, is a simulated one in an environment consistent with the climate and topography of Canton, Oklahoma ((latitude, longitude) approximately (36.00063,-98.63319)), over a 6-month period, between August 2010 and March 2011, at the sampling rate of one measurement per hour. This data is generated by a land surface hydrology simulation MOBIDIC [23], and has been calibrated using location- and time-specific variable exogenous forcings (e.g., rainfall, temperature, cloud cover, and solar radiation) and landscape parameters (e.g., vegetation cover, soil type, and topography), as well as actual data collected at this location. The farm data contains one depth per location; traces of 3 locations are shown in Figure 2, in a similar progression with increasing resolution.

The reason for using two different sets of data is to provide some diversity in the type of soil moisture processes we use for evaluation. We see that the soil moisture peaks shortly after a rainfall event, with the corresponding moisture level primarily determined by the precipitation. The moisture then slowly dissipates and evaporates, following a roughly monotonic non-increasing pattern. Over a period of dry weather, the soil moisture level stays relatively constant, resulting in a piece-wise smooth curve between two successive rainfall events. Except for the up-shoot at the onset of a rainfall, the moisture variation exhibits fairly high temporal correlation.

3. COMPRESSIVE SENSING

In this section we briefly summarize the part of the compressive sensing (CS) literature most relevant to the study presented in this paper.

Consider a discrete signal given by the vector $\mathbf{x}$ of size N. Results in compressive sensing [24] have shown that if $\mathbf{x}$ is sparse, i.e., if $||\mathbf{x}||_o \ll N$, then it is possible to reconstruct it from M random samples produced by a suitably chosen linear transform Φ of $\mathbf{x}$: $\mathbf{y}_{M \times 1} = \Phi \mathbf{x}$, where $M < N$. The $M \times N$ matrix Φ is usually referred to as the *measurement matrix*. In other words, we can recover signal $\mathbf{x}$ from $\mathbf{y}$ if $\mathbf{x}$ is sufficiently sparse, subject to some pre-conditions on Φ (more discussed below). In practice, $\mathbf{x}$ is usually non-sparse. However, it can often be sparsely represented in an alternative domain. Specifically, $\mathbf{x}$ may be further written as $\mathbf{x} = \Psi \mathbf{s}$, for some $N \times N$ matrix Ψ, where $\mathbf{s}$ is the $N \times 1$ coefficient vector in the Ψ-domain with $||s||_o = K$, where $K \ll N$. The matrix Ψ will also be referred to as the *representation basis*. The measurement vector can thus be written as

$$\mathbf{y} = \Phi \Psi \mathbf{s} \,, \tag{1}$$

and the associated signal recovery problem is to determine $\mathbf{s}$ for given measurement $\mathbf{y}$ and known matrices Φ and Ψ. The reconstruction of the original signal is given by $\mathbf{x} = \Psi \mathbf{s}$. Clearly, Equation (1) is an under-determined linear system, as the number of equations M is much smaller than the number of variables N (i.e., number of entries of $\mathbf{s}$). Finding the solution to this ill-conditioned system has been the subject of extensive study in recent years.

There are in general the following classes of approaches. The first class seeks $\mathbf{s}$ with the smallest l_o norm:

$$\min_{\mathbf{s} \in \mathbb{R}^N} \| \mathbf{s} \|_o \quad \text{s.t.} \quad \mathbf{y} = \Phi \Psi \mathbf{s}. \tag{2}$$

Directly solving the above is intractable [25, 26], but fast approach exists by using smoothed l_o norm, see e.g. the SL0 method proposed in [27]. A second class of approaches bypasses the original l_o minimization problem and instead seeks to solve the l_1 norm minimization problem to reduce complexity, also known as Basis Pursuit (BP), see e.g., [28, 29]:

$$\min_{\mathbf{s} \in \mathbb{R}^N} \| \mathbf{s} \|_1 \quad \text{s.t.} \quad \mathbf{y} = \Phi \Psi \mathbf{s}, \tag{3}$$

which can be easily solved using linear programming (LP) methods. The justification for solving (3) is that for large systems of equations, the solution to either minimization is the same [28]. Algorithms exist to solve the above problem in polynomial time, including interior-point methods; there are also faster algorithms aimed at large-scale systems, see e.g., [30, 31, 32, 27]. In addition to LP, the algorithms we will examine include Iterative Re-weighted Least Squares (IRWLS) [30], and Matching Pursuit (MP), see e.g. OMP

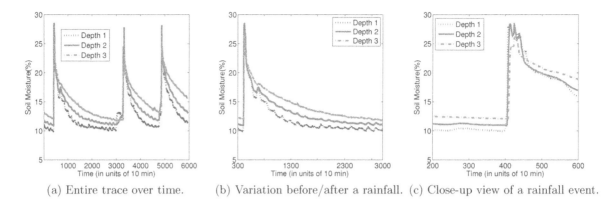

(a) Entire trace over time. (b) Variation before/after a rainfall. (c) Close-up view of a rainfall event.

Figure 1: Real soil moisture evolution collected from a botanical garden.

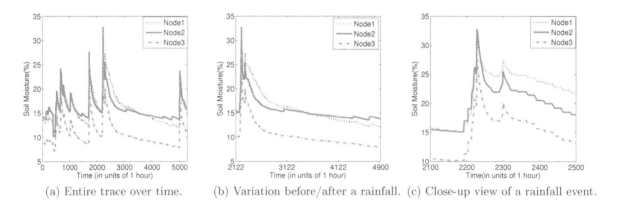

(a) Entire trace over time. (b) Variation before/after a rainfall. (c) Close-up view of a rainfall event.

Figure 2: Simulated soil moisture evolution on a farm in Oklahoma.

[31] and ROMP [32]. They are considered faster than LP but with worse estimation quality, especially if the signal is not sufficiently sparse.

Using any of the above mentioned recovery algorithm, a K-sparse signal can be reconstructed from M measurements with higher probability if M is such that:

$$M \geq C\mu^2(\Phi, \Psi)K \log N, \qquad (4)$$

where C is a positive constant, N is the dimension of the signal, and $\mu(\Phi, \Psi)$ is the coherence between the two matrices Φ and Ψ. Given a pair (Φ, Ψ) of orthobases of $\mathbb{R}^N$, $\mu(\Phi, \Psi)$ can be defined as

$$\mu(\Phi, \Psi) = \sqrt{N} \max_{1 \leq i,j \leq N} | < \phi_i, \psi_j > | \in [1, \sqrt{N}]$$

where ϕ_i and ψ_j are row and column vectors of Φ and Ψ, respectively. Thus given Φ and $\mathbf{x}$, Ψ must be chosen carefully: it is desirable to represent $\mathbf{x}$ in Ψ domain sparsely (small K); at the same time, it is also desirable to have $\mu(\Phi, \Psi)$ as small as possible. The selection of Ψ to meet both criteria is in general non-trivial, especially when Φ is constrained, as we discuss next.

4. DESIGN OF MEASUREMENT AND REPRESENTATION BASIS

In this section we discuss the selection of a measurement matrix Φ and a representation basis Ψ. The measurement matrix Φ directly corresponds to a measurement scheduling policy, whereas the representation basis Ψ is used in a reconstruction algorithm so we can first determine $\mathbf{s}$ and then recover the original signal $\mathbf{x}$.

4.1 Measurement Scheduling Matrix Φ

Recall that the original soil moisture signal in time is denoted by the $N \times 1$ vector $\mathbf{x}$. The $M \times N$ measurement matrix Φ specifies a measurement scheduling policy: it contains a "1" in the (m, n) position ($1 \leq m \leq M, 1 \leq n \leq N$) if the m-th measurement is taken at time n. The physical nature of the instrument is such that only a single measurement is taken at any scheduled time, i.e., upon actuation, the soil moisture probe takes one measurement of the soil moisture process at the time of actuation; the same point in the process cannot be measured more than once due to causality. This implies, regardless of the schedule, Φ contains one and only one "1" element in any row, and at most one "1" in any column, and "0" everywhere else.

As $M < N$, there will be exactly $N - M$ empty (all-0) columns, making the Φ matrix extremely sparse. This is very different from what is commonly studied in the literature, e.g., the Gaussian measurement matrix which is very dense with virtually no 0-entries. This poses a significant challenge, since in general the measurement matrix is required to be dense with at least one non-zero entry in each column [24, 15]. This same challenge also arose in a routing problem studied in [21], where the authors reported less than satisfying results due to the difficulty in finding the right Ψ matrix to match the highly constrained Φ matrix.

With the above constraint in mind, we will consider two types of schedules. The first has periodic sampling times, where measurements are taken at intervals of $\lfloor \frac{N}{M} \rfloor$ discrete units of time; this will also be referred to as the *uniform schedule* (US), and the corresponding matrix denoted as Φ_U. The second follows random sampling times generated using certain probability distribution with an average sampling rate of M/N; this will be referred to as the *random schedule* (RS), and the corresponding matrix denoted as Φ_R. Note that since N is not always an integer multiple of M, in such cases under the uniform schedule the first measurement point is randomly selected within a small range $[1, \lfloor \frac{N}{M} \rfloor]$, with subsequence measurements taken every $\lfloor \frac{N}{M} \rfloor$ time units till we exhaust N.

The reason we consider these two relatively simple schedules is due to their ease in implementation. We do compare their performance with more complex schedules (see below and the closed-loop scheduling in Section 6). As we shall see the estimation accuracy of our method turns out to be highly robust against the measurement schedule.

For comparison purposes, we will also consider the commonly studied Gaussian scheduling (GS) matrix Φ_G mentioned above. It should be emphasized that this matrix is *not* practical in our scenario: since each row in this matrix has typically many non-zero entries, it requires each measurement be a linear combination of multiple samples from the soil moisture process. More importantly, as there are virtually no empty columns, this matrix essentially requires the collection of nearly all samples of the original signal. This obviously defeats our basic objective of minimizing the amount of measurements taken.

4.2 Representation Basis Ψ

As mentioned, there are two main criteria in selecting a good representation basis Ψ: (1) its corresponding inverse has to sufficiently sparsify the signal $\mathbf{x}$, and (2) it has to be sufficiently incoherent with the measurement matrix Φ. This is highly non-trivial due to the sparse nature of our Φ matrix. In general the basis Ψ can be generated without assuming a priori knowledge of the signal, other than its size (which determines the size of the matrix). However, to generate a basis that meets the above two criteria without exploiting any feature of the signal can take a large amount of trial-and-error. Thus typically certain known features of the signal are taken into account in searching for a suitable basis to speed up this design process.

To this end, we observe that the soil moisture process (seen earlier in Figures. 1 and 2) is relatively smooth and slow changing, except at the onset of a rainfall. This suggests that the signal might be sparsely represented if we consider the difference between two adjacent sample values. This motivates the following *difference matrix* M_D:

$$M_D = \begin{bmatrix} -1 & 1 & 0 & \cdots & 0 & 0 \\ 0 & -1 & 1 & \cdots & 0 & 0 \\ 0 & 0 & -1 & \cdots & 0 & 0 \\ \vdots & \cdots & \cdots & \cdots & & \vdots \\ 0 & 0 & 0 & \cdots & -1 & 1 \\ 0 & 0 & 0 & \cdots & 0 & -\gamma \end{bmatrix} \quad (5)$$

Table 1: Comparison of approximate sparsity.

N	Sparsity			
	Garden data		Farm data	
	Ψ_D	Ψ_H	Ψ_D	Ψ_H
64	24.9	1.0	15.4	1.1
128	28.4	1.1	21.0	1.1
256	23.1	1.3	19.8	1.3
512	12.4	1.6	17.2	1.3
1024	7.5	1.8	10.0	1.3
2048	7.0	2.5	10.0	2.0

where the last element $\gamma, 0 < \gamma < 1$, ensures that M_D is invertible.

Ideally, one would like the projection of $\mathbf{x}$ on M_D, $\mathbf{s} = M_D \mathbf{x}$, to be a vector containing many zero/near-zero entries. If this is the case, then the original signal $\mathbf{x}$ can be sparsely represented in the M_D-domain as $\mathbf{x} = M_D^{-1} \mathbf{s}$. In the numerical experiments presented in the next section we will use M_D^{-1} as a choice for the representation basis and denote $\Psi_D = M_D^{-1}$ [^2].

The temporal correlation and piece-wise smooth feature of the soil moisture process also suggests that it may be more compactly represented through a Haar (wavelet) transformation M_H. We will thus use $\Psi_H = M_H^{-1}$ as a second choice for the representation basis Ψ in our experiment.

We now check the quality of these two matrix choices against the two criteria outlined earlier. It turns out that neither Ψ_D nor Ψ_H can produce a precisely K-sparse signal for $K \ll N$ (the amount of non-zero elements are above 50% in both cases). However, the resulting $\mathbf{s}$ are approximately K-sparse if we neglect small elements. Table 1 shows the approximate sparsity of Ψ_D and Ψ_H under different scale N, the signal size. Here the entire data set is segmented into signals of size N, and the transformation is applied over each signal. The overall sparsity is calculated as the sum of all entries of the normalized $\mathbf{s}$ with values of at least 0.1, and averaged over all signals. We see that as expected the Haar transform is much more effective than the difference matrix at sparsifying the signal.

We next examine the incoherence between these two representation bases and our measurement matrices. As the notion of coherence is not defined for non-orthogonal matrices, in the following we will use its dual-incoherence to indirectly measure the correlation between the proposed Φ_U (Φ_R) and Ψ_D (Ψ_H). The incoherence of two matrices are measured as follows [21]. Projecting each row of Φ onto the space spanned by the columns of Ψ we get:

$$\zeta_j = (\Psi^T \Psi)^{-1} \Psi^T \phi_j^T, \quad (6)$$

where ϕ_j is the jth row of Φ and ζ_j is the vector of coefficients corresponding to its projection on the space spanned by the columns of Ψ. A measure of the incoherence is then defined as

$$\mathbf{I}(\Phi, \Psi) = \min_{j=1,\cdots,N} \left[\sum_{i=1}^{N} 1\{\rho_i^j \neq 0\} \right] \in [1, N], \quad (7)$$

where ρ_i^j is the ith entry of vector ζ_j and $1\{A\}$ is the indicator function: it is 1 when A is true and 0 otherwise. The

[^2]: A similar operation aiming to sparsify a spatial 2D signal was used in [21], but as mentioned in the introduction it did not lead to very good performance.

Table 2: Comparison of incoherence.

N	$\mathbf{I}(\Phi_R, \cdot)$	
	Ψ_D	Ψ_H
64	63	11
128	125	34
256	255	66
512	512	130
1024	1024	258
2048	2048	514

larger this quantity, the more incoherent the two matrices. In Table 2, we show the incoherence obtained from Equation (7), for the random measurement matrix Φ_R with the two choices of Ψ at different scales. We see Ψ_D has much higher incoherence with our measurement matrix than Ψ_H does. Thus we have two representation bases, one (Ψ_H) better at sparsifying the signal while the other (Ψ_D) much more incoherent with the measurement matrix. In the next section we examine which choice leads to better reconstruction performance.

5. NUMERICAL EXPERIMENTS

In this section we evaluate the effectiveness of using compressive sensing techniques to solve the soil moisture measurement problem using the matrices introduced in the previous section, through extensive numerical experiments. In the remainder of this section, the garden data refers to the surface level (top level) soil moisture process shown in Figure 1, and the farm data refers to the soil moisture process of Node 3 as shown in Figure 2. Unless otherwise specified, we trim the real and simulated data to 4096 observations (or discrete times steps) in total, for the convenience of the experiment. To perform the experiments, we divide each data set into W windows (or signal) of N points each. Our sampling and recovery algorithms are applied to each window separately and similarly. The $N \times 1$ discrete signal within the w-th window ($1 \leq w \leq W$) is denoted as $\mathbf{x}_w$. Within each window, $M < N$ measurements are taken. The goal is to reconstruct $\mathbf{x}_w$ from the M direct observations.

Breaking the data set into windows of N allows us to balance the computational complexity/delay and estimation accuracy. If the measurement and reconstruction is done in a close-to-real time fashion, then it is desirable to perform these operations over a smaller N. On the other hand, larger N generally results in better estimates, though at the expense of increased computational complexity.

The quality of the reconstruction is measured by the following average error criterion:

$$AvgError = \frac{1}{NW} \sum_{w=1}^{W} ||\mathbf{x}_w - \hat{\mathbf{x}}_w||_1 , \qquad (8)$$

where W is the number of windows ($W = 4096/N$); $\mathbf{x}_w$ and $\hat{\mathbf{x}}_w$ are the true and estimated signal of window w; $||\mathbf{x}_w - \hat{\mathbf{x}}_w||_1$ is the sum of absolute errors in the estimate. This error is further averaged over 20 random trials when the measurement schedule is generated randomly. The scale-down rate (γ) used in the difference matrix M_D is 0.001. The sampling times under a random schedule (RS) is generated using a uniform probability distribution.

The overall quality of signal reconstruction is determined by three elements: the choice of measurement scheduling

matrix Φ, the choice of the representation basis Ψ, and the choice of a recovery algorithm (also referred to as a *solver* below). In the following, we will first examine what types of solvers work best with our choices of Φ (Φ_U and Φ_R) and and Ψ (Ψ_D and Ψ_H). We then compare the performance of different combinations of these matrices.

5.1 Effect of recovery algorithms

We first investigate what CS recovery algorithms or solvers work best with our selection of Φ and Ψ. A candidate list of these algorithms is discussed in Section 3, and they include SL0, IRWLS, OMP and BP (using LP). Of these, SL0 aims to minimize the l_o norm, while the others aim at minimizing the l_1 norm. The Matlab code of IRWLS, OMP, and LP is obtained from Sparse Lab [33] and SL0 from [34].

A set of experiments are run by increasing the window size N. For each window, the number of measurement M is set to 10% of N. As the Haar basis requires N to be a power of two, we set $N = 2^p, p = 6, 7, 8, 9, 10, 11$. For each value of N we evaluate the average estimation error in applying one of the above algorithms to the two data sets while using Φ_R as the measurement matrix, and Ψ_D and Ψ_H respectively as the representation basis. The results are shown in Figure 3. Our main observations are as follows.

Firstly, compared to Haar, the difference matrix Ψ_D shows significant advantage regardless of the data used and the solver used: the $AvgError$ of Ψ_H is at least 10 orders of magnitude higher than Ψ_D. As discussed earlier, Ψ_H sparsifies the data better than Ψ_D, while the later has much higher incoherence with the measurement matrix Φ_R. This observation thus suggests that in this case incoherence is more critical in determining the effectiveness of these solvers.

Secondly, we see that there are substantial performance gaps among different recovery algorithms. When Ψ_D is used, we see from Figure 3(a) and 3(c) that SL0 and LP perform the best (these two curves almost completely overlap) and they significantly outperform IRWLS and OMP. When Ψ_H is used, Figure 3(b) and 3(d) (the two curves of OMP and IRWLS almost completely overlap as well) again show that LP performs the best and significantly so. Furthermore, since the soil moisture content is measured between 10 and 35 (in %), an estimation procedure effectively fails if its $AvgError$ exceeds 10. In this sense except for LP, all other solvers do not work successfully with Ψ_H. These observations suggest that the estimation quality of LP and SL0 is much more robust to the level of sparsity than the faster solvers (OMP, IRWLS) when there is sufficient incoherence (in the case of Ψ_D. At the same time, LP is also robust to weak incoherence when there is sufficient sparsity (in the case of Ψ_H).

Based on these results, for the rest of our numerical evaluation we will limit our attention to SL0 and LP. As LP is more computationally costly than SL0, we will only use SL0 when Ψ_D is used, and LP when Ψ_H is used.

5.2 Effect of measurement matrices

We next study the impact of scheduling methods on the reconstruction quality. The three measurement matrices we examine are random (Φ_R), uniform (Φ_U) and Gaussian (Φ_G) introduced in Section 4.1. Note again that the Gaussian matrix is used as a point of comparison; it is not a practical scheduling policy for our problem.

Figure 4 illustrates the reconstruction quality under these

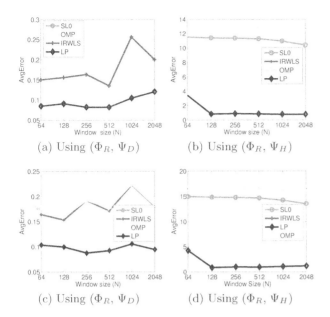

(a) Using (Φ_R, Ψ_D) (b) Using (Φ_R, Ψ_H)

(c) Using (Φ_R, Ψ_D) (d) Using (Φ_R, Ψ_H)

Figure 3: Comparison of reconstruction performance: (a)(b) Garden data; (c)(d) Farm data

Table 3: Comparison of scheduling methods.

$(\Psi$, solver$)$	Data	Range	Φ_R	Φ_U	Φ_G
$(\Psi_D$, SL0$)$	Garden	Total	0.0827	0.0623	0.1040
		Peak1	0.8738	0.7682	1.5367
		Peak2	0.2340	0.3795	0.3732
	Farm	Total	0.0909	0.0688	0.1280
		Peak1	0.4712	0.2552	0.3628
		Peak2	0.2156	0.3148	0.4973
$(\Psi_H$, LP$)$	Garden	Total	0.8553	0.7537	0.6473
		Peak1	12.9222	0.1744	7.1455
		Peak2	4.2919	4.1016	2.0057
	Farm	Total	0.9797	0.9537	1.3647
		Peak1	2.7720	0.5587	1.8389
		Peak2	4.0324	4.5034	13.3529

should perform the best, such results often rely on the signal being precisely sparse, but in our case the signal **x** is only approximately sparsified.

5.3 Comparison with interpolation

So far all solvers we tested are taken from the literature on compressive sensing. It is also natural to consider simple interpolation as an alternative to reconstructing the original signal using a small set of samples. In the following we provide an additional comparison point and examine the performance of using spline interpolation (referred to as SP in Figure 6).

In general, spline interpolation is preferred over polynomial interpolation because the interpolation error can be made small even when using low degree polynomials for the spline. Figure 6 illustrates the difference between CS and SP while using the uniform sampling matrix Φ_U. For CS we use Ψ_D as the representation basis and $SL0$ the solver. Clearly, CS performs better than SP, and especially so when the measurement cost (M) and estimation window (N) are low; low values of M and N are preferred as they lead to low computational complexity and estimate delay. However, note that the SP performance is far better than if we had used Ψ_H as the representation basis. This highlights the importance of selecting the right matrix, for otherwise one might do better by simply using standard interpolation.

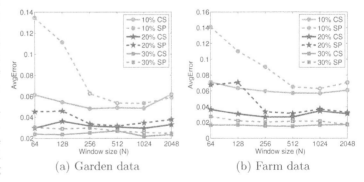

(a) Garden data   (b) Farm data

Figure 6: Performance comparison of CS and Spline recovery using Φ_U.

three scheduling methods, with respect to the true soil moisture values (denoted as TV in the figure). In this set of results, the representation basis and solver used are Ψ_D and SL0, respectively, the window size is $N = 128$, and the sampling rate is $M = 10\%N$. To observe the finer differences among these methods, Figure 4 also provides zoomed-in views around two peaks in the original data. Overall, all three scheduling methods perform very closely, and all of them reconstruct the original signal to very high accuracy.

To be more precise in quantitative comparison, Table 3 further shows the corresponding *AvgError* calculated over different time segments in the data. Here, a range of "Total" includes the entire period (i.e, from 1 to 4096), while the ranges "Peak1" and "Peak2" refer to the two peaks amplified in Figure 4 within each data set. Peak 1 is given by the time intervals [400, 500] and [600, 750] for the garden and farm data, respectively. Peak 2 is given by the time intervals [3300, 3400] and [2200, 2400] for the garden and farm data, respectively. As a comparison point, we also present the same set of results when the Haar basis matrix Ψ_H and the LP solver are used in same table. We repeat the same calculation at different sampling rates, from 10% to 30%, and present these results in Figure 5.

When the same $(\Psi$, solver$)$ pair is used, the main factor affecting the final reconstruction performance is the incoherence between Ψ and the measurement matrix Φ. The incoherence between (Φ_R, Φ_U, Φ_G) and Ψ_D is 125, 127, and 128, respectively, at $N = 128$. Thus it is not surprising that we see very close performance as evidenced in Figure 4. In particular, we see that the uniform (periodic) scheduling provides the best overall performance.

It is however interesting to see, from Table 3, that both uniform and random scheduling outperform Gaussian scheduling, especially under the pair $(\Psi_D$, SL0$)$. This is somewhat surprising, because the Gaussian measurement matrix has the highest incoherence with Ψ_D though by a small amount. This is possibly due to the fact that while in theory Ψ_G

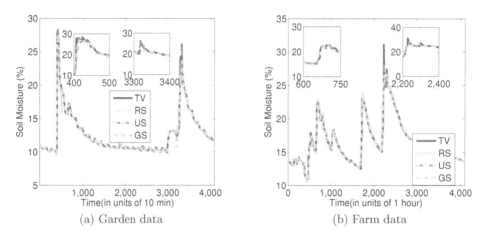

(a) Garden data   (b) Farm data

Figure 4: Performance comparison of different scheduling methods, using Ψ_D and SL0.

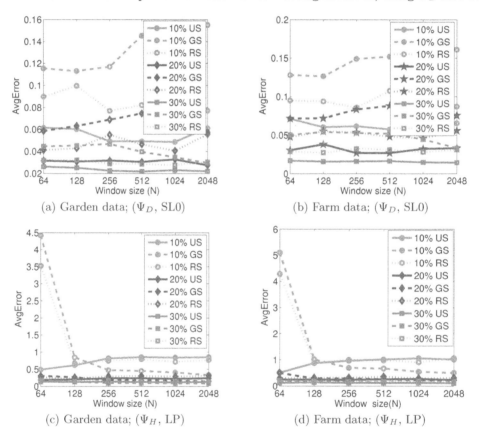

(a) Garden data; $(\Psi_D, \text{SL0})$ (b) Farm data; $(\Psi_D, \text{SL0})$

(c) Garden data; (Ψ_H, LP) (d) Farm data; (Ψ_H, LP)

Figure 5: Performance comparison of different sampling rate.

6. CLOSED-LOOP MEASUREMENT SCHEDULING

As pointed out in the introduction, the type of scheduling policies studied so far (uniform, random, Gaussian) are all open loop ones, i.e., the scheduling decision is independent of the past and current state of the soil moisture process, independent of past scheduling decisions, and does not exploit any physics in the soil moisture dynamics. If one possesses statistical information on the underlying random process, then a conceptually more desirable approach is a closed-loop one, where the physics of the process, as well as the past observations and decisions are taken into account when making the next measurement decision. Note however that unlike the compressive sensing based open-loop approach developed in the preceding section, this closed-loop approach in general requires training in order to learn the statistics from past data. In this section we describe such an approach which formulates a partially observable Markov decision problem (POMDP); more details on this method can be found in [10]. We then compare its performance with compressive sensing based open-loop approach.

We further examine whether there is performance gain in combining these two approaches.

Under a closed-loop framework, the soil moisture evolution (again at a single location) is modeled as a discrete-time stochastic process $\{X_t\}_{t=0,1,2,\cdots}$. A decision U_t, $t = 1, 2, \cdots$, is made at time t: $U_t = 1$ denotes taking a measurement at time t and $U_t = 0$ otherwise. If a measurement is taken, then a perfect observation $Y_t = X_t$ is made at time t, otherwise; a "blank" observation results.

An estimated process $\hat{X}_t$ of the soil moisture is formed, with each new observation, using all past observations (some of which are blanks) and all past scheduling decisions:

$$\hat{X}_t = h_t\big(Y_0, Y_1, \cdots, Y_t; U_1, U_2, \cdots, U_t\big). \quad (9)$$

Similarly, the scheduling decision for time $t + 1$ is based on all prior observations and scheduling decisions:

$$U_{t+1} = g_t\big(Y_0, Y_1, \cdots, Y_t; U_1, U_2, \cdots, U_t\big) \in \{0, 1\}. \quad (10)$$

The sequences $\mathbf{h} := (h_1, h_2, \cdots)$ and $\mathbf{g} := (g_1, g_2, \cdots)$ are the *estimation* and *scheduling* policies, respectively. The optimal policy pair $(\mathbf{g}^*, \mathbf{h}^*)$ may be derived by adopting a certain cost (or reward) objective; below is an example of an infinite horizon expected discounted cost:

$$(\mathbf{g}^*, \mathbf{h}^*) = \arg\min_{(\mathbf{g},\mathbf{h})} \mathbb{E}^{\mathbf{g},\mathbf{h}}\left\{ \sum_{t=1}^{\infty} \alpha^{t-1} \cdot \left[c(U_t) + \rho\big(X_t, \hat{X}_t\big) \right] \right\} \quad (11)$$

where $\alpha \in \{0, 1\}$ is the discount factor, $c(U_t)$ is the measurement cost, and $\rho\big(X_t, \hat{X}_t\big)$ is a penalty on estimation error, e.g., the mean squared error. The expectation is over known statistics of the process X_t.

Compared to an open-loop approach, the above closed-loop framework is conceptually precise (it has an explicit and well-defined optimization criterion), and it allows one to adjust the tradeoff between the measurement cost and the estimation error (by for instance introducing weights for the two cost terms). The main disadvantage of such an approach lies in (1) it requires a priori statistical knowledge of $\{X_t\}$, which may only be available through training and is often an approximation, and (2) it may be computationally intractable due to the large state space.

In the experiments below, we will assume $\{X_t\}$ to be first-order Markov, with which the above problem becomes a POMDP. This allows us to limit our attention to the class of Markov policies. We will further assume that X_t can only take on a finite number of values (i.e., soil moisture is quantized), to limit the state space. Specifically, the quantization levels used are given by $Q = [8, 9.5, 11, 12.5, 13.25, 14, 14.75, 15.5, 16, 17.5]$ (all in %).

With these assumptions, the soil moisture data is first quantized, and then the first T quantized values are used as a training set to generate a state transition matrix $\mathbb{P}$ that describes the evolution of the discrete-time discrete-valued process $\{X_t\}$. The POMDP problem defined in Eqn (11) is solved using Cassandra's pomdp-solve package [35]. The cost function $c(U_t)$ is set to 0.05, 0.10, 0.50 and 1.00 for $U_t = 1$ and 0 otherwise in different experiments. This is intended to control the sampling cost. The penalty $\rho()$ is set to be the sum of absolute error. The discount factor (α) is set to 0.99. An interested reader is referred to [10] for more on parameter options. The amount of data in the training set (T) is set to 1000 and 3000, respectively. These are referred to as T1

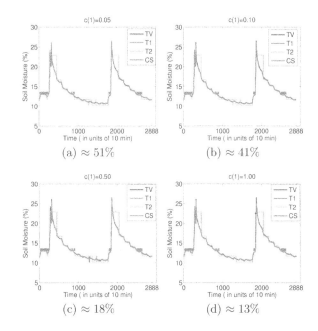

(a) $\approx 51\%$ (b) $\approx 41\%$

(c) $\approx 18\%$ (d) $\approx 13\%$

Figure 7: **Performance under different sampling rates.**

Table 4: Open-loop vs. closed-loop.

Method	T	Sampling rate (%)	AvgError
$(\Phi_U, \Psi_D, \text{SL0})$	0	51	0.018
$c(1) = 0.05$	1000	51	0.481
	3000	51	0.418
$(\Phi_U, \Psi_D, \text{SL0})$	0	41	0.018
$c(1) = 0.10$	1000	47	0.523
	3000	38	0.460
$(\Phi_U, \Psi_D, \text{SL0})$	0	19	0.040
$c(1) = 0.50$	1000	22	0.652
	3000	17	0.594
$(\Phi_U, \Psi_D, \text{SL0})$	0	13	0.049
$c(1) = 1.00$	1000	16	0.691
	3000	11	0.646

and T2 in Figure 7, respectively. The solution to (11), in the form of a policy pair is then applied to the segment of garden data [3001, 5888], with the resulting estimation error reported in Figure 7 and Table 4. For comparison, we also present results on the same data set (garden data, [3001, 5888]) by using uniform scheduling Φ_U, representation basis Ψ_D and solver SL0, with a window size of $N = 128$.

We see that compressive sensing based reconstruction performs significantly better than the closed-loop approach, under a range of cost levels and sampling rates (the rates cannot be perfectly controlled in the experiments, and are organized into groups of similar values). Furthermore, the open-loop approach improves much faster as the sampling rate increases. The reason for the performance difference, as well as the slow improvement of the closed-loop approach, lies in the fact that in order to be computationally tractable, we had to quantize the soil moisture in solving (11). As a result the output of the estimation/reconstruction is also quantized, which contributed to a significant part of the error; this phenomenon is also visible in Figure 7. We also examine the effect of combining closed-loop scheduling (the output scheduling policy $\mathbf{g}^*$ from (11)), and the reconstruc-

Table 5: Closed-loop scheduling, open-loop estimate

Method	T	Sampling rate (%)	$c(1)$	AvgError
$(\Phi_U, \Psi_D, \text{SL0})$	0	11	1.0	0.0763
$(\mathbf{g}^*, \Psi_D, \text{SL0})$	3000	11	1.0	0.0750
$(\Phi_U, \Psi_D, \text{SL0})$	0	17	0.5	0.0533
$(\mathbf{g}^*, \Psi_D, \text{SL0})$	3000	17	0.5	0.0607
$(\Phi_U, \Psi_D, \text{SL0})$	0	37	0.1	0.0241
$(\mathbf{g}^*, \Psi_D, \text{SL0})$	3000	37	0.1	0.0285
$(\Phi_U, \Psi_D, \text{SL0})$	0	51	0.05	0.0191
$(\mathbf{g}^*, \Psi_D, \text{SL0})$	3000	51	0.05	0.0195

tion based on Ψ_D and SL0, i.e., to replace the measurement given by Φ with $\mathbf{g}^*$. The comparison results over the same data segment are shown in Table 5.

We conclude that using closed-loop scheduling adds very little, if any at all, to the reconstruction accuracy. This shows that the compressive sensing method developed in the previous sections performs very well indeed, with relatively little room to improve. It also suggests that the combination of Ψ_D and SL0 is extremely robust to the type of measurement schedules used.

7. CONCLUSION AND FUTURE WORK

In this paper, we considered the problem of monitoring soil moisture evolution using a wireless network of in-situ sensors. We showed that at the cost of small estimation error we can significantly reduce energy consumption by taking a sparser set of measurements. We discussed how to apply compressive sensing techniques to achieve this. With very strict constraints imposed on the measurement matrix, we investigated what types of representation basis can successfully sparsify the soil moisture signal while being sufficiently incoherent with the measurement matrix. We showed that a difference matrix attains a good tradeoff for these objectives. The effectiveness of this combination is validated through extensive numerical experiments over real soil moisture data as well as simulated soil moisture data, and through comparison with the often-used Gaussian measurement matrix and a closed-loop approach. We showed that with these choices we can achieve very low estimation error at no more than 10% of the standard sampling rate.

To give a more concrete sense of how much this level of reduction in sampling rate can ultimately contribute to the overall energy saving in the operation of an entire monitoring system, we quote below some quantities based on a soil moisture monitoring system Ripple-2 developed at the University of Michigan. The design and development of this system have been partially documented in [4]. We estimate that the lifetime of a wireless node under our system implementation would be significantly increased, from around 6 months to nearly 5 years by sampling at an average of 100-min intervals compared to 10-min intervals. This is because the amount of transmitted data is reduced by 10-fold, and nodes can be in sleep mode for much longer periods of time. It however should be cautioned that such quantitative estimates are clearly heavily dependent on other elements of the system design. For instance, in our implementation the uniform sampling method is particularly appealing because the periodic scheduling is extremely easy to implement and amenable to simple sleep scheduling as well.

There are many future directions to pursue. One question is whether it is possible to obtain more precise performance guarantee or a quantitative relationship between estimation error and the sampling rate. A second is whether there are other interesting measurement techniques to explore. For instance, the estimation error under the current scheme is mainly due to the failure in capturing the peak in the signal after a rainfall. Thus the recovery performance can be improved if the sensors can be alerted to the onset of a rainfall. This is in fact feasible in practice through the use of a rain gauge or similar sensors. Such instrumentation can allow the wireless nodes to wake up upon rainfall and start taking measurements. Similarly, one can also set higher sampling rate immediately following the peak and let it gradually decrease while maintaining the same average rate. We are actively working to include these in the next deployment of our system. Finally, joint design of sampling at multiple locations may be beneficial. This is done naturally in a closed-loop approach. Under a compressive sensing framework it would be interesting to combine closed-loop scheduling for multiple locations with CS based recovery and examine its potential benefit.

Acknowledgment

This work was carried out at the University of Michigan as part of the following two projects: "Soil Moisture Smart Sensor Web Using Data Assimilation and Optimal Control" (NASA grant NNX06AD47G) and "Ground Network Design And Dynamic Operation For Near Real-Time Validation of Space-Borne Soil Moisture Measurements" (NASA grant NNX09AE91G), both through the Earth Science Technology Office, Advanced Information Systems Technologies program (AIST). The authors would like to thank other members of the project team: Profs. M. Moghaddam, D. Teneketzis, and D. Entekhabi, and Y. Goykhman, Q. Wang, Y. Liu, A. Silva, M. Burgin, A. Kakhbod, and A. Castillo. The authors would also like to thank the anonymous reviewers for comments and suggestions that greatly helped improve the quality of the paper.

8. REFERENCES

[1] (2006) Nasa strategic plan. [Online]. Available: http://www.nasa.gov/

[2] I. F. Akyildiz, W. Su, Y. Sankarasubramaniam, and E. Cayirci, "A survey on sensor networks," *IEEE Communications Magazine*, vol. 40, no. 8, pp. 102–114, August 2002.

[3] N. Ramanathan, T. Schoellhammer, and E. Kohler, "Suelo: Human-assisted sensing for exploratory soil monitoring studies," in *SenSys'09*, November 2009, pp. 197–210.

[4] M. Moghaddam, D. Entekhabi, Y. Goykhman, K. Li, M. Liu, A. Mahajan, A. Nayyar, D. Shuman, and D. Teneketzis, "A wireless soil moisture smart sensor web using physics-based optimal control: Concept and initial demonstrations," *IEEE Journal of Selected Topics in Applied Earch Observations and Remote Sensing (JSTARS)*, vol. 3, no. 4, pp. 522–535, December 2010.

[5] L. Meier, J. Peschon, and R. M. Dressler, "Optimal control of measurement subsystems," *IEEE Transactions on Automatic Control*, vol. 12, no. 5, pp. 528–536, January 2003.

[6] M. Athans, "On the determination of optimal costly measurement strategies for linear stochastic systems," *Automatica*, vol. 8, no. 1972, pp. 397–412, August 1972.

[7] M. Athans and C. Schweppe, "Optimal waveform design via control theoretic concepts," *Information and Control*, vol. 10, no. 1967, pp. 335–37, October 1967.

[8] H. Kushner, "On the optimum timing of observations for linear control systems with unknown initial state," *IEEE Transactions on Automatic Control*, vol. 9, no. 2, pp. 144–150, April 1964.

[9] M. S. Andersland and D. Teneketzis, "Measurement scheduling for recursive team estimation," *Journal of Optimization Theory and Applications*, vol. 89, no. 3, pp. 615–636, April 1996.

[10] D. Shuman, A. Nayyar, A. Mahajan, Y. Goykhman, K. Li, M. Liu, D. Teneketzis, M. Moghaddam, and D. Entekhab, "Measurement scheduling for soil moisture sensing: From physical models to optimal control," *Proceedings of the IEEE Special Issue on Sensor Networks and Applications*, vol. 98, no. 11, pp. 1918–1933, November 2010.

[11] J. Evans and V. Krishnamurthy, "Optimal sensor scheduling for hidden markov model state estimation," *International Journal of Control*, vol. 74, no. 18, pp. 1737–1742, December 2001.

[12] V. Krishnamurthy, "Algorithms for optimal scheduling and management of hidden markov model sensors," *IEEE Transactions on Signal Processing*, vol. 50, no. 6, pp. 1382–1397, June 2001.

[13] J. S. Baras and A. Bensoussan, "Optimal sensor scheduling in nonlinear filtering of diffusion processes," *SIAM Journal of Control and Optimization*, vol. 27, no. 4, pp. 786–813, July 1989.

[14] L. W. K. Y. Li, E. K. P. Chong, and K. N. Groom, "Approximate stochastic dynamic programming for sensor scheduling to track multiple targets," *Digital Signal Processing*, vol. 19, no. 6, pp. 978–989, December 2009.

[15] E. J. Candés, J. Romberg, and T. Tao, "Robust uncertainty principles: exact signal reconstruction from highly incomplete frequency information," *IEEE Transactions on Information Theory*, vol. 52, no. 4, pp. 489–509, February 2006.

[16] D. Donoho, "Compressed sensing," *IEEE Transactions on Information Theory*, vol. 52, no. 2, pp. 4036–4048, February 2006.

[17] E. Candés and T. Tao, "Near optimal signal recovery from random projections: Universal encoding strategies?" *IEEE Transactions on Information Theory*, vol. 52, no. 12, pp. 5406–5425, December 2006.

[18] D. Baron, M. Wakin, M. Duarte, S. Sarvotham, and R. Baraniuk, "Distributed compressed sensing," *IEEE Transactions on Information Theory*, vol. 52, no. 12, pp. 5406–5425, December 2006.

[19] E. Candés and T. Tao, "Decoding by linear programming," *IEEE Transactions Information Theory*, vol. 51, no. 12, pp. 4203–4215, Decemeber 2006.

[20] Z. Tian and G. Giannakis, "Compressed sensing for wideband cognitive radios," in *Proceedings of IEEE International Conference on Acoustics, Speech and Signal Processing (ICASSP)*, April 2007, pp. 1357–1360.

[21] G. Quer, R. Masiero, D. Munaretto, M. Rossi, J. Widmer, and M. Zorzi, "On the interplay between routing and signal representation for compressive sensing in wireless sensor networks," in *Information Theory and Applications Workshop (ITA 2009)*, February 2009, pp. 206–215.

[22] C. Luo, F. Wu, C. W. Chen, and J. Sun, "Compressive data gathering for large-scale wireless sensor networks," in *Proceedings of the 15th annual international conference on Mobile computing and networking*, September 2009, pp. 145–156.

[23] A. Castillo, "Parallelizing the Distributed Hydrologic Model MOBIDIC," Environmental Engineering,Massachusetts Institute of Technology, Tech. Rep., May 2010.

[24] E. J. Candés, "Compressive sampling," in *Proceedings of the International Congress of Mathematicians*, August 2006, pp. 265–272.

[25] D. L. Donoho, M. Elad, and V. Temlyakov, "Stable recovery of sparse overcomplete representations in the presence of noise," *IEEE Transactions Information Theory*, vol. 52, no. 1, pp. 6–18, January 2006.

[26] E. J. Candés and T. Tao, "Decoding by linear programming," *IEEE Transactions Information Theory*, vol. 51, no. 12, pp. 4203–4215, December 2005.

[27] H. Mohimani, M. Babaie-Zadeh, and C. Jutten, "A fast approach for overcomplete sparse decomposition based on smoothed l0 norm," *IEEE Transactions On Signal Processing*, vol. 57, no. 1, pp. 289–301, January 2009.

[28] D. L. Donoho, "For most large underdetermined systems of linear equations the minimal l1-norm solution is also the sparsest solution," Technology Report, 2004.

[29] (2005) l1-magic: Recovery of sparse signals via convex programming. [Online]. Available: www.acm.caltech.edu/l1magic/downloads/l1magic.pdf.

[30] I. F. Gorodnitsky and B. D. Rao, "Sparse signal reconstruction from limited data using focuss, a re-weighted minimum norm algorithm," *IEEE Transactions on Signal Processing*, vol. 45, no. 3, pp. 600–616, March 1997.

[31] J. A. Tropp and A. C. Gilbert, "Signal recovery from random measurements via orthogonal matching pursuit," *IEEE Transactions on Information Theory*, vol. 53, no. 12, pp. 4655–4666, December 2007.

[32] D. Needell and R. Vershynin, "Signal recovery from inaccurate and incomplete measurements via regularized orthogonal matching pursuit," *IEEE Journal of Selected Topics in Signal Processing*, vol. 4, no. 2, pp. 310–316, February 2010.

[33] (2007) Sparse lab. [Online]. Available: http://sparselab.stanford.edu/

[34] (2008) Sl0. [Online]. Available: http://ee.sharif.ir/ SLzero/

[35] G. E. Monahan, "A survey of partially observable markov decision processes: Theory, models, and algorithms," *Management Science*, vol. 28, no. 1, pp. 1–16, January 1982.

Efficient Cross-Correlation Via Sparse Representation In Sensor Networks

Prasant Misra[1,2], Wen Hu[2], Mingrui Yang[2], Sanjay Jha[1]
[1]School of Computer Science and Engineering, The University of New South Wales, Sydney, Australia.
[2]Autonomous Systems Laboratory, CSIRO ICT Centre, Brisbane, Australia.
{pkmisra, sanjay}@cse.unsw.edu.au {Wen.Hu, Mingrui.Yang}@csiro.au

ABSTRACT

Cross-correlation is a popular signal processing technique used in numerous localization and tracking systems for obtaining reliable range information. However, a practical efficient implementation has not yet been achieved on resource constrained wireless sensor network platforms. We propose *cross-correlation via sparse representation*: a new framework for ranging based on ℓ^1-minimization. The key idea is to compress the signal samples on the mote platform by efficient random projections and transfer them to a central device, where a convex optimization process estimates the range by exploiting its sparsity in our proposed *correlation domain*. Through sparse representation theory validation, extensive empirical studies and experiments on an *end-to-end* acoustic ranging system implemented on resource limited off-the-shelf sensor nodes, we show that the proposed framework, together with the proposed correlation domain achieved up to *two order of magnitude* better performance compared to naive approaches such as working on DCT domain and downsampling. Furthermore, compared to cross-correlation results, 30-40% measurements are sufficient to obtain precise range estimates with an additional bias of only 2-6 cm for high accuracy application requirements, while 5% measurements are adequate to achieve approximately 100 cm precision for lower accuracy applications.

Categories and Subject Descriptors

C.3 [**Special-Purpose and Application-Based Systems**]: Signal processing systems

General Terms

Algorithms, Design, Experimentation

Keywords

Cross-Correlation, Sparse Representation, ℓ^1-Minimization, Compressed Sensing, Ranging, Localization

1 Introduction

Location awareness is an important requirement for many applications in the field of binaural science, acoustic source detection, location-aware sensor networking, target motion analysis, mobile robot navigation, etc. However, location estimation still remains a fundamental problem, especially for indoor and outdoor environments where GPS does not work well. Localization is a two-step process that involves obtaining the separation distance of the unknown entity from at least three positioned entities (or known locations), which are then triangulated or multilaterated to obtain a location estimate. Therefore, obtaining accurate and reliable range measurement is a crucial prerequisite for localization.

There has been a significant progress in the related areas of acoustic and radio ranging technology, wherein high accuracy results have been achieved by measuring the time-of-arrival (TOA) of the ranging signal. However, the resources required for signal detection are a deciding factor for the cost, size and weight of the sensing platform, and this essentially strikes a trade-off between localization accuracy/coverage range and energy efficiency. Low-cost systems [1–4] utilize simple detection methods to estimate the arrival time of the pulse, but they tend to be less reliable due to their limited capability to counter environmental noise and multipath reflections [5].

A well established technique is to broaden the range of signal frequencies and distribute the energy between the various multiple paths, wherein the received signal is processed using a matched filter implemented by cross-correlating with a locally stored copy of the transmitted pulse. This mechanism not only resolves the different propagation paths, but also, increases the signal-to-noise ratio (SNR) of the direct path (which gives the range) without increasing the transmission power. It has been widely used in air [6–10] and underwater ranging systems, and is also a prime component of radars for tracking fast moving objects. While their performance (i.e., accuracy vs. range) is impressive, these systems require hardware components (such as DSP or other specialized processors and units) that are costly and power exhaustive. This is a major drawback for the new fields of pervasive computing and wireless sensor networks (WSN) that aim to achieve similar functional capability on low-cost and low-power hardware [11, 12]. Generally, resource constraints of WSNs (i.e., data sensing rates, link bandwidth, computational speed, battery life and memory capacity which typically offer less than 50 kB of code memory and 10 kB RAM) limit the implementation of complex algorithms. Therefore, the main focus of this paper is to design a lightweight detection and post-processing algorithm that is suitable for low-cost and low-power sensor platforms.

We introduce cross-correlation via sparse representation: a new computing framework for ranging based on ℓ^1- minimization [13]. The key idea is to compress the received signal samples and transmit the condensed data to a more resourceful device (or base-station) that can estimate the range by solving the ℓ^1-convex optimization problem efficiently. We make use of the theoretical results in sparse representation, which show that a signal can be recovered by ℓ^1- minimization [13], when its *representation is sufficiently sparse* with respect to an over-complete dictionary of base elements. Similar to Lasso in statistics [14, 15], the resulting optimization problem penalizes the ℓ^1-norm of the sparse coefficients in the linear combination, instead of penalizing the number of nonzero coefficients directly (e.g., ℓ^0-norm) [16]. We propose a new sparse representation dictionary termed as the *correlation domain*, which provides significantly better sparse depiction of the underlying signals compared to traditional domains such as discrete cosine transform (DCT).

This approach has several merits. It substitutes the computationally intensive cross-correlation function by a simpler dimensionality reduction operation that is implementable on a WSN node. It is independent of the physical signal (radio/acoustic) and medium (air/water). Most importantly, it requires processing a significantly smaller datasets (proportional to the logarithmic count of the acquired signal samples) to obtain accuracies comparable to cross-correlation. This useful feature provides a scope for greater savings in radio (where typically sample counts are of the order of 10^9) than acoustic ranging, and so, requires fewer compressed measurements to obtain the desired accuracy. However, the requirement for centralized processing is its prime drawback. We argue that it is a reasonable trade-off for achieving the performance of cross-correlation on mote-class devices that may be suitable for many applications. Besides having an impact on current localization systems, we envision that it would also create a new drive for WSN applications where the requirements for reliable location information using wearable (lightweight) sensors hold more importance than centralized computation. The proposed concept of sparse correlation can also be extended into additional applications such as speech recognition and power signature matching.

This paper makes the following primary contributions:
• We establish a new computing model for ranging: cross-correlation via sparse representation, and propose a new representation dictionary: correlation domain, which achieved up to *two order of magnitude* better performance compared to naive approaches such as working on DCT domain and downsampling.

• We empirically validate our hypothesis in real-world indoor and outdoor experiments. With respect to cross-correlation, we show that the proposed method obtains range estimates with a relative error of less than 2 cm by using 30% compressed measurements, and aproximately 100 cm relative error with 5% measurements only. We also address the problems of slower compression speed and incorrect peak identification (important for estimating range) by devising a divide-and-conquer method.

• We present the design and implementation of an *end-to-end* acoustic ranging system consisting of Tmote Invent (receiver) nodes and a custom built audio (transmitter) node. The results of the different system tests show a maximum ranging and 2D position error of less than 22 cm with a relative error of 5-6 cm over cross-correlation using 30-40% compressed measurements.

The rest of the paper is organized as follows: In the next section, we introduce the theory of sparse representation followed by empirical studies in Section 3. We describe the architecture of the acoustic ranging system in Section 4 and present evaluation results in Section 5. We outline the related work in Section 6, and finally, conclude in Section 7.

2 Cross-correlation via Sparse Representation

In this section, we discuss the theory of ℓ^1- minimization in contrast to compressive sensing. We discuss the general approach of broadband ranging, and then, establish the system model for cross-correlation via sparse representation.

2.1 Theoretical Basis of ℓ^1-Minimization

Given a dictionary $\Psi \in \mathbb{R}^{n \times d}$, any discrete time signal $\mathbf{x} \in \mathbb{R}^n$ can be linearly represented as:

$$\mathbf{x} = \Psi \mathbf{s} = \sum_{i=1}^{d} s_i \psi_i \qquad (1)$$

where $\mathbf{s} \in \mathbb{R}^d$ is a coefficient vector of $\mathbf{x}$ in the Ψ domain, and ψ_i is a column of Ψ. If $\mathbf{s}$ is sparse, then the solution to an underdetermined system of the form $\mathbf{x} = \Psi \mathbf{s}$ (where the unknowns d are greater than the observations n) can be solved using the following ℓ^0-minimization problem, where the ℓ^0-norm counts the number of nonzero entries in a vector.

$$(\ell^0): \quad \hat{\mathbf{s}}_0 = \arg\min \|\mathbf{s}\|_0 \text{ subject to: } \mathbf{x} = \Psi \mathbf{s} \qquad (2)$$

However, this problem of finding the sparsest solution (ℓ^0-minimization) of an underdetermined system of linear equations is NP-hard [17].

DEFINITION 2.1. *An $m \times n$ matrix A satisfies (k, δ_k)-RIP if*

$$(1 - \delta_k)\|x\|_2 \leq \|Ax\|_2 \leq (1 + \delta_k)\|x\|_2$$

for all k-sparse vector $x \in \mathbb{R}^n$.

Candes et al. in [18] and Donoho in [19] show that if $\mathbf{s}$ is sparse enough, and Ψ satisfies the Restricted Isometry Property (RIP), then the ℓ^0-minimization problem (Eq. 2) has the same sparse solution as the following ℓ^1- minimization problem that can be solved in polynomial time by linear programming methods.

$$(\ell^1): \quad \hat{\mathbf{s}}_1 = \arg\min \|\mathbf{s}\|_1 \text{ subject to: } \mathbf{x} = \Psi \mathbf{s} \qquad (3)$$

However, due to noise (white Gaussian) $\mathbf{v} \in \mathbb{R}^n$ present in real data, $\mathbf{x}$ may not be exactly expressed as a sparse superposition of $\mathbf{s}$, and so, Eq. 1 needs to be modified to:

$$\mathbf{x} = \Psi \mathbf{s} + \mathbf{v} \qquad (4)$$

where $\mathbf{v}$ is bounded by $\|\mathbf{v}\|_2 < \epsilon$. The sparse $\mathbf{s}$ can still be recovered accurately by solving the following *stable* ℓ^1- minimization problem via the second-order cone programming.

$$(\ell^1_s): \quad \hat{\mathbf{s}}_1 = \arg\min \|\mathbf{s}\|_1 \text{ subject to: } \|\Psi \mathbf{s} - \mathbf{x}\|_2 \leq \epsilon \qquad (5)$$

Notice that RIP is only a sufficient but not a necessary condition. Therefore, ℓ^1-minimization may still be able to recover the sparse **s** accurately, even if the sensing matrix Ψ does not satisfy RIP. In fact, the use of ℓ^1-minimization to find sparse solutions has a rich history. It was first proposed by Logan [20], and later developed in [13, 21–26]. Here, we use ℓ_1-minimization to solve the cross-correlation problem via sparse representation.

Dimensionality Reduction by Random Linear Projections: As shown in [27] by the Johnson-Lindenstrauss Lemma, the ℓ^2 distance is preserved in the projection domain with high probability by random projections. In other words, all the useful information is preserved in the projection domain. Hence, ℓ^1-minimization can still be used to recover the sparse **s** from the projected measurements with an overwhelming probability, even though, its dimension is significantly reduced. More precisely, this projection from high to low dimensional space can be obtained by using a random sensing matrix $\Phi \in \mathbb{R}^{m \times n}$ as:

$$\mathbf{y} = \Phi\mathbf{x} = \Phi(\Psi\mathbf{s}) \qquad (6)$$

where $m \ll n$ and $\mathbf{y} \in \mathbb{R}^m$ is the measurement vector. In practice, if **s** has $k \ll d$ nonzero coefficients, then the number of measurements is usually chosen to be [28]:

$$m \geq 2k\log(d/m) \qquad (7)$$

The sparsity level of **s** can be verified if the reordered entries of its coefficients decay like the power law; i.e., if **s** is arranged in the decreasing order of magnitude, then the dth largest entry obeys $|s|_{(d)} \leq Const \cdot d^{-r}$ for $r \geq 1$. For sparse **s**, the ℓ^2-norm error between its sparsest and approximated solution also obeys a power law, which means that a more accurate approximation can be obtained with the sparsest **s**. Ensembles of random matrices sampled independently and identically (i.i.d.) from Gaussian and ± 1 Bernoulli distributions permit computationally tractable recovery of **s** [13,18].

Application of Sparse Representation: This theory is applicable to a sensing problem if the underlying signal can be sparsely represented in some dictionary. A useful feature is that the dimensionality reduction operation is completely independent of its recovery via ℓ^1-minimization. A sparse signal can be captured efficiently using a limited number of random measurements that is proportional to its information level. The ℓ^1-minimization process does its best to correctly recover this information with the knowledge of only the dictionary that sparsely describes the signal of interest.

2.2 Problem Statement

The cross-correlation method of detection and range estimation finds the position of the first tallest peak, which signifies the time-delay of the received signal $x(t)$ with respect to its transmitted replica $p(t)$. Cross-correlation of $p(t)$ and $x(t)$ is a sequence $s(l)$ defined as:

$$s(l) = \sum_{t=-\infty}^{\infty} p(t+l)x(t) \quad l = 0, \pm 1, \pm 2, \dots \qquad (8)$$

where the index of l is the (time) shift (or lag) parameter. The position of the peaks in $s(l)$ provide a measure of the arrival time of the different multipaths, with the first tallest peak corresponding to the direct path.

Generally, $x(t)$ is acquired for a (finite) minimum time $t = t_a$ given by:

$$t_a \geq \left(\frac{d_c}{v_s} + t_p + t_r\right) \qquad (9)$$

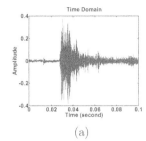 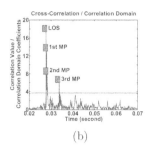

(a)   (b)

Figure 1: Equivalent representations of the same waveform in (a): time domain and (b): correlation domain.

where, d_c is the channel length between the transmitter and the receiver, v_s is the speed of the ranging signal in the medium, t_p is the time-period of the transmitted signal $p(t)$, and t_r is the approximate reverberation time within which the echoes from the transmitted pulse should have fallen below an acceptable level before the next pulse is emitted. The corresponding discrete-time signal of $p(t)$ and $x(t)$ obtained at a sampling rate (hertz/samples per second) of F_s is given as: $p[n_p] = p[t_p F_s]$ and $x[n_a] = x[t_a F_s]$ $0 \leq n_p, n_a \leq \infty$. Therfore, $p(t)$ and $x(t)$ can be represented as vectors $\mathbf{p} \in \mathbb{R}^{n_p}$ and $\mathbf{x} \in \mathbb{R}^{n_a}$. Fig. 1(a) shows a received signal trace recorded for a duration of 0.1 s sampled at 48 kHz, and its cross-correlation with the reference copy (a linear chirp of [1-20] kHz/0.01 s) is depicted in Fig. 1(b).

Although, obtaining the range using Eq. 8 and Eq. 9 is efficient, it requires the total knowledge (or samples n_a) of the received signal **x**. Therefore, our objective (problem statement) is: *Given significantly fewer (known) observations of **x**, obtain the cross-correlation result (unknown) **s** and estimate the range by finding the position of the first tallest peak.*

2.2.1 Design of Dictionary for Cross-Correlation

The problem can be casted into the framework of sparse approximation (for solving underdetermined systems) by designing a dictionary that sparsely describes the received signal. With respect to ranging, the dictionary should also (precisely) capture the characteristic of the ranging pulse

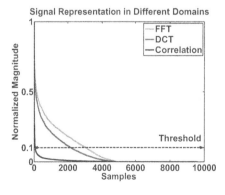

Figure 2: The signal has a more sparse representation in the correlation domain than the FFT and DCT domains by an order of more than 2.

that includes channel multipaths and low-noise signals, and facilitates the derivation of the range estimate from the reconstruction process *without* recovering the signal entirely.

We propose a new dictionary Ψ for ranging: *correlation domain* that satisfies all of the three requirements.

1. Sparsity: It can be explained by Fig. 1(b), where only 4 samples (corresponding to the direct and other multipaths) out of the total 4800 samples are of significance as their peak heights are the most dominant among others that take on zero or negligible values resulting in a sparse depiction of the received waveform.

2. Preservation of channel profile: The index of the nonzero elements (i.e., correlation peak positions) define the multipath characteristic, and their coefficient values (i.e., correlation peak heights) provide an estimate of their contribution.

3. Implicit TOA: The (correlation) coefficient vector obtained from the recovery algorithm provides the measure of time-delay without further processing.

In contrast, other popular dictionaries such as the FFT and DCT do not provide as good a sparse approximation as the proposed correlation domain, and also, do not satisfy the remaining two requirements (important for ranging). Fig. 2 compares their sparsity levels (for an indoor high multipath channel) by sorting the samples by their magnitudes. The fastest decay characteristic (or the smallest k) is observed in the correlation domain, and so, offers the most sparse representation; which means that the most accurate approximations (or range estimates) can be obtained in this dictionary using the smallest number of measurements m (Eq. 7).

2.2.2 Compression and Recovery

Compression: The dimensions of $\mathbf{x} \in \mathbb{R}^{n_a}$ are significantly reduced at the receiver by multiplying it with a random sensing matrix $\Phi \in \mathbb{R}^{m \times n_a}$ resulting in the measurement vector $\mathbf{y} \in \mathbb{R}^m$ ($m \ll n_a$) as: $\mathbf{y} = \Phi\mathbf{x}$. m is related to n_a by the compression factor α given as: $m = \alpha\, n_a$ where $\alpha \in [0,1]$. For example, $\alpha = 0.10$ means that the information in $\mathbf{x}$ has been compressed by 90%. Φ is a binary sensing matrix with its entries identically and independently (i.i.d.) sampled from a symmetric Bernoulli distribution.

$$\Phi = \frac{1}{\sqrt{m}}\bar{\Phi} \quad \text{where } \bar{\Phi}_i \text{ i.i.d. } \mathbf{Pr}(\bar{\Phi}_{i,j} = \pm 1) = 0.5 \quad (10)$$

Binary ensembles have a shorter memory representation than Gaussian ensembles, and also, alleviate operational complexity; hence, are economical for sensor platforms. The receiver transfers m samples of $\mathbf{y}$ to the base-station (BS) for post-processing.

Recovery: The BS requires a-priori knowledge of the seed that generates Φ and the dictionary Ψ. Ψ is the positive and negative time shifted Toeplitz matrix of the transmitted signal vector $\mathbf{p}$.

Case-1 ($t_a = t_p$) : Vectors $\mathbf{p}$ and $\mathbf{x}$ are of equal dimensions with n_a samples. The elements of $\Psi \in \mathbb{R}^{n_a \times (2n_a - 1)}$ are given as:

$$\Psi(:,i) = \begin{cases} [zeros(n_a - i)\ p(1:i)]^T & 1 \leq i \leq n_a \\ [p(i+1-n_a:n_a)\ zeros(i-n_a)]^T & \\ & (n_a+1) \leq i \leq (2n_a - 1) \end{cases}$$
$$(11)$$

where $\Psi(:,i)$ denotes the ith column, $[\ ]$ denotes a vector of length n_a, $zeros(i)$ denotes a zero vector of length i, $\cdot^T$ denotes the transpose of a vector (matrix), and $p(i:j)$ denotes a vector of elements with indices from i to j of the input sample set $\mathbf{p}$. For example, if $\mathbf{p} = [x_1\ x_2\ ...\ x_{n-1}\ x_n]$, then:

$$\Psi^T = \begin{bmatrix} 0 & 0 & . & . & 0 & x_1 \\ 0 & 0 & . & . & x_1 & x_2 \\ . & . & . & . & & \\ x_1 & x_2 & . & . & x_{n-1} & x_n \\ . & . & . & . & & \\ x_{n-1} & x_n & . & . & 0 & 0 \\ x_n & 0 & . & . & 0 & 0 \end{bmatrix}$$

Case-2 ($t_a > t_p$) : The size of $\mathbf{x}$ is greater than $\mathbf{p}$, and so, the system is balanced by right zero-padding ($n_a - n_p$) entries to $\mathbf{p}$.

Since, $\mathbf{x}$ can be represented sparsely as $\mathbf{s}$ in the dictionary Ψ and $\mathbf{x}$ (the received signal) is known, the desired sparse solution $\mathbf{s}$ can be recovered by solving the ℓ^1-minimization problem Eq. 5 (with dimensions of $\mathbf{x}$ reduced significantly via Eq. 6[1]) that results in the following *reduced* ℓ^1- minimization problem for a given tolerance ϵ:

$$(\ell^1_r): \quad \hat{\mathbf{s}}_1 = \arg\min \|\mathbf{s}\|_{\ell_1} \text{ s.t: } \|\Phi\Psi\mathbf{s} - \mathbf{y}\|_2 \leq \epsilon \quad (12)$$

(ℓ^1_r) is a stable version of ℓ^1-minimization. It is known as Lasso[2] in statistical literature, and regularizes highly undetermined linear systems when the desired solution is sparse. *The correlation domain coefficients $\hat{\mathbf{s}}_1$ are related to the various propagation (direct and reflected) paths, where the index of the first tallest correlation coefficient peak is the estimate of the pulse arrival time of the direct path, and thus, provides the range.*

3 Empirical Study and Analysis

In this section, we validate the proposed detection method on a proof-of-concept (POC) acoustic ranging system (Fig. 3), explore performance improvements, and present results of various characterization studies.

---

[1] Direct cross-correlation in the projection domain (using $\mathbf{y}$) did not produce desirable ranging results because $\mathbf{y}$ consists of random projections.

[2] The minimizer of $\|x - \Psi s\|_2^2 + \lambda\|x\|_1$ is defined as the Lasso solution; where λ can be referred as the inverse of the Lagrange multiplier associated with a constraint $\|x - \Psi s\|_2^2 \leq \epsilon$. For every λ, there is an ϵ such that the two problems have the same solution.

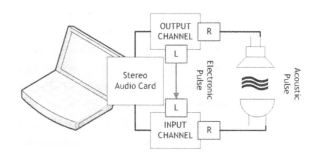

Figure 3: POC System Architecture.

3.1 POC System Architecture

Hardware: The transmitting front-end consisted of a ribbon (speaker) transducer driven by an external wideband (power) amplifier with a tunable gain controller [5x-20x]. The receiving front-end consisted of a custom designed receiver mounted with Knowles microphone (SPM0404UD5) attached to a preamplifier PCB.

Ranging: The synchronization and ranging signals were generated, captured and analyzed using a laptop. A linear chirp [01-20] kHz/0.01 s was generated and directed into two separate streams: left input channel of the ADC of the audio card and wideband amplifier. The electronic chirp (directed into the ADC) is equivalent to an RF pulse and marks the time of transmission of the acoustic chirp when its amplified version is emitted by the speaker. The acoustic chirp is detected by the receiver and directed into the right input channel of the ADC. The final acoustic signal is considered from the TOA of the electronic chirp. The processing stage replicates the working of the receiver and BS, wherein the acquired samples are first compressed and subsequently recovered to estimate the range.

In the experimental setup, the transmitter and the receiver were placed 1.5 m apart. The ranging process was performed with the receiver configured to record for 0.03 s - just long enough to capture the ranging signal along with its multipaths. The audio card was configured to sample at 48 kHz; hence, the transmitted signal $\mathbf{p}$ and the acquired trace $\mathbf{x}$ consisted of 480 and 1440 samples respectively. Using $\alpha = 0.30$, $\mathbf{x}$ was compressed to obtain the measurement vector $\mathbf{y}$ of 432 samples followed by its recovery to obtain $\mathbf{s}$ (Section 2.2.2). Its accuracy was validated against standard cross-correlation (Eq. 8).

Fig. 4(a) and Fig. 4(b) show the respective results, where we observe that both the methods obtain exactly the same estimate for the position of the first tallest peak at a negative lag of 220 samples along with the remaining multipath profile. The generation of the domain coefficients and cross-correlation peaks are in the negative lag part since we have reversed the order of operation, wherein the reference signal was operated with the acquired signal. Although, the remaining reconstructed peaks do not follow the same height-to-position relationship (observe the position of peak-2 & 3 in Fig. 4(a)) as is expected from the corresponding cross-correlation result (Fig. 4(b)), they are not important parameters for distance estimation. This study validates our proposed algorithm for detection and ranging.

3.2 Performance Analysis and Improvement

A vital point of difference between existing techniques and the proposed method is the functionality algorithm on the receiver: cross-correlation vs. compression. Conventional systems execute the cross-correlation algorithm on the receiver, whose implementation has a running time of $O(n^2)$ in the time domain (TD-CC) and $O(n \log n)$ in the frequency domain (FD-CC). However, due to no hardware divide or floating point support on WSN nodes, additional signal processing platforms have to be added. We propose an alternate data compression functionality that has a similar time complexity ($mn \approx O(n \log n)$), but a much smaller space complexity (competent with the mote constraints).

In order to compare their performance on the POC system, we performed the same ranging process but configured the receiver to record for 0.1 s (i.e., 4800 acquired samples). Table 1 shows the individual running time of the TD-CC, FD-CC and compression for different compression factors α. We note that FD-CC is $\approx$ 30 times faster than TD-CC as expected from their asymptotic results. However, the compression time (shown as 'Compression 1-Buf') varies for different α, and is slower than FD-CC for all except $\alpha = 0.05$.

We overcome this drawback by using the simple idea of buffer-by-buffer compression rather than one-step compression. This method divides the acquired signal vector $\mathbf{x}$ of length n_a across b buffers of equal sizes, compresses the information in each buffer, and finally, assembles the measurements in their correct order. The signal in each buffer $\tilde{\mathbf{x}}$ is of length $\tilde{n}$, where $\tilde{n} = n_a/b$. The random sensing matrix Φ for compressing the data in each buffer is of size $[\tilde{m} \times \tilde{n}]$, where $\tilde{m} = \alpha \, \tilde{n} = \alpha \, (n_a/b) = m/b$. The resultant measurement vector $\tilde{\mathbf{y}}$ (for each buffer) is of length of $\tilde{m}$. The number of iterations required to process each buffer is ($\tilde{m}\tilde{n}$). Therefore, the compression time for b buffers take ($b\tilde{m}\tilde{n}$) = (mn_a/b) iterations. This improvement can be identified in Table 1 (shown as 'Compression 10-Buf'), where we divide the 4800 samples across 10 buffers and record their individual compression time for different α. The results show a worst-case to best-case improvement of 6× to 60× over FD-CC. A greater improvement is expected on sensor platforms (shown in Section 5) than PC as they do not support floating point operation.

3.3 Signal Detection and Post-processing

The process of detection is not without errors as the reconstructed coefficients $\mathbf{s}$ may have been wrongly approximated due to measurement noise that contributes to higher coefficient values at incorrect locations. To overcome these inaccuracies, we use the same principle of buffer-by-buffer reconstruction at the BS as well, which not only provides an additional clue for correct detection, but also, serves as a guideline to choose the buffer count b.

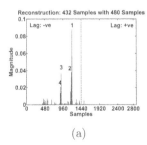
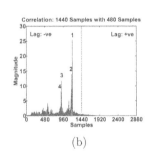

(a)   (b)

Figure 4: Correlation Domain Coefficients and standard Cross-Correlation obtain the same result for the position of the LOS peak.

Table 1: Performance Analysis: PC

α	TD-CC (sec)	FD-CC (sec)	Compression 1-Buf (sec)	Compression 10-Buf (sec)
0.05	0.1932	0.0062	0.0042	0.0001
0.10	0.1932	0.0062	0.0077	0.0003
0.30	0.1932	0.0062	0.0218	0.0006
0.50	0.1932	0.0062	0.0361	0.0010

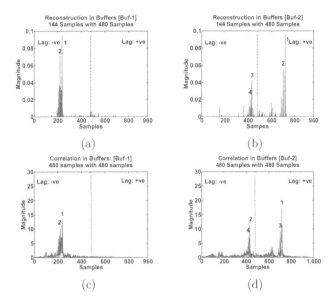

(a)   (b)

(c)   (d)

Figure 5: Buffer-by-Buffer Processing: Reconstruction of Correlation Coefficients and Cross-Correlation obtain the same result for the position of the LOS peak, and the tallest peak in each buffer.

The number of buffers b is chosen such that the number of samples in each buffer is the same as the sample count of the reference signal $\mathbf{p}$, i.e., $\tilde{n} = t_p F_s$. For example, if $\mathbf{p}$ contains 100 samples and $\mathbf{x}$ consists of 1000 samples, then b is 10. There are two benefits in making this choice. First, it restricts the direct path signal (in the total acquired trace) to be spread across a maximum of 2 buffers, and so, guarantees that the magnitude of the corresponding recovered coefficient would always remain at least 50% above its original estimate. Increasing b beyond 2 buffers decreases the individual peak heights to smaller magnitudes that poses a difficult detection task to differentiate them from the noise-floor. Second, it provides easy processing at the BS, where the operation of right zero-padding $\mathbf{p}$ to make its dimensions equal to $\mathbf{x}$ is substituted by fragmenting $\mathbf{x}$ into b buffers to match the size of $\mathbf{p}$ (Section 2.2.2).

The reconstruction process is performed on all b buffers, which is followed by the signal detection and range estimation algorithm.

Phase-1: It identifies the various correlation domain coefficient peaks and selects the first tallest peak in each of the b buffers that is atleast 6 standard deviations above the mean. The detection is considered to have failed for those buffers where no point qualifies as a peak. This reduces the validation space for phase-2 to $\tilde{b}$ ($\leq b$) buffers.

Phase-2: If there are valid peaks in more than one buffer (i.e., $\tilde{b} > 1$), then the tallest peak (across all $\tilde{b}$ buffers) among them is selected as the ranging peak. The detection is correct, if this peak in buffer b_i has a lag that is:

• Positive: ⇒ The peak in the previous buffer b_{i-1} must have a negative lag.

• Negative: ⇒ The peak in the next buffer b_{i+1} must have a positive lag.

This relationship is a result of the manner in which the signal gets aligned in different buffers and its equivalent representation in the correlation domain/cross-correlation (Fig. 5).

If $\tilde{b} = 1$ (i.e., only a single buffer has a valid peak), then the peak identified in phase-1 qualifies as the ranging peak. The estimated range r is obtained as:

$$r = ((\tilde{n}b_{i-1} + \hat{l})/F_s) \times v_s \tag{13}$$

where b_{i-1} is the buffer count before the detection buffer, $\hat{l}$ is the lag (in samples) of the ranging peak in the detection buffer, and v_s is the temperature compensated speed of sound in air.

3.4 Characterization of Compression Factor

One of the key decisions is to choose the optimal compression factor α thats achieves the best accuracy with the least measurements (or projections) m, where a smaller m leads to lower storage and transmission cost. α depends on the sparsity k (Eq. 7) of the received signal in the correlation domain, which in turn depends on the received SNR that varies with transmission power and ranging distance. In this subsection, we empirically study the relationship between SNR and α. The study was conducted in the following environments.

Case-A - Outdoor, Very low multipath: A less frequently used urban walkway, and the weather being sunny with occasional mild breeze.

Case-B - Indoor, Low multipath: A quiet lecture theatre ($[25 \times 15 \times 10]$ m) with a spacious podium at one end of the large room.

Case-C - Indoor, High multipath: A quiet meeting room ($[7 \times 6 \times 6]$ m) with a big wooden table in the center and other office furnitures.

The transmitter and the receiver were fixed at a constant separation distance of 5 m. The transmit power was varied such that the received SNR were recorded within the limits: [0-5] dB, [5-10] dB, [10-20] dB, [20-30] dB. For reasons that will be explained in the next subsection, we slightly modified the peak selection criteria of the detection algorithm to choose the tallest peak if there was no valid peak (6 standard deviation above the mean). 100 observations were collected for every experiment. *We show the relative mean error and its deviation with respect to the (best-case) standard cross-correlation in all the results in this subsection.*

Fig. 6(a), Fig. 6(b) and Fig. 6(c) shows the dependence of α-compression and its recovery accuracy on the SNR of the ranging signal. Across all figures, we observe that applying a higher α on a lower SNR signal results in an increase in estimation error. Fig. 6(a) for Case-A presents the most clear characterization by negating the effect of channel multipaths (though introducing an increased background noise level), where observations with a high SNR of [20-30] dB provide reliable range estimates by using only 15% projections while those having low SNR of [0-5] dB show confident result only with $\alpha = 0.30$ (i.e., using more projections). Fig. 6(b) and Fig. 6(c) show the results for Case-B and Case-C. Due to a less dominant multipath profile and background noise in Case-B, the accuracy levels show high confidence for $\alpha \geq 0.20$. The situation is challenging in Case-C (due to high multipath), and so, the errors are as large as 1 m with $\alpha = 0.05$, but attain stability after $\alpha = 0.25$. The cumulative probability results suggest that there is a 95% probability of incurring an additional error of < 1.5 cm in indoors and < 3 cm in outdoors with $\alpha = 0.30$ with respect to its standard cross-correlation estimate. Using $\alpha > 0.30$ does not improve the accuracy significantly considering the

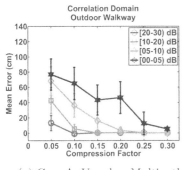
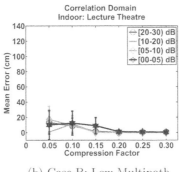
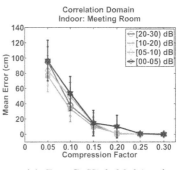

(a) Case-A: Very-low Multipath   (b) Case-B: Low Multipath   (c) Case-C: High Multipath

Figure 6: Characterization of Compression Factor α with SNR.

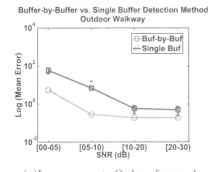
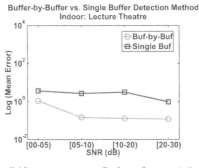
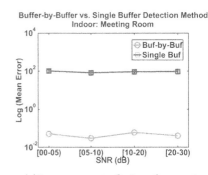

(a)Improvement: Order of mag. 1   (b)Improvement: Order of mag. 1.5   (c)Improvement: Order of mag. 4

Figure 7: For a compression factor of 0.30, the Buffer-by-Buffer detection shows an order of magnitude 1-4 improvement over Single Buffer detection method.

additional overheads. Fig. 6 also shows that for applications that require lower accuracy (e.g., 100 cm), α as less as 0.05 is sufficient.

We also performed ranging experiments with changes in distance over 1-10 m. Although, smaller values of α (i.e., lesser projections) were good for high SNR levels, the results with $\alpha = 0.30$ were optimal, even in the worst case to obtain higher accuracy (< 2 cm). Fig. 7 compares the detection accuracy between our proposed buffer-by-buffer method versus processing all the samples in a single buffer. From reasons explained in Section 3.3, the results show at least 1 order of magnitude improvement.

The sparse representation in the proposed correlation domain shows significantly better accuracy of an order of magnitude 2 (Fig. 8) compared to the DCT domain (for α=0.30) due to the most sparse depiction of the ranging signal (Fig. 2). For DCT domain processing, the recovered coefficients $\hat{s}_1$ were multiplied with the DCT basis Ψ (Eq. 1) to obtain an estimate of the received signal $\hat{x}_1$, and then cross-correlated with the reference signal $\mathbf{p}$.

Another simple (but deterministic) method of reducing the sample count is to downsample $\mathbf{x}$ by a factor F_d resulting in $\hat{y}$. We verify its detection accuracy in the correlation domain by using two different algorithms: (a) standard cross-correlation and (b) sparse approximation problem formulated as:

$$(\ell_r^1): \quad \hat{\mathbf{s}}_1^d = \min \|\mathbf{s}\|_{\ell_1} \quad \text{subject to:} \|\Psi^{'}\mathbf{s} - \hat{\mathbf{y}}\|_2 \leq \epsilon \quad (14)$$

The comparison results in Fig. 8 show that neither of these two methods based on downsampling provide better estimates than the proposed method of ℓ^1-minimization in the correlation domain where the improvement is of an order of magnitude 2 across all experimental environments. This improvement is the result of information embedding in random ensembles that preserves the ℓ^2-norm (or energy) of its respective higher dimension representation, as opposed to deterministically choosing samples and discarding information (i.e., frequency components) by downsampling. It supports the theoretical result that there is an overwhelming probability of correct recovery via ℓ^1-minimization for dimensionality reduction by random linear projection (Section 2.1).

3.5 Adaptive α-Estimation

The design of an adaptive mechanism for α requires estimating the received SNR. We propose two different approaches: first, with a BS feedback to receiver, and second, on the receiver itself.

For the BS-feedback mechanism, we utilize empirical information from the peak detection algorithm. In Section 3.3, we considered the scenarios where the valid buffer count $\tilde{b} \geq 1$. If a valid peak (i.e., at least 6 standard deviations above the mean) is not detected in any buffer (i.e., $\tilde{b} = 0$), then the detection is considered to have failed. This implies that the recovered coefficients are noisy due to a non-optimal α for the respective measurements (characterized by its SNR). It was precisely the reason for modifying the peak

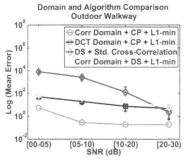

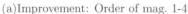

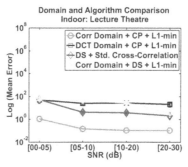

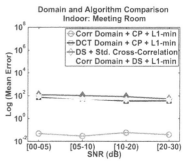

(a)Improvement: Order of mag. 1-4   (b)Improvement: Order of mag. 2-4   (c)Improvement: Order of mag. 4

Figure 8: For a compression(CP)/downsampling(DS) factor of 0.30, the proposed sparse approximation method based on compression with ℓ^1-min in the correlation domain shows an order of magnitude 1-4 higher detection accuracy compared to: (i) compression with ℓ^1-min in the DCT domain (ii) downsampling with cross-correlation (iii) downsampling with ℓ^1-min in the correlation domain.

selection criteria in the previous subsection, where we observed large errors in peak positions for magnitudes below the specified threshold. The BS-feedback algorithm starts with the initial knowledge of whether a valid peak was determined with $\alpha = 0.30$. If the detection succeeds, then α is decremented by a step size of 0.05 and compressed. This process is iterated until the detection fails, in which case, the previous α values is selected. On the other hand, if no valid peaks were encountered for the starting case, α is incremented in steps of 0.05 and the entire process is repeated until the detection succeeds.

A major drawback of the feedback approach is the additional measurements (that translate to transmission overhead), and its associated delay and power usage for deriving α. Therefore, we introduce this functionality on the receiver by a simple power estimation algorithm. The ratio ρ of the peak signal amplitude to the average of the absolute values in the sampled signal is calculated, and a corresponding α is selected according to the following empirically chosen criteria. $\alpha = \{\{0.05 : \rho > 30\}, \{0.10 : 20 < \rho \le 30\}, \{0.10 : 20 < \rho \le 30\}, \{0.20 : 15 < \rho \le 20\}, \{0.30 : 10 < \rho \le 15\}, \{0.50 : 05 < \rho \le 10\}, \{1.00 : \rho \le 05\}\}$.

For our analysis, we randomly selected 1000 measurements pertaining to different SNR levels in the indoor lecture theatre (Case-B). The respective α was estimated using the above two methods and their performance was compared against our empirically selected threshold value of $\alpha = 0.30$. Table 2 reports their performance trade-off where the BS-feedback obtains high accuracy but requires 2 times more measurements, while the receiver estimation approach takes fewer measurements and obtains only a 5% worse accuracy.

Table 2: Projections vs. Accuracy: A positive value indicates higher projections or reconstruction error compared to the threshold $\alpha = 0.30$

Scenario	Projections (%)	Accuracy (%)
BS-Feedback	101.16	-1.75
Receiver	-17.55	5.26

4 End-to-End System Architecture

In this section, we present the implementation of an end-to-end acoustic ranging system. Its design was driven by the specific goal of *fast* data acquisition and compression on the receiver node, which could be achieved by performing all operations on the mote's RAM without involving its external flash that would introduce additional latency. Therefore, all design decisions were guided towards maximum RAM utilization.

4.1 System Design: Hardware & Software

The system comprised of the TmoteInvent (as listener), our designed sensor mote (as beacon) and a network interface to the base-station (Fig. 9).

Transmitter: The beacon node (Fig. 10) comprised of our WSN platform along with a custom designed audio daughter board that included four TI TLV320AIC3254 audio codecs, each providing two audio I/O channels and a connector to hold the Bluetechnix CM-BF537E digital signal processor module. The transmitting front-end of the beacon mote consisted of a power amplifier driving a tweeter (speaker) transducer (VIFA 3/4" tweeter module MICRO). The tweeter (size: $[2 \times 2 \times 1]$ cm) had a fairly uniform and high frequency response of ≈ 22 dB above the noise-floor between 1-10kHz.

Receiver: TmoteInvent [29] was used as the listener node, due to its low-cost and low-power (100 times more power efficient than the DSP on the transmitter) features that are expected from a WSN platform. The receiving front-end consisted of an omni-directional electret microphone (Panasonic WM-61B) attached to an Analog Devices SSM2167 preamplifier. It allows omni-directional acquisition in the range 20 Hz - 10 kHz, and has a near-flat frequency response between 3-7 kHz that is 10 dB above the noise floor. High-rate audio data collection was achieved using the DMA controller packaged with the MSP430 MCU. The driver for the acoustic daughter board performs DMA acquisition to coordinate the transfer of samples from the ADC conversion registers to sequential words in RAM, and generates an interrupt on filling the assigned RAM buffer with data. Delay between fetching a new buffer for the DMA to fill was minimized by prefetching an additional spare buffer and making it available at the instant it was requested. However, the MSP430 DMA causes truncation of the 12 bits ADC data

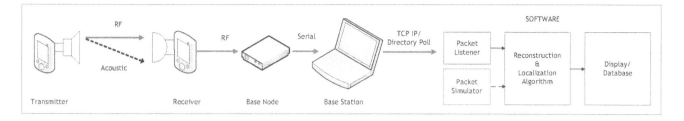

Figure 9: System Architecture of the End-to-End Acoustic Ranging System.

Figure 10: Transmitter Node: CSIRO Audio Mote.

to 8 bits rather than to two bytes, and so, results in a data resolution loss of 4 bits.

4.2 Ranging and Detection Methodology

The system uses the time-difference-of-arrival (TDOA) of RF and acoustic signals to measure the beacon-to-listener distance. The beacon initiates the ranging process by periodically transmitting a RF signal followed by a acoustic pulse after a fixed time interval. The fast propagating RF pulse reaches the listener almost instantaneously and synchronizes the clocks on both the devices, following which, the TDOA is measured after the arrival of the acoustic pulse. The ranging signal was a linear chirp of [3-7] kHz/0.01 ms and was transmitted at an acoustic pressure level of 70 dB. The DAC on the audio codec of the beacon node was programmed to sample at 48 kHz, while the ADC on the receiver Tmote was configured to acquire at 15 kHz.

If the time taken for sound to travel a maximum range d_c at a speed v_s is at most $\frac{d_c}{v_s}$, and if the transmitted chirp length is t_p, then the signal must reach the receiver within $\left[\frac{d_c}{v_s} + t_p\right]$. For $t_p = 0.01$ s and $d_c \approx 10$ m, the recording of the signal must be completed by 0.03 s. We include an additional 0.01 s to compensate for reverberation time (t_c), and setup the recording time to 0.04 s (Eq. 9). Following the buffer-by-buffer compression method, the signal was spread across 5 buffers. A measurement matrix $\bar{\Phi}$ was stored in the RAM that contained i.i.d. entries sampled from a symmetric Bernoulli distribution (Eq. 10). We postponed the multiplication operation on the matrix entities with the constant $(1/\sqrt{m})$ until the recovery stage at the BS.

The listener acquires the audio samples, compresses and stores these measurements in the RAM over a period of 5 iterations, and then, transfers them to the BS. These measurements are again divided into their respective buffers and reconstructed to obtain the coefficients. The detection process is the same as explained in Section 3.3, however we

made two minor modifications. First, due to a higher receiver noise floor, we set the criteria for selecting the first tallest peak to 3 (instead of 6) standard deviations above the mean. Second, as each sample corresponds to 2.2 cm of distance (at a sampling rate of 15 kHz), we used a simple parabolic interpolation method to obtain finer resolution. This additional step identifies the position of the first neighboring peak on the left and right of the selected ranging peak, finds the parabola that passes through these points, and calculates the time coordinate of the maximum of this parabola that estimates the range.

5   Evaluation: Experimental and Performance

Ranging: The ranging experiments were performed in the same three environments as mentioned in Section 3.4: (a) Case-A: outdoor walkway, (b) Case-B: lecture theatre, and (c) Case-C: meeting room. In all the setups, the listener node was fixed while the beacon node was moved along the direct LOS in a controlled manner. The correct ground truth was established using a measuring tape and markers.

The evaluation results are shown in Fig. 11, where we plot the absolute mean error and standard deviation for both standard and ℓ^1-min cross-correlation with respect to the ground truth. The best results were obtained in Case-B (Fig. 11(b)) where the mean error for ℓ^1-min was recorded as ≈ 9 cm at the maximum measured distance of 10 with a maximum deviation of ≈ 11 cm with respect to ground truth. Its maximum deviation from standard cross-correlation was ≈ 2 cm. Due to the decrease in the sparsity levels with lower SNR, the measurements from $[6 - 10]$ m were compressed with a higher α of 0.35.

Fig. 11 (a) and Fig. 11 (c) show the results for Case-A and Case-C, where the mean errors and deviations are significantly higher than Case-B (even at short range $[1 - 5]$ m). The sparsity of the received signal was affected by the high background noise and multipath in the respective environments, and hence, resulted in incorrectly approximated range values. Also, we observe a maximum error difference of ≈ 5-6 cm between the two algorithms. In Case-A, $\alpha = 0.40$ was used for compressing data after 5 m of measurement distance. The audio recordings after 8 m were highly noisy and required an even higher α value for compression. However, due to non-availability of RAM memory space for storing the additional entries of the new measurement matrix $\bar{\Phi}$, range estimates beyond 8 m could not be processed. There was no scope for adaptive α-estimation (Section 3.5) as the empirically chosen values were the absolute minimum required for reliable recovery.

Localization: In these experiments, 5 listener nodes were placed at fixed (known) locations in a $[4 \times 5]$ m area of the

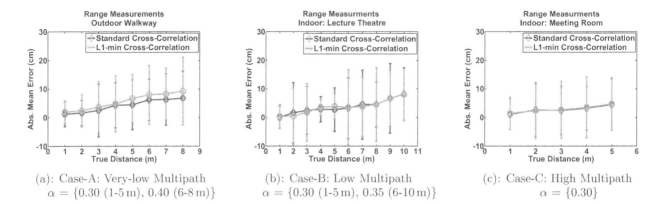

(a): Case-A: Very-low Multipath
$\alpha = \{0.30 \ (1\text{-}5\,\text{m}), \ 0.40 \ (6\text{-}8\,\text{m})\}$

(b): Case-B: Low Multipath
$\alpha = \{0.30 \ (1\text{-}5\,\text{m}), \ 0.35 \ (6\text{-}10\,\text{m})\}$

(c): Case-C: High Multipath
$\alpha = \{0.30\}$

Figure 11: End-to-End Acoustic Ranging System: Ranging results.

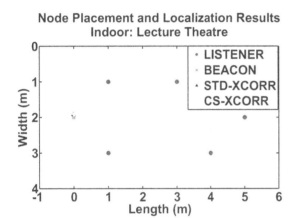

Figure 12: Localization result.

Table 3: Performance Analysis: TmoteInvent

Operation	Time (s)	Energy (mJ)
Audio Acquisition	00.0665	0020.50
Compression	00.0060	0001.85
Radio Transfer (Compressed Data)	00.0580	0017.88
Cross-correlation (Time-domain)	15.6250	4816.00

Energy Consumption: Table 3 reports the time and energy consumed for each operational step on the listener node. The cumulative time spent in compression and radio transfer is $\approx 0.0640\,\text{s}$, which is more than 100 times faster than performing time-domain cross-correlation on the node itself. Its equivalent frequency-domain cross-correlation requires 2*FFT and IFFT operation steps. When optimized for speed, a FFT over 512 sample window of an 8 kHz signal takes 0.5 s execution time on TelosB [30], and so, for our case of 750 samples would take $\approx 2.2\,\text{s}$, which is still 34 times slower.

With respect to compression performance, the popular LZ77-based algorithm 'gzip' achieves slightly better compressibility of $\alpha = 0.27$ (Table 4). However, due to its lossless nature of compression, it is not robust to information loss (packet drops) that are common in low-power sensor networks. In contrast, the performance degradation by our approach is less severe and has the same effect as compressing with a smaller α (Fig. 6). A similar, but energy efficient algorithm proposed by Sadler et al. [31]: S-LZW reports an execution time of approximately 0.05 s for 528 bytes of data, and therefore, its equivalent compressing cost

indoor lecture theatre (Case-B) to obtain the (unknown) location coordinates of the beacon node. The speaker had a fairly uniform signal strength within the directionality cone of $\pm 45^o$ (with a 2 dB decrease from $0^o - 45^o$), therefore, all the 5 listeners were confined within this perimeter with their microphones facing the speaker.

The beacon initiated the ranging process and the corresponding acoustic chirp was recorded by the 5 listeners. A simple time division multiple access (TDMA) approach was followed for orderly data transfer wherein each listener transferred the compressed data in a preset time slot. The distances between the beacon and the receivers were estimated at the BS, which was followed by the linear least square localization algorithm to calculate the 2D location of the beacon node. Fig. 12 shows the node placements, where the listener and beacon node(s) have been depicted as circle and square respectively along with the estimated beacon location using the two methods. The standard and ℓ^1-min cross-correlation show similar results with a mean localization error of 18 cm and 17 cm with a deviation of 6 cm and 7 cm respectively. As the localization error is upper bounded by its ranging errors, we expect similar relative performance in Case-A and Case-C that show a maximum ranging error difference of 5 cm.

Table 4: Compression Factor (α) for LZ77-based Compression Algorithm 'gzip': Dataset collected by the POC System (Section 3.4).

Scenario	Mean α	Deviation α
Case-A: Very-low Multipath	0.27	0.005
Case-B: Low Multipath	0.27	0.005
Case-C: High Multipath	0.28	0.009

for 750 bytes would be approximately 0.075 s ($\approx$ 12 times slower than our technique). These statistics suggest that although compression by random ensembles is not the best compression method, it benefits of greater energy savings along with faster data processing is a good trade-off between compression and computation time, accuracy (in case of data loss), energy consumption. For example, if applications can tolerate 100 cm localization accuracy, the proposed method requires approximately 5% of measurements only (Fig. 6). Furthermore, in the event of packet loss, S-LZW needs to either retransmit the entire compressed data segment, or employ expensive end-to-end reliable communication protocol. On the other hand, the performance of the proposed protocol degrades gracefully with packet losses as it can still recover the ranging information, but with larger errors (Fig. 6).

6 Related Work

We broadly categorize the related work based on the detection mechanism used in existing acoustic, ultrasound and RF localization systems in WSN.

Non Cross-correlation: Active Bat [1], Cricket [2], Medusa [3] and SpiderBat [32] are ultrasound positioning systems. Range measurements are performed by calculating the TDOA between two synchronously sent RF and ultrasonic pulses at the receiver. The ranging pulse is a single frequency (40 kHz) sinusoidal and its arrival is detected by triggering an interrupt pin of the microcontroller when its leading edge exceeds a preset threshold. Due to the functional simplicity, low-power microcontrollers (Atmega/MSP430 series) used in these platforms are efficient in managing the on-board processing. Kusy et al. in [33] introduced radio inferferometry to design a low-cost RF-based positioning system on the Mica2 platform. This method measures the relative phase offsets of the interference field (created by two nodes transmitting RF pulses at slightly different frequencies) at different locations to obtain the position estimate of the transmitters. However, these techniques are not robust against multipath characteristics, and so, no results have been published for complex cluttered environments.

Cross-correlation: The system proposed by Kushwaha et al. in [7], Hazas et al. in [6], AENSBox [8], Beep-Beep [9] and TWEET [10] are existing acoustic broadband systems. Despite their difference in signal design, synchronization schemes and methods to improve the received SNR, they share a common detection mechanisms:cross-correlation. These systems have been reported to withstand considerable channel multipath and environmental noise, and so, benefit in providing reliable and precise distance estimates for long coverage range. However, the capability of these systems have been upgraded by using DSP/smart phones that typically consume higher power and resources.

The theory of sparse representation [13] helps to efficiently embed information without much loss (which serves the purpose of storage and transmission) followed by its recovery from an underdetermined system. Although, we follow a similar approach as Wright et al. [28] in face recognition, the scope of our problem is completely different. We design a new dictionary, specifically, for cross-correlation based detection and ranging, as opposed to feature extraction for face classification.

Previous work by Whitehouse et al. in [11] and Sallai et at. in [12] on acoustic ranging in resource constrained sensor networks (using MICA platform) categorically state that the limited availability of RAM was the most serious constraint in their system implementation. The ranging results reported by [12] have an average error of 8.18 cm over a distance of 1-9 m by repeating the ranging signal 16 times, which results in significant runtime and energy overhead. Using cross-correlation via sparse representation, our acoustic ranging system was able to confront this problem, and also, was able to provide similar performance (mean error of < 10 cm over 1-10 m) with fewer samples.

7 Conclusion and Discussion

We presented a new information processing approach for range estimation: cross-correlation via sparse representation. We showed that exploiting sparsity is critical for high-performance signal processing operations of high-dimensional data such as cross-correlation. The sparsity of the underlying signal in our proposed correlation domain aids in the recovery mechanism to obtain reliable range estimates. The main idea was to use a Toeplitz matrix with the time-shifted reference signal as the dictionary that leads to sparser representation than processing in other domains such as DCT. We designed its theoretical framework and validated its working through empirical system tests and characterization studies. Considering the implementation simplicity in the acoustic domain, we developed an end-to-end acoustic ranging system using COTS sensor platforms to verify our hypothesis.

The theoretical foundation of this work is based on sparse approximation, and not on compressive sensing that mandates strict adherence to the RIP condition. As explained in Section 2, RIP is only a sufficient but not a necessary condition for reconstruction accuracy; therefore, a stable solution is still recoverable by ℓ^1-minimization.

It is well understood that cross-correlation only solves a small part of the ranging problem, and therefore, our work is preliminary in the sense that we have not yet entirely evaluated the consequences of externalities. An intriguing question for future work is whether this framework can be useful with other challenges such as directional receivers, limited range and signal penetration, noisy background conditions and high-stress environments [34], scalability issues, etc. In addition, an indepth analysis of the properties of a Toeplitz matrix with respect to spare approximation and compressive sensing is also required for better design of sensing matrices. Furthermore, its ability to adapt to mobile conditions (for object tracking) needs to be evaluated, and executing it in a principled manner remains an important future direction.

Our work in this paper is guided by the current hardware limitations of low-cost and low-power sensor platforms. We believe that the key observations and principles derived here will find their application in location sensing systems that have constrained hardware resources to handle the bulk of data processing.

8 Acknowledgment

We would like to thank the anonymous reviewers for their helpful comments; and Dr. Brano Kusy (CSIRO) and Dr. Philipp Sommer (CSIRO) for being internal reviewers. This work is supported by Sensors and Sensor Networks Transformational Capability Platform, CSIRO.

9 References

[1] Andy Harter, Andy Hopper, Pete Steggles, Andy Ward, and Paul Webster. The anatomy of a context-aware application. In *MobiCom*, pages 59–68. ACM, 1999.

[2] Nissanka Bodhi Priyantha. *The Cricket Indoor Location System*. PhD thesis, MIT, 2005.

[3] Andreas Savvides, Chih-Chieh Han, and Mani B. Strivastava. Dynamic fine-grained localization in ad-hoc networks of sensors. In *MobiCom*, pages 66–179. ACM, 2001.

[4] Evangelos Mazomenos, Dirk De Jager, Jeffrey S. Reeve, and Neil M. White. A two-way time of flight ranging scheme for wireless sensor networks. In *EWSN*. Springer-Verlag, 2011.

[5] P. Misra, D. Ostry, and S. Jha. Improving the coverage range of ultrasound-based localization systems. In *WCNC*, pages 605–610. IEEE, 2011.

[6] M. Hazas and A. Hopper. Broadband ultrasonic location systems for improved indoor positioning. *IEEE TMC*, 5(5):536–547, 2006.

[7] M. Kushwaha, K. Molnar, J. Sallai, P. Volgyesi, M. Maroti, and A. Ledeczi. Sensor node localization using mobile acoustic beacons. In *MASS*, pages 9pp.–491. IEEE, 2005.

[8] Lewis Girod, Martin Lukac, Vlad Trifa, and Deborah Estrin. The design and implementation of a self-calibrating distributed acoustic sensing platform. In *SenSys*, pages 71–84. ACM, 2006.

[9] Peng Chunyi, Shen Guobin, Zhang Yongguang, Li Yanlin, and Tan Kun. Beepbeep: a high accuracy acoustic ranging system using cots mobile devices. In *SenSys*, pages 1–14. ACM, 2007.

[10] P. Misra, D. Ostry, N. Kottege, and S. Jha. Tweet: An envelope detection based ultrasonic ranging system. In *MSWiM*, pages 409–416. ACM, 2011.

[11] Kamin Whitehouse and David Culler. Calibration as parameter estimation in sensor networks. In *WSNA*. ACM, 2002.

[12] János Sallai, György Balogh, Miklós Maróti, Ákos Lédeczi, and Branislav Kusy. Acoustic ranging in resource constrained sensor networks. In *ICWN*, page 04. CSREA Press, 2004.

[13] David L. Donoho. For most large underdetermined systems of linear equations the minimal ℓ_1-norm solution is also the sparsest solution. *Communications on Pure and Applied Mathematics*, 59(6):797–829, 2006.

[14] P. Zhao and B. Yu. On model selection consistency of lasso. *J. Machine Learning Research*, 7:2541–2567, 2006.

[15] R. Tibshirani. Regression shrinkage and selection via the lasso. *J. Royal Statistical Soc. B*, 58(1):267–288, 1996.

[16] E. Amaldi and V. Kann. On the approximability of minimizing nonzero variables or unsatisfied relations in linear systems. *Theoretical Computer Science*, 209:237–260, 1998.

[17] Edoardo Amaldi and Viggo Kann. On the approximability of minimizing nonzero variables or unsatisfied relations in linear systems. *Theoretical Computer Science*, 209(1-2):237 – 260, 1998.

[18] E. J. Candes and T. Tao. Near-optimal signal recovery from random projections: Universal encoding strategies? *IEEE Trans. on Inf. Theory*, 52(12):5406–5425, 2006.

[19] D.L. Donoho. Compressed sensing. *IEEE Trans. on Inf. Theory*, 52(4):1289–1306, april 2006.

[20] B. F. Logan. Properties of high-pass signals. *Ph.D. Thesis*, 1965.

[21] Donoho D. L. and B. F. Logan. Signal recovery and the large sieve. *SIAM J. APPL. MATH.*, 52(2):577–591, 1992.

[22] S. S. Chen, D. L. Donoho, and M. A. Saunders. Atomic decomposition by basis pursuit. *SIAM J. Scientific Computing*, 20(1):33–61, 1999.

[23] D. L. Donoho and X. Huo. Uncertainty principles and ideal atomic decomposition. *IEEE Trans. Inf. Theory*, 47(7):2845–2862, 2001.

[24] R. Gribonval and M Nielsen. Sparse representations in unions of bases. *IEEE Trans. Inf. Theory*, 49(12):3320–3325, 2003.

[25] David L. Donoho and Michael Elad. Optimally sparse representation in general (nonorthogonal) dictionaries via ℓ_1 minimization. *Proceedings of the National Academy of Sciences*, 100(5):2197–2202, 2003.

[26] M. Elad and A.M. Bruckstein. A generalized uncertainty principle and sparse representation in pairs of bases. *IEEE Trans. on Inf. Theory*, 48(9):2558 – 2567, sep 2002.

[27] R. Baraniuk, M. Davenport, R. DeVore, and Wakin M. A simple proof of the restricted isometry property for random matrices. *Constr Approx*, 28:253–263, 2008.

[28] J. Wright, A. Y. Yang, A. Ganesh, S. S. Sastry, and Ma Yi. Robust face recognition via sparse representation. *IEEE PAMI*, 31(2):210–227, 2009.

[29] http://sentilla.com/files/pdf/eol/tmote-invent-user-guide.pdf.

[30] Ben Greenstein, Christopher Mar, Alex Pesterev, Shahin Farshchi, Eddie Kohler, Jack Judy, and Deborah Estrin. Capturing high-frequency phenomena using a bandwidth-limited sensor network. In *SenSys*. ACM, 2006. 279-292.

[31] Christopher M. Sadler and Margaret Martonosi. Data compression algorithms for energy-constrained devices in delay tolerant networks. In *SenSys*, pages 265–278. ACM, 2006.

[32] G. Oberholzer, P. Sommer, and R. Wattenhofer. Spiderbat: Augmenting wireless sensor networks with distance and angle information. In *IPSN*, pages 211–222. ACM/IEEE, 2011.

[33] Kusy Branislav, Sallai Janos, Balogh Gyorgy, Ledeczi Akos, Protopopescu Vladimir, Tolliver Johnny, DeNap Frank, and Parang Morey. Radio interferometric tracking of mobile wireless nodes. In *Mobisys*. ACM, 2007.

[34] P. Misra, S. Kanhere, D. Ostry, and S. Jha. Safety assurance and rescue communication systems in high-stress environments: A a mining case study. *IEEE Communication Magazine*, 48(4):66–73, 2010.

Closing the Loop: A Simple Distributed Method for Control over Wireless Networks *

Miroslav Pajic
Dept. of Electrical & Systems Eng.
University of Pennsylvania
pajic@seas.upenn.edu

Shreyas Sundaram
Dept. of Electrical & Computer Eng.
University of Waterloo
ssundara@uwaterloo.ca

Jerome Le Ny
Dept. of Electrical & Systems Eng.
University of Pennsylvania
jeromel@seas.upenn.edu

George J. Pappas
Dept. of Electrical & Systems Eng.
University of Pennsylvania
pappasg@seas.upenn.edu

Rahul Mangharam
Dept. of Electrical & Systems Eng.
University of Pennsylvania
rahulm@seas.upenn.edu

ABSTRACT

We present a distributed scheme used for control over a network of wireless nodes. As opposed to traditional networked control schemes where the nodes simply route information to and from a dedicated controller (perhaps performing some encoding along the way), our approach, Wireless Control Network (WCN), treats the network itself as the controller. In other words, the computation of the control law is done in a fully distributed way inside the network. We extend the basic WCN strategy, where at each time-step, each node updates its internal state to be a linear combination of the states of the nodes in its neighborhood. This causes the entire network to behave as a linear dynamical system, with sparsity constraints imposed by the network topology. We demonstrate that with observer style updates, the WCN's robustness to link failures is substantially improved. Furthermore, we show how to design a WCN that can maintain stability even in cases of node failures. We also address the problem of WCN synthesis with guaranteed optimal performance of the plant, with respect to standard cost functions. We extend the synthesis procedure to deal with continuous-time plants and demonstrate how the WCN can be used on a practical, industrial application, using a process-in-the-loop setup with real hardware.

---

*This work has been partially supported by NSF-CNS 0931239 and NSF-MRI 0923518 grants. It has also been funded by a grant from the Natural Sciences and Engineering Research Council of Canada (NSERC).

Categories and Subject Descriptors

C.2.1 [**Computer-Communication Networks**]: Network Architecture and Design— *Wireless communication*; C.3 [**Special-purpose and Application-based Systems**]: *Process control systems*

General Terms

Algorithms, Design, Theory, Performance, Reliability

Keywords

Cooperative control, decentralized control, networked control systems, wireless sensor networks

1. INTRODUCTION

Improvements in the capabilities and cost of wireless technologies have allowed multi-hop wireless networks to be used as a means of (open-loop) monitoring of large-scale industrial plants [1, 2]. With this technology, sensor measurements of plant variables can be transmitted to controllers, data centers and plant operators without the need for excessive wiring, thereby yielding gains in efficiency and flexibility for the operator. However, the use of multi-hop wireless networks in closed-loop feedback control is in its infancy, and is an active area of research [3, 4]. Wireless Networked Control Systems (WNCSs) fundamentally differ from standard wired distributed systems in that the dynamics of the *network* (variable channel capacity, probabilistic connectivity, topological changes, node and link failures) can change the operating points and physical dynamics of the *closed-loop system* [3, 5]. The most important objective of WNCSs is to provide stability of the closed-loop system. An additional requirement is optimality with respect to some appropriate cost function. It is therefore necessary for the network (along with its interfaces to sensors and actuators) to be able to provide some form of guarantee of the control system's stability in the face of the non-idealities of the wireless links and the communication constraints of the wireless network.

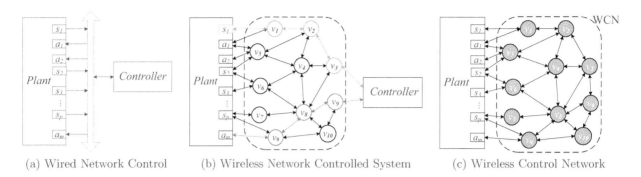

(a) Wired Network Control   (b) Wireless Network Controlled System   (c) Wireless Control Network

Figure 1: Standard architectures for Networked Control Systems; (a) Wired system with a shared bus and dedicated controller; (b) Red links/nodes - routing data from the plant's sensors to the controller; Blue links/nodes - routing data from the controller to the plant's actuators; (c) A multi-hop wireless control network used as a distributed controller.

The most common approach to incorporating WNCSs into the feedback loop is to use it primarily as a communication medium: the nodes in the network simply route information to and from one or more *dedicated controllers*, which are usually specialized CPUs capable of performing computationally expensive procedures (see Fig. 1(b)). The use of dedicated controllers imposes a routing requirement along one or more fixed paths through the network, which must meet the stability constraints, encapsulated by end-to-end delay requirements [6, 7]. However, this assignment of routes is a static setup, which commonly requires global reorganization for changes in the underlying topology, node population and wireless link capacities.

Routing couples the communication, computation and control problems [4, 8, 9]. Therefore, when a new route is required due to topological changes, the computation and control configurations must also be recalculated. Merely inserting a WNCS into the standard network architecture "sensor → channel → controller/estimator → channel → actuator" requires the addition of significant software support [7, 10], as the overhead of completely recomputing the computation and control configurations, due to topological changes or packet drops, is too expensive and does not scale.

1.1 Wireless Control Design Challenge

It should be noted that providing closed-loop stability and performance guarantees for wireless control networks is a challenging problem. On one hand, the control systems community typically abstracts away the systems details and solves the problem for semi-idealized networks with approximated noise distributions and link perturbations [3, 5]. While this approach provides mathematical certainty of the properties of the network, it fails to provide a systematic path to real-world network design. On the other hand, the network systems community uses hardware and software approaches to address open-loop issues, but these fail to provide any guarantees to maintaining stability and performance of closed-loop control. We propose a control scheme over wireless networks that provides closed-loop stability or optimality with respect to standard metrics, while maintaining ease of implementation in real-world networks.

The applications of interest in this work are industrial process control systems (such as natural gas refineries and paper pulp manufacturing plants) and building automation systems. In general, the plant time-constants are on the order of several seconds to a few minutes and the control network is expected to operate at rates of hundreds of milliseconds. While such plants may have as many as 80,000 to 110,000 control loops, they are organized in a hierarchal manner such that networks span 10-20 wireless nodes (per gateway) for low-level control [6]. Therefore, in this work we focus on the networks with up to a few tens of nodes.

Furthermore, the networks might be shared among control loops (i.e., a node may be involved in several feedback loops), and new feedback loops may be added at run-time. Adding new communication loops in a standard WNCS could affect the performance of the existing loops, and the system must be analyzed as a whole. Although techniques have been developed for compositional analysis of WNCS (e.g., [4]), their complexity limits their use in these applications. Therefore, it is necessary to derive a *composable* control scheme, where control loops can be easily added and a simple compositional analysis can be performed at run-time, to ensure that one loop does not affect performance of other loops.

Finally, with the use of asynchronous event triggered network substrates, it is difficult to design, model and analyze control networks and also hard, if not impossible, to verify performance of a system that consists of several event-triggered loops. On the other hand, full network synchronization allows the use of Time-Triggered Architectures (TTAs) where communication and computation are scheduled at particular instances of time (i.e., time slots) [11]. This simplifies modeling of the closed-loop system, which now consists of continuous-time physical dynamics and a communication network. With TTA, the closed-loop system can be modeled as a switched control system [4], allowing the use of existing techniques for switched-system analysis. Therefore, when communication and computation schedules are derived, it is possible to determine if the closed-loop system is stable (i.e., asymptotically stable or mean square stable) for channel errors, with and/or without permanent link or node failures.

1.2 Contributions

In this effort, we build on the work from [12], in which we introduced the Wireless Control Network (WCN), a fundamentally new concept where the network *itself* acts as the controller. We proposed a basic scheme that can be used to guarantee closed-loop system stability. We henceforth refer to this as the "basic WCN". Our contribution is focused specifically on four major extensions to the basic WCN, making it optimal, more robust and practical:

1.) While the basic WCN in [12] provided closed-loop stability, the key issue of *optimality* was not investigated. We present here a method to extract an optimal WCN configuration, thus providing a greater incentive to adopt WCN in industrial control applications.

2.) The basic WCN was able to provide stable network configurations for a large class of wireless network topologies. However, it was highly susceptible to packet drops greater than 1%. In this work, we present significant robustness improvements, maintaining stability for packet drop rates *up to 20%* for a specific network topology and plant. This bridges the gap between the basic WCN and the theoretical upper bound of robustness to packet drops [13].

3.) Furthermore, we propose a method to extract WCN configurations that maintain stability of the closed-loop system even in presence of node failures.

4.) Finally, we illustrate the use of the improved WCN in an industrial process control case study. Using a process-in-the-loop test-bed we demonstrate its ability to optimally control continuous-time physical processes, and to maintain system stability under the presence of node and link failures.

In this paper, we consider scenarios where the network topology is already set, and we present algorithms to configure the WCN to guarantee stability (optimality) for the pre-defined topology. In [14] we have investigated a dual problem, how to synthesize the network so that a stable WCN configuration exists. The topological conditions from [14], along with the results from this work allow for an integrated decentralized wireless control network design framework.

1.3 Organization of the Paper

The rest of the paper is organized as follows: Sec. 2 describes the concept of the WCN. In Sec. 3 we present a method used to extract optimal WCN configurations. Sec. 4 and 5 extend the WCN scheme to improve its robustness to link and node failures. Sec. 6 describes an approach to employ WCN for control of continuous-time process. Finally, in Sec. 7 we show how the WCN can be used in an industrial, process control application.

1.4 Notation

We use $\mathbf{I}_N$ to denote the $N \times N$ identity matrix, while $\mathbf{I}$ denotes the identity matrix of appropriate dimensions. The notation $\operatorname{diag}(\cdot)$ indicates a square matrix with the quantities inside the brackets on the diagonal, and zeros elsewhere. For a vector $\mathbf{x}$, $\|\mathbf{x}\|$ denotes the Euclidean norm (i.e., $\|\mathbf{x}\| = \sqrt{\mathbf{x}^T\mathbf{x}}$). Finally, $\mathbf{A} \succ \mathbf{0}(\succeq \mathbf{0})$ indicates that matrix $\mathbf{A}$ is positive (semi)definite.

2. WIRELESS CONTROL NETWORKS

2.1 An Intuitive Overview of the WCN

The role of feedback control is to apply inputs to the plant (based on observed outputs) in order to elicit the desired behavior. The exact mapping between observed behavior and applied inputs depends on a mathematical model of the plant, describing how inputs affect the system (over time). Here, we start with a common discrete-time, linear time-

invariant model of the form:[1]

$$\mathbf{x}[k+1] = \mathbf{A}\mathbf{x}[k] + \mathbf{B}\mathbf{u}[k] + \mathbf{B_w}\mathbf{u}_w[k]$$
$$\mathbf{y}[k] = \mathbf{C}\mathbf{x}[k], \tag{1}$$

where $\mathbf{x} \in \mathbb{R}^n$ and $\mathbf{y} \in \mathbb{R}^p$ denote the plant's state and output, $\mathbf{u} \in \mathbb{R}^m$ is the plant's (controllable) input, and $\mathbf{u}_w \in \mathbb{R}^{m_w}$ is the disturbance input.[2] Accordingly, the matrices $\mathbf{A}, \mathbf{B}, \mathbf{B}_w, \mathbf{C}$ have suitable dimensions.

Standard dynamical feedback controllers collect the observed plant outputs $\mathbf{y}[k]$ and generate the control input $\mathbf{u}[k]$ as the output of a linear system of the form:

$$\mathbf{x_c}[k+1] = \mathbf{A_c}\mathbf{x}_c[k] + \mathbf{B_c}\mathbf{y}[k]$$
$$\mathbf{u}[k] = \mathbf{C_c}\mathbf{x}_c[k] + \mathbf{D_c}\mathbf{y}[k]. \tag{2}$$

The vector $\mathbf{x}_c[k]$ denotes the state of the controller, and the matrices $\mathbf{A}_c, \mathbf{B}_c, \mathbf{C}_c$ and $\mathbf{D}_c$ are designed using standard tools from control theory, to ensure that the control inputs are stabilizing. Depending on the control method used, the state of the controller can often be as large as the state of the system itself.

In the above traditional approach to controller design, a wireless network would simply be placed between the controller and the plant to carry information back and forth. The goal of our work is to derive a truly networked and fully distributed control scheme, where the collective computation and communication capabilities of the wireless nodes are fully leveraged to compute the control inputs *in-network*. Intuitively, we propose a simple scheme for each node in the network to follow (using only information from its nearest neighbors at each time-step) that results in the desired network behavior. Essentially, we would like each wireless node to act as a small dynamical controller, with two main differences: (i) the state of the controller at each node will be constrained to be rather small (in order to account for resource and computational constraints), and (ii) in its updates, each node only uses the states of its nearest neighbors (which could include the plant's outputs, if the node is within transmission range of the outputs). Note that the latter condition precludes the need to route information from the plant to each controller in order for it to perform its update. In the rest of this section, we will make these conditions more mathematically precise.

2.2 Model of the Wireless Control Network

To model the WCN we consider the basic WCN setup from Fig. 1(c), where the plant is to be controlled using a multi-hop, fully synchronized wireless network with N nodes. In this paper, we extend the proposed scheme to allow for the design of a WCN that applies inputs in an 'optimal' manner (according to a cost function that we will define later). The plant model is given by (1), where the output vector $\mathbf{y}[k]$ contains the plant's output measurements provided by the sensors $s_1, \ldots, s_p$, while the input vector $\mathbf{u}[k]$ corresponds to the signals applied to the plant by actuators $a_1, \ldots, a_m$. The wireless network is described by a graph $\mathcal{G} = \{\mathcal{V}, \mathcal{E}\}$, where $\mathcal{V} = \{v_1, v_2, \ldots, v_N\}$ is the set of N nodes and $\mathcal{E} \subseteq \mathcal{V} \times \mathcal{V}$ represents the radio connectivity (communication topology) in the network (i.e., edge $(v_j, v_i) \in \mathcal{E}$, if node v_i can receive information directly from node v_j).

---

[1] In Section 6 we will show how continuous-time plants can be cast in this framework using discretization.

[2] We do not have any control over the disturbances.

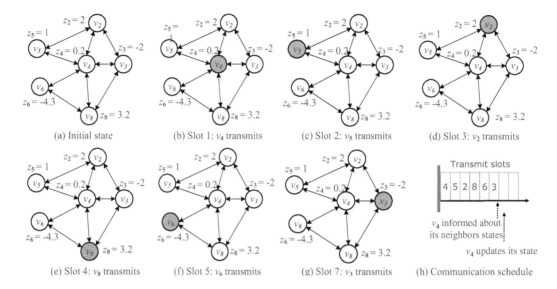

| (a) Initial state | (b) Slot 1: v_4 transmits | (c) Slot 2: v_5 transmits | (d) Slot 3: v_2 transmits |

| (e) Slot 4: v_8 transmits | (f) Slot 5: v_6 transmits | (g) Slot 7: v_3 transmits | (h) Communication schedule |

Figure 2: An illustration of the WCN scheme for a simple network.

As mentioned earlier, our scheme views each node v_i as a (small) linear dynamical controller, with (possibly vector) state z_i. Each node updates the state of its controller as a linear combination of the states of its neighbors and its own state. The state update for node v_i can also include a linear combination of the plant outputs from all plant sensors in v_i's neighborhood.

For example, consider the network presented in Fig. 2, where at the beginning of a time frame each node has an initial state value denoted by z_i (Fig. 2(a)). If each node maintains a scalar state, the size of the state is just **2 bytes**.[3] In the first time slot of a frame (Fig. 2(b)) node v_4 transmits its state, and in the second slot node v_5 transmits the state, etc. Finally, in the 6th slot node v_3 is the last node in the frame to transmit its state (Fig. 2(g)). This results in a communication schedule as depicted in Fig. 2(h). After slot 6, node v_4 is informed about all its neighbors' states, which enables it to update its state by activating the WCN task. The task has to compute the updated state value before the node is scheduled for transmission in the next frame.

In the general case, if $z_i[k]$ denotes the ith node's state at time step (i.e., communication frame) k, the **runtime update procedure** is:

$$z_i[k+1] = w_{ii}z_i[k] + \sum_{v_j \in \mathcal{N}_{v_i}} w_{ij}z_j[k] + \sum_{s_j \in \mathcal{N}_{v_i}} h_{ij}y_j[k], \quad (3)$$

where the neighborhood of a vertex v is represented as $\mathcal{N}_v$ and $y_j[k]$ is the measurement provided by sensor s_j. We will model the resource constraints of each node in the network by limiting the size of the state vector that can be maintained by each node.[4] Note the similarity of the update (3) to the state update equation for traditional dynamical controllers of the form (2); the state $z_i[k]$ plays the role of $x_c[k]$,

[3]Given that standard analog-to-digital converters have a precision of 12-16 bits, two bytes suffice for scalar values.
[4]To present our results, we will focus on the case where each node's state is a scalar. The general case, where each heterogeneous node can maintain a vector state with possibly different dimensions, can be treated with a natural extension of our approach (e.g., see [12]).

the weights w_{ii} and w_{ij} play the role of $\mathbf{A}_c$ and the columns of $\mathbf{B}_c$, respectively.

To enable interaction between the network and the plant, each actuator a_i applies input $u_i[k]$, which is computed as a linear combination of states from the nodes in the neighborhood of the actuator:

$$u_i[k] = \sum_{j \in \mathcal{N}_{a_i}} g_{ij}z_j[k]. \quad (4)$$

Once again, note the resemblance of this applied input to the input applied by a standard controller of the form (2). Therefore, the behavior of each node in the network is determined by values w_{ij}, h_{ij} and g_{ij}. Aggregating the state values of all nodes at time step k into the value vector $\mathbf{z}[k]$, we see that the above individual controllers at each node collectively cause the entire network to act as a dynamical controller of the form:

$$\mathbf{z}[k+1] = \underbrace{\begin{bmatrix} w_{11} & w_{12} & \cdots & w_{1N} \\ w_{21} & w_{22} & \cdots & w_{2N} \\ \vdots & \vdots & \ddots & \vdots \\ w_{N1} & w_{N2} & \cdots & w_{NN} \end{bmatrix}}_{\mathbf{W}} \mathbf{z}[k] +$$

$$+ \underbrace{\begin{bmatrix} h_{11} & h_{12} & \cdots & h_{1p} \\ h_{21} & h_{22} & \cdots & h_{2p} \\ \vdots & \vdots & \ddots & \vdots \\ h_{N1} & h_{N2} & \cdots & h_{Np} \end{bmatrix}}_{\mathbf{H}} \mathbf{y}[k]$$

$$= \mathbf{W}\mathbf{z}[k] + \mathbf{H}\mathbf{y}[k] \ ,$$

$$\mathbf{u}[k] = \underbrace{\begin{bmatrix} g_{11} & g_{12} & \cdots & g_{1N} \\ g_{21} & g_{22} & \cdots & g_{2N} \\ \vdots & \vdots & \ddots & \vdots \\ g_{m1} & g_{m2} & \cdots & g_{mN} \end{bmatrix}}_{\mathbf{G}} \mathbf{z}[k] = \mathbf{G}\mathbf{z}[k]$$

for all $k \in \mathbb{N}$. Since for all $i \in \{1, \ldots, N\}$, $w_{ij} = 0$ if $v_j \notin \mathcal{N}_{v_i}$, $h_{ij} = 0$ if $s_j \notin \mathcal{N}_{v_i}$, and $g_{ij} = 0$ if $v_j \notin \mathcal{N}_{a_i}$ the matrices $\mathbf{W}, \mathbf{H}$ and $\mathbf{G}$ are *structured*, with sparsity constraints determined by the network topology at design time.

Throughout the rest of the paper, we will define Ψ to be the set of all tuples $(\mathbf{W}, \mathbf{H}, \mathbf{G}) \in \mathbb{R}^{N \times N} \times \mathbb{R}^{N \times p} \times \mathbb{R}^{m \times N}$ satisfying the aforementioned sparsity constraints. Denoting the overall system state (plant's state and states of all nodes in the network) by $\hat{\mathbf{x}}[k] = \begin{bmatrix} \mathbf{x}[k]^T & \mathbf{z}[k]^T \end{bmatrix}^T$, the closed-loop system evolves as:

$$
\hat{\mathbf{x}}[k+1] = \underbrace{\begin{bmatrix} \mathbf{A} & \mathbf{BG} \\ \mathbf{HC} & \mathbf{W} \end{bmatrix}}_{\hat{\mathbf{A}}} \underbrace{\begin{bmatrix} \mathbf{x}[k] \\ \mathbf{z}[k] \end{bmatrix}}_{\hat{\mathbf{x}}[k]} + \underbrace{\begin{bmatrix} \mathbf{B}_w \\ \mathbf{0} \end{bmatrix}}_{\hat{\mathbf{B}}} \mathbf{u}_w \tag{5}
$$
$$
= \hat{\mathbf{A}}\hat{\mathbf{x}}[k] + \hat{\mathbf{B}}\mathbf{u}_w[k].
$$

To use the WCN runtime scheme it is essential to determine an appropriate set of link weights $(w_{ij}, h_{ij}$ and $g_{ij})$ at **design-time**, so that the closed loop system is asymptotically stable.[5] When there are no disturbances (i.e., $\mathbf{u}_w[k] \equiv \mathbf{0}$), an initial procedure was proposed for the basic WCN that guarantees that the closed-loop system is stable, or Mean Square Stable (MSS) if the communication links are unreliable.[6]

2.2.1 Advantages of the WCN

The WCN introduces very low communication and computation overhead. The linear iterative runtime procedure (3) is computationally very inexpensive as each node only computes a linear combination of its value and values of its neighbors. This makes it suitable for resource constrained, low-power wireless nodes (e.g., Tmote). Furthermore, the communication overhead is also very small, as each node needs to transmit only its own state once per frame. In the case when a node maintains a scalar state it transmits only *2 bytes* in each message, making it suitable to combine this scheme with periodic message transmissions in existing wireless systems.

Another key benefit is that the WCN can easily handle plants with multiple geographically distributed sensors and actuators, a case that is not easily handled by the "sensor $\rightarrow$ channel $\rightarrow$ controller/estimator $\rightarrow$ channel $\rightarrow$ actuator" setup commonly adopted in networked control design. The existence of a centralized controller might impose a requirement that the sampling time of the plant is greater than or equal to the sum of communication delays, from sensors to the controller and from the controller to the actuator, along with the time required for the computation of the control algorithm. The WCN does not rely on the existence of centralized controllers, and inherently captures the case of nodes exchanging values with the plant at various points in the network. Therefore, when the WCN is used, the network diameter does not affect the sampling period of the plant.

Finally, the WCN utilizes a simple transmission schedule where each node is active only once during a TDMA cycle and the control-loop does not impose end-to-end delay requirements. This allows the network operator to decouple the computation schedule from the communication sched-

ule, which significantly simplifies closed-loop system design and enables compositional design and analysis. As long as each node can send additional states in a single transmission packet, and schedule computation of additional linear procedures, adding a new control loop will not affect the performance of the existing control loops. For example, consider IEEE 802.14.5 networks that have the maximal packet size of 128 bytes. If each plant is controlled using the WCN scheme where all nodes maintain a scalar 16 bit state value, then up to 64 plants can be controlled in parallel.

In this paper, we provide an enhanced WCN scheme that maintains all of these desirable properties, and further incorporates optimality and robustness metrics into the basic scheme.

2.2.2 Synchronization Requirements

For the network sizes considered here, it is necessary to use either hardware-based out-of-band synchronization or some of the built-in synchronization protocols that guarantee low synchronization error between neighboring nodes (e.g., the approach described in [17] guarantees that the maximal synchronization error between neighboring nodes is less than $1 \mu s$). Even for $10 \mu s$ synchronization error between neighboring nodes, for large scale networks with the network diameter less than 100 nodes, maximal synchronization error between nodes is less than 1ms, which is significantly smaller than standard sampling rates of the plant when WCN is used. For example, if communication frames that consist of 16 slots are used, where each slot is 10 ms wide, the sampling period of the plant equals to 160 ms. In this case, synchronization errors would take less than 1% of the sampling period. We employ a synchronized network and use the RT-Link [18] time synchronized protocol in our evaluation. Time synchronized network protocols are the norm in the control automation industry, and two recent standards, WirelessHART[1] and ISA 100.11a [19] utilize a time division multiplexing link protocol.

3. SYNTHESIS OF AN OPTIMAL WCN

In this section we present a design-time method to determine a WCN configuration (i.e., link weights for a network with predefined topology) that minimizes effects of the disturbances acting on the system. More specifically, consider the model of the closed-loop system from (5), and assume that we want to minimize the influence of the disturbance input $\mathbf{u}_w$ on the vector $\hat{\mathbf{y}} = \hat{\mathbf{C}}\hat{\mathbf{x}}[k]$, for some matrix $\hat{\mathbf{C}}$. For example, if we would like to focus on minimizing the effects on the plant's state $\mathbf{x}$, we would define $\hat{\mathbf{C}} = \begin{bmatrix} \mathbf{I} & \mathbf{0} \end{bmatrix}$. Thus, we can consider the vector $\hat{\mathbf{y}}$ as the 'output' of the system:

$$
\hat{\mathbf{x}}[k+1] = \hat{\mathbf{A}}\hat{\mathbf{x}}[k] + \hat{\mathbf{B}}\mathbf{u}_w[k]
$$
$$
\hat{\mathbf{y}} = \hat{\mathbf{C}}\hat{\mathbf{x}}[k]. \tag{6}
$$

To determine the effect of the disturbance on the system's outputs, it is necessary to define a unit of measure to capture the 'size' of discrete-time signals. We will use the norms: $\|\mathbf{v}\|_{\ell_2} \triangleq \left(\sum_{k=0}^{\infty} \|\mathbf{v}[k]\|^2 \right)^{1/2}$ and $\|\mathbf{v}\|_{\ell_\infty} \triangleq \sup_{k \geq 0} \|\mathbf{v}[k]\|$. Furthermore, the notion of a *system gain* is introduced to classify the worst-case system response to limited energy input disturbances.

DEFINITION 1 ([20]). *System gains for the discrete-time system* (6) *are defined as:*

---

[5] A linear system $\mathbf{x}[k+1] = \mathbf{A}\mathbf{x}[k]$ is asymptotically stable if for any $\mathbf{x}[0]$, $\lim_{k \to \infty} \mathbf{x}[k] = \mathbf{0}$. This is equivalent to saying that all eigenvalues of $\mathbf{A}$ have magnitude less than 1.

[6] The system $\mathbf{x}[k+1] = \mathbf{A}_{\theta(k)}\mathbf{x}[k]$, where subscript $\theta(k)$ describes time-variations caused by (probabilistic) drops of communication packets, is mean-square stable if for any initial state $(\mathbf{x}[0], \theta(0))$, $\lim_{k \to \infty} \mathbb{E}\left[\|\mathbf{x}[k]\|^2\right] = 0$, where the expectation is with respect to the probability distribution of the packet drop sequence $\theta(k)$ [15, 16].

- **Energy-to-Peak Gain:** $\gamma_{ep} = \sup_{\|\mathbf{u}_w\|_{\ell_2} \leq 1} \|\hat{\mathbf{y}}\|_{\ell_\infty}$
- **Energy-to-Energy Gain:** $\gamma_{ee} = \sup_{\|\mathbf{u}_w\|_{\ell_2} \leq 1} \|\hat{\mathbf{y}}\|_{\ell_2}$

We will require the following result from [21].

THEOREM 1. *Suppose that the system* (6) *is asymptotically stable and consider any nonnegative* $\gamma \in \mathbb{R}$.
(a) $\gamma_{ep} < \gamma$ *if and only if there exist matrices* $\mathcal{X} \succ 0, \Upsilon \succeq 0$ *and* $\mathcal{Z}$ *such that* $\Upsilon \prec \gamma\mathbf{I}$ *and*

$$\mathcal{R}(\mathcal{X}, \mathcal{Z}, \Upsilon, \mathcal{X}^{-1}) = \begin{bmatrix} \mathcal{X} & \mathcal{Z} & \hat{\mathbf{A}} & \hat{\mathbf{B}} \\ \mathcal{Z}^T & \Upsilon & \hat{\mathbf{C}} & 0 \\ \hat{\mathbf{A}}^T & \hat{\mathbf{C}}^T & \mathcal{X}^{-1} & 0 \\ \hat{\mathbf{B}}^T & 0 & 0 & \mathbf{I} \end{bmatrix} \succ 0 \quad (7)$$

(b) $\gamma_{ee} < \gamma$ *if and only if there exists matrices* $\mathcal{X} \succ 0, \Upsilon \succeq 0$ *such that* $\Upsilon \prec \gamma^2\mathbf{I}$ *and* (7) *holds for* $\mathcal{Z} = \mathbf{0}$.

Only the matrix $\hat{\mathbf{A}}$ contains the WCN parameters, aggregated in the structured matrices $\mathbf{W}, \mathbf{G}, \mathbf{H}$ (from (5)). Our goal is to determine matrices $\mathbf{W}, \mathbf{G}, \mathbf{H}$ that satisfy the imposed structural constraints, along with matrices $\mathcal{X}, \mathcal{Z}, \Upsilon$, for which the value γ is minimized.

The constraint (7) is linear with respect to all variables, except the matrix $\mathcal{X}$ (due to the presence of the term $\mathcal{X}^{-1}$). This term causes the problem of solving the matrix inequality to be non-convex. To ameliorate this issue and efficiently solve the optimization problem, we linearize the $\mathcal{X}^{-1}$ term. As shown in [21], the Taylor series expansion of $\mathcal{X}^{-1}$ 'around' any matrix $\mathcal{X}_k$ is

$$LIN(\mathcal{X}^{-1}, \mathcal{X}_k) = \mathcal{X}_k^{-1} - \mathcal{X}_k^{-1}(\mathcal{X} - \mathcal{X}_k)\mathcal{X}_k^{-1}. \quad (8)$$

With the above linearization we obtain a linear matrix inequality (LMI) for the constraint 7. As in [21, 22], we can now define an iterative algorithm to minimize γ, while ensuring that the constraint from (7) is satisfied. This is achieved by replacing the term $\mathcal{X}^{-1}$ with $LIN(\mathcal{X}^{-1}, \mathcal{X}_k)$ in each iteration, which results in Algorithm 1. Note that $\hat{\mathbf{A}}(\mathbf{W}, \mathbf{H}, \mathbf{G})$ denotes the matrix $\hat{\mathbf{A}}$ obtained from matrices $\mathbf{W}, \mathbf{H}, \mathbf{G}$ as defined in (5). Finally, for γ obtained from Algorithm 1, $\sqrt{\gamma}$ should be used if we had optimized for γ_{ee}.

Consider the sequence $\{\gamma_k\}_{k \geq 0}$ obtained from Algorithm 1. As shown in [21], the linearization from (8) guarantees that for each $k \geq 0$, in step $k + 1$ there exists a feasible matrix in an open neighborhood of the point $\mathcal{X}_k$ for which there exists γ, such that $\gamma \leq \gamma_k$. Since γ_{k+1} is the minimum in that iteration, it follows that $\gamma_{k+1} \leq \gamma$. Thus, the sequence $\{\gamma_k\}_{k \geq 0}$ is non-increasing and bounded ($\gamma_k \geq 0$), meaning that it will always converge. Since we are optimizing a convex function over a non-convex set, by linearizing the constraints we might obtain a sub-optimal WCN configuration. The final result and the convergence rate depend on the initial point (from Step 1. of the algorithm). Finally, the smallest ϵ for which we can find an optimal controller can be obtained using bisection on the parameter ϵ.

4. ROBUSTNESS TO LINK FAILURES

We now describe the main limitation of the basic WCN, and extend the WCN scheme to improve its robustness to link failures.

The unreliability of wireless communication links is one of the main drawbacks when wireless networks are used for control. When communication links in the feedback loop fail according to a given probability distribution, the notion of

---

Algorithm 1 *Design-time* procedure used to extract optimal WCN configuration

1. Set $\epsilon > 0, k = 0$. Find a feasible point $\mathcal{X}_0, \mathcal{Y}_0, \Upsilon_0 \succ 0$, $\hat{\mathbf{A}}(\mathbf{W_0}, \mathbf{H_0}, \mathbf{G_0})$, such that $\mathcal{R}(\mathcal{X}_0, \mathcal{Z}, \Upsilon_0, \mathcal{Y}_0) \succ 0$, $\mathcal{X}_0 \succeq \mathcal{Y}_0^{-1}$ and $(\mathbf{W_0}, \mathbf{H_0}, \mathbf{G_0}) \in \Psi$. If a feasible point does not exist, it is not possible to stabilize the system with this network topology.

2. At iteration k ($k \geq 0$), from $\mathcal{X}_k$ obtain the matrix $\mathcal{X}_{k+1}$ and scalar γ_{k+1} by solving the LMI problem

$$\mathcal{X}_{k+1} = \arg \min_{\mathcal{X}, \mathcal{Z}, \Upsilon, \mathbf{W}, \mathbf{H}, \mathbf{G}, \gamma_{k+1}} \gamma_{k+1} \quad (9)$$

$$\mathcal{R}(\mathcal{X}, \mathcal{Z}, \Upsilon, LIN(\mathcal{X}^{-1}, \mathcal{X}_k)) \succ 0, \quad (10)$$

$$\Upsilon \prec \gamma_{k+1}\mathbf{I}, \quad (11)$$

$$(\mathbf{W}, \mathbf{H}, \mathbf{G}) \in \Psi, \quad \mathcal{X} \succ 0, \Upsilon \succeq 0 \quad (12)$$

if γ_{ee} is being optimized, add the constraint $\mathcal{Z} = \mathbf{0}$.

3. If $\gamma_{k+1} < \epsilon$ stop the algorithm. Otherwise, set $k = k+1$ and go to the step **2.**

---

asymptotic stability is typically relaxed to settle for *mean square stability* (MSS), where the expected value of the norm of the state stays bounded. For the basic WCN, we proposed a design-time procedure that can be used to extract a stabilizing configuration that guarantees MSS despite unreliable communication links [12]. For example, consider the system from Fig. 3 with a scalar plant, where $\alpha = 2$ (the plant is unstable), and assume that the link between node v_2 and the actuator is reliable (i.e., never drops packets). The basic WCN scheme, where each node maintains a scalar state, guarantees that the closed-loop system is MSS for probabilities of packet drops $\leq 1.18\%$.

To place this result in context, it is worth comparing it with the theoretical limit of robustness in lossy networks from [13]. The work in [13] considers a system with a plant controlled by a centralized controller, which is connected to the plant using a single wireless link between a sensor and the controller. In addition, the controller is connected to the actuators with a set of wired connections. It was shown that for this setup, the system can not be stabilized with a linear controller for probability of message drops p greater than $\frac{1}{|\lambda_{max}|^2}$, where $|\lambda_{max}|$ denotes the maximal norm of the plant's eigenvalues (i.e., eigenvalues of $\mathbf{A}$ from (1)). For the plant from Fig. 3, this would mean that a centralized controller in the aforementioned setup cannot provide MSS of the plant if the probability of message drops is higher than 25% (since $\alpha = 2$). This value is significantly larger than the 1.18% value obtained when the basic WCN scheme is used. We now show how the basic WCN formulation presented in (3), (4) can be modified to significantly improve tolerance to packet drops.

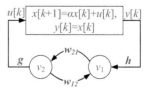

Figure 3: An example of the WCN: A plant with a scalar state controlled by a WCN.

4.1 WCN with Observer Style Updates

To improve WCN robustness to independent link failures, we now allow each node in the network to use different weights in each time step, depending on which neighbors' transmissions were successfully received. Thus, we define the update procedure as:

$$z_j[k+1] = \tilde{w}_{jj}z_j[k] + \sum_{i \in \mathcal{N}_{v_j}} \tilde{w}_{ji}z_i[k], \,^7 \qquad (13)$$

where $\tilde{w}_{ji} = 0$ if the message from the node v_i was not received, or w_{ji} otherwise.[8] More importantly, $\tilde{w}_{jj}$ depends on a newly introduced set of link weights (q_{ji}): $\tilde{w}_{jj} = w_{jj} - \sum_{i \in \mathcal{N}_{v_j}} \tilde{q}_{ji}$. Here, $\tilde{q}_{ji} = 0$ if the message from the node v_i was not received, and q_{ji} (a free parameter that will be carefully designed) otherwise.

To model the WCN that employs the above scheme, we need to model the links in the network. We utilize the approach proposed in [16], where each unreliable link $\xi_{ji} = (v_i, v_j)$ (i.e., $v_i \to v_j$) can be modeled as a memoryless, discrete, independent and identically distributed (IID) random process ξ_{ji}. Here, IID implies that the random variables $\{\xi_{ji}[k]\}_{k \geq 0}$ are IID.[9] For each link, these random processes map each transmitted value t_{ji} into a received value $\xi_{ji}[k]t_{ji}$ (see Fig. 4).

With this link model, (13) can be described as:

$$z_j[k+1] = (w_{jj} - \sum_{i \in \mathcal{N}_{v_j}} \xi_{ji}q_{ji})z_j[k] + \sum_{i \in \mathcal{N}_{v_j}} \xi_{ji}w_{ji}z_i[k],$$

REMARK 1. *If we consider the case with reliable communication links, the update procedure for each node v_j in the network can be described as:*

$$z_j[k+1] = w_{jj}z_j[k] + \sum_{i \in \mathcal{N}_{v_j}} (w_{ji}z_i[k] - q_{ji}z_j[k]), \qquad (14)$$

Since the above equation has the standard observer structure [23], we refer to this scheme as the WCN with observer style updates (as in [24]).

Following the approach from [16], each link described with a random process ξ_{ji} can be specified with a fixed gain, corresponding to the mean value of the random variable, and the zero-mean random part: $\xi_{ji} = \mu_{ji} + \Delta_{ji}$. For example, if each link (i.e., random process ξ_{ji}) is described as a Bernoulli process with probability $p_{ji} \leq 1$ (i.e., the link delivers the transmitted message with probability p_{ji}), then $\mu_{ji} = p_{ji}$ and Δ_{ji} can have values $-p_{ji}$ and $1 - p_{ji}$, with probabilities $1 - p_{ji}$ and p_{ji}, respectively. Therefore, the above procedure becomes:

$$z_j[k+1] = (w_{jj} - \sum_{i \in \mathcal{N}_{v_j}} \mu_{ji}q_{ji})z_j[k] + \sum_{i \in \mathcal{N}_{v_j}} \mu_{ji}w_{ji}z_i[k]$$
$$+ \sum_{i \in \mathcal{N}_{v_j}} \Delta_{ji}(w_{ji}z_i[k] - q_{ji}z_j[k]).$$

We define $r_t[k] := (w_{ji}z_i[k] - q_{ji}z_j[k])$, for each link $t = (v_i, v_j)$. Also, for each link $t = (s_i, v_j)$ we denote $r_t[k] := (h_{ji}y_i[k] - q_{ji}z_j[k])$. After aggregating all of the $r_t[k]$'s in a

---
[7]A similar update is introduced for nodes that receive sensor values. This part has been omitted for ease of exposition.
[8]Although these weights are technically time varying (i.e., they depend on k), we use this notation for simplicity.
[9]We will address these assumptions later in this section.

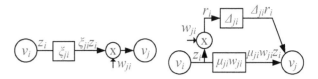

Figure 4: Communication over a non-deterministic channel; (a) A link between nodes v_i and v_j; (b) Link transformation into a robust control form.

vector $\mathbf{r}[k]$ of length N_l (where N_l is the number of links), we obtain:

$$\mathbf{r}[k] = \mathbf{J}^{or} \begin{bmatrix} \mathbf{y}[k] \\ \mathbf{z}[k] \end{bmatrix} = \underbrace{\mathbf{J}^{or} \begin{bmatrix} \mathbf{C} & 0 \\ 0 & \mathbf{I}_N \end{bmatrix}}_{\hat{\mathbf{J}}^{or}} \hat{\mathbf{x}}[k]. \qquad (15)$$

Each row of the matrix $\mathbf{J}^{or} \in \mathbb{R}^{N_l \times (N+p)}$ contains up to two nonzero elements, equal to a gain w_t, h_t, g_t or $-q_t$.

This allows us to model the behavior of the closed-loop system with unreliable communication. Specifically, the update equation for each node v_j is:

$$z_j[k+1] = (w_{jj} - \sum_{i \in \mathcal{N}_{v_j}} \mu_{ji}q_{ji})z_j[k] + \sum_{t=(v_i,v_j)} \mu_t w_t z_i[k]$$
$$+ \sum_{t=(s_i,v_j)} \mu_t h_t y_i[k] + \sum_{t=(v_i,v_j)} \Delta_t[k]r_t[k] + \sum_{t=(s_i,v_j)} \Delta_t[k]r_t[k]$$

Similarly, the input value applied by each actuator at time k is:

$$u_j[k] = \sum_{t=(v_i,a_j)} \mu_t g_t z_i[k] + \sum_{t=(v_i,a_j)} \Delta_t[k]r_t[k].$$

Finally, denoting $\Delta[k] = \text{diag}(\{\Delta_t[k]\}_{t=1}^{N_l})$, the above expressions can be written in vector form as:

$$\mathbf{z}[k+1] = \mathbf{W}_\mu \mathbf{z}[k] + \mathbf{H}_\mu \mathbf{y}[k] + \mathbf{J}_v^{dst}\Delta[k]\mathbf{r}[k], \qquad (16)$$
$$\mathbf{u}[k] = \mathbf{G}_\mu \mathbf{z}[k] + \mathbf{J}_u^{dst}\Delta[k]\mathbf{r}[k], \qquad (17)$$

where all elements of matrices $\mathbf{W}_\mu, \mathbf{H}_\mu$ and $\mathbf{G}_\mu$ (except the diagonal entries of $\mathbf{W}_\mu$) are of the form $\mu_{ji}w_{ji}, \mu_{ji}h_{ji}$ and $\mu_{ji}g_{ji}$, respectively. The diagonal entries of $\mathbf{W}_\mu$ are of the form $w_{jj} - \sum_{i \in \mathcal{N}_{v_j}} \mu_{ji}q_{ji}$. The binary matrices $\mathbf{J}_v^{dst}$ and $\mathbf{J}_u^{dst}$ are designed in a way that each row of the matrices selects elements of the vector $\Delta[k]\mathbf{r}[k]$ that are added to the linear combinations calculated by the nodes and the actuators. If we denote $\mathbf{J}^{dst} = \begin{bmatrix} \mathbf{J}_u^{dst} \\ \mathbf{J}_v^{dst} \end{bmatrix}$ the overall system with unreliable links can be modeled as:

$$\hat{\mathbf{x}}[k+1] = \underbrace{\begin{bmatrix} \mathbf{A} & \mathbf{B}\mathbf{G}_\mu \\ \mathbf{H}_\mu\mathbf{C} & \mathbf{W}_\mu \end{bmatrix}}_{\hat{\mathbf{A}}_\mu} \hat{\mathbf{x}}[k] + \underbrace{\begin{bmatrix} \mathbf{B} & 0 \\ 0 & \mathbf{I}_N \end{bmatrix}\mathbf{J}^{dst}}_{\hat{\mathbf{J}}^{dst}} \Delta[k]\mathbf{r}[k],$$
$$(18)$$

with $\mathbf{r}[k]$ given by (15). Now, using the same approach as in [16, 12], the following theorem can be proven.

THEOREM 2. *The system from (18) is MSS if and only if exist matrices $\mathcal{X}, \mathcal{Y} \succ 0$ and scalars $\alpha_1, ..., \alpha_{N_l}$ such that*

$$\begin{bmatrix} \mathcal{X} - \hat{\mathbf{J}}^{dst}diag\{\alpha\}(\hat{\mathbf{J}}^{dst})^T & \hat{\mathbf{A}}_\mu \\ \hat{\mathbf{A}}_\mu^T & \mathcal{Y} \end{bmatrix} \succ 0 \qquad (19)$$

$$\mathcal{Y} = \mathcal{X}^{-1} \qquad (20)$$

$$\alpha_i \geq \sigma_i^2(\hat{\mathbf{J}}^{or})_i \mathcal{Y}^{-1}(\hat{\mathbf{J}}^{or})_i^T, \; \forall i \in \{1, ..., N_l\} \qquad (21)$$

where $(\hat{\mathbf{J}}^{or})_i$ denotes the ith row of the matrix $\hat{\mathbf{J}}^{or}$.

A procedure based on LMIs, with the same structure as Algorithm 1, can be used in this case to compute a WCN configuration that guarantees MSS of the closed-loop system with error-prone links. The difference from Algorithm 1 is that in Step 2, the following problem should be solved:

$$\mathcal{X}_{k+1} = \arg \min_{\mathcal{X}, \mathcal{Y}, \Upsilon, \mathbf{W}, \mathbf{H}, \mathbf{G}} tr(\Upsilon)$$

$$\mathcal{Y} - LIN(\mathcal{X}^{-1}, \mathcal{X}_k) \prec \Upsilon, \quad \mathcal{X} \succeq \mathcal{Y}^{-1}$$

such that the constraints from (19),(21),(12) are valid,

where $tr(\mathbf{A})$ denotes the trace of the matrix $\mathbf{A}$. Note that the above algorithm adds only one additional LMI constraint for each link in the network.

4.1.1 Validity of the Assumptions

While developing the model of the WCN from (16), we have assumed that all links in the network are memoryless and independent. Memoryless channels can be obtained if channel hopping is used at the network layer [25]. However, the physical placement of the nodes might introduce correlation between some of the network links.

If these IID assumptions are not valid (or too simplistic), we must model correlation between links along with more complex link failures (such as those induced by a Markov process). In these cases, an approach similar to [15] can be used, which would result in an exponential number of additional constraints introduced to deal with link failures (compared to the linear number of additional constraints introduced under the IID assumption of independent and memoryless channels). Except for very large scale systems, the observer style update procedure is practical as the computation of WCN configurations $(\mathbf{W}, \mathbf{H}, \mathbf{G})$ is only required at design time.

4.1.2 Evaluation

We evaluated the performance of the proposed scheme by modeling all links as independent Bernoulli processes. To analyze robustness of the WCN with observer style updates, we first analyzed the performance of WCNs with $N \geq 2$ nodes that create a complete graph. The WCN is used for control of a single-state plant shown in Fig. 3 (with $\alpha > 1$). Node v_1 receives the plant output $y[k] = x[k]$ at each time-step k, and the input to the plant is derived as a scaled version of the transmission of the node v_2 (i.e., $u[k] = gz_2[k]$ for a scalar g). Using the bisection method from [15], we extracted the maximal probabilities of message drops (p_m) for which there exists a stabilizing configuration that ensures MSS.

We considered two scenarios: In the first scenario, we have compared the performance of the basic WCN with that of the WCN with observer style updates (denoted oWCN). We analyzed networks where all the links are unreliable, described with the same probability of packet drops p (including the links between the plant and the network nodes). The results are presented in Fig. 5(a). In addition, we have investigated the case where the link between node v_2 and the plant's actuator is reliable (without any packet drops). The results are shown in Fig. 5(b). As can be observed, the proposed scheme **significantly** improves system robustness to link failures. *For example, the WCN with observer style updates guarantees MSS for the system from Fig. 3 even when*

	WCN (scalar state)	WCN ($\mathbb{R}^2$ state)	oWCN (scalar state)	oWCN ($\mathbb{R}^2$ state)
$N = 2$	$p_m = 0.69\%$	$p_m = 0.72\%$	$p_m = 1.64\%$	$p_m = 1.82\%$
$N = 3$	$p_m = 0.74\%$	$p_m = 0.77\%$	$p_m = 1.66\%$	$p_m = 1.88\%$
$N = 4$	$p_m = 0.77\%$	$p_m = 0.79\%$	$p_m = 1.66\%$	$p_m = 1.88\%$

(a) With all links being unreliable

	WCN (scalar state)	WCN ($\mathbb{R}^2$ state)	oWCN (scalar state)	oWCN ($\mathbb{R}^2$ state)
$N = 2$	$p_m = 1.18\%$	$p_m = 1.30\%$	$p_m = 10.46\%$	$p_m = 17.82\%$
$N = 3$	$p_m = 1.32\%$	$p_m = 1.46\%$	$p_m = 11.24\%$	$p_m = 17.88\%$
$N = 4$	$p_m = 1.41\%$	$p_m = 1.54\%$	$p_m = 11.46\%$	$p_m = 17.88\%$
		oWCN ($\mathbb{R}^3$ state)	oWCN ($\mathbb{R}^4$ state)	oWCN ($\mathbb{R}^5$ state)
$N = 2$		$p_m = 20.40\%$	$p_m = 20.48\%$	$p_m = 20.64\%$

(b) With a reliable link between the node v_2 and actuator

Figure 5: Maximal probabilities of link failures for which the closed-loop system from Fig. 3 ($\alpha = 2$) is MSS, when controlled without (WCN) and with observer style updates (oWCN).

the probability of link failures is more than 20% (compared to 1.5% for the basic WCN). Similarly, going back to the discussion from the beginning of the section, we have shown in this simple example that the WCN performance is much closer to that of the optimal centralized controllers used for control over wireless links (guaranteeing MSS with up to 25% packet drops).

Using the observer style updates, similar significantly improved results were obtained for the more complex examples from [12], including larger plants with multiple inputs and outputs, controlled by a mesh network with 9 nodes.

5. ROBUSTNESS TO NODE FAILURES

The stability of the closed-loop system, described by (5), can be affected by node crash failures (i.e., nodes that stop working and drop out of the network). Currently, we have considered two approaches to deal with the node failures. One obvious method to deal with up to k node failures is to precompute at the design-time a set of $N_k = \sum_{j=0}^{k} \binom{N}{j}$ different stabilizing configurations $(\mathbf{W}, \mathbf{H}, \mathbf{G})$ that correspond to all possible choices of k or fewer failed nodes. In this case, each node would need to maintain N_k different sets of link weights for all its incoming links. For example, if each node in the WCN maintains a scalar state, a node with d neighbors would have to maintain on the order of $d \cdot N_k$ different scalar weights. The switching between the precomputed stabilizing configurations could be done either by implementing the detection algorithm from [26], or by having the neighbors of failed nodes broadcast the news of the failures throughout the network, which will prompt all nodes to switch to the appropriate choice of $(\mathbf{W}, \mathbf{H}, \mathbf{G})$.

A more sophisticated method for dealing with the node failures would be to design the WCN in a way that even if some of the nodes fail, the closed-loop system remains stable. For simplicity, consider a WCN that can deal with a single node failure. Let us denote with $\hat{\mathbf{A}}_i$ the matrix $\hat{\mathbf{A}}$ from (5) in the case when node i dies. This is equivalent to setting to zero the ith row of matrices $\mathbf{W}$ and $\mathbf{H}$, along with the ith column of $\mathbf{W}$ and $\mathbf{G}$:

$$\hat{\mathbf{A}}_i \triangleq \begin{bmatrix} \mathbf{A} & \mathbf{BGI}_N^i \\ \mathbf{I}_N^i \mathbf{HC} & \mathbf{I}_N^i \mathbf{WI}_N^i \end{bmatrix}, \quad i = 1, \dots, N, \quad (22)$$

Here, $\mathbf{I}_N^i$ denotes $N \times N$ diagonal matrix, with all ones on the diagonal except at the ith position. A sufficient condition for system stability in this case is that there exists a positive definite matrix $\mathcal{X}$ (and, thus, a common Lyapunov function $V(\hat{\mathbf{x}}) = \hat{\mathbf{x}}^T \mathcal{X} \hat{\mathbf{x}}$) such that $\mathcal{X} - \hat{\mathbf{A}}^T \mathcal{X} \hat{\mathbf{A}} \succ \mathbf{0}$ and

$$\mathcal{X} - \hat{\mathbf{A}}_i^T \mathcal{X} \hat{\mathbf{A}}_i \succ \mathbf{0}, \; i = 1, 2, \ldots N. \quad (23)$$

Therefore, the procedure from the previous section with additional N LMI constraints, can be used to extract a stabilizing configuration that can deal with a single node failure. However, in this case it is necessary to design the network in a way that guarantees that such a stabilizing configuration exists. Initial results on these topological conditions have been presented in [14].

6. CONTROL OF CONTINUOUS-TIME PLANTS

Optimal and stabilizing WCN configurations can be obtained using algorithms developed from the closed-loop system model (5) that contains a discrete-time model of the plant (1). However, a similar framework can be used for control of continuous-time plants by discretizing the controlled plant, while taking into account a subtle delay introduced by the communication schedule. To illustrate this, consider a standard continuous-time plant model:

$$\dot{\mathbf{x}}(t) = \mathbf{A}_c \mathbf{x}(t) + \mathbf{B}_c \mathbf{u}(t)$$
$$\mathbf{y}(t) = \mathbf{C}_c \mathbf{x}(t), \quad (24)$$

with input $\mathbf{x}(t) \in \mathbb{R}^n$, output $\mathbf{y}(t) \in \mathbb{R}^p$, $\mathbf{u}(t) \in \mathbb{R}^m$ and matrices $\mathbf{A}_c, \mathbf{B}_c, \mathbf{C}_c$ of the appropriate dimensions.[10] We denote the sampling period of the plant by T, and we assume that all sensors sample the plant outputs at the beginning of the zero-th slot (as shown in Fig. 6(a)). We also assume that all actuators are scheduled to apply their newly calculated inputs at the beginning of the hth time slot. Note that $h > 0$, because from (4) each actuator has to first receive state values from all of its neighbors, before calculating its next plant input. Similarly, from (4) $h \geq \max(d_{a_i})$, where d_{a_i} denotes the number of neighbors of the actuator a_i.

Therefore, the new inputs will be applied to the plant with the delay $\tau = hT_{sl}$, where T_{sl} is the size of communication slots. This results in the input signal with the form shown in Fig. 6(b). Denoting the number of slots in a communication frame by F, we can write $T = FT_{sl}$. Using the approach from [3, 5], we describe the system:

$$\dot{\mathbf{x}}(t) = \mathbf{A}_c \mathbf{x}(t) + \mathbf{B}_c \mathbf{u}(t),$$
$$\mathbf{y}(t) = \mathbf{C}_c \mathbf{x}(t), \quad t \in [kT + \tau, (k+1)T + \tau), \quad (25)$$
$$\mathbf{u}(t^+) = \mathbf{G}\mathbf{z}[k], \quad t \in \{kT + \tau, k = 0, 1, 2, \ldots\}$$

where $\mathbf{u}(t^+)$ is a piecewise continuous function and only changes values at time instances $kT + \tau$, $k = 0, 1, \ldots$. From the above equation, the discretized model of the system with the sampling period T can be represented as [23]:

$$\mathbf{x}[k+1] = \mathbf{A}\mathbf{x}[k] + \mathbf{B}\mathbf{G}\mathbf{z}[k] + \mathbf{B}^-\mathbf{G}\mathbf{z}[k-1]$$
$$\mathbf{y}[k] = \mathbf{C}\mathbf{x}[k], \quad (26)$$

[10] For simplicity we do not model disturbance inputs to the plant. However, the approach presented in this section can readily handle that scenario.

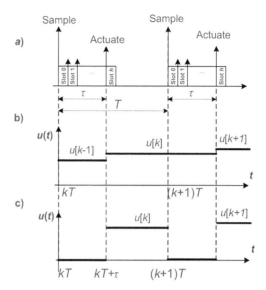

Figure 6: (a) Scheduling sampling/actuation at the start of the slots; (b) Timing diagram for the first type of plant inputs; (c) Plant inputs when actuators reset the inputs at the beginning of the frames.

where $\mathbf{x}[k] = \mathbf{x}(kT)$, $k \geq 0$ and

$$\mathbf{A} = e^{\mathbf{A}_c T}, \; \mathbf{B} = \int_0^{T-\tau} e^{\mathbf{A}_c \delta} \mathbf{B}_c d\delta, \; \mathbf{B}^- = \int_{T-\tau}^T e^{\mathbf{A}_c \delta} \mathbf{B}_c d\delta. \quad (27)$$

When the communication schedule is extracted and the network is configured, the matrices $\mathbf{A}, \mathbf{B}$ and $\mathbf{B}^-$ obtain fixed-values that depend on the continuous-time plant dynamics, communication frame size T (i.e., the sampling period of the plant) and the utilized communication schedule (as it determines the value for h).

If each actuator applies its current input only until the end of the corresponding frame and then forces its input to zero until the next actuation slot (i.e., h^{th} slot), the input signals would have the form shown in Fig. 6(c) (instead of the form from Fig. 6(b)). In this case, the discretized system could be specified as in (26), (27), with the difference that $\mathbf{B}^- = \mathbf{0}$. Therefore, the discrete-time system takes the form from (1), and stabilizing and optimal configurations can be obtained using the procedures described in the previous sections. However, due to the delay τ, the resulting discrete-time system could be uncontrollable, which in the general case would mean that there is no stabilizing configuration for the closed-loop system.

In situations where $(\mathbf{A}, \mathbf{B})$ is not controllable it is necessary for all actuators to apply their 'old' inputs until new inputs are available (as shown in Fig. 6(b)). This results in a discrete-time plant that does not have the form from (1), and the previous algorithms cannot be directly employed. However, by defining a new vector $\tilde{\mathbf{x}}[k] \triangleq \begin{bmatrix} \mathbf{x}[k]^T & \mathbf{u}[k-1]^T \end{bmatrix}^T$ the discrete-time system can be described as:

$$\tilde{\mathbf{x}}[k+1] = \underbrace{\begin{bmatrix} \mathbf{A} & \mathbf{B}^- \\ \mathbf{0} & \mathbf{0} \end{bmatrix}}_{\tilde{\mathbf{A}}} \tilde{\mathbf{x}}[k] + \underbrace{\begin{bmatrix} \mathbf{B} \\ \mathbf{I} \end{bmatrix}}_{\tilde{\mathbf{B}}} \mathbf{u}[k] = \tilde{\mathbf{A}}\tilde{\mathbf{x}}[k] + \tilde{\mathbf{B}}\mathbf{u}[k],$$

$$\mathbf{y}[k] = \underbrace{\begin{bmatrix} \mathbf{C} & \mathbf{0} \end{bmatrix}}_{\tilde{\mathbf{C}}} \tilde{\mathbf{x}}[k] = \tilde{\mathbf{C}}\tilde{\mathbf{x}}[k]$$

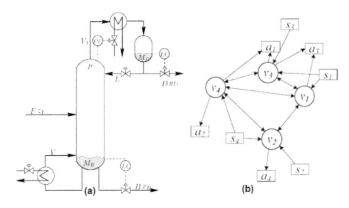

Figure 7: (a) Structure of the distillation column; (b) The network topology of the WCN corresponding to the sensor and actuator positions.

The above system has the same form as (1) and, therefore, we can use the aforementioned algorithms to obtain a stabilizing or optimal configurations of the WCN.

7. PROCESS CONTROL APPLICATION

The WCN has been deployed on a process-in-the-loop testbed with a plant running in Simulink and the plant's sensors and actuators connected to analog interfaces (see Fig. 8(a)). We first describe the plant's model, then the closed-loop wireless control test-bed and finally demonstrate the WCN use for control of the plant.

7.1 Case Study Description

To illustrate the use of the WCN, we consider the distillation column control (Fig. 7(a)), a well-known process control problem described in [27]. Four input flows (in $[mols/s]$) are available for the column control: reflux (L), boilup (V), distillate (D) and bottom flow (B). The goal is to control four outputs: x_D - top composition, x_B - bottom composition, M_D - liquid levels in condenser, and M_B - liquid levels in the reboiler (in $[mol]$). Finally, the column has two disturbances, feed flow-rate F and feed composition z_F. The columns are described using the continuous-time Linear Time Invariant (LTI) model from [27], where the state-space contains 8 states.

7.2 WCN Experimental Platform

We have implemented the WCN scheme on FireFly embedded wireless nodes [28] and TI's MSP430F5438 Experimenter Boards, both equipped with IEEE 802.15.4 standard-compliant radio transceivers. FireFly is a low-cost, low-power platform based on Atmel ATmega1281 8-bit microcontroller, while the experimenters board uses a 16-bit MSP430 microcontroller. Both platforms can be used for TDMA-based communication with the RT-Link protocol [18], and support in-band synchronization provided as a part of the protocol.

The WCN procedure on each wireless node was implemented as a simple task executed on top of the nano-RK, a Real-Time Operating System (RTOS) [29]. The WCN task had a 140.64ms period, equal to the RT-Link frame size (RT-Link was configured to use 16 slots of size 8.79 ms). Since the WCN requires a TTA, nano-RK has been modified to enable scheduling of sensing and actuation at the start of

the desired slots. This guarantees synchronized actions at all sensors and all actuators.

The column, modeled as a continuous-time LTI system along with disturbances and measurement noise was run in Simulink in real-time using Real-Time Windows Target [30]. The interface between the model and the real hardware were two National Instruments PCI-6229 boards which provided analog outputs that correspond to the Simulink model's outputs (see Fig. 8(a)). The output signals were saturated between -4V and 4V, due to NI boards limitations. Also, to provide inputs to the Simulink model, the boards sampled the analog input signals within range [-4V, 4V], at a 1 kHz rate. Finally, Simulink's input and output signals were monitored and controlled with 4 sensors and 4 actuators positioned according to the distillation column structure (Fig. 7(a)). In addition, 4 real wireless controller nodes ($v_1 - v_4$) were added, resulting in the topology shown in Fig. 7(b).

7.3 Results

From the communication and computation schedules, we obtained the discrete-time plant model using the discretization procedure from Section 6 (Eqs. (26),(27)), with sampling rate $T = 140.64\ ms$ (RT-Link frame size).

We first investigated the problem of providing MSS of the closed-loop system with uncorrelated random link failures and single node failures. Assigning each node to maintain a scalar state, using the procedures from Sections 4 and 5 we derived a stabilizing WCN configuration for the topology presented in Fig. 7(b) and the discretized LTI plant model. To solve the convex optimization problems we used the CVX, a package for specifying and solving convex programs [31].

We were able to obtain only WCN configurations that maintain stability if one of the nodes v_1-v_3 fails, meaning that the constraint from (23) for the node v_4 was violated (without v_4 the topology violates the conditions from [14], for existence of a stabilizing configuration). Fig. 9 shows obtained measurements where the disturbance inputs F, z_F were set to zero, while we provided periodical pulses to the input L. Although the output of the plant degrades when the node v_1 is turned off, the WCN maintains system stability. However, if the node v_4 is turned off, the system becomes unstable (shown in Fig. 10 - after the node is turned back

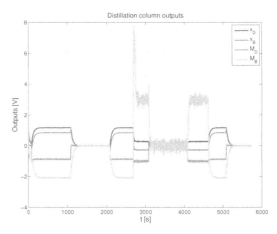

Figure 9: Plant outputs for a stabilizing WCN configuration. Node v_1 has been turned off at time $t = 1680\ s$ and turned back on at $t = 4560\ s$.

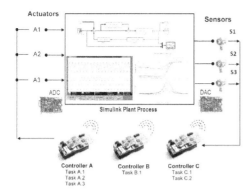 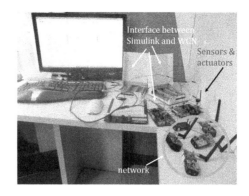

Figure 8: Process-in-the-loop simulation of the distillation column control; (a) The plant model is simulated in Simulink, while the WCN is implemented on FireFly nodes; (b) Experimental setup used for the WCN validation.

on, the system slowly, due to the output saturation, returns to stability). Finally, we showed that if a node was added, connected to actuator a_2, sensor s_4 and nodes v_2, v_4, we could maintain stability if one of the node fails.

We also considered optimal WCN design that minimizes effects of disturbance inputs F, z_F. Using Algorithm 1 we computed an optimal WCN configuration for energy to peak minimization. The obtained measurements for a setup with periodical F impulses are shown in Fig. 11. Fig. 11(b) and Fig. 11(a) present the plant outputs for the optimal and stable WCN configurations. As shown in Fig. 11(c), the norm of the output controlled with the optimal configuration is almost 5 times smaller than the norm with the stabilizing WCN.

8. CONCLUSION

We have extended the concept of the Wireless Control Network, where the network itself acts as a fully distributed controller. We have first addressed the WCN synthesis problem to guarantee *optimal* performance of the plant with respect to standard cost functions. Second, by including the observer style updates in the simple, linear iterative procedure, we have been able to significantly increase *robustness*

of the closed-loop system to link failures. We have also proposed a method to extract a stabilizing configuration for the WCN that can deal with node failures. Finally, we have extended the synthesis procedure to deal with continuous-time plants, and demonstrated how the WCN can be used on an industrial application, using a process-in-the-loop setup with real hardware. In future, we aim to introduce complex control operations (e.g., Kalman filtering, model predictive control) and investigate heterogeneous nodes with varied computation/communication capabilities.

9. REFERENCES

[1] HART Communication Foundation. Why WirelessHART? White Paper, Oct. 2007.

[2] S. Amidi and A. Chernoguzov. Wireless process control network architecture overview. White Paper, Mar. 2009.

[3] J. P. Hespanha, P. Naghshtabrizi, and Y. Xu. A survey of recent results in networked control systems. *Proceedings of the IEEE, Special Issue on Technology of Networked Control Systems*, 95(1):138 – 162, 2007.

[4] R. Alur, A.D'Innocenzo, K. H. Johansson, G. J. Pappas, and G. Weiss. Compositional modeling and analysis of multi-hop control networks. *IEEE Transactions on Automatic Control*, 56(10):2345–2357, Oct. 2011.

[5] W. Zhang, M.S. Branicky, and S.M. Phillips. Stability of networked control systems. *IEEE Control Systems Magazine*, 21(1):84–99, 2001.

[6] A. Saifullah, Y. Xu, C. Lu, and Y. Chen. Real-Time Scheduling for WirelessHART Networks. In *31st IEEE Real-Time Systems Symposium*, pages 150 –159, 2010.

[7] M. Pajic and R. Mangharam. Embedded virtual machines for robust wireless control and actuation. In *RTAS'10: 16th IEEE Real-Time and Embedded Technology and Applications Symposium*, pages 79–88, 2010.

[8] G. Fiore, V. Ercoli, A.J. Isaksson, K. Landernäs, and M. D. Di Benedetto. Multi-hop Multi-channel Scheduling for Wireless Control in WirelessHART Networks. In *IEEE Conference on Emerging Technology & Factory Automation*, pages 1 – 8, 2009.

[9] A. D'Innocenzo, G. Weiss, R. Alur, A.J. Isaksson, K.H. Johansson, and G.J. Pappas. Scalable scheduling

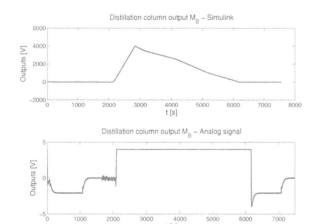

Figure 10: Distillation column output M_B. Node v_4 has been turned off at $t = 2140 \ s$ and back on at $t = 2860 \ s$. Top - Simulink signal; bottom - analog signal, saturated at 4V.

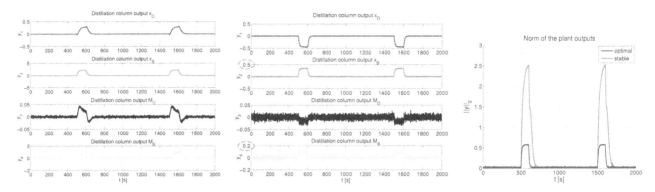

Figure 11: Distillation column outputs; (a) For a stable WCN configuration; (b) For an optimal WCN configuration (note the axes scales); (c) Comparison of the output vector norms for the stable and the optimal WCN configurations.

algorithms for wireless networked control systems. In *CASE'09: IEEE International Conference on Automation Science and Engineering*, pages 409–414, 2009.

[10] S. Graham, G. Baliga, and P.R. Kumar. Abstractions, architecture, mechanisms, and a middleware for networked control. *IEEE Transactions on Automatic Control*, 54(7):1490–1503, 2009.

[11] H. Kopetz and G. Bauer. The Time-Triggered Architecture. *Proceedings of the IEEE*, 91(1):112–126, 2003.

[12] M. Pajic, S. Sundaram, G. J. Pappas, and R. Mangharam. The Wireless Control Network: A New Approach for Control over Networks. *IEEE Transactions on Automatic Control*, 56(10):2305–2318, 2011.

[13] C. N. Hadjicostis and R. Touri. Feedback control utilizing packet dropping network links. In *Proceedings of the 41st IEEE Conference on Decision and Control*, pages 1205–1210, 2002.

[14] M. Pajic, S. Sundaram, G. J. Pappas, and R. Mangharam. Topological Conditions for Wireless Control Networks. In *Proceedings of the 50th IEEE Conference on Decision and Control*, pages 2353–2360, 2011.

[15] P. Seiler and R. Sengupta. Analysis of communication losses in vehicle control problems. In *Proceedings of the American Control Conference*, pages 1491–1496, 2001.

[16] N. Elia. Remote stabilization over fading channels. *Systems & Control Letters*, 54(3):237–249, 2005.

[17] Thomas Schmid, Prabal Dutta, and Mani B. Srivastava. High-resolution, low-power time synchronization an oxymoron no more. In *Proceedings of the 9th ACM/IEEE International Conference on Information Processing in Sensor Networks*, IPSN'10, pages 151–161, 2010.

[18] A. Rowe, R. Mangharam, and R. Rajkumar. Rt-link: A time-synchronized link protocol for energy-constrained multi-hop wireless networks. In *SECON'06: IEEE Conference on Sensor, Mesh and Ad Hoc Communications and Networks*, pages 402–411, 2006.

[19] ISA100.11a: Wireless systems for industrial

automation: Process control and related applications. Standard, 2009.

[20] R. E. Skelton, T. Iwasaki, and K.M. Grigoriadis. *A unified algebraic approach to linear control design*. CRC Press, 1998.

[21] J. Han and R.E. Skelton. An LMI optimization approach for structured linear controllers. In *Proceedings of the 42nd IEEE Conference on Decision and Control*, pages 5143–5148, 2003.

[22] L. El Ghaoui, F. Oustry, and M. Ait Rami. A cone complementarity linearization algorithm for static output-feedback and related problems. *IEEE Transactions on Automatic Control*, 42(8):1171–1176, Aug. 1997.

[23] P.J. Antsaklis and A.N. Michel. *Linear Systems*. McGraw Hill, 1997.

[24] V. Gupta, A. F. Dana, J. Hespanha, R. M. Murray, and B. Hassibi. Data transmission over networks for estimation and control. *IEEE Transactions on Automatic Control*, 54(8):1807–1819, Aug. 2009.

[25] K. S.J. Pister and L. Doherty. Tsmp: Time synchronized mesh protocol. In *International Symposium on Distributed Sensor Networks (DSN)*, pages 391–398, 2008.

[26] S. Sundaram, M. Pajic, C.N. Hadjicostis, R. Mangharam, and G.J. Pappas. The Wireless Control Network: Monitoring for malicious behavior. In *Proceedings of the 49th IEEE Conference on Decision and Control*, pages 5979–5984, 2010.

[27] S. Skogestad and I. Postlethwaite. *Multivariable Feedback Control: Analysis and Design*. Wiley, 1996.

[28] R. Mangharam, A. Rowe, and R. Rajkumar. FireFly: A Cross-layer Platform for Real-time Embedded Wireless Networks. *Real-Time System Journal*, 37(3):183–231, 2007.

[29] The nano-RK Sensor Real-Time Operating System. http://nanork.org.

[30] Real-Time Windows Target - Run Simulink models on a PC in real time. http://www.mathworks.com/products/rtwt/.

[31] M. Grant and S. Boyd. CVX: Matlab software for disciplined convex programming, http://stanford.edu/ boyd/cvx, 2009.

@scale: Insights from a Large, Long-Lived Appliance Energy WSN

Stephen Dawson-Haggerty[†], Steven Lanzisera[‡], Jay Taneja[†], Richard Brown[‡], and David Culler[†]

[†]Computer Science Division   [‡]Environmental Energy Technologies Division
University of California, Berkeley   Lawrence Berkeley National Lab
Berkeley, CA 94720   Berkeley, CA

Abstract

We present insights obtained from conducting a year-long, 455 meter deployment of wireless plug-load electric meters in a large commercial building. We develop a stratified sampling methodology for surveying the energy use of Miscellaneous Electric Loads (MELs) in commercial buildings, and apply it to our study building. Over the deployment period, we collected over nine hundred million individual readings. Among our findings, we document the need for a dynamic, scalable IPv6 routing protocol which supports point-to-point routing and multiple points of egress. Although the meters are static physically, we find that the set of links they use is dynamic; not using such a dynamic set results in paths that are twice as long. Finally, we conduct a detailed survey of the accuracy possible with inexpensive AC metering hardware. Based on a 21-point automated calibration of a population of 500 devices, we find that it is possible to produce nearly utility-grade metering data.

Categories and Subject Descriptors

H.4 [**Information Systems Applications**]: Miscellaneous; J.7 [**Computers in Other Systems**]: Industrial Control

General Terms

Design, Measurement, Performance

Keywords

Energy, Audit, Building, Power, Wireless, Sensor Network

1. INTRODUCTION

More than a decade after wireless sensor networks emerged as a topic of research, much progress has been made in understanding the contours of the field. There is now a large body of work from which to draw inspiration and ideas. From the early "let chaos reign" days to the current state-of-the-art, the field has evolved to the point where it is possible to deploy large-scale applications over a long period

with the expectation that they will work to produce useful, scientifically-relevant data. Deploying these systems at scale requires rigorous attention to both engineering and deployment management. Recent studies have begun to show successes and failures [4, 11, 17] as well as offering practical guidance on deployments, continuing the sequence of papers performing science in the real world [31, 35].

In this paper, we present results and insights from a massive application, developed and deployed over the past two years. This application consists of 455 wireless energy plug-load meters and 7 load-balancing routers deployed across four floors of a commercial building for the past year. It was motivated by a need for a better understanding of the power consumption and usage patterns of electric plug-loads, or "miscellaneous electric loads." These are estimated to make up nearly 30% of the electric load in commercial buildings [32], but are difficult to study because they are so numerous and diverse. They are a good target for a wireless sensor network because they require both high density and a large number of metering elements.

When conducting our deployment, we took care to heed the lessons of the past, and thus avoided many of the pitfalls of previous deployments. By considering both the innovative aspects of our system (the density and scale) while limiting our innovation in other areas, we have been able to develop a system which performed well and met our science goals, while developing new insights in the types of applications and practices which work well at scale.

One set of insights relates to the networking technology used. Our networking stack uses 6loWPAN/IPv6 to form all meters into a single subnet, the largest such deployment we are aware of. This results in a variety of lessons about the **routing requirements** needed for this scale, validating the need for point-to-point routing and support for multiple egress routers. We discuss **data loss** at both the routing layer and the application layer, and distinguish them where possible, as well as issues which arise when a low-power subnet is connected to other networks. Finally, even though there is little node mobility in this deployment, the usage model implies that nodes intermittently disappear, resulting in interesting **network dynamics** that emerge. We find that the set of intermittent links even in a static deployment is large, many times the size of the set of "good" links. Ignoring links that disappear due to changing noise conditions results in path lengths twice as long as using routes that incorporate variable links.

We also take to a new level inexpensive energy metering technology similar to that used in the past. The science goals of the deployment require consideration of the **accuracy** required by the meters; we developed an extensive automated calibration procedure that could be efficiently applied to hundreds of meters to achieve better than 2% accuracy. Furthermore, previous studies have not explicitly considered the importance of **sampling methodology** in choosing which plug-loads to monitor; we propose that *staged stratified sampling* is the proper methodology for observing usage patterns and power states across a broad range of devices.

In the remainder of the paper we first present an overview of the science goals and methodology of our study. We then present our system design, noting where we have learned from mistakes published in the past and pointing out how simplicity is key to conducting large deployments with limited resources. In the body of the paper, we examine the lessons learned by deploying our large system, and how being driven by energy science (in addition to computer science) goals led to new insights.

2. MISCELLANEOUS ELECTRIC LOADS

Auditors of commercial buildings and residences typically attribute energy to end uses such as heating, cooling, hot water, and lighting. All other energy use is attributed to the "miscellaneous" category (MELs). As major categories of electric usage are reduced through more stringent efficiency requirements and better design practice, this category of load becomes more of the overall energy spend and thus a larger target for reduction. However, MELs are both difficult to study and difficult to reduce, because they comprise a large number of relatively small loads, many of which are infrequently used. Our goal was to conduct a representative sampling of the energy used by this category of devices to build usage models of many different types of devices, as well as energy models for particular devices.

To do so, we conducted a large-scale sensor network deployment in a typical commercial office. The study building is a 1960s-era facility largely used as a traditional office space. It has a total floor area of 89,500 square feet, with approximately 450 occupants in six working groups located among four floors and a basement. Certain aspects of the study presented challenges which are not immediately apparent; for instance, although the study building was located only a few miles from our campus, due to human subjects regulations we were not supposed to enter the building to diagnose particular devices. Physical contact with individual meters was restricted to our on-site partners. This limited our opportunities for diagnosing or fixing problems with the deployment.

2.1 MELs Device Inventory

The first phase of the study consisted of a full inventory of the MELs devices in the office to serve as ground truth when comparing various sampling approaches. Due to the diversity of devices, a standardized system of identifying and recording MELs is essential for inventory and energy data analysis. We updated an extensive taxonomy developed in [23] to include new device types found today, such as tablet computers. The taxonomy consists of three levels: End Use, Category, and Product Type. MELs are divided into three major end uses – Electronics, Miscellaneous, and Traditional. Each end use is in turn composed of categories, and each category contains many product types.

For example, an "LCD computer display" is a product type in the "Display" category, which is part of the end use "Electronics." The inventory categorized every plug-load in the building according to this taxonomy, resulting in the identification of almost 5,000 devices. The inventory was collected by two-person teams and recorded in a relational database.

2.2 Device Sampling Methodology

With such a large number of MELs in our study building, metering all devices would be time- and cost-prohibitive, and not all data generated would provide useful insights. The sampling must be driven by science criteria, not networking expedience. The selection of an appropriate sampling method is driven by the multi-fold purpose of our energy data collection and analysis:

- Provide a statistically-relevant survey of power and energy measurements of the population of MELs devices in a typical commercial setting; and

- Capture traces and derive usage patterns of MELs to build an appliance energy signature database and construct models for future analysis; and

- Study usage correlations between devices, *e.g.*, computer, display, and lighting within the same occupant's office.

We developed a multi-stage, stratified random sampling approach to select devices for metering. Devices were first divided into stages by physical location or organization owning the devices. For each stage, a subset of devices were then selected from a stratified sample by Device Category to meet our data collection objectives. A stratified sample is critical because a simple random sample would result in metering a large number of uninteresting devices (*e.g.*, computer speakers, external disk drives) instead of devices with significant energy use such as computers or LCD displays.

In the second phase of the study, we deployed a total of 455 meters on the selected devices. The deployment took approximately 120 person-hours. No effort was made to deploy meters to ensure network connectivity, but load-balancing routers (LBRs) were placed with connectivity and hop count in mind. Once the meters were in place, we had only limited opportunities to perform on-site troubleshooting. This made our remote debugging setup more important.

Figure 2.2 shows meter locations from the third floor of the deployment; a couple features are evident. First, the deployment was physically dense, with several meters often placed within a single office. Second, the meters are well distributed spatially. This was intentional, since the stratified sampling procedure was performed within each physical area and administrative unit.

3. SYSTEM DESIGN

We developed the metering system for this deployment using a mix of existing and custom software, combined with a custom hardware platform. Figure 2 shows a schematic of the overall metering system design, with particular emphasis on the networking. Overall, the system can be decomposed into three tiers: the metering tier, the backhaul tier, and the database.

The **metering tier** is made up of a large number of low-cost electric meters, each designed around a custom hardware platform similar to the ACme [14]. They contain an

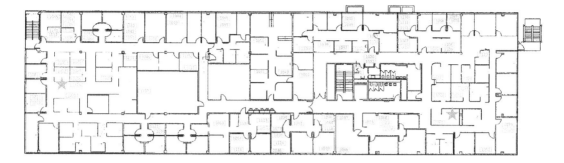

Figure 1: The third floor of the deployment. Small boxes are meters, while the two stars are LBRs.

msp430 microcontroller integrated with an 802.15.4 radio and Analog Devices ADE7753 energy metering chip. Each device runs the TinyOS operating system and uses blip, an IPv6/6loWPAN stack to provide IPv6 network connectivity [7].

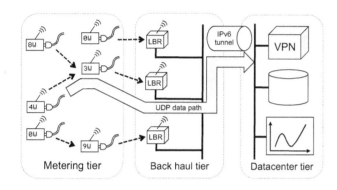

Figure 2: System design. The metering tier, left, forms an IPv6 mesh network of 802.15.4 links and transmits metering data through the backhaul tier comprised of load-balancing routers, center; these routers communicate with each other using the building's Ethernet. The UDP data packets travel over an IPv6 tunnel from the building to the Internet where they reach the database, located in a datacenter.

To provide scalability to hundreds of nodes, the back haul tier consists of a number of LBRs that provide connectivity to and from the metering elements. Unlike a deployment with multiple gateways, *these LBRs are transparent to the other tiers*. Additional units can be deployed without any extra configuration. This is a key result of our use of the IP architecture. Along with the meters, these devices make up a single IPv6 subnet where all devices participate in the routing protocol called HYDRO [8], designed to provide efficient any-to-any IPv6 routing over constrained links. Each LBR communicates with neighboring meters using an 802.15.4 interface, and distributes the topology it learns from them to the other routers using the building's Ethernet. We ultimately deployed seven LBRs over the four floors of the building. Each LBR advertises a minimum-cost path to neighboring meters. Each meter then chooses the closest LBR as its default router, and sends all traffic to the selected LBR. This allowed us to increase both network and backhaul capacity by deploying new meters and routers at will.

Data generated by the meters are sent in UDP packets, destined to a machine in our datacenter. This **datacenter tier** makes up the final part of the system, which runs as a hosted web application. Data packets from the meters traverse several network segments en route to the data center, moving from the 6loWPAN network out over a local subnet before traveling through an IPv6 tunnel to the open IPv6 Internet. By extending our deployment to the Internet, we are able to share backend infrastructure between this and other meter deployments.

3.1 Embedded Application

Due to the large scale and long duration of the planned deployment, key goals were simplicity and reliability while maintaining enough flexibility to accommodate shifting deployment conditions and science requirements. Although there are sophisticated techniques available for over-the-air reprogramming, time synchronization, and distributed debugging, the reality is that each of these components add code size and testing complexity. Therefore, we either simplified or eliminated many complicated services. An invaluable simplification was to extract the most commonly changed configuration parameters like sampling rate and calibration parameters, and make them settable without reprogramming. Although we also included a simple over-the-air image update utility, in practice it was rarely used since we could update parameters without reflashing the entire image. Since we used an IPv6 routing protocol to support point-to-point and multicast traffic, implementing this functionality in the application was much simplified, yet extremely valuable to debugging. For instance, over-the-air reprogramming is implemented using TFTP instead of a complicated epidemic protocol [12].

3.2 Data Generation

The metering devices sample average power and total energy every 10 seconds, and send a packet every 20 seconds with the previous two readings. This period was chosen to be the highest we could reasonably support in high-density deployments. We pack two readings into a single packet. One of the most important aspects of sensing is the notion of time. It allows correlation of readings across meters. Even though approaches to time synchronization of various sophistication have been used successfully [4, 19, 25], problems with it are well documented [35]. Given our requirements, our approach was very simple. Therefore, we included redundant clocks and counters to distinguish the various events we expected in such a large deployment; these counters are presented in Table 1.

Clock	Rate	Purpose
LocalTime	32kHz	Time since reset or rollover
GlobalTime	1Hz	Unix timestamp
SequenceNumber	1/pkt	Monotonic value for the life of the meter
InsertTime	1/pkt	Timestamp at database

Table 1: Counters stored with each data packet.

In normal operation and for energy analysis, only GlobalTime is needed, since data are timestamped at the meter with the number of seconds since January 1, 1970. Other timestamps become useful for *post facto* analysis. For instance, packet delivery ratio (PDR) is a commonly-reported metric of network performance: it consists of the ratio between packets delivered and packets originated. In a large system where there is uncertainty about device state (*e.g.*, some devices may be broken or off), it is not possible to compute a "true" PDR. However, using SequenceNumbers which are stored in non-volatile flash memory, we approximated the number of packet originations even when the device is frequently rebooted. In another example, device reboots in our study change the set of motes available over time, and may indicate end-user attempts to save energy. The LocalTime clock quickly indicates reboot events, which would otherwise need to be inferred from data loss and could not be distinguished from network outages.

3.3 Design Takeaways

In reviewing recent deployment literature, we found numerous instances of malfunctioning networking stacks. By using a well-tested existing stack rather than starting from scratch, we avoided many of the networking bugs that plague deployments. By constraining the system to a single use and a set of protocols that have been tested together, we avoid the need for more complicated resource-sharing arrangements [13].

Our key insight was the value of *configuration, not reprogramming*. In the two or so years since our mote software was "released to manufacturing," we have not developed a new image; instead we have been able to work around the few, minor, and well-understood bugs in the existing software. Because of the ability to change parameters, we have been able to deploy meters in other systems not discussed here with differing needs but the same software. This results in a significantly smaller testing surface. Reprogramming hundreds of meters by unscrewing the case and using a wired programmer only needs to be experienced once to motivate a better solution. Second, although only a global clock is needed for data analysis, *you can never have enough clocks*. Since there are several notions of ordering, it is difficult or impossible to compute metrics like data yield independent of power failure, or node uptime without multiple counters.

Finally, IPv6 allowed us to develop compact implementations of many services wished for in previous deployments, like a configuration manager and a software updater. Although some of these were less efficient than the state-of-the-art, they worked when required at a very large scale.

4. NETWORKING INSIGHTS

An important component of our network is the routing protocol that provisions routes from the individual meters towards the edge of the access network. The protocol needed to be reliable and perform at a scale of hundreds of individual meters. We used HYDRO [8], a conceptual predecessor to the RPL protocol currently being advanced in the IETF [36]. HYDRO builds a directed acyclic graph (DAG) towards a set of load-balancing routers (LBRs). Traffic originating from inside the network is routed down this DAG to one of the LBRs, where further routing decisions are made. Traffic originating from an LBR or another network is first routed to the "nearest" LBR, and then source-routed to its final destination.

HYDRO contains numerous mechanisms to improve reliability and scalability in the face of shifting link conditions and deployment sizes. Each router maintains a list of potential next-hop default routes and will attempt delivery to several of them, using link-layer acknowledgements to determine whether a particular packet was delivered. Each embedded router also maintains only a subset of its neighbor set to limit the amount of state and periodically attaches this information to outgoing data packets. The LBRs use this information to build a view of the link state of the network and construct source routes back into the network.

At its peak, our network consisted of 455 nodes spread across four floors, routing through 7 LBRs. The average node density was at least 16; we estimate this by counting the number of distinct links reported over the life of the deployment.

4.1 Routing Requirements

When in production, our application collects data using a typical multipoint-to-point (MP2P) traffic pattern, which is well-known to be a key traffic pattern for embedded networks [20]. This traffic pattern is optimized in HYDRO by maintaining a DAG towards egress routers with a large amount of redundancy. Point-to-point routing in this type of network is less common. We made use of unicast routing primarily for management. For example, during meter calibration, we sent calibration parameters to be written to non-volatile flash, and during deployment, commands were sent to change the destination of data.

The ability to communicate with each meter *in situ* to troubleshoot was valuable, but infrequently used. This leads us to the main insight: *point-to-point routing should be available, but may be expensive*. In the case of HYDRO, all unicast traffic is source-routed from an LBR. Since most traffic flows out of the network to an LBR, adding a small amount of extra data to maintain the topology is inexpensive, and eliminates the need for a flood of discovery messages as would be required in an on-demand protocol. This is somewhat in opposition to the networking structure that has emerged in recent years in TinyOS, positing that *collection* (MP2P) and *dissemination* (P2MP) are the dominant traffic patterns. Although these are invaluable and common traffic patterns, at times it is simply convenient to contact a single node individually.

A second requirement was the ability to *scale using multiple LBRs*. HYDRO supports this by extending the routing topology over a backhaul link; in our case, this was the building Ethernet. This allowed us to have multiple, redundant LBRs; indeed, it was common for one or two of them to be offline for various reasons. Until protocols and implementations support this functionality, they should not be considered for large-scale deployments.

4.2 Data Loss

Since our network was situated in a real environment for upwards of a year with a large number of devices, we experienced practically every form of data loss at one time or another. Table 4.2 summarizes the causes of missing data which we diagnosed at various points in time. Although protocol loss is the most well-studied form of loss, we found that the amount of data missing from other causes dwarfed the amount dropped due to routing errors or forwarding path errors. The high-level insight is that *if perfect reliability is required, buffering must be present between every link which may fail.* This is a notable consequence of our use of IPv6, the data path spanning multiple links, and the end-to-end principle. Given that there are devices of varying capabilities and links with varying reliabilities on the path from a meter to the database, it may be worthwhile in the future to use an application protocol with support for intermediate caching proxies.

One of the most unexpected sources of missing data was that of device unpluggings. During the deployment, occupants were instructed that meters were attached to devices, not receptacles. Therefore, they frequently unplugged the meter along with the device. Figure 3 shows the frequency of these "on" and "off" events in time. An on event is when a meter begins reporting after having been turned off, while an off event is when it stops sending data because it is unplugged. After interviewing several study participants, we discovered that it was common for a meter to be plugged into a power strip, which was turned off at the end of each workday. This behavior was intended to reduce the leakage power consumed by devices plugged into the strip, but also caused network churn and gaps in the data!

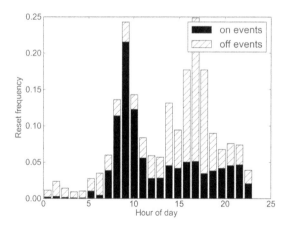

Figure 3: Not all network dynamics are caused by link and node failure or mobility; some devices were turned off or unplugged during nights. These events correlate strongly with working hours.

Once data loss due to LBR connectivity problems and meter unpluggings is filtered out, we can observe the overall data yield in the month of April, shown in Figure 4. The 5th percentile yield across all devices was over 99% nearly every

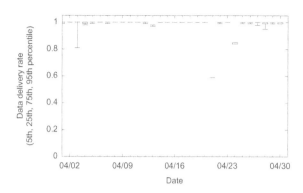

Figure 4: Observed data yield distribution in April, with losses due to mote shutdowns removed. Losses due to database maintenance are clearly visible as days with lower yield but little variation. For many days, the 5th percentile yield was above 99%. Boxes show 25th and 75th percentiles, whiskers show 5th and 95th percentiles. Data were delivered using UDP datagrams with no end-to-end mechanisms.

day, and the best value was 99.91%; the median was 98.7%. Because we did not deploy meters with an eye towards connectivity, certain meters had consistently poor connectivity; however the deployment was dense enough that the size of this set was only 12 meters, or less than 3% of meters deployed. These numbers refer to drop rates of the best-effort UDP datagrams sent from meters to the database and compare favorably with published estimates of Internet-wide packet loss [5, 33].

4.3 Network Dynamics

Running a routing protocol in a large network over a year gives us a rich set of data with which to observe link dynamics. First, we have application-layer data reported by the motes to the data repository. These UDP packets are sent every 20 seconds, traversing several network segments. These contain the local time, global time, sequence number, current default next hop and link estimate, and the current path cost estimate. These data provide the ultimate metric of application-layer performance. Second, HYDRO routers apprise the LBRs of their link-state at regular intervals so that they can build source routes back into the network. We stored a snapshot of this state every five minutes, which consists of the top four entries in each router's neighbor table, along with corresponding link estimates (ETX). These estimates are kept fresh by a periodic exploration process each router conducts to sample neighboring links.

Using these data, we are able to confirm several previously proposed hypotheses about link dynamics: *intermittent links are prevalent, their uses reduced routing stretch by a factor of 2,* and *networks experience significant diurnal and weekly variations.*

4.3.1 Daily Variations

Figure 5(a) shows a basic look at the collected topology for March. In most of these analyses we focus on March and April when the set of meters was stable and there were infrequent database or connectivity outages. The dashed line shows the mean shortest path between all pairs of nodes in

Loss cause	Description
Network loss	Packets dropped by the link layer or routing protocol due to exceeding the number of retransmissions or hop limit.
Device shutdowns	Devices attached to power strips were frequently turned off overnight.
Building shutdowns	The facilities organization disconnected power for maintenance, resulting in a 14-hour outage and subsequent network reinitialization.
LBR connectivity	The LBRs were networked through an Ethernet VPN, and connected to the IPv6 Internet with a tunnel. Both of these network components were subject to failure.
Software faults	We observed a software failure rate of approximately 10 nodes per month, or one every 3.5 mote-years. This could be improved through better software engineering.
Database failures	Months of data were lost when MySQL tables were corrupted during a software upgrade.
Meter attrition	Over a period of time, some devices were removed from the system by maintenance workers or occupants. Approximately 100/455 of our meters disappeared over the course of the study.

Table 2: Missing data in real deployments are caused by many factors beyond the control of the deployment staff.

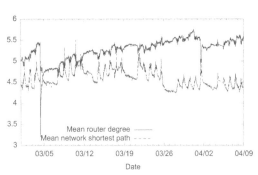

(a) HYDRO quickly builds a rough link-state database, and then slowly improves its view as individual routers explore new links during this 1.5 month-long section of the deployment. Routes become approximately 10% longer during the workday, and then relax at night. Reported degree gradually increases while path length decreases, as HYDRO discovers new links. Furthermore, a subset of meters are only on during working hours. The network was reinitialized on 3/5/2011.

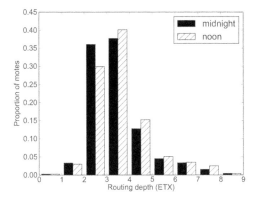

(b) Compared to the topology at midnight, routes during the day are approximately 10% longer. This shift occurs each day as changing noise conditions cause the routing protocol to evict grey links and search for better candidate parents.

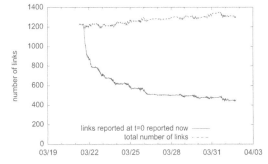

(c) The link set is actually quite dynamic. At the start of the analysis we snapshot the link set reported at that time, and compare the size of its intersection into the future. Less than half of the links appear after a week. Without this dynamic set of links, the network diameter increases by a factor of 2.

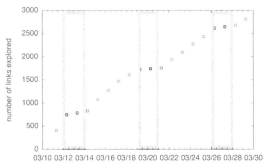

(d) The set of links undergoing exploration continues to grow, rather than stabilize. The network is quite dense, and each router has many more potential default routes than can fit in the neighbor table. The exploration process halts on weekends (in grey) when better conditions no longer force the routing protocol to adapt.

Figure 5: Running a routing protocol over a long period of time in a real environment confirms many hypotheses about link behavior over time.

the network, while the solid line shows the mean reported router degree. Since HYDRO reports only a partial subset of neighbors it is using for routing, this degree is not the "true" degree of the network. The weekend to weekday distinction is clearly visible, with path lengths remaining stable on weekends but increasing by 5-10% on weekdays. Figure 5(b) shows this effect more clearly, contrasting node routing depth in terms of ETX at midnight with depth at noon; the shift to deeper ranks is clearly visible.

4.3.2 Routing Churn

There are numerous possible explanations for these daily variations. Many studies suggest that there are links with bimodal behavior [29], alternating between "good" and "bad" states with various frequencies. One difference with these studies is that we do not have ground truth data about these links. Rather, we have link data filtered through the actions of a routing protocol. However, it is interesting to consider the actions of the protocol by examining the links it selected in a real-world setting. Figure 5(c) shows the result of an analysis designed to uncover how much churn there is in the nodes' next hop choices. At the start of the analysis (chosen arbitrarily after the network had been initialized for several weeks), we form a set containing all links reported by the network. At each subsequent time step, we find the size of the intersection of the set of reported links at that time with the original link set.

We find that the protocol consistently reports a set of about 500 links, which we call the **static links**. The remainder of the original set of links disappear after about a week. Since HYDRO removes links which are not useful for routing as well as poorly-performing links, there is a subset of links that are both consistently useful and reliable. However, HYDRO also discovers and reports a constantly changing set of other links, which we call the *churn links*. The total number of links reported by the network (from all nodes) is consistently around 1200; each router was configured to report a maximum of 4. This indicates that the density of this deployment provided each router with ample choice of next-hop, although not all were consistently available.

Figure 5(d) addresses whether the churning set of links is of a fixed size or is dynamic. At the beginning of our analysis we remove all static links and at each time step add all new links which are not part of the static set. HYDRO consistently tries new links; the number of links it tries does not stabilize in the time frame of the experiment. Over 20 days it tries almost 3000 discrete links; we infer that this churn is caused by changes in noise floor and interference conditions, since *the exploration process comes to a virtual halt on weekends.*

The final question was whether the effort to discover and track these variable links was "worth it." That is, does the set of churn links improve routes to the LBRs? The answer is a resounding "yes." If we were to consider only the links in the static set, *i.e.*, those continuing to appear after a week, *the network diameter increases by a factor of 2.1: from an ETX of 4.6 to 9.9.*

4.4 Networking Takeaways

We chose not to use TCP, opting instead for UDP, to use only the best-tested code and because the reliable delivery by the raw network was sufficient. The introduction of so many parallel TCP flows in a large deployment was an untested proposition. Furthermore, even TCP's end-to-end acknowledgements are not a panacea for data reliablity problems unless much care is taken managing send buffers on the mote to guarantee all data is delivered in the face of connection resets and timeouts. Transport- and application-layer protocol designs currently in development (for instance, CoAP [26]) should be evaluated to ensure that they provide appropriate mechanisms for caching between network segments, especially if they are designed to work over UDP. *It is an open question of how to merge the buffering and end-to-end demands of TCP with the constrained resources of embedded systems.*

Furthermore, we have largely validated earlier studies about the importance of grey links to routing, We infer that the churn links which are coming and going from the routing table must have varying quality. Even in a very dense deployment, failing to take advantage of links that are not consistently high-quality would have resulted in paths twice as long as we experienced. Even in a deployment with no mobility, we must maintain a continuous process of routing table maintenance and discovery to achieve good performance.

5. ENERGY SCIENCE

A mark of good system design and construction in a sensor networking deployment is the collection of scientific data that enable better visibility into a phenomenon that could not previously be observed. In this section, we document the domain-specific lessons derived from the preparations taken to collect the data, including the calibration of meters for accurate collection of data, stratified appliance sampling for guiding the deployment strategy, and share insights gained from the data.

5.1 Accuracy Analysis

For energy meters, calibration transforms measurements taken by the device into engineering units usable for scientific comparison. This process presents a number of challenges. First are accuracy requirements: in the MELs regime, loads seldom consume more than $300W$, with a large proportion below $60W$. We are not aware of a documented testing regimen that covers low load levels. For example, the California Public Utilities Commission requires expensive, utility-grade electric meters to be accurate to within 2% of load from $60W$ to $3.6kW$, ignoring the lowest range. [30] A second requirement is simple, yet individualized calibration: there are differences among metering devices caused by variations in the manufacturing process, but the calibration equations need to be simple enough to be computed on the devices themselves. Thus, each device needs to be tested, calibrated, and programmed separately. Last, to ensure that the process of calibrating all 455 meters is not cost- or time-prohibitive, it should be quick and automated.

We used these goals to guide the design and development of an automated calibration process. It uses eight different resistive loads from $2W$ to $100W$, actuated by a computer-controlled relay to create 21 calibration points between $0W$ and $300W$. A reference power meter [10] is used for ground truth. Additionally, the process is designed to handle five meters plugged in concurrently, accelerating the calibration process. Each calibration run takes 5 minutes, reducing the time per meter to 1 minute.

The process of developing a calibration function revealed a couple of key insights. First after analyzing raw data from several hundred meters, the raw values exhibited highly linear behavior *but only over limited domains*. In fact, a single linear function over the entire range of loads cannot meet our accuracy target. Therefore, *single-point calibration is insufficient*. Instead, a piecewise linear function using multi-point calibration as shown in Figure 6 may be used, consisting of three portions, where the first only ensures that the meter returns a zero reading at zero load, and the boundary between the second and third segment is chosen to minimize the overall error in the calibration. Although more segments in the function would decrease error, there is risk of overfitting as well as unnecessary complexity. The calibration coefficients are stored on each meter so that future readings are provided in engineering units (mW) for easier analysis.

The second insight is that despite larger percentage error at lower load levels, absolute error remains quite low when examined across all meters. The error of this calibration procedure for the entire population of 455 meters is shown in Figure 7. The plot shows cumulative distribution functions at four load levels. At low loads, we achieve absolute errors of less than $1W$ for virtually all of the meters calibrated. Additionally, more than 75% of meters are within 2% of the measured load at $60W$, the standard for "utility-grade" metering, with improved accuracy as the load increases. These results demonstrate that inexpensive metering hardware can be calibrated both quickly as well as reasonably accurately.

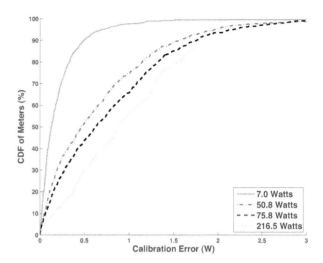

Figure 7: **Error of calibrated meters at four load levels.**

consumption of devices in the top seven energy-consuming categories and all other devices for the commercial study building.

Energy estimates for the entire population are projected from the metered sample of devices using sample probability weights, and energy is projected from the metering period to the entire year. Computers clearly use both the most energy overall and the most per unit, whereas the Other category of devices shows the opposite behavior. Because the building is primarily office space, displays, imaging, networking and miscellaneous (*i.e.*, task) lighting are the next largest energy users. Space heating and fans make up most of miscellaneous HVAC, and the appliances are primarily refrigerators found in break rooms and a few offices. The energy breakdown shows that information technology equipment consumes over 75% of annual MELs energy but comprises less than half of total devices, emphasizing that *IT devices should be disproportionately metered more when studying MELs energy use in offices*. This finding corresponds well with surveyed sources of these data [32].

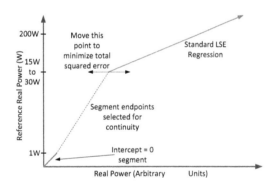

Figure 6: **Selection of piecewise linear calibration coefficients.**

5.2 Energy Results

The detailed metering of MELs enabled by this work provides an opportunity to understand MELs energy use in a way previously not possible. In a sub-metered building, which is still rare, MELs energy use is typically a single number for the entire building because only the primary end-uses (*i.e.*, heating, cooling, ventilation, lighting and water heating) are metered, and MELs consumption is found by subtraction from the building total. On the other hand, in this study, the fine resolution in device type and time resolution allows energy to be divided by device type, operational mode, or a variety of other parameters.

Section 2.2 described the methodology for selecting a stratified sample of devices for metering. Here we provide the quantitative justification for that experimental design decision. Figure 8 presents the count as well as annual energy

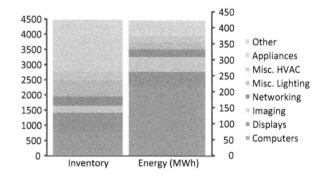

Figure 8: **Comparison of the device inventory to annual energy use by device category.**

Another dimension in which to view the data is temporally. The average weekday load shape divided by category is shown in Figure 9, providing insight into typical energy usage patterns. The largest energy-consuming category, computers, uses about 60% of its energy outside working hours at this facility. Considering that only 10% of the computers in this facility must remain on at all times, this presents an enormous opportunity for energy efficiency via power management on computers. In fact, this facility could save over $100,000kWh$ ($\approx$ \$15,000) annually without loss of access or productivity by reconfiguring operating systems [1] or installing widely-available software [2, 15, 22] for this purpose.

Additionally, it is clear that significant energy is used in most other device categories outside of working hours. Timer-controlled plug strips could shut off power to office devices except appliances and network equipment during non-working hours. If used, they provide a relatively inexpensive solution that would save 30% of non-computer energy use. Even though these changes have a negligible cost and despite the popularity of energy efficiency in commercial settings, there is still huge potential for saving money and energy in the MELs end-use category.

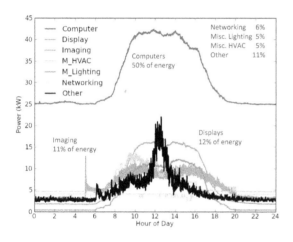

Figure 9: Device category average load shapes.

A cost effective way to save energy is to ensure that only energy-efficient products are used in a building. For IT equipment, price and efficiency are not tightly correlated. Consider computer displays. A comparison of the on-mode power of the metered devices shows that the average power is $33W$ for displays smaller than 24". However, the 10th percentile on-mode power of 24" displays is only $20W$. If all of the smaller monitors were replaced with $20W$ 24" displays during the next upgrade cycle, users would not only have greater screen area, but total display energy use would decrease by 40%.

6. RELATED WORK

Our study of a large-scale, long-lived energy metering wireless sensor network benefits from previous efforts in two key areas: WSN deployment science and studies of routing and link behavior in low-power, lossy networks.

Though a range of studies document the design, development, and evaluation of large-scale and occasionally long-lived WSNs [3, 6, 9, 18, 21, 34], there are a notable few that provide systematic guidance based on difficulties experienced in deploying large-scale, long-lived WSNs. We designed our system and methodology considering these valuable insights. For example, Langendoen, *et al.* "advocate

the manifold use of statistics" to have frequent state reports available for potential debugging efforts [17]. In our study, node and LBR state are continuously logged. Each data packet provides a number of different time counters for *post hoc* assessments; further, routing state and periodic snapshots of LBR link-state allows reconstruction of network dynamics. These data have been invaluable for diagnosing protocol behavior and connectivity issues. Barrenetxea, *et al.* draw from years of experience deploying networks in the Swiss Alps to provide guidance through the entire development, testing, and deployment process [4]. They thoroughly summarize issues described in previous deployments augmented with their own experiences to provide a "hitchhiker's guide" to outdoor WSN deployments. In the development phase, they advocate "keeping it simple" and avoiding complexity wherever possible, particularly to circumvent unexpected interactions between software components especially in the communications stack. Many of our design decisions reflect this parable, including our selection of a well-tested routing protocol. Hnat, *et al.* provide a similar guide aimed towards indoor deployments [11]. A particular insight is that despite common belief, deployment in buildings still presents significant connectivity and access challenges. In our case, the ability to cope with a consistently varying noise floor by using an adaptive routing protocol as well as our range of remote debugging and reconfiguration services enabled us to address these challenges.

Adherence to the lessons in the literature coupled with thorough planning and understanding of the deployment environment allowed us to avoid many of the issues that plague WSN deployments, resulting in a successful long-lived and large-scale deployment. It is this combination of long life, large scale, and good planning that sets us apart from previous work in plug-load energy metering. The PowerNet project deployed 85 wireless electricity meters for 3 months to examine IT-related electricity consumption [16]. Also, Jiang, *et al.* deploy 39 plug-load meters in an office space for several months and look at disaggregation of appliances as well as decomposition on different parameters [15]. However, both of these studies lack the rigor in sample design and long time-scale needed to understand overall MELs usage in their respective settings. Additionally, neither describe calibration processes to ensure the accuracy of the collected data.

There is also a body of work related to the understanding of link dynamics. Zhao and Govindan characterize the size and behavior of "grey zones" of intermittent performance in low-power links, while Son, *et al.* extend this understanding to multiple contending senders [27, 37]. Srinivasan, *et al.* synthesize these results into a more detailed understanding of these link dynamics, and finally propose a metric called β which is used to characterize the temporal variation in links [28, 29]. Finally, Ortiz attempts to quantify the value of variable links and multiple channels for reliability when routing is also an option [24]. These studies informed our understanding of the HYDRO protocol, and also allowed us to infer what was happening inside of our network from the external signals it presented to us, like routing state. They also confirm the importance of using a protocol which expects significant temporal variation from the links in use.

7. CONCLUSION

Our results present several new findings and insights. For instance, the design decision to explore and use links that become unstable at certain parts of the day was essential to achieving low path costs. Using these links results in path costs half of what would be achieved using exclusively very stable links. In general, we found that although there was almost no mote mobility, there were still dynamics caused by a changing noise floor and a shifting set of devices which are on the network: the interior of a commercial building is indeed a dynamic environment. We also confirm the value of point-to-point routing in a real sensor network deployment.

There are also several takeaways which should inform future protocol design. It is still somewhat unusual to connect large subnetworks of devices directly to the broader Internet but gave us host of advantages in terms of debugging and visibility; this may cause researchers in the embedded space to examine transport protocols which can provide better end-to-end guarantees than either UDP or TCP while continuing to impose a very low burden on the low-power and lossy network segments. Incorporating reliability at every layer of design is common practice in other domains; we expect it to become common here as well.

The result of this work is to allow deployments at larger scales. We have presented results from @scale; one of the largest deployment in terms of mote-years yet published. We were successful in achieving our science goals while testing several hypotheses about network dynamics, and reinforced emerging design practice on the construction of this type of network.

Acknowledgements

We would like to thank Ken Lutz, Albert Goto, and Xiaofan Jiang of Berkeley and Iris Cheung, Judy Lai, and Margarita Kloss of LBNL for their help with the design, manufacture, calibration, and deployment of the @scale system. Alice Chang and Shelley Kim provided able assistance in calibrating and programming the meters; Sara Alspaugh of Berkeley contributed Figure 2. Ray Woodfin and Joann Nguyen of Megaforce Corporation provided support in manufacturing these devices. This work was supported by the DOE Building Technologies Program and the National Science Foundation under grants CPS-0932209 and CPS-0931843.

8. REFERENCES

[1] Advanced configuration and power interface specification – revision 4.0a. http://www.acpi.info.

[2] Y. Agarwal, S. Hodges, R. Chandra, J. Scott, P. Bahl, and R. Gupta. Somniloquy: augmenting network interfaces to reduce pc energy usage. In *Proceedings of the 6th USENIX symposium on Networked systems design and implementation*, NSDI'09, Berkeley, CA, USA, 2009. USENIX Association.

[3] A. Arora, P. Dutta, S. Bapat, V. Kulathumani, H. Zhang, V. Naik, V. Mittal, H. Cao, M. Gouda, Y. Choi, T. Herman, S. Kulkarni, U. Arumugam, M. Nesterenko, A. Vora, and M. Miyashita. A line in the sand: A wireless sensor network for target detection, classification, and tracking. *Computer Networks (Elsevier*, 46:605–634, 2004.

[4] G. Barrenetxea, F. Ingelrest, G. Schaefer, and M. Vetterli. The hitchhiker's guide to successful wireless sensor network deployments. In *Proceedings of the 6th ACM conference on Embedded network sensor systems*, pages 43–56, New York, NY, USA, 2008. ACM.

[5] J.-C. Bolot. End-to-end packet delay and loss behavior in the internet. *SIGCOMM Comput. Commun. Rev.*, 23:289–298, October 1993.

[6] M. Ceriotti, L. Mottola, G. P. Picco, A. L. Murphy, S. Gunã, M. Corrà, M. Pozzi, D. Zonta, and P. Zanon. Monitoring heritage buildings with wireless sensor networks: The torre aquila deployment. In *In Proc. of the 8th ACM/IEEE Int. Conf. on Information Processing in Sensor Networks*, 2009.

[7] S. Dawson-Haggerty. Design, implementation, and evaluation of an embedded ipv6 stack. *Masters Thesis, University of California at Berkeley*, 2010.

[8] S. Dawson-Haggerty, A. Tavakoli, and D. Culler. Hydro: A hybrid routing protocol for low-power and lossy networks. In *First IEEE International Conference on Smart Grid Communications*, October 2010.

[9] P. Dutta, J. Hui, J. Jeong, S. Kim, C. Sharp, J. Taneja, G. Tolle, K. Whitehouse, and D. Culler. Trio: Enabling sustainable and scalable outdoor wireless sensor network deployments. In *IEEE SPOTS*, pages 407–415, 2006.

[10] Electronic Product Design, Inc. Plm-1 power meter. http://epd.com/power_meters.html#PLM-1.

[11] T. W. Hnat, V. Srinivasan, J. Lu, T. Sookoor, R. Dawson, J. Stankovic, and K. Whitehouse. The hitchhiker's guide to successful residential sensing deployments. In *Proceedings of the 9th ACM Conference on Embedded Networked Sensor Systems*, SenSys '11, New York, NY, USA, 2011. ACM.

[12] J. W. Hui and D. Culler. The dynamic behavior of a data dissemination protocol for network programming at scale. In *SenSys '04: Proceedings of the 2nd international conference on Embedded networked sensor systems*, pages 81–94, 2004.

[13] J. Il Choi, M. A. Kazandjieva, M. Jain, and P. Levis. The case for a network protocol isolation layer. In *Proceedings of the 7th ACM Conference on Embedded Networked Sensor Systems*, SenSys '09, pages 267–280, New York, NY, USA, 2009. ACM.

[14] X. Jiang, S. Dawson-Haggerty, P. Dutta, and D. Culler. Design and implementation of a high-fidelity ac metering network. In *Proceedings of the 2009 International Conference on Information Processing in Sensor Networks*, pages 253–264, Washington, DC, USA, 2009. IEEE Computer Society.

[15] X. Jiang, M. Van Ly, J. Taneja, P. Dutta, and D. Culler. Experiences with a high-fidelity wireless building energy auditing network. In *Proceedings of the 7th ACM Conference on Embedded Networked Sensor Systems*, New York, NY, USA, 2009. ACM.

[16] M. Kazandjieva, O. Gnawali, B. Heller, P. Levis, and C. Kozyrakis. Identifying energy waste through dense power sensing and utilization monitoring. Technical report, Stanford University, 2010.

[17] K. Langendoen, A. Baggio, and O. Visser. Murphy loves potatoes: Experiences from a pilot sensor network deployment in precision agriculture. In *In Int. Workshop on Parallel and Distributed Real-Time Systems*, 2006.

[18] C.-J. Liang, J. Liu, L. Luo, A. Terzis, and F. Zhao. Racnet: A high-fidelity data center sensing network. In *Proceedings of the 7th ACM Conference on Embedded Networked Sensor Systems*, SenSys '09, New York, NY, 2009.

[19] M. Maróti, B. Kusy, G. Simon, and Ákos Lédeczi. The flooding time synchronization protocol. In *SenSys '04: Proceedings of the 2nd international conference on Embedded networked sensor systems*, New York, NY, USA, 2004. ACM Press.

[20] J. Martocci, P. D. Mil, N. Riou, and W. Vermeylen. RFC 5867: Building automation routing requirements in low-power and lossy networks, 2010.

[21] L. Mo, Y. He, Y. Liu, J. Zhao, S.-J. Tang, X.-Y. Li, and G. Dai. Canopy closure estimates with greenorbs: sustainable sensing in the forest. In *Proceedings of the 7th ACM Conference on Embedded Networked Sensor Systems*, New York, NY, USA, 2009. ACM.

[22] S. Nedevschi, J. Ch, S. Ratnasamy, and N. Taft. Skilled in the art of being idle: reducing energy waste in networked systems. In *In Proceedings of the 6th USENIX Symposium on Networked Systems Design and Implementation*, 2009.

[23] B. Nordman and M. Sanchez. Electronics come of age: A taxonomy for miscellaneous and low power products. http://eetd.lbl.gov/ea/nordman/docs/taxonomy.pdf.

[24] J. Ortiz and D. Culler. Multichannel reliability assessment in real world wsns. In *Proceedings of the 9th ACM/IEEE International Conference on Information Processing in Sensor Networks*, New York, NY, USA, 2010. ACM.

[25] T. Schmid, Z. Charbiwala, Z. Anagnostopoulou, M. B. Srivastava, and P. Dutta. A case against routing-integrated time synchronization. In *Proceedings of the 8th ACM*

Conference on Embedded Networked Sensor Systems, New York, NY, USA, 2010. ACM.

[26] Z. Shelby, K. Hartke, C. Bormann, and B. Frank. Constrained Application Protocol (CoAP). Internet-Draft draft-ietf-core-coap-07, Internet Engineering Task Force, July 2011. Work in progress.

[27] D. Son, B. Krishnamachari, and J. Heidemann. Experimental Analysis of Concurrent Packet Transmissions in Low-Power Wireless Networks. Tech Report ISI-TR609, Viterbi School of Engineering, University of Southern California, 2005.

[28] K. Srinivasan et al. Understanding the causes of packet delivery success and failure in dense wireless sensor networks. Tech Report SING-06-00, Department of Electrical Engineering, Stanford University, 2006.

[29] K. Srinivasan, M. A. Kazandjieva, S. Agarwal, and P. Levis. The β-factor: measuring wireless link burstiness. In *Proceedings of the 6th ACM conference on Embedded network sensor systems*, New York, NY, USA, 2008. ACM.

[30] State of California Division of Measurement Standards. Device enforcement program manual, 2008. http://www.cdfa.ca.gov/dms/programs/devices/DeviceProgramManual2008.pdf.

[31] G. Tolle, J. Polastre, R. Szewczyk, D. Culler, N. Turner, K. Tu, S. Burgess, T. Dawson, P. Buonadonna, D. Gay, and W. Hong. A macroscope in the redwoods. *ACM Sensys*, 2005.

[32] U.S. Department of Energy. *Buildings Energy Data Book*. 2009.

[33] A. Wang, C. Huang, J. Li, and K. W. Ross. Queen: Estimating packet loss rate between arbitrary internet hosts. In *10th International Conference on Passive and Active Network Measurement*, volume 5448 of *Lecture Notes in Computer Science*. Springer, 2009.

[34] T. Wark, C. Crossman, W. Hu, Y. Guo, P. Valencia, P. Sikka, P. Corke, C. Lee, J. Henshall, K. Prayaga, J. O'Grady, M. Reed, and A. Fisher. The design and evaluation of a mobile sensor/actuator network for autonomous animal control. In *Proceedings of the 6th international conference on Information processing in sensor networks*, New York, NY, USA, 2007. ACM.

[35] G. Werner-Allen, K. Lorincz, J. Johnson, J. Lees, and M. Welsh. Fidelity and yield in a volcano monitoring sensor network. *USENIX OSDI*, 2006.

[36] T. Winter et al. draft-ietf-roll-rpl-19: RPL: IPv6 routing protocol for low power and lossy networks. (in progress), 2011.

[37] J. Zhao and R. Govindan. Understanding packet delivery performance in dense wireless sensor networks. In *Proceedings of the 1st international conference on Embedded networked sensor systems*, New York, NY, USA, 2003. ACM.

Simbeeotic: A Simulator and Testbed for Micro-Aerial Vehicle Swarm Experiments

Bryan Kate
Harvard University
Cambridge, MA, USA
bkate@eecs.harvard.edu

Jason Waterman
Harvard University
Cambridge, MA, USA
waterman@eecs.harvard.edu

Karthik Dantu
Harvard University
Cambridge, MA, USA
kar@eecs.harvard.edu

Matt Welsh
Google, Inc.
Seattle, WA, USA
mdw@mdw.la

ABSTRACT

Micro-aerial vehicle (MAV) swarms are an emerging class of mobile sensing systems. Simulation and staged deployment to prototype testbeds are useful in the early stages of large-scale system design, when hardware is unavailable or deployment at scale is impractical. To faithfully represent the problem domain, a MAV swarm simulator must be able to model the key aspects of the system: actuation, sensing, and communication. We present Simbeeotic, a simulation framework geared toward modeling swarms of MAVs. Simbeeotic enables algorithm development and rapid MAV prototyping through pure simulation and hardware-in-the-loop experimentation. We demonstrate that Simbeeotic provides the appropriate level of fidelity to evaluate prototype systems while maintaining the ability to test at scale.

Categories and Subject Descriptors

I.6.3 [**Simulation and Modeling**]: Applications; I.2.9 [**Artificial Intelligence**]: Robotics—*Autonomous Vehicles*

General Terms

Design, Experimentation, Measurement

Keywords

Swarm, Micro-Aerial Vehicle, Simulation, Testbed

1. INTRODUCTION

Simulation is often used in systems research for rapid prototyping, emulation of future architectures, and testing at scale. In this paper we present a simulator and hardware testbed that facilitate the development of micro-aerial vehicle (MAV) swarms.

MAV swarms are an emerging class of mobile sensing systems. As opposed to a single, more capable robot, MAV swarms employ a group of autonomous micro-robots to accomplish a common goal. Research platforms include quadrotors [15], fixed-wing aircraft [9], small "flying motes" [20], and insect-scale ornithopters [25]. Like sensor networks, MAV swarms rely on spatial diversity and collective sensing to explore a target area. However, MAVs must also be concerned with classic robotics challenges such as obstacle avoidance, navigation, planning, and environmental manipulation.

Our research is focused on MAV swarms comprised of thousands of smaller, less capable vehicles [21]. In this subset of the MAV swarm space the challenges faced by individual MAVs are similar to those of static sensor network nodes; computation is limited, sensing is minimal, and energy is scarce. However, there are differences between the two domains that invalidate some of the assumptions made in static sensor network deployments. For example, the radio is no longer the primary energy sink – it is dwarfed by the energy needed for actuation. Additionally, duty cycling the hardware to save energy is not an option when the vehicle is in flight. We contend that conducting research in this domain necessitates treating autonomous mobility as a first class concern in simulation tools and testbeds.

The main contribution of this work is a new simulation environment and MAV testbed. The core requirements for building a holistic MAV swarm simulator in the vein of other simulators [13] are defined as follows:

- **Scalability** The simulator must be able to simulate thousands of MAVs in a single scenario. Scale of deployment is an important aspect of swarm research. Without the ability to study algorithms at true swarm scale, some of the hard problems will be missed.

- **Completeness** Simulations should model as much of the problem domain as possible. Though research may be conducted on a subset of swarm design (e.g. flight control or networking), it is advantageous to construct a holistic view of the problem in which complex interactions are revealed. For MAV swarms, this means modeling *actuation*, *sensing*, and *communication* for each application.

- **Variable Fidelity** The desire to improve the accuracy of models is often at odds with simulation performance (scalability in this case). Users should be free to construct models with the appropriate level of fidelity to capture the subtleties of their problem. For example, researchers working on emergent algorithms may not require realistic flight control loops, whereas those working on controls will require accurate sensor and flight dynamics models but may not be concerned with network protocols. Using the same simulator, these researchers can work to improve the modeling of their domain while retaining the ability to combine their efforts and simulate the system as a whole.

- **Staged Deployment** No matter how detailed, simulation cannot completely capture every situation that will be encountered in the real world. While the ultimate goal is to deploy a swarm of MAVs, building hardware can be expensive and time consuming. The simulator can facilitate the development of control software and inform the hardware design process by providing a staged deployment feature, allowing prototype hardware to respond to both real and simulated inputs.

We present Simbeeotic, a simulation framework constructed from the above requirements. Simbeeotic supports both pure simulation and hardware-in-the-loop (HWIL) experimentation with a radio controlled (RC) helicopter testbed. The simulator relies on modular software design principles and a commitment to deployment-time configuration to provide modeling flexibility and ease of use. It is highly extensible and is designed for repeated experimentation. With Simbeeotic we demonstrate that whole-system modeling is feasible for the MAV swarm domain. The primary contribution of Simbeeotic is the tool itself, which is available to the community at http://robobees.seas.harvard.edu.

2. RELATED WORK

The MAV swarm domain intersects with other research areas, including biologically-inspired algorithms, robotics, and sensor networks. There are high fidelity simulators that exist in each of these communities. Prior to implementing Simbeeotic, we investigated the possibility of using these tools. In general, we were unable to find a simulator that satisfied our completeness requirement. We considered combining multiple simulators to satisfy this goal, but determined that performance would suffer due to the high fidelity of some of the tools. Each simulator uses considerable machine resources to model its own domain for thousands of agents, making our scalability goal untenable with this approach. Finally, we considered the engineering cost of repurposing multiple simulators to be too high, given that these tools are written in a number of languages and are not uniformly maintained.

Implementing a new simulator has several advantages. We can ensure that our requirements are satisfied and make design decisions that suit our needs. Our approach also allows us to evolve the fidelity of each subdomain (e.g. actuation, sensing, communication) as more accuracy is needed. However, we do not want to reinvent what is considered state-of-the-art in each domain. Whenever possible, we leverage open source tools and learn from existing models to avoid duplication of effort. In the rest of this section we discuss the relevant simulation tools from the swarm intelligence, robotics, and sensor networking communities.

The first set of tools considered come from the multi-agent systems and swarm intelligence communities. These simulators are appealing because they can generally model thousands of agents at once. Swarm [10], MASON [14] are two such tools. The main drawback of these simulators is that the they do not faithfully model the environment and actuation, opting for cell-based or 2D continuous worlds. In Swarm and MASON, a significant amount of effort would be put into modeling a three dimensional, physics-based world that is accurate enough to support the staged deployment requirement. MASON provides a builtin 3D space (known as a field

in MASON-speak), but leaves manipulation of objects in the field (e.g. kinematics, collision detection) to the modeler. Breve [12] is very similar to Simbeeotic in that it is a discrete event simulator with an embedded physics engine. Unfortunately, models are written in a domain specific language called Steve (there is limited support for Python), which hinders adoption and limits the number of existing math and science packages available to modelers.

The robotics community has long used simulators as design tools since building hardware is often expensive and time consuming. In many cases, the hardware and software are co-designed, driving the need for accurate modeling of the physical environment. Thus, the strength of robot simulators is generally in modeling the interaction of the robot with the environment (e.g. actuation and sensing). Two commonly used tools are Webots [17] and Player-Stage [5] [23]. Webots models the environment as a three dimensional continuous space and has physics-based sensor models. It is an excellent teaching tool with support for many commercial robot platforms, but fails to meet our scalability requirements. In addition, its commercial nature does not allow for arbitrary modification, as would likely be the case for modeling communication networks and bridging with our testbed. Player-Stage consists of a robot driver interface, Player, and a simulated environment, Stage. Player is used in a client/server fashion to control robot and sensor hardware. Stage is used to simulate robots in a virtual environment, but exports a Player interface so that code can be migrated to a hardware platform. Stage is a 2.5D simulator that scales to handle hundreds of robots in real time for realistic workloads and thousands of robots for simple workloads. Its key limitation as mentioned by the authors [23] is that it is a first-order geometric simulator that does not model acceleration or momentum. Our approach to MAV swarm simulation requires a more comprehensive treatment of vehicle dynamics.

The Robot Operating System (ROS) is a collection of hardware drivers, algorithms, and tools for building robotic applications [22]. ROS users compose agent behaviors from a large set of open source packages that provide functionality for data acquisition and processing, planning, and locomotion. For the most part, ROS is a complementary technology to Simbeeotic. It is primarily used to construct a fully functioning software stack that can be deployed on one or more robots. There are packages that integrate ROS with simulators (including Player-Stage) to execute a robot in a virtual world, but these packages are insufficient for our needs due to shortcomings mentioned above. However, it should be possible to integrate ROS with our simulator in a similar way - a topic that is discussed further in Section 6.

The construction of the GRASP Micro UAV Testbed [16] is similar to Simbeeotic in that an offboard computer remotely controls the vehicles, relying on accurate position and orientation information from a motion capture system. One difference between the two testbeds is fidelity. The researchers using the GRASP testbed are interested in vehicle control, so the simulation includes a dynamics model and accounts for aerodynamic effects. Though we have performed a system identification on our helicopters and constructed a dynamics model, our efforts in simulation have focused on modeling larger swarms with lower fidelity vehicle movements. If researchers are interested in the aggregate behavior of a large swarm, foregoing the simulation of control loops can significantly improve simulation scalability.

The wireless networking and sensor network communities have invested heavily in simulation tools. GloMoSim [26] and ns-3 [19] are widely adopted simulators that model the OSI seven layer architecture. While they do an excellent job of implementing RF propagation, radio models, and network protocols, these tools are singu-

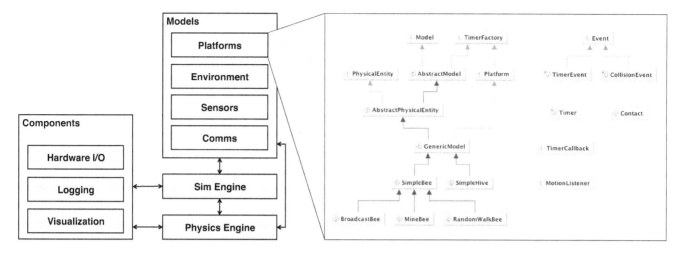

Figure 1: The Simbeeotic architecture. Domain models are plugged into a discrete event simulation engine. The kinematic state of models with physical presence is managed by an integrated physics engine. Several levels of abstraction in the model layer provide flexibility and convenience to modelers. The simulation architecture can be augmented by user-supplied plugin components.

larly focused on networking. A significant effort would be needed to model actuation and sensing to meet our completeness requirement. Rather, our approach is to start with a physical simulation and add networking fidelity as needed. This strategy allows us to selectively integrate the parts of these tools that are useful in our domain.

TOSSIM [13] and EmStar [6] are two popular wireless sensor network simulators. TOSSIM takes the completeness and bridging requirements to an extreme by providing a virtual environment in which the embedded mote software (running TinyOS) is executed. Though the whole-system approach is appealing, TOSSIM restricts users to writing applications in TinyOS. We borrow the idea of staged deployment from EmStar, which allows virtual models (e.g. radios) to be replaced by physical hardware in a testbed. Our staged deployment goal is derived from a desire to iterate on software and hardware designs using virtualized representations prior to building a deployable system. We do not consider EmStar a viable starting point for a MAV swarm simulator because the software is no longer maintained.

3. SIMULATOR DESIGN

At its core, Simbeeotic is a general purpose discrete event simulator. A simulation execution consists of one or more *models* that schedule *events* to occur at a future point in time. The virtual time of the simulation is moved forward by an executive that retrieves the next event from a queue of causally ordered pending events and passes it to the intended recipient for processing. In effect, time passes in between events – the events themselves represent discrete points in time. Since we are interested in modeling the MAV swarm domain, Simbeeotic builds upon the basic discrete event mechanism to provide convenient abstractions for building MAV swarm simulations, such as a virtual environment, robotic platforms, sensors, and radios.

Simbeeotic is written in the Java programming language. Java was chosen for a number of reasons. First, it is widely understood amongst our team and easily learned by neophytes. Second, it is for the most part a cross-platform language. We have confidence that Simbeeotic can be compiled on or distributed in binary form with little effort to the most popular (and some esoteric) operating systems. Third, there exists a large repository of high quality,

open source libraries that can be leveraged by our modelers. At present, Simbeeotic consists of 13,387 lines of Java code in 148 classes and 506 lines of XML schema. Of this code base, 48% makes up the core (including the simulation executor, modeling interfaces, base classes, and common model implementations), 26% is for testbed integration, 13% is example code, 6% defines tools that generate random enclosed environments (such as mine shafts and office buildings), 6% is for visualization components, and 1% is for the main entry point. This codebase builds atop a collection of open source libraries that provide support for physics simulation, linear algebra, statistics, 3D visualization, plotting, message serialization, code generation, and logging.

3.1 Architecture

We have constructed Simbeeotic to fulfill the requirements established in Section 1 (scalability, completeness, variable fidelity, and staged deployment). In addition, we are careful to provide repeatability and promote ease of use and extensibility throughout our design. Scenario repeatability is of utmost importance; experiments must be reproducible given identical inputs. As such, our framework provides seeded random number streams to models and causally orders scheduled events using a set of deterministically generated tiebreak fields. Ease of use improvements include the elimination of boilerplate code through convenience mechanisms and a simple configuration system.

Figure 1 shows an overview of the simulation architecture (lefthand side) and a partial class diagram of the modeling abstractions (righthand side). The heart of the simulation is the simulation engine, which manages the discrete event queue and dispatches events to models, pushing virtual time forward. Prior to the start of the scenario, the simulation engine populates the virtual world from a supplied configuration and initializes all of the models by calling a model-specific initialization routine. The simulation engine is also responsible for answering queries about the model population. It provides an API for locating models based on type or ID.

The model layer sits on top of the simulation engine. The majority of user-supplied code will use model layer interfaces to implement features of the target domain. Simbeeotic employs a layered strategy to provide extension points within the model space. The layered approach API is one way that Simbeeotic fulfills the vari-

```
compass = getSensor("compass", Compass.class);

// a timer that takes a compass reading periodically
Timer compTimer = createTimer(new TimerCallback() {

    public void fire(SimTime time) {

        float h = compass.getHeading();
        ...
    }
}, 0, TimeUnit.SECONDS,
   sensorTimeout, TimeUnit.MILLISECONDS);
```

Figure 2: A code snippet from a model initialization routine demonstrating how to query for attached equipment and schedule a periodic timer (starting immediately and firing every `sensorTimeout` ms).

able fidelity design goal outlined in Section 1. Modelers introduce new functionality by building on layer with the interface that most closely matches the desired level of fidelity of the new model.

At the very bottom are the `Model` and `Event` interfaces. All models implement the `Model` interface, but few do so directly. The `AbstractModel` base class provides a default implementation that introduces other useful mechanisms, such as a seeded random number generator and a timer abstraction. We have committed to a continuous, three dimensional representation of space in Simbeeotic. The `PhysicalEntity` interface is defined to standardize the representation of a physical object (its size, shape, and mass), the information that can be queried about its kinematic state, and how its state can be manipulated (by applying forces, torques, and impulses). While it is possible for users to directly implement the `PhysicalEntity` interface, there exists a base class, `AbstractPhysicalEntity`, that implements the interface by delegating to a rigid body physics engine (described below).

The next level of abstraction, the `GenericModel` class, treats the established physical body as a robotic platform, allowing equipment (e.g. sensors and radios) to be associated with the platform. The attached equipment models do not implement the `PhysicalEntity` interface. Rather, they are granted access to the host platform's physical presence and are attached using a body-relative position and orientation (e.g. antenna position and pointing direction). It is possible for a modeler to develop a new robotic platform by extending `GenericModel`, attaching sensors and radios, and defining custom agent logic using the timer mechanism. We introduce a final abstraction layer with the `SimpleBee` base class. This class provides a simple actuation API (e.g. `turn`, `setLinearVelocity`, `setHovering`) that makes the simulation more accessible to modelers who do not require high fidelity actuation modeling. The `SimpleBee` carries out the actuation commands with an internal kinematic update loop, translating the desired motion into the appropriate forces and torques and applying them to the body.

Modelers do not generally use the event scheduling mechanism directly. Rather, they implement agent logic using the `Timer` mechanism introduced by the `AbstractModel` class. Timers are a familiar abstraction that most modelers are comfortable using. Timers can be scheduled periodically or for single use. A custom callback is provided by the modeler, to be fired when the timer expires (Figure 2). Timers are implemented with a self-scheduled `TimerEvent` under the covers.

We also discourage the use of events for inter-model communication. We feel that in-domain communication mechanisms (e.g.

the radios) should be used for the sake of realism and consistency. These mechanisms expose a familiar API to the modeler and are implemented internally with events.

In addition to building models in the target domain, users can extend the functionality of the simulator by providing *components*. Component implementations can interact with the simulation engine and physics engine directly, or with models by scheduling events. Two components that have received heavy use in our research are the 3D visualization component and a component used to communicate with our MAV testbed (discussed in Section 4). Component instances are created prior to model initialization and can operate in a separate thread of execution. This way it is possible to provide asynchronous I/O components, such as buffered loggers.

The final piece of the Simbeeotic architecture is the physics engine. As described above, the physics engine is used as the backing implementation for the `PhysicalEntity` interface, which is implemented by all models with a physical presence in the simulation. The physics engine we use is JBullet [11], a six degrees of freedom (6DoF) rigid body physics engine written in pure Java. JBullet provides a number of features that are useful in modeling MAV swarms at high fidelity:

- **Rigid Bodies** The MAV platforms and the virtual environment are composed from simple shapes (e.g. box, sphere, cone) and complex geometries (e.g. convex hull, triangular mesh).

- **Dynamics Modeling** The kinematic state of every object is maintained by integrating the forces and torques (e.g. rotor thrust, gravity, wind) applied to physical entities over time.

- **3D Continuous Collision Detection** Physical interactions between objects, such as environmental manipulation by a robot or bump sensors, are easily modeled.

- **Ray Tracing** Used primarily to implement sensors, such as range finders and optical flow.

When a descendant of `AbstractPhysicalEntity` is initialized, a representative rigid body is registered with the physics engine. The information associated with the body include its size, shape, mass, inertial properties, initial position, and orientation. As the rigid body is manipulated over time, its kinematic state is updated. During the course of an event, a model can query the kinematic state of an `AbstractPhysicalEntity`, which delegates the request to the rigid body. The simulation engine invokes JBullet in between events to push the dynamics simulation forward to the time of the next discrete event. We modified the JBullet library to break out of the dynamics simulation if a collision is detected during an update. In this case, the simulation engine checks a registry of interested collision listeners (registered by the models). If found, an event is generated to inform the listener (e.g. a bump sensor) of the collision. If no listener is interested in the collision, the dynamics simulation is resumed.

JBullet integration enables high fidelity actuation and sensor models, but this fidelity comes at a cost. Most of the routines in JBullet execute sequentially, therefore the performance of the simulator is explicitly coupled with the size of the swarm and complexity of the environment (i.e. the number of states that must be integrated and bodies checked for collisions). Section 5.1 evaluates the effect of environmental complexity and swarm size on simulation performance. Our conclusion is that the performance tradeoff is acceptable given the corresponding increase in fidelity.

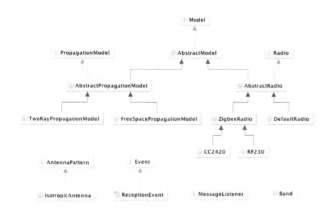

Figure 3: A class diagram for the RF communications package in Simbeeotic. The abstraction defines a physical layer packet-driven radio.

3.2 MAV Domain Models

Modelers contribute new functionality to the community codebase using the extension points described above. Simbeeotic constructs the virtual world from the rigid bodies defined by the physical entities and object definitions supplied in a world configuration file. The configuration file contains definitions of obstacles, structures, and environmental features to be inserted into the environment. Weather is modeled in the simulation by an abstract model (one without physical presence) that can be queried for the current weather state with respect to location. High fidelity models can simulate the effects of weather on themselves (e.g. by applying a wind force to a physical entity) or other models using the information provided (e.g. wind speed and direction).

Most of the builtin sensors provided by Simbeeotic are based on information provided by the physics engine. At present, interfaces and default implementations exist for inertial (accelerometer, gyroscope, optical flow), navigational (position, compass), and environmental (camera, range, bump) sensors. The inertial and navigational sensors use the kinematic state of the host platform, whereas the environmental sensors (and the optical flow sensor) use advanced features of the physics engine, such as ray tracing and collision detection. All of the default sensor models can be configured to produce inaccurate readings from truth state using a Gaussian noise model. Modelers can introduce new implementations of sensors that closely reflect the accuracy, precision, and error profile of real hardware.

Modeling RF communication is something that is done well by community standard simulators [19]. As such, the philosophy for RF in Simbeeotic has been to implement the smallest portion of the OSI seven layer architecture as possible and evolve the fidelity of the models (or integrate another simulator) when the need arises. Figure 3 shows a class diagram for the communications package in Simbeeotic. We implement a simple physical layer abstraction that includes the radio, antenna, and path loss model interfaces. Modelers are free to implement layers on top of the packet-driven radio abstraction.

3.3 Software Engineering Tricks

Simbeeotic relies on two features of the Java programming language, reflection and runtime annotation processing, to provide convenient interfaces to the end user. Though not necessary to achieve our original design goals, these features provide usability improvements over alternative implementations.

```
@Inject
private double maxVel;
private boolean useRadio = false;

@Inject(optional=true)
public void setUseRadio(@Named("use-radio")
                        boolean use) {
    this.useRadio = use;
}
```

Figure 4: A code snippet demonstrating the usage of the `@Inject` annotation for model parameterization.

Both reflection and runtime annotation processing are used to provide a flexible configuration system in Simbeeotic. Our design treats models and components as plugins to the simulator and configures them through dependency injection. Specifically, we use Java reflection to construct scenarios from an arbitrary number and type of models. We define an XML schema for our scenario configuration file that allows users to specify the fully qualified name of Java classes they wish to load and execute. When the scenario file is parsed, the user supplied type is checked for compliance (that it implements the required interfaces) and the specified number of instances are instantiated, registered with the simulation engine, and initialized. Other simulation frameworks, such as Player-Stage, allow for an arbitrary number of user defined scenarios to be loaded based on a configuration file. However, users are restricted to a preexisting set of known model types. By using reflection, any class or component on the Java classpath is eligible for inclusion in the simulation.

The second part of configuration is parameterization. As a convenience to the user, we allow for a set of key-value pairs to be associated with each model or component definition in the scenario file. We use an open source dependency injection library, Google Guice [7] to configure the newly instantiated objects using the supplied parameters. After an object is instantiated, Guice inspects the instantiated class for injection sites (annotated fields or setters). To identify parameters for a model or component, users simply annotate their classes with the `@Inject` annotation, which can be attached to fields and methods. Guice uses the type of the field or method argument to match the injection site with a supplied configuration parameter. An additional `@Named` annotation that is used to disambiguate between parameters of the same type. Figure 4 depicts the usage of these annotations on fields and methods to prepare a model for parameter injection. With the ability to load arbitrary model and component implementations and inject parameters, many decisions regarding scenario construction can be pushed to deployment time.

Figures 11 and 12 of Appendix A list example Java model code and scenario configuration XML that leverage many of the features mentioned above. More comprehensive examples are available in the Simbeeotic source code.

4. HELICOPTER TESTBED

In addition to Simbeeotic, we maintain an indoor MAV testbed for conducting small-scale experiments. The testbed is primarily used to test algorithms in a more realistic environment. Despite our best effort, the simulator cannot form a complete representation of the real world. Our approach is to develop new systems and algorithms at scale in simulation and experiment with smaller deployments in the testbed.

We chose the E-flite Blade mCX2 [4] RC helicopter as the aerial platform for the testbed. The mCX2 is a low cost ($100), off-the-shelf vehicle. The mCX2 is quite limited in its capabilities; it has a payload of up to 5 grams and a flight time on the order of 5-10 minutes. It carries a proprietary control board that processes RC commands and stabilizes flight with an embedded gyroscope (yaw axis only). As a stock system it has no other processors, sensors, or radios. There are several advantages to using this platform. First, building a swarm from these helicopters is not prohibitively expensive. Second, the small size (20cm in length) allows multiple helicopters to be flown in our 7m x 6m laboratory space. The helicopter serves as a convincing prototype for the intended target of our research, insect-scale MAVs, in terms of flight time and capability. One disadvantage of the mCX2 is that it is a toy, not a research robot. Processing, sensing, and communication hardware must be added to make the vehicle into an autonomous swarm agent.

4.1 Remote Control

The helicopter testbed is instrumented with a Vicon [24] motion capture system. The Vicon sensors are capable of capturing the position and orientation of an object (adorned with reflective markers) in our testbed with sub-millimeter accuracy at 100Hz. This information is made available to programs that remotely control the helicopters. We achieve computer control by disassembling the supplied joystick and removing the radio transmitter daughterboard. Though the wireless protocol between the transmitter and helicopter is proprietary, the transmitter board is driven by a serial interface. The input signal to the transmitter is composed of four RC command values; yaw, pitch, roll, and throttle. We connect the transmitter to a PC with a USB-serial cable and allow the RC commands to be generated programmatically.

A testbed gateway machine mediates access to the observed helicopter state and RC transmitters. For helicopter state (measured by Vicon) the gateway provides a publish-subscribe mechanism for pushing updates to interested clients. Clients receive updates via messages that are serialized using Google Protocol Buffers [8]. The information in each update includes the Vicon frame number (essentially a timestamp) along with the object's identifier, position, orientation, and an occlusion flag (indicating that Vicon has lost track of the object in this frame). The gateway also provides a server for controlling each helicopter, which accepts <yaw, pitch, roll, throttle> command tuples. The server ensures that at most one client is connected to each helicopter and sends the latest RC commands to the transmitter at the required 50Hz. Clients communicate with the testbed gateway machine over a Gigabit Ethernet LAN.

4.2 Simbeeotic Integration

It is possible to write a standalone program that communicates with the testbed gateway to control the helicopters in the testbed. However, we realize that writing such programs would result in significant overlap with Simbeeotic, given that virtual sensor outputs would need to be constructed from the absolute position and orientation information provided by Vicon. We chose instead to integrate the helicopter testbed with Simbeeotic, allowing the modeler to leverage the virtual sensor implementations that already exist and conduct hybrid experiments with simulated and real MAVs. We refer to this operating mode as hardware-in-the-loop (HWIL) simulation. This technique is similar to the staged deployment mechanism in EmStar [6], which allows a simulated network to be transparently backed by real hardware.

We accomplish the testbed integration, depicted in Figure 5, by introducing *ghost models* in the simulator for physical objects that

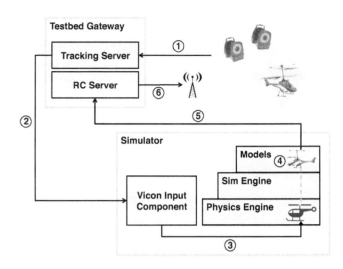

Figure 5: The HWIL cycle in Simbeeotic. Vicon cameras track the position and orientation of a helicopter and push frames to a tracking server (1), which pushes updates (2) to registered clients. A Vicon input component in Simbeeotic receives the update and overrides the kinematic state (3) of the corresponding object in the physics engine. When the ghost model executes an event (4) it has the most recent state of the helicopter. If a command is issued, it is sent to the RC command server (5) where it is dispatched by the RF transmitter (6) to the helicotper.

are tracked by Vicon. The ghost models implement the same PhysicalEntity interface as the simulated models, so interaction between the two is unchanged. The difference is that the ghost model's kinematic state is derived from the Vicon input, not the physics engine. However, the virtual sensors and other models that interrogate the virtual environment rely on the presence of an object in the physics engine for every physical entity. To fulfill this requirement, we simply create an object with the correct size, shape, and mass in the physics engine and periodically override its kinematic state with the information from Vicon. We introduce a new component that is responsible for connecting to the testbed gateway and receiving state updates. The simulation allows for the internal state of tracked objects in the physics engine to be updated prior to executing each event. Thus, whenever an event is executed, the state of all physical entities in the simulation is correctly represented by the physics engine. Some minor modifications to JBullet were required to allow the state to be set and to integrate the new state forward correctly in between Vicon updates.

Sending RC commands is similar. Upon initialization, each ghost MAV model opens a socket that connects to the testbed gateway. The RC commands are fed over the wire to the transmitter, which controls the helicopter in turn. The effects of the commands are witnessed by the Vicon, and the loop is closed.

Simbeeotic processes events as fast as possible when executing a pure simulation. However, the simulator must make an effort to run in realtime when hardware is attached. We make the assumption that the wallclock time necessary to execute an event is less than the virtual time between the current event and its immediate successor. If this assumption holds then it is trivial to maintain a soft realtime schedule by delaying the processing of an event until a corresponding system time has passed. When event processing violates this assumption, events are processed as fast as possible to catch up. This approach works in practice, though it compels modelers to keep events simple (arguably a good thing) and avoid scheduling simultaneous events.

4.3 HWIL Discussion

The testbed integration allows us to fly real vehicles using virtual sensors in a simulated environment. This arrangement allows us to transform our laboratory space into an arbitrarily complex proving ground, with virtual obstacles and features. One advantage of this setup is the ability to test the limits of proposed hardware and software payloads. The physics engine cannot always capture subtleties like aerodynamic ground effects and servo actuation error. The HWIL tests can aid in the iterative design process by observing these phenomena early on.

Our HWIL arrangement has some disadvantages as well. First and foremost, we are completely coupled to Vicon. Without a very accurate measurement of position and orientation, we would not be able to write sensors that convey the truth about the physical object. Second, we cannot fly outdoors. This is not a severe limitation at the moment, but our laboratory can only accommodate a handful of physical helicopters. Third, the control software for the helicopter is running in the simulator on a PC-class system. We run the risk of developing software that uses far too many resources for the eventual platform to handle. A TOSSIM-like approach to whole-system simulation may be needed to keep the modelers honest. Finally, our current setup does not allow for any processing or sensing to occur on the physical helicopter. This is why we refer to the remote-control HWIL solution as staged deployment. It is merely a stepping stone to truly autonomous MAVs. Section 6 discusses the possibility of extending the HWIL approach to communication hardware and how Simbeeotic can facilitate a move toward autonomous MAVs.

There are multiple sources of latency in the HWIL loop described above, including capture and processing time for Vicon frames, the transmission of MAV tracks to Simbeeotic over the LAN, processing events in Simbeeotic, sending RC commands to the testbed gateway over the LAN, and broadcasting the RC commands via the wireless link. If needed, the tracking server, RC server, and simulation could be co-located, eliminating the LAN. However, our experiments have shown that the round-trip loop latency in the testbed does not cause control instability or a substantive delay in MAV reaction time. We speculate that the latency introduced by the processing loop is absorbed by the relatively slow update rate of the RC helicopters (50Hz). In addition, if a command is delayed there is not a noticeable impact on the position and orientation of the MAV. Unlike the GRASP testbed, which focuses on fast, complicated maneuvers, our MAVs typically move at a rate of 0.5–$1.0 \frac{m}{s}$. At this velocity a 20ms latency might result in a positional drift of a few centimeters. Since the HWIL loop latency is not an observable hindrance to our experiments, little effort has been put into characterizing and minimizing the delay in our testbed.

When we first integrated the testbed MAVs into Simbeeotic we defined a common helicopter interface with the intention of creating HWIL-agnostic control behaviors. We defined two implementations of the interface, one that is purely simulated and one that interacts with the testbed hardware. The simulated helicopter implements control commands by applying a force (derived from a dynamics model) on its body in the physics engine. The HWIL helicopter implementation forwards the command to the testbed gateway as described above. However, our users never embraced the simulated helicopter model, preferring to try new behaviors at scale atop models based on `SimpleBee` and produce a separate behavior that interacts with the helicopter interface (for HWIL experiments) if needed. We conclude that the fidelity afforded by the simulated helicopter implementation is not required for the swarm experiments conducted by most members of our group.

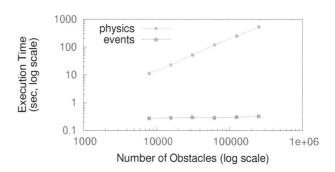

Figure 6: The overhead of collision detection in Simbeeotic. A fixed number of MAVs are simulated with a varying number of static obstacles. The amount of time to execute the event logic is constant. The number of required collision checks between MAVs and obstacles (and the time spent in the physics engine) grows linearly as obstacles are introduced.

5. EVALUATION

We have used Simbeeotic for over two years (one year with HWIL) to conduct research on MAV swarms. In this section we evaluate the performance of the simulator and present two applications that use Simbeeotic to explore the MAV swarm domain.

5.1 Simulation Performance

Since Simbeeotic is used in daily experimentation, we can state from experience that the tool meets our needs. However, it is beneficial to know the limits of the simulator, how modeler and user decisions can impact performance, and how the tool might be improved with future work. We evaluate the performance of the simulator and our ability to meet our scalability objectives based on three challenges:

- **Environment Complexity** The number of objects defined in the environment (e.g. obstacles, structures) determines how much collision checking is necessary during each physics update. Complicated scenarios can slow down the simulator.

- **Swarm Size** As more MAVs are introduced there is more work to be done by the physics engine to maintain the kinematic states of the moving objects. In addition, each new MAV represents an additional workload (events to process) to execute the agent's logic.

- **Model Complexity** Higher fidelity agent logic is likely to impact performance since complex events take longer to simulate.

Defining a single performance goal for the simulator is difficult given that modelers can construct scenarios that contain models of varying fidelity and execute in arbitrarily complex environments. Our motivation for constructing the simulator was to study large swarms of less capable MAVs. Thus, we focus on a performance goal of simulating one thousand MAVs executing a typical workload in soft realtime or better[1]. Our experiments show that Simbeeotic is capable of simulating thousands of MAVs executing a typical workload and hundreds of MAVs executing a complex workload in

---

[1]The scalability goal is lowered for HWIL scenarios to ensure that RC commands are issued as close as possible to a realtime schedule (i.e. the helicopters do not crash).

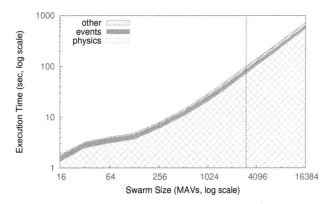

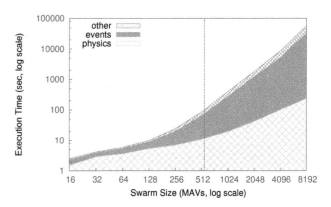

Figure 7: The number of events to process and kinematic states to integrate increases linearly with swarm size. The corresponding event and physics execution times reflect this increase. The dashed vertical line indicates the point above which soft realtime cannot be achieved with this workload (3,074 MAVs).

Figure 8: The simulation runtime does not increase linearly for the broadcast scenario. A nontrivial amount of work is undertaken for each radio transmission event, which may also generate reception events on all other MAVs. The event execution time dominates this scenario as the swarm scales. The dashed vertical line indicates the point above which soft realtime cannot be achieved with this workload (550 MAVs).

soft realtime. As with other discrete event simulators, Simbeeotic is capable of simulating faster than realtime when there is no testbed hardware in the loop.

We define a typical MAV workload to consist of a random walk (10Hz kinematic update rate) and a periodic sensor reading (1Hz compass). In all of the following experiments the MAVs operate for 100 virtual seconds and start from random locations within 20m of the origin. We instrument Simbeeotic to record the amount of wallclock time necessary to simulate the physics (in between events) and run the agent logic (the events themselves). All measurements are taken on a 2.2GHz quad-core laptop with 8GB of RAM using the HotSpot JVM version 1.6.0_26.

We begin with an experiment that addresses the environmental complexity challenge. We measure the overhead of collision detection by simulating a small swarm (32 MAVs) executing the workload defined above. A variable number of static obstacles are introduced into the environment at each iteration of the experiment. As the number of obstacles grows, we expect the collision detection routines to take more time. Performing naive collision detection is $O(n^2)$ in time. Fortunately, JBullet employs more sophisticated collision detection routines that reduce the number of compared objects. Since the kinematic state of a static object in JBullet is not integrated forward at each time step, we can attribute any increase in the physics simulation time to increased collision checks (and likely some added overhead). Further, we expect this increase to be linear with respect to the number of obstacles (as opposed to quadratic) because two statically placed objects are not checked for collisions. Thus, the only collisions being checked are between the MAVs and the obstacles. The results in Figure 6 show that the amount of time to execute the events (agent logic) is constant through the course of the experiment (the swarm size does not change). However, the overall time spent in the physics simulator increases linearly with the number of objects introduced. MAV swarm modelers must be informed that environmental complexity, not just swarm size, can have a significant impact on the performance of the simulation.

The next experiment aims to characterize the scalability of the simulator with respect to swarm size. With each iteration of this experiment we vary the number of MAVs deployed into a constant environment (no obstacles). The MAVs execute the typical workload defined above. We expect increased collision checks (between

MAVs) and a linear increase in the time needed to update the kinematic states of the MAVs. Figure 7 shows the results of this experiment. The simulation scales roughly linearly as the swarm size is increased. The number of events (and the corresponding event execution time) scales linearly as well. Using this workload, it is possible to simulate 3,074 MAVs in soft realtime. These scalability results are comparable to the performance of Player-Stage using a similarly defined "simple" workload [23].

We address the final performance challenge, model complexity, by introducing an additional element to the workload – each MAV broadcasts a radio message at 1Hz. The result of this addition is a significant increase in the event execution time. The increase in event time has two main causes, event complexity and message explosion. The former refers the nontrivial amount of work that must be done to send each packet. The propagation model considers every other radio-equipped model as a potential recipient and performs path loss calculations between the two radios. This includes determining the antenna positions and orientations, extracting the gains from the antenna patterns, and computing the signal strength at the recipient. Though there is a cutoff distance in the path loss model, this optimization is not useful in the scenario under test because the MAVs are closely spaced. Message explosion refers to the number of receive events that will be generated as a result of each packet transmitted. It is possible that n^2 events are generated each second in the simulation. In this case, some events are not generated due to low signal strength at the recipient. Despite the relative simplicity of the receive event processing, the sheer number that need to be processed can add significant overhead. The results of this experiment are shown in figure 8. The overhead of creating and enqueuing these events is likely the source of the increase in the 'other' category. With this workload, we can simulate 550 MAVs in soft realtime.

We set out to create a complete simulator for the MAV swarm domain. These experiments demonstrate that Simbeeotic meets our scalability goals for typical workloads (thousands of MAVs in soft realtime). They also reaffirm the premise that environment complexity and model fidelity can significantly impact performance. Section 6 discusses potential modifications to improve the scalability of the simulator.

(a) Virtual World

(b) Helicopter Testbed

Figure 9: A HWIL deployment of a MAV swarm. Five testbed MAVs are deployed alongside 45 simulated MAVs to search a space for flowers. The circle in the virtual world represents a flower patch (also visible in the testbed floor), and the box at the center denotes the MAV hive.

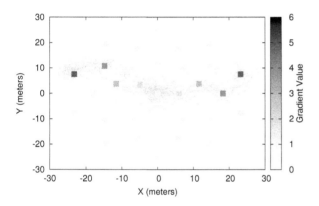

Figure 10: An overhead trace of five simulated MAVs navigating through the environment with the assistance of a gradient field provided by RF beacons (square dots). The gradient in this case specifies two paths away from the center. The MAVs use the value and the signal strength of beacon packets as input to a biased random walk (chemotaxis) algorithm. The MAVs are successful in traveling between the hive and the edge of the gradient field along the two paths.

5.2 Example Scenarios

We describe two MAV swarm scenarios that we have simulated using Simbeeotic. The main goal of the first scenario is coverage. The MAV swarm is deployed to search a space for features of interest (e.g. flowers) and manipulate the environment where the features are located (e.g. chemical sampling, pollination). There are many possible solutions to the swarm coordination problem, including static task assignment, cooperative planning, and emergent behavior. We employ a system that coordinates the actions of the swarm from a centralized location called the hive [2]. We discretize the world into cells and dispatch MAVs from the hive to perform a specific task until they are low on energy, at which point they return to recharge. A planner at the hive analyzes the results of the trip (the information collected) and determines which cells require more attention. Figure 9 shows a snapshot of our swarm management system executing a search and survey scenario using 45 virtual MAVs and 5 testbed helicopters. The lefthand panel shows a

Simbeeotic visualization of the virtual world, while the righthand panel shows the helicopters flying under PC control. This example demonstrates that Simbeeotic has adequate modeling fidelity in actuation and sensing to fly real hardware, and that the staged deployment goals are satisfied.

The second scenario explores the possibility of using RF beacons embedded in the environment as navigational aids for flying MAVs. Figure 10 shows an overhead trace of MAVs using a biased random walk algorithm in a gradient field [3] to navigate along two preferred paths. The MAVs and beacons are equipped with virtual CC2420 radios and isotropic antennas. The two-ray RF propagation model is used to calculate path loss. The MAVs use the value and signal strength of beacon packets to determine the direction of travel in the gradient. This example demonstrates one way that RF communication can be used in a MAV swarm.

6. ONGOING WORK

There are three main directions for future work – scalability, fidelity, and autonomy. From the results in Section 5.1 it is clear that the the physics engine is a bottleneck. We rely heavily on JBullet for modeling actuation (dynamics, collision detection) and sensing (ray tracing). Though it has satisfied our needs thus far, we may consider replacing JBullet with Bullet [1] as we move toward modeling swarms with tens of thousands of MAVs. JBullet is a pure Java port of Bullet, which is written in C++. In addition to being written in a native language, newer versions of Bullet support hardware acceleration on the GPU. The potential performance improvement may be worth the modest engineering effort to create Java wrappers for the subset of the Bullet interfaces used by Simbeeotic.

Though we model the breadth of the MAV swarm domain, the fidelity of the networking models in Simbeeotic could be improved. To date, our work on MAV swarms has not focused on communication. It is likely that the networking interfaces will need to evolve beyond the simple physical layer implementation. We will look to leverage community standard tools and models such as ns-3 as our needs develop. In addition, we may expand our HWIL capabilities to include real radios in a mote testbed, much link in EmStar. On first inspection, it appears that the ghost model approach will work well with a radio interface. Packets sent on a ghost interface would be transmitted on the physical radio in addition to the virtual radio, and packets received on the physical radio would be captured and injected as a virtual packet reception. Some care must be taken to prevent duplicate transmission and reception events by ghost radio models participating in both domains.

A major limitation of our testbed is the dependence on an accurate motion capture system. We expect to phase out this dependence as our MAV platform evolves. For example, our MAVs may soon be equipped with enough sensors to stabilize themselves and perform local obstacle avoidance but lack the computing power for path planning. In this case a Simbeeotic model may simulate the higher levels of the MAVs software stack (e.g. planning, coordination) while the lower levels (e.g. control, obstacle avoidance) are executed onboard. With such a deployment we can no longer rely on a purely simulated environment. Obstacles must be represented in both worlds, a feat that can be accomplished by adding Vicon markers to physical objects and creating a corresponding ghost representation. Ideally, we would want to feed virtual sensor information wirelessly to the testbed MAVs, allowing them to sense purely virtual objects. However, this might not be feasible considering the bandwidth and latency requirements of the sensors.

As we develop the software stack that will execute on the autonomous MAVs, it may be possible to leverage ROS [22]. This presents an opportunity for Simbeeotic to be used as a virtual input to software that will be embedded on a vehicle. We view this TOSSIM-like approach as another (purely simulated) intermediate step toward MAV autonomy that is orthogonal to HWIL operation.

On our path toward fully autonomous MAVs we may relax the requirement that physical objects and virtual objects are co-visible. Instead, we could construct a virtual world to match the physical world and ignore interactions between MAVs. This would allow us to experiment outside of the testbed and obviate the need for accurate tracking once the MAVs are fully autonomous (other than for ground truth during experimentation). We have considered constructing a less accurate tracking system using Microsoft Kinect [18] sensors that can be deployed outside of our testbed. This system would be used for collecting ground truth positional information of indoor exploration experiments. Simbeeotic would remain as a useful tool, allowing physical MAVs to coordinate with simulated MAVs via HWIL in the communication layer, as described above.

7. CONCLUSIONS

MAV swarms are an emerging class of mobile sensor systems with strong ties to the robotics, sensor networking, and swarm intelligence communities. We present Simbeeotic, a simulation environment and testbed for MAV swarms to support research effort in this area. Simbeeotic is designed to be flexible and easy to use. The domain modeling interfaces are designed to cover a complete view of the application space, including actuation, sensing, and communication. We show that Simbeeotic is capable of simulating MAV swarms at scale, and demonstrate its usefulness in exploring new concepts with real hardware. Simbeeotic is available as open source at http://robobees.seas.harvard.edu.

8. ACKNOWLEDGEMENTS

We would like to thank the anonymous reviewers for their insight and detailed feedback. Special thanks to Eddie Kohler for his encouragement and editorial contributions. This work was partially supported by the National Science Foundation (award number CCF-0926148). Any opinions, findings, and conclusions or recommendations expressed in this material are those of the authors and do not necessarily reflect the views of the National Science Foundation.

9. REFERENCES

[1] Bullet Physics Library. http://bulletphysics.org/wordpress.

[2] K. Dantu, B. Kate, J. Waterman, P. Bailis, and M. Welsh. Programming micro-aerial vehicle swarms with karma. In *Proceedings of the 9th ACM Conference on Embedded Networked Sensor Systems*, SenSys '11, pages 121–134, New York, NY, USA, 2011. ACM.

[3] A. Dhariwal, G. Sukhatme, and A. Requicha. Bacterium-inspired robots for environmental monitoring. In *Proceedings of the 2004 IEEE International Conference on Robotics and Automation (ICRA '04)*, volume 2, pages 1436–1443, May 2004.

[4] E-flite Blade MCX2. http://www.e-fliterc.com.

[5] B. Gerkey and R. Vaughan. The player/stage project: Tools for multi-robot and distributed sensor systems. In *Proceedings of the International Conference on Advanced Robotics (ICAR 2003)*, pages 317–323, 2003.

[6] L. Girod, J. Elson, A. Cerpa, T. Stathopoulos, N. Ramanathan, and D. Estrin. EmStar: a software environment for developing and deploying wireless sensor networks. In *Proceedings of the annual conference on USENIX Annual Technical Conference (ATEC '04)*. USENIX Association, 2004.

[7] Google Guice. http://code.google.com/p/google-guice.

[8] Google Protocol Buffers. http://code.google.com/apis/protocolbuffers.

[9] S. Hauert, L. Winkler, J. Zufferey, and D. Floreano. Ant-based swarming with positionless micro air vehicles for communication relay. *Swarm Intelligence*, 2(2-4):167–188, 2008.

[10] D. Hiebeler. The Swarm simulation system and individual-based modeling. In *Proceedings of Decision Support 2001: Advanced Technologies for Natural Resource Management*, Toronto, Sept. 1994.

[11] JBullet. http://jbullet.advel.cz.

[12] J. Klein. Breve: A 3d simulation environment for the simulation of decentralized systems and artificial life. In *Proceedings of Artificial Life VIII, the 8th International Conference on the Simulation and Synthesis of Living Systems*, 2002.

[13] P. Levis, N. Lee, M. Welsh, and D. Culler. TOSSIM: accurate and scalable simulation of entire tinyos applications. In *Proceedings of the 1st international conference on Embedded networked sensor systems (SenSys '03)*, Nov. 2003.

[14] S. Luke, C. Cioffi-Revilla, L. Panait, and K. Sullivan. MASON: A new multi-agent simulation toolkit. In *Proceedings of the 2004 SwarmFest Workshop*, 2004.

[15] N. Michael, J. Fink, and V. Kumar. Cooperative manipulation and transportation with aerial robots. *Autonomous Robots*, 30(1):73–86, Sept. 2010.

[16] N. Michael, D. Mellinger, Q. Lindsey, and V. Kumar. The GRASP Multiple Micro-UAV Testbed. *Robotics & Automation Magazine, IEEE*, 17(3):56–65, 2010.

[17] O. Michel. WebotsTM: Professional mobile robot simulation. *International Journal of Advanced Robotic Systems*, 1(1):40–43, 2004.

[18] Microsoft Kinect. http://www.xbox.com/kinect.

[19] ns-3. http://www.nsnam.org.

[20] A. Purohit, Z. Sun, M. Salas, and P. Zhang. SensorFly: Controlled-mobile sensing platform for indoor emergency response applications. In *Proceedings of the 10th International Conference on Information Processing in Sensor Networks (IPSN '11)*, Apr. 2011.

[21] RoboBees. http://robobees.seas.harvard.edu.

[22] Robot Operating System. http://www.ros.org.

[23] R. T. Vaughan. Massively multi-robot simulations in stage. *Swarm Intelligence*, 2(2-4):189–208, 2008.

[24] Vicon Motion Capture Sytems. http://www.vicon.com.

[25] R. Wood. The first takeoff of a biologically inspired at-scale robotic insect. *IEEE Transactions on Robotics*, 24(2):341–347, 2008.

[26] X. Zeng, R. Bagrodia, and M. Gerla. GloMoSim: a library for parallel simulation of large-scale wireless networks. In *Proceedings of the twelfth workshop on Parallel and distributed simulation (PADS '98)*, pages 154–161. ACM, July 1998.

APPENDIX

A. EXAMPLE MODEL AND CONFIG

```java
public class InstrumentBee extends SimpleBee
                      implements MessageListener {

private Compass compass;
private Radio radio;

@Inject(optional=true)
@Named("max-vel")
private float maxVelocity = 2.0f;    // m/s
private float velocitySig = 0.2f;    // m/s
private float headingSig = 0.2f;     // rad
private long sensorTimeout = 1000;   // ms
private long radioTimeout = 1000;    // ms

@Override
public void initialize() {

  super.initialize();
  setHovering(true);

  compass = getSensor("compass", Compass.class);
  radio = getRadio();

  createTimer(new TimerCallback() {

    public void fire(SimTime time) {
      compass.getHeading();
    }
  }, 0, TimeUnit.SECONDS,
     sensorTimeout, TimeUnit.MILLISECONDS);

  createTimer(new TimerCallback() {

    public void fire(SimTime time) {
      radio.transmit(new byte[] {1, 2, 3, 4});
    }
  }, 0, TimeUnit.SECONDS,
     radioTimeout, TimeUnit.MILLISECONDS);
}

@Override
public void finish() {
}
```

```java
@Override
protected void updateKinematics(SimTime time) {

  // randomly vary the heading (rot. about Z axis)
  turn(getRandom().nextGaussian() * headingSig);

  // randomly vary the velocity in X & Z dirs
  Vector3f newVel = getDesiredLinearVelocity();

  newVel.add(new Vector3f(getRandom().nextGaussian() *
                          velocitySig,
                          0,
                          getRandom().nextGaussian() *
                          velocitySig));

  // cap the velocity
  if (newVel.length() > maxVelocity) {

    newVel.normalize();
    newVel.scale(maxVelocity);
  }

  setDesiredLinearVelocity(newVel);
}

@Override
public void messageReceived(SimTime time, byte[] data,
                            double rxPower) {
  // do nothing
}

@Inject(optional=true)
public final void setVelSig(@Named("vel-sigma")
                            final float sigma) {
  this.velocitySig = sigma;
}

@Inject(optional=true)
public final void setHeadSig(@Named("heading-sigma")
                             final float sigma) {
  this.headingSigma = sigma;
}

@Inject(optional=true)
public final void setSensorTO(@Named("sensor-timeout")
                              final long t) {
  this.sensorTimeout = t;
}

@Inject(optional=true)
public final void setRadioTO(@Named("radio-timeout")
                             final long t) {
  this.radioTimeout = t;
}
}
```

Figure 11: A listing of the Java code for the MAV used in the experiment from Figure 8. The MAV is based on the `SimpleBee`, which provides a simplified locomotion interface (used in `updateKinematics` to implement a random walk). Timers are established at initialization to take a sensor reading and send a message periodically. Both long and short forms of parameter injection (method and field annotation) are demonstrated. This code demonstrates the basic Simbeeotic APIs but serves no useful purpose other than to instrument the simulator in our experiments.

```xml
<?xml version="1.0"?>

<scenario xmlns:xsi="http://www.w3.org/2001/XMLSchema-instance"
          xmlns="http://harvard/robobees/simbeeotic/configuration/scenario">

    <master-seed>
        <constant value="111982"/>
    </master-seed>

    <simulation>
        <end-time>100.0</end-time>
    </simulation>

    <models>
        <model>
            <java-class>harvard.robobees.simbeeotic.model.comms.FreeSpacePropagationModel</java-class>
            <properties>
                <prop name="noise-floor-mean" value="-100"/>
                <prop name="noise-floor-sigma" value="10"/>
                <prop name="range-thresh" value="30"/>
            </properties>
        </model>
        <model>
            <java-class>harvard.robobees.simbeeotic.model.SimpleHive</java-class>
            <start-position x="0" y="0" z="0"/>
        </model>
        <model count="8192">
            <java-class>harvard.robobees.simbeeotic.example.InstrumentBee</java-class>
            <properties>
                <prop name="kinematic-update-rate" value="100"/>
                <prop name="use-random-start" value="true"/>
                <prop name="random-start-bound" value="20"/>
                <prop name="allow-bee-collisions" value="true"/>
                <prop name="radio-timeout" value="1000"/>
                <prop name="sensor-timeout" value="1000"/>
            </properties>
            <sensor name="compass">
                <java-class>harvard.robobees.simbeeotic.model.sensor.DefaultCompass</java-class>
            </sensor>
            <radio>
                <java-class>harvard.robobees.simbeeotic.model.comms.CC2420</java-class>
                <properties>
                    <prop name="tx-power-level" value="31"/>
                </properties>
                <!-- by default an isotropic antenna will be attached -->
            </radio>
            <start-position x="0" y="0" z="0"/>
        </model>
    </models>

    <!-- if you want to see what is happening, uncomment this component
    <components>
        <variation>
         <java-class>harvard.robobees.simbeeotic.component.VisComponent3D</java-class>
         </variation>
    </components>
    -->
</scenario>
```

Figure 12: The scenario configuration file used in the experiment from Figure 8. Users can control the global simulation properties (e.g. master random seed, simulation end time), and add models and components. The structure of a model entry (which must conform to the scenario XML schema) allows users to specify the type of the model to instantiate along with the number of instances. In addition, equipment such as sensors and a radio can be attached. The key-value properties are passed to Guice for injection into user classes that contain @Inject annotations. A description of the virtual world in which these models operate is supplied in a separate configuration file.

TriopusNet: Automating Wireless Sensor Network Deployment and Replacement in Pipeline Monitoring

Ted Tsung-Te Lai[1]   Wei-Ju Chen [1]   Kuei-Han Li[1]   Polly Huang[2,3]   Hao-Hua Chu[1,2]

Department of Computer Science and Information Engineering[1], Graduate Institute of Networking and Multimedia[2],
Department of Electrical Engineering[3]
National Taiwan University, Taipei, Taiwan
{tedlai, r99922148, r98922022}@csie.ntu.edu.tw, phuang@cc.ee.ntu.edu.tw, hchu@csie.ntu.edu.tw

ABSTRACT

This study presents TriopusNet, a mobile wireless sensor network system for autonomous sensor deployment in pipeline monitoring. TriopusNet works by automatically releasing sensor nodes from a centralized repository located at the source of the water pipeline. During automated deployment, TriopusNet runs a sensor deployment algorithm to determine node placement. While a node is flowing inside the pipeline, it performs placement by extending its mechanical arms to latch itself onto the pipe's inner surface. By continuously releasing nodes into pipes, the TriopusNet system builds a wireless network of interconnected sensor nodes. When a node runs at a low battery level or experiences a fault, the TriopusNet system releases a fresh node from the repository and performs a node replacement algorithm to replace the failed node with the fresh one. We have evaluated the TriopusNet system by creating and collecting real data from an experimental pipeline testbed. Comparing with the non-automated static deployment, TriopusNet is able to use less sensor nodes to cover a sensing area in the pipes while maintaining network connectivity among nodes with high data collection rate. Experimental results also show that TriopusNet can recover from the network disconnection caused by a battery-depleted node and successfully replace the battery-depleted node with a fresh node.

Categories and Subject Descriptors

C.3 [Special-Purpose and Application-Based Systems]: Real-time and Embedded Systems, Signal Processing Systems.

General Terms

Design, Experimentation, Performance.

Keywords

Pipeline monitoring, sensor deployment, wireless sensor network.

1. INTRODUCTION

Pipelines are used everywhere to transport substances for human living. For example, water pipelines deliver water to support hu-

man daily activities. Oil pipelines carry valuable natural resources for fuel, electricity generation, or petrochemical production. Flow assurance is a major safety concern for pipelines. For example, water pipelines must deliver clean and uncontaminated water to ensure human health. Therefore, proper monitoring of these pipelines is important.

Traditional monitoring method requires humans to manually place sensors along pipelines. However, this approach has several drawbacks. First, pipelines can be hundreds or even thousands of miles long. Because most pipelines have been built underground or underwater, it is difficult for humans to access these pipelines and install sensors. Second, directly sensing flows inside the pipelines often require either breaking a pipe or limiting sensing points to locations at pipe exits or joints. These challenges in pipeline monitoring motivate the need for automated sensor deployment and replacement.

To overcome these challenges, we have developed TriopusNet, a mobile wireless sensor network system for autonomous pipeline monitoring. Figure 1 illustrates the overview of TriopusNet. Human effort is strictly needed only at the start of the deployment to prepare and deposit mobile sensors at the source of the water pipeline. The system then automates in-field deployment and replacement of mobile sensors by releasing them from the water inlet and leveraging natural water flow propulsion inside pipes to carry sensor nodes. Creating water flow propulsion might also require human to manually turn on the faucet or use a remote-control actuation device to automate this step. Each mobile sensor node in TriopusNet is equipped with one motor that drives three arms. These arms can be extended for the purpose of latching a traveling sensor node onto the pipe's inner surface, thereby fixing the node placement. Because of its mechanical resemblance to octopus, the mobile sensor node is referred to as Triopus, pronounced tree-o-pus.

TriopusNet runs a sensor deployment algorithm, which considers both the sensing coverage in the pipes and the network connectivity among sensor nodes, and computes the deployment location for each released sensor node. Upon arrival at its deployment location, a traveling sensor activates its latching mechanism and attaches itself to the pipe inner surface. As more sensor nodes are released and deployed, the system gradually builds an interconnected wireless sensor network covering the entire pipeline, forming TriopusNet. Automated sensor deployment enables large-scale sensor deployment in pipeline because it reduces the level of human effort to only depositing sensor nodes at the start of the infrastructure deployment.

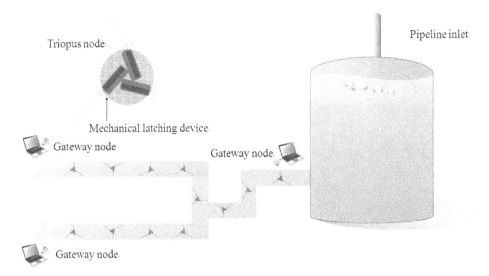

Figure 1. An overview of TriopusNet. The sensor nodes are released from the water inlet points. Each node equips with mechanical arms that can latch to fix a sensor node onto the pipe's inner surface, thereby controlling node deployment inside the pipeline. Sensor network data is wirelessly transmitted to nearby gateway nodes.

Upon detection of low battery level (or a fault), the sensor node retracts its mechanical arms to detach itself from the pipe's inner surface. Flow in the pipes carries the battery-depleted sensor node to exit to a pipe outlet. To repair the network disconnection created by the departed sensor node, the TriopusNet system releases a fresh sensor node and runs the sensor replacement algorithm to position the fresh sensor node and adjust the locations of existing sensor nodes to fill any sensing area and repair any network disconnections.

Previous research [9] addresses the sensor deployment problem in wireless sensor networks. They formulated this as an optimization problem of how and where to place a minimum number of sensor nodes to achieve the maximum sensing coverage and maintain the best possible network connectivity while consuming the least amount of communication energy. They developed optimizing deployment algorithms to solve this problem. However, previous studies fail to directly address the human effort problem, i.e., human effort is still needed for any in-field sensor deployment (and replacement) at the locations determined by their optimizing deployment algorithms. Though some previous systems [16][15] assume sensor nodes capable of physical mobility, their mobility models are often simulated [16] or require continuously traveling sensor nodes without fixed deployment [15]. TriopusNet complements previous work by leveraging water propulsion to carry sensor nodes from water inlet to scale down human effort, and by creating mobile sensor nodes capable of positioning themselves at locations determined by any optimizing deployment algorithm developed by previous systems.

Many related systems [10][19] address fault management in wireless sensor networks. These systems use various techniques to detect sensor node faults and errors, including information fusion for fault detection, collaborative fault detection, etc. However, these techniques do not eliminate the need for human effort to perform in-field replacement of faulty sensor nodes. TriopusNet complements previous work by using free water propulsion to facilitate in-field sensor node replacement. Other previous techniques [17] implement autonomic computing, in which systems self-heal by activating redundant (or backup) components near faulty components. These techniques deploy dense and/or redun-

dant sensor nodes which increases the deployment cost. TriopusNet shares the autonomic computing concept such that a small number of backup sensor nodes (i.e., equal to the number of expected battery-depleted or faulty sensors) are deposited at a pipeline inlet storage and released on an as-needed basis.

The main contributions of this work are:

- Different from traditional sensor network deployment in which human effort is needed to place and replace sensors manually, TriopusNet automates sensor deployment and replacement by leveraging natural water propulsion to carry sensor nodes throughout pipes, thus scales down human effort in deploying and maintaining WSN in pipeline monitoring.

- This study tests and evaluates TriopusNet by developing a real prototype and pipeline testbed. Results show that automated sensor deployment in TriopusNet successfully produced quality deployment using no more sensor nodes than non-automated static deployment. Results also indicate that automated replacement in TriopusNet successfully replaced a battery-depleted sensor node with a fresh sensor node while recovering data collection rate from the departure of a battery-depleted sensor node.

The rest of this study is organized as follows. Section 2 provides the system overview, assumptions, and limitations. Section 3 describes hardware design. Section 4 presents sensor deployment and replacement algorithms. Section 5 describes the experimental testbed. Section 6 gives experimental results. Section 7 discusses limitations and future extensions. Section 8 reviews related work. Finally, Section 9 concludes the study.

2. SYSTEM OVERVIEW, ASSUMPTIONS, AND LIMITATIONS

To understand system assumptions and limitations, this section first provides an overview of how the system dispatches and places sensor nodes in pipelines (Fig. 1). The pipelines interconnect a set of vertical and horizontal pipes, starting with a single water inlet and ending at multiple water outlets (i.e., faucets). In

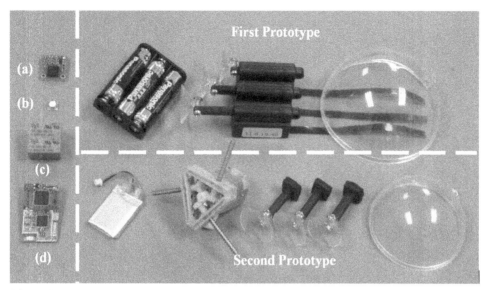

Figure 2. A TriopusNet node contains (a) gyroscope, (b) water pressure sensors, (c) relays, and (d) Kmote CPU board. The first prototype uses three AAA batteries and three linear actuators. The second prototype uses a lithium battery and one customized motor to drive three arms, resulting in a significant size reduction.

other words, pipelines form a virtual tree in which the inlet is the root node, each faucet outlet is a leaf node, a pipe branch point is an intermediate node, each pipe tube is an edge between parent and child nodes, and each flow path is a downward path from the root node to each leaf node. The inlet also serves as the storage point where sensor nodes are deposited into a dispatch queue at the start of deployment. The TriopusNet releases sensor nodes from the dispatch queue while running the sensor deployment algorithm. This approach forms an interconnected wireless network that covers all possible flow paths with sensors.

The proposed system involves the following four steps.

1. *Preparation Step*: The pipeline spatial topology must be measured a-priori as an input for automated sensor deployment. Interested readers may refer to the PipeProbe system [4] on obtaining pipeline spatial topology. The dispatch queue at the inlet must be filled with sensor nodes ready to be released into the pipeline. Each faucet in the pipeline is turned on, one after another, to create a running flow path from the inlet to each outlet. That is, each faucet must be turned on at least once such that sensor nodes can travel and cover all possible flow paths in the pipelines. Each faucet could be turned on either manually (i.e., by the user) or automatically (i.e., by installing a remote-control actuation device). This preparation step constitutes a one-time manual effort at the start of deployment.

2. *Sensor Deployment Step*: Prior to releasing each sensor node, TriopusNet runs the sensor deployment algorithm to compute its deployment position. Sections 4.1 and 4.2 describe the sensor deployment algorithm. The system then sends the "release" message including the deployment position, to the head sensor node in the dispatch queue. The head sensor node retracts its mechanical arms from the dispatch tube and starts its pipe journey. Note that the sensor node requires no power for its physical movement as it uses water flow for propulsion.

3. *Sensor Latching Step*: The sensor node continuously computes its current location as it travels through the pipeline. Section 4.4 describes the sensor localization algorithm. When the sensor node approaches its deployment position, it extends mechanical arms to attach itself to the pipe's inner surface. The sensor node then reports latch completion to the system, and TriopusNet releases the next sensor node (i.e., repeats Step 2). Thus, the deployment of sensor nodes continues until TriopusNet covers all possible flow paths in the pipeline.

4. *Sensor Replacement Step*: Sensor nodes consume battery power during the data collection phase. At some time point, some sensor node may report low-battery to the system. A low-battery sensor node uses its remaining battery power to retract its mechanical arms and detach itself from the pipe's inner surface. The sensor node is then carried by the water current to a faucet, where it exits the pipeline. To recover from the sensing area and network disconnection caused by the departed sensor node, TriopusNet releases fresh sensor nodes (from the dispatch queue) during replacement. Section 4.7 describes the sensor replacement algorithm.

To communicate with sensor nodes inside the pipelines, gateway nodes must be installed prior to any sensor node deployment inside the pipelines. Figure 1 shows that gateway nodes are placed at the inlet and each endpoint in pipelines. To ease manual deployment effort, gateway nodes can be installed outside pipes. To collect data from in-pipe sensor nodes, gateway nodes must have wireless communication with at least one in-pipe sensor node. Gateway nodes must also have a network connection to a laptop (or desktop) computer for remote control, data logging, and automated sensor deployment and replacement algorithms.

The following list summarizes TriopusNet's assumptions (particularly where manual effort is needed) and limitations below:

- The spatial topology of pipelines must be known, including the pipe length, the pipe's internal diameter, horizon-

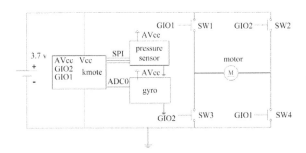

Figure 3. TriopusNet node schematic. An H-arrangement of Switch 1 – 4 is used to control the motor.

Figure 4. The final TriopusNet node prototype

tal/vertical turns, and the faucet size. Interested readers may refer to the PipeProbe system [4] on obtaining pipeline spatial topology.

• In the absence of automatic faucets, manual effort is required to open each faucet in turn and at least once, such that water runs through all pipelines to ensure complete sensor deployment. In addition, manual effort is required to open each faucet when a battery-depleted or faulty node needs to flow out for replacement. Section 7 discusses how to reduce this manual effort.

• The current sensor node measures 6 cm in diameter, which does not fit inside all pipes or may get stuck in some pipes. Given a limited budget in making this proof-of-concept prototype, further engineering efforts may reduce its size. Section 7 discusses how to further reduce the prototype size in the future.

The current sensor prototype uses 2.4 GHz radio (CC2420) to send/receive messages. High frequency radio is not the ideal choice in water, as water absorbs radio waves and limits its transmission range. In water, sonar and light are better communication media than radio [12]. Given this study focuses on the deployment method, we leave the choice of radio an issue to be addressed in the future.

3. HARDWARE DESIGN

Figure 2 shows the components of a Triopus node, and figure 3 presents its block diagram and circuit design. The Triopus node consists of (1) a wireless sensor mote called Kmote [6], (2) a motor that drives three mechanical arms for latching onto and delatching from the pipe's inner surface, (3) a spherical case that encapsulates and waterproofs the node's electrical components, and (4) pressure and gyroscope sensors used for node localization. The details of these components are described as follows.

The Kmote circuit is a clone of a standard TelosB mote, which features a MSP430 microcontroller and CC2420 radio stack. It is Tiny-OS compatible. The main difference between Kmote and TelosB mote is that Kmote separates the CPU circuit board from the USB program uploader circuit broad. In a field deployment, Kmote needs only the CPU board, thus reducing the form factor size of the Triopus node. The CPU board measures 35 mm (L) x 21 mm (W) x 7 mm and weighs approximately 4 grams.

For the latching & delatching mechanism, the first version of Triopus node contains three linear actuators (model PQ-12) made

by Firgelli Technologies [7]. A linear actuator controls a mechanical arm following a linear push and pull motion. To activate a linear actuator for the push motion, the Kmote turns on switch (SW) 1 and 4 to make current flow from left to right on the H-bridge (the right-hand side of Fig. 3). To activate the linear actuator for the pull motion, the Kmote turns on switch (SW) 2 and 3 to reverse the current from flow right to left on the H-bridge. The switches are simply relays controlled by GPIO. To reduce the Triopus node size that is primarily occupied by three PQ-12 linear actuators, the 2nd prototype replaced three motors (each driving a separate mechanical arm) with one motor driving all three mechanical arms and replaced the three AAA batteries with a lithium battery. Motor calibration was achieved by adding a spiral gear that connects and pushes three separate gears moving all three mechanical arms simultaneously. When a Triopus node needs to attach to a pipe location, it extends mechanical arms until they touch the pipe's inner surface. To ensure that the latching mechanism works well, three arms of a Triopus node point to three different angles and form a triangle. Because pipes have different diameters, the arm's stroke length must be long enough to touch the pipe's inner surface on three sides.

To localize in a vertical pipe segment, a Triopus sensor node measures water pressure using an Intersema MS5541C [21] water pressure sensor. The Intersema MS5541C pressure sensor gives pressure readings within a range of 0 to 14 bars (with a resolution of 1.2 mbars) and consumes less than 5 uA operating current. To detect the horizontal pipe turns, the Triopus sensor node uses a gyro-scope sensor [22] to measure the rotational motion along the yaw (z) axis with a ±300°/s range. The gyroscope sensor module is fixed precisely at the top of the upper half of the node's hemispheres such that the gyroscope lays flat on the horizontal plane to obtain an accurate z-axis measurement. Figure 4 shows the final prototype of a Triopus Node.

4. SYSTEM DESIGN

This section describes key software components that support automated sensor deployment and maintenance in TriopusNet. The process of automating sensor deployment and maintenance involves calculating the sensor deployment order, sensor deployment positions, etc. The goal of sensor deployment is two-fold: (1) blockage-free movement and fixation of the sensors in the pipelines, and (2) full sensing and network coverage. The following subsections detail the individual software components as they are activated in the process of a complete deployment and replacement of a battery-depleted node.

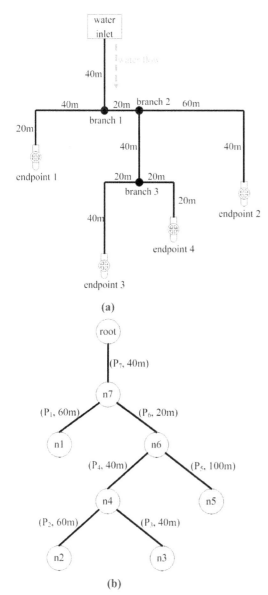

Figure 5. An example pipeline structure (a) with the corresponding virtual tree (b).

4.1 Sensor Deployment Order

This initial phase determines the deployment order of the sensor nodes. Placing nodes close to the releasing point early may result in blockage and hinder the movement of nodes destined for downstream positions. To avoid this problem, the sensor deployment algorithm first transforms the physical layout of the pipelines into a virtual tree, in which the inlet is the root node, each endpoint is a leaf node, each pipe branch point is an intermediate node, and each pipe segment is an edge between parent and child nodes. Figure 5(b) shows the resulting virtual tree transformed from the physical layout (Fig. 5(a)).

The algorithm subsequently runs a *post-order* traversal of the virtual tree, in which the resulting node traversal sequence is also the order of node deployment in pipe segments. Consider the example in Figure 5(b). The post-order traversal sequence is $\{n_1, n_2, n_3, n_4, n_5, n_6, n_7\}$. Following that traversal order, the algorithm

starts the first sensor deployment at the pipe segment p_1 (ending at n_1) then the pipe segment p_2 (ending at n_2), and so forth until reaching pipe segment p_7. This post-order deployment sequence is important for two reasons. (1) It assures that sensor deployment covers all pipe segments. (2) It orders the deployment of a downstream sensor to precede the deployment of its upstream sensors. This prevents a newly released sensor from traveling past one or more latched sensors that may cause knocking-off or blocking in narrow pipes.

4.2 Sensor Deployment

Before sensor nodes can be released, the sensor deployment algorithm computes first the coarse-grain positions – the pipe segment and the approximate latching point. This computation process ensures satisfactory sensing coverage. A Triopus node's capabilities can be modeled as a coverage function of radio distance and sensing quality. A sensing quality utility function can thus be defined based on the sensor capability or application requirement. This study uses a simple coverage function in which each sensor monitors a disk area with a sensing range (radius) R. In this study, full sensing coverage over the monitored pipelines requires any pipe distance between two neighbor sensors to be less than or equal to $2*R$. Sensing coverage means that the sensor network is able to monitor the health of the pipelines in full. Note that this sensor deployment algorithm is not limited to a simple sensor coverage function, but can perform other sensor coverage functions as well.

Assume that the new sensor node is placed in segment S and the sensing range is R. Subtracting $2*R$ distance from the most recently deployed sensor node in segment S gives the position of the new sensor node. If segment S is not long enough to accommodate the new sensor node, the new sensor node is placed in the next segment on the sensor deployment order sequence (Sec 4.1). To bootstrap for the leaf segments, the gateway node at the faucet is considered the only node at the beginning. For intermediate segments, i.e., segments with multiple downstream branches, the first sensor node in an intermediate segment is placed at the position such that the distances to all immediate downstream nodes are less than or equal to $2*R$.

4.3 Sensor Movement

Because sensor mobility leverages the force of water flow within the pipe, an endpoint faucet must be turned on to generate a running flow path. The sensor movement algorithm computes first the flow paths from the inlet to each outlet. The algorithm then selects a path intersecting the pipe segment the node is positioned to. Consider the example in Fig. 5(b). A sensor deployment at the pipe segment p_3 requires the running flow path ($root \rightarrow n_7 \rightarrow n_6 \rightarrow n_4 \rightarrow n_3$) to power its movement. Turning on the endpoint faucet n_3 and turning off all other faucets create this flow path.

4.4 Sensor Localization

As a sensor node travels along its flow path, it continuously calculates and updates its location so that it knows when it has arrived at its assigned location. This study adopts the pipeline localization technique from the PipeProbe system [4], which uses a combination of pressure and gyroscope sensors to detect vertical and horizontal pipe turns. As pipelines have many segments, a flowing sensor node can track its location by counting the number of turns encountered on the flow path between the root inlet and the leaf faucet. To determine the segment offset distance from the last turn, the algorithm infers vertical distance offset from the change in water pressure and horizontal distance offset by multiplying node velocity by the traveled time. Since the sensor node was designed

Figure 6. Pipeline Testbed

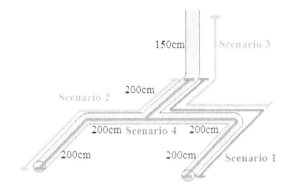

Figure 7. The lengths (cm) of testbed and 4 test scenarios

with its weight density equal to the water density, the node's flow velocity approximates the water flow velocity.

4.5 Sensor Latching

When a sensor arrives at its assigned location, it latches onto the pipe's inner surface and turns on its radio to listen to beacon packets from downstream sensor nodes or gateway node. The sensor node measures the packet received rate for the link quality. Stable link quality is important because a single link failure may lead to a network partition in a tree-based network topology. Upon detecting a low packet received rate, the sensor node moves one increment closer to its downstream sensor node. This sensor downstream movement requires unlatching from the pipe inner surface, moving forward for t seconds, and re-latching onto the pipe's inner surface. The sensor node repeats this latching step until a pre-defined link quality threshold is met.

A tricky case is to ensure the first sensor node of an intermediate segment is connected to the sensor nodes of all downstream segments. This sensor node moves downstream until all immediate downstream sensor nodes from all branches are reachable. If a sensor node arrives at the exact branching point but is still unable to reach all downstream sensor nodes, the sensor node moves into one of the unreachable downstream segment until it connects to a sensor node in that segment.

Upon successful attachment to a pipe location, the sensor node sends a "latching completion" packet to the system, including its latching position. The system continues to re-lease and deploy

sensor nodes over other segments until it reaches full sensing and network coverage.

4.6 Data Collection

Upon completion of the sensor deployment, TriopusNet enters the data collection phase and runs the collection tree protocol (CTP) [5] implemented in TinyOS 2.1. To balance the load over its network traffic, this study uses the support for anycast to multiple sinks provided by CTP. In the pipeline scenario, each gateway node acts as a sink for data collection. To reduce the hop count and packet loss rate, a sensor node forwards packets to the gateway node with the least CTP routing cost. Previous study in tunnel monitoring [11] shows that multi-sink collection trees work effectively in node deployments with linear topology.

4.7 Sensor Replacement

Each sensor node continues to monitor its battery level and network connectivity while the system collects pipeline health data. Network connectivity can break as the node battery runs low. This issue is particularly disruptive due to TriopusNet's tree-like connectivity. A single node failure in such a network can easily result in network partitions, i.e., persistent data losses. Therefore, the system must be able to recover when the battery of a sensor node runs out.

The replacement mechanism requires collaboration between the battery-depleted node and good nodes. First of all, the battery-depleted node informs the downstream gateway at the endpoint, so the faucet can be turned on to allow node movement. The battery-depleted node retracts its mechanical arms to flow to an endpoint for node retrieval. At the same time, the battery-depleted node's downstream nodes are also flushed out to prevent clogging inside the pipeline. This is due to the size of the current prototype being too big for a node to pass through its downstream nodes. For the node retrieval method, we adopt a similar approach from the SmartBall commercial product [23]. A fishing net with a tail is inserted at the ends of pipelines to catch any outgoing sensor nodes. Therefore, a sensor node will not remain inside the pipe when its battery dies.

Flushing out the battery-depleted sensor node and its downstream nodes produces an uncovered monitoring area in the system. To repair this uncovered area, each upstream node unlatches itself from the pipe sequentially and flows downstream to find the gateway node or its downstream neighbor node. Each sensor node repeats the process of detachment, movement, localization, and reattachment until the uncovered area reaches the root location. The system then releases fresh nodes from the dispatch queue to cover the remaining area.

With a smaller prototype in the future, it is possible that the Triopus node can pass through any upstream and downstream nodes. Therefore, the new node can replace the battery-depleted node without having to move the entire set of nodes in the network. Section 7 discusses how to further reduce the prototype size in the future.

To determine battery depletion, a sensor node simply uses its battery voltage to estimate residual energy and sets a low-battery threshold that triggers node replacement.

Table 1. Results for automated sensor deployment

Scenarios	# of test runs	Node-to-node coverage distance (cm)		# of node deployed		Data collection rate (%)	Positional error (cm)	Time to deployment (sec)	# of latching per node
		Mean	Std.	TriopusNet	Static				
1	5	193.7	65.1	3.6	7	97.6	6.1	103.7	2.3
2	5	156.8	35.4	4	7	98.4	8.0	117.5	1.6
3	5	166.3	45.4	4	4	98.7	7.94	139.1	2
4	5	173.4	69.3	6	12	98.8	12.6	185.9	2.2
Overall	20	172.7	58.0	4.35	7.5	98.4	9.22	136.5	2.1

5. EXPERIMENTAL DESIGN

This section describes the experimental testbed, procedure, and performance metrics.

5.1 Experimental Testbed

Figure 6 shows the pipeline testbed used to evaluate performance of TriopusNet. This testbed connects 6 transparent pipe tubes and 2 water valves and forms a pipeline network that starts with one vertical path, followed by a horizontal path, and forks into two paths in the middle of horizontal path. These 6 transparent pipe tubes, each measuring 10 cm in diameter, enable direct observation of how well the sensor nodes flow and latch/de-latch inside the pipes. The two valves at the end of each horizontal path control the volumetric flow rate on each flow path. Figure 7 lists the lengths of each pipe tube segment in the testbed.

5.2 Performance Metrics

The following list defines the metrics used to evaluate the performance of TriopusNet.

- *Data collection rate*: This measures the percentage of data packets successfully received by the gateway nodes compared to all packets sent from sensor nodes.
- *Coverage distance:* This measures the total pipeline length covered by the deployed nodes.
- *Number of nodes deployed:* This counts the number of nodes deployed to cover a given sensing area.
- *Time to deployment*: This measures the time to complete the node deployment for a test scenario.
- *Time to replacement*: This measures the time to replace a battery-depleted node.
- *Energy Consumption*: This measures the energy to complete the node deployment for a test scenario or to replace a battery-depleted node.

5.3 Experimental Procedure

This study uses four test scenarios in Figure 7 to test TriopusNet's performance. Each scenario has different pipe area coverage. Scenarios #1, #2, and #3 have the single-outlet sensing areas, and Scenario #4 involves a multi-outlet sensing area. System parameter settings are: the packet received rate (PRR) threshold = 95%, water flow velocity = 12.5 cm/sec, and each node's sensing range $R >=$ radio range.

To measure node deployment performance, each test scenario was repeated five times for a total of 20 (= 4 scenarios * 5 runs per scenario) test runs. The procedure for each test run involved the following steps. (1) All sensor nodes were returned to the water inlet point. (2) In the current testbed, opening and closing a faucet

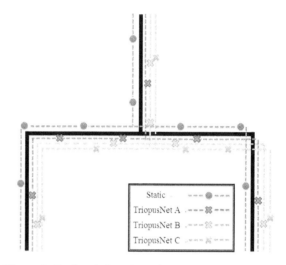

Figure 8. Real node locations of three test runs from Scenario 4. It shows the dynamic of each deployment.

to create a running flow path is manual. For the single-outlet scenarios (#1, #2, and #3), the target faucet was turned on to create a flow path before starting the node deployment. In the multi-outlet scenario (#4), each of two faucets was turned on to create two different flow paths for node deployment. (3) After the system deployed all nodes in the pipes, data collection was performed by running the multi-sink collection tree protocol (CTP). During data collection, sensor nodes transmitted data packets back to the gateway nodes/sinks. The gateway is a laptop computer wired to Kmote. Data was logged during both node deployment and data collection for performance analysis.

To measure sensor node replacement performance, scenario #4 began from a 6-node configuration. Each of the last two downstream sensor nodes was selected in turn by setting its battery level to low. When the test began, the selected node reported a "low-battery level" message and triggered the system's node replacement. For each low-battery node replacement, we repeated the test 5 times. Over all, there were 10 test runs of node replacement. Each test run involved the following steps. (1) All nodes were restored to their initial configuration. (2) The system started the data collection phase. (3) The selected node reported low-battery level and triggered node replacement. Data were recorded before, during, and after node replacement for performance analysis.

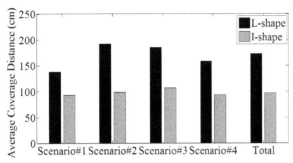

Figure 9. Coverage distances in L-shape and in I-shape pipe

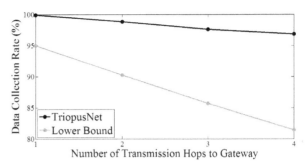

Figure 11. Data collection rate vs. number of transmission hops to gateways.

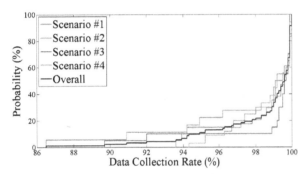

Figure 10. CDF of data collection rate

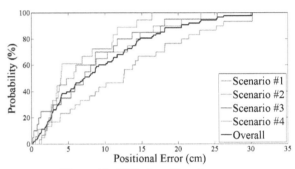

Figure 12. CDF of positional errors

6. EXPERIMENTAL RESULTS

This section describes the results collected from test runs in the experimental testbed.

6.1 Results for Automated Sensor Deployment

Table 1 shows the results collected from 20 test runs of automated sensor deployment. To evaluate the quality and efficiency of the automated sensor deployment, this study first shows the node locations and then measures the coverage distance, the number of nodes deployed, the data collection rate, the node's positional error, the time to deployment, and energy overhead from mechanical latching.

6.1.1 Node Locations

Figure 8 shows the locations of deployed nodes in three test runs (labeled A, B and C) in Scenario #4. This figure also draws the node locations of a static deployment, where nodes are fixed 90 cm apart. This 90 cm measurement is based on repeated measurements for an average radio range between two sensor nodes in a straight pipe. Static deployment is a good baseline for performance comparison because it is the most commonly-used method in sensor deployment. It might have better data collection ratio, but it would need a lot more redundant nodes to hop the data.

In the TriopusNet system, each test run produces different node locations. The average node-to-node distance over all scenarios is 172.7 cm, with a standard deviation of 58 cm. This large variation implies that the radio range varies significantly from location to location. Examining the dataset reveals that the average radio range is approximately 90 cm for connecting nodes in the same pipe tube. However, the radio range can reach up to 170 cm for nodes placed in different tubes. Figure 9 provides statistics supporting this observation. The I-shape in this figure indicates radio range for adjacent nodes in the same tube, whereas the L-shape indicates nodes in different tubes. The reason for variation in the radio range is when two adjacent nodes are in different pipe segments (L-shape case), radio signals can travel through air, and therefore travel far. In comparison, for two adjacent nodes within the same pipe segment, radio signals travel mostly in water, which absorbs energy and limits its range. This highlights the benefits of using an online sensor deployment algorithm over a static sensor deployment. In comparison to the static deployment which on average uses 7.5 nodes for deployment, TriopusNet uses only 4.35 nodes.

6.1.2 Data Collection Rate (DCR)

To quantitatively evaluate whether a network is well connected, this study measures the ratio of data being successfully collected at the gateway. In each test run of each scenario, each sensor node sent 1000 data packets to a gateway node. In other words, if a scenario involved 5 sensor nodes, a total of 5000 data packets were sent from all sensor nodes. Based on four scenarios and 20 test runs, this study logs the ratio of successfully received packets at the gateway nodes over all transmitted packets from each individual node. Figure 10 depicts the cumulative density function (CDF): 80% of the sensor nodes show a data collection rate exceeding 99%, and all sensor nodes have a data collection rate higher than 86.5%.

The data collection rate varies depending on how far the sensor node is from the gateway. Figure 11 plots the average data collection rate for nodes with different transmission hop counts to the gateway node. This figure also plots the lower-bound data collection rate assuming an exact 95% data collection rate (DCR) for every hop. This can be calculated by taking the n-th power of the DCR threshold in the sensor deployment algorithm, where n is the transmission hop count to reach a gateway node. Note that the sensor nodes only latch when the measured per-hop DCR exceeds the threshold. This result also supports that the latching is reliable

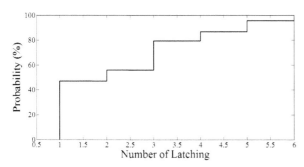

Figure 13. CDF of the number of latching for all nodes

Table 2. Time to replacement

The low battery node	# of test run	Time to replacement (sec) Mean	Std.	# of latching per node	Transmission hops to inlet
2nd last	5	223.4	38.8	2.2	3
Last node	5	152.3	24.1	2.3	4

and the data collection rate does not go below the lower-bound data collection rate.

6.1.3 Positional Accuracy

Figure 12 shows the (CDF) of positional errors in each of the 4 scenarios and an assemblage of all scenarios. The dataset for the CDF is based on 18 location estimates of the node in scenario #1, 20 estimates in scenario #2, 20 estimates in scenario #3, and 30 estimates in scenario #4, for a total of 88 location estimates. The overall median error is 7.14 cm, and 90% of the errors are less than 20.45 cm. Node positional accuracy is important for achieving sensing coverage in node deployment, as sensing range and coverage are calculated from node locations. From a practical viewpoint, this positional accuracy is sufficient for most pipeline applications, such as pinpointing the location of pipe leakage.

6.1.4 Time to Deployment

Table 1 summarizes the average time required to fully deploy nodes in each of the four scenarios. Note that the deployment time excludes the time required for humans to manually turn on/off faucets, because these steps could be automated in the future. If the flow velocity is set at 12.5 cm/sec, the average time to deploy nodes is less than 2.5 minutes.

6.1.5 Energy Consumption

The primary energy consumer in the sensor node is in the motor and relays that drive the three mechanical arms. To quantify the energy spent on the mechanical motor and relays, the energy consumed by a single act of latching was measured first. This step consumes 1.01W and takes two seconds, which is less than 1% of the overall energy budget given a 3.7V Polymer Lithium Ion Battery at 600mAh. Subsequently, the number of latching processes required to fix a node deployment was measured (e.g., this may involve repeating the data collection rate measurement and node movement as described in Section 4.5). In total, data were collected from deploying 88 nodes over 20 test runs in four scenarios. Figure 13 shows the CDF on the numbers of required latching per node deployment. The average is 2.35 (latching), whereas 90% of nodes required less than 5 (latching).

6.2 Results for Automated Sensor Replacement

Scenario #4 was selected to determine the effects of automated sensor replacement, as it is the most representative scenario among the four scenarios. Each of the last two downstream nodes was set to low battery to trigger automated node replacement five times. The resulting data was then measured to determine the data collection rate and time to replacement.

6.2.1 Data Collection Rate

The data collection rates of the system before a node reported low-battery level and after the node was replaced were 0.989 and 0.984 respectively. This small difference suggests the effectiveness of the automated replacement. The data collection rate without automated replacement was 0.81. The reasons for the high data loss rate without automated replacement were: (1) In the presence of a network hole or an uncovered area, some sensor nodes selected a new route to reach the gateways. These new routes were longer than the original routes, and hence increased the chance of packet losses. (2) In the cases of network partition, isolated nodes reported zero data collection rate.

6.2.2 Time to Replacement

The time to recover from a battery-depleted node depends on the location of the node and the size of the network. If the node is far from the root node, the system must repeat the cycle of detecting an uncovered area and then progressively shifting each upstream node to fill a moving area toward the root node. Table 2 shows the average time to replacement. Note that replacing the 2nd last node requires flushing and replacing its downstream node (i.e., the last node). As a result, replacing the 2nd last node has a longer average time to replacement than replacing the last node.

7. DISCUSSION

The prototype evaluation in this study demonstrates the feasibility of the TriopusNet system. However, there are several assumptions and limitations that require future extensions before practical in-field deployment.

The size of the current TriopusNet node prototype is too big to be flushed out independently in small-diameter pipes. In the experiment, when a battery-depleted node detaches from the pipes, its downstream nodes must be flushed out first such that the battery-depleted node does not get clogged by any downstream nodes in the pipe. Flushing good downstream nodes can be prevented by further minimizing the node size such that the battery-depleted node can easily pass through any downstream nodes without clogging the pipes. In addition, the upstream nodes do not have to move downstream for network coverage hole repair because the new node would be able to flow directly to the coverage hole to fix the network disconnection without being blocked by nodes already inside the pipeline. It would also benefit the time to replacement in section 6.2.2. For example, in our current testbed, the time for a node to travel from inlet to outlet is 44 seconds on average. In other word, it means that to replace a battery-depleted node only require 44 seconds at most. Reducing the node size is possible with current micro-mechanical design, particularly on folding the mechanical arms that occupy majority of the space in a sensor node.

Since the mobility of TriopusNet node relies on water flow in pipes, node placement requires controlling or obtaining the direction of the water flow in the pipes. In our experiment, we manually turn on one water outlet at a time, so each released node flows on the path leading to its assigned pipe location. Removing this manual effort is possible with automatic touch-free faucets. By attaching a sensor-trigger node to activate/deactivate the infrared sensor in each automatic faucet, the TriopusNet gateway controls each faucet by sending signals to the sensor-trigger node.

We envision an opportunistic node placement scheme in which each deployed sensor node is equipped with a water flow sensor. By gathering water flow information from all deployed nodes inside pipes, the system can infer the current flow path. The system opportunistically releases new nodes whose destinations must match the current water flow path.

8. RELATED WORK
Related research can be categorized into 2 classes: (1) mobile WSN deployment and (2) WSN in pipeline monitoring.

8.1 Mobile WSN Deployment
Deployment has been a notorious issue in successful sensor network application. Previous research [8] provides a guideline for successful sensor network deployment. The human effort involved in installing and maintaining sensors is a tremedous cost, especially in remote on-site field deployment. There have been related systems that automate sensor deployment. For examples, Liu et al. [20] developed a breadcrumb system that leverages the mobility of a firefighter to deploy sensors in an environment. A firefighter carries a lightweight dispenser device that automatically drops and releases sensor nodes along a firefighter's path. These dropped sensors automatically form a WSN and localize the fireflighter without human attention and effort.

Purohit et al. developed the SensorFly system [18], which is a controlled-mobile aerial sensor network platform for indoor emergency response. When SensorFly is deployed, the nodes perform collaborative localization during flying, which is similar to the deployment algorithm in Section 4. Unlike the current project, SensorFly mobility relies on a battery to power the helicopter-like device, whereas the proposed Triopus node mobility relies on water flow. A Triopus node only consumes energy when it performs latching and delatching tasks.

8.2 Wireless Sensor Network for Pipeline Monitoring
Recent projects involving WSN technologies for monitoring water pipelines include the PipeNet project [1], the NAWMS project [2], the HydroSense project [3], and the PipeProbe project [4].

The PipeNet project [1] detects, localizes, and quantifies leaks and bursts in water pipelines. PipeNet attaches a variety of acoustic, vibration, pressure, and flow sensors to wireless sensor nodes mounted on pipelines, externally and internally, to detect faults and anomalies. The signals received from these sensor nodes are analyzed to identify and locate leaks. In PipeNet's deployment, human effort is required to install and repair each sensor node on-site. In contrast, the proposed TriopusNet releasing method eliminates these human efforts to install and maintain sensors in the pipes.

The NAWMS project [2] detects the water outflow rate for each pipe and outlet. This method attaches a vibration (accelerometer) sensor to each pipe to separate the water outflow rate for an individual pipe from the master household water meter. By calibrating and deriving the relationship between the standard deviation of pipe vibration and the mean flow rate in the pipe, the NAWNS system can infer a pipe's water flow rate from the sensed vibration level produced by each flowing pipe. In TriopusNet, the lo-

calization algorithm needs to obtain the water flow rate at each pipe to compute the location of Triopus node. The NAWNS project's method can be used to calculate the water flow rate.

HydroSense [3] proposes a novel single-point sensing technique that identifies the water usage activities of each water outlet using a single pressure sensor installed at one point within a building.

The HydroSense system senses and recognizes the unique "water hammer" pressure fingerprint produced by each water fixture. By training and recognizing individual fixture's fingerprint, the system can accurately infer which water fixture is turned on or off. The idea of single-point sensing also eliminates the human cost of a sensing system. However, HydroSense does not focus on sensor network deployment, whereas TriopusNet aims to reduce human effort in deploying a network.

The PipeProbe project [4] developed a mobile sensor node for determining the spatial topology of hidden water pipelines behind walls. It works by dropping a tiny sensor capsule into pipeline. As this capsule traverses the pipeline, it collects water pressure and gyroscope readings to determine the 3D spatial pipeline layout. The proposed system assumes the pipeline layout is known. Thus, PipeProbe can be used first to discover the pipeline layout if such information is not available.

9. CONCLUSION
This study presents TriopusNet, a mobile wireless sensor network system for autonomous sensor deployment in pipeline monitoring. TriopusNet scales down human effort in deploying and maintaining WSN infrastructure inside pipes. To show the benefits and feasibility of TriopusNet, we have prototyped and tested the system in a real pipeline testbed. Experimental results have demonstrated that automated sensor deployment was able to produce quality node placement using no more nodes than non-automated static sensor deployment. Results have also demonstrated that automated sensor replacement was able to successfully restore sensing and network coverage from the departure of a battery-depleted node. We believe that TriopusNet provides an alternative and promising strategy to automate sensor deployment and replacement in pipeline monitoring.

10. ACKNOWLEDGMENTS
We would like to thank our shepherd Gian Pietro Picco and the anonymous reviewers for their insightful comments to improve the quality of this paper.

11. REFERENCES
[1] I. Stoianov, L. Nachman, S. Madden and T. Tokmouline. PIPENET: A Wireless Sensor network for pipeline monitoring. In *IPSN*, 2007.

[2] Y. Kim, T. Schmid, Z. M. Charbiwala, J. Friedman and M. B. Srivastava. NAWMS: Non-Intrusive Autonomous Water Monitoring System. In *SenSys*, 2008.

[3] J. Froehlich, E. Larson, T. Campbell, C. Haggerty, J. Fogarty, and S. Patel. HydroSense: Infrastructure- Mediated Single-Point Sensing of Whole-Home Water Activity. In *Ubicomp*, 2009.

[4] T. S. Lai, Y. H. Chen, P. Huang and H. H. Chu. PipeProbe: A Mobile Sensor Droplet for Mapping Hidden Pipeline. In *SenSys*, 2010.

[5] O. Gnawali, R. Fonseca, K. Jamieson, D. Moss and P. Levis. Collection Tree Protocol. In *SenSys*, 2009.

[6] Kmote, INTECH http://www.tinyosmall.com/product_p/100-101.htm

[7] PQ12-P Linear Actuator, Firgelli.
http://store.firgelli.com/pq12-p-linear-actuato12.html

[8] G. Barrenetxea, F. Ingelrest, G. Schaefer and M. Vetterli. The hitchhiker's guide to successful wireless sensor network deployments. In *SenSys*, 2008.

[9] A. Krause, C. Guestrin, A. Gupta, and J. Kleinberg. Near-optimal Sensor Placements: Maximizing Information while Minimizing Communication Cost. In *IPSN*, 2006.

[10] K. Ni, N. Ramanathan, M. N. H. Chehade, L. Balzano, S. Nair, S. Zahedi, E. Kohler, G. Pottie, M. Hansen and M. Srivastava. Sensor Network Data Fault Types. *ACM Trans. on Sensor Networks, Vol. 5, No. 3, Article 25*, May 2009.

[11] M. Ceriotti, M. Corra, L. D'Orazio, R. Doriguzzi, D. Facchin, S. T. Guna, G. P. Jesi, R. L. Cigno, L. Mottola, A. L. Murphy, M. Pescalli, G. P. Picco, D. Pregnolato and C. Torghele. Is there light at the ends of the tunnel? Wireless sensor networks for adaptive lighting in road tunnels. In *IPSN*, 2011.

[12] I. Vasilescu, K. Kotay, D. Rus, M. Dunbabin and P. Corke. Data collection, storage, and retrieval with an underwater sensor network. In *SenSys*, 2005.

[13] G. Chen, S. Hanson, D. Blaauw and D. Sylvester. Circuit Design Advances for Wireless Sensing Applications. *Proceedings of the IEEE, Vol.98, No.11, pp.1808-1827*, Nov. 2010.

[14] Y. C. Wang, C. C. Hu and Y. C. Tseng. Efficient Placement and Dispatch of Sensors in a Wireless Sensor Network. *IEEE Trans. on Mobile Computing, Vol. 7, No. 2. pp. 262-274*, Feb, 2008.

[15] M. Laibowitz and J. A. Paradiso. Parasitic mobility for pervasive sensor networks. In *Pervasive*, 2005.

[16] K. Dantu, B. Kate, J. Waterman, P. Bailis and M. Welsh. Programming Micro-aerial vehicle swarms with Karma. In *SenSys*, 2011.

[17] T. Bourdenas, M. Sloman and E. C. Lupu. Self-healing for Pervasive Computing Systems. *Architecting Dependable Systems VII*, Springer-Verlag 2010.

[18] A. Purohit, Z. Sun, F. Mokaya and P. Zhang. SensorFly: Controlled-mobile Sensing Platform for Indoor Emergency Response Applications. In *IPSN*, 2011.

[19] S. Guo, Z. Zhong and T. He. FIND: faulty node detection for wireless sensor networks. In *SenSys*, 2009.

[20] H. Liu, J. Li, Z. Xie, S. Lin, K. Whitehouse, J. A. Stankovic and D. Siu. Automatic and Robust Breadcrumb System Deployment for Indoor Firefighter Applications. In *MobiSys*, 2010.

[21] MS5541C Pressure Sensor
http://www.intersema.ch/products/guide/calibrated/ms5541

[22] The STMicroelectronics LISY300AL gyroscope chip
http://www.st.com/stonline/books/pdf/docs/14753.pdf

[23] SmartBall, Pure Technologies
http://www.puretechltd.com/products/smartball/smartball_leak_detection.shtml

[24] ROBOBEES project
http://robobees.seas.harvard.edu

Collaborative Calibration and Sensor Placement for Mobile Sensor Networks

Yun Xiang[†], Lan S. Bai[‡], Ricardo Piedrahita[*],
Robert P. Dick[†], Qin Lv[◦], Michael Hannigan[*], Li Shang[△]

[†]EECS Department, University of Michigan, Ann Arbor, U.S.A.
[‡]EMC, Pleasanton, CA 94566, U.S.A.
[◦]Dept. of Computer Science, University of Colorado Boulder, CO 80309, U.S.A.
[△]Dept. of ECEE, University of Colorado Boulder, CO 80309, U.S.A.
[*]Dept. of Mechanical Engineering, University of Colorado Boulder, CO 80309, U.S.A.

[†]xiangyun@umich.edu, [‡]lanceybai@hotmail.com, [†]dickrp@eecs.umich.edu,
{[*]ricardo.piedrahita, [◦]qin.lv, [*]hannigan, [△]li.shang}@colorado.edu

ABSTRACT

Mobile sensing systems carried by individuals or machines make it possible to measure position- and time-dependent environmental conditions, such as air quality and radiation. The low-cost, miniature sensors commonly used in these systems are prone to measurement drift, requiring occasional re-calibration to provide accurate data. Requiring end users to periodically do manual calibration work would make many mobile sensing systems impractical. We therefore argue for the use of collaborative, automatic calibration among nearby mobile sensors, and provide solutions to the drift estimation and placement problems posed by such a system.

Collaborative calibration opportunistically uses interactions among sensors to adjust their calibration functions and error estimates. We use measured sensor drift data to determine properties of time-varying drift error. We then develop (1) both optimal and heuristic algorithms that use information from multiple collaborative calibration events for error compensation and (2) algorithms for *stationary sensor placement*, which can further decrease system-wide drift error in a mobile, personal sensing system. We evaluated the proposed techniques using real-world and synthesized human motion traces. The most advanced existing work has 23.2% average sensing error, while our collaborative calibration technique reduces the error to 2.2%. The appropriate placement of accurate stationary sensors can further reduce this error.

Categories and Subject Descriptors

C.2.1 [**Computer-Communication Networks**]: Network Architecture and Design

General Terms

Algorithms, design

Keywords

Mobile sensing, Collaborative, Calibration, MILP

1. INTRODUCTION

Mobile sensing applications are increasingly popular. The fast development of smartphones and sensor technology makes many such applications possible, e.g., mobile noise pollution sensing networks [14] and mobile personalized air quality sensor networks [10]. Compact, light, and energy-efficient sensors are now becoming available at prices that permit widespread use by non-scientists (and scientists). In the future, individuals will carry multiple unobtrusive sensors with them, within or networked with their smartphones, forming dense and interconnected sensor networks. Mobile sensing applications will soon become mainstream.

Mobile sensing systems have many advantages over conventional systems composed of a few accurate, low-drift, stationary, and expensive sensing stations. For example, in the personal air quality sensing application, many pollutants have nonuniform spatial distributions [22]. As a result, personal exposure is poorly estimated by using sparsely distributed stationary sensors. If each participant in a sensing system were to carry a sensor, we would be able to better understand human exposure and provide more relevant information to users.

Temporal drift is generally not a concern for expensive stationary sensors, since they are regularly calibrated by experts. However, low cost and compact sensors can accumulate substantial errors in short time spans [8, 17]. Our own measurements of 15 volatile organic compound (VOC) sensors kept in a controlled environment showed up to 20% drift in a single day. Erroneous measurements caused by sensor drift can result in incorrect scientific conclusions, false alarms, and bad decisions. Therefore, low cost sensors require frequent re-calibration.

Manually calibrating sensors to compensate for drift is time-consuming and burdensome; it can annoy users and limit their desire to use the sensors, which will result in an ineffective system. Automatic calibration (which requires no explicit user intervention) has the potential to solve these problems, thereby increasing mobile sensing opportunities.

We propose a system supporting automatic, opportunistic, and collaborative calibration among mobile sensors. Our solution takes into account the gradual increase in sensor drift error with time, and appropriately weights different calibration events based on the time-dependent estimated errors of the other sensors, i.e., we consider the temporal and spatial properties of the graph formed by (transitive) calibration events. Although we do not require the presence of stationary sensors, we support their inclusion in the system, and also provide algorithms for determining their best locations. Our evaluation makes use of controlled sensor drift studies as well as measured human motion patterns.

The proposed collaborative calibration approach is appropriate for applications with the following characteristics.

1. Spatial variation of sensor readings are low within certain physical distance.

2. Sensor nodes are able to communicate with each other and detect when they are within calibration distance, e.g., either by tracking their own locations or by measuring signal attenuation between nodes.

3. Sensor drift can be compensated for using a drift predictor. The residual error of this predictor has a Gaussian distribution with variance that increases as a function of time, as explained in Section 4.2 and demonstrated in Section 6.1.

Our technique can potentially be used in many mobile sensing applications, such as radiation sensing applications in which sensors are carried by individuals and unmanned aerial vehicles, remote sensing applications in which detailed data are available from in-field sensors and sparse data are available from satellites, and personal environmental sensing. Although the concepts we develop apply to a broader range of mobile sensing systems susceptible to drift error, in the rest of paper, we focus our discussion on a personal air quality sensing application.

It should be noted that collaborative calibration minimizes the increase in the rate of uncompensable drift error, but does not eliminate error. Without the stationary accurate sensors, the mobile sensor network's overall accuracy degrades over time. The use of a few stationary accurate sensors to augment mobile collaborative calibration is beneficial; it allows the drift error to be bounded.

Our work makes the following main contributions.

1. We formulate and solve the opportunistic collaborative mobile sensor calibration problem.

2. We formulate and solve the mobility aware stationary sensor placement problem to augment collaborative calibration.

3. We propose a sensor drift model built using experimental data from 15 VOC sensors.

To better understand and characterize the effects of real-world human motion on calibration, we also carried out an indoor human motion pattern study on a university campus. Compared with our collaborative calibration scheme, the most advanced existing auto-calibration technique has an average error of 23.2%, while our efficient heuristic has an error of 2.2%. We also present two algorithms for placing stationary sensors to further improve mobile collaborative calibration. The use of well-placed stationary sensors within the collaborative calibration system techniques reduces sensing error significantly, e.g., by about 40% for a density of 1 stationary sensors per 25 mobile sensors. The approximation algorithm based placement technique results in only 6.2% more error than an MILP based technique.

The rest of this paper is organized as follows. Section 2 gives a motivating example. Section 3 summarizes the related work on collaborative calibration and stationary sensor placement. Section 4

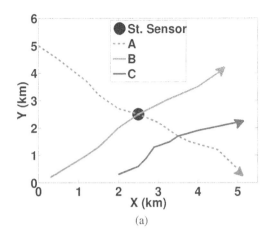

(a)

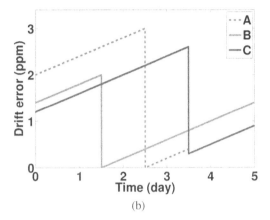

(b)

Figure 1: (a) Human motion traces and calibration events and (b) drift errors for three sensors.

describes the sensor random drift model and our collaborative calibration method. Section 5 generalizes the human mobility model, and provides an MILP based solution for the human motion aware stationary sensor placement problem as well as an approximation algorithm. Section 6 describes our controlled-environment experiments for sensor drift and the data analysis results. It also evaluates the performance of our techniques using simulations based on real-world and synthesized human motion traces. Section 7 concludes the paper.

2. MOTIVATING EXAMPLE

Consider a mobile sensor network formed by sensing devices carried by individuals to monitor their air pollution exposures. Each device houses small, energy efficient, and inexpensive metal oxide gas sensors that measure various air pollutants. The sensor measurements gradually drift over time. Drift rates can vary greatly; to minimize error, the sensors must be re-calibrated frequently. In many cases, accurate stationary sensors are not readily accessible for users, and the occasional calibration opportunities they provide are insufficient to cover all the participants in the sensing system. By using collaborative calibration together with optimized placement of stationary sensors, accuracy can be significantly improved.

Figure 1 illustrates an example of our mobile sensor network calibration technique. Figure 1(a) shows the trajectories of three mobile sensors (A, B, and C). Figure 1(b) shows their uncompensable drift errors over time. Each vertical drop in Figure 1(b) corresponds to one calibration event. Between calibration events, the drift error increases with time as a result of reduced drift prediction accuracy. Given the mobile sensor motion traces, our sensor placement approach decides where to put accurate stationary sensors to maximize the probabilities of mobile sensors being calibrated against the stationary sensor. In this example, the stationary sensor is located at a position both sensor A and B visit, thus providing ground truth calibration for two sensors. When sensor A and B get close to the accurate stationary sensor, their errors drop due to calibration (refer to Figure 1(b)). Our problem formulation and solution also consider a realistic human mobility model that considers individual motion traces able to represent day-to-day variation. With our collaborative calibration technique, even though sensor C never directly calibrates with any (accurate) stationary sensor, its drift error still reduces in the third day by calibrating with sensor A, which has a smaller error due to recent calibration with an accurate stationary sensor.

3. RELATED WORK

This section summarizes prior work on auto-calibration and placement for distributed sensor networks.

Bychkovskiy et al. [3] proposed a two-phase post-deployment calibration technique for dense stationary sensor networks. In the first phase, linear relative calibration relations are derived for pairs of co-located sensors. In the second phase, the consistency of the pair-wise calibration functions among groups of sensor nodes is maximized. Their technique requires a dense deployment of stationary sensors. In contrast, our work focuses on mobile sensor networks.

Miluzzo et al. [15] proposed an auto-calibration algorithm for mobile sensor networks, called CaliBree. In their approach, uncalibrated mobile nodes opportunistically calibrate themselves when interacting with stationary sensors. In their work, calibration events always involve stationary sensors. Our work supports calibration with stationary sensors, but in contrast also supports calibration among mobile sensors, allowing either higher accuracy or a reduction in the number (and therefore cost) of stationary sensors.

Tsujita et al. [21, 22] studied calibration for air pollution monitoring networks. They [22] observed that at a certain time of day, the nitrous oxide pollutant concentration becomes low and uniform in certain areas. They use these opportunities to calibrate mobile sensors using the pollutant concentration reported from nearby environment monitoring stations. In their other work [21], when multiple sensors are close to each other, the average of their readings is used as ground truth to estimate sensor drift. In contrast, we account for the gradual increase in drift error as a function of time, allowing an optimal weighting for each of the many calibration events used to determine drift compensation parameters. Our experimental results show that the technique proposed by Tsujita et al. technique has 23.2% error relative to the optimal result; our proposed heuristic only has 2.2% error.

Berry et al. [2] used an MILP based method to solve the $\mathcal{NP}$-hard problem of placing sensors in water networks for optimal contamination detection. Chakrabarty et al. [4] tried to find an optimal sensor placement scheme to minimize the cost of sensors while meeting coverage constraints. Our problem formulation differs in that mobile sensors are carried by individuals. A realistic human mobility model is therefore necessary to solve our placement problem. We build our human mobility model based on previous research and our indoor human motion study, and solve the stationary sensor placement problem using a high quality but potentially slow MILP method and an efficient approximation algorithm based technique.

4. COLLABORATIVE CALIBRATION

This section describes our collaborative calibration technique. We present the problem definition, mathematical analysis, and our algorithm to solve this problem optimally.

4.1 Overview

Our collaborative calibration technique uses drift modeling and sensor fusion to reduce drift-related sensor measurement error. Sensor drift models, or drift predictors, are built based on past measured or estimated drift errors. They are used to estimate sensor drift at any point of time and (partially) compensate for drift errors in sensor measurements. In addition, the drift model allows the *residual error* of the drift predictor to be predicted as a function of time. Sensor fusion uses measurements from co-located sensors to improve the accuracy of the combined results. The fusion algorithm determines how to combine multiple sensor measurements based on their residual errors in order to maximize the combined accuracy. In implicit mobile calibration, sensor fusion happens whenever sensors happen to be close to each other; our calibration technique is opportunistic and collaborative.

Actual sensor drifts are only known when sensor measurements are compared with a highly accurate sensor (ground truth). Such opportunities are rare in most personal sensing applications. At most times, drifts must be estimated using models based on prior calibration events with other sensors having varying accuracies. The temporal correlation in sensor drift decreases with temporal distance. Therefore, all other things being equal, the uncertainty of the model (i.e., the residual error of the predictor) increases with the elapsed time since the last drift measurement.

Since nearby sensors are exposed to similar physical conditions, readings from co-located sensors can be combined to statistically improve accuracy. As mentioned before, each sensor has a residual error associated with its post-drift-compensation measurement. Each calibration event allows this error to be reevaluated and potentially reduced. If the two residual errors are independent, the measurement with the smaller residual error should be given more weight during combination. Calibration relationships introduce correlations in sensors' residual errors that the calibration algorithm must account for. Section 4.3 describes our correlation-aware fusion algorithm in detail.

4.2 Collaborative Calibration Problem Definition

Our analytical framework can handle classes of mobile and stationary sensors with arbitrary drift rates. However, we will focus our discussions on systems composed of inexpensive, high drift rate mobile sensors, and expensive but accurate stationary sensors with low drift rates. Although our collaborative calibration technique does not rely on accurate (and most likely stationary) sensors, the use of a few stationary sensors will allow network-wide drift error to be reduced. We assume that these stationary sensors provide accurate readings, either because they are inherently resistant to error or because they are maintained by experts.

Mobile sensors are generally calibrated before deployment but they drift over time. Drift is a function of various factors such as sensing material, exposure to sulfur compounds or acids, aging, or condensate on the sensor surface [1, 8]. It is reported that short-term sensor drift can be modeled accurately with simple models but long-term drift is less predictable [5]. We assume only that (1) there exists an unbiased drift predictor whose residual error has Gaussian distribution and that (2) we have knowledge of how its variance increases over elapsed time since the most recent calibration event.

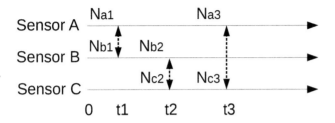

Figure 2: An example of sensor error correlation as a result of previous calibration events.

As explained in Section 6.1, we observed that high-quality predictors for our sensors have this property.

Our goal is to develop a distributed technique that automatically compensates for sensor drift error; there is no notion of a central controller that has access to data from all sensors. Avoiding dependence on a central controller can reduce sensing system energy consumption, cost, and security problems.

We now present the formal problem definition. Given N mobile sensors and M accurate stationary sensors, the location of a mobile sensor i at time t is $L_i(t), i \in N$. The location of accurate stationary sensor j is $L_j, j \in M$. Sensor i's raw reading (including drift error) at time t is $r_i(t)$. Its drift prediction function is $f_i(t, k_1, k_2, ..., k_n)$. The parameters of this function may be different for each sensor and may change over time. The error associated with the drift predictor $e(t)$ changes over time. The drift-compensated sensor reading is $R_i(t) = r_i(t) - f_i(t)$. The accurate value of the monitored parameter at location l and time t is G_l^t. Let $C_i(t)$ be the post-calibration sensor reading. In other words, $C_i(t)$ is the sensor reading after drift compensation and sensor fusion. The goal is to determine $k_1, k_2, ..., k_n$ for each sensor to minimize its total mean squared error, i.e., $\sum_t (G_l^t - C_i(t))^2$. Each sensor i at time t, only has access to $R_j(t)$ of sensor j when $|L_i(t) - L_j(t)| < D_c$ (D_c is the calibration range).

Our measurements in several rooms suggest that in well-ventilated rooms with no obvious pollution sources, the pollutant mixture is spatially homogeneous within 2 m distance. We will use this distance as calibration range D_c in simulations. Note that the spatial distributions of air pollutant concentrations vary based on nearby pollution sources and ventilation conditions, thus the calibration range depends on circumstances.

4.3 Error Estimation and Error Propagation

As we mentioned before, each sensor has a residual error that is adjusted after each calibration event. In this section, we describe how this residual drift error is calculated and minimized via calibration and prediction. We address the problem of predictor design for one particular type of sensor in this paper. In general, the predictor should be provided by the sensor manufacturer or determined by pre-deployment lab calibration.

We start with a simple scenario where errors of two sensors are independent. Assume two co-located sensors A and B. Sensor A's current error estimate is n_a and sensor B's current error estimate is n_b, where n_a and n_b are random numbers with Gaussian distributions N_a and N_b and standard deviations E_a and E_b (in the rest of the paper, we use N to represent a Gaussian distribution, n to represent a random number following distribution N, and E to represent its standard deviation). Assume this is the first time sensors A and B calibrate with other sensors. N_a and N_b are independent and their standard deviations, E_a and E_b, are determined by how long the sensors remain uncalibrated. Let G be the ground truth

value of the physical condition measured by the sensors. Readings from these two sensors can be represented as $R_a = G + n_a$ and $R_b = G + n_b$. The weighted sum of R_a and R_b is $R_{ab} = \alpha \cdot R_a + (1 - \alpha) \cdot R_b = G + N(0, \sqrt{\alpha^2 \cdot E_a^2 + (1 - \alpha)^2 \cdot E_b^2})$. It is easy to prove that when

$$\alpha = E_b^2 / (E_a^2 + E_b^2), \qquad (1)$$

the weighted sum has minimal standard deviation for both calibrated sensors, i.e., $G + N(0, E_a E_b / \sqrt{E_a^2 + E_b^2})$. A reading from the sensor with smaller error is given more weight. After calibration, both sensors should adjust their readings to R_{ab} and use R_{ab} to estimate their current ground truth readings as well as to predict future drifts.

Now we consider the scenario in which N_a and N_b are correlated. This may happen as a result of both sensors directly or transitively calibrating with the same mobile sensor prior to their calibration with each other. In this case, we need to know the correlation between N_a and N_b to compute the optimal combination of their readings. Let us consider the example shown in Figure 2. Assume three sensors A, B, and C all start operating at time 0. At time t_1, sensors A and B calibrate. Their calibration parameters are independent of each other at that time and thus the analysis in the previous paragraph for independent errors can be applied. Assume weights of 0.2 and 0.8 are used, thus the error after calibration is $0.2n_{a1} + 0.8n_{b1}$. At time t_2, sensors B and C calibrate. Assume sensor B's drift prediction error increased by n_{b12} from time t_1 to t_2. The errors of B and C are still independent. Assume the optimal weight is 0.5 in this case. After calibration, B's and C's errors are $0.1n_{a1} + 0.4n_{b1} + 0.5n_{b12} + 0.5n_{c2}$. At time t_3, sensors A and C calibrate. A's error is now $n_{a3} = 0.2n_{a1} + 0.8n_{b1} + n_{a13}$ and C's error is $n_{c3} = 0.1n_{a1} + 0.4n_{b1} + 0.5n_{b12} + 0.5n_{c2} + n_{c23}$. Note that at that moment, these two sensors contain the same errors generated from the previous calibration, which are n_{a1} and n_{b1}. Now N_a and N_c are correlated and Equation 1 cannot be directly applied. However, it is still possible to use the weight assignment technique to find an optimal solution. To do that, we can remember all the independent distributions and weight assignments from previous calibration events.

Now we present the general approach that accounts for correlation introduced by transient calibration events among sensors. Each sensor's error distribution is represented as a weighted sum of multiple independent error distributions. Each independent distribution is from the other sensor's or its own increased prediction error over the uncalibrated time interval. Label the two calibrating sensors as sensor 1 and 2. Let S_1 and S_2 be the sets of independent error distributions for sensors 1 and 2. Let C be the intersection of S_1 and S_2, i.e., $C = S_1 \cap S_2$. Let C_1 and C_2 be S_1 and S_2's non-overlapping regions, i.e., $C_1 = S_1 - C$, $C_2 = S_2 - C$. Let W_{1i} and W_{2i} be the weights associated with the error distributions for sensors 1 and 2, δ_i be the standard deviation of each distribution, and G be the ground truth value of measured object. Sensor 1's reading after drift compensation is

$$R_1 = G + \sum_{i \in C} W_{1i} N(0, \delta_i) + \sum_{j \in C_1} W_{1j} N(0, \delta_j). \qquad (2)$$

Sensor 2's reading is

$$R_2 = G + \sum_{i \in C} W_{2i} N(0, \delta_i) + \sum_{k \in C_2} W_{2k} N(0, \delta_k). \qquad (3)$$

In order to generate more accurate results by combining the readings of sensor 1 and 2, we use a linear weighted sum function to combine their drift-compensated measurements. Assuming the weights are α and $1 - \alpha$ for sensor 1 and 2 respectively, the combined result is

$$
\begin{aligned}
R_{12} &= \alpha R_1 + (1 - \alpha) R_2 \\
&= G + \sum_{i \in C} [\alpha W_{1i} + (1 - \alpha) W_{2i}] N(0, \delta_i) \\
&\quad + \sum_{j \in C_1} \alpha W_{1j} N(0, \delta_j) + \sum_{k \in C_2} (1 - \alpha) W_{2k} N(0, \delta_k). \quad (4)
\end{aligned}
$$

The variance of the error for the combined reading is

$$
\begin{aligned}
Var &= \sum_{i \in C} [\alpha W_{1i} + (1 - \alpha) W_{2i}]^2 \delta_i^2 + \sum_{j \in C_1} W_{1j}^2 \alpha^2 \delta_j^2 \\
&\quad + \sum_{k \in C_2} W_{2k}^2 (1 - \alpha)^2 \delta_k^2. \quad (5)
\end{aligned}
$$

The derivative of the variance is

$$
\begin{aligned}
\frac{dVar}{d\alpha} &= 2\alpha \sum_{i \in C} (W_{1i} - W_{2i})^2 \delta_i^2 + 2 \sum_{i \in C} W_{2i}(W_{1i} - W_{2i}) \delta_i^2 \\
&\quad + 2\alpha \sum_{j \in C_1} W_{1j}^2 \delta_j^2 + 2\alpha \sum_{k \in C_2} W_{2k}^2 \delta_k^2 - 2 \sum_{k \in C_2} W_{2k}^2 \delta_k^2.
\end{aligned}
$$

$$(6)$$

To minimize the variance, we have $\frac{dVar}{d\alpha} = 0$, therefore

$$
\alpha =
$$
$$
\frac{\sum_{i \in C} W_{2i}(W_{2i} - W_{1i}) \delta_i^2 + \sum_{k \in C_2} W_{2k}^2 \delta_k^2}{\sum_{i \in C} (W_{1i} - W_{2i})^2 \delta_i^2 + \sum_{j \in C_1} W_{1j}^2 \delta_j^2 + \sum_{k \in C_2} W_{2k}^2 \delta_k^2}.
$$

$$(7)$$

Equation 7 gives the general expression for weight assignment. In the case of two independent sensors (C is empty), we have

$$
\alpha = \frac{\sum_{k \in C_2} W_{2k} \delta_k^2}{\sum_{j \in C_1} W_{1j}^2 \delta_j^2 + \sum_{k \in C_2} W_{2k}^2 \delta_k^2} = \frac{E_2^2}{E_1^2 + E_2^2}, \quad (8)
$$

which is consistent with Equation 1.

Note that the above analysis applies only to the scenario where collaborative calibration involves two sensors. It is possible to extend the evaluation to an arbitrary number of co-located sensors, although this would increase the complexity of the weight assignment expression.

4.4 Collaborative Calibration Algorithm

We have presented the key concept allowing the optimal calibration algorithm to combine readings from co-located sensors. Now we present the complete algorithm for collaborative calibration, which includes drift compensation, weight assignment, and drift reevaluation. Note that calibration opportunity detection is not part of our algorithm. There are multiple existing approaches to discover calibration opportunities, including radio communication (e.g., Bluetooth), ultrasound, and passive audio environment based proximity detection schemes [10, 16, 20].

The key data structure used is a table that stores all the independent error distributions and their corresponding weight assignments for each sensor. Each entry is a tuple of name, weight, and standard deviation. The names are used to distinguish independent error distributions. The calibration algorithm for a mobile sensor labeled i that calibrates with sensor j is shown in Algorithm 1.

Mobile sensors participating in the collaborative calibration system carry out three actions every time a calibration event happens: (1) estimate its current drift with its drift predictor and use the result to compensate its raw reading, (2) estimate the ground truth

value and update its error table, and (3) use the estimated ground truth value to recompute its drift, residual error, and drift predictor. The type of co-located sensor determines the details of step (2). If the co-located sensor is an accurate stationary sensor, its reading can be directly used as ground truth to estimate the mobile sensor's drift. The mobile sensor ignores its own reading and directly overwrites its own reading with the reading from the stationary sensor and its current error immediately drops to zero. As a consequence, it can forget all previous calibration errors as they become irrelevant (clear the table). Otherwise, if the co-located sensor is also a mobile sensor with a non-zero error, its drift-compensated reading is combined with the mobile sensor's drift-compensated reading according to Equation 7 to generate an estimate of ground truth and the error distribution table will be updated accordingly.

Algorithm 1 Collaborative calibration algorithm for mobile sensor i

---

Require: r_i // i's raw reading
Require: R_j // j's calibrated reading
Require: T_i // i's error table
Require: T_j // j's error table
Require: t // current time
  if j is accurate stationary sensor **then**
    $R_i \leftarrow R_j$
    $Di'(t) \leftarrow r_i - R_i$
    Update drift model
    T_i.clear()
  else
    Predict current drift D_i
    $R_i \leftarrow r_i - D_i$
    $T_i.insert(i.t, g(t - last\_cali\_t), 1)$
    $C \leftarrow T_i \bigcap T_j$
    $C_1 \leftarrow T_i - C$
    $C_2 \leftarrow T_j - C$
    Compute α using Equation 7
    $R_{ij} \leftarrow \alpha R_i + (1 - \alpha) R_j$
    Update current drift $D_i'(t) \leftarrow r_i - R_{ij}$
    Update drift model
    for $k \in C$ **do**
      $T_i[k].weight \leftarrow T_i[k].weight \times \alpha + T_j[k].weight \times (1-\alpha)$
    end for
    for $k \in C_1$ **do**
      $T_i[k].weight \leftarrow T_i[k].weight \times \alpha$
    end for
    for $k \in C_2$ **do**
      $T_i[k] \leftarrow (T_j[k].name, T_j[k].var, T_j[k].weight \times (1 - \alpha))$
    end for
  end if
  $last\_cali\_t \leftarrow t$

---

5. STATIONARY SENSOR PLACEMENT

In this section, we consider placement of stationary sensors to further assist the collaborative calibration of mobile sensors. Our discussion will focus on human-carried sensors.

5.1 Overview

Adding stationary sensors to a system composed of collaboratively calibrating mobile sensors can further improve accuracy. The number of stationary sensors is constrained by cost; they must be carefully positioned to enable frequent calibration opportunities with mobile sensors. Fortunately, humans move with patterns that can

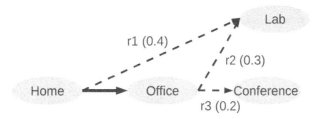

Figure 3: Example human motion trace with 3 patterns.

be used to our benefit; some locations are more frequently visited than others [13].

Recent research has shown that most people's daily motion patterns are predictable [7, 18, 19]. We present a stochastic human mobility model capable of capturing the most relevant motion patterns for the stationary sensor placement problem. The field for stationary sensor deployment is modeled as a grid in which implicit calibration may occur among sensors in the same grid element. It is possible to eliminate discretization problems by making grid elements arbitrarily small and permitting calibration between nodes in multiple grid elements within the calibration distance. We define a motion pattern as a set of locations (grid elements) that a person is likely to visit on a particular day. An individual's mobility model is a probability-weighted collection of possible motion patterns. Extreme sensor drift typically occurs on a timescale of days, not hours, enabling a simplified model that neglects the order of visited locations within a single day. In our evaluation, these models are extracted from measured motion traces as well as those generated by software provided by human motion pattern researchers [13].

Daily motion patterns are weighted with probabilities. For example, as shown in Figure 3, there are three distinct patterns: r_1, r_2, and r_3. A value ranging from 0 to 1 is associated with each pattern to indicate its probability. It is possible for multiple stationary sensors to be encountered by a person in a day. However, encountering one is sufficient for calibration.

5.2 Sensor Placement Problem Definition and MILP-Based Solution

We now define the problem of stationary sensor placement to assist calibration of mobile sensors.

Problem Definition: The field for stationary sensor deployment can be represented by a grid G. A set of people S move within the grid. Each person $s \in S$ carries a mobile sensor. A person's motion pattern for a particular day, r_s, is a set of locations. R is the set of all motion patterns, and the motion patterns associated with a particular person s are represented with R_s. Each motion pattern r is associated with a value p_{sr}, which is the probability of person s having pattern r. The sum of the calibration probabilities of all patterns of person s is P_s. A total number of k sensors are deployed in the field. The optimization objective is to find a set of grid elements in which stationary sensors should be placed to maximize the average daily probability of mobile sensor calibration, i.e., $\frac{\sum_{s \in S} P_s}{k}$.

This problem is $\mathcal{NP}$-hard. Let each pattern be represented by an element associated with a probability weight and each possible stationary sensor placement location be represented by a subset. An element belongs to a subset if and only if the corresponding pattern contains the placement location. Given a resource constraint, k, the original problem can be stated as selecting at most k subsets such that the covered elements have maximum total weight. This is the

weighted maximum coverage problem [11]. We will now describe an MILP formulation for the problem.

Maximize

$$\frac{\sum P_s}{k}, \forall s \in S,$$

subject to

$$\sum_{(i,j) \in G} x_{ij} \leq k, \tag{9}$$

$$\forall r \in R, \sum_{(i,j) \in r} x_{ij} - M d_r \leq 0, \tag{10}$$

$$\forall r \in R, \sum_{(i,j) \in r} x_{ij} - m d_r \geq 0, \tag{11}$$

$$P_s - \sum_{r \in R_s} d_r * p_{sr} = 0, \tag{12}$$

$$1 \geq x_{ij}, \text{ and } d_r \geq 0. \tag{13}$$

x_{ij}, d_r are integers. M and m are constants and are set to $k + 1$ and 0.5. The probabilities p_{sr} are known. The properties of binary indicators x_{ij} and d_r are described below.

$$x_{ij} = \begin{cases} 1 & \text{if a sensor is placed at grid element } (i, j) \\ 0 & \text{otherwise,} \end{cases} \tag{14}$$

and

$$d_r = \begin{cases} 1 & \text{if pattern } r \text{ is covered by at least one sensor} \\ 0 & \text{otherwise.} \end{cases} \tag{15}$$

M is greater than the largest possible value of $\sum_{(i,j) \in r} x_{ij}$ (which is satisfied by setting M to be $k + 1$) and m is less than the smallest possible non-zero value of $\sum_{(i,j) \in r} x_{ij}$ (which is satisfied by setting m to be 0.5).

5.3 Approximation Algorithm Based Placement Technique

Algorithm 2 Approximation based placement technique

Require: G // deployment field grid
Require: R // set of all patterns
Require: P // probabilities
Require: k // stationary sensor count constraint
   $C \leftarrow \{\}$ // output set
   while size(C) $\leq k$ **do**
      Select $g \in G$ s.t. $\sum_{r \in g} P_r$ is maximized
      Remove the covered patterns from R
      $C \leftarrow C \cup g$
   end while

Normally MILP-based solutions are not tractable for large instances of hard problems. Fortunately, the number of patterns per person is limited: it is possible to directly use the MILP formulation for substantial problem instances. The solver performance is further improved because human motion traces tend to be spatially clustered [13]. We will show in Section 6.3 that our algorithm can be applied to deployment cases with up to $840\,\text{km}^2$ area or 200 patterns. It is conceivable that some problem instances will exceed

Figure 4: Calibration chamber used for sensor drift experiments.

the size tractable for MILP solvers. Therefore, we also present an approximation algorithm based polynomial time heuristic.

The maximum coverage problem can be solved with the polynomial time $(1 - \frac{1}{e})$-approximation algorithm shown in Algorithm 2. This is minimum achievable bound [11]. However, the $(1 - \frac{1}{e})$-approximation bound only applies for the average calibration probability between stationary and mobile sensors. There are many other factors influencing the network sensing accuracies, such as collaborative calibration events, calibration time, and calibration order. Section 6.3 evaluates the approximation algorithm based technique in detail.

6. EXPERIMENTAL RESULTS

In this section, we first describe our controlled drift experiments (Section 6.1), which support the hypothesis in Section 4.2. Section 6.2 presents simulation results for our optimal and efficient collaborative calibration techniques and compares them with two existing works that are most related. Section 6.3 reports on the performance of our MILP based stationary sensor placement algorithm and compares it with the efficient approximation algorithm we propose.

6.1 Calibration Procedure and Drift Experiments

Section 4.2 describes our sensor drift model. We assume that drift can be (partially) compensated for by an unbiased predictor, and the residual error can be modeled using a Gaussian distribution with a variance that predictably increases with time. To test this hypothesis, we have conducted a drift experiment in our controlled chamber.

Before the drift experiment, we manually calibrated all sensors. Calibrations were performed using de-humidified zero grade air (i.e., air with less than 1 ppm total hydrocarbons) and controlled-concentration iso-butylene (a VOC unlikely to damage graduate students when used at low concentration). The purpose of this calibration is to compensate for initial measurement offsets, possibly due to variation in the manufacturing process. During calibration and drift experiments, sensors are mounted on a custom printed circuit board enclosed in the $250 \, \mathrm{cm}^3$ polycarbonate chamber as shown in Figure 4. A fan is mounted inside the chamber to improve mixing and make convection heat loss from the sensors uniform. The temperature and humidity inside the chamber are stabilized at

$43.8 \pm 1.3 \,^\circ$C, and $7.8 \pm 1.7\%$ respectively. A LabVIEW interface controls the gas mixture using mass flow controllers. During calibration runs, the sensors are held at concentrations of 0, 0.25, and 1.0 ppm (parts per million by volume) of iso-butylene in a total volume flow of 4 liters per minute, for 20 minutes each. The sensors are powered continuously throughout the experiment period, and were warmed up for two weeks prior to starting the experiments to allow the sensors to reach an initial equilibrium, as recommended by the manufacturer.

During the drift experiment, 15 pre-calibrated Figaro TGS 2602 VOC sensors are placed in the controlled gas chamber and exposed to 4 liters per minute air. These exposure tests last 120 minutes and are performed daily. Since the sensors are powered continuously, they should drift constantly during the experiment. The drift data are calculated by averaging the last 30 minutes of readings from each test to avoid any warm-up effects from changes in the air flow rate.

We use the analog to digital converter on Labjack U3 data acquisition modules to measure the voltage output of the TGS sensors, at a sampling frequency of 0.5 Hz. We use log-based transfer function to convert the voltages to VOC concentrations, based on calibrations performed before the experiment. The concentration readings after conversion are shown in Figure 5. Since the ground truth reading should be 0 ppm, the readings after the conversion already represent drift. Seven of the 48 measurements were discarded due to inconsistent air flow rate or relative humidity levels due to transient problems with the testing chamber air supply.

We now evaluate a simple drift predictor based on linear extrapolation of two consecutive drift errors to predict future errors. The difference between the predicted drift value and the measured drift is the portion of the drift error that is not captured by the drift model. We have also evaluated higher-order non-linear predictors but they did not have higher prediction accuracies than the linear predictor. The linear predictor compensated for 94.1% and 87.7% of the drift on average when predicting one day and two days ahead. We therefore consider it to be a good predictor for this kind of sensor. Note that for different sensor types, the forms of the predictor function may be different. In some cases, a higher order non-linear fitting function might be necessary.

We applied the Lillie normality test to the residual error of the linear predictor. The residual error has a Gaussian distribution, with an exception for predictions eight days in advance. For most cases, the linear predictor meets Gaussian residual requirement posed in Section 4.2. For specific sensors and time offsets passing the normality test, we perform t-tests to assess whether the distributions have means of 0 ppm. The significance levels used in the Lillie test and t-test are both 0.05 and the test results are shown in Figure 6(a). Figure 6(b) shows the standard deviation of the remaining drift error after applying the linear predictor for up to 10 days in the future. The results clearly show an increasing trend for all the sensors, consistent with our hypothesis in Section 4.2 that the variance increases over time. The standard deviations of the short-term drift errors can be well predicted using simple linear functions.

With one possible anomaly at an eight-day offset, the drift experiment results confirm our hypothesis that the residual error after drift prediction has a Gaussian distribution with mean 0 and predictable variance that increases over time.

6.2 Evaluation of Collaborative Calibration

To evaluate our collaborative calibration algorithm, we compare it with two other approaches proposed in relevant and recent work. In the first approach, Calibree [15], all mobile sensors calibrate with stationary accurate sensors. In contrast, our calibration tech-

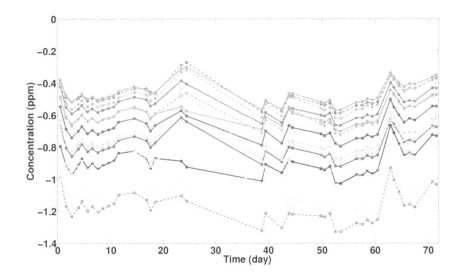

Figure 5: Measured drift error as a function of time for Figaro TGS2602 VOC sensors.

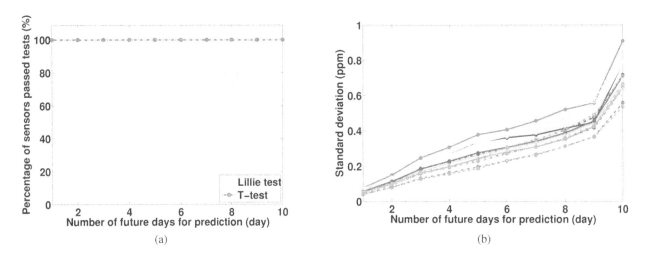

Figure 6: (a) The normality test results and (b) the standard deviations of prediction errors using the 2-day linear predictor to compensate for 1 to 10 days of future drift.

Table 1: Aggregated Sensor Error with Synthesized Human Motion Traces

Trace	Num. of cali. events			Total aggregated mean squared error			
	Total	Uncorrelated	Stationary	CaliBree	Averaging	Heuristic	Optimal
1	44,290	5,072	21,818	964.6	393.6	321.9	312.1
2	43,378	3,368	20,144	1,716.6	559.0	454.9	434.8
3	9,701	1,722	4,429	3,059.0	1,461.1	1,244.3	1,229.8
4	5,659	1,048	2,589	6,805.8	2,359.6	1,984.0	1,966.3
5	14,308	2,496	4,398	8,610.6	3,234.7	2,681.8	2,643.6
Average overhead (%)				224.8	23.2	2.2	0

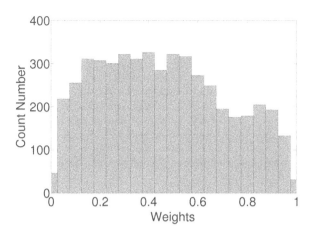

Figure 7: Histogram of assigned weights for an example trace using the optimal collaborative calibration scheme.

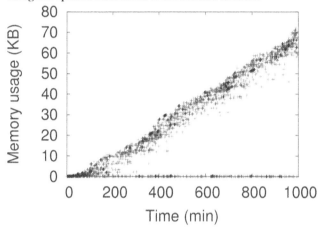

Figure 8: Memory use of the optimal collaborative calibration scheme.

nique allows sensors to calibrate with each other as well as stationary sensors. In the second approach [21], readings from co-located sensors are averaged to estimate the ground truth value. In contrast, our technique enables more accurate drift compensation by considering the differing drift prediction errors of calibration events, i.e., sensors. We also propose and evaluate a *calibration heuristic* that reduces computation complexity and memory use at the cost of a very slight reduction in calibration accuracy. This heuristic ignores correlations between prediction errors. Instead tracking independent error distributions from previous calibration events and temporal error growth, this algorithm only stores an aggregated error for each sensor. During calibration, it uses Equation 1 to assign weights to readings from co-located sensors. We evaluate the four approaches with the same set of motion traces and sensor placements, and compare the resulting accumulated mean squared error. For this experiment, we use 10 stationary accurate sensors placed at the most frequently visited locations and use a random walk model for sensor drift.

Table 1 shows the results for the four approaches with five synthesized motion traces generated using the SLAW human mobility model [13]. The second to the fourth columns present statistics for calibration events for the optimal algorithm. The second column shows the total number of calibration events. A pair-wise calibration between two sensors is considered to be two calibration events. The third column shows the number of calibration events in which

Table 2: Statistics for Human Mobility Case Study

Participant	Duration (days)	On campus prob. (%)	# of patterns	# of locations
1	30	90.0	12	11
2	30	86.7	5	5
3	22	77.3	4	4
4	23	100.0	5	4
5	21	76.2	7	6
Average	25.3	85.2	6.6	6

the errors from two sensors are independent. The fourth column shows the number of calibrations with stationary accurate sensors. The last four columns show the aggregated mean squared errors of all sensors during the entire experiment.

On average, CaliBree [15] has 224.8% more error than optimal. This is because it only considers calibration events between stationary and mobile sensors, and thus misses opportunities for calibration between mobile sensors. 43.6% of calibration events occur between mobile and stationary sensors; the rest occur between pairs of mobile sensors.

Tsujita's technique (averaging) has 23.2% more error than optimal result. Figure 7 shows the distribution of the weights generated with the optimal algorithm for Trace 5. The weights are widely distributed from 0 to 1. Only 25.4% are in the range from 0.4 to 0.6. The structure of this histogram has implications for the effectiveness of Tsujita's approach: the closer weights are to 0.5, the more effective Tsujita's approach.

Our heuristic produces results with accuracy that deviates from optimal by only 2.2%. Even though the percentage of correlated events is fairly large (41.8%), ignoring the correlation does not significantly degrade accuracy. However, this algorithm greatly reduces required memory compared with the optimal algorithm. With the optimal algorithm, the memory use increases linearly with time for most sensors. Figure 8 shows the memory use over time for all sensor nodes in our experiment with trace 1. Each point corresponds to a sensor node involved in a calibration event. We therefore conclude that the heuristic is more efficient and likely to be appropriate for most practical applications.

The optimal algorithm allows us to evaluate the quality of various calibration approaches. In summary, utilizing the interactions among mobile sensors improves the accuracy by 224.8% compared to only permitting mobile sensors to calibrate with stationary sensors. The accuracy is improved by 23.2% by considering the heterogeneity of drift estimation parameters among different sensors. Considering correlations among sensors due to calibration imposes large computation complexity and memory use with a relatively small gain (2.2%). In summary, a technique using collaborative calibration among mobile sensors that considers heterogeneity in drift estimation parameters but ignores calibration event induced inter-sensor correlations represents a good trade off between accuracy and run-time overhead/complexity.

6.3 Evaluation of Stationary Sensor Placement

This section introduces our human motion pattern case study and evaluates our stationary sensor placement algorithms with both measured and synthesized human mobility traces.

6.3.1 Measured Human Mobility Case Study

Much human mobility modeling research is based on outdoor GPS data [7, 13, 19]. However, GPS is inaccurate indoors, where humans spend 90% of their time [6]. According to a survey-based model, office worker indoor activities can be modeled using a few

Table 3: Statistics for Measured and Synthesized Human Motion Traces and Solver Performance

Trace	Area (km^2)	Total pat.	Sensor no.	Cand. loc.	Runtime (s)
Case study	N/A	33	5	17	0.01
KAIST	840.1	92	92	41,270	1.2
NCSU	142.3	35	35	10,691	0.13
New York	618.8	39	39	12,180	0.05
Orlando	122.0	41	41	26,662	0.07
State fair	1.2	19	19	4,422	0.03
1	0.01	200	50	1,225	0.13
2	0.01	200	50	1,001	0.24
3	1.0	200	50	26,448	2.44
4	1.0	200	50	39,695	5816.10
5	4.0	400	100	101,891	>6 h

patterns [12]. In our evaluation, we use mobility traces generated using algorithms proposed by other researchers as well as data gathered in our real-world human mobility study, which was conducted on the campus of University of Colorado Boulder.

In our study, five graduate students, undergraduate students, and professors used their mobile phones to record their daily motion patterns. Participants manually entered locations and times into their smart phones as they moved and these data were sent to a server via the Internet. Locations in which users spent fewer than five minutes were omitted from the motion patterns. The study was conducted between August 3rd, 2011 and September 12th, 2011. Statistics from the study are shown in Table 2. Motion patterns contain 1.94 locations on average, which implies that the indoor activities of the participants were spatially concentrated, which is consistent with the findings of other human motion studies [12,19].

6.3.2 Experiment on Measured and Synthesized Human Motion Traces

To solve the MILP problem, we use the CPLEX v.12.2 solver [9] on an Intel 4-core Xeon E31230 CPU running at 3.2 GHz with 8 GB of memory. The evaluation is performed on both real-world and mobility model generated [13] human motion traces.

The statistics of the real-world and synthesized human motion traces [13], as well as our case study trace, and their MILP solver performances are shown in Table 3. The case study trace does not contain detailed location information, but lasts for multiple days. The rest of the real-world traces contain detailed location information, but are finished within a day each, i.e., each person has one motion pattern. The duration for each trace is 4 days, i.e., each person has 4 patterns. According to our real-world case study, the average probabilities of the top 4 patterns are 0.48, 0.2, 0.1, and 0.08. The same probability values are used in the synthesized traces. The fourth column of the table shows the total number of mobile sensors in each trace. The fifth column shows the total number of candidate locations where stationary sensors may be placed. Grid elements visited by one or more person are considered as placement location candidates. The total number of the candidate locations is equal to the number of variables x_{ij} in Equation 9.

The MILP placement algorithm quickly solves all the problem instances, except for synthesized trace 5. For this trace, the solver terminated after six hours without producing a solution. This trace contains 400 patterns and 101,891 candidate placement locations. We conclude that the MILP solution is suitable for many useful-scale problem instances, but there may be some real-world cases for which a more efficient solution is required, e.g., that in Section 5.3.

The results of the MILP placement algorithm are shown in Figure 9. For most of the solutions, the number of sensors is far less than the number of patterns. This is consistent with the hypothesis that people's motion traces tend to be clustered, repetitive, and frequently overlap each other. The synthesized human motion traces typically required fewer sensors despite having more motion patterns because a relatively small geographical area was considered in these traces. In summary, although personal mobile sensors are needed to monitor the conditions experienced by many individuals, the accuracy of these sensors can be improved substantially by using a few accurate stationary sensors to assist a collaborative calibration technique.

The results of evaluating the algorithms on both real-world and synthesized human motion traces are shown in Table 4. We assume that repeated calibration with a stationary sensor during the same day does not further reduce error. The aggregated network error (the sum of mean square errors of all the sensors in the network for readings taken every 30 seconds) is measured when both placement algorithms are permitted to use the number of stationary sensor listed in the second column of Table 4. For the synthesized traces, we assume that all the patterns occur with the same probability. The fifth column of Table 4 shows the aggregated network error using our optimal collaborative calibration technique, assuming there are no stationary sensors. The results show that the approximation algorithm based technique increases aggregated network error by 6.2% compared to the MILP placement algorithm. Note that for Trace 4, the approximation algorithm based technique outperforms the MILP solution. In that case, the approximation algorithm had already reached 99% average calibration probability, making its solution essentially equivalent to the MILP solution. Note that in our placement problem formulation, the error caused by calibration order is neglected. However, since the uncompensable drift error within a day is small (less than 0.1 ppm as shown in 6(b)), this simplification has very little impact on solution quality.

7. CONCLUSIONS

We have presented a collaborative calibration and sensor placement framework for mobile sensor networks. We developed a random sensor drift model based on controlled experiments and developed a collaborative calibration technique to compensate for drift error. We also describes placement techniques for stationary sensors used to augment collaborative calibration among mobile sensors. We conducted a human motion study on a university campus to build these models and evaluate our placement algorithms. Experimental results indicate that, compared with our collaborative calibration algorithm, the most advanced existing work has an average sensor error of 23.2%. Our stationary sensor placement algorithms further reduce the effects of drift error.

8. ACKNOWLEDGEMENTS

We would like to thank Yifei Jiang and Xin Pan for help with the human mobility case study. This work was supported in part by the National Science Foundation under awards CNS-0910995, CNS-0910816, and CNS-1059372.

9. REFERENCES

[1] K. Arshak, E. Moore, G. M. Lyons, J. Harris, and S. Clifford. A review of gas sensors employed in electronic nose applications. *Sensor Review*, 24(2):181–198, 2004.

[2] J. Berry, L. Fleischer, W. Hart, C. Phillips, and J. Watson. Sensor placement in municipal water networks. *J. of water resources planning and management*, 131(3):237–243, 2005.

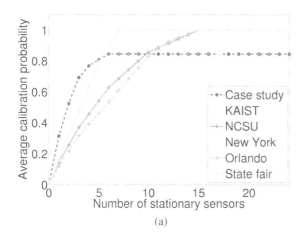

(a)

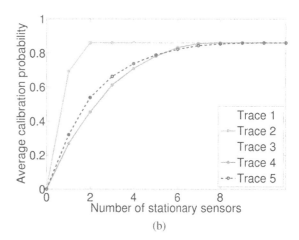

(b)

Figure 9: The MILP stationary sensor placement results for (a) measured human motion traces and (b) synthesized human motion traces.

Table 4: Aggregated Sensor Errors for Different Placement Algorithms

Trace	Sensor number			Aggregated error			
	MILP	Approx. Algo.	Improvement	All Mobile	MILP	Approx. Algo.	Improvement
KAIST	16	19	18.8%	9,880	7,875	8,465	7.5%
NCSU	15	15	0.0%	6,075	3,095	3,333	7.7%
New York	23	26	13.0%	4,720	2,076	2,504	20.6%
Orlando	15	16	6.7%	7,208	3,683	3,954	7.4%
State fair	7	7	0.0%	5,303	2,649	2,786	5.2%
1	2	2	0.0%	910	523	551	5.4%
2	2	3	50.0%	1,083	701	738	5.3%
3	5	5	0.0%	2,326	1,783	1,831	2.7%
4	8	9	12.5%	3,370	2,522	2,511	-0.4%
5*	10	11	10.0%	3,924	3,195	3,205	0.3%

*The MILP solution is derived by setting the relative tolerance of the MILP solver to be 0.3%.

[3] V. Bychkovskiy, S. Megerian, D. Estrin, and M. Potkonjak. A collaborative approach to in-place sensor calibration. In *Proc. Int. Conf. Information Processing in Sensor Networks*, pages 301–316, Apr. 2003.

[4] K. Chakrabarty, S. Iyengar, H. Qi, and E. Cho. Grid coverage for surveillance and target location in distributed sensor networks. *IEEE Trans. Computers*, 51(22):1448–1453, Dec. 2002.

[5] A. Emami-Naeini, M. Akhter, and S. Rock. Effect of model uncertainty on failure detection: the threshold selector. *IEEE Trans. Automatic Control*, 33(12):1106–1115, Dec. 1988.

[6] EPA. Buildings and their impact on the environment: a statistical summary, 2009.

[7] M. Gonzalez, C. Hidalgo, and A.-L. Barabasi. Understanding individual human mobility patterns. *Nature*, 453(7196):779–782, 2008.

[8] J.-E. Haugen, O. Tomic, and K. Kvaal. A calibration method for handling the temporal drift of solid state gas-sensors. *Analytica Chimica Acta*, 407(1–2):23–39, Feb. 2000.

[9] IBM ILOG CPLEX Division. IBM ILOG CPLEX 12.0 user manual, 2008.

[10] Y. Jiang, K. Li, L. Tian, R. Piedrahita, Y. Xiang, O. Mansata, Q. Lv, R. P. Dick, M. Hannigan, and L. Shang. MAQS: A personalized mobile sensing system for indoor air quality monitoring. In *Proc. Int. Conf. Ubiquitous Computing*, pages 271–280, Sept. 2011.

[11] S. Khuller, A. Moss, and J. Naor. The budgeted maximum coverage problem. *Information Processing Letters*, 70(1):39–45, 1999.

[12] J. Kim, V. Sridhara, and S. Bohacek. Realistic mobility simulation of urban mesh networks. *Ad Hoc Networks*, 7(2):411–430, 2009.

[13] K. Lee, S. Hong, S. J. Kim, I. Rhee, and S. Chong. SLAW: a mobility model for human walks. In *Proc. Int. Conf. Computer Communications*, pages 855–863, Apr. 2009.

[14] N. Maisonneuve, M. Stevens, M. Niessen, P. Hanappe, and L. Steels. Citizen noise pollution monitoring. In *Proc. Int. Conf. Digital Government Research*, pages 96–103, 2009.

[15] E. Miluzzo, N. D. Lane, A. T. Campbell, and R. Olfati-saber. CaliBree: a self-calibration system for mobile sensor networks. In *Proc. Int. Conf. Distributed Computing in Sensor Networks*, pages 11–14, June 2008.

[16] N. Priyantha, A. Chakraborty, and H. Balakrishnan. The cricket location-support system. In *Proc. MOBICOM*, pages 32–43, 2000.

[17] A. Romain and J. Nicolas. Long term stability of metal oxide-based as sensors for e-nose environmental applications: an overview. *Sensors and actuators, B, Chemical*, 146(2):502–506, Apr. 2010.

[18] U. Schlink, K. Strebel, M. Loos, R. Tuchscherer, M. Richter, T. Lange, J. Wernicke, and A. Ragas. Evaluation of human mobility models, for exposure to air pollutants. *Science of The Total Environment*, 408(18):3918–3930, Aug. 2010.

[19] C. Song, Z. Qu, N. Blumm, and A.-L. Barabasi. Limits of predictability in human motion. *Science*, 327:1018–2021, Feb. 2010.

[20] S. P. Tarzia, P. A. Dinda, R. P. Dick, and G. Memik. Indoor localization without Infrastructure using the acoustic background spectrum. In *Proc. Int. Conf. on Mobile Systems, Applications, and Services*, pages 155–168, June 2011.

[21] W. Tsujita, H. Ishida, and T. Moriizumi. Dynamic gas sensor network for air pollution monitoring and its auto-calibration. In *IEEE Proc. Sensors*, pages 56–59, Oct. 2004.

[22] W. Tsujita, A. Yoshino, H. Ishida, and T. Moriizumi. Gas sensor network for air-pollution monitoring. *Sensors and Actuators, B, Chemical*, 110(2):304–311, Oct. 2005.

Poster Abstract:

Detecting Faulty Street Lamps with Illumination Maps

Huang-Bin Huang, Huang-Chen Lee

Department of Communications Engineering and
Advanced Institute for Manufacturing with High-tech Innovations (AIM-HI),
National Chung-Cheng University, Taiwan

hbhuang212@hotmail.com, huclee@ccu.edu.tw

ABSTRACT

Badly lit roads usually lead to vehicle accidents and encourage crime in the area. Therefore, it is important to detect faulty street lamps rapidly and report them to related authorities to keep roads safe. Currently, communities still mostly depend on electrical inspectors to check street lamps regularly, which may result in long time delays for repair. Recent studies focus on add networking capability into street lamp poles to enable real-time reports on the healthy status of lamps. However, such a smart system increases costs to add sensors and network modules in every street lamp; therefore, it is nearly impossible to realize this kind of system in a short term. We propose a new method to detect faulty lamps. We designed equipment that could be installed on fixed bus routes and collect the lighting intensity along the routes. We created illumination maps in meter-level resolution. The differences between illumination maps created at different times can help identify the changes of lighting intensity in specific locations. We executed a proof-of-concept experiment that shows our method is feasible. This method can be extended to a city-wide scale at low cost. As a result, this would detect faulty street lamps along main roads and prevent accidents and crime by shortening the duration of badly lit streets.

Categories and Subject Descriptors

C.3 [Special-Purpose and Application-Based Systems]: Real-time and Embedded Systems

General Terms

Design, Experimentation, Measurement, Performance.

Keywords: fault, street lamp, failure detection.

1. INTRODUCTION

A recent study [1] has shown that street lighting may prevent vehicle accidents and injuries. However, maintaining street lamps and ensuring they work correctly is labor intensive. Communities still mostly depend on the electrical inspectors of local authorities or residents to report faulty street lamps. Some studies focus on the addition of sensing and networking capability to street lamps, which enables remote monitoring and automatic reporting of a street lamp's healthy condition via Wi-Fi, Zig-Bee, Power Line Communication, or GPRS, i.e., [2]. However, this approach requires adding sensing components and networking modules on every street lamp, which significantly increases the costs and prohibits this kind of system to be realized in a short term. A practical solution is desperately needed to detect faulty street lamps at a low cost with a minimum of human labor.

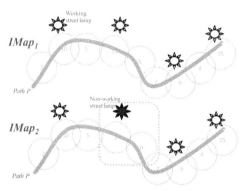

Fig. 1 Two illumination maps, *IMap₁* and *IMap₂*, describe the changes of illumination intensity on the same path, *P*. The numbers in the red-dotted circles indicate the illumination intensity at different locations.

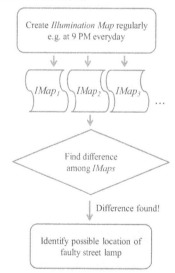

Fig. 2 The procedure of the proposed method.

We propose a novel method to detect faulty street lamps by using *Illumination Maps* (hereafter denoted by *IMap*). An *IMap* describes the illumination intensity over several two-dimensional locations. Fig. 1 shows two illumination maps, *IMap₁* and *IMap₂*, which were created at *Time₁* and *Time₂*, respectively, and describe the illumination intensities along the same path, *P*. The numbers in the red-dotted circles indicate the illumination intensity at different locations. The basic assumption of our method is that, if the illumination in this area is the same in *Time₁* and *Time₂*, the illumination maps *IMap₁* and *IMap₂* should be identical. That is, in an ideal case, for any location, *p*, on the path, *P*, the illumination intensity of *p* in *IMap₁* and *IMap₂* should be the same.

However, if a specific street lamp at a location, q, works at $Time_1$ but not at $Time_2$, the illumination intensity near q should change significantly (as the green-dotted rectangle in $IMap_2$ indicates). Therefore, by comparing several $IMaps$ created at different times, the location with a significant change in illumination intensity may help point out the location of a faulty street lamp.

2. PROOF-OF-CONCEPT EXPERIMENT

We executed a proof-of-concept experiment to create an illumination map. We built special equipment to collect the illumination intensity and its GPS location at 10-Hz frequency. This equipment was installed on the top of a car roof to collect the illumination intensity as we drove along the loop road for several rounds, as shown in Fig. 3. This experiment was executed from 7:33:46 PM to 7:42:58 PM on December 13, 2011, on the campus of National Chung Chen University, Chia-Yi County, Taiwan. Note that all the street lamps along the loop road were working while we executed this experiment. Therefore, we can use this illumination map as the "control group" for later comparison. If the light intensity in a specific location, q, had significant changes, we could infer that the street lamp near q was possibly out and may need repair soon.

Fig. 3 The bird's-eye view shows the area we executed the proof-of-concept experiment. The red line is the path where we collected light intensity.

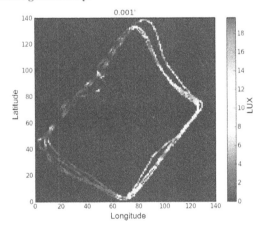

Fig. 4 The illumination map in 0.001-min resolution.

The illumination map in Fig. 4 shows the average illumination intensity in 0.001-min resolution in both longitude and latitude. Because the position error of consumer-grade GPS receivers is about 5 m, the collected GPS traces did not overlap perfectly, even though we drove on the same loop road several times. However, Fig. 4 shows that the illumination intensity measured has a high correlation in a small area. To alleviate the problem caused by GPS position error, we adjusted the resolution to 0.01 min. The result is shown in Fig. 5.

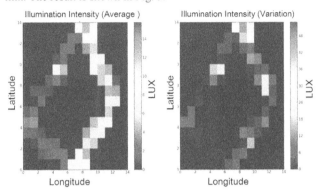

Fig. 5 The illumination map (in 0.01-min resolution in both longitude and latitude).

The illumination map in Fig. 5 shows the average and variation of illumination intensity and can be used as the control group illumination map now. By repeating the procedure to create more illumination maps at different time points, we can apply the statistical hypothesis test to analyze whether the later illumination map significantly differed from the control group illumination map, and point out the location of possible faulty street lamps.

3. SUMMARY AND FUTURE WORKS

We proposed a novel method to create illumination maps and use them to detect possible faulty street lamps. The proposed method brings significant advantages: 1) Additional sensors and networking modules do not need to be installed on every street lamp. The costs of our specially designed equipment to sense illumination were low; thus, this method may be realized in the near future. 2) The equipment can be used on fixed bus routes to collect illumination intensity and create illumination maps regularly without extra effort and cost. 3) The automatic procedure to detect and report faulty lamps can reduce the time between street lamp repairs. We are planning to install this system on a local fixed bus route to create town-scale illumination maps. This system should be able to help detect faulty street lamps and keep roads safer.

4. ACKNOWLEDGMENTS

The authors acknowledge support from the National Science Council, Taiwan, under grant 100-2218-E-194-006-MY3, and from the Ministry of Economic Affairs, Taiwan, under grant 98-EC-17-A-04-S1-044. The authors would like to thank Pei-Jyi Lee and Pin-Chen Kuo for excellent technical assistance.

5. REFERENCES

[1] F. R. Beyer; K. Ker, "Street lighting for prevention of road traffic injuries", *Injury Prevention*, vol.15, issue 4, pp.282-282, August 2009

[2] Y. Chen; Z. Liu, "Distributed Intelligent City Street Lamp Monitoring and Control System Based on Wireless Communication chip nRF401," *Networks Security, Wireless Communications and Trusted Computing, 2009. NSWCTC '09. International Conference on* , vol.2, no., pp.278-281, 25-26 April 2009

Fault Detection in Wireless Sensor Networks: A Hybrid Approach

Ehsan Warriach, Tuan Anh Nguyen, Marco Aiello
University of Groningen
Groningen, The Netherlands
{e.u.warriach, t.a.nguyen, m.aiello}@rug.nl

Kenji Tei
National Institute of Informatics
Tokyo, Japan
tei@nii.ac.jp

ABSTRACT

Wireless Sensor Network (WSN) deployment experiences show that data collected is prone to be imprecise and faulty due to internal and external influences, such as battery drain, environmental interference, sensor aging. An early detection of such faults is necessary for the effective operation of the sensor network. In this preliminary work, we propose a hybrid approach to the detection of faults and we illustrate its performance on data coming from a real sensor deployment. The proposal is a first step to have a hybrid method towards automated on-line fault detection and classification in context-aware WSNs middleware framework.

Categories and Subject Descriptors

B.8.1 [**Hardware**]: Metrics—*Performance and Reliability - Reliability, Testing and Fault-tolerance*

General Terms

Algorithm, Experimentation, Measurement, Reliability

Keywords

Data & System faults, Hybrid Fault detection

1 Introduction

Wireless Sensor Networks (WSN) has been widely employed for enabling various monitoring and control applications such as environment surveillance, industrial sensing, traffic monitoring, etc [4]. Many mobile and pervasive applications deliver us with information about phenomena or events at a much higher level of detail by continuously collecting and processing information from the physical world. The cornerstone for its success lies in the ability to draw meaningful and precise inferences from the collected data which in turn requires to have high data quality coming from the sensors. In general, wireless sensor nodes may experience two broad categories of faults that lead to the degradation of performance such as function and data faults. On the one hand, there is the data centric view comprising faults such as outlier, spike, stuck-at and noise. On the other hand, there is the system centric view with faults such as calibration, hardware, low battery and clipping [3].

To illustrate examples of fault, consider two specific sensors such as pressure sensor to detect chair occupancy status and designed by Advantic Systems uses the Tekscan® A201-100 FlexiForce® sensor. It provides force and load measurements. Another is Passive InfraRed (PIR) sensor detects the motion of users inside the office. The sensor uses the Perkin Elmer Optoelectronics® LHI878 sensor. We study the sensors in the context of an activity recognition effort part of the EU FP7 project GreenerBuildings [1]. For the project we set up a Smart Office Living Lab at the University of Groningen (RUG) where a number of simple sensors are used [2]. If we consider individual sensor readings over a period of time, we notice that faults can have a diversity of lengths, magnitudes, and patterns. For instance, some faults show a long-duration, relatively gradual change in sensor reading, whereas others exhibit a short duration, quite sudden change. Take for instance two PIR sensors. They can report value significantly deviating for short intervals from the expected values, resulting in a noticeable short in the graph (see Figure 1(a)). If instead we consider a pressure sensor, it reports value with much higher rate of change than expected over a period of time which may not return to the normal afterwords, resulting in a noticeable spike(see Figure 1(b)). So not a single mathematical fault model is perfect for detecting these kinds of faults.

Given the general impossibility to install a perfectly calibrated and robust network of sensors, we consider the paramount problem of run-time detection and classification of faults. We couple it with root-cause analysis of sensor faults, as well as techniques that can automatically scrub collected sensor data to ensure high quality in context-aware WSNs middleware framework. A first step in this direction is to obtain an understanding of the occurrence of faulty sensor readings in existing real-world deployments by using more than one detection method. Here, we propose to firstly explore three qualitatively different techniques for automatically detecting faults from a trace of sensor readings: rule-based, estimation, and learning based methods. Our proposal is based on (1) by artificially injecting faults of varying intensity into sensor datasets, we are able to study the detection performance of these methods. We find that these methods sit at different points on the accuracy and robustness spectrum; (2) we evaluate the methods on real-world datasets, where we observe the actual frequency of fault occurrence; (3) we define heuristics rules to identify faults dynamically in WSNs. This study lays the foundations for the definition of a hybrid approach to fault detection in WSNs.

2 Faults Detection Approach

To define a hybrid approach, we begin by over-viewing three prominent methods.

Detection Methods: While there are numerous methods for detecting faults, we consider three qualitatively diverse methods Rule-

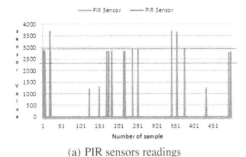

(a) PIR sensors readings

(b) Pressure sensor readings

Figure 1: Visual faults in RUG dataset

based, Linear Least-Square Estimation (LLSE) and Hidden Markov Model (HMM - learning-based) to define heuristics rules for detecting and identifying faults dynamically. Rule-based methods are based on domain and expert knowledge to define heuristic rules for identifying and classifying faults. Estimation methods predict normal sensor behavior by leveraging sensor correlation. Finally, learning-based methods are able to statistically identify and classify classes of faults. The system heuristics rules built on expert and domain knowledge and data from activity recognition in smart office Lab. Next we describe such heuristic rules.

Rules: Upon getting a data point, the system applies the set of rules developed to identify inconsistent data. Consequently all rules are applied to all data points, a few of them are listed below:

• Noise: There is always some amount of noise in the measurements. We take the average of readings in the noise window N. If the standard deviation of points within the noise window is greater than some threshold specified by the noise parameter, the samples are corrupted by the noise fault. Clearly, the performance of this rule depends on the threshold value.

• Constant: Compute the standard deviation of sample readings within a window N. If it is zero, the samples are corrupted by constant faults. The window size N can be in terms of number of sample or time, so the performance of this rule depends on the window size N.

• Outlier: The most common features to model an outlier are distance from other readings and gradient but first needs to model the expected underlying behavior. For that purpose we use simple methods of determining the expected range based upon previous data sample points and also expert and domain knowledge. Contextual information about the sensor plays a larger role in this fault meanwhile we are modeling expected behavior in a struggle to identify outliers.

• Short: Compute the rate of change of the physical phenomenon being sensed between two successive sensors readings. If the rate of change is above a threshold, it is an instance of a short fault.

Once the rules have been applied to each data-point and recovery required for the various identified faults to resolve them dynamically. The recovery and reconfiguration techniques that would either isolate or resolve identified faults remain also to be investigate in future.

3 Preliminary Evaluation and Conclusion

Our preliminary evaluation of the approach on the occurrence of faults in real world datasets coming from the GreenerBuildings project shows promise. The major fault in the readings was of the type short. We applied the short rule, LLSE and HMM methods, and a Hybrid (combination of Rule, LLSE and HMM) method to identify short faults in pressure, acoustic and PIR sensors readings. Figure 2 shows the occurrence of short faults for different sensors in the GreenerBuildings dataset. The Hybrid method removes false positives reported by the Short, LLSE or HMM methods. From Figure 1(a) one notices that short faults are relatively common. They are most predominant in the PIR sensor data (almost 1 fault every 70 samples). In this data set, spike faults were infrequent. Only one node had spike fault but it last for long time. If we consider it as a system fault then it will be either low battery or node broken as shown in the Figure 1(b).

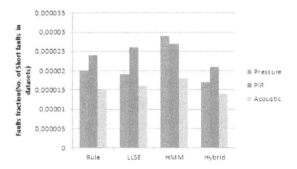

Figure 2: Short Faults in GreenerBuildings Dataset

In summary, we propose a hybrid approach for the detection of data faults in wireless sensor network which shows promise when applied to real sensor data. We plan to continue by integrating well-known mathematical fault models to make more robust and dynamic Hybrid method to identify data faults as well as system faults in context-aware WSNs and to thoroughly evaluate them.

4 References

[1] *GreenerBuildings*. http://www.greenerbuildings.eu.

[2] T. Nguyen and M. Aiello. Beyond indoor presence monitoring with simple sensors. In *Proc. 2nd Int. Conf. on Perv. & Embedded Comp. and Comm. Sys.*, 2012.

[3] K. Ni, N. Ramanathan, M. N. H. Chehade, and M. Srivastava. Sensor network data fault types. *ACM Trans. Sen. Netw.*, 5:25:1–25:29, June 2009.

[4] C. yee Chong, Ieee, S. P. Kumar, and S. Member. Sensor networks: evolution, opportunities, and challenges. *Proceedings of the IEEE*, 2003.

Poster Abstract:

Cyclic Network Automata For Indoor Sensor Network

Yiqing Cai
Department of Mathematics
University of Pennsylvania
Philadelphia, PA 19104
yiqcai@sas.upenn.edu

Robert Ghrist
Department of Mathematics and Electrical &
System Engineering
University of Pennsylvania
Philadelphia, PA 19104
ghrist@math.upenn.edu

ABSTRACT

Following Baryshnikov-Coffman-Kwak [1], we use network cyclic cellular automata to generate a decentralized protocol, with only a small fraction of sensors awake. The work here shows that waves of awake-state nodes turn corners and automatically solve *pusuit/evasion*-type problems without centralized coordination.

Categories and Subject Descriptors

D.2.1 [**Network Architecture and Design**]: Distributed networks

Keywords

cyclic cellular automata, wireless sensor network

1. INTRODUCTION

A very common application of wireless sensor networks is intrusion-detection. One may try to minimize the energy consumption, considering that sensors are battery driven. A natural way is to construct a sleep-wake protocol for the network, allowing sensors to alternate between higher and lower energy cost states. This paper is motivated by the work in [1], which applies a specific type of **cyclic cellular automata** (CCA), named Greenberg-Hastings automata (GHA), to sensor networks, instead of lattice spaces [2]. By applying this easily computable automata to a randomly generated dense enough sensor network on a two dimensional plane, barriers consisting of wake-sensors (wavefronts) will appear periodically after a certain amount of time, and sweep the whole domain. For spaces with small obstacles, the waves just ignore them, behaving like physical waves (see Figure 1). However, for spaces with huge obstacles (*e.g.*, indoor environment), wavefronts turn at corners and propagate, while still being able make intruders inescapable.

The system is not only energy conserving, but also inherits other advantages from CCA: parameters such as wavelengths are controllable; no coordinates or identification of sensors is needed; computations are distributed.

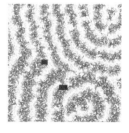

Figure 1: Greenberg-Hastings model in square with blocks

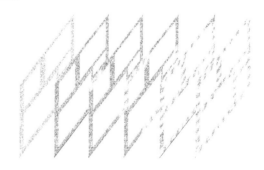

Figure 2: GHM for Narrow hallways space at time 0, 20, 45, 90, 150, 250

2. GREENBERG-HASTINGS MODEL AND EXPERIMENTS

The Greenberg-Hastings model (GHM) is a CCA first invented to study the spatial patterns in excitable media [3], with the dynamics taking values in $\mathbb{Z}_n$, under modular arithmetic. One denotes the (discrete) collection of nodes in network as X and denotes a **state** at time t as $u_t : X \to \mathbb{Z}_n$, then the update rule $\mathcal{G}$ is given as follows:

$$u_{t+1}(x) = \begin{cases} u_t(x) + 1 & : \quad u_t(x) \neq 0 \\ 1 & : \quad u_t(x) = 0; \exists \text{ a neighbor in 1} \\ 0 & : \quad \text{else} \end{cases}$$

Figure 2 illustrates the dynamic of the GHM of a specific indoor network. The network is built on narrow hallways modeled as a metric space with Euclidean metric; neighborhood of a node is defined as nodes within distance r.

In application we set states $2, 3, \ldots, n-1$ as sleeping states, 0 as awake state, and 1 as broadcasting state. Following $\mathcal{G}$, every sensor is supposed to sleep for $n-2$ time steps and then wake up, until hearing from a neighbor. As in simulation, only a small proportion (about $\frac{1}{n}$) of sensors are awake, which requires low energy cost.

3. ASYMPTOTIC BEHAVIOR CLASSIFICATIONS

We re-prove certain results from the CCA literature [2] in the more general setting of network (as opposed to lattice) systems. From observation, the interesting dynamical features associated with the GHM are time-periodic. We therefore focus our efforts on understanding time-periodic states.

A state u on a subgraph $X' \subset X$ is **continuous** if for every pair of neighbors $x, y \in X'$, $|u(x) - u(y)| \leq 1$. For a given network X and a state u, if u is continuous on a cycle $(x_i)_0^{k-1}$, then the **degree** of u on this cycle is defined as $\frac{1}{n}\sum_{i=0}^{k-1}(u(x_{i+1}) - u(x_i))$ where the summands are forced to be -1, 0, or 1, and the sum is ordinary addition (not mod n). Intuitively, the term degree defined here is an analogy of degree in topology, which is a homotopy invariant [4]. Here, it is the discrete version of "winding number". Degree is proved to be invariant under $\mathcal{G}$. We call a cycle $(x_i)_0^{k-1}$ a **defect** for some state u if the degree of u on this cycle is none zero. A **seed** is a special kind of defect with states in cyclic order.

THEOREM 1. *For a state u on a connected compact network X, if u contains at least one seed, the system will eventually reach a periodic state. If u is continuous on X, the system eventually turns to all-0 state (die out) if and only if it does not contain a defect.*

Since degree is invariant under the updating rule G, the theorem is saying a continuous state dies out eventually if and only if it is of a trivial first cohomology class, in topological sense.

4. EVASION GAME MODEL

Definition 1. Let the domain where sensors and evaders live be $\mathcal{D} \subset \mathbb{R}^2$. For each sensor $x \in X$, its covers a subset of $\mathcal{D}$, noted as U_x. Suppose at time slot $[t, t+1)$, $t \in \mathbb{Z}^+$, the set of sensors that are turned on is $X(t)$, then we define the "Evasion Game" between, the pursuer and the evader as follows: The strategy for pursuer is to update the network following GHM, and the strategy for the evader is to follow a continuous path in $\mathcal{D}$: $f : [0, \infty) \to \mathcal{D}$. If $\exists \tau \in [0, \infty)$, such that

$$f(\tau) \in \bigcup_{x \in X(\lfloor \tau \rfloor)} U_x,$$

then the pursuer wins. Otherwise, the evader wins.

The simplified case we consider is a limiting version when every hallway is narrow enough compared to the walls, so that the $\mathcal{D}$ could be treat as a 1-d space with the same homotopy type. We assume those sensors are located in $\mathcal{D}$ such that the union of two neighbors' coverages, which are one dimensional convex sets around each, covers the convex hall of them. We also assume the union of convex halls of neighbors (subspace of $\mathcal{D}$) is good enough to cover $\mathcal{D}$, in which case the whole space is covered when every sensor is turned on.

THEOREM 2. *For a GHM on network X with communication distance r in a compact and connected supper narrow hallways $\mathcal{D}$, if there exist a subnetwork X' with a sub-domain $\mathcal{D}'$, which is the union of convex halls of neighbors in X', such that there is a moment when every node in X' is in state 0, an evader will always lose in the evasion game in $\mathcal{D}'$.*

In narrow hallways case, we will prove that the same results hold, for a sufficiently dense network, with existence of controlling boundary paths.

5. REFERENCES

[1] Y. Baryshnikov, E. Coffman, and K. Kwak. High performance sleep-wake sensor systems based on cyclic cellular automata. In *Information Processing in Sensor Networks, 2008. IPSN '08. International Conference on*, pages 517 –526, april 2008.

[2] R. Durrett and J. E. Steif. Some rigorous results for the greenberg-hastings model. *Journal of Theoretical Probability*, 4:669–690, 1991. 10.1007/BF01259549.

[3] J. M. Greenberg and S. P. Hastings. Spatial patterns for discrete models of diffusion in excitable media. *SIAM Journal on Applied Mathematics*, 34(3):pp. 515–523, 1978.

[4] A. Hatcher. *Algebraic Topology*. Cambridge, 2002.

TDOA Sensor Pairing in Multi-hop Sensor Networks

Wei Meng, Lihua Xie
EXQUISITUS, Centre for E-City, School of
Electrical and Electronic Engineering,
Nanyang Technological University, Singapore
{meng0025, elhxie}@ntu.edu.sg

Wendong Xiao
School of Automation and Electrical Engineering
University of Science and Technology
Beijing, China
wendongxiao68@gmail.com

ABSTRACT

Acoustic source localization based on time difference of arrival (TDOA) measurements from spatially separated sensors is an important problem in wireless sensor networks (WSNs). While extensive research works have been performed on algorithm development, limited attention has been paid in how to form the sensor pairs. In the literature, most of the works adopt a centralized sensor pairing strategy, where only one common sensor node is chosen as the reference. However, due to the multi-hop nature of WSNs, it is well known that this kind of centralized signal processing method is power consuming since raw measurement data is involved in the transmissions. To reduce the requirements for both network bandwidth and power consumptions, we propose an in-network sensor pairing method to collect the TDOA measurements while guaranteeing the quality of source localization. The solution involves finding a minimal sized dominating set (MSDS) for a graph of the muti-hop network. It has been proved that in-network sensor pairing can result in the same Cramer-Rao-Bound (CRB) as the centralized one but at a far more less communication cost. Furthermore, the structure of the proposed in-network sensor pairing coincides with the decentralized source localization, which is an important application of our method.

Categories and Subject Descriptors

C.2.1 [**Computer-Communication Networks**]: Network Architecture and Design-Wireless Networks

General Terms

Algorithms, Performance, Design

Keywords

Wireless Sensor Networks, Time Difference of Arrival, Source Localization, Sensor Pairing.

1. INTRODUCTION AND MOTIVATION

Source localization using measurements from spatially separated sensors is an important application of wireless sensor networks (WSNs) [3]. The time-difference-of-arrival (TDOA) based method has a high estimation accuracy for source localization which has wide applications. TDOA based methods usually proceed in a two-step fashion. Firstly, TDOA measurements between sensor pairs are extracted by using a generalized cross correlation (GCC) method

[1]. Then in the second step, the estimated TDOA information will be utilized for final location estimation.

While extensive research works have been performed on algorithm development, limited attention has been paid in how to form the TDOA sensor pairs, especially in the multi-hop networks, which is the main concern of this work. Traditionally, the TDOA sensor pairs are formed in a centralized way which we call centralized sensor pairing. One common sensor node is chosen as the reference node. Then the other nodes need broadcast their raw measurement data to this reference node. However, due to the multi-hop nature of WSNs, most of the nodes can not communicate with the reference node directly. Hence, data relaying is demanded which will burn much energy since the raw measurement data is involved in the transmissions. In addition, this kind of methods requires a high bandwidth which is generally limited in WSNs and also may cause a large processing delay. Hence, in practice, a new TDOA sensor pair information collection method with low requirements for both network bandwidth and power consumptions is highly desirable.

It is well known that decentralized in-network signal processing and aggregation is more energy efficient than the centralized methods. It can reduce the amount of energy and bandwidth used for communications. In this paper, we propose an in-network sensor pairing method to collect the TDOA measurements. The basic idea is to find a minimal sized dominating set (MSDS) for a graph of a muti-hop network. It has been proved that the proposed decentralized in-network sensor pairing can result in the same Cramer-Rao-Bound (CRB) as the centralized one but at a far more less communication cost. Furthermore, the structure of the proposed sensor pairing method can be directly applied to the decentralized source localization and tracking problem which is also new for the TDOA based source localization method.

2. SENSOR PAIRING

2.1 Measurement Model

We consider a multi-hop sensor network. Given a team of M nodes performing a source localization task. For M sensors, there are a total number of $M(M-1)/2$ possible sensor pairs and TDOA measurements. Each sensor pair can estimate TDOA between them by using GCC methods [1]. The TDOA estimate by a sensor pair $\{i, j\}$ can be written as: $\hat{t}_{ij} = \frac{d_{ij}}{v} + e_{ij}$, where $d_{ij} = \|\mathbf{x}_i - \theta\| - \|\mathbf{x}_j - \theta\|$. $\mathbf{x}_i = [x_i, y_i]^T$ denotes the coordinates of sensor i, $\theta = [\theta_x, \theta_y]^T$ is source's coordinates; v denotes the propagation speed of signal; $e_{ij} \sim (0, \sigma_{ij}^2)$ denotes the TDOA estimation error, whose error variance σ_{ij}^2 depends on the signal bandwidth, observation time and SNRs [1]. For simplicity, in this paper, we assume that the error variances of all the sensor pairs are identical, i.e., $\sigma_{ij}^2 = \sigma^2$. The cross covariance of $\hat{t}_{ij}$ and $\hat{t}_{kl}$ denoted by $\text{cov}(\hat{t}_{ij}, \hat{t}_{kl})$ is

$$cov(\hat{t}_{ij}, \hat{t}_{kl}) = \begin{cases} \frac{1}{2}\sigma^2, & i = k \text{ and } j \neq l \text{ or } i \neq k \text{ and } j = l, \\ -\frac{1}{2}\sigma^2, & i = l \text{ and } j \neq k \text{ or } i \neq l \text{ and } j = k, \\ 0, & \text{otherwise.} \end{cases}$$

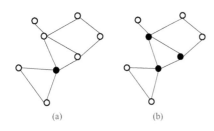

(a)   (b)

Figure 1: Sensor Pairing

2.2 TDOA Sensor Pairing in Multi-hop Networks

2.2.1 Network Model

Let us represent a multi-hop wireless sensor network (WSN) as an undirected graph defined by $\mathcal{G} := (\mathcal{N}, \mathcal{E})$, where $\mathcal{N}$ is the node set, $\mathcal{N} := 1, \ldots, N$ and $\mathcal{E} \subseteq \mathcal{N} \times \mathcal{N}$ is the edge set. If node k and node l can communicate with each other directly, we define the undirected link by $(k, l) \in \mathcal{E}$.

Several definitions from graph theory are used in this paper.

Definition 1. Maximum Degree is the maximum count of edges emanating from a single node.

Definition 2. Dominating Set: S is defined as a subset of $\mathcal{N}$ such that each node in $\mathcal{N} - S$ is adjacent to at least one node in S.

Definition 3. Minimal Sized Dominating Set (MSDS): G is the dominating set with minimum cardinality.

2.2.2 Proposed TDOA Sensor Pairing Method

To reduce the requirements for both network bandwidth and power consumptions, we propose an in-network sensor pairing method to collect the TDOA measurements while guaranteeing the quality of source localization. The solution involves finding a minimal sized dominating set (MSDS) for graph of the network which is a NP-hard problem [2]. A sequential greedy algorithm is used in this paper to find a MSDS. Note that the MSDS for a graph may not be unique. We modify the existing algorithm stated in [2] considering the communication costs between the nodes in the MSDS, which is presented in Algorithm 1.

Algorithm 1 Sequential Greedy Algorithm

1: Coloring all nodes white.
2: Selecting a node that causes the maximum reduction of the number of white nodes (or selecting a node with a maximal degree to the white nodes). Once a node is selected, it is marked black and its white neighbors are marked gray.
3: Repeat step (2). Note that if there are several nodes satisfying the condition in step (2) simultaneously, then the sensor chosen should be the one with minimal sum of hops(which is related to communication cost) with existing black nodes.
4: Algorithm terminates when there is no white node left.

Algorithm 2 In-network Sensor Pairing in Multi-hop Networks

1: Finding a minimal sized dominating set using Algorithm 1.
2: The nodes in the dominating set (black nodes) broadcast **raw measurement data** to their corresponding one-hop neighbors (gray nodes), respectively.
3: The gray nodes do the TDOA estimation using their local processor.
4: The gray nodes transmit the estimated TDOA information (which is a **scalar**) back to their neighboring black node.
5: The black nodes estimate the source location cooperatively in a centralized or a sequential mode.

In real applications, the dominating set of a sensor network can be determined offline if the topology of the network remains fixed during the online sensing tasks. Once the MSDS is determined, the TDOA measurements can be collected by using the following in-network sensor pairing method presented in Algorithm 2.

2.2.3 Performance Analysis

Estimation Accuracy.

THEOREM 1. *If $\sigma_{ij} = \sigma_{ji}, \forall i, j$ and the network is connected, then the proposed in-network sensor pairing results in the same CRB with the centralized one.*

Communication Cost.

LEMMA 1. *Defining E_{ce} and E_{in} as the communication cost for the centralized and proposed in-network sensor pairing methods, respectively, then we have $E_{in} \leq E_{ce}$.*

3. CONCLUSIONS AND FURTHER WORK

In this paper, we have proposed an in-network sensor pairing method to collect the TDOA measurements. Compared with the centralized paring method, it requires lower requirements for both network bandwidth and power consumptions involved in the data transmission. It has been proved that in-network sensor pairing can result in the same Cramer-Rao-Bound (CRB) as the centralized one but at a less communication cost.

We are currently studying the distributed localization algorithms based on the proposed in-network sensor pairing structure. How to fuse the TDOA information in a distributed way is still an open problem.

4. ACKNOWLEDGMENTS

This work was supported in part by the National Natural Science Foundation of China under grant NSFC 61120106011.

5. REFERENCES

[1] M. Azaria and D. Hertz. Time delay estimation by generalized cross correlation methods. *IEEE Transactions On Acoustics, Speech, and Signal Processing*, 32(2):280–285, 1984.
[2] J. Blum, M. Ding, A. Thaeler, and X. Cheng. Connected dominating set in sensor networks and MANETs. *Handbook of Combinatorial Optimization*, pages 329–369, 2004.
[3] W. Meng, W. Xiao, and L. Xie. An efficient EM algorithm for energy-based multisource localization in wireless sensor networks. *IEEE Trans. Instrum. Meas.*, 60(3):1017–1027, Mar. 2011.

Poster Abstract:

The Low-Power Wireless Bus:
Simplicity is (Again) the Soul of Efficiency

Federico Ferrari*   Marco Zimmerling*   Lothar Thiele*   Luca Mottola†

*Computer Engineering and Networks Laboratory, ETH Zurich, Switzerland
†Swedish Institute of Computer Science (SICS), Kista, Sweden
{ferrari, zimmerling, thiele}@tik.ee.ethz.ch   luca@sics.se

ABSTRACT

We present the *low-power wireless bus* (LWB), a simple yet efficient communication support for low-power wireless networks. The LWB maps different communication demands onto fast Glossy network flooding, effectively turning the wireless network into a bus-like infrastructure. The LWB requires no information of the network topology, thus drastically reducing the control overhead of common solutions such as route maintenance, and natively supports many-to-many communication and mobile nodes in addition to more traditional static, one-to-many scenarios. For instance, experiments on a 90-node testbed show that on average the LWB reduces packet loss by a factor of 231 and energy consumption due to communication by a factor of 11 compared to a state-of-the-art many-to-many routing protocol.

Categories and Subject Descriptors

C.2.1 [**Computer-Communication Networks**]: Network Architecture and Design—*wireless communication*

Keywords

Wireless Sensor Networks, Multi-Sink, Flooding, Shared Bus

1. OVERVIEW

Common communication support for low-power wireless networks mostly battled one of the defining features of the wireless channel: that of being a broadcast medium. Existing network-layer protocols build and maintain routes connecting sources to destinations, in an attempt to spare efforts from nodes that may be excluded from processing. The routes tend to be tailored to specific traffic patterns (*e.g.*, one-to-many or many-to-many) and application scenarios (*e.g.*, presence or absence of mobile nodes). However, route maintenance may require significant control traffic against link fluctuations and topology changes. Moreover, existing solutions typically require multiple functionality at different layers, whose interactions may be difficult to understand [1].

A different take on the problem. Owing to the broadcast nature of the wireless channel, the LWB incarnates a different approach, intuitively described in Fig. 1. It maps all communication requests onto network flooding by using Glossy, which provides 99.99 % flooding reliability with millisecond latencies in networks of hundreds of nodes, requir-

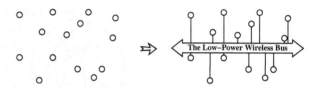

Figure 1: The LWB provides connectivity in multi-hop wireless networks similar to a shared bus.

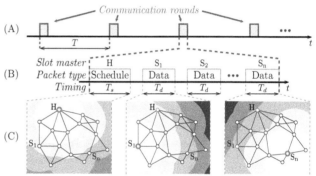

Figure 2: Communication rounds (A); communication slots in a round (B); Glossy floods in a slot (C).

ing no information of the network topology [2]. This effectively turns a multi-hop wireless network into a bus-like infrastructure. As a result, building and maintaining distributed routing state becomes unnecessary. Glossy's global time synchronization allows to integrate radio duty-cycling into the LWB, sparing the need for multiple network layers.

The absence of network state allows the LWB to (*i*) natively support multiple communication patterns with the *same* implementation, and (*ii*) be inherently resilient to topology changes. For instance, no changes to the protocol operation are required to support communication to multiple sinks, typical of control scenarios [9], or in presence of mobile nodes. The integrated design and simplicity of the LWB's functioning also make it straightforward to set the (few) protocol parameters and to understand its operation.

The LWB in a nutshell. Nodes in the LWB communicate in a *time-triggered* fashion [6] based on Glossy's built-in time synchronization. At most one *master* node at a time puts a message on the bus (*i.e.*, initiates a Glossy flood), whereas the other *slave* nodes read the message from the bus (*i.e.*, receive and relay the flooding packet). Communication complies with a *global schedule* that rotates the master role over time among all source nodes. A dedicated *host* node periodically announces the schedule. Depending on the application scenario, the schedule can be static or dynamically

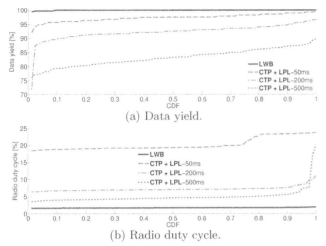

(a) Data yield.

(b) Radio duty cycle.

Figure 3: CDFs showing the performance of the LWB against CTP + LPL on Twist with a single sink.

re-computed, for example, based on bandwidth demands. We are currently investigating several scheduling policies.

In our current prototype, communication over the LWB occurs within *communication rounds* repeated with period T, as shown in Fig. 2(A). Nodes keep their radio off between two rounds to save energy. At the beginning of a round, the host node H transmits the current schedule, as illustrated in Fig. 2(B). This initial Glossy flood also time-synchronizes the nodes. The rest of the round is divided into non-overlapping *communication slots* wherein every source node S_i is granted access to the bus. Each communication slot then corresponds to a distinct Glossy flood, as shown in Fig. 2(C).

To ensure exclusive bus access by the master node against communication failures, a node is permitted to initiate a flood *only* if it received the last schedule from the host, which also provides time synchronization.

2. PRELIMINARY RESULTS

Our preliminary results from several diverse scenarios confirm that *"simplicity is the soul of efficiency"* [3]; that is, the cost of acquiring and maintaining distributed routing state often outweighs the benefits it possibly brings.

Experimental settings. We consider periodic data collection applications and corresponding performance metrics [4]: (*i*) *data yield* as the fraction of packets successfully received at the sink over those sent; and (*ii*) *radio duty cycle* as the fraction of time a node keeps the radio on, which provides a measure of a protocol's energy efficiency.

We compare the current LWB prototype with state-of-the-art routing and MAC protocols in both many-to-one and many-to-many scenarios. We use the Collection Tree Protocol (CTP) [4] available in TinyOS 2.1.1 as a baseline for the former and Muster [7] for the many-to-many case. Both protocols run atop the low-power listening (LPL) layer [8]. We repeat the experiments with 50 ms, 200 ms, and 500 ms LPL wake-up intervals. In all experiments, the application payload is 15 bytes. In the LWB, the round period T is set to 1 min, equal to the inter-packet interval. All operational parameters of CTP and Muster are at their default values.

The experiments run on the Twist [5] testbed, a 90 TelosB nodes installation densely spread across three floors in a university building. We set the transmit power to -7 dBm, yielding a maximum network diameter of 3 hops, and use

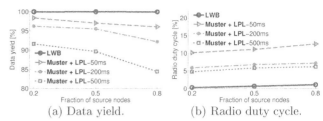

(a) Data yield. (b) Radio duty cycle.

Figure 4: LWB against Muster + LPL on Twist, with varying number of source nodes and 8 sinks.

channel 26 to limit the interference with co-located WiFi. We employ Contiki's power profiler to measure the radio duty cycle of the LWB prototype in software, and adopt a similar approach in TinyOS for all other protocols.

Results. Fig. 3 shows CDFs comparing the performance of the LWB prototype against CTP + LPL in a setting where all nodes funnel data to a single sink. The LWB outperforms CTP + LPL for all wake-up intervals we tested. It achieves a data yield of 100 % for most nodes (see Fig. 3(a)) with an average of 99.97 %, and performs evenly in radio duty cycle with an average of 1.69 % (see Fig. 3(b)). In comparison, CTP trades data yield for radio duty cycle, achieving the highest average data yield of 97.31 % at 50 ms wake-up interval, but at 20.18 % average radio duty cycle. Longer wake-up intervals result in significantly lower data yield, averaging 83.19 % at 500 ms wake-up interval.

Fig. 4 depicts the LWB performance against Muster + LPL in a setting with 8 sinks and a varying number of source nodes. The *unmodified* LWB used for the single-sink experiments outperforms a protocol conceived for multi-sink scenarios. The average data yield across all sinks with the LWB is steadily at 99.97 %, whereas with Muster it starts at 98.32 % and decreases to 96.01 % with more sources due to route maintenance overhead (see Fig. 4(a)). Moreover, the LWB achieves between 0.31 % and 1.07 % radio duty cycles, whereas Muster's highest data yield corresponds to an average duty cycle between 10.14 % and 12.57 % (see Fig. 4(b)).

Acknowledgments. This work was supported by Nano-Tera, the National Competence Center in Research on Mobile Information and Communication Systems under SNSF grant number 5005-67322, the Swedish Foundation for Strategic Research, and the Cooperating Objects Network of Excellence under contract number EU-FP7-2007-2-224053.

3. REFERENCES

[1] J. Choi, M. Kazandjieva, M. Jain, and P. Levis. The case for a network protocol isolation layer. In *ACM SenSys*, 2009.

[2] F. Ferrari, M. Zimmerling, L. Thiele, and O. Saukh. Efficient network flooding and time synchronization with Glossy. In *ACM/IEEE IPSN*, 2011.

[3] A. Freeman. *The eye of Osiris*. Cambridge University Press, 1996.

[4] O. Gnawali, R. Fonseca, K. Jamieson, D. Moss, and P. Levis. Collection tree protocol. In *ACM SenSys*, 2009.

[5] V. Handziski, A. Köpke, A. Willig, and A. Wolisz. TWIST: A scalable and reconfigurable testbed for wireless indoor experiments with sensor networks. In *ACM REALMAN*, 2006.

[6] H. Kopetz. The time-triggered model of computation. In *IEEE RTSS*, 1998.

[7] L. Mottola and G. P. Picco. Muster: Adaptive energy-aware multi-sink routing in wireless sensor networks. *IEEE Trans. on Mobile Computing*, 10(12), 2011.

[8] J. Polastre, J. Hill, and D. Culler. Versatile low power media access for wireless sensor networks. In *ACM SenSys*, 2004.

[9] J. A. Stankovic, I. Lee, A. Mok, and R. Rajkumar. Opportunities and obligations for physical computing systems. *Computer*, 38, 2005.

Poster Abstract:

Effectively Modeling Data from Large-area Community Sensor Networks

Saket Sathe[§]   Sebastian Cartier[§]   Dipanjan Chakraborty[‡]   Karl Aberer[§]

[§]EPFL, Switzerland.   [‡]IBM Research India,
{name.surname}@epfl.ch   cdipanjan@in.ibm.com

ABSTRACT

Effectively managing the data generated by Large-area Community driven Sensor Networks (LCSNs) is a new and challenging problem. One important step for managing and querying such sensor network data is to create abstractions of the data in the form of models. These models can then be stored, retrieved, and queried, as required. In our OpenSense[1] project, we advocate an *adaptive model-cover* driven strategy towards effectively managing such data. Our strategy is designed considering the fundamental principles of LCSNs.

We describe an adaptive approach, called *adaptive k-means*, and report preliminary results on how it compares with the traditional grid-based approach towards modeling LCSN data. We find that our approach performs better to model the sensed phenomenon in spatial and temporal dimensions. Our results are based on two real datasets.

Categories and Subject Descriptors

I.5.3 [**Clustering**]: Algorithms

General Terms

Algorithms, Design, Performance

Keywords

adaptive clustering, community sensing, data management

1. INTRODUCTION

OpenSense[1] is a LCSN whose major scientific objective is to investigate challenges in efficiently and effectively monitoring environmental parameters (e.g., air pollution) using community-driven sensors, mounted on buses and cars. In this context, our work investigates different approaches of synthesizing the data generated by LCSNs. At its core, LCSNs form a dynamic new form of mobile geosensor networks, characterized by uncontrolled or semi-controlled mobility of vehicles or people, moving over a large geographical area. For this reason, we treat the underlying sensor network as a disconnected component, which is collecting data using local policies and principles.

Although, there is significant literature on model-based query processing, both in-network [1] or in the back-end [3], on mobile sensor networks, there is a lack of understanding of approaches to determine high quality and concise models of the phenomenon from LCSNs. Most prior work [4, 5] implicitly assumes that the sensors are relatively homogeneously distributed and/or their sensing behavior can be tuned, considering the phenomenon being sensed.

[1]http://opensense.epfl.ch/

Unfortunately, this is not true for LCSNs. Hence, it is difficult to produce a homogeneous, good quality view of the phenomenon. The community-sensing pattern often leads to spatio-temporal irregularities in sensing. Therefore, a challenging question is: *how do we efficiently create quality-controlled models that cover the sensed data, spatially and temporally?*

Towards this, we propose adaptive strategies that discover spatial areas that can be modeled using single or multiple models. Our strategies adapt to the changing nature of the sensed phenomenon by adjusting the geographical granularity of the models to capture the phenomena with high fidelity. Through user-defined approximation error thresholds, we determine the quality of the models demanded.

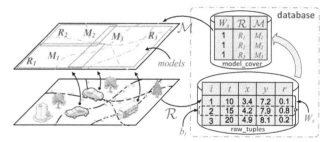

Figure 1: Architecture of the framework.

We compare our approach with a grid-based model cover strategy called GRIB, where the area under consideration $\mathcal{R}$ (refer Figure 1) is divided into equal size grid cells and a model is estimated for each grid cell. We find that adaptive approaches are significantly better with respect to the tradeoff between computational complexity and model quality, and also towards modeling the temporal evolution of the phenomenon.

2. ADAPTIVE MODELS

Our adaptive modeling approach provides a multi-model abstraction or a *model cover* over the raw tuples dumped in the region $\mathcal{R}$ (refer Figure 1). A model cover is a set of models $\mathcal{M} = \{M_1, \ldots, M_p\}$ that are respectively responsible for modeling the sub-regions $R_1, R_2, \ldots, R_p$ of $\mathcal{R}$. The sub-regions, taken together, cover the entire region $\mathcal{R}$. Specifically, the model cover is responsible for two tasks: (i) estimate the models $M_1, M_2, \ldots, M_p$, such that the approximation error per model and the total number of models (p) are minimized, and (ii) efficiently maintain the model cover as and when there are changes to the observed phenomena.

Estimating the Model Cover. For our first task, we present an adaptive method, called *adaptive k-means* or Ad-KMN, that gave us the best results amongst many candidates we designed [2]. This method partitions the region $\mathcal{R}$ adaptively (i.e., only when and where it is necessary) and estimates the models $M_1, M_2, \ldots, M_p$. The standard k-means algorithm uses the Euclidean distance for creating the clusters. Instead, in the Ad-KMN method, we use the model approximation error as an additional clustering criteria.

We denote the raw tuple as $b_i = (t_i, x_i, y_i, r_i)$, where r_i is the raw sensed value, and t_i and (x_i, y_i) are time and position corresponding to the sensed value r_i. We assume that the model cover is computed using a window of raw tuples W_s. W_s is a set of raw tuples b_i, whose time t_i is in between sH and $(s+1)H$, where s is a positive integer and H is the window length.

An example of the Ad-KMN method on toy data is shown in Figure 2. Assume that before executing the Ad-KMN method, we compute two centroids μ_1 and μ_2 by executing the standard k-means algorithm using the positions (x_i, y_i) found in the raw values of the window W_s (refer Figure 2(a)). We, then, (a) partition the raw values in W_s, such that R_1 and R_2 contain raw values that are nearest to μ_1 and μ_2 respectively, and (b) for the raw values in R_1 and R_2 we estimate linear regression models M_1 and M_2 and compute the approximation error [2].

Next, we check whether the approximation error is within a user-defined threshold τ_n. If, for instance, the error in both the regions R_1 and R_2 is greater than τ_n, then we introduce an additional cluster centroid for each region R_1 and R_2 and re-estimate the four centroids μ_1, μ_2, μ_3, and μ_4 using the standard k-means algorithm (refer Figure 2(b)). This procedure is continued until all regions meet the approximation error threshold τ_n.

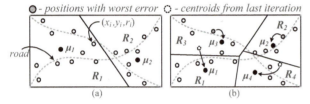

Figure 2: Example on toy data: (a) initial regions, and (b) two new regions R_3 and R_4 added after an Ad-KMN iteration.

Efficiently Maintaining the Model Cover. Furthermore, we are interested in maintaining the model cover as new windows of raw tuples are streamed into the system. Given several windows of raw tuples W_s, where $s = (1, 2, \ldots, S)$, we are interested in continuously maintaining the model cover, while reducing the number of additional computations required for its maintenance.

We start by estimating the cluster centroids $\mu_1, \mu_2, \ldots, \mu_p$ over a training window W_D of size $D \gg H$ using the Ad-KMN method. The Ad-KMN method returns the regions R_α and models M_α, where $\alpha = (1, \ldots, p)$. Now, assume that the first window of raw values W_1 is available. W_1 is first partitioned according to the cluster centers μ_α, such that W_1^α contains the raw tuples nearest to μ_α. Next, if the approximation error obtained using the raw values in the partition W_1^α is greater than a user-defined model retain threshold τ_r, then we invalidate the model M_α and re-estimate it from scratch. We perform a similar test for all the other W_1^α. We use flops[3] to measure the re-estimation cost of the model cover.

3. PRELIMINARY EXPERIMENTS

We demonstrate results obtained using our Ad-KMN method on two real datasets collected from large geographical areas. The *opensense* dataset contains 110k raw tuples measuring the Ozone (O_3) concentration in Zurich, Switzerland over a period of seven weeks, through bus-mounted sensors. The *safecast*[4] dataset contains 970k raw tuples of radiation values collected by the community in Eastern Japan after the Fukushima Daiichi nuclear disaster.

Error Analysis. Figure 3 shows the approximation error as a function of the number of regions p, where τ_n is set to 1% and H is

---

[2] *approximation error* is the average percentage error compared to the normal range of r_i in the environment (pollutant specific).

[3] A *flop* represents either an addition or a multiplication of two floating point numbers.

[4] http://blog.safecast.org/

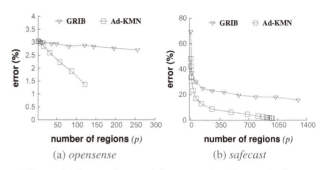

(a) *opensense* (b) *safecast*

Figure 3: Comparing model cover estimation methods.

6 hours. Linear regression models are fitted to the data in each grid cell for GRIB (or R_α for Ad-KMN). For both the approaches the approximation error decreases with increase in the number of regions. The decrement rate, however, is faster for Ad-KMN, leading to better quality models at lesser number of regions p. Notably, for *safecast* the Ad-KMN method delivers *12.5 times less error* as compared to the GRIB method for $p = 1000$.

Analyzing Temporal Validity of Ad-KMN and GRIB. We choose τ_r as 1%, a training window W_D of length 6 hours and 88 testing windows W_s of length 30 minutes. W_D and W_s are consecutive in time. Figure 4 shows the cumulative number of flops required to maintain the model cover on *opensense* for different p. Although per-operation cost of the Ad-KMN method is higher, the Ad-KMN method requires a factor of 2.7 less number of flops, when amortized over time. Notice, the Ad-KMN method requires zero flops for the first 34 windows as opposed to the 1874 flops required by the GRIB method. This empirically demonstrates the regions produced by the Ad-KMN method are valid for a longer time.

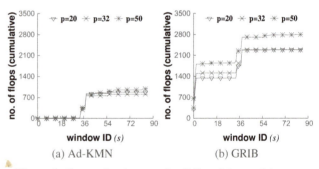

(a) Ad-KMN (b) GRIB

Figure 4: Comparing temporal validity of the model cover.

4. CONCLUSIONS

In this poster, we demonstrated that adaptive model cover estimation methods, namely Ad-KMN, exhibit promising performance gains in terms of accuracy and efficiency as compared to the grid-based methods for modeling data obtained from LCSNs. Future work will focus on efficient storage and query processing using adaptive model covers.

5. REFERENCES

[1] A. Bhattacharya and A. Meka, Singh. MIST: Distributed indexing and querying in sensor networks using statistical models. In *VLDB*, 2007.

[2] S. Cartier, S. Sathe, D. Chakraborty, and K. Aberer. ConDense: managing data in community-driven mobile geosensor networks. EPFL Technical Report, 2012. http://infoscience.epfl.ch/record/174752.

[3] A. Deshpande and S. Madden. MauveDB: Supporting model-based user views in database systems. In *SIGMOD*, 2006.

[4] M. Mokbel. The new Casper: query processing for location services without compromising privacy. In *TODS*, 2009.

[5] S. Nittel. A survey of geosensor networks: advances in dynamic environmental monitoring. In *Sensors*, 2009.

MARS: A Muscle Activity Recognition System Using Inertial Sensors

Frank Mokaya
Carnegie Mellon University
5000 Forbes Avenue
Pittsburgh, PA 15213
fmokaya@andrew.cmu.edu

Cynthia Kuo
Nokia Research Center
955 Page Mill Road,
Palo Alto, CA 94304
cynthia.kuo@nokia.com

Pei Zhang
Carnegie Mellon University
5000 Forbes Avenue
Pittsburgh, PA 15213
peizhang@cmu.edu

ABSTRACT

We present MARS, a muscle activity recognition system that uses inertial sensors to capture the vibrations of active muscles. Specifically, we show how accelerometer data capturing these vibrations in the quadriceps, hamstrings and calf muscles of the human leg, can be leveraged to create muscle vibration signatures. We finally show that these vibration signatures can be used to distinguish these muscles from each other with greater than 85% precision and recall.

Categories and Subject Descriptors

J.3 [**Life and Medical Sciences**]: Medical infomation systems

Keywords

Muscle activity recognition, inertial sensors, body sensors

1. INTRODUCTION

Human activity depends largely on functioning, active muscles. As a consequence, sensing and monitoring of muscle activity is important for many reasons. For instance, in sports medicine, information about the fatigue level of a muscle is useful for preventing over-exertion of muscles which might lead to muscle-based injuries. In addition, sensing muscle activity could be leveraged for precision training, allowing athletes to monitor progress on targeted muscle groups as needed. Finally, other ubiquitous applications such as muscle controlled prosthetics could also be enabled by muscle activity data. To be complete, however, a muscle sensing system needs to both detect muscle activity and use this data to distinguish the different groups of active muscle on the human body. This means first and foremost that the system must consist of a highly sensitive set of distributed sensors capable of sensing the relevant physical and physiological traits of muscle. Secondly, the system must be capable of processing the sensed data so as to be able to infer and distinguish different muscle groups from each other. In this paper, we present MARS, a system designed along these requirements, that uses inertial sensors to uniquely distinguish and identify muscle activity. Specifically, our work focuses on how muscle activity can be detected and muscle groups distinguished, using inertial sensors. The contributions of our work are as follows:

1. We investigate the feasibility of inertial sensors in sensing and distinguishing muscles based on muscle vibrations during an active workout.

2. We compare the performance of two different classifiers in distinguishing the muscle groups of the human leg.

1.1 Related Work

There are two main methods for detecting and monitoring muscle activity. The first is electromyography (EMG) [2] which accurately measures the electrical potential of active muscle fibers. However EMG requires perfect contact with the skin, necessitating the use of gels or small needles. This makes use of EMG complicated and invasive.

Mechanomyographic (MMG) methods on the other hand use vibration transducers such as fabric stretch sensors, force sensitive resistors (FSR) or inertial sensors (accelerometers, gyroscopes and magnetometer) to detect muscle activity. Fabric stretch sensors contain conductive carbon-loaded rubber whose resistance changes as it is stretched and relaxed when the muscle is active. Their susceptibility to hysteresis however complicates their use [1]. FSRs contain a polymer thick film device which changes its resistance according to the force applied to its active surface by the muscle belly as it contracts and expands in size. The major drawback of FSRs is that since the sensors vary highly and since they depend on change in size of muscle belly circumference, they are highly susceptible to placement on the body [4].

MARS is based on inertial sensors due to their ability to measure the muscle vibrations resulting from actively working muscle, as well as the motion of skeletal body segments. This allows for the possibility of integrating muscle activity recognition with skeletal motion categorization to realize a more holistic body activity recognition system.

2. THE EXPERIMENT

Muscle vibrations arise during muscle contraction and relaxation, as muscle fibers slide over each other, changing the shape and size of the muscle belly [1, 6]. These are the vibrations that MARS targets for sensing.

The inertial sensors used in MARS consist of a triaxial accelerometer, gyroscope and magnetometer. The sensors are all consolidated into a circular inertial measurement unit and linked to an onboard ATmega328P chip via an I^2C bus. We place MARS sensors at the estimated center of the muscle belly of each major leg muscle (quadricep, hamstring and calf), where muscle inflation and vibrations are largest. We estimate the center of the muscle belly visually by noting

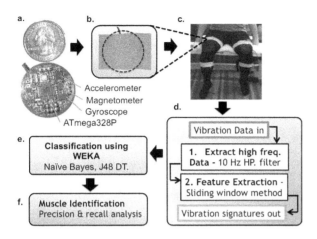

Figure 1: Overview of MARS system. (a) shows a sample sensor. (b), (c) show sensor placement during performed exercises. (d) shows processing of raw vibration data to extract features. In (e) Weka Naïve Bayes, J48 Decision Tree (DT) classifiers are used to distinguish muscles. Identification of muscles in (f) is the last step.

the position of the largest bulge in muscle when a subject flexes their muscle. We secure and place the sensors using an elastic bandage. The overview of the system, its components and overall flow is shown in Figure 1.

To facilitate extraction of vibration signatures, subjects perform five sets of exercises, selected with the help of a fitness trainer: three isolation exercises and two compound exercises. The first isolation exercise is a leg extension that works only the quadriceps. The second is a standing leg curl, which exercises only the hamstrings. Finally, calf raises work the calf muscle. For compound exercises, we select a squat which works all these 3 muscle groups as well as the gluteus. We also choose the 'bridge' which works the gluteus and to a lesser extent the hamstrings. As each participant performs each of these exercises in turn, MARS samples its sensors at 90 Hz. Exercises last about 3 minutes each. Subjects are allowed a 2 minute rest period in between exercises. In total we collect data from 12 participants: 5 female and 7 male.

3. EVALUATION AND RESULTS

For our initial round we use only accelerometer data, passed through a 10Hz high pass filter as shown in Figure 1d. 10Hz was sufficient to eliminate skeletal movement data, but low enough not to interfere with muscle vibration frequencies which are above 10Hz [5]. Next, we use a sliding window approach with a 50% overlap to calculate a set of 6 features over each of the axes of the remaining filtered data, for a total of 18 features. The features are signal standard deviation, mean, cosine correlation, correlation coefficients, power, and entropy, selected based on related work in muscle activity recognition [1, 2]. The features serve as the 'vibration signature' of the muscle group associated with the specific sensor data. We use Weka [3], to train two classifiers: the J48 decision tree and Naive Bayes classifier, on the extracted features, as shown in Figure 1e. We perform a 10-fold cross validation when identifying each leg muscle and report the precision and accuracy results of the classification. A subset of the obtained results are shown in Figure 2.

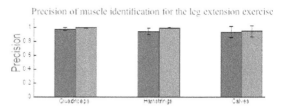

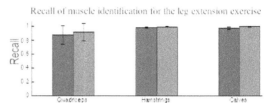

Figure 2: Preliminary classification results for the quadriceps, hamstring and calf muscle by MARS. Blue bars are the results of the Naive Bayes classifier. Red are the results of the J48 decision tree classifier.

These results show that MARS can leverage detected muscle vibrations to distinguish leg muscles with upwards of 85% precision and recall.

4. CONCLUSION AND FUTURE WORK

We have shown the preliminary results of MARS, an inertial sensor-based system of muscle activity recognition. The results show that MARS can be used to sense muscle vibrations and distinguish muscle groups with greater than 85% precision and recall. In future, we will incorporate gyroscope and magnetometer data in order to increase performance in MARS. Finally, we will extend the technique shown here to identifying the level of fatigue within muscle.

5. REFERENCES

[1] O. Amft, H. Junker, and P. Lukowicz. Sensing muscle activities with body-worn sensors. *Body Sensor*, pages 6–9, 2006.

[2] H. Ghasemzadeh, R. Jafari, and B. Prabhakaran. A body sensor network with electromyogram and inertial sensors: multimodal interpretation of muscular activities. *IEEE transactions on information technology in biomedicine*, 14(2):198–206, Mar. 2010.

[3] M. Hall, H. National, E. Frank, G. Holmes, B. Pfahringer, P. Reutemann, and I. H. Witten. The WEKA Data Mining Software : An Update. *SIGKDD Explorations*, 11(1):10–18, 2009.

[4] G. Ogris, M. Kreil, and P. Lukowicz. Using FSR based muscle activity monitoring to recognize manipulative arm gestures. *2007 11th IEEE International Symposium on Wearable Computers*, pages 1–4, Oct. 2007.

[5] M. T. Tarata. Mechanomyography versus electromyography, in monitoring the muscular fatigue. *BioMedical Engineering Online*, 10:1–10, 2003.

[6] J. Wood and D. Barry. Time-frequency analysis of skeletal muscle and cardiac vibrations. *Proceedings of the IEEE*, 84(9):1281–1294, 1996.

Poster Abstract:

Sensorcam: An Energy-Efficient Smart Wireless Camera for Environmental Monitoring

Zichong Chen, Paolo Prandoni, Guillermo Barrenetxea, and Martin Vetterli

{zichong.chen, paolo.prandoni, guillermo.barrenetxea, martin.vetterli}@epfl.ch
School of Computer and Communication Sciences
Ecole Polytechnique Fédérale de Lausanne (EPFL), Lausanne CH-1015, Switzerland

ABSTRACT

Reducing energy cost is crucial for energy-constrained smart wireless cameras. Existing platforms impose two main challenges: First, most commercial smart phones have a closed platform, which makes it impossible to manage low-level circuits. Since the sampling frequency is moderate in environmental monitoring context, any improper power management in idle period will incur significant energy leak. Secondly, low-end cameras tailored for wireless sensor networks usually have limited processing power or communication range, and thus are not capable of outdoor monitoring task under low data rate. To tackle these issues, we develop *Sensorcam*, a long-range, smart wireless camera running a Linux-base open system. Through better power management in idle period and the "intelligence" of the camera itself, we demonstrate an energy-efficient wireless monitoring system in a real deployment.

Categories and Subject Descriptors

C.2.1 [**Computer-Communication Networks**]: Wireless communication

1. INTRODUCTION

Wireless sensor networks are becoming the new paradigm for environmental data gathering. In this context, a visual feedback from the monitored area can prove indispensable to access the potentially critical environmental situation (avalanches, rock slides, fires, etc.) or to better interpret the telemetry data (snow vs. rain, clouds vs. sun, and so on). To this end, an autonomous, low-power camera could be installed in conjunction with the sensor network to deliver on-site images or video. However, a monitoring camera generates much higher data volume than the traditional environmental data, while it still suffers from the same challenges including i) low communication rate and ii) limited energy budget.

Ideally, the setup would be similar to that of the sensing stations, i.e., a wireless camera delivers the scene of interest periodically to the base station, using the energy from a rechargeable battery and a solar panel. The camera would need to work autonomously for long periods of time, while it achieves a desired sampling frequency (1-200 images/hour in our case). In order to minimize power consumption and

bandwidth requirements, the camera must be "intelligent" to process large amounts of raw data and transmit as minimum bits as possible.

There are some off-the-shelf solutions for wireless cameras, however, all prove to be impractical for this task:

1) Commercial smart phones with image sensor: closed platform and impossible for low-level power management.
2) Image sensing nodes developed for wireless sensor networks like Cyclops [5], CITRIC [1]: limited computing capability or insufficient communication range for outdoor monitoring.

To address these problems, we developed *Sensorcam*, a fully flexible, long-range, smart wireless camera running a Linux-base open system. In Section 2, we first briefly introduce the *Sensorcam* prototype. To demonstrate the advantage of smart cameras over conventional ones, in Section 3, we implement on *Sensorcam* three video coding schemes with increasing "intelligence". The energy profiling at a real deployment shows substantial benefits in overall consumption, including both communication and computation.

2. SENSORCAM PROTOTYPE V.2

Sensorcam includes a master board capable of embedded computing, GSM radio communication and GPS localization. A solar power system is equipped as the energy source. The master board runs an embedded Linux system and is able to control all the hardware peripherals from the software level. The main benefit of the Linux system is that, it can directly adopt libraries and programs from the open-source community. For instance, OpenCV library [4] is extensively used by us for image processing programming. It is also worth to mention that the developers of such libraries have started to release optimized codes for embedded platform, thanks to the emergence of mobile computing.

Fig. 1a shows the master board and its main components. Particularly, it includes: 1) MSP430 micro-controller for power management; 2) Colibri PXA270 module that runs Linux system; 3) Telit GM862 GSM/GPRS module for data communication and GPS localization; 4) Camera interface that connects to a camera module (e.g., Omnivision OV7720); 5) UART/Ethernet interface for debugging during software development; 6) SD card for data storage.

Fig. 1b shows the solar power system we used. Using solar radiation data collected from the deployed system, we calculate the average energy supply during the winter period (most adverse period) from 15th Jan 2011 till 17th Mar 2011. The energy budget and other important specifications of *Sensorcam* are listed in Table 1. Particularly, through

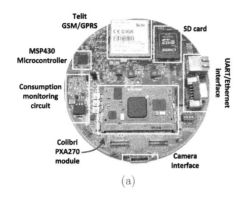 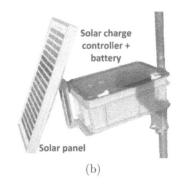

(a)   (b)

Figure 1: *Sensorcam* v.2 prototype: (a) Master board. (b) Solar power system.

Table 1: Specifications of *Sensorcam* v.2

CPU	520 MHz
SDRAM	64 MBytes
Flash memory	32 MBytes
GSM/GPRS uplink speed	~16 Kbps
Resolution of camera OV7720	640×480
average energy supply in winter	
2.4W solar panel	12.6 KJ/day
typical system consumption	
CPU normal, radio on (Transmitting)	900~3000 mW
CPU busy, radio off (Computing)	900 mW
CPU sleep, radio off (Idle)	40 mW

precise power management of all hardware peripherals before the system goes to sleep state, we minimize the system consumption in idle mode to 40 mW (250 mW for commercial product like EZ camera [3]).

3. BENEFIT OF INTELLIGENCE

Due to considerable complexities of video coding algorithms like H.264, most of standalone cameras in market cannot afford real-time encoding at 30fps. However, even in the scenarios where real-time is not a requirement (e.g., lower fps or latency permitted), current wireless surveillance cameras does not fully take advantage of the computation power on board. For instance, at a similar consumption rate of *Sensorcam*, EZ camera [3] employs the simplest Motion JPEG to compress captured image sequences. To demonstrate the benefit of using computation power of a camera, we implement three video coding schemes on *Sensorcam* with increasing "intelligence" to deliver potential events of interest to the end-user, namely: (1) Motion JPEG (MJPEG); (2) H.264/AVC High Profile; (3) Event-driven video coding (EVC) as proposed in our work [2].

In the experiments, the camera is programmed to capture an image of a parking lot at every T minutes. During standby period, the minimum configuration of the circuits is put into sleep mode and the rest is shut down. We connect an energy meter at the power source to measure the overall energy consumption during each experiment. Figure 2 shows the consumption per frame of three schemes. We can see that the overall consumption decreases substantially as the "intelligence" of camera increases.

4. CONCLUSIONS

We present *Sensorcam*, a smart wireless camera designed

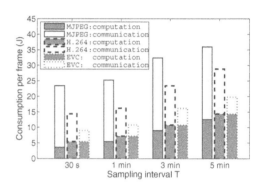

Figure 2: Energy profiling of EVC, H.264 and MJPEG on *Sensorcam*.

for environmental monitoring. Unlike existing platforms, it is fully flexible in both software and hardware levels. To minimize the energy leak during the idle period, we keep the minimum configuration of circuits in sleep mode and all the rest is shut down. In a real deployment, we show that the energy efficiency can be achieved by exploiting the "intelligence" of the camera itself. Despite its original motivation, using the on-board GPS, *Sensorcam* has also the potential to be used in a broader range of applications like outdoor surveillance, mobile sensing, etc..

5. REFERENCES

[1] P. Chen, P. Ahammad, C. Boyer, S. Huang, L. Lin, E. Lobaton, M. Meingast, S. Oh, S. Wang, P. Yan, et al. Citric: A low-bandwidth wireless camera network platform. In *Proc. ICDSC '08*, pages 1–10. IEEE, 2008.

[2] Z. Chen, G. Barrenetxea, and M. Vetterli. Event-driven video coding for outdoor wireless monitoring cameras. 2012. submitted to IEEE ICIP 2012.

[3] EZcam. Outdoor GSM 2Mega pixel Colour Camera. http://www.ezcam.co.uk/.

[4] OpenCV. A library of programming functions for real time computer vision. http://opencv.willowgarage.com/wiki/.

[5] M. Rahimi, R. Baer, O. Iroezi, J. Garcia, J. Warrior, D. Estrin, and M. Srivastava. Cyclops: in situ image sensing and interpretation in wireless sensor networks. In *Proc. SenSys '05*, pages 192–204. ACM, 2005.

Poster Abstract:
Extreme Learning Machine for Wireless Indoor Localization

Wendong Xiao[1], Peidong Liu[2], Wee-Seng Soh[2], Yunye Jin[3]

[1]School of Automation and Electrical Engineering, University of Science and Technology Beijing, China
[2]Department of Electrical & Computer Engineering, National University of Singapore, Singapore.
[3]Institute for Infocomm Research, A*STAR, Singapore

wendongxiao68@gmail.com, {u0804128, elesohws}@nus.edu.sg, yjin@i2r.a-star.edu.sg

ABSTRACT

Due to the widespread deployment and low cost, WLAN has drawn much attention for indoor localization. In this poster, an efficient indoor localization algorithm, which utilizes the WLAN received signal strength from each Access Point (AP), has been proposed. The algorithm is based on the Extreme Learning Machine (ELM), a Single layer Feed-forward neural Network (SLFN). It is competitive fast in offline learning and online localization. Also. compared with existing fingerprinting approach, it does not need the fingerprinting database in the online phase, which can substantially reduce the required storage space of the terminal devices.

Categories and Subject Descriptors

C.2.1 [Computer-Communication Networks]: Network Architecture and Design – *wireless Communication*

General Terms

Algorithms

Keywords

Indoor localization, fingerprinting, neural network, ELM

1. INTRODUCTION

The accurate location estimation or positioning is a key research task to any location aware system. The Global Positioning System (GPS) is most widely used outdoors [3]. However, due to the multipath effect and other technical limitations, GPS is unsuitable for complex indoor environment. Some solutions utilize the angle of arrival (AoA), the time of arrival (ToA) and the time difference of arrival (TDoA) for indoor localization. Although these solutions can provide high accuracy, they require special hardware, which increases the cost and complexity of the systems. Some other solutions make use of the Received Signal Strength (RSS). The most common approach is to build a radio map, and then apply nearest neighbor or probabilistic fingerprinting methods to do localization. Although these approaches do not need special hardware, they suffer from the noise greatly and require the fingerprinting database in the online phase. It is critical to terminal devices, which have limited storage capability. Another solution is to utilize the propagation model. Although, this solution does not need fingerprinting database and special hardware, the localization accuracy highly depends on the model, which is difficult to be built accurately [2]. In this poster, an efficient localization algorithm based on the Extreme Learning Machine (ELM) is being proposed. The algorithm utilizes the Received Signal Strengths. It does not need special hardware and fingerprinting database for online localization. It has also shown competitive fast offline learning and online localization speed.

2. ELM BASED INDOOR LOCALIZATION

2.1. Extreme Learning Machine

An ELM is a Single-hidden Layer Feed-forward neural Network (SLFNs), which has n input nodes, N hidden nodes and m output nodes. It can be represented as

$$Y_N(X) = \sum_{i=1}^{N} \beta_i G(a_i, b_i, X), X \in R^{n \times 1}, \beta_i \in R^{m \times 1}, a_i \in R^{n \times 1}, \quad (1)$$

where X are the inputs, a_i is the weight connecting the input nodes and the ith hidden node, b_i is the bias of ith hidden node, β_i is the weight connecting the ith hidden node and the output nodes, and G( ) is the activation function of the hidden nodes. In supervised learning, the number of training samples is finite. Assuming there are K arbitrary distinct samples (X_j, t_j), j=1,2…K, is used for training, equation (2) gives the relationship between the inputs and targets for each sample:

$$y_N(X_j) = \sum_{i=1}^{N} \beta_i G(a_i, b_i, X_j), X_j \in R^{n \times 1}, \beta_i \in R^{m \times 1}, a_i \in R^{n \times 1}, \quad (2)$$

where $y_N(X_j)$ is t_j, and $t_j \in R^{m \times 1}$. For all samples, the equations can be written in matrix form as

$$H * \beta = Y, \quad (3)$$

where $H(a, b, X) = \begin{bmatrix} G(a_1, b_1, X_1) & \cdots & G(a_N, b_N, X_1) \\ \vdots & \ddots & \vdots \\ G(a_1, b_1, X_k) & \cdots & G(a_N, b_N, X_k) \end{bmatrix}, \quad (4)$

$$\beta = \begin{bmatrix} \beta_1^T \\ \vdots \\ \beta_N^T \end{bmatrix}, \quad (5)$$

$$Y = T = \begin{bmatrix} t_1^T \\ \vdots \\ t_N^T \end{bmatrix} \quad (6)$$

Unlike the traditional training algorithms, which requires to adjust the input weights a and hidden layer biases b iteratively, it has been proved that the input weights and hidden layer biases can be randomly assigned if only the activation function is infinitely differentiable [1]. Thus, H is fixed once a and b are initialized randomly. To train a SLFN is simply equivalent to find a least square solution β of the equation $H * \beta = T$.

2.2. Algorithm Formulation

The localization algorithm consists of two phases: offline phase and online phase. During the offline phase, an empirical database is being built. The database consists of many fingerprints. For each fingerprint, it consists of two vectors: the signal strength vector and the corresponding location information vector. The ELM is being trained based on this database. The input of the ELM is the signal strengths, and the location information is considered as the output. Each fingerprint is considered as a training sample. Thus, β can be obtained by solving equation (3). After the network is being trained, the terminal devices only need to store the parameters of the ELM instead of the huge fingerprinting database. During the online phase, new collected signal strengths from each AP are fed into the trained ELM, an output will be given by the trained network. This output is thus considered as the estimated location.

3. PRELIMINARY EVALUATION

The data used to evaluate the performance was collected in the NUS Communication Lab. Three Linksys-WRT54G wireless routers are deployed in the test-bed as APs, broadcasting beacon frames periodically in channel 1, 6 and 11. A Fujitsu S6410 notebook equipped with an Intel Wi-Fi 4965AGN adapter, is used for RSS measurements. The Linux packet sniffer, tcpdump, is used to monitor the beacon frames transmitted by the APs. The MAC addresses of APs, timestamps, and the Received Signal Strength are retrieved from the radiotap header of the captured packet. Although the beacon frames from each AP arrives asynchronously, we can still use the timestamps of the arriving packets to align the reported RSS values and form the fingerprints.

The size of the test-bed is approximately $130m^2$. Within the accessible area of the test-bed, 251 locations are uniformly selected, such that the spacing between adjacent locations is 0.6m. At each location, 50 RSS fingerprints are collected.

All the evaluations are carried out in MATLAB 7.11 environment running in an Intel® Core™ i5, 2.4GHz CPU.

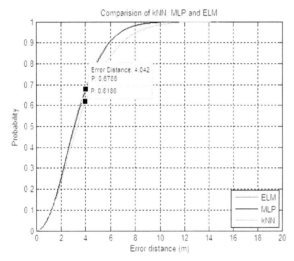

Figure 1: CDF Plots of ELM, MLP and kNN

Table 1. Time consumption of ELM, MLP and kNN

Training Sample size	Testing Sample Size	ELM		kNN		kNN/ELM
		Training Time	Testing time	Training Time	Testing time	Testing time
17x50	234x50	46.8ms	31.2ms	N.A	2.34s	75
20x50	231x50	15.6ms	12.2ms	N.A	2.574s	210
72x50	179x50	31.2ms	13.7ms	N.A	8.52s	621

Figure 1 shows that the proposed algorithm performs similar as the Back Propagation (BP) method. Both of the algorithms perform a little better than kNN regarding to the localization accuracy. However, Table 1 shows that the proposed algorithm has a relatively hundred times faster real-time localization speed than kNN. Moreover, the relative speed keeps increasing as the size of the database increases.

4. CONCLUSION AND FUTURE WORKS

This poster proposes an efficient novel indoor localization algorithm. It has been shown that the proposed algorithm is fast in offline learning and online localization. Furthermore, the proposed algorithm substantially reduces the required storage space since it does not need the fingerprinting database in the online phase. In the future, the application of ELM to larger scale localization will be explored.

5. REFERENCES

[1] G.-B. Huang, Q.-Y. Zhu, C.-K. Siew, Extreme learning machine: theory and applications, *Neurocomputing* 70 (1–3) (2006) 489–501.

[2] H. Liu, Houshang Darabi, P. Banerjee, and Jing Liu. Survey of Wireless Indoor Positioning Techniques and Systems. *IEEE Transactions on Systems, Man, and Cybernetics, Part C*, 37(6):1067–1080, 2007.

[3] National Research Council (U.S.). Committee on the Future of the Global Positioning System and National Academy of Public Administration, "The global positioning system: a shared national asset", National Academies Press, Chapter 1, p. 17, 1995.

Efficient Background Subtraction for Tracking in Embedded Camera Networks

Yiran Shen[†‡], Wen Hu[‡], Mingrui Yang[‡], Junbin Liu[‡], and Chun Tung Chou[†]

[†]School of Computer Science and Engineering, University of New South Wales, Sydney, Australia
[‡]Autonomous Systems Laboratory, CSIRO ICT Centre, Australia
{yrshen, ctchou}@cse.unsw.edu.au, {wen.hu, mingrui.yang, Junbin.liu}@csiro.au

ABSTRACT

Background subtraction is often the first step in many computer vision applications such as object localisation and tracking. It aims to segment out moving parts of a scene that represent object of interests. In the field of computer vision, researchers have dedicated their efforts to improve the robustness and accuracy of such segmentations but most of their methods are computationally intensive, making them nonviable options for our targeted embedded camera platform whose energy and processing power is significantly more constrained. To address this problem as well as maintain an acceptable level of performance, we introduce Compressive Sensing (CS) to the widely used Mixture of Gaussian to create a new background subtraction method. The results show that our method not only can decrease the computation significantly (a factor of 7 in a DSP setting) but remains comparably accurate.

Categories and Subject Descriptors

C.2.4 [**Distributed Systems**]: Distributed Systems

General Terms

Algorithm, Experimentation, Performance

Keywords

Compressive Sensing, Mixture of Gaussian, Background Subtraction, Object Tracking

1. INTRODUCTION

Many recent real-time object tracking methods require significant computation and energy consumption. These methods are difficult to implement on embedded camera networks because of the resource consumption. Robust background subtraction, such as Mixture of Gaussian (MoG)[2], is typically the dominant factor. The MoG models every pixel with a mixture of $3 \sim 5$ Gaussian distributions for the complex background and a pixel will be marked as foreground if it fits none of these background Gaussian models.

We propose a new background subtraction method that preserves the robustness of MoG meanwhile dramatically decreases the computation. We introduce Compressive Sensing (CS) in MoG to build a computation efficient background

subtraction method by reducing data dimensions (termed CS-MoG).

The process of CS-MoG can be divided into three steps: In the first step, it segments the image into small blocks (e.g., 8×8 pixels) then it produces random projection vectors (e.g., 8 projections) for each image block, as

$$Y = \Phi X \qquad (1)$$

where, X is from vectorising one of the 64-pixel blocks by row; Φ is ± 1 Bernoulli matrix (e.g., 8×64); Y is the projection vector whose dimension is significantly less than the block size (e.g., $1/8$). In the second step, CS-MoG models every projection in Y as a MoG. For every projection CS-MoG will check if its value belongs to the recent background model. Finally, to make a final decision, we design a higher level fusion strategy to determine if this block contains foreground. We evaluate the decision strategy such as max, min and majority voting and we find that the best method is min voting.

2. RESULTS

In this section we firstly compare CS-MoG with an existing method based on CS for background subtraction [1] (termed CSBS). CSBS employs direct comparison between

 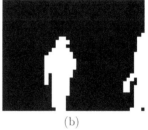

(a)   (b)

Figure 1: a) is a sample image of our dataset (b) is background subtracted image with 8-projections CS-MoG

consecutive images to subtract background. We evaluate the performance of proposed CS-MoG with CSBS in an outdoor pedestrian tracking dataset which consists of 400 images (resolution is 320×240), and Fig. 1(a) is one example image. Fig.1(b) is the result of CS-MoG for Fig.1(a). The number of projections is $1/8$ of image size. Fig. 2 shows the performance results with different parameters settings. False Alarm (FA) is the probability that we mistakenly decide the background as foreground and Probability of Detection (PD) is probability of correct detection for the foreground. Fig. 2 shows that CS-MoG outperforms CSBS significantly in term of subtraction accuracy. For example, CS-MoG achieves more than 98% PD when the FA is below 3%. Meanwhile CSBS only achieve about 75% of PD with the same FA.

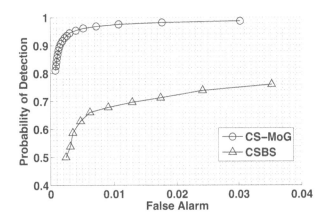

Figure 2: Performance comparison between CS-MoG with CSBS

We also compare CS-MoG with two other efficient MoG subtraction method using the same dataset. The results are shown in Fig. 3. Mean-MoG is to further divide the 8 × 8 blocks into smaller sub-blocks and calculate the mean of pixel values to represent a sub-block. Then, the mean values are modelled as MoG. RS-MoG is to randomly choose parts of the pixels to represent the whole block. They all have same dimension reduction ratio as CS-MoG. Fig.3(a) shows the performance of CS-MoG with different number of projections for one block. It demonstrates that when the number of projections increases above 8, CS-MoG will not obtain significant performance gain. Fig.3(b) shows that the performance of CS-MoG is the best among efficient methods and very close to original MoG method. All efficient MoG produce 8 measurements for one block.

To evaluate its efficiency, we implement the CS-MoG with 1/8 dimension reduction and the original MoG in a Blackfin BF-537 DSP camera node (see Fig.4) using fixed point arithmetics. The results show that with the original MoG it takes approximately $250 \sim 280$ms for the camera node to process one 320×240 image meanwhile with CS-MoG it takes approximately $37 \sim 42$ms only. Therefore, CS-MoG is approximately 7 times faster than the original MoG and makes it suitable for real-time tracking applications in embedded camera networks.

3. FUTURE WORK

we plan to further process the blocks containing both background and foreground in order to directly obtain the pixel scale results from compressed projections. Moreover, we plan to evaluate proposed CS-MoG with more datasets before implementing the whole tracking system in an embedded camera network.

4. REFERENCES

[1] Cevher, Volkan, and etc. Compressive sensing for background subtraction. In *Computer Vision ECCV 2008.*, pages 155–168, 2008.

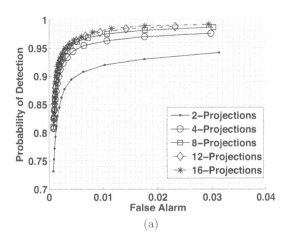

(a)

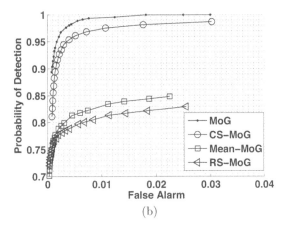

(b)

Figure 3: a) is the results of CS-MoG with different number of projections and (b) is the comparison of different methods

Figure 4: Picture of a Blackfin DSP camera node

[2] C. Stauffer and W. Grimson. Adaptive background mixture models for real-time tracking. In *Computer Vision and Pattern Recognition, 1999.*, volume 15, pages 246–252, 1999.

Poster Abstract:

Distributed Sparse Approximation for Frog Sound Classification

Bo Wei[†‡], Mingrui Yang[‡], Rajib Kumar Rana[‡], Chun Tung Chou[†], and Wen Hu[‡]

[†]School of Computer Science and Engineering, University of New South Wales, Sydney, Australia
[‡]Autonomous Systems Laboratory, CSIRO ICT Centre Australia
{bwei, ctchou}@cse.unsw.edu.au, {mingrui.yang, rajib.rana, wen.hu}@csiro.au

ABSTRACT

Sparse approximation has now become a buzzword for classification in numerous research domains. We propose a distributed sparse approximation method based on ℓ_1 minimization for frog sound classification, which is tailored to the resource constrained wireless sensor networks. Our pilot study demonstrates that ℓ_1 minimization can run on wireless sensor nodes producing satisfactory classification accuracy.

Categories and Subject Descriptors

C.2.1 [**Computer Communication Networks**]: [Network Architecture Design]

General Terms

Algorithms, Design, Experimentation, Performance

Keywords

ℓ_1 minimization, sparse approximation

1. INTRODUCTION

Sparse approximation, more precisely ℓ_1 minimization has recently been adopted largely by the researchers in the image processing and computer vision domain for efficient classification. In particular, researchers from the field of face classification [2] have reported that ℓ_1 minimization offers better classification accuracy compared to the state of the art classification algorithms such as Support Vector Classification. Motivated by this promising outcome we are interested in investigating the performance of ℓ_1 minimization for frog sound classification within a wireless sensor network platform.

There are two key challenges that need to be addressed before ℓ_1 minimization can be used for frog sound classification in wireless sensor networks. First, scaling down the minimization problem so that it can be solved on a wireless sensor network node. Second, unlike the test samples in the face or facial expression application, test samples may consist of multiple frog sounds. Therefore, ℓ_1 minimization is expected to classify multiple classes simultaneously. In our work, we seek to address these two key challenges.

2. CLASSIFICATION BY ℓ_1 MINIMIZATION

In this paper we propose a system for conducting frog sound classification using wireless sensor networks. In the proposed system, collaborative or cooperative classification is conducted locally at the sensor nodes. Upon detecting a frog sound, a sensor node organizes a cluster including other wireless sensor nodes and decides a cluster head. The cluster head distributes the classification task among the cluster nodes. Each cluster node conducts a part of the classification tasks and transmits the classification result to the cluster head. The cluster head joins the individual classification results to a complete result and identify the frog class(es).

Before describing our proposed method for frog sound classification, let us describe the general model for classification using ℓ_1 minimization. Consider we have c training classes and each class has t number of training subjects or samples. Let us define a matrix A containing the entire training set. Therefore $A = [a_{1,1}, a_{2,1}, \ldots, a_{t,c}] \in \mathbb{R}^{m \times (t \times c)}$. A test subject or sample $y \in \mathbb{R}^m$ belonging to the ith class can be represented as a linear combination of the training samples:

$$y = A\alpha \in \mathbb{R}^m, \qquad (1)$$

where $\alpha = [0, 0, \ldots, \alpha_{1,i}, \alpha_{2,i}, \ldots, \alpha_{t,i}, 0, 0, \ldots]^T$, $\alpha_{j,i} \in \mathbb{R}$, is a coefficient vector whose elements are zeros except for the ith training class.

Since it is now well known that ℓ_1 minimization can be used to find the sparse solution to Eq. (1) and the solution can be calculated in polynomial time, [2] used this idea for face recognition. However, notice that classification is not based on the largest sparse coefficients, but is given by

$$\arg\min_i r_i(y) = \|y - A\delta_i(\alpha)\|_2, \qquad (2)$$

where $\delta_i(\alpha)$ selects only the nonzero coefficients belonging to class i.

In our frog song classification problem, audio stream of a given class of frog is segmented into smaller windows and the Fourier transform of each window ($a_{i,j}$) of the sound is used as a column of the training matrix A. A test frog sound is first segmented by the window and then transformed to the frequency domain. Then the residual with respect to each class is calculated using Eq. (2) and the class with the minimum residual is identified as the match.

Notice that the dimension of the training matrix is typically very large. Finding the solution to Eq. (1) requires to run an ℓ_1 minimization problem, which is already computationally expensive for wireless sensor nodes. Therefore, in order to use the ℓ_1 based classification on wireless sensor nodes we propose to segment the training matrix into smaller parts where each part forms an Eq. (1) and is solved in a separate sensor node. For example, if p nodes take part in the classification, the training matrix A is divided into p parts as $[A_1, A_2, \ldots, A_p]$ and the observation made by the initiating node is transmitted to all the participating nodes. Then each node solves for α

$$y = A_i\alpha_i, \quad i = 1, \ldots, p.$$

$\{\alpha_i\}_{i=1}^p$ are then transmitted back to the initiating node, which forms the coefficient vector $\alpha = [\alpha_1^T, \alpha_2^T, \ldots, \alpha_p^T]^T$, and calculates the residuals using Eq. (2) to identify the frog sound.

3. RESULTS

We perform the frog sound classification in Matlab R2010b. Gradient Projection for Sparse Reconstruction (GPSR) (see [1]) is applied to calculate the coefficients for the training set.

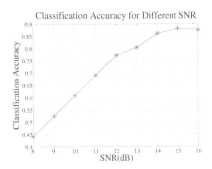

Figure 1: Accuracy Rate for Different SNR

In the simulation environment, the sample rate is 15,000Hz, and the window size is 0.5 seconds. Fig. 1 shows the accuracy rate of our ℓ_1 minimization approach using GPSR with respect to different signal to noise ratio (SNR). The noise is collected from the frog's living environment. We vary its amplitude and add it to the original test sound to get different SNR. The test sound sample set has 14 species whose call duration varies from 7.0 seconds to 43.4 seconds. We segment the test sample according to the window size and count the correct number of windows of the test sound, and compare it to the total number of windows to get the accuracy. As we expect, the accuracy rate increases to near 90% as SNR increases from 8 to 16.

Next, we show some preliminary results of the distributed frog sound classification. We want to classify the testing sound from Cyclorana cryptotis (class 2). Fig. 2 shows the classification residual by using one node, two nodes, and three nodes respectively. As we can see from these plots, Cyclorana cryptotis always has the smallest residual among all training species. The main concern here is how far we can go. It is clear that we can not go through this process forever, based on both the resource limitation and the accuracy concern. We are still working on finding a critical point to balance the trade off between efficiency and accuracy.

We also tested the performance of our approach on multi-frog detection. Encouragingly, when multi-class frog sounds appear simultaneously in the test sample, we are still able to detect these classes using this approach. As we can see from

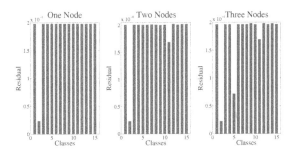

Figure 2: Residual Plots for Multi-node Classification

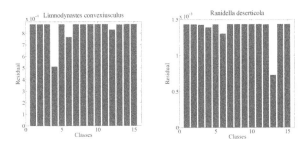

Figure 3: Residual Plots for Multi-frog Detection

the residual plots, Fig. 3, when Limnodynastes convexiusculus and Ranidella deserticola are singing simultaneously, we are still able to classify them using ℓ_1 minimization and Eq. (2). Therefore, ℓ_1 minimization also makes the simultaneous classification for multi-class test samples feasible.

4. CONCLUSION AND FUTURE WORK

In this paper, we propose a novel distributed frog sound classification method based on ℓ_1 minimization. We scale down the typical ℓ_1 base classification problem to be solvable on resource improvised wireless sensor nodes. We also demonstrate that ℓ_1 minimization is feasible to classify multiple classes simultaneously. To the best of our knowledge we are the first to propose and evaluate the above two features of ℓ_1 based classification.

The key issue that we are to address in the full bloomed version of our work is, how to define the number of segments of the training matrix. Our simulation shows that increasing the number of segments improves the computation time. However, after certain number of segments, the classification accuracy diminishes. We seek to find the optimal number of segments that offers a good trade-off of classification accuracy and computation time.

5. REFERENCES

[1] M. Figueiredo, R. Nowak, and S. Wright. Gradient projection for sparse reconstruction: Application to compressed sensing and other inverse problems. *Selected Topics in Signal Processing, IEEE Journal of*, 1(4):587–596, 2008.

[2] J. Wright, A. Yang, A. Ganesh, S. Sastry, and Y. Ma. Robust face recognition via sparse representation. *Pattern Analysis and Machine Intelligence, IEEE Transactions on*, 31(2):210–227, 2009.

Poster Abstract:

Ambulatory Real-time Micro-sensor Motion Capture

Shuai Huang[1], Shuyan Sun[1,2], Zhipei Huang[1], Jiankang Wu[1,2], Xiaoli Meng[1,2],
Guanhong Tao[1], Nan Zhang[1] and Li Yang[3]

[1] Graduate University of Chinese Academy of Sciences, Beijing, China
[2] China-Singapore Institute of Digital Media, Singapore
[3] Western Michigan University, Michigan, United States
{huangshuai09, sunshuy09b}@mails.gucas.ac.cn, jkwu@gucas.ac.cn

ABSTRACT

Commercial optical human motion capture systems perform well in studio-like environments, but they do not provide solution in daily-life surroundings. Micro-sensor motion capture has shown its potentials because of its ubiquity and low cost. We present an ambulatory low-cost real-time motion capture system using wearable micro-sensors (accelerometers, magnetometers and gyroscopes), which can capture and reconstruct human motion in real-time almost everywhere. It mainly consists of three parts: a sensor subsystem, a data fusion subsystem and an animation subsystem. The sensor subsystem collects human motion signals and transfers them into the data fusion subsystem. The data fusion subsystem performs sensor fusion to obtain motion information, i.e., the orientation and position of each body segment. Using the motion information from the data fusion subsystem, the animation subsystem drives the avatar in the 3D virtual world in order to reconstruct human motion. All the processes are accomplished in real-time. The experimental results show that our system can capture motions and drive animations in real-time vividly without drift and delay. And the output from our system can be made use of in film-making, sports training and argument reality applications, etc.

Categories and Subject Descriptors

H.1.1 [**Models and Principles**]: User/Machine Systems—*Human Information Processing*

General Terms

Design

Keywords

Human motion capture, micro-sensor, data fusion, motion reconstruction, real-time animation.

1. INTRODUCTION

Human Motion capture (Mocap) has wide applications in many areas, such as virtual reality, interactive game, sports training and film-making, etc. Among all the motion capture techniques, optical Mocap is one of the most mature ones, such as Vicon [1]. In optical Mocap, a subject is asked

to wear retro-reflective or light emitting markers. Exact 3D locations of these markers are computed from the images which are recorded by certain number of high resolution surrounding cameras, in order to form the motion of the subject. Optical Mocap systems are of high accuracy and fast update rates. However, they need multiple high speed and high resolution cameras structured and calibrated in a dedicated studio, which restricts applications into a studio-like environment; the systems are quite complex and have the line-of-sight problem.

We present an ambulatory low-cost real-time motion capture system using wearable micro-sensor nodes (accelerometers, magnetometers and gyroscopes), which can capture and reconstruct human motion in real-time almost everywhere. Several micro-sensor nodes are placed on body segments to measure human motion signals. The collected motion signals are used to estimate orientations and positions of body segments by fusion algorithms. A sensor data-driven hierarchy human motion model is developed and driven by the estimated orientations and positions for real-time motion reconstruction. The experimental results have shown that our motion capture system can capture human motion and drive animation in real-time without drift and delay.

2. PROTOTYPE SYSTEM

The prototype system of our micro-sensor motion capture mainly consists of three parts: the sensor subsystem, the data fusion subsystem and the animation subsystem, as depicted in Figure 1. The sensor subsystem samples and gathers human motion signals, and transmits the sensory data to the data fusion subsystem. The data fusion subsystem fuses sensory data to obtain the motion information, and sends the motion information to the animation subsystem. The animation subsystem visualizes the motion information using an avatar in the 3D virtual space in real-time.

The sensor subsystem mainly includes two parts: a base station and several micro-sensor nodes. The sensor nodes sample and collect human motion signals, and send them to the base station through wired communication. On each body segment a sensor node is fixed. Each sensor node contains a tri-axis accelerometer, a tri-axis magnetometer, and a tri-axis gyroscope. The base station gathers the motion signals from all the sensor nodes, packets the data and sends the packages to the data fusion subsystem for further processing. The sampling rate can be adjusted according to applications, and up to 200Hz. We use rechargeable Li-ion battery pack to provide power for the sensor subsystem. The

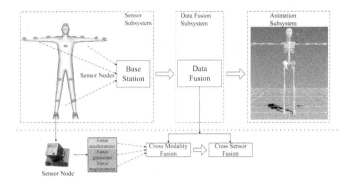

Figure 1: The prototype of MMocap system contains three parts: sensor subsystem, data fusion subsystem and animation subsystem.

system sends data between the base station and the data fusion subsystem with Bluetooth or WiFi.

The data fusion subsystem receives sensor signals and fuses them to obtain motion information. The motion information mainly includes orientation and position of each body segment. The data fusion subsystem first performs cross-modality fusion, which estimates the body segment orientation from the three different modalities of sensors. A quaternion-based Complementary Kalman Filter (CKF) is designed to combine these complementary data sources. Under this filtering framework, the integrated quaternion from gyroscope signals is corrected by the gravity and earth magnetic direction. To optimize the performance under interference, the CKF fuses gyroscope, accelerometer and magnetometer signals adaptively based on their information confidence, which are evaluated by computing their interference level [2]. However, strong and continuous magnetic distortion will eventually cause some estimation errors. After the orientation estimation, the fusion subsystem performs cross-sensor fusion, which estimates Center of Mass (CoM) displacement of the subjects based on gait analysis and forward kinematics. Then, each joint's relative positions are obtained from hierarchical transformations, where the pelvis is taken as root, and then is spread to limbs and head [3].

The motion information from the data fusion subsystem will be sent to the animation subsystem to drive the avatar in the 3D virtual space for real-time human motion reconstruction [4]. During the motion reconstruction, an articulated anatomic skeleton human model is built to represent the subject's body structure. The model is composed of chains of bone segments linked by joints. We assume that each bone segment is rigid and their shape does not change during the motion. When we reconstruct the human motion animation in real time, the orientation and position of each body segment drive the respective joint of the digital model directly along the hierarchical chain.

3. EXPERIMENTAL RESULTS

For the evaluation of our MMocap system, each micro-sensor node is mounted on the mechanical calibration platform (rate and position tables) to run multiple times, and the orientation measurements are compared with the standard platform readings. Based on the comparative experiments, the root mean square error of the average orientation

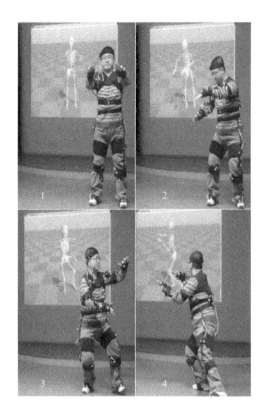

Figure 2: Real-time motion reconstruction

estimation accuracy of all sensors reaches 1.73 degree. Moreover, real motion recorded by a camera and reconstructed motion by our system are compared in real-time. During the experiment, the subject first stood still to get the initial orientation, and then he did Tai Chi Quan. As we can see from Figure 2, the 3D human model animation driven by our MMocap system performs the exact same actions vividly and reliably compared to the real human motion without delay and drift. This verified the effectiveness of our system. The full video results can be found in the website [5].

4. ACKNOWLEDGMENTS

This paper is supported by the National Natural Science Foundation of China (Grant No. 60932001), K. C. Wong Education Foundation of Hong Kong, and partially supported by CSIDM project 200802.

5. REFERENCES

[1] Vicon. http://www.vicon.com.
[2] S. Y. Sun, X. L. Meng, L. Y. Ji, J. K. Wu and W. C. Wong. Adaptive Sensor Data Fusion in Motion Capture. *Fusion*, 26-29 July 2010. EICC, Edinburgh, UK.
[3] X. L. Meng, S. Y. Sun, L. Y. Ji, J. K. Wu and W. C. Wong. Estimation of Center of Mass Displacement based on Gait Analysis. *BSN*, 23-25 May 2011. Dallas, US.
[4] G. H. Tao, S. Y. Sun, S. Huang, Z. P. Huang and J. K. Wu. Human modeling and real-time motion reconstruction for micro-sensor motion capture. *VECIMS*, 19-21 Sept. 2011. Ottawa, Canada.
[5] http://snarc.ia.ac.cn.

Light-weight Network Health Monitoring

Yi-Hsuan Chiang*   Matthias Keller†   Roman Lim†   Polly Huang*   Jan Beutel†

*Graduate Institute of Communication Engineering, National Taiwan University, Taiwan
†Computer Engineering and Networks Laboratory, ETH Zurich, Switzerland
{junctionQQ, huang.polly}@gmail.com   {kellmatt, lim, beutel}@tik.ee.ethz.ch

ABSTRACT

As the application of WSNs for long-term monitoring purposes becomes real, the issue of WSN system health monitoring grows increasingly important. Manually understanding the root causes of an observed behavior is time-consuming and difficult, often knowledge of prior behavior is necessary for understanding the potential risk on the long-term system performance. The challenges lie in the balance between the amount of system data collected and the level of detail in which state can be inferred from this data. In this paper, we propose a lightweight runtime logging and corresponding network state inference mechanism that enables scalable WSN health monitoring. Concretely, we propose that nodes only report their internal state on the occurrence of important events. Having a very low computational complexity and message overhead within the sensor network, reported events are analyzed at a less constrained network sink.

Categories and Subject Descriptors

C.2.1 [**Computer-Communication Networks**]: Network Architecture and Design—*Wireless communication*

Keywords

Wireless Sensor Networks, Environmental Monitoring, Health Monitoring, Long Term, Data Analysis

1. INTRODUCTION

Wireless sensor networks are well-suited for long-term data collection applications [4]. Not only being challenged by highly unpredictable, fast-changing conditions for wireless communication, the system performance is also at risk due to many other external factors [1], *e.g.*, mechanical damage. While short-term dynamics in the structure of a network are tolerable subject to the latency requirements of an application, a severe decrease in system performance, *e.g.*, long-lasting node isolations, might even need human intervention, *e.g.*, a hardware replacement.

Detecting and localizing anomalies is essential for a timely assessment of potential risks. Given a snapshot of the current system state, understanding the underlying root causes for the observed behavior can be a difficult problem [5].

In this paper, we propose a novel runtime health monitoring system that runs at the sink of a wireless sensor network.

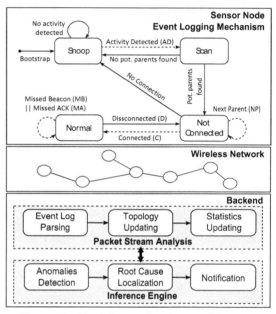

Figure 1: Health monitoring architecture

Based on a logging mechanism that only generates data on the occurrence of important events, internal network state is efficiently captured and transported to the sink. Monitoring algorithms running at the sink continuously analyze reported events to understand the system behavior, to infer root causes of undesired behavior, and to notify a network operator if a situation is severe. The usefulness of the proposed system is demonstrated using long-term data that has been collected at a real-world deployment.

2. SYSTEM ARCHITECTURE

The proposed event logging mechanism is tightly integrated into the Dozer [2] cross-layer communication stack used. The operation of Dozer on a sensor node can be described as a state machine with four states [4], see Figure 1. Here, dashed lines denote state transitions in which an event is emitted. The occurrences of two classes of events are recorded: 1) Internal transitions of the network protocol, *e.g.*, a transition from connected to disconnected operation. 2) Communication errors, *e.g.*, failed packet transmissions. An event has three properties: 1) Event_ID: denoting the type of event, 2) Event_Time: the time of event occurrence and 3) Event_Value: additional information, *e.g.*, the address of a new child node. Available event types are listed

Event_ID	meaning	Event_Value
10	Connected (C)	Parent ID
11	Disconnected (D)	*N/A*
13	Missed Beacon (MB)	#. times
14	Missed ACK (MA)	#. times
16	Next Parent (NP)	#. pot. parents

Table 1: Event types

in Table 1. Up to seven events are transmitted within a single event log packet. In contrast to periodically generated application data packets, *aperiodic* event log packets are only produced on the occurrence of interesting events.

3. HEALTH MONITORING

We propose two components for monitoring incoming traffic at the backend, see Figure 1. According to the event feedback, the *Packet Stream Analysis* component rebuilds the network topology and reassembles a global state composed of each node's current status. Those accumulated events of each node provide valuable diagnostic information. Hence, the *Packet Stream Analysis* component also extracts events from the packet stream and statistically updates high-level metrics. Three of them are listed as follows:

- **Disconnection Duration**: Time difference between event *D* and the next event *C*. It reflects the time needed for the node returning to the network.

- **Number of Potential Parents**: The Event_Value returned by the event *NP* reflects the node's tolerance to topology changes.

- **Number of Handshaking Attempts**: Since *NP* would be recorded when a node attempts to establish a connection with a potential parent node while traversing the list of potential parents, the number of reported *NP* events is used as an index of connection recovering ability.

The *Inference Engine* is responsible for detecting anomalies and inferring the root cause using above mentioned diagnostic metrics. In detail, when the application data throughput decreases, the *Inference Engine* is triggered to localize isolated nodes in the network. Here, a node is diagnosed as isolated if the symptom persists longer than the learned 90th percentile of its *Disconnection Duration*. If the throughput from several sensor nodes decreases at the same time, the *Inference Engine* tries to locate a potentially faulty link including potentially affected nodes. If the throughput of all nodes dropped at once, there is likely a failure at the sink.

4. CASE STUDY

The data used here originates from a real-world PermaSense [3] deployment that is located at the Matterhorn. The WSN consists of 22 nodes and a base station. We extract one month of data from Oct. 2010 for evaluating our proposed health monitoring mechanism.

Depending on the sensor configuration, every 120 seconds each node generates up to six kinds of application data packets. During the analyzed month, we find 500 event log packets out of in total 65,000 received packets. Thus, the introduced overhead is less than 1%.

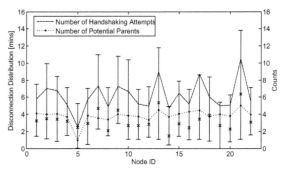

Figure 2: Diagnostic metrics that have been inferred from packets recorded at 22 nodes in Oct. 2010

In Figure 2, we show the statistics of the used diagnostic metrics. The y-axis on the left side represents the *Disconnection Duration* of each node. The 30th, 50th, and 70th percentile of the *Disconnection Duration* are plotted respectively along the error bar. The dashed and dotted curves denote the average counts of found potential parents and needed handshaking attempts until a node successfully (re)connected to the network, respectively.

Distinctively, we are able to diagnose node 5 being isolated repeatedly in Oct. 2010 due to the observations that (1) there is a persistent application data throughput drop, and (2) that the drop in throughput persists longer than the 90th percentile of the historical *Disconnection Duration* of node 5. Additionally, we can also observe that the communication ability of node 5 is dependent on the availability of only one available potential parent.

5. CONCLUSIONS

This preliminary results demonstrate that we can benefit from the light-weight logging mechanism. Our intention is to further evaluate available metrics for improving our algorithms for automated diagnosis at the backend.

6. ACKNOWLEDGEMENTS

The work presented was supported by NCCR-MICS, a center supported by the Swiss National Science Foundation under grant number 5005-67322, and from the Swiss Nano-Tera.ch initiative.

7. REFERENCES

[1] G. Barrenetxea, F. Ingelrest, G. Schaefer, and M. Vetterli. The hitchhiker's guide to successful wireless sensor network deployments. In *Proc. of the 6th ACM Conference on Embedded Networked Sensor Systems (SenSys'08)*, 2008.

[2] N. Burri, P. von Rickenbach, and R. Wattenhofer. Dozer: ultra-low power data gathering in sensor networks. In *Proc. 6th Int'l Conf. Information Processing Sensor Networks (IPSN '07)*, pages 450–459, 2007.

[3] A. Hasler, I. Talzi, J. Beutel, C. Tschudin, and S. Gruber. Wireless sensor networks in permafrost research – concept, requirements, implementation and challenges. In *Proc. 9th Int'l Conf. on Permafrost (NICOP)*, 2008.

[4] M. Keller, M. Woehrle, R. Lim, J. Beutel, and L. Thiele. Comparative performance analysis of the permadozer protocol in diverse deployments. In *Proc. 6th IEEE Int'l Workshop on Practical Issues in Building Sensor Network Applications (SenseApp '11)*, pages 969–977, 2011.

[5] Y. Liu, K. Liu, and M. Li. Passive diagnosis for wireless sensor networks. *IEEE/ACM Transactions on Networking*, 18(4):1132–1144, 2010.

Poster Abstract:

Understanding City Dynamics by Manifold Learning Correlation Analysis

Wenzhu Zhang
Department of Electronic Engineering
Tsinghua University
zhwz@tsinghua.edu.cn

Lin Zhang
Department of Electronic Engineering
Tsinghua University
linzhang@tsinghua.edu.cn

ABSTRACT

Cities have long been considered as complex entities with nonlinear and dynamic properties. Pervasive urban sensing and crowd sourcing have become prevailing technologies that enhance the interplay between the cyber space and the physical world. In this paper, a spectral graph based manifold learning method is proposed to alleviate the impact of noisy, sparse and high-dimensional dataset. Correlation analysis of two physical processes is enhenced by semi-supervised machine learning. Preliminary evaluations on the correlation of traffic density and air quality reveal great potential of our method in future intelligent evironment study.

Categories and Subject Descriptors

I.2.6 [**Learning**]: [Knowledge acquisition]; I.4.8 [**Scene Analysis**]: [Sensor fusion]

1. INTRODUCTION

Sensors have become an essential part of urban lives. Transdomain usage of sensor data and new emerging paradigms can change urban lives and policy-making processes by revealing hidden connections. Urban dynamics is the social behavior of human beings, which is known to relate strongly to environmental changes and resource consumption. Exploring the correlation between human activities, environmental change and resource consumption will be beneficial in many aspects including city plan, resource utility optimization, convenience improvement etc.

There has been a great shift by methodologies on urban dynamic study: from model-driven paradigm to data-driven paradigm[2]. The major challange now is how to perform efficient analysis with regard to oceans of data(if available) to obtain informative knowledge. To be specific, three aspects should not be neglected.

1) *The unavoidable presence of noise or imprecision in training data adds uncertainty to the reconstruction process.*

2) *The sparsity of data obtained from crowd urban sensing cause incompleteness and heterogeneity of dataset both in space and time.*

3) *Quantitive analysis among different physical process in different measurement is difficult. Semantic abstraction are needed to gain meaningful information.*

Our goal is to develope proper methods which could allevi-

IPSN'12, April 16–20, 2012, Beijing, China.
ACM 978-1-4503-1227-1/12/04.

ate the impact of noisy, sparse and high-dimensional dataset. We propose manifold learning based method to perform semantic abstraction, as well as spatial-temporal correlation to understand the implicit relationship between two phenomena.

2. SEMANTIC ABSTRACTION BASED ON MANIFOLD LEARNING

Suppose that in a city, there are N adjacent but not intersect areas $A_1, A_2, \ldots, A_N$. Each A_i, $i \in \{1, 2, \ldots, N\}$, contains m blocks $B_1, B_2, \ldots, B_m$. For every A_i, there are m measurement(sensory data) coming from m blocks respectively, denoted by $X_i(t)$. Define the learning result(output) as scalar $d_i^X(t)$. So we have we have m-dimensional input $X_i(t)$ and one scalar output $d_i^X(t)$ at time-step t in area A_i.

Suppose we have only partial knowledge about the input-output mapping. And there are two inter-related process $X_i(t)$ and $Y_i(t)$, $i \in \{1, 2, \ldots, N\}$. If we want to explore the implicit relationship between them, traditional methods adopt statistical methods such as canonical correlation analysis(CCA). However, it is hard to justify the meaning or significance of study results. Here we propose a new paradigm to perform correlation analysis. Firstly, for each dataset, we adopt manifold learning methods to reduce the dimension of data and obtain more 'abstract' information, which we could interperet as semantic level knowledge. Then spatial-temporal analysis could be used to gain higher level knowledge or prediction model. This approach is illustrated by Fig. 1.

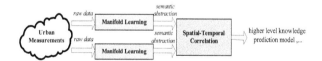

Figure 1: Manifold Learning Correlation Analysis

To overcome the problem of overfitting by a learning machine, regularization is usually used to restrict the solution of the hypersurface reconstruction problem by minimizing the augmented cost function. Generalized regularization theory extend classical theory by incorporating a second penalty function that reflects the intrinsic geometric structure of the input space. To be specific, the augmented cost function can be expressed by

$$\Psi(F) = \Psi_s(F) + \lambda_A \Psi_c(F) + \lambda_I \Psi_I(F) \qquad (1)$$

Here, $\Psi_s(F)$ denotes empirical cost function. While $\Psi_c(F)$ denotes regularizer, which is dependent on certain geometric properties of the approximating fuction. Thus, we propose a manifold based method to find proper $\Psi_I(F)$, which implies the intrinsic geometric structure of the input space. Here, we pursue the kernel approach based on manifold regularization. We use spectral graph theory to model a manifold.

Given this training sample, we proceed by constructing a weighted undirected graph graph consisting of N vertices, one for each input data point, and a set of edges connecting adjacent vertices. Let any two nodes i and j are connected, provide that the Euclidean distance between their respective data point $\mathbf{x}_i$ and $\mathbf{x}_j$ is small enough. Let w_{ij} denote the weight of an undirected edge connecting nodes i and j. Hereafter, we refer to the undirected graph, characterized by the weight matrix $\mathbf{W}$, as graph G. Let $\mathbf{T}$ denote an N-by-N diagonal matrix whose ii-th element is defined by $t_{ii} = \sum_{j=1}^{N} w_{ij}$, which is called the degree of node i. We define the *Laplacian* of graph G as $\mathbf{L} = \mathbf{T} - \mathbf{W}$.

Let $\Psi_I(F) = \mathbf{f}^T \mathbf{L} \mathbf{f}$ in equation (1).Define the vector valued function $\mathbf{f}$ in terms of the training sample X:$\mathbf{f} = [F(\mathbf{x}_1), F(\mathbf{x}_2), \ldots, F(\mathbf{x}_N)]^T$. According to generalized representer theorem[1], optimization of the cost function $\Psi(F)$ admits the form $F(\mathbf{x}) = \sum_{i=1}^{N} a_i k(\mathbf{x}, \mathbf{x}_i)$, where $k(\cdot, \cdot)$ could be Gaussian kernel function.

3. CORRELATION OF TRAFFIC DENSITY AND AIR QUALITY

There are two datasets that we used for analysis, within the range of Beijing city (E116.209-E116.544, N39.76-N40.02). For traffic density, we use Beijing taxi dataset with involves totally more than 20,000 taxi trajectories in one month. For the air quality, we used the dataset from our prototype system[3].

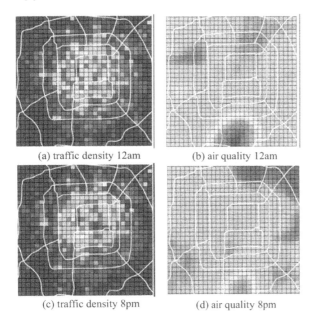

(a) traffic density 12am   (b) air quality 12am

(c) traffic density 8pm   (d) air quality 8pm

Figure 2: Traffic Density and Carbon Distribution

Fig.2 shows the density of vehicles and carbon-monoxide levels, where each small cell denotes 1km×1km area. We can see from Fig.2 that in downtown (inside the 3rd ring

road), the traffic density is usually higher than that of other places, with the west region's higher than the east region's in downtown. We can see an obvious 'hot zone' of air quality, which indicates severe air pollution in that region. We find that there are several chemical plants in the south of Beijing city, which are reasonably responsible for the local air pollution.

Fig.3 shows the learning results at selected area (Dong Tie Ying Bridge, a 9 km^2 region with center E116.43, N39.856). We use a real value as uniformed index to represent the learning outputs for this specific area. The blue real line denotes traffic density, while red dotted line denotes air quality. It is inferred that the air quality is probably influenced by population density. For the selected area, we can predict with confidence the air pollution peak will occur approximately three hours later after the rush hour.

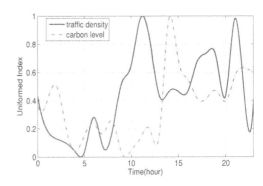

Figure 3: A Semantic Abstract of Traffic Density and Air Pollution in 24 hours

4. CONCLUSION

In this paper, we report our work progress on urban dynamics study. The major contribution of this paper is to use manifold learning on city phenomena correlation analysis. It reveals the intrinsic structure of dataset by spectral graph theory to achieve dimension reduction. In futhur study, spatial-temporal correlation methods can be developed to obtain non-trivial results. Interesting applications will be emerging towards better understanding of the cities.

5. REFERENCES

[1] M. Belkin, P. Niyogi, and V. Sindhwani. Manifold regularization: A geometric framework for learning from labeled and unlabeled examples. *J. Mach. Learn. Res.*, 7:2399–2434, December 2006.

[2] I. Benenson. Modeling population dynamics in the city: from a regional to a multi-agent approach. *Discrete Dynamics in Nature and Society*, 3:149–170, 1999.

[3] W. Zhang, L. Zhang, Y. Ding, T. Miyaki, D. Gordon, and M. Beigl. Mobile sensing in metropolitan area: Case study in beijing. In *Mobile Sensing Workshop in 13th International Conference on Ubiquitous Computing (UbiComp'11)*, 2011.

Poster Abstract:
Cybermussels: A Biological Sensor Network using Freshwater Mussels

Henry Baidoo-Williams[1], Jeremy Bril[2], Mehmed Diken[1], Jonathan Durst[2], Josiah McClurg[1]
Soura Dasgupta[1], Craig Just[2], Anton Kruger[1], Raghuraman Mudumbai[1], Teresa Newton[3]

[1]Electrical & Computer Engineering, University of Iowa, Iowa City, IA
[2]Civil & Environmental Engineering, University of Iowa, Iowa City, IA
[3]Upper Midwest Environmental Sciences Center, US Geological Survey, La Crosse, WI

[henry-baidoo-williams, jeremy-bril, mehmed-diken, jonathan-durst, Josiah-mcclurg]@uiowa.edu
[soura-dasgupta, craig-just, anton-kruger, raghuraman-mudumbai]@uiowa.edu, [Tnewton]@usgs.gov

ABSTRACT

In this paper, we describe our ongoing work on designing an underwater sensor network for monitoring the ecosystem of the Mississippi river using freshwater mussels as biological sensors.

One of the most extensive manifestations of anthropogenic mismanagement of nitrogen is eutrophication of the Gulf of Mexico. Our vision is to create a biosensor network of native freshwater mussels in the Mississippi river to monitor and model key components of the nitrogen cycle.

Categories and Subject Descriptors

C.2.1 [**Network architecture and design**]: Wireless Communication

General Terms

Design, Experimentation, Verification

Keywords

Bio-sensor, wireless sensor network, freshwater mussel

1. INTRODUCTION

Native freshwater mussels are a guild of long-lived, suspension feeding bivalves that can influence nutrient cycling by transferring nutrients from the water column to the riverbed. There is a long history of monitoring the response of individual mussels to changes in their environment. These range from biological investigations of mussels to complete commercial systems that use mussels as biological sensors, such as *Mosselmonitor* [1]. Our work goes beyond this previous literature in networking individual mussel sensors to create a wireless biosensor network. The gape, a rhythmic opening and closing of a mussel's valve, is by far the most commonly studied/used behavior, however we are exploring sensors for three additional variables: heart rate, valve pumping, and burrowing.

2. IMPLEMENTATION OF FRESHWATER MUSSEL SENSOR NETWORK

As a preliminary step towards this vision, our interdisciplinary team has built a mussel microhabitat with a constant river water feed stock, solar simulator, and a variety of water chemistry sensors. We have also designed simple, compact "backpacks" to be glued to a number of mussels; these backpacks each include a Hall-effect sensor to monitor the gape response of the mussel, memory, and a low-power wireless transceiver to connect the mussels into a wireless sensor network. It is well-known that RF wireless signals suffer very high attenuation underwater and therefore it has been assumed that underwater wireless networks are not feasible. However, we take advantage of the fact that freshwater mussels tend to congregate together in closely-packed clusters, and our preliminary experimental work has shown that off-the-shelf wireless transceivers work quite well underwater over distances of up to 1.2 meters (~4 feet).

Our poster will report on our initial results with the design of the backpack, experimental work with underwater wireless networking, design of the mussel microhabitat and our ongoing work on modeling the role of mussels in the freshwater ecosystem.

Figure 1 shows the sensors to be instrumented onto the mussels in our experimental setup; these include a mounted Hall-effect sensor which performs gape sensing, a digital thermometer chip providing both temperature and a unique "silicon id" for each mussel, and a pressure sensor to weigh the water column above the mussel which can provide information about vertical movement (burrowing) of the mussels.

Figure 2 also shows a tracking system used to track the mussels in our experimental microhabitat. It consists of a high resolution camera that is controlled via a custom application residing on computer. Continuously acquired pictures of the tanks are processed using image processing techniques that can identify and calculate the location of each mussel. In addition, the system utilizes a RFID tracking setup that traverses a reader under the tanks along the x/y-plane to detect and log unique mussel locations. Both processed images and RFID data are stored in a central database and we plan to make these available on the web along with time-lapse videos.

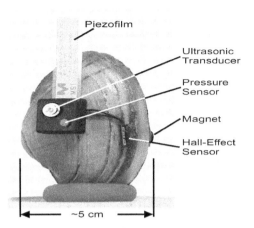

Figure 1. A mock-up of an instrumented freshwater mussel.

Piezofilm

Ultrasonic Transducer

Pressure Sensor

Magnet

Hall-Effect Sensor

~5 cm

Our objective with the setup in Figure 2 is to validate and profile Mussel behavior both with and without backpacks in a controlled environment through autonomous tracking of identification of RFID tags on the mussels.

We also plan to use the mussel location data obtained from the setup in Figure 2 to develop simple analytical models to describe the observed spatial aggregation behavior of mussels [2][3].

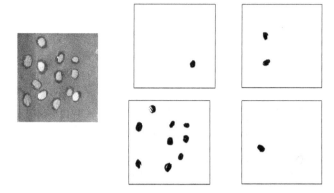

Figure 2. A sample image of mussel identification scheme using different colors and the masks generated to detect each color. These masks are further processed to find centroid information that is stored in a central database for further analysis.

3. REFERENCES

[1] de Zwart, D., Kramer, K. J. M. and Jenner, H. A. (1995), Practical experiences with the biological early warning system "mosselmonitor". Environmental Toxicology and Water Quality, 10: 237–247. doi: 10.1002/tox.2530100403

[2] van de Koppel J, Gascoigne J. C, Theraulaz G, Rietkerk M, Mooij W. M, et al. (2008) Experimental evidence for spatial self-organization and its emergent effects in mussel bed ecosystems. Science 322: 739–742

[3] M. de Jager et al, Levy walks evolve through interaction between movement and environmental complexity, Science 322, 1551 (2011)

Poster Abstract: Direct Multi-hop Time Synchronization with Constructive Interference

Yin Wang[†§], Gaofeng Pan[§], Zhiyu Huang[*]

[†]MOE Key Lab for Information System Security, School of Software, TNLIST, Tsinghua University
[§]Science and technology on communication information security control laboratory
[*]Institute of Software, Chinese Academy of Sciences
wangyin00@gmail.com, jec@jec.com.cn, huangzy@gmail.com

ABSTRACT

Multi-hop time synchronization in wireless sensor networks (WSNs) is often time-consuming and error-prone due to random time-stamp delays for MAC layer access and unstable clocks of intermediate nodes. Constructive interference (CI), a recently discovered physical layer phenomenon, allows multiple nodes transmit and forward an identical packet simultaneously. By leveraging CI, we propose direct multi-hop (DMH) time synchronization by directly utilizing the time-stamps from the sink node instead of intermediate nodes, which avoids the error caused by the unstable clock of intermediate nodes. DMH doesn't need decode the flooding time synchronization beacons. Moreover, DMH explores the linear regression technique in CI based time synchronization to counterbalance the clock drifts due to clock skews.

Categories and Subject Descriptors

C.2.1 [**Computer Communication Networks**]: Network Architecture Design

General Terms

Design, Performance

Keywords

multi-hop, time synchronization, constructive interference

1. INTRODUCTION

The main objective of multi-hop time synchronization in wireless sensor networks (WSNs) is to propagate synchronized time-stamps across the entire network as fast as possible and keep the global synchronization error small. However, multi-hop time synchronization remains a crucial task due to the unstable clocks of intermediate nodes [1] and large propagation delay across the entire network of flooding time synchronization messages [2]. Directly utilizing the standard time-stamps from the sink node is most beneficial for the time synchronization accuracy of a remote node multi-hop away. However, due to the undeterminate message transmission delay caused by the CSMA/CA protocol, a remote node must relay on the time-stamps from intermediate nodes to provide reference times. Let N_h denote a node which is h hops away from the sink node S. To synchronize N_h, previous protocols first synchronize one of its neighbor node N_{h-1} and then transmit the synchronized time-stamps of node N_{h-1} to node N_h. If the clock of node N_{h-1} is unsteady (e.g. due to fluctuant temperature), it will greatly influence node N_h's synchronization accuracy [1].

Constructive interference (CI) allows multiple senders transmit an identical packet simultaneously, which helps improve the packet reception ratio (PRR) of a common receiver rather than causing mutual interference. We design the direct multi-hop (DMH) time synchronization protocol by further exploiting CI, which can straightly employ the standard reference time-stamps from the sink node. DMH need not decode the time synchronization messages, which indicates the software delay due to MCU processing can be completely eliminated and the period between a reception and a retransmission can be reduced. Moreover, DMH compensates the clock skews, which is essential for CI based time synchronization to be deployed in real world WSN applications.

2. BACKGROUND

Constructive interference comes from the physical layer design to tolerate multi-path effects and has been utilized to alleviate the ACK storm problem, reduce the transmission latency of acknowledge packets, and improve the reliability of packet transmissions. By taking considerable care to transmit data packets with precise timing, Glossy [3] exploits CI by quickly propagating a packet from the sink node to all the other nodes across the entire network. When Glossy time synchronization starts, the sink node first inserts a reference time-stamp T_s and a packet relay counter $c = 0$ in the synchronization beacon, and broadcasts it to all its one hop neighbors. The intermediate nodes forward overheard packets immediately after receiving them. They trigger more nodes to receive the packets simultaneously, and the receivers also start to relay the same packets concurrently. Glossy decodes the synchronization packet and increases the relay counter c by 1 before initiating a new round transmission. Since the time slot T_{slot} between each hop is a network-wide constant, Glossy synchronizes the receiver by utilizing the reference time-stamp T_s and relay counter c to adjust the clock offset. In this way, Glossy realizes $0.4\mu s$ time synchronization accuracy for clock offsets in 8 hops.

3. DESIGN AND THEORETICAL ANALYSIS

DMH improves on Glossy from two aspects: first, DMH need not the relay counter c in the synchronization beacons, which indicates that DMH doesn't decode the flooding packets; second, DMH counterbalances the clock skews and thus reduces the period of resynchronization. DMH captures the time L_i with local on-chip timer at the instant when the start of frame delimiter (SFD) interrupt for the ith synchronization beacon is generated. DMH forwards the beacon immediately after each successful packet reception. After that, DMH decodes the synchronization beacon, fetches the reference time-stamp G_i inserted by the sink node and acquires a synchronization pair (G_i, L_i) for linear regression. DMH reduces the time slot T_{slot} between each hop by not decoding the packets and hence decreases the entire synchronization delay. In fact, if the radio supports the automatic switch to transmission mode at the end of a packet reception, DMH can completely eliminate the indeterministic software delay brought from hardware interrupts and software processing by not requiring the participation of MCU. We use linear regression technique to estimate the frequency error $\hat{\delta}$ and offset error $\hat{o}$ relative to the sink node.

Assume the initial true offset o relative to the sink node is within $\left[-\frac{T_{slot}}{2}, \frac{T_{slot}}{2}\right]$. The compensated time $\hat{L}$ for node N_h after linear regression can be expressed as

$$\hat{L} = L(1 + \frac{\hat{\delta}}{f_0}) - \hat{o} + \left[\frac{G_0 - L_0}{T_{slot}}\right] T_{slot}. \qquad (1)$$

Here, L and f_0 denote the local time of node N_h and the standard clock frequency of the sink node respectively, while G_0 and L_0 represents the first synchronization time pair.

As its name indicates, DMH straightly employs the reference time-stamps from the sink node instead of intermediate synchronized nodes, which is different from traditional protocols [2, 1]. If we use the Gaussian random walk model [4] to describe a clock, the MSE (mean square error) of clock skew of node N_h with linear regression can be calculated as:

$$\text{var}(\delta_h) = \frac{T_p^2 f_0^2}{4}\sigma_\eta^2 + 2\sigma_o^2 \frac{f_0^2}{T_p^2}, \qquad (2)$$

where σ_η^2 indicates the clock instability, σ_o^2 represents the MSE of clock offset measurement and T_p stands for the synchronization period. It can be indicated from Eq. 2 that DMH benefits from not being influenced by the synchronization accuracy of intermediate nodes. The assumption that the initial true offset between the node N_h and the sink node is within $\frac{T_{slot}}{2}$ can be satisfied by firstly synchronizing the offset of the entire network with Glossy protocol. The pseudo-code of DMH is illustrated in algorithm 1.

Algorithm 1: DMH protocol

/*init the offset synchronization with Glossy*/
ScheduleGlossy();
/*whenever receives ith beacon G_i at local time L_i;*/
  retransmit();
  store(G_i, L_i);
  delete($[G_{i-N}, L_{i-N}]$);/*N the regression table size*/
  $[\hat{\delta}, \hat{o}]$=linearRegression();
  $\hat{L}$=compensate($L, \hat{\delta}, \hat{o}$);/*use Eq. 1*/

---

4. EVALUATION AND CONCLUSION

We use five Tmote Sky nodes, one sink node N_0, three receivers N_1, N_2, N_3 and one observer N_4. We adjust the

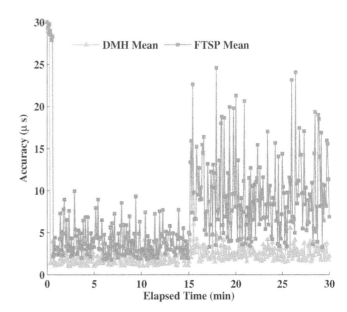

Figure 1: Average network synchronization error

transmission power of the sink node and three receivers, and form a two hops path $N_0 \rightarrow \{N_1, N_2\} \rightarrow N_3$ We implement FTSP and DMH protocol to compare the performance. We set the synchronization period $T_p = 30s$ and the linear regression table size $N = 4$. The observer N_4 sends querying messages every 5s to the above four nodes. They record the time when they successfully receive the querying messages, and store them in the external flash for off-line process. To compare the performance influenced by the clock uncertainty of intermediate nodes, we heat node N_1 for 60s at 15 minutes. The accuracy measurement of three receivers during an interval of 30 minutes are illustrated in Fig. 4.

In this poster abstract, we presented the DMH time synchronization protocol by exploiting CI. DMH is a new class of multi-hop time synchronization protocol, which directly utilizes the time-stamps from the sink node instead of intermediate nodes, and avoids the synchronization error caused by the unstable clock of intermediate nodes. Preliminary experiment shows that DMH is faster and more accurate than the state-of-the-art FTSP protocol. Future works includes the measurement study of DMH in real world large-scale WSN (CitySee project in Wuxi, China, 4000+ nodes).

5. REFERENCES

[1] T. Schmid, Z. Charbiwala, Z. Anagnostopoulou, M. B. Srivastava, and P. Dutta. A case against routing-integrated time synchronization. In *Proc. of ACM SenSys*, Nov. 2010.

[2] M. Maróti, B. Kusy, G. Simon, and À. Lèdeczi. The flooding time synchronization protocol. In *Proc. of ACM SenSys*, November 2004.

[3] F. Ferrari, M. Zimmerling, L. Thiele, and O. Saukh. Efficient network flooding and time synchronization with Glossy. In *Proc. of ACM/IEEE IPSN*, Apr. 2011.

[4] Z. Zhong, P. Chen, and T. He. On-demand time synchronization with predictable accuracy. In *Proc. of IEEE INFOCOM*, Apr. 2011.

Pair-wise Reference-free Fault Detection in Wireless Sensor Networks

[Extended Abstract]

Chun Lo
Dept. of Electrical Engineering
and Computer Science
University of Michigan
Ann Arbor, Michigan 48109
chunlo@umich.edu

Jerome P. Lynch
Dept. of Civil and
Environmental Engineering
University of Michigan
Ann Arbor, Michigan 48109
jerlynch@umich.edu

Mingyan Liu
Dept. of Electrical Engineering
and Computer Science
University of Michigan
Ann Arbor, Michigan 48109
mingyan@umich.edu

ABSTRACT

This poster presents a distributed reference-free fault detection algorithm which is based on local pair-wise verification. We show there exist a linear relationship between the output of any pair of sensors if the system excitations can be aggregated as a single system input. Using this relationship, faulty sensors suffering from sparse spike errors can be identified with high accuracy by our algorithm. An appealing feature of our method is that existence of reference sensors and knowledge of system input are not required. preliminary performance analysis shows that the algorithm is scalable, robust and able to detect most of the faults exist in the sensors. Communication power is also greatly reduced by the distributed nature of the algorithm.

Categories and Subject Descriptors

B.2.3 [**Arithmetic and Logic Structures**]: Reliability, Testing, and Fault-Tolerance—*Diagnostics, Error-checking*

Keywords

Sensor fault detection, Wireless sensor networks, spike error, nonlinearity

1. INTRODUCTION

With continuous improvements of sensor units over the past decade, wireless sensor networks (WSNs) are now being adopted in many applications, such as structural health monitoring, environmental monitoring , animal tracking, etc, for pervasive and affordable sensing and monitoring. In spite of being widely recognized in many applications, WSNs still have many issues to be addressed to ensure its reliability and scalability. One major problem of WSNs is the sensor unit used are usually simple structured and thus are more prone to fault and failure.

Over the past decade, sensor failure detection has been extensively studied. Most of the studies are based on analytical redundancy. The main idea of this approach is that when multiple sensors are attached to the same physical system should possess common system dynamics and thus correlation exist among sensors. Such correlation can be utilized to

reveal the abnormal sensors. Different detection algorithms based on this idea can be found at Li et al. [3] , Da and Lin [2], and Ricquebourg et al. [5]. However, most of the above studies require the knowledge of accurate system model parameters which are difficult to obtain in most system. Li's method further requires large number of expensive reference sensors. Furthermore, all of above methods are centralized, which means all the data is required to send back to a base station before running the fault detection. This communication intense algorithm is unfavorable in power limited WSNs. Chen et al. [1] presented an iterative and distributive detection algorithm. Nevertheless, it requires each sensor to be evaluated by large number of neighbour sensors which implies the communication cost and detection delay are still high.

This study presents a distributed reference-free fault detection algorithm. This algorithm divides the whole sensor network into pairs of two sensors. Under an assumption of the system input , the relationship between any two sensors can be learnt accurately with an autoregressive model with exogenous input (ARX) through training. After training, each pair of sensors can make use of the trained ARX model to evaluate each other. We proposed two different methods for detecting two major faults in sensor units, which are spike error and nonlinearity error. As a result, the failure detection happens locally, and only detection result are being sent back to the base station.

2. PAIR-WISE LINEAR RELATIONSHIP

Consider a set of monitoring sensors attached to a physical system and that form a connected multi-hop wireless network. Each sensor can potentially suffer from error at any time, and there are no reference sensor. The objective is to detect which sensor has error and when did it occurred. The mathematical state space model of the physical system and the output of the sensors (after Z-tranform) can be represented by:

$$zX(z) = AX(z) + BU(z)$$
$$Y(z) = CX(z) + DU(z) , \qquad (1)$$

where $Y(z)$ is the output vector of sensors.

By eliminating $X(z)$ in the second equation using the first equation, the transfer function between the output of sensor

i and sensor j is:

$$\frac{\boldsymbol{Y}_i(z)}{\boldsymbol{Y}_j(z)} = \frac{(\boldsymbol{C}_i(z\boldsymbol{I} - \boldsymbol{A})^{-1}\boldsymbol{B} + \boldsymbol{D}_i)\boldsymbol{U}(z)}{(\boldsymbol{C}_j(z\boldsymbol{I} - \boldsymbol{A})^{-1}\boldsymbol{B} + \boldsymbol{D}_j)\boldsymbol{U}(z)} . \qquad (2)$$

It shows that there exists a linear relationship between any pair of sensors. If the excitation of the system can be aggregated as a single source, i.e., $\boldsymbol{U}$ is a scalar, we can have a linear relationship between any two sensors which is independent of the system input.

If we represent the equation explicitly in terms of delays, Equation. 2 is exactly the representation of the ARX which has the following form:

$$y_1(t) = \sum_{i=1}^{n} -a_i y_1(t-i) + \sum_{j=0}^{n} b_j y_2(t-j) . \qquad (3)$$

3. FAULT DETECTION WITH ARX MODEL

By using the established relationship between a pair of sensors, any discrepancies between these two sensors can now be detected. First, define an error function of a sensor to be the difference between the observed output $\tilde{y}$ and the estimated output $\hat{y}$ (from the ARX model) of the sensor. Then define the error function (e_{12}) of sensor 1, using sensor 2 as reference, has the following form

$$e_{12}(t) = \boldsymbol{a}^T \boldsymbol{e}_1 - \boldsymbol{b}^T \boldsymbol{e}_2 ,$$

where $\boldsymbol{a}^T = [1, a_1, a_2, \ldots, a_n]$, $\boldsymbol{b}^T = [b_0, b_1, \ldots, b_n]$ and $\boldsymbol{e}_i = [e_i(t), e_i(t-1), \ldots, e_i(t-n)]$.

The error function represents the error characteristics within the sensor pair. In general, since either or both sensors may be faulty, it is impossible to determine weather both, or which sensor is faulty solely by inspecting the error function alone. Consequently, we developed two identification methods specially for spiky errors and nonlinearity errors.

Spike errors is a common fault in WSNs, especially for the motion sensors. One reason that causes this fault is by the vibration of loose electrical contact inside the sensor unit. Spike errors usually have short duration of time and have sparse occurrence. We thus assume $\boldsymbol{e}_1$ or $\boldsymbol{e}_2$ will have all zero entries except one component for spike error.

With the above assumption, $e_{12}(t)$ will be equal to $a_i d$ if a single spike occurred in sensor 1 at time $t-i$ with amplitude d and no spike occurred in sensor 2. As a result, a spike error in sensor $1(2)$ will appear in error function as a length n signal proportional to coefficient $\boldsymbol{a}(\boldsymbol{b})$. For the case $\boldsymbol{a} \neq k\boldsymbol{b}, k \in \mathbb{R}$, spike fault detection can be regarded as signal detection because a spike in different sensors will have different signals in the error function. A widely used signal detection technique, matched filter [4], in telecommunication is adopted here to identify the spikes. To detect spikes in sensor 1, the error function is passed through a filter identical to the coefficient $\boldsymbol{a}$. This filter will match the signal caused by a spike in sensor 1 and give a high signal in the output while the signal caused by a spike in sensor 2 will be suppressed. For the same idea, spikes in sensor 2 can be identified by a matched filter identical to the coefficient $\boldsymbol{b}$. For the case $\boldsymbol{a} \approx k\boldsymbol{b}$, the matched filter loses the ability to classify error function signals from different sensors. However, the algorithm is still able to detect errors within the sensor pairs as the error function is not equals to zero.

Nonlinearity fault means the output of a sensor units is not linearly related to its input, which is a very common

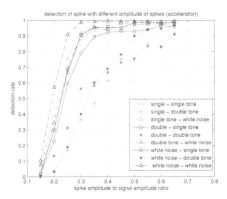

Figure 1: Detection rate VS spike amplitude.

error in sensor units. It can be occurred when the input or output exceeds the linear response region of the sensor or the sensor is not attached firmly to a physical structure. As this fault usually has long time duration, we cannot use the matched filter technique as in detecting spike errors. Assume the sensor only fall into the nonlinearity region occasionally, the error function of a sensor pair will have some time period equals to zero when both sensors are in the linear response region and have other time periods not equals to zero. The corresponding outputs of the sensors when the error functions is zero give information of the linear region of the sensors while the outputs corresponding to the transition from zero to non-zero of error function give information about the nonlinearity region.

4. RESULTS AND CONCLUSIONS

The performance of the algorithm was tested by a 5-degree-of-freedom spring-mass structure via simulation. The detection rate verses spike amplitude with different combinations of training and testing input signals are presented in Fig. 1. The algorithm performs well and the detection rate increases with the amplitude of spikes. For the nonlinearity fault, preliminary results show that the algorithm is able to identify at least on faulty sensor in a sensor pair. The condition of other sensor is uncertain and subject to another analysis. An sequential testing algorithm is preferred to optimize the number of comparisons.

5. REFERENCES

[1] J. Chen, S. Kher, and A. Somani. Distributed fault detection of wireless sensor networks. In *DIWANS, Proceedings of*, pages 65–71, September 2006.

[2] R. Da and C.-F. Lin. Sensor failure detection with a bank of kalman filters. volume 2, pages 1122–1126, June 1995.

[3] Z. Li, B. H. Koh, and S. Nagarajaiah. Detecting sensor failure via decoupled error function and inverse input-output model. *Journal of Eng. Mech.*, 133(11):1222–1228, November 2007.

[4] J. G. Proakis. *Digital Communiations 5th edition*. McGraw-Hill, 2007.

[5] V. Ricquebourg, D. Menga, M. Delafosse, B. Marhic, L. Delahoche, and A. Jolly-Desodt. Sensor failure detection within the tbm framework: A markov chain approach. In *Proceedings of IPMU*, 1991.

Poster Abstract: Crane Charades: Behavior Identification via Backpack Mounted Sensor Platforms

William P. Bennett, Jr.† Megan Fitzpatrick†† David Anthony† Mehmet C. Vuran† Anne Lacy‡

†CPN Laboratory, Computer Science and Engineering, University of Nebraska-Lincoln, Lincoln, NE
{wbennett,danthony,mcvuran}@cse.unl.edu
††Zoology Department, University of Wisconsin-Madison, Madison, WI
mjfitzpatric@wisc.edu
‡International Crane Foundation, Baraboo, WI
anne@savingcranes.org

ABSTRACT

The Whooping Crane is an endangered species native to North America and there are approximately 575 in existence. There have been recent efforts to provide ecologists with a tool to study the multifaceted behavior of the endangered species. Like many species, cranes display distinctly identifiable movements while being threatened, acting territorial, migrating, or preening. The preliminary experiments described in this poster provide evidence that sensor data presented by a novel sensing platform, the CraneTracker, can be used to identify crane behaviors on-board. With the ability to identify these behaviors, ecologists will have a more granular insight on what occurs during a crane's life on a daily basis.

Categories and Subject Descriptors

C.2.1 [**Computer-Communication Networks**]: Wireless communication

General Terms

Experimentation

Keywords

Wireless sensor networks, tracking, behavior identification

1. INTRODUCTION AND MOTIVATION

The Whooping Crane (Grus americana) is one of the most endangered species native to North America. Of the 575 in existence, 279 are from the original migratory Aransas-Wood Buffalo population (AWBP). These birds conduct a 4,000km annual migration from southern Texas to northern Canada, often flying 950 km/day during migration. The other portion of the cranes exist in captivity or re-introduced in Wisconsin, Florida, and Louisiana.

Recently, conservation efforts have centered on utilizing new tracking and monitoring technology to assist researchers in answering concerns regarding the newly re-introduced population in WI. The data collected from these efforts is intended to reveal potential causes of mortality, inability to reproduce in the wild, and possible impact a human dominated landscape on these birds.

Presently, Whooping Cranes' inability to reproduce is the most pressing threat to the success of the reintroduction efforts. There are a several explanations for these problems. First, it has been suggested that black-flies in the breeding grounds in Canada may be harassing birds, forcing them to flee from their nests. Second, the birds may be physically unable to complete incubation due to the lack of energy resources. They are compelled to leave their eggs to find food resources away from their territory.

The cranes exhibit distinct movements related to the behaviors they are engaging in. These behaviors are typically broken into comfort, locomotion, foraging, and social behaviors. These behaviors can be identified using state-of-the-art sensors, while recording time and location. The frequency of behaviors occurring or lack thereof, could be used to flag irregular behavior. Using MEMS sensors, there has been studies to identify animal behavior [3–6], which rely on data loggers [6]. Consequently, the studies rely on the recovery of devices to extract information. The improbable chance of crane recapture, high device energy consumption and lack of wireless data recovery make these tools unsuitable for monitoring Whooping Cranes. Instead, ecologists rely on direct observations, a task that is often difficult in field conditions.

In our recent work, we have developed the CraneTracker platform [1], which provides a rich set of sensors coupled with multi-modal communication to satisfy the data requirements of ecologists. Deployments with captive and wild cranes have provided measurements that never existed before for crane monitoring. Moreover, the deployed platforms have successfully survived 5 months of operation and a migration of 1,725 km. In this work, we discuss the preliminary data collected on captive birds that provide evidence that the basic movements can be classified on-board using the developed Crane Tracker platform [1].

2. EXPERIMENT RESULTS

To exploit the behavioral sensing capability of the Crane-Tracker platform [1], a set of controlled experiments were carried out at the International Crane Foundation, Baraboo, Wisconsin in July 2011. For the experiments, a tracker was programmed to collect solid-state compass readings at a sampling rate of 10 Hz for 30 seconds every 3 minutes. The readings from this sensor consist of acceleration in three axes, heading, pitch, roll and ambient temperature. To ensure their safety, crane were handled by experienced ecologists. The tracker was harnessed to a crane as a backpack and monitored over a closed circuit camera Fig. 1(a). The

 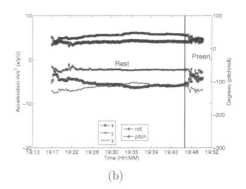 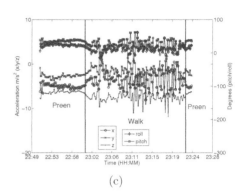

(a)   (b)   (c)

Figure 1: (a) CraneTracker on captive Siberian Crane (top), close-up view (bottom). Behavioral movements (b) rest to preen and (c) preen to walk to preen.

data were transmitted using the Zigbee radio interface to a base station, which was equipped with a directional antenna. The goal of the experiments was to correlate well-known crane behaviors with the solid-state compass readings. The behaviors from the camera feed were corroborated by an ecologist.

Data from the compass were collected over 4 hours and 21,882 records were received. In post processing, the video recording was played in sync with and the plotted data was annotated at points where basic behavior changed. In Figs. 1(b) and 1(c), the tri-axial acceleration (m/s^2) noted on the left y-axis and orientation (pitch/roll in degrees) noted on the right y-axis, are plotted over time. In the burst depicted in Fig. 1(b), the crane begins in a resting behavior then at 19 : 47 changes to a preening behavior. In Fig. 1(c), the crane is preening, then at time 23 : 00 starts to walk around the cage, and then at 23 : 22 returns back to preening behavior. The collected data supports that distinct behaviors can be differentiated.

3. FUTURE WORK

In the future, our goal is to identify cranes' behavior using the on-board processing capabilities of the CraneTracker, instead of logging an immense amount of data for post processing. The experiment results shown in Figs. 1(b) and 1(c) motivate the feasibility of this approach. Moreover, our initial work shown in a demonstration [2], proves that processing behavior on the mote is possible. The next steps in this process includes constructing a behavioral model, that correctly identifies common behaviors and obscure behaviors from sensor readings with great probability. The development of this model will require more experiments with captive and free-living cranes, over longer sensing periods.

Effective on-board processing enabled by this model, will be beneficial by reducing data stored and transmitted during sensing missions. In addition, the reduction of data transmitted could save a considerable amount of energy, extend sensing mission life-time, and more importantly, be more effective in the conservation of Whooping Cranes.

4. REFERENCES

[1] D. Anthony and et. al., "Sensing through the continent: Towards monitoring migratory birds using cellular sensor networks," in *Proc. ACM/IEEE IPSN '12*, Beijing China, April 2012.

[2] W. Bennett and et. al., "Cranetracker: A multi-modal platform for monitoring migratory birds on a continental scale." in *ACM MobiCom '10 Demo*, Las Vegas, NV, September 2011.

[3] A. Gleiss and et. al., "Making overall dynamic body acceleration work: on the theory of acceleration as a proxy for energy expenditure," *British Ecological Society, Methods in Ecology and Evolution*, vol. 2, pp. 23–33, Aug. 2011.

[4] E. Shepard and et al., "Identification of animal movement patterns using tri-axial accelerometry," *Endangered Species Research*, vol. 10, pp. 47–60, March 2008.

[5] R. Wilson and et al., "Moving towards acceleration for estimates of activity-specific metabolic rate in free-living animals: the case of the cormorant," *British Ecological Society, Journal of Animal Ecology*, vol. 75, pp. 1081–1090, Sept. 2006.

[6] ——, "Prying into the intimate details of animal lives: use of a daily diary on animals," *Endangered Species Research*, vol. 4, pp. 123–137, Jan. 2008.

Poster Abstract:

Exploiting Human Mobility Trajectory Information In Indoor Device-Free Passive Tracking

Chenren Xu, Bernhard Firner, Yanyong Zhang, Richard Howard and Jun Li

WINLAB, Rutgers University, 671 route 1 South, North Brunswick, NJ, USA

{lendlice,bfirner,yyzhang,reh,jonjunli}@winlab.rutgers.edu

ABSTRACT

Device-free passive (DfP) localization is proposed to localize human subjects indoors by observing how the subject disturbs the pattern of the radio signals without having the subject wear a tag. In our previous work, we have proposed a probabilistic classification based DfP technique, which we call PC-DfP in short, and demonstrated that PC-DfP can classify which cell (32 cells in total) is occupied by the stationary subject with an accuracy as high as 97.2% in a one-bedroom apartment. In this poster, we focus on extending PC-DfP to track a mobile subject in indoor environments by taking into consideration that a human subject's locations should form a continuous trajectory. Through experiments in a 10×15 meters open plan office, we show that we can achieve better accuracies by exploiting the property of continuous mobility trajectories.

Categories and Subject Descriptors

C.3 [**Special-Purpose and Application-Based Systems**]: Real-time and embedded systems

Keywords

Device-free Passive Tracking, Linear Discriminant Analysis, Trajectory

1. INTRODUCTION

The ability to continuously track human subjects in indoor environments can enable a large array of important applications. Among the existing localization methods, radio-frequency (RF) based device-free passive (DfP) localization does not inconvenience people, is unobtrusive, and offers good privacy protection [3, 2]. In our previous work [2], we propose PC-DfP, a probabilistic classification based device-free passive localization technique by formulating the localization problem as a linear classification problem. To achieve high classification accuracies, we take extra care to mitigate the adverse impact of indoor multipath. Our results show that PC-DfP can classify which cell (32 cells in total) is occupied by the stationary subject with an accuracy as high as 97.2% in a one-bedroom apartment, and an accuracy of 93.8% in an open-plan office.

In this paper, we focus on tracking mobile subjects using PC-DfP. We argue that mobility can introduce new opportunities for optimizing the localization accuracies. First, people usually move on continuous trajectories, and as a result their locations should exhibit continuity with time. Second, various obstacles in an indoor environment also bound human movement, further reducing

(a)

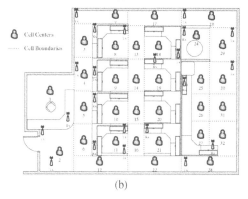

(b)

Figure 1: In (a), we show the first author's lab in which we deployed our system. In (b), we show the experimental topology. The office deployment region is partitioned into 32 cubicle-sized cells. Thirteen transmitters and nine receivers are deployed. We show the cell boundaries in this plot.

the problem space. With preliminary experimental results in a 10×15 meters office environment, we demonstrate that we can track a subject's movement with a cell estimation accuracy of 95.3%.

2. TRACKING STRATEGIES

To mitigate multi-path effect, we use training data to characterize the deployed room. In our approach [2], we first slice a deployed region into cells, and then we localize a subject to a cell. For this purpose, we obtain the training data by collecting the Received Signal Strength (RSS) of each radio link when the subject moves around within each of these cells. Based on this training information, we can determine the cell with the maximum likelihood of containing

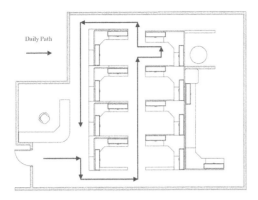

Figure 2: Experimental trajectory simulating a subject's daily path in a office's environment.

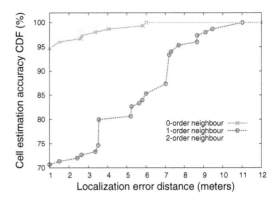

Figure 3: Tracking performance of a daily path when different number of order neighbor are adopted.

the subject. We treat all the possible RSS vectors from all the radio links when a subject is located in a cell as a class. We treat each class as a multi-variate Gaussian, construct a multi-class training dataset, and use Linear Discriminant Analysis (LDA) [1] as our classification algorithm to solve the indoor localization problem.

This approach can be used to not only localize a static subject's position, but also track his/her moving trajectory. Tracking a moving subject actually introduces new optimization opportunities - we can improve our localization results by considering the fact that human's locations from adjacent time intervals should form a continuous trajectory. In our cell-based approach, we define neighbors and rings for each cell. A cell's neighbors is defined as the cells which are possibly reachable by a subject in next reasonable time interval. For an arbitrary cell c, its 1-order neighbors are its immediate adjacent cells in physical space, and its 2-order neighbors are all the immediate adjacent cells of its 1-order neighbors, etc. Further, the i-th ring of cell c is the area consisting of the following cells: c itself, its 1-order neighbors, ..., up to its i-order neighbors. In particular, we define the 0-order neighbors as not considering its neighbors, and 0-th ring of cell is the cell itself. If the subject appears in a specific cell in an interval, then we assume the subject can only appear within this cell's rth ring in the next time interval. In more detail, suppose the subject is in cell c in the previous interval, and we are using PC-DfP to estimate in which cell the subject is in the current interval. In our previous work, PC-DfP only returns the cell with the highest likelihood. In this paper, we search for the cell with the highest likelihood from cell c's rth ring. We believe the tracking performance can be improved by adding this additional constraint. When we say we adopt the r-order neighbor, each estimated cell comes from the cells inside the previous cell's rth ring. The value r is an important parameter that we are going to study and evaluate through experiments in this paper.

3. EXPERIMENTAL RESULTS

Our experimental setup consists of a centralized PC serving as the system manager, thirteen wireless transmitters and nine wire-

less receivers. Each transmitter broadcasts a packet with its unique id every 0.25 second. The receivers receive the packets, extract the RSS values and forward them to the centralized PC for data collection and analysis.

The deployment takes place in an office room with the total area of 10×15 meters, which contains office furniture as shown in Figure 1(a). The room is spatially divided into 32 cubicle-size cells as shown in Figure 1(b). In the training phase, the first author moves around within each of these cells and makes 100 RSS measurements for all the links. Then, in the testing phase, as shown in Figure 2, the first author follows a daily path: enters the room, crosses an aisle, prints paper in his cubicle, and walks through another aisle to retrieve his paper. We consider a tracking interval successful if the estimated cell is the same as the occupied cell. We sample the RSS measurements every second. To evaluate our tracking performance, we define cell estimation accuracy as the success rate among all the tracking intervals, and localization error distance as the average distance between the actual location and the center of the estimated cell. We test our tracking performance when we adopt 0-order, 1-order, and 2-order neighbors respectively. For instance, in Figure 1(b), cell 28 is cell 22's 1-order neighbor, and cell 32 is cell 22's 2-order neighbor.

Table 1 shows that tracking performance of 1-order neighbor case is worse than 0-order neighbor. We found that most of the mis-estimated cells are the neighbors of the actual cell. In this way, if the mis-estimated cell's 1-th ring does not cover the actual cell for the next interval, then this single mistake in one interval may cascade to subsequent intervals. This problem, however, can be solved by adopting 2-order neighbor. Our experimental results show that we achieve 95.3% cell estimation accuracy and 1.0 m localization error distance in the 2-order neighbor case, which is the best among these three cases. In addition, Figure 3 shows 2-order neighbor case has a shorter tail than 0-order and 1-order cases, which suggest 2-order neighbor performs the best in the worst case.

4. REFERENCES

[1] T. Hastie, R. Tibshirani, and J. H. Friedman. *The Elements of Statistical Learning.* Springer, 2nd edition, July 2003.

[2] C. Xu, B. Firner, Y. Zhang, R. Howard, J. Li, and X. Lin. Improving rf-based device-free passive localization in cluttered indoor environments through probabilistic classification methods. In *Proceedings of the 11th ACM/IEEE International Conference on Information Processing in Sensor Networks*, IPSN '12, New York, NY, USA, 2012. ACM. to appear.

[3] M. Youssef, M. Mah, and A. Agrawala. Challenges: device-free passive localization for wireless environments. In *Proceedings of the 13th annual ACM international conference on Mobile computing and networking*, MobiCom '07, pages 222–229, New York, NY, USA, 2007. ACM.

Neighbor Order	Cell Estimation Accuracy (%)	Localization Error Distance (m)
0	94.7	1.2
1	70.7	2.5
2	95.3	1.0

Table 1: Comparison of tracking performance when different number of order neighbor are adopted.

Poster Abstract: A Beamforming Method for Multiple Source DOA Estimation, Spectrum Separation and Localization from Field Data

Juo-Yu Lee
Electrical Engineering Department
University of California,
Los Angeles, CA, USA

juoyul@ucla.edu

Zac Harlow, Travis C. Collier,
Charles E. Taylor
University of California,
Los Angeles, CA, USA

{zac.harlow, travcollier}@gmail.com,
taylor@biology.ucla.edu

Kung Yao
Electrical Engineering Department
University of California,
Los Angeles, CA, USA

yao@ee.ucla.edu

ABSTRACT

In this abstract, we present a beamforming method for estimating the directions and locations of multiple sources and separating each source's spectrum from field data collected by a wireless acoustic sensor network. Each acoustic sensor is equipped with four microphones that receive acoustic signals in a time-synchronized manner. The difference in time-of-arrival of proximal signals depends on the source direction with respect to the geometry of the microphone array. We show that by using beamforming in the frequency domain, the locations and Direction-Of-Arrivals (DOAs) of multiple 3D sources may be estimated, and the source spectrum may be separated from the audio data spectra.

Categories and Subject Descriptors

C.3.5 [**Special-Purpose and Application-based Systems**]: Signal processing systems

General Terms

Algorithms, Design, Measurement

Keywords

Acoustic sensor, DOA, Localization, Source Separation

1. INTRODUCTION

We consider the problem of localization, DOA estimation and source separation for multiple near-field wideband sources using a wireless acoustic sensor network and the maximum likelihood (ML) estimator. In our approach, we first apply Discrete Fourier transform (DFT) to the received wideband acoustic signals, and obtain the narrowband signals in each frequency bin [1]. We then explore all frequency bins of our interest and derive the optimal parametric ML solution to estimate DOAs of wideband sources. ML-based optimization for the source DOAs may be made possible without explicitly calibrating the relative time delay. The number of sources has been determined by techniques such as principal component analysis (PCA) independent of the underlying ML estimator. To reduce computation complexity, we only consider frequency bins of significant energy levels, which yield a reasonable approximate ML solution.

2. SYSTEM MODEL

Suppose the reference waveform $s(\cdot)$ in our system model is a signal arriving at the origin of the coordinate system O at time zero. Without loss of generality, we consider an array (centered at the origin) of P microphones equipped on a sensor. In Cartesian coordinate system, each microphone is located at the position $r_p = [u_p, y_p, z_p]^T$, $1 \leq p \leq P$, where superscript T denotes matrix transposition. We assume M wideband sources in the near-field of the array are located at unknown points $[u_m, y_m, z_m]^T$, $1 \leq m \leq M$. The relative time delay of the mth source is given by

$$t_{cp}^{(m)} = t_c^{(m)} - t_p^{(m)} = \frac{1}{v}\sqrt{(u_m - u_p)^2 + (y_m - y_p)^2 + (z_m - z_p)^2} \qquad (1)$$

where $t_c^{(m)}$ and $t_p^{(m)}$ are the absolute time delays from the mth source to the coordinate origin and to the pth microphone, respectively, and v is the speed of sound (nominally, 345 m/s at room temperature). Hence, the data received by the pth microphone at sample time $t = t_n$ is given by

$$x_p(t_n) = \sum_{m=1}^{M} s^{(m)}(t_n - t_{cp}^{(m)}) + w_p(t_n), n = 0,...,N-1, \qquad (2)$$

where N is the number of signal samples, $s^{(m)}(n)$ is the mth source signal at the array center, and w_p is the zero mean white Gaussian noise with variance σ^2. Note that in the above equation, $t_{cp}^{(m)}$ can be an arbitrary positive or negative scalar.

The majority of the data processing performed by the ML estimator takes place in the frequency domain. Given the N point DFT $X_p(\omega_l)$ and $S^{(m)}(\omega_l)$ of $x_p(n)$ and $s^{(m)}(n)$, we aim to search for optimal $[u_m, y_m, z_m]^T$ by minimizing the residual error defined as follows.

$$J(\{u_m, y_m, z_m\}_{m=1}^{M})$$
$$= \sum_{l=1}^{N/2} \sum_{p=1}^{P} | X_p(\omega_l) - \sum_{m=1}^{M} e^{\frac{-j2\pi l t_{cp}^{(m)}(u_m,y_m,z_m)}{N}} S_p^{(m)}(\omega_l) |^2 \qquad (3)$$

We first cancel the residual error dependency on $S^{(m)}(\omega_l)$ and solve for optimal locations, which can be used to solve for $S^{(m)}(\omega_l)$, hence completing source separation. For each source, we perform search over all possible points in a hypothesized 3D grid to find the optimal $[u_m, y_m, z_m]^T$. We apply an efficient alternating projection procedure [2] by sequentially estimating the location of one source while nulling out the estimate of other source locations from the previous iteration.

3. FIELD DATA COLLECTION

We deployed an acoustic sensor network of eight nodes for field data collection (Fig. 1). A self-survey procedure was activated to localize each sensor's microphones [3]. Fig. 1 (left) shows the network topology projected onto a 2D plane. Fig. 1 (right) shows the interior view of an acoustic sensor. Each sensor receives audio signals through four microphones and stores the audio streams into WAV files with four channels. Each single channel audio stream was sampled at 48 kHz. The spectrum carrying significant acoustic energy ranges from 1295 Hz to 2259 Hz.

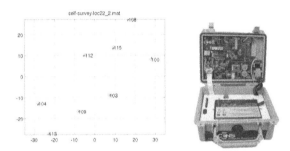

Figure 1. An acoustic sensor network of eight nodes. Left: network deployment. Right: an acoustic sensor node.

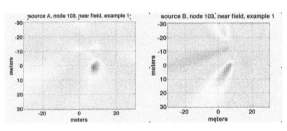

Figure 2. Location estimation (projected on one horizontal plane) for source A (left) and source B (right) based on the field data received by node #103. Actual localization results: source A is located at [8, 1, 11] (meters) and source B is located at [12, -11, 1] (meters).

4. RESULTS AND CONCLUSION

The ML estimator yields estimated locations based on segmented audio streams. Source DOAs may be computed, and source spectra may be separated. Three audio segments were chosen that contain overlapped multiple source audio streams. Figure 2 shows the localization results based on the field data collected by node #103 (in Fig. 1, left). The example described herein yields location estimates for one source at [8, 1, 11] (meters) and for a second source at [12, -11, 1] (meters). Given the received audio spectrum and localization results, one can separate source spectrum (as if measured at the estimated locations). Fig. 3 shows recovered and separated waveforms and

spectra based on one sample audio segment (of 0.5 seconds) from the data set "Example 1" collected by Node 103. The DOA of source A (Table 1) with respect to node #103 is 85.6962 (degrees, azimuth)/33.1974 (degrees, elevation). The DOA of source B (Table 1) with respect to node #103 is -22.8344 (degrees, azimuth)/-33.7003 (degrees, elevation).

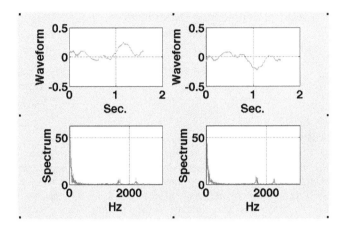

Figure 3. Source separation for two sources, based on data ("Example 1") collected by node #103.

Table 1. DOAs of two sources (A and B in Figure 2) with respect to node #103.

	Azimuth (degrees)	Elevation (degrees)
Source A	85.6962	33.1974
Source B	-22.8344	-33.7003

5. ACKNOWLEDGMENT

This work was supported in part by the U.S. National Science Foundation (NSF) grant IIS1125423. The authors acknowledge the valuable comments from anonymous reviewers and Dr. Lewis Girod. Dr. Girod is one of the main developers of the acoustic nodes used in the experiments.

6. REFERENCES

[1] J. Chen, R. Hudson, and K. Yao. Maximum-likelihood source localization and unknown source localization estimation for wideband signals in the near-field. *IEEE Trans. On Signal Processing, 2002*, 50(8): 1843 - 1854.

[2] A.M. Ali, et al. An empirical study of collaborative acoustic source localization. J. of SP Systems, 2009, 415-435

[3] http://lecs.cs.ucla.edu/wiki/index.php/Acoustic_Platform

Poster Abstract: Multi-Channel Communication vs. Adaptive Routing for Reliable Communication in WSNs

Antonio Gonga[1], Olaf Landsiedel[*][2], Pablo Soldati[1], Mikael Johansson[1]
gonga@kth.se, olafl@chalmers.se, soldati@kth.se, mikaelj@kth.se

[1]KTH Royal Institute of Technology, Sweden
[2]Chalmers University of Technology, Sweden

ABSTRACT

Interference and link dynamics constitute great concerns for stability and performance of protocols in WSNs. In this paper we evaluate the impact of channel hopping and adaptive routing on delay and reliability focusing on delay critical applications.

Categories and Subject Descriptors

C.2.1 [**Network Architecture and Design**]: Wireless Communication

Keywords

Wireless Sensor Network, Interference, Channel Hopping

1. INTRODUCTION

Interference and link dynamics constitute great concerns for stability and performance of wireless sensor network protocols, especially for delay critical applications [1]. These phenomena normally manifest in link burstiness, i.e, prolonged periods of time where packet transmissions from sender to receiver are lost [10]. Such loss bursts cause delays and instability in communication protocols with potentially severe consequences in, *e.g.*, critical processes in industrial automation [7] and health care [6, 2].

A number of papers show that frequency diversity, *e.g.*, by employing channel hopping, increases the resilience to interference and link dynamics [9, 11, 12, 14], while others argue that adaptive routing provides sufficient, or even superior, results [7]. This paper presents our ongoing work on filling this gap. Overall, we believe that it is important to understand the advantages and limitations of channel hopping as it is increasingly adapted by standard bodies such as IEEE 802.15.4e [4], ISA100.11a [5], and WirelessHART [13].

2. CONTRIBUTION

Experimental Setup: The data in our analysis is collected from a testbed consisting of 32 TelosB motes scattered throughout the ceiling of offices in the following way: In

[*]Work done while at ACCESS Linnaeus Center, KTH Royal Institute of Technology, Sweden

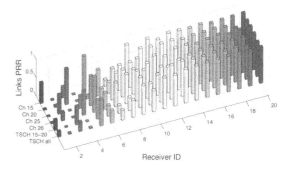

Figure 1: Average links PRR for a random source node to all its neighbors in our testbed: for channels c_{15}, c_{20}, c_{25} and c_{26}, and for the hopping sequences $\{c_{15}, c_{20}\}$ and $\{c_{15}, c_{20}, c_{25}, c_{26}\}$.

round robin, each node transmits $10{,}000$ consecutive packets with inter-packet interval of 10ms (the time slot length used by standards such as *Wireless*HART). All other nodes log which of these packets they received. We collected traces for three scenarios: single channel, two-channel hopping, and n-channel hopping (hopping sequences of increasing length, i.e, 2, 4, 8, 12, and 16 channels). Figure 1 shows typical results for a single node transmitting 10,000 consecutive packets on ISM-band channels 15, 20, 25 and 26 along with TSCH sequences $\{15, 20\}$ and $\{15, 20, 25, 26\}$. The packet reception ratios shown are averaged over 100 consecutive trials.

Experimental Metrics: The intuition behind the use of multi-channel communication is that different channel are subject to different interference patterns. Thus, transmitting a packet on alternating channels decreases the impact of interference and reduces the (re)transmission count until a packet is successfully received. In this paper we evaluate how channel hopping decreases the duration of burst losses and increases their statistical independence, i.e., their β-*factor* [10]. β quantifies the temporal correlation of packet losses. A value of $\beta = 0$ identifies a link with independent packet losses (following a Bernoulli process), while a value of $\beta = 1$ indicates a bimodal link, i.e., a link that exists either in a good or a bad state.

Adaptive routing, however, allows the network to adapt its routing topology to interference sources and thus choose next hops that are highly reliable and show only limited impact of interference. We evaluate this claim, and compare

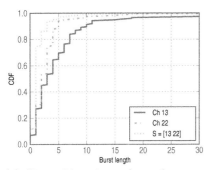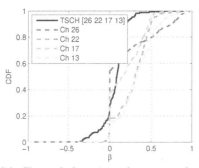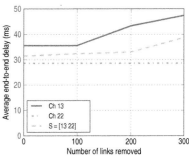

(a) Channel hopping reduces the maximum burst loss duration on WIFI-interfered channels.

(b) Channel hopping decreases the correlation of packet loss (β-factor).

(c) Routing delay: single-channel vs. channel-hopping on Wifi-interfered channels.

Figure 2: Comparing channel hopping and routing in terms of packet loss and delay.

adaptive multi-path routing to channel-hopping in topologies of different densities.

Experimental Results: Figure 2(a) depicts the CDF of the maximum burst loss for two Wi-Fi-interfered channels (we plot links with at least 90% PRR): It shows that channel hopping reduces the duration of burst losses. Figure 2(b) compares the CDF of β for a data set collected with a length-4 channel hopping sequence $S = \{c_{26}, c_{22}, c_{17}, c_{13}\}$, against the CDF of β for data sets collected on each individual channel. The major insight from this result is that channel hopping strongly reduces the packet loss correlation in time, with over 95% of links having a value of $\beta \leq 0.2$ corresponding to roughly independent packet losses.

In Figure 2(c), we explore the impact of network density on end-to-end reliability and delay. To create networks with varying density, we eliminate links from the experimental traces. Starting from the best link in terms of PRR, we remove links until the network becomes disconnected. We compare the multi-hop end-to-end delay and reliability between the two strongly interfered channels and their channel hopping combination. Routing on top of channel hopping yields an average end-to-end delay that is essentially the average of the delay experience when routing on each individual channel.

3. DISCUSSION AND CONCLUSIONS

We analyzed single-channel and multi-channel communication over a single-hop in terms of maximum burst loss, temporal correlation of losses, and end-to-end delay. Our results show that, on a single-hop, multichannel communication via channel hopping significantly reduces link burstiness and decorrelates packet losses in time, to the point that 95% of links show independent packet losses for hopping sequences with more than two channels. In multi-hop networks, multi-channel communication and adaptive routing yield similar end-to-end reliability in dense and medium dense deployments. This can be explained since routing protocols tend to use good long-term stable links, thus avoiding the intermediate links where burstiness is more dominant.

Overall, our results indicate two key observations: (1) Channel hopping de-correlates packet losses both across time and frequency domain, thus reducing the number of consecutive packet losses compared to the corresponding individual channels. Therefore, in single-hop communication, or on fixed topologies where adaptive routing is not an option

(such as preplanned WirelessHART deployments) frequency diversity can yield significant reliability improvements. (2) However, when routing topologies can be adapted to link dynamics and interference, our results indicate that adaptive routing without channel hopping provides on-par reliability. Unless the deployment is very sparse, there are sufficiently many good links on every channel to provide end-to-end connectivity that is comparable with the multi-channel solution, or even better, in terms of end-to-end delay. These paths would readily be found using standard routing protocols, such as CTP [3] or RPL [8].

4. REFERENCES

[1] C. A. Boano, T. Voigt, C. Noda, K. Romer, and M. Zuniga. JamLab: Augmenting sensornet testbeds with realistic and controlled interference generation. *IPSN'11, April 12-14, 2011, Chicago , IL*, 2011.

[2] O. Chipara, C. Lu, T. C. Bailey, and G.-C. Roman. Reliable Clinical Monitoring using Wireless Sensor Networks: Experiences in a Step-down Hospital Unit. *ACM Sensys'10, November 3-5, 2010, Zurich, Switzerland*, 2010.

[3] O. Gnawali, R. Fonseca, K. Jamieson, D. Moss, and P. Levis. Collection Tree Protocol. *ACM Sensys'09, November 4-6, 2009, Berkeley, CA, USA*, 2009.

[4] IEEE802154e, Last Access January 2012.

[5] ISA10011a, Last Access January 2012.

[6] J. Ko, C. Lu, M. B. Srivastava, J. A. Stankovic, A. Terzis, and M. Welsh. Wireless Sensor Networks for Healthcare. *In Proc. of the IEEE*, 2010.

[7] J. Ortiz and D. Culler. Multichannel Reliability Assessment in Real World WSNs. *IPSN10, April 12-16, 2010, Stockholm, Sweden*, 2010.

[8] RPL Draft 19, Last Access January 2012.

[9] M. Sha, G. Hackmann, and C. Lu. ARCH. Practical Channel Hopping for Reliable Home-Area Sensor Networks.

[10] K. Srinivasan, M. A. Kazandjieva, S. Agarwal, and P. Levis. The β Factor: Measuring Wireless Link Burtiness. *Sensys 08*, 2008.

[11] T. Watteyne, S. Lanzisera, A. Mehta, and K. S. J. Pister. Mitigating Multipath Fading Through Channel Hopping in Wireless Sensor Networks. *ICC, 2010, Cape Town, South Africa*, 2010.

[12] T. Watteyne, A. Mehta, and K. Pister. Reliability Through Frequency Diversity: Why Channel Hopping Makes Sense. In *PE-WASUN*, 2009.

[13] WirelessHART, Last Access January 2012.

[14] Y. Wu, J. A. Stankovic, T. He, J. Lu, and S. Lin. Realistic and Efficient Multi-channel Communications in Wireless Sensor Networks. *INFOCOM'08*, pages 1193 – 1201, 2008.

Shipping Data from Heterogeneous Protocols on Packet Train

Chieh-Jan Mike Liang
Microsoft Research Asia
5 Dan Ling Street
Beijing, 100080 China
liang.mike@microsoft.com

Kaifei Chen
Microsoft Research Asia
5 Dan Ling Street
Beijing, 100080 China
v-kaiche@microsoft.com

Jie Liu
Microsoft Research
One Microsoft Way
Redmond, WA 98052 USA
liuj@microsoft.com

Nissanka Bodhi Priyantha
Microsoft Research
One Microsoft Way
Redmond, WA 98052 USA
bodhip@microsoft.com

Feng Zhao
Microsoft Research Asia
5 Dan Ling Street
Beijing, 100080 China
zhao@microsoft.com

ABSTRACT

The maturity and availability of network protocols have enabled wireless sensor networks (WSN) designers to build heterogeneous applications by composing different protocols. A common heterogeneous application combines data collection and dissemination for environmental monitoring with node retasking. While these co-located protocols on the same node have different goals, many of them share requirements and characteristics. Examples of commonalities include the use of bi-directional traffic for reliable transmissions and tree for packet routing. This work explores how the MAC layer can reduce the network transmission overhead of heterogeneous applications by taking advantage of protocol commonalities to aggregate outgoing packets. In other words, this aggregation creates a train of packets destined to the same receiver. Finally, we discuss a strawman implementation of packet train and how our data center monitoring deployment leverages it.

Categories and Subject Descriptors

C.2.2 [**Computer-Communication Networks**]: Network Protocols

General Terms

Design, Performance, Experimentation

Keywords

Link protocols, MAC protocols, Wireless sensor networks

1. INTRODUCTION

After a decade of active research, the wireless sensor networks (WSN) community has developed and published many open-source implementations of networking protocols. These protocols fall under different categories according to their objectives (e.g., data collection vs. dissemination), delivery latency requirement (e.g., real-time vs. delay-tolerant), energy requirement (e.g., duty-cycled vs. always-on) and so on. One

observation from these work is the difficulty in architecting a single protocol that can address all application requirements. Therefore, one common practice in developing WSN applications is composing multiple network protocols to form the application logic. In other words, these protocols co-locate on the same node and result in a heterogeneous application. For example, one could combine data collection and dissemination protocols for an environmental monitoring application with code retasking [1, 3, 8].

Previous work have looked at various aspects of building such heterogeneous WSN applications: reducing the complexity in development [6], minimizing the interference among multiple co-located protocols [5], optimizing the node energy costs [2] and so on.

This work aims to improve the link latency and bandwidth usage by aggregating and scheduling outgoing packets with common parameters to create a packet train. Our contributions are identifying the advantages and challenges in integrating packet train, and presenting a real-world use of packet train in a data center monitoring WSN deployment.

2. PACKET TRAIN

Section 1 uses the trend of heterogeneous applications in WSN deployments to motivate our interests on packet train. This section first describes the idea of packet train, and argues that packet train can improve the network performance by reducing various overheads. Then, we present design considerations for implementing packet train.

Packet train builds on the idea of piggy-backing small control packets onto data packets. TCP is an example that piggy-backs packet acknowledgment onto data packets [7]. In addition to merging packets, packet train can also treat packets with common parameters as a group and send these packet back-to-back. Effectively, this group of packets can be considered as one "mega" packet, and the transmission costs would be amortized over these sub-packets. While common parameters can include the destination address, radio channel and so on, this paper focuses on the destination address. As one requirement of packet train is the global view on outgoing packets, we propose that packet train should be a MAC-layer feature.

Advantages. Packet train can reduce the transmission over-

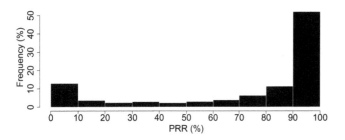

Figure 1: Packet reception ratios (PRR) across all the links from a 52-node data center site survey. Many links have a PRR above 70%

head in both latency and bandwidth. First, most WSN deployments rely on CSMA to resolve contentions among concurrent senders. However, CSMA incurs overhead due to the backoff and wait times. By sending packets destined to the same receiver back-to-back, the sender can simply perform CSMA once at the beginning of the packet train. In fact, the sender also takes advantage of the short-term link stability and transmits packets in burst. Second, a typical WSN packet consists of preambles, header and footer, in addition to the data payload. The preambles, header and foot are control information that do not carry application data, and thus lower the goodput. For example, in TinyOS, 802.15.4 packet preambles, header and footer occupy about 15% of the space with respect to the maximum-sized packet. Considering the case of multiple small data payloads, packet train can merge them in one packet to share one set of preambles, header, and footer. Third, packet train can amortize the energy expenditure across co-located protocols. Dunkels et al. presented the case where aggregating broadcast beacons of co-located duty-cycling protocols can significantly reduce energy costs incurred on each beacon [2].

Design Considerations. Packet train breaks some of the radio and protocol assumptions on the packet structure and delivery. We discuss the implications and design considerations in implementing packet train. First, packet train breaks most radio PHYs' assumption that one incoming radio frame represents a single packet. Therefore, certain radio features may not always work. For example, if a packet contains two payloads where one requires acknowledgment, the radio PHY might not be able to look at all embedded headers to trigger the hardware acknowledgment properly. Second concern is the protocol fairness. As the MAC-layer shuffles the outgoing queue to aggregate outgoing packets with common parameters, the order of packet transmission is not the same as the order of submission from protocols. This reordering can delay pending packets that do not have common parameters with previous pending packets in the queue. Finally, merging payloads increases the packet size. The networking community has shown that the larger the packet size the higher the chance of packet corruption. Therefore, packet train may not be suitable under all conditions.

3. IMPLEMENTATION

We have integrated packet train with our data center monitoring application, MeshNet (based on our previous work, RACNet [4]). MeshNet is a heterogeneous deployment of upstream QoS-aware data collection and downstream selective dissemination protocols. Figure 1 shows that a larger percentage of links in our network have a fairly good packet reception ratios (PRR). This represents opportunities for nodes to take advantage of a larger network MTU, and short-term link stability. MeshNet uses packet train in the following two ways.

All co-located protocols rely on acknowledgments for packet delivery reliability. Since acknowledgment packets are small, they are suitable candidate for merging with other data packets or acknowledgment packets. To improve the chance of merging, we delay low-priority data packets in the outgoing queue for 100 ms. And, before transmitting an acknowledgment packet, the MAC layer scans through the MAC layer buffer for packets with the same destination address. As upstream data traffic dominate in MeshNet, we expect that the acknowledgment packets for different upstream packets can often be merged. Another opportunity for packet train is to merge acknowledgment packets with downstream protocol traffic, similar to TCP.

MeshNet also actively groups data packets destined to the same receiver. Experiment results suggest that the different requirements in end-to-end delivery latency can result in outgoing packets being queued, which in turn increases the opportunities for packet train.

4. REFERENCES

[1] G. W. Allen, K. Lorincz, J. Johnson, J. Lees, and M. Welsh. Fidelity and Yield in a Volcano Monitoring Sensor Network. In *OSDI*, 2006.

[2] A. Dunkels, L. Mottola, N. Tsiftes, F. Osterlind, J. Eriksson, and N. Finne. The Announcement Layer: Beacon Coordination for the Sensornet Stack. In *EWSN*, 2011.

[3] K. Langendoen, A. Baggio, and O. Visser. Murphy Loves Potatoes: Experiences from a Pilot Sensor Network Deployment in Precision Agriculture. In *WPDRTS*, 2006.

[4] C.-J. M. Liang, J. Liu, L. Luo, A. Terzis, and F. Zhao. RACNet: A High-Fidelity Data Center Sensing Network. In *SenSys*, 2009.

[5] C.-J. M. Liang and A. Terzis. Rethinking Multi-Channel Protocols in Wireless Sensor Networks. In *HotEmNets*, 2010.

[6] J. Polastre, J. Hui, P. Levis, J. Zhao, D. Culler, S. Shenker, and I. Stoica. A Unifying Link Abstraction for Wireless Sensor Networks. In *SenSys*, 2005.

[7] A. Tanenbaum. *Computer Networks*. Prentice Hall Professional Technical Reference, fourth edition, 2002.

[8] G. Tolle and D. Culler. Design of an Application-Cooperative Management System for Wireless Sensor Networks. In *EWSN*, 2005.

Demo Abstract: Histogram Distance-Based Radio Tomographic Localization

Yang Zhao and Neal Patwari[*]
Department of Electrical and Computer Engineering
University of Utah, Salt Lake City, Utah, 84112
yang.zhao@utah.edu, npatwari@ece.utah.edu

ABSTRACT

We present an interactive demonstration of histogram distance-based radio tomographic imaging (HD-RTI), a device-free localization (DFL) system that uses measurements of received signal strength (RSS) on static links in a wireless network to estimate the locations of people who do not participate in the system by wearing any radio device in the deployment area. Compared to prior methods of RSS-based DFL, using a histogram difference metric is a very accurate method to quantify the change in RSS on the link compared to historical metrics. The new method is remarkably accurate, and works with lower node densities than prior methods.

Categories and Subject Descriptors

H.4 [**Information Systems Applications**]: Miscellaneous

Keywords

Localization, Sensor networks

1. INTRODUCTION

Localization of people in wireless sensor networks has significant benefits for elder care, security, and smart facilities. An emerging technique is to use radio signal changes caused by the human body to locate people who do not carry any radio devices. Since this new technique does not require people to wear any devices, we call it device-free localization (DFL). Recent research work has focused on DFL using received signal strength (RSS) measurements from a wireless mesh network [3], due to the fact that RSS measurements are inexpensive and available in almost all wireless devices. However, the reported methods are ad hoc and incomplete. For example, methods that use the change in mean of RSS measurements require calibration measurements to be made when the area is empty in order to provide the baseline mean RSS, and are not robust to non-line-of-sight (non-LOS) environments. Variance-based DFL methods such as [4] do not require an empty calibration period. However, they cannot locate stationary people, since they use certain forms of RSS

[*]This material is based upon work supported by the National Science Foundation under Grant Nos. #0748206 and #1035565.

variance to locate human motion, and stationary people do not cause much RSS variance. Thus, we need a new DFL method that is capable of locating both moving and stationary people without an empty-area calibration.

Our proposed approach is built upon two innovations designed to improve current DFL systems: (1) histogram difference to quantify change in RSS, rather than using change in mean or using variance as a metric, which allows DFL systems to locate both moving and stationary people; (2) online calibration, which allows DFL systems to operate without an empty-room calibration. The use of histogram differences is motivated by experimental observations in a variety of environments. A person in motion on or near the line between two wireless devices tends to increase the variance of RSS measurements, but may or may not significantly change the mean. A person standing still at a location tends to change the mean of the RSS, but may show very little variance while the person is stationary. Using either the variance or the change in mean of the RSS value will measure their presence in the "in motion" or stationary case, respectively, but not both. Using a measure of histogram difference captures both changes. In terms of online calibration, we show that online RSS measurements allow one to keep a long-term histogram in memory without significant computational complexity. This long-term histogram is close enough to the histogram which would have been measured in an empty-room calibration to perform as well as, or better than, with empty-room calibration.

We demonstrate some initial results for the use of histogram difference in RTI, and call this new method histogram distance-based radio tomographic imaging (HD-RTI). Compared to VRTI, which cannot detect or locate people without any motion, our HD-RTI can capture the difference caused by stationary human body on RSS histograms, and thus is able to locate stationary people. Compared to mean-based RTI, which needs offline calibration, in which measurements are made without any people present in the network, our HD-RTI does not need such offline calibration measurements, and works well using online calibration measurements. Finally, HD-RTI provides a significantly more accurate radio tomographic images than previous RTI methods, and works successfully with lower node densities.

2. METHODS

2.1 Distance between histograms

From many indoor experiments, we have observed that when a person (either stationary or moving) is present near

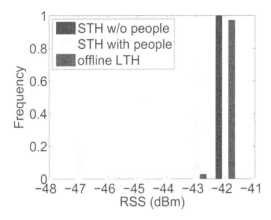

Figure 1: Long-term histogram (LTH) and short-term histograms (STH) with and without moving people near the LOS of a link.

the line-of-sight (LOS) of a link, the RSS histogram of that link in a short-time window (we call short-term histogram) is significantly different from the RSS histogram from the calibration period without any people present in the network (long-term histogram). For example, in an indoor experiment, a person walks across a link between two nodes at a particular time, and the short-term histogram (STH) from a three-sample window (about 0.2 seconds) is shown in Figure 1. We see that due to human motion, RSS measurements are quite variable. For the same link, the long-term histogram (LTH) from an offline calibration period (about 60 seconds) is also shown in Figure 1, and it is significantly different from STH with people. However, with no people near the link, there is not much difference between STH and LTH. For example, when the person is several meters away from the link, all three RSS measurements in the window are -42 dBm. As shown in Figure 1, STH without people is similar to LTH.

To quantify the difference between STH and LTH. We need a metric to measure the difference between two histograms. A well known way to measure the difference between two distributions is the Kullback-Leibler divergence, which is a bin-to-bin distance assuming the histograms are aligned. Another metric is the earth mover's distance, which does not require aligned histograms. However, it involves solving an optimal transportation problem, and is computationally expensive. Finally, the kernel distance has been used to compare shapes and distributions in the field of computational geometry, it has nice mathematical properties and is easy to compute [2]. We explore using these histogram difference metrics in our demo.

2.2 Histogram distance-based RTI (HD-RTI)

Let $\mathbf{d} = [d_1, d_2, \cdots, d_L]^T$ denote the histogram distance vector from L directional links of a network, we estimate the P dimensional position vector $\mathbf{x}$ representing human presence as:

$$\hat{\mathbf{x}} = (W^T W + \alpha Q^T Q)^{-1} W^T \mathbf{d} \qquad (1)$$

where Q is the Tikhonov matrix, α is a regularization parameter, and W is an $L \times P$ matrix representing the weighting of motion in each voxel on each link measurement, which is formulated as [3]. Note that although HD-RTI uses the

same formulation as mean-based RTI, it does not need offline calibration, which is necessary for mean-based RTI to obtain the baseline mean RSS.

3. DEMO DESCRIPTION

We plan to use radio nodes made with TI's CC2531 system-on-chip powered by two AA batteries. All nodes are placed on fixed locations (either on stands or on tables) to form a static sensor network. The initial network deployment plan is that we deploy 16 nodes around a 4 m by 4 m square area with a node density of 1 per m^2. The distance between each two adjacent nodes along each side is 1 m so that we have 5 nodes (including one node at each corner) at each side of the square. All 16 nodes are programmed with Spin [1] – a token passing protocol which enables each node to broadcast pairwise RSS measurements between itself and all the other nodes at a particular time. The transmission interval between two nodes is set by the Spin protocol so that more than one link measurement can be recorded each second to match the speed of normal human motion (i.e., 1 m/s). For fast human motion, we can increase the transmission frequency in Spin protocol at the cost of more power consumption. A basestation connected to a laptop is used to collect pairwise RSS measurements from all nodes of the network.

The demo will be performed following procedures below. First, a calibration is performed with people (online calibration) or without people (offline calibration) present in the deployment area. Then, we run different RTI algorithms on two laptops, and ask participators to interact with our RTI systems. Since our RTI algorithms can be implemented in real time, participators can see the RTI images shown on the laptop immediately after they enter the network. We will have a variety of RTI algorithms including mean-based RTI [3], variance-based RTI (VRTI) [4] and HD-RTI in the demo, so that participators can judge their relative performances in different conditions. For example, if we use offline calibration, both mean-based RTI and HD-RTI may work well. However, if online calibration is used, our HD-RTI may still work, but mean-based RTI may not work at all. As another example, a demo participator can keep motionless in the network so that he or she disappears in the motion images from VRTI. However, HD-RTI can locate a person no matter he is moving or not, and the participator can always see his locations from the HD-RTI images. We can also allow multiple people to interact with our RTI systems at the same time and they can test ideas that they have with different RTI algorithms.

4. REFERENCES

[1] Sensing and Processing Across Networks (SPAN) Lab, Spin website. http://span.ece.utah.edu/spin.

[2] J. M. Phillips and S. Venkatasubramanian. A gentle introduction to the kernel distance. Technical Report arXiv:1103.1625, Arxiv.org, 2011.

[3] J. Wilson and N. Patwari. Radio tomographic imaging with wireless networks. *IEEE Transactions on Mobile Computing*, 9(5):621–632, May 2010.

[4] J. Wilson and N. Patwari. See-through walls: Motion tracking using variance-based radio tomography networks. *IEEE Transactions on Mobile Computing*, 10(5):612–621, May 2011.

Demo Abstract: BlimpProbe:
An Aerial Surveillance Platform

Cheng-Yuan Li
Department of Computer Science
& Information Engineering
National Taiwan University
D99922035@csie.ntu.edu.tw

Hao-Hua Chu
Department of Computer Science
& Information Engineering
National Taiwan University
hchu@csie.ntu.edu.tw

ABSTRACT
This paper proposes a blimp-based vehicular sensing system, called BlimpProbe, which travels above ground to perform environmental monitoring. We describe an application in atmosphere science that is suitable for this blimp-based sensing system.

Categories and Subject Descriptors
C.3 [Special-Purpose and Application-Based Systems]: Real-time and Embedded Systems.

General Terms
Design, Experimentation.

Keywords
Unmanned aerial vehicles, mobile sensors, environmental monitoring

1. INTRODUCTION
Recently, we have seen the development of a variety of vehicular-based mobile sensing systems that travel on the ground [3], in the air [2][3], or in the water [1] while performing environmental sensing. This paper proposes an aerial vehicular sensing system, called BlimpProbe, which travels above ground to monitor the environmental. Blimps have interesting properties that give them unique advantages over other aerial vehicles based on micro-airplanes and helicopters: (1) Blimps incur a lower cost than micro-airplanes and helicopters. (2) Blimps can hover above a target area for an extensive time with little or no energy expenditure, enabling long-term aerial surveillance. (3) Blimps can carry a heavier equipment load, including additional battery packs, sensors and actuators, than micro-airplanes and helicopters.

Given its advantages, BlimpProbe provides an aerial surveillance platform to enable atmospheric science applications that demand long-term and wide-area environment sensing. For example, one possible application is to find optimal placements of wind turbines which maximize the amount of renewable energy generation. Since wind and

Figure 1. BlimpProbe Prototype

weather patterns are dynamic and often change across seasons, finding these optimal placements require long-term data collection and development of an accurate three-dimensional wind model over a wide geographical area. Another application is in detecting and tracking of air pollution. Depending on wind and weather patterns, air pollutants can travel and disperse over a wide geographical area.

2. SYSTEM OVERVIEW
Figure 1 shows our BlimpProbe prototype. When inflated with helium, the blimp is 4.5 meters long and 1.1 meters in diameter. Its net lift is 2.3 kilograms. The tail of the blimp has three fins. A turbofan motor, placed at the tail of the blimp, adjusts the blimp's heading direction. Additionally, two turbofan motors are mounted on two sides of the blimp's gondola. Each turbofan can change its orientation and vary its speed, enabling the blimp to propel forward, hover, ascend and descend.

Figure 2 shows the system architecture of the BlimpProbe. Almost all electric devices are housed in the blimp's gondola, which contains the following components. (1) The primary component is an Android-based smart phone. The phone comes with various built-in sensors, including a GPS receiver to obtain the blimp's location, a digital compass to sense the blimp's heading, an accelerometer to detect the blimp's movement, and a camera to capture ground images. (2) An IOIO board is used to connect the smart phone to an

Arduino board as well as to the motors. The smart phone runs the blimp's navigation program. The navigation program changes the headings and speed of the blimp by generating PWM (Pulse Width Modulation) signals to control the motor. (3) The Arduino Pro mini board connects to three off-phone weather sensors: temperature, humidity, and barometric pressure, as well as a three-axis gyroscope sensor. (4) When the blimp travels within the radio range of 3/3.G cell towers, the smart phone acts as a gateway to transmit any collected sensor data to the PC on the ground. The PC then displays (real-time) sensor readings on its screen and stores them in a database.

3. CHALLENGES

We have identified the following research challenges for BlimpProbe.

- *Energy.* For efficient use of energy in aerial sensing, planning the blimp's flight route to optimize sensing coverage is an important issue. In particular, when multiple blimps are deployed in an area for collaborative environmental sensing, further optimization is possible by planning their flight routes collaboratively.

- *Communication.* In aerial sensor networks, flight information is exchanged among BlimpProbes in real time in order to compute optimal flight route planning. Additionally, sensor data is sent to the sink (i.e., the PC on the ground) through mobile phones' radios. Power consumption, reliability and connectivity are foremost consideration in wireless communication.

- *Sensor noises.* Sensors all have noises. For example, the GPS sensor has positional error. These noisy sensor data would have to be processed and filtered.

4. DEMO SCRIPT

In this demonstration, we will exhibit our BlimpProbe prototype and demonstrate its operation. Conference attendants will be able to see the maneuverability of the BlimpProbe and to watch BlimpProbe's real-time sensor data collection on the PC's screen.

5. REFERENCES

[1] Tsung-te Lai, Yu-han Chen, Polly Huang, and Hao-hua Chu.. PipeProbe: a mobile sensor droplet for mapping hidden pipeline. *In SenSys '10.*

[2] GD, Shipley, ST, S. Greco and SA Wood, 2008: Airborne DopplerWind Lidar: Recent Results and In-Flight Visualization Using Google Earth, Presentation to Working Group on Space-Based Lidar Winds, Wintergreen, VA, 8 July.

[3] Jude Allred, Ahmad Bilal Hasan, Saroch Panichsakul, William Pisano, Peter Gray, Jyh Huang, Richard Han, Dale Lawrence, and Kamran Mohseni. 2007. Sensor-Flock: an airborne wireless sensor network of micro-air vehicles. *In SenSys '07.*

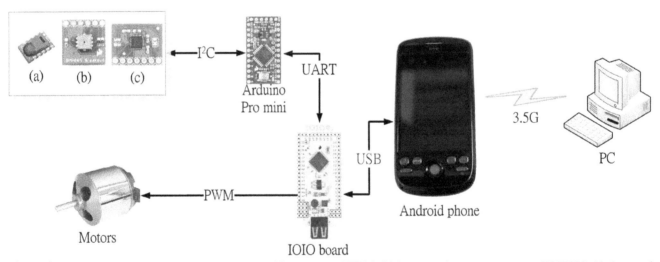

Figure 2. System overview. (a) temperature and humidity sensor - SHT11. (b) barometric pressure sensor - BMP085. (c) three-axis gyroscope - ITG-3200.

Demo Abstract: MiDebug: Microcontroller Integrated Development and Debugging Environment *

Chenguang Shen
Software School
Fudan University
No. 825 Zhangheng Road
Shanghai, 201203, China
cgshen.fudan@gmail.com

Henry Herman, Zainul Charbiwala,
Mani B. Srivastava
Networked and Embedded Systems Laboratory
Electrical Engineering Department
University of California, Los Angeles
Los Angeles, 90095, CA, USA
{hherman,zainul,mbs}@ucla.edu

ABSTRACT

e present MiDebu a web-base Inte rate Development
nvironment ID for embe e system pro rammin with
in-browser ebu in capabilities This web application reatly
re uces the time an e ort re uire for rapi prototypin
of microcontroller base   evices

Categories and Subject Descriptors

D   **Software Engineering** : Pro rammin   nvironments—
Integrated Environments D   **Software Engineering** :
Testin an Debu in —*Debugging aids*

General Terms

Desi n   perimentation

Keywords

Microcontroller Pro rammin Debu in Inte rate Development nvironment

1. INTRODUCTION

Cyber-physical systems have become ubi uitous completely
chan in how we interact an sense the worl   ith the
continuin   rop in price of mass pro uce inte rate   e-
vices that contain processors sensors an ra io transceivers
the ma or cost of early evelopment an   eployment of sensor networ s has shifte from har ware esi n to software
 esi n   arly clou -base   evelopment systems are showin
promise in lowerin the barriers of entry to microcontroller
software evelopment

MiDebu is a convenient browser-base ID that allows
remote ebu in of eeply networe embe e systems
with limite physical access while minimizin the re uire
time for wor station toolchain installation

*This research was con ucte while Chen uan Shen was
a research intern at the etwor e an   mbe e Systems
 aboratory C A

2. BACKGROUND

There are primarily two approaches to creatin binaries
for a microcontroller application cross-compilin on a local client wor station or a server base approache via an
 nline ID

2.1 Local Cross-compile

Cross-compilin re uires a local toolchain on the eveloper s wor station   owever the installation of a toolchain
can be comple an time consumin Settin up a toolchain
re uires pro cient un erstan in of the interrelate components compiler lin er ebu er river libraries an etc
 or a software en ineer unfamiliar with a har ware architecture a si ni cant time investment is nee e to overcome
the re uire learnin curve

2.2 Online IDE

 XP an A M have sponsore a pro ect that utilizes
web   technolo ies to create an online compiler an ID
 - mbe or   sers can write co e an compile throu h
a web browser then ownloa an   ash the e ecutable le
onto the microcontroller Movin the toolchain to the clou
 reatly re uces the installation time re uire for microcontroller pro rammin

 hile easy to use the mbe ID has limitations It lac s
har ware ebu in capability as the microcontroller is separate from the ID when runnin pro rams Therefore the
JTA   ebu in interface of the tar et processor is not e -
pose to the en ineer eliminatin the possibility of usin
this in ustry stan ar   ebu in interface As a result a
 eveloper must write e tra co e e blin the D to
show the runnin state of the microcontroller The mbe
platform is har ware speci c - only supportin two evelopment boar s with two processors   XP PC 7XX an
 PC u

In contrast by usin the JTA   ebu in interface the
architecture of MiDebu allows the system to easily support
other common microcontroller platforms MiDebu also has
JTA   ebu in capabilities

3. SYSTEM DESIGN

3.1 Overview

 i ure shows the overall system architecture of MiDebu   MiDebu consists of the server-base toolchain the
web-base co e e itor shown in i ure   an the local

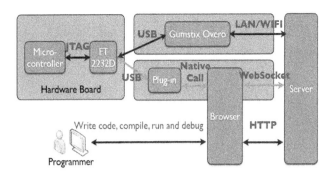

Figure 1: System Architecture of MiDebug

Figure 2: Code Editor of MiDebug

browser plu -in n the server si e MiDebu a re ates toolchains for i erent har ware architectures enablin the software en ineer to choose the tar et platform MiDebu also provi es the interfaces to a a itional platforms an users can simply install pro rammin support for other ar- chitectures by lo in into the a ministration console The web-base co e e itor is written purely in JavaScript base on the Co eMirror pro ect sers can write their co e in the e itor then clic a button to compile run or ebu a pro ram

In or er to ash an ebu an e ecutable le on the tar et microcontroller an a itional interface between the server an the tar et is re uire e ivi e the tar et evices into two cate ories: networ -connecte evices an local wor - station attache evices

Scientists an en ineers often nee to pro ram an ebu the microcontrollers in eploye no es If these no es are connecte to the eveloper s networ the MiDebu server can pro ram an ebu them throu h the client computers local networ connection MiDebu is e ible an can access S har ware irectly connecte to the client wor station

Clou base evelopment tools can be an asset in embe - e systems courses ith a microcontroller-base evice which supports JTA stu ents can lo into the MiDebu website to compile run an ebu their pro rams Clou base tools are inherently platform in epen ent an can eas- ily support multiple operatin systems This allows stu ents to focus on the pro ram itself instea of settin up the en- vironment

3.2 Network-Connected Device

To ebu a networ -connecte evice we utilize the um- sti vero ire Computer-on-Mo ule an the umsti oboVero base boar The oboVero has a T D IC that enables S -JTA pro rammin the tar et micro- controller buntu is run on the vero as well as pen CD 7 provi in a pro rammin interface between the vero an the tar et microprocessor

n the other en the vero communicates with the server throu h the onboar A an I I mo ule The cross- D on MiDebu server can therefore interact with the pen CD on vero

3.3 Local Device

Due to JavaScript security restrictions we use the ire- reath plu -in framewor to achieve ebu in of local

evices This framewor enables native system calls throu h the JSAPI The browser plu -in connects to pen CD run- nin on the local computer an the cross- D runnin on server The ebSoc et protocol is use to transmit ata between the plu -in an the server The plu -in supports multiple operatin systems an browsers e are currently inte ratin pen CD into the plu -in so that no a itional installation is re uire

3.4 GitHub Support

A notable tren to ay is the emer in pro rammer com- munity such as it ub e have inte rate MiDebu with it ub pro rammers can use it ub as a version control tool an share their co e on it ub with others Currently MiDebu uses it ub s Auth to authenticate users ma in it ub repositories accessible to lo e in users

4. CONCLUSION AND FUTURE WORK

MiDebu is a convenient tool for microcontroller pro rammin sers can simply evelop an ebu rmware for mi- crocontrollers on a client wor station throu h a web-browser To the best of our nowle e MiDebu is the rst clou - base microcontroller inte rate evelopment environment to support ebu in of local evices In the future we are oin to release MiDebu for testin an fee bac e are a in support for a itional platforms an MiDebu will be evaluate as a evelopment platform in an embe e systems course

5. REFERENCES

Co emirror http://codemirror.net/
irebreath framewor http://www.firebreath.org/
t - ual usb uart fo ic http://www.ftdichip. com/Products/ICs/FT2232D.htm
ithub: Social co in https://github.com/
umsti overo https://www.gumstix.com/store/ product_info.php?products_id=227
umsti robovero https://www.gumstix.com/store/ product_info.php?products_id=262
7 pen on-chip ebu er http://openocd. sourceforge.net/
api prototypin for microcontrollers | mbe http:// mbed.org

Demo Abstract: Sensor-enabled Yo-yos as New Musical Instruments

Jung-Hyun Jun[1]
peterjun@sutd.edu.sg

Sunardi[1]
sunardi@sutd.edu.sg

Lijuan Wang[1]
wanglijuan@sutd.edu.sg

Joel W. Matthys[2]
joel@matthysmusic.com

Simon Lui[1]
simon_lui@sutd.edu.sg

Yu Gu[1]
jasongu@sutd.edu.sg

[1]Singapore University of Technology and Design, 20 Dover Drive, Singapore 138682
[2]College Conservatory of Music, University of Cincinnati, Cincinnati OH, U.S.A. 45221-0003

ABSTRACT

An interactive and reprogrammable musical yo-yo system is designed. The aim of it is to demonstrate the feasibility of converting any sensor-enabled objects into potential musical instruments. This involves three design phases. First, the physical yo-yo is designed to house Iris sensors. The software is developed to sense the movement of yo-yo and transmit its measurements to Max/MSP for corresponding music generation. Finally, aurally pleasing and real-time musical sounds are designed and generated in effect of yo-yo by the computer music composer.

Categories and Subject Descriptors

H.4 [**Computer Applications**]: Miscellaneous; D.2.8 [**Design**]: Performance—*Sensor-enabled instruments*

Keywords

Wireless sensor networks, MaxMSP, Yo-yo, Musical instrument, Cyber-physical objects

1. INTRODUCTION

Wireless Sensor Networks and Internet of Things have potentials to turn ordinary objects into programmable and interactive devices with networking capability. We envision that these technological advances will open up a possibility of transforming sensor nodes and cyber-physical objects into tunable and programmable musical instruments that are aurally pleasing, interactive, and fun to play.

In today's market, there exist some interactive musical toys and software which can convert portable electronics like smartphones into simple musical instruments. However, they often do not support the sophisticated needs of computer music composers. Smartphones, for all their versatility, provide a restricted and unintuitive interface for musical performers with limited choice of sounds and capability to interact with other musical objects. Also, they are not readily programmable and, most importantly, smartphones and tablets lack the tactile and kinesthetic feedback necessary for complex instrument design. But, with help of wireless sensor network and Max/MSP [2], a visual programming language

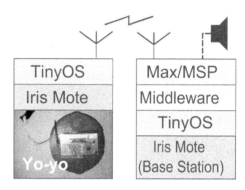

Figure 1: Musical yo-yo system architecture.

for music and multimedia, it is now feasible to transform a non-instrumental object like a yo-yo into a complete musical performance.

Our contributions here are twofold: (1) we have successfully developed a working musical yo-yo system and (2) we make it simple for computer music composers to use this system.

2. MUSICAL YO-YO SYSTEM

We selected the yo-yo as our platform because of its playful and familiar form. Capable of a wide range of complex motion in three dimensions, as well as rotation, the yo-yo shows great potential as a musical instrument, while also being inviting and children friendly. The motion of the yo-yo provides both tactile feedback to the performer and strong visual interest to an observer. The musical yo-yo system is of a three-layered architecture as shown in Figure 1.

a. Yoyo Hardware Design : The model of musical yo-yo is designed to house two Iris motes as shown as Figure 2. The Iris mote [1] with an external 3-axis accelerometer and 2-axis gyroscope is used to measure the force exerted from a hand tossing the yo-yo. The Iris sensors are placed close to the center of yo-yo, which helps to balance the yo-yo while it is spinning. The yo-yo is materialized by the 3D printer using polyester. Four metal rings are implanted onto the yo-yo to balance the misaligned weight caused by two AA batteries that supply power to Iris sensors. Although, the size and overall weight of this yo-yo is bigger and heavier than the regular yo-yos, it still functions like a real yo-yo.

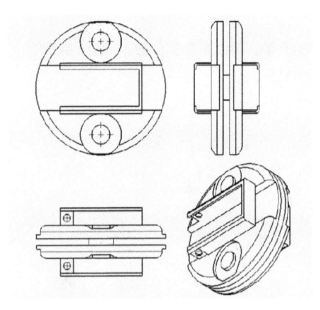

Figure 2: Yo-yo 3D layout model.

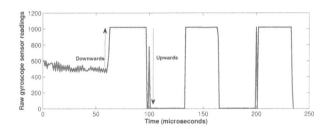

Figure 3: Gyroscope sensor readings and corresponding directions where yo-yo is spinning.

We had many failures while designing the musical yo-yo that can hold wireless sensors without disturbing the balance of its weight. However, this would not have been a challenge if wireless sensors were smaller and lighter-weighted.

b. Sensor Software Design : To the best of our knowledge, there is no formally published software/middleware which integrate the tinyOS with Max/MSP that accepts commands from the composers and outputs the data into Max/MSP. Our custom middleware is designed to translate commands and outputs between tinyOS to Max/MSP. It is an extended Java object running inside the virtual java machine (MXJ). It lists a set of available sensors to Max/MSP for the composer. Then, it enables sensors and adjusts their sampling rate and transmission rate of the musical yo-yo according to the composer's command. Sensors transmit a stream of raw sensor data to middleware periodically. Typically, the period is set to 1 (msec) for its responsiveness.

When the yo-yo system is executed the data received at the middleware is forwarded to Max/MSP and makes the data available for the composers. The data mining was done at the composers' end to optimize their usage of the sensor data.

c. Transformation from Sensory Data to Music : Four or five yo-yos are intended to be used simultaneously in a live performance as fully independent musical instruments. In designing the sound in Max/MSP, we decided to craft a kind of generative techno-music, rhythmic but not strictly repetitive, which is able to use as much of the yo-yo's motion data as possible. This gives the performer the maximal potential for musical variety and control.

Using John Chowning's frequency modulation techniques, we created a set of synthetic bells whose pitches would rise and fall with the extension of the yo-yo. Combining the X, Y, and Z values, with respect to the 3-axis acceleration from the sensor, the total velocity is normalized and mapped onto one of two alternating pitch sets: {C,D,E,G,A} and {C,Eb,F,G,Bb}, commonly known as the major and minor pentatonic scales, spanning three octaves. The tone pans from left to right based on the X values and the notes are

quantized rhythmically to occur twice per second, or 120 beats per minute. The Z value is used to generate a bass line, whose tone is a sine wave altered through amplitude modulation. This bass instrument is mapped on the same scale as the treble bells, but at half the tempo.

Other musical data is derived from higher-order sensor data. A sampled drum set (kick drum, snare, and hi-hat) is triggered by aspects of acceleration in the gyroscope and velocity data as shown as Figure 3. The bass drum is triggered by a trough in the acceleration data, which occurs when the yo-yo reaches either the top or the bottom of the string.

Every 8 bass drum hits triggers a change of harmony, which provides a sense of development and complexity to the music. Usually this involves alternating between the two pentatonic scales, but occasionally a different scale is randomly triggered. This scale, the traditional American blues scale {C, Eb, F, F#, G, Bb}, introduces a new harmonic element to the music.

3. CONCLUSION AND FUTURE WORK

The rehearsal of musical yo-yos was recorded and uploaded onto www.youtube.com [3] and it was first demonstrated for openhouse at Singapore University of Technology and Design. Due to its flexibility and user friendliness, any composers can use it for their professional performances. It is expected to be performed as a part of The Cincinnati Composers Laptop Orchestra Project (CiCLOP).

As for the future work, we will map the sensor inputs to trigger and produce more controllable music pattern. For example, using drum-loop rather than individual drum sound as atomic element, or using certain thresholds of spinning speed to trigger drum pattern instead of using signal crest and trough, or just performing a sequence of drum loop, but the spinning will trigger and switch to other loop.

4. ACKNOWLEDGMENTS

This work is supported by SUTD SRG ISTD 2010 002 and Singapore-MIT International Design Center IDG31000101.

5. REFERENCES

[1] Crossbow iris datasheet at.
    http://bullseye.xbow.com:81/Products.
[2] Max/msp - a visual programming language for music and multimedia. http://cycling74.com/whatismax.
[3] Musical yo-yo rehearsal video.
    http://www.youtube.com/watch?v=Y_Dceb3S_tM.

Demo Abstract: A Compact, Inexpensive, and Battery-Powered Software-Defined Radio Platform

Ye-Sheng Kuo
EECS Department
University of Michigan
Ann Arbor, MI 48109
samkuo@umich.edu

Thomas Schmid
ECE Department
University of Utah
Salt Lake City, UT 84112
thomas.schmid@utah.edu

Prabal Dutta
EECS Department
University of Michigan
Ann Arbor, MI 48109
prabal@umich.edu

ABSTRACT

We present μSDR, a compact, inexpensive, and battery-powered software-defined radio (SDR) platform built on a single-chip, flash-based FPGA fabric and ARM Cortex-M3 processor, enabling lower power and tighter hardware/software integration than prior commodity SDR platforms. Our architecture, unlike prior designs, is well-suited to hand-held or battery-operated systems and also supports cleaner partitioning since hardware can be easily mapped into the software addresses space, and vice versa. Building on this flexibility, we show how highly time-critical MAC protocols can be implemented on this platform and deployed using just AAA batteries.

Categories and Subject Descriptors

B.4.2 [**HARDWARE**]: Input/Output and Data Communications—*Input/Output Devices*; C.3 [**COMPUTER-COMMUNICATION NETWORKS**]: Special-Purpose and Application-Based Systems

General Terms

Design, Experimentation, Measurement, Performance

1. INTRODUCTION

Software-defined radios are fully-programmable radio systems which enables a wide range of applications in wireless communication. Some predict that they will become the standard approach to radio design by 2020 for military and commercial radios, whether the systems are stationary or mobile handheld devices [4]. However, modern SDRs target high performance, which are poorly suited to future mobile and handheld operation.

Modular design and high performance hardware results in high cost and large size. Beside, SRAM-based FPGAs offer high performance, but also draw high power and cannot be duty-cycled. The need to strike a balance between power and performance is critical for future application, but today's architectures fail to strike this balance.

In a low-power communications device, duty-cycle is critical to reducing the system power. We present μSDR, based on flash-based FPGA technology which offers low *static power*, *dynamic power*, and *fast wakeup*.

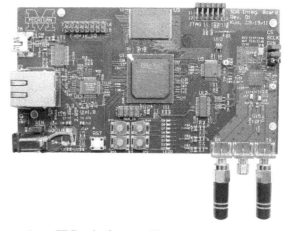

Figure 1: μSDR platform. The main components are Microsemi's SmartFusion A2F500 for baseband processing and higher-level protocol processing, Maxim MAX2831 RF transciever, Analog Devices AD9288 high-speed ADC and Maxim MAX5189 high-speed DAC.

2. SYSTEM ARCHITECTURE

The μSDR platform is based on Microsemi's SmartFusion mixed-signal FPGA which integrates 500 K gate flash-based FPGA, a hardcore ARM Cortex-M3, and an Analog Compute Engine (ACE) into a single chip. The FPGA and CPU sit on the same high-speed bus that offers up to 16 Gbps of aggregate throughput, which offers a low-latency path between the CPU and FPGA. The high speed bus allows architects to allocate computing resource across the FPGA or CPU freely, to broaden the design space. The μSDR is composed of four major components – SmartFusion, RF front-end, and two data converters. Instead of using the built-in data converters, we use external high speed ADCs/DACs to generate high fidelity waveforms and support higher data rate communication protocols. The radio, a MAX2831, is a highly integrated RF front-end that operates around 2.4 GHz incorporates almost all RF functional blocks within a small form factor. These advantages benefit low-power communication. The AD9288/MAX5189 ADC/DAC provide 8-bit parallel high speed data conversion with low cost. More importantly, all of these chips support sleep/shutdown mode to further reduce the power when the radio goes to sleep.

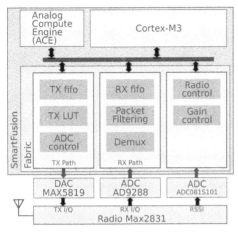

Figure 2: System architecture of our μSDR platform with IEEE 802.15.4 signal conditioning blocks and control flow.

3. DEMONSTRATION

In this demo, we propose to showcase the capability of our μSDR and how the platform enhances the low-power wireless communication research. Our platform leverages both the FPGA and Cortex-M3 as major computing resources; thus, architects are are able to split the communication tasks across hardware and software. Nychis, et al., noted that radio operations that have sensitive timing constraints should be implemented close to radio, which we do [2]. Many reliable communication protocols require ACK frames with tight timing constraints. Therefore, basic packet recognition should be implemented close to the radio.

3.1 Rich Hardware Support

Researchers working on low-power communications have recently proposed several receiver-initiated link layer protocols which offer a better reliability and energy-efficiency than transmitter-initiated protocols [1]. However, some protocols require hardware support which is non-exist in today's off-the-shelf radio hardware. Without such support, receiver-initiated protocols cannot be realized fully. However, with the μSDR, it is possible to provide the tight timing needed for these (and other) protocols in a compact and low-power architecture. The interface between the radio and processor is often on the critical path for performance. Therefore, overall radio performance is limited by the latency, throughput, and loading/offloading of the data between the radio and processor. With our platform, hardware support for backcast [1] enhances network performance through efficent neighbor polling. Moreover, off-the-shelf radios only filter the incoming packet in specific fields like *destination address, or limited source address*. To implement receiver-initiated protocols, prior work abused address fields. As a result, the transmitter was limited in it concurrency support. Using μSDR, is possible to offer greater flexibility on frame filtering, dramatically improving efficiency and throughput. The frame could be filtered on source address, destination address, or any arbitrary field concurrently. In a multi-node network, packet forwarding relies on loading and offloading the radio's TX/RX FIFOs. Therefore, the processor-radio bus can become the bottleneck, limiting total network throughput [3]. However, the μSDR supports hardware zero-copy, improving communications latency and throughput.

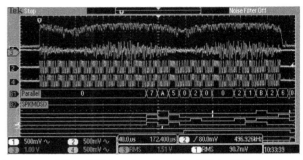

Figure 3: CH1: RX baseband. CH2,CH4: TXs baseband. CH3: RX RSSI. Two ACKs arrive at the receiver at the same time. Different carrier frequencies results in envelope modulation on the receiver baseband signal (yellow).

3.2 Research Enabling Research

/sdr allows radio designers to access crucial low-level transceiver information from RX baseband, RSSI, VCO, and CLK signals. For example, researchers can design a circuit that focus on fast wake-up by resonating the oscillator to reduce the time to stabilize the PLL. Also, clock drifts over environmental change results in synchronization issues, but designers could observe or quantitatively analyze them. The μSDR also allows us to visualize low-level operations like the envelope modulation from packet collisions, as Figure 3 shows. It also allows us to mitigate the effect of collisions by tight AGC loop control on μSDR on the order of a few μS. It could also improves the BER and improve scheduling.

4. CONCLUSION

We present μSDR, a compact (3" by 5"), inexpensive ($150), and battery-operated (4x AAA) software-defined radio platform. This fully programmable platform provides a wide range of hardware support which enables much higher performance, receiver-initiated protocols to be finally realized. Designers also have the access to low-level radio signals which facilitates better understanding of radio communications and control.

5. ACKNOWLEDGMENTS

This material is supported by NSF Award #0964120.

6. REFERENCES

[1] P. Dutta, S. Dawson-Haggerty, Y. Chen, M. Liang, and A. Terzis. Design and Evaluation of a Versatile and Efficient Receiver-Initiated Link Layer for Low Power Wireless. In *Proceedings of the 8th ACM Conference on Embedded Networked Sensor Systems (SenSys)*, November 2010.

[2] G. Nychis, T. Hottelier, Z. Yang, S. Seshan, and P. Steenkiste. Enabling MAC Protocol Implementations on Software-defined Radios. In *Proceedings of the USENIX NSDI*, Boston, MA, April 2009.

[3] F. OSTERLIND and A. DUNKELS. Approaching the maximum 802.15.4 multi-hop throughput. In *Proceedings of the 5th ACM Workship on Embedded Networked Sensors (HotEmNets)*, June 2008.

[4] C. Patridge. Realizing the future of wireless data communications. *COMMUNICATIONS OF THE ACM*, 54(9):62–68, September 2011.

Demo Abstract:

Simbeeotic: A Simulation-Emulation Platform For Large Scale Micro-Aerial Swarms

Jason Waterman
Harvard University
Cambridge, MA, USA
waterman@eecs.harvard.edu

Bryan Kate
Harvard University
Cambridge, MA, USA
bkate@eecs.harvard.edu

Karthik Dantu
Harvard University
Cambridge, MA, USA
kar@eecs.harvard.edu

Matt Welsh
Google, Inc.
Seattle, WA, USA
mdw@mdw.la

ABSTRACT

Micro-aerial vehicle (MAV) swarms are an emerging class of mobile sensing systems. Designing the next generation of such swarms requires the ability to rapidly test algorithms, sensors, and support infrastructure at scale. Simulation is useful in the early stages of such large-scale system design, when hardware is unavailable or deployment at scale is impractical. To faithfully represent the problem domain, an MAV swarm simulator must be able to model all key aspects of the system: *actuation, sensing, and communication.* Further, it is important to be able to quickly test swarm behavior using different control algorithms in a varied set of environments, and with a variety of sensors.

We demonstrate Simbeeotic, a simulation framework that is capable of modeling large-scale MAV swarms. Simbeeotic enables algorithm development and rapid prototyping through both simulation and hardware-in-the-loop experimentation. We demonstrate Simbeeotic running simulated applications and videos demonstrating hybrid experiments with simulated MAVs as well as helicopters flying in our testbed that show the power and versatility required to assist next generation swarm design.

Categories and Subject Descriptors

I.2.9 [**Artificial Intelligence**]: Robotics—*Autonomous Vehicles*; I.6.3 [**Simulation and Modeling**]: Applications

General Terms

Design, Experimentation, Measurement

Keywords

Swarm, Micro-Aerial Vehicle, Simulation, Testbed

1. INTRODUCTION

MAV swarms are an emerging class of mobile sensing systems. As opposed to a single, more capable robot, MAV swarms employ a group of autonomous micro-robots to accomplish a common goal. Research platforms include quadro-

Figure 1: Simbeeotic includes a realtime 3D visualization of running applications.

tors [4], fixed-wing aircraft [2], small "flying motes" [5], and insect-scale ornithopters [6]. Such MAVs might be equipped with a variety of sensors such as cameras, optic flow sensors, accelerometers, magnetometers, UV range finders, compasses, and positioning sensors such as GPS. They could be deployed in diverse environments such as collapsed buildings, commercial farms, forests, mountains, or disaster areas such as after a flood. MAV swarms could consist of many individuals ranging from one to hundreds of MAVs. Considering the diversity of their deployment, it is extremely hard to deploy MAV swarms at scale to understand their behavior. This posits the requirement of a simulation environment capable of simulating such diverse scenarios. To this end, we have built Simbeeotic, a simulation platform for MAV swarms.

Work in MAV swarms is inherently inter-disciplinary, with research opportunities in a variety of areas including embedded systems, control theory, robotics, artificial intelligence, wireless networking, and distributed systems. Most researchers are interested in one aspect of the design (such as control algorithms or network connectivity). To accommodate this requirement, Simbeeotic comes with an extensive library of components that can be dropped in for features that are not directly interesting to the user (e.g., modeling of an optic flow sensor) while being able to customize aspects of the simulation that the designer cares about (e.g., con-

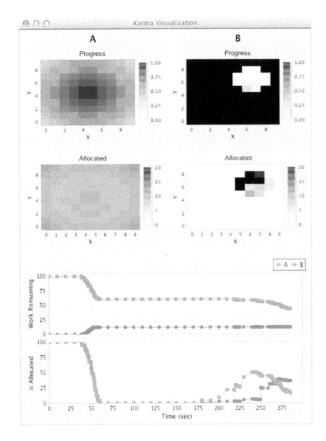

Figure 2: Diagnostic task allocation graphs for a Simbeeotic application.

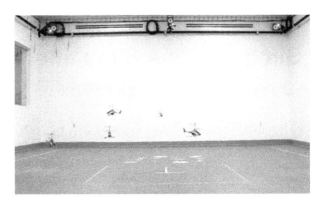

Figure 3: Simbeeotic simulations can interact with and control hardware devices.

trol of individual MAVs). We have been using it in our own research for over two years [1] and have found it extremely useful.

Simbeeotic is written in the Java programming language. Java was chosen for a number of reasons. First, it is widely understood in our team and easily learned by neophytes. Second, it is a cross-platform language so Simbeeotic can be compiled or distributed in binary form for most popular (and some esoteric) operating systems. Third, there exists a large repository of high quality, open source libraries that can be leveraged by our modelers. Finally, native code can be integrated through mechanisms such as JNA [3], allowing us to take advantage of legacy or optimized native code, should the need arise. At present, Simbeeotic consists of 13,387 lines of Java code in 148 classes and 506 lines of XML schema. Of this code base, 48% makes up the core (including the simulation executor, modeling interfaces, base classes, and common model implementations), 26% is for testbed integration, 13% is example code, 6% defines tools that generate random enclosed environments (such as mine shafts and office buildings), 6% is for visualization components, and 1% is for the main entry point. This codebase builds atop a collection of open source libraries that provide support for physics simulation, linear algebra, statistics, 3D visualization, plotting, message serialization, code generation, and logging.

Simbeeotic relies on modular software design principles and a commitment to deployment-time configuration through easy to read XML files, which provides modeling flexibility

and ease of use. It is highly extensible and is designed for repeated experimentation. With Simbeeotic we demonstrate that whole-system modeling is feasible for the MAV swarm domain. Simbeeotic is available as open source software at http://robobees.seas.harvard.edu.

2. DEMONSTRATION

Our demonstration consists of a laptop running live simulations in Simbeeotic. The demonstration shows Simbeeotic's 3D visual realtime output, as shown in Figure 1. We show Simbeeotic running at scale with an application that allocates tasks to a large MAV swarm over a gridded area. A snapshot of the visualization of this task allotment is shown in Figure 2.

Our simulation framework provides for both pure software simulation and hardware-in-the-loop (HWIL) experimentation with a radio controlled (RC) helicopter testbed, as shown in Figure 3. We also show a video of Simbeeotic's integration with our hardware testbed.

3. REFERENCES

[1] K. Dantu, B. Kate, J. Waterman, P. Bailis, and M. Welsh. Programming micro-aerial vehicle swarms with karma. In *Proceedings of the 9th International Conference on Embedded Networked Sensor Systems (Sensys '11)*, November 2011.

[2] S. Hauert, L. Winkler, J. Zufferey, and D. Floreano. Ant-based swarming with positionless micro air vehicles for communication relay. *Swarm Intelligence*, 2(2-4):167–188, 2008.

[3] Java Native Access. http://github.com/twall/jna.

[4] N. Michael, J. Fink, and V. Kumar. Cooperative manipulation and transportation with aerial robots. *Autonomous Robots*, 30(1):73–86, Sept. 2010.

[5] A. Purohit, Z. Sun, M. Salas, and P. Zhang. SensorFly: Controlled-mobile sensing platform for indoor emergency response applications. In *Proceedings of the 10th International Conference on Information Processing in Sensor Networks (IPSN '11)*, Apr. 2011.

[6] R. Wood. The first takeoff of a biologically inspired at-scale robotic insect. *IEEE Transactions on Robotics*, 24(2):341–347, 2008.

Free-form Text Summarization in Social Sensing

Hongzhao Huang, Sam Anzaroot, Heng Ji
City University of New York
{hengjicuny}@gmail.com

Hieu Khac Le, Dong Wang, Tarek Abdelzaher
University of Illinois at Urbana-Champaign
{zaher}@illinois.edu

ABSTRACT

This demonstration illustrates an information aggregation and summarization service for social sensing applications. Social sensing, using mobile phones and other networked devices in the possession of individuals, has gained significant popularity in recent years. In some cases, the information collected is structured, such as numeric data from temperature sensors, accelerometers, or GPS devices. Aggregate statistical properties, such as expected values, standard deviations, and outliers, can be easily computed, and can be used to summarize the data set. In other cases, however, the collection includes unstructured data types such as text or images with textual annotations. The concepts of expected values and outliers are harder to define, yet it is still important to be able to aggregate and summarize the data. We demonstrate a system which can automatically summarize real-time textual data common to social sensing applications. Specifically, we focus on text messages that describe events in the environment. The output of our service provides a reliable summary of observations that can be used in many contexts from military intelligence to participatory sensing campaigns.

Categories and Subject Descriptors

H.4 [**Information Systems Applications**]: Miscellaneous

Keywords

Social Sensing, Information Summarization, Free-form Text

1. INTRODUCTION

Our work is motivated by the emerging needs of social sensing applications. It is clear that significant enhancements are possible to the capabilities of social sensing systems if they were able to process and summarize unstructured data types. Consider, for example, a participatory sensing campaign that allows individuals to geo-tag locations of relevance to the campaign (e.g., using their GPS

phone), and add a short annotation to explain the reason for geo-tagging. For example, in a "clean campus" campaign, individuals might be asked to geotag locations where they observed a need for maintenance or upkeep, and add a text message that explains the nature of the problem. For another example, in a military or peace-keeping scenario, a friendly local population might be encouraged to report observations of relevance to the military or peace-keeping mission in the form of text.

In this demonstration, we use microblogs as a way of sharing observations. Twitter already offers an easy way to report short observations, as well as a way to include pointers to visual and location information. It has exhibited advantages over traditional news agencies in the success of reporting news more timely, for instance, in reporting the Chilean earthquake of 2010 [1]. A comparative study [2] shows that Twitter users tend to seek more temporally relevant information than those of general web search engines. This makes Twitter an ideal vehicle for real-time dissemination of observations in social sensing applications.

As with numeric data types (such as temperature), it is useful to summarize a large body of reported textual observations in order to convey the information more efficiently. This is especially important in large-scale applications, where in the absence of summarization, users of the data collection service might be overwhelmed by the sheer amount of collected observations. The main contribution of the demonstrated service lies in the implementation of novel (i) clustering and (ii) ranking techniques for summarizing unstructured *textual* observations in social sensing. The components of the service are described below.

2. A DATA SUMMARIZATION SERVICE

Our service addresses the need for summarization in the context of free-form textual sensing data. The service has three components:

Clustering: In the case of numeric data, one way to summarize a data set would be to report statistical properties such as average and standard deviation. Since textual data does not have an inherent order (unlike numeric data types), in the text domain, the corresponding solution is to (i) perform clustering of data, and (ii) report representatives of different clusters. For example, if several individuals describe the same event, one should be able to cluster those observations and report one or a few representative descriptions only. Our service uses clustering as a way to significantly reduce the size of input data and offer a quick representative view of the entire observation set. Our contribution lies not in how clusters are formed (which is borrowed from natural language processing), but how their credibility is evaluated. Cluster size alone is not a good indication of authenticity of data. For example, it does not eliminate rumors where, a significant number of observers may report the same event because they heard it from others.

Ranking: When the collected observations are noisy, it is important to eliminate statistical outliers, since they are more likely to represent measurement noise. This is straightforward to do in the case of numeric data, but is needed when handling unstructured data as well. Outlier elimination, in the context of unstructured data, requires algorithms for data ranking that help sort the observations by statistical likelihood, such that less likely ones can be ignored. Our ranking techniques are novel in opportunistically exploiting heterogeneous *relations* between observations. For example, if we happened to observe (from reported textual annotations or from a map) that individuals reporting litter at some locations were frequently at a stop for Bus 13, other bus stops on the same route may be considered more likely candidates for having litter as well. Finally, if individuals reporting an observation are not at the location of the observed event, they are likely not observing the event first-hand. Hence, understanding relations between observations, sources, and locations can improve ranking. In general, if observation attributes (such as locations and reported events) were nodes, and their different semantic relations were (heterogeneous) links, we call the resulting network an *information network*. Our main contribution lies in information-network-assisted summarization of textual sensing data.

Query engine: Given the generated summary view, we make it possible to answer queries about the data. For example, much like a person can ask for all locations where the average daily temperature is above a threshold, we allow a user to ask about all locations where excessive litter was commonly observed. The former is a standard query on a numeric data type. The latter, in contrast, requires processing of textual annotations of geo-tagged locations, clustering, ranking, and returning the best representatives of the most statistically credible clusters.

3. TECHNICAL APPROACH

Given a set of textual observations (in our implementation, we use Twitter to share the data), we cluster them by linking together those pairs with similarity larger than a threshold, then assign initial credibility weights to each cluster using an expectation maximization approach (published in this IPSN [3]).

We then exploit linguistic lexical, syntactic and semantic analysis to extract pre-specified types of facts and entities from written text, and convert them into structured representations (i.e., information networks). An information network is a heterogeneous network that includes a set of "information graphs" $G = G_i(V_i, E_i)$, where V_i is the collection of entity nodes, and E_i is the collection of edges linking one entity to the other, labeled by relation or event attributes, such as "hometown", "employer", or "spouse". We adopt the taxonomy defined in the ACE2005[1] Information Extraction system [4, 5], which includes 7 types of entities (such as persons, locations, and organizations), 18 types of relations, and 33 distinct types of events.

[1]http://www.itl.nist.gov/iad/mig/tests/ace/

One can think of the resulting information network as one that encodes inter-dependencies among various types of observations, from which certain regularities, called *association rules*, are mined. These regularities can be thought of as latent constraints. We then rank the observations based on the following hypothesis: an observation is more likely to be correct if it's more consistent with other extracted regularities [6]. Observations that are the most inconsistent are removed.

4. SCRIPT OUTLINE

In the demonstration, the audience will be presented with raw textual data sets collected from observations of recent events of interest, such as Hurricane Irene, and recent riots. We shall ask the users to summarize what happened in those events. It will be evident that the raw amount of information received makes it impossible to do so in a reasonable amount of time, and in fact makes it easy to miss important observations in the deluge of raw reported data.

We shall then demonstrate our summarization service. The service will automatically cluster tweets, extract information units from tweet clusters, and construct an information network to express relations between such clusters. It will then mine the constructed information network for regularities (the association rules), and use these to rank the individual tweet clusters based on conformance with these regularities. A summary consisting of individual tweets representing the highest ranked clusters will then be displayed. This will be compared to other information summarization techniques that do not exploit relations between clusters. It will be shown that the new summarization technique offers a more relevant picture of what transpired, making it a good candidate for summarizing unstructured (textual) data in social sensing.

5. REFERENCES

[1] Marcelo Mendoza, Barbara Poblete, and Carlos Castillo. Twitter under crisis: Can we trust what we rt? In *Proc. 1st Workshop on Social Media Analytics*, 2010.

[2] Jaime Teevan, Daniel Ramage, and Meredith Ringel Morris. Twittersearch: A comparison of microblog search and web search. In *Proc. WSDM11*, 2011.

[3] Dong Wang, Lance Kaplan, Hieu Le, and Tarek Abdelzaher. On truth discovery in social sensing: A maximum likelihood estimation approach. In *ACM/IEEE IPSN*, 2012.

[4] Heng Ji, Ralph Grishman, Zheng Chen, and Prashant Gupta. Cross-document event extraction and tracking: Task, evaluation, techniques and challenges. In *Proc. Recent Advances in Natural Language Processing 2009*, 2009.

[5] Zheng Chen, Suzanne Tamang, Adam Lee, Xiang L, Wen-Pin Lin, Matthew Snover, Javier Artiles, Marissa Passantino, and Heng Ji. Cuny-blender tac-kbp2010 entity linking and slot filling system description. In *Proc. TAC 2010 Workshop*, 2009.

[6] Qi Li, Sam Anzaroot, Wen-Pin Lin, Xiang Li, and Heng Ji. Joint inference for cross-document information extraction. In *Proc. 20th ACM Conference on Information and Knowledge Management (CIKM2011)*, 2011.

Demo Abstract:

PhotoNet+: Outlier-resilient Coverage Maximization in Visual Sensing Applications

Md Yusuf S Uddin
University of Illinois
Urbana, IL 61801, USA
mduddin2@illinois.edu

Md Tanvir Al Amin
University of Illinois
Urbana, IL 61801, USA
maamin2@illinois.edu

Tarek Abdelzaher
University of Illinois
Urbana, IL 61801, USA
zaher@illinois.edu

Arun Iyengar
IBM T.J. Watson Research
Center, NY 10598, USA
arun@us.ibm.com

Ramesh Govindan
University of Southern
California, CA 90089, USA
ramesh@usc.edu

ABSTRACT

This demonstration illustrates a service for collection and delivery of images, in participatory camera networks, to maximize coverage while removing outliers (i.e., irrelevant images). Images, such as those taken by smart-phone users, represent an important and growing modality in social sensing applications. They can be used, for instance, to document occurrences of interest in participatory sensing campaigns, such as instances of graffiti on campus or invasive species in a park. In applications with a significant number of participants, the number of images collected may be very large. A key problem becomes one of data triage to reduce the number of images delivered to a manageable count, without missing important ones. In prior work, the authors presented a service, called PhotoNet [2], that reduces redundancy among delivered images by maximizing diversity. The current work significantly extends our previous effort by recognizing that diversity maximization often leads to selection of outliers; images that are visually different but not necessarily relevant, which in fact reduces the quality of the delivered image pool. We demonstrate a new prioritization technique that maximizes diversity among delivered pictures, while also reducing outliers.

Categories and Subject Descriptors

H.4 [**Information Systems Applications**]: Communications Applications

Keywords

Redundancy reduction, outlier detection, visual sensing

1. INTRODUCTION

We define a participatory camera (sensor) network as one where participants contribute pictorial data, either on their own initiative or through participation in a corresponding data collection campaign. For example, in the aftermath of a natural disaster, relief workers and other first responders might survey an area in search of damage that is then pictorially documented and reported. Alternatively, residents of a neighborhood might pictorially document issues that require attention (e.g., graffiti on walls, trash piles, or hazardous potholes). Yet a third application might be to compile a list of most visited tourist landmarks from pictures contributed by local tourists. Participatory camera sensing applications are made popular by the vast proliferation of cameras and camera phones in the possession of the average individual, not to mention the richness of information contained in pictures compared to other sensing modalities [1].

Our camera sensing service runs on participants' phones (the clients) and on a destination server (the collection point). When pictures are taken using our application, they are locally stored on the phone. When two participant phones meet, they may gossip by exchanging a portion of their pictures. Similarly, when a phone connects to the destination server it uploads a portion of its pictures. The contribution of the service lies in prioritizing transmission of pictures both when two phones meet or when a phone meets the server, such that the most *representative subset* is sent (instead of sending all), in order to conserve resources. Resources may need to be conserved for many reasons. For example, participants, who upload pictures from their mobile phones, may have to pay for their data plans. Network resource constraints may also require data triage to fit the available capacity. In DTN-style communication and military scenarios, groups of soldiers in the field may have only a low or intermittent bandwidth channel to a remote base.

We do not make inherent assumptions regarding the type of network in which our service operates. For example, it could be a star network, where all phones have a direct way of connecting to the server. Alternatively, it could be a DTN, where the primary data propagation occurs via phone-to-phone gossiping. Either way, the decision we are concerned with is which pictures to send in what order when two nodes meet (either two clients, or a client and the server).

In this demonstration, we show that algorithms that maximize diversity to improve coverage, such as those proposed in previous literature [2], favor outliers as opposed to more representative content. The main contribution of our new prioritization scheme lies in combining coverage maximization with outlier elimination, to handle picture sets of poor quality in participatory camera sensing networks.

It is worth noting, at this point, that outlier elimination is not always a goal in a participatory camera network. In some applications, such as anomaly detection, outliers are in fact what carries the relevant information. For example, an in-store security camera might report the same view all night, except when an intruder breaks in. A frame with the intruder in view might be the outlier, but it is also the frame that contains the most interesting information. Our service considers a different type of applications, where a community of users document relatively static conditions in the environment, such as damage or points of interest. In such cases, one is not looking for anomalies in reporting, but rather for *representative* depiction.

2. THE OPERATING PRINCIPLE

The contribution of our new service lies in maximizing diversity while removing outliers in the delivered subset of collected images. An explicit goal is to estimate relevance of a picture to the mission *without having to understand the semantics* of what is in a picture, since this would be very complex and application-specific. The scheme has two components; one for maximizing coverage and one for outlier elimination, as discussed below.

Coverage maximization: Our scheme separates out the application-specific notion of "similarity" between images into the definition of a *distance metric*, $d(x, y)$, defined on any pair of images x and y to denote the degree of similarity in their visual content and metadata (such as location). The distance metric allows images to be represented as points in a logical multidimensional feature space, where the proximity of points designates information overlap between the corresponding objects. If two points lie very close to each other, they are partially redundant. We further assume that there exists a certain distance threshold beyond which there is no information overlap. Let this constant be τ. Hence, it is useful to imagine that each object logically covers a hyper-sphere with radius $\frac{\tau}{2}$ so that the spheres of two objects overlap when their distance is smaller than τ. The volume of a sphere is called the *coverage* of the object.

Note that, due to overlap, the total coverage of a set of objects is generally less than the sum of the coverages of the individual objects. The total coverage of all objects in a set can thus be treated as a quantitative estimation of the diversity of the set. The diversity maximization problem is then to chose a subset of objects whose total coverage is maximum, subject to an aggregate resource constraint (e.g., storage capacity) that limits the number of objects chosen.

In practice, pictures taken by participants would typically fall into groups (each group representing pictures of the same scene at the same place), such that logical distances between pictures within the same group (or cluster) are much smaller than those among different groups. This naturally leads to partitioning objects into a set of *clusters*. Our service implements a coverage-maximizing algorithm for picture selection that leverages clustering to reduce problem complexity. The details of the algorithm are beyond the scope of this abstract.

Outlier elimination: It turns out that clustering offers an elegant way of separating the concern of outlier detection from the concern of diversity maximization. Intuitively, by assigning appropriate *relevance weights* to clusters, we can first get rid of low-ranked clusters (the outliers) to address relevance, then collect objects from the remaining clusters, thereby maximizing diversity for non-outlier clusters.

Short of "understanding" each picture, we can only approximately *estimate* relevance, which we do from the behavior of data collection agents themselves. Presumably,

they are motivated to collect relevant information. Hence, if more sources report an observation, it is more likely that the observation is relevant. Note, however, that the converse is not true. Sometimes items may be isolated not because they are irrelevant and do not generate interest, but rather because they are in the vicinity of only very few observers. If there were more people in their vicinity, more pictures may have been taken of them. Hence, some consideration to the level of isolation of the *location* of pictures needs to be made in outlier determination. Intuitively, a scene should be considered an outlier not only because it is different but because others who are present at the scene are not taking pictures of it. Correspondingly in our context, a picture is treated as an outlier, if it is geographically collocated with a popular picture set, but is *visually* significantly different from the group.

3. THE DEMONSTRATION SCRIPT

In this demonstration, the audience will be presented with a table-top landscape comprised of different "damage scenes" in an imaginary city that has just witnessed a natural disaster, as well as some scenery that is less relevant to damage documentation and response efforts. The audience will be presented with smart phones and asked to imagine that they are volunteer first-responders in that virtual city, instructed to document and report urgent concerns of relevance to the rescue mission by taking pictures of them and sending those to the local rescue center. They will be allowed to take as many or as few pictures as they like. For example, they can choose to photograph one or many of the table-top scenes. They can take multiple pictures of the same scene, or not. They can also choose to "confuse" the system by advertantly taking pictures of no relevance to the mission. A base-station (at the demo location) will receive all pictures, run our algorithm and choose a small subset to represent the "most urgent" rescue needs. These will be displayed and compared to the subset of pictures chosen by other baselines, such as random selection and FIFO, to show that our service provides better coverage without outliers.

Acknowledgment

Research reported in this paper was sponsored by ONR grant N00014-10-1-0172, DTRA grant HDTRA-1-10-1-0120, NSF grants CNS 06-26825 and 1040380, and the Army Research Laboratory under Cooperative Agreement Number W911NF-09-2-0053. The views and conclusions contained in this document are those of the authors and should not be interpreted as representing the official policies, either expressed or implied, of the Army Research Laboratory or the U.S. Government. The U.S. Government is authorized to reproduce and distribute reprints for Government purposes notwithstanding any copyright notation here on.

4. REFERENCES

[1] Mani Srivastava, Tarek Abdelzaher, and Boleslaw Szymanski. Human-centric sensing. *Philosophical Transactions of the Royal Society, A*, 370(1958):176–197, 2012.

[2] Md Yusuf Uddin, Hongyan Wang, Fatemeh Saremi, Guo-Jun Qi, Tarek Abdelzaher, and Thomas Huang. Photonet: a similarity-aware picture delivery service for situation awareness. In *Proc. of RTSS*, 2011.

Demo Abstract:

Collaborative Indoor Sensing With The SensorFly Aerial Sensor Network

Aveek Purohit, Frank Mokaya and Pei Zhang
Department of Electrical and Computer Engineering
Carnegie Mellon University
{aveek.purohit|frank.mokaya|pei.zhang}@sv.cmu.edu

ABSTRACT

The SensorFly is a novel, low-cost, miniature (29g) controlled-mobile aerial sensor networking platform. Mobility permits a network of SensorFly nodes, unlike fixed networks, to be autonomous in deployment, maintenance and adapting to the environment, as required for emergency response situations such as fire monitoring or survivor search.

We demonstrate the ability of the SensorFly system to collaboratively sense the environment (floor temperature) in a demonstration scenario. The SensorFly nodes are tasked to explore the area and transmit sensed data back to a base station. The system partitions tasks among SensorFly nodes based on their capabilities (location, sensors, energy) to achieve concurrent and faster coverage. The real-time sensor data is presented to the user on a display terminal at the base station.

Categories and Subject Descriptors

C.2 [**Computer-Communication Networks**]: Network Architecture and Design—*Wireless communications*; I.2 [**Artificial Intelligence**]: Robotics—*Autonomous vehicles, Sensors*

General Terms

Design, Experimentation, Measurement

Keywords

Wireless Sensor Networks, Applications

1. INTRODUCTION

Indoor emergency response situations, such as urban fire or survivor search, are characterized by dangerous constantly-changing operating environments with little access to situational information for first responders. In-situ information about the conditions can augment rescue efforts and reduce risk to emergency personnel. Static sensor networks that are pre deployed or manually deployed have been proposed [1, 2, 6], but are less practical due to need for large infrastructure, lack of adaptivity and limited coverage. Controlled mobility in sensor networks, i.e. the capability of nodes to move as per network needs can provide the desired autonomy to overcome these limitations.

The SensorFly is a controlled-mobile sensor network for indoor sensing. The network comprises of aerial sensor nodes,

Figure 1: Airborne Sensorfly node

each of which is capable of autonomous flight and can be directed as per the sensing objectives of the network.

Moreover, the SensorFly system takes a network-centric view to collectively achieve sensing goals. The system trades-off more accurate sensing, navigation and processing abilities on individual nodes for a lower cost and a very small form-factor(29g). Communication and co-ordination between nodes is used to offset the per-device resource limitations. Consequently, a large number of nodes can be deployed in indoor environments to provide greater robustness, better access, and faster concurrent coverage.

In this demonstration, we present an illustrative indoor temperature monitoring scenario consisting of a SensorFly network with 6-nodes collaboratively sensing the floor temperature of the demo arena. 4 nodes land(and remain stationary) to setup a communication and localization infrastructure, while 2 nodes move and sense temperature.

The major features shown in the demo are as follows:

- We present the second generation SensorFly node hardware with on-board 9-axis sensor fusion that enables the nodes to hold a direction and move as per the networks' needs.

- The communication and radio-based ranging capability of the aerial as well as ground based nodes in the SensorFly network.

- The task partitioning capability of the network that assigns sub-tasks to nodes based on their location and battery capacity.

2. DEMONSTRATION

The demonstration is aimed at illustrating the potential of the SensorFly system in emergency response scenarios such as fire monitoring or survivor search.

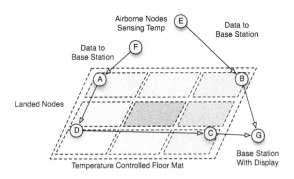

Figure 2: Demonstration setup with 4 deployed SensorFly nodes and 2 exploring airborne nodes measuring floor temperature of the demo arena.

The demonstration shows three major components of the SensorFly system: the hardware platform, the communication and co-ordination protocol and the task partitioning scheme to assign sub-tasks to individual nodes as per their capability.

This demonstration builds on and shows the advances since our previous work [5] that demonstrated the hovering capability of SensorFly node and a Round-trip Time-of-Flight(RToF) based localization system. The notable new features are as follows:

- The SensorFly nodes hold direction and are capable of controlled movement as per the programmed algorithm as opposed to hovering in place.

- The aerial SensorFly nodes are localized by stationary landed nodes and the location information is used to guide their motion. This demonstration shows how the network uses the RToF-based localization capability demonstrated earlier [5] to close-the-loop and guide mobile nodes.

- Multiple SensorFly nodes move and sense the environment. The sensed data is routed back to the base station illustrating the ad-hoc communication protocol. The collaborative coverage achieved is visualized at base station.

2.1 Hardware Platform

The SensorFly [4] node uses a miniature dual-rotor helicopter design as the movement mechanism with minimal weight to reduce increase flight time and maximize coverage.

Each node includes a 16MHz microprocessor, a 802.15.4a radio [3] with short distance time-of-flight ranging capabilities, 9-axis motion sensors (3-axis accelerometer + 2-axis gyro + magnetic compass), motor control, helicopter mechanical drive, and sensor extension port. The design of this node is limited by the liftoff weight of the helicopter, which in our current implementation is 35 grams. With the basic set of sensors mentioned above the platform weighs 29 grams. Figure 1 shows a SensorFly node hovering in the university hallway.

In the demonstration, each SensorFly node is equipped with a non-contact infra-red thermometer to measure the floor temperature.

2.2 Communication Protocol

The SensorFly networks' goal is to route all sensed data from mobile nodes to the base station. Consequently, the system implements aggregate and broadcast communication

for the airborne explorer nodes while peer-to-peer routing is supported on landed anchor nodes. The constant motion of exploring nodes makes establishing routes and running explicit node discovery service impractical. Nodes therefore periodically broadcast messages containing their sensor data. Neighboring nodes, on hearing the broadcast message aggregate the node's sensor data with their message.

2.3 Task Partitioning

The SensorFly system consists of nodes with heterogeneous capabilities. They may differ in their location, battery charge capacity, the type of sensors. The system must divide the global sensing task into sub-tasks that can be executed by the individual nodes keeping in mind their individual resource constraints.

The system designates some nodes as anchors that land and remain stationary. The anchors act as relays for data communication and provide reference beacons for location estimates. The remaining mobile nodes are tasked with exploring the area and periodically take sensor measurements. The co-ordination between multiple nodes exploring the area is achieved through both peer-to-peer communication/range measurements as well as centralized directions from the base station. For example, the base station directs nodes with lower remaining battery charge to relay their collected data and limit movement.

2.4 Demo Script

Our demonstration setup consists of a demo arena with a $4m \times 4m$ floor mat equipped with heating elements to create a varying temperature profile. 6 SensorFly nodes equipped with infra-red sensors collaboratively move and explore the demo arena to sense and achieve coverage.

4 SensorFly nodes acting as anchors are placed on the ground at arbitrary locations. At least 2 airborne SensorFly nodes move in the arena as per the exploration algorithm and transmit sensed temperature measurements to the base station. The setup is illustrated in Figure 2.

The coverage is ascertained and presented to the users on a visual display in real-time as the SensorFly nodes obtain updated measurements.

3. REFERENCES

[1] X. Jiang, N. Y. Chen, J. I. Hong, K. Wang, L. Takayama, and J. A. Landay. Siren: Context-aware Computing for Firefighting. In *Proceedings of the 2nd International Conference on Pervasive Computing*, pages 87–105, 2004.

[2] M. Klann, T. Riedel, H. Gellersen, C. Fischer, G. Pirkl, K. Kunze, M. Beuster, M. Beigl, O. Visser, and M. Gerling. LifeNet: an Ad-hoc Sensor Network and Wearable System to Provide Firefighters with Navigation Support. In *Proceedings of the 9th International Conference on Ubiquitous Computing*, 2007.

[3] Nanotron Tecnologies Gmbh. nanoLOC AVR Module Technical Description, 2008.

[4] A. Purohit, Z. Sun, F. Mokaya, and P. Zhang. SensorFly: Controlled-mobile sensing platform for indoor emergency response applications. In *In Proceeding of the 10th International Conference on Information Processing in Sensor Networks (IPSN)*, pages 223–234, 2011.

[5] A. Purohit and P. Zhang. SensorFly: a controlled-mobile aerial sensor network. In *Proceedings of the 7th ACM Conference on Embedded Networked Sensor Systems*, SenSys '09, pages 327–328, New York, NY, USA, 2009. ACM.

[6] R. Upadhyay. Towards a Tailored Sensor Network for Fire Emergency Monitoring in Large buildings. In *Proceedings of the 1st IEEE International Conference on Wireless Emergency and Rural Communications, Rome*, 2007.

Demo: Ultra-Constrained Sensor Platform Interfacing

Pat Pannuto, Yoonmyung Lee, Ben Kempke, Dennis Sylvester, David Blaauw, Prabal Dutta
Electrical Engineering and Computer Science Department
University of Michigan
Ann Arbor, MI 48109
{ppannuto, sori, bpkempke, dmcs, blaauw, prabal}@umich.edu

ABSTRACT

In this work we expose the challenges of interfacing both conventional and new systems with an extremely resource constrained platform. We find that even when attempts are made to utilize an industry standard protocol (I2C), necessary protocol modifications for ultra-low power design means that interfacing remains non-trivial.

We present a functional 0.4mm x 0.8mm ARM Cortex M0 with 3KB of RAM, 24 GPIOs, and an ultra-low power I2C interface. This chip is part of the Michigan Micro Mote (M3) project, which is designed to build a complete software and hardware platform for general purpose sensing at the millimeter scale. We demo an I2C interface circuit allowing commercial hardware to program and interact with the chip and present the beginning of the millimeter scale sensing revolution.

Categories and Subject Descriptors

B.4.3 [**HARDWARE**]: Input/Output and Data Communications—*Interconnections (subsystems)*

Keywords

Bus Protocols, Low Power, Smart Dust

1. INTRODUCTION

In the design of ultra-low power systems, communication is of paramount importance. While great emphasis is often placed on *inter*-node communication – via wireless, light, et al – the challenges of *intra*-node communication are often neglected. Traditionally, this issue is relegated to existing solutions such as I2C or SPI. However, there are several important limitations when working in this space. A significant concern for our design is wire count as the integrated configuration has very limited physical space for interchip bond wires. In addition, common open-drain bus architectures impose a relatively high constant leakage through their pull-up resistors, bounded in the other extreme by maintaining a reasonably fast bus frequency. Despite these challenges, we find it undesirable and unnecessary to impose a completely novel protocol on system designers. Instead we preserve the semantics of the I2C protocol, while developing a significantly more power efficient implementation.

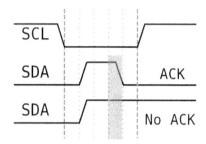

Figure 1: The ACK cycle of the modified I2C protocol. The negative clock edge is divided into 5 cycles: wait, pulse up, wait, pulse data, wait. These cycles are all 250ns long, permitting any clock rate up to 400kHz. The shaded region marks the only period in a I2C transaction the slave is responsible for driving.

1.1 Ultra-low Power I2C

The M3 system developed an ultra-low power I2C variant. Instead of the traditional pull-up resistor, a weak keeper circuit made up of a pair of inverters preserves the current value of the clock and data lines. During communication, the I2C master is responsible for pulsing the clock line both high and low. The negative clock cycle is divided into 5 separate states: wait, pulse high, wait, pulse data, wait. The master is responsible for driving the SDA line high every cycle, allowing either the master or slave to pull down the SDA line as appropriate. A waveform of the more-interesting ACK cycle (which requires a slave device to drive the SDA line) is shown in Figure 1.

2. MICHIGAN MICRO MOTE

The Michigan Micro Mote (M3) project is a collaborative effort to develop a general purpose millimeter-scale sensor platform [2]. The current work builds a five chip stack composed of a 96x96 pixel imager, solar energy harvester, control CPU with 3KB of retentive memory, DSP CPU with 16KB of non-retentive memory, energy storage, and UWB radio.

2.1 M3 as a Platform

The main utility of M3 is as a development platform for new sensors and systems. It provides the builing blocks for the creation of a diverse array of sensors at the millimeter scale. Much like the development of the Epic core faciliatated the rapid development and deployment of sensors at the several inch scale [1], it is our hope that the M3 platform can springboard a new class of sensors at the millime-

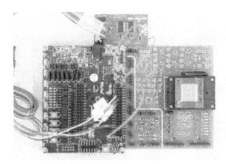

(a) The complete system: A commercial I2C device the BusPirate (top), the interface circuit realized in an IGLOO nano FPGA (left), and a breakout of the M3 control CPU board (right)

(b) A die shot of the M3 control CPU board

Figure 2: The ultra-low power and commerical devices

Figure 4: A combinational approach to interfacing the two divergent I2C systems. The M3 pull-up signal is supplied to a monostable multivibrator acting as a one-shot timer

ter scale. The ultra-low power I2C to commercial I2C bridge presented in this work will allow for iterative development and utilization of the M3 platform immediately with existing hardware and enable other hardware devices to utilize our ultra-low power I2C variant.

3. INTERFACE

Figure 3 gives a high level overview of the differing I2C implementations. The following sections highlight the challenges of interfacing these two distinct I2C designs.

3.1 A Purely Combinational Approach

Our first interface attempt was the combinational circuit presented in Figure 4. The circuit latched who had pulled a line low and held the opposite signal line low until it was

released, using a one-shot timer to pulse the M3 signal lines high when the commercial chip was the master.

While nearly correct, this circuit suffered from an insurmountable timing glitch. If the commercial line was acting as the master and the LSB of a transaction was 0, it would not pulse the SDA line high until the pull-up resistor had pulled the line high, typically between 550 and 800ns after the negative edge. Referring back to Figure 1, this would cause the SDA pull-up to drown out the M3's attempt to acknowledge the transaction. In addition to the RC delay, a further 50ns of delay came from a level converter and the discrete logic components. As more challenges became apparent, it became clear that a purely combinational circuit would have been untenably complex.

3.2 Enter the FPGA

Our final solution takes the form of a state machine realized in an Actel IGLOO Nano FPGA. The state machine is able to act as a 'proper' M3 master, pulsing the SDA line high 250–500ns after each falling clock edge. Care must be taken while communicating from the M3 to the commercial side as well. Since the M3 data is not available until 1000ns after the negative clock edge, it leaves only 250ns to drive the commercial I2C network. In practice this requires the FPGA to hold the commercial line at about half voltage and actively drive it high or low for the last 250ns to ensure timing constraints are met.

4. DEMONSTRATION

In this demo, we present a functional 0.4mm x 0.8mm ARM Cortex M0 with an ultra-low power I2C network interfaced to traditional commercial I2C components. We will show bus-based DMA programming of the M3 chip using commercial I2C interfaces and communication with commercial sensors not yet adapted or optimized for millimeter scale computing, including a TI TMP101 temperature sensor.

5. REFERENCES

[1] P. Dutta and D. Culler. Epic: An open mote platform for application-driven design. In *IPSN'08 Proceedings of the Seventh International Conference on Information Processing in Sensor Networks (IPSN'08)*, Apr. 2008.
[2] Y. Lee, G. Kim, S. Bang, Y. Kim, I. Lee, P. Dutta, D. Sylvester, and D. Blaauw. A modular 1mm3 die-stacked sensing platform with optical communication and multi-modal energy harvesting. In *ISSCC'12 International Solid-State Circuits Conference*, Feb. 2012.

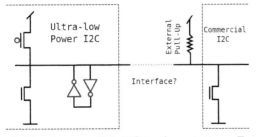

Figure 3: Two incompatible I2C implementations. Extreme care must be taken to not overpower the weak keeper. Driving signals to the low-power side requires manually driving the SDA line high both when writing and reading.

An Energy Harvesting Nonvolatile Sensor Node and Its Application to Distributed Moving Object Detection

Yongpan Liu, Yiqun Wang, Hongyang Jia, Shan Su, Jinghuan Wen, Wenzhu Zhang,
Lin Zhang and Huazhong Yang

Dept. of Electronic Engineering, Tsinghua University
Tsinghua National Laboratory for Information Science and Technology
Beijing, 100084, P.R.China
ypliu@tsinghua.edu.cn, yanghz@tsinghua.edu.cn

ABSTRACT

Energy harvesting sensor nodes based on real nonvolatile processors are demonstrated to show the desirable characteristics of those systems, such as no battery, zero standby power, microsecond-scale sleep and wake-up time, high resilience to random power failures and fine-grained power management. Furthermore, we show its applications to a distributed moving object detection system, one of novel nonvolatile computing systems.

Categories and Subject Descriptors

C.3 [**Special-Purpose and Application-Based Systems**]: Microprocessor/microcomputer applications

Keywords

Nonvolatile Sensor Node, Object Detection

1. INTRODUCTION

Energy harvesting techniques [1] provide a possible way to eliminate the need for a battery from wireless sensor nodes. However, power variations and intermittent availability patterns from the energy harvesting module make the traditional sensor nodes unreliable and even fail. This limitation comes from the restriction of volatile processors. Given a volatile processor based sensor node, the system state will become lost when powered off. Though it may be possible to store the system state to the off-chip nonvolatile memory, it would be both time and energy consuming. As a result, such back-up scheme is not fast enough and inefficient to follow the power intervals in a real energy harvesting module. In many applications, it is desirable for the processor to remember its state quickly and efficiently before powered off. When powered on, the processor can resume computing and sensing at the exact place before the power failure. In this way, the sensor node can work effectively in an energy harvesting environment.

Next, we will demonstrate the prototype of an energy-driven sensor node based on a nonvolatile processor. The proposed node consists of an energy harvesting module, a nonvolatile computing and sensing module and a power efficient wireless transceiver. It addresses the above challenges

facing the self-power sensor node based on the volatile processor. Based on the ferroelectric nonvolatile memory technologies, the nonvolatile processor [2] based sensor node has the following advantages: I) zero-standby power, II) instant on and off, III) high resilience to power failures, IV) fine-grained power management supported. To show the system's high resilience to power intervals and its continuous operation in an energy driven mode, a demo is built where the sensor node works continuously under a 1Khz square wave power supply. The setup is depicted in Fig. 1. Here, the sensor node is running a counter program. After each power failure, the system restarts from the value before the nearest power break point, instead of the initial system state. This system is one of our demonstration platforms.

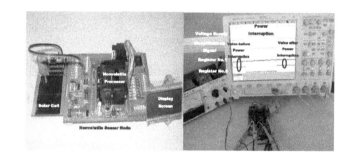

Figure 1: Proposed Energy Driven Nonvolatile Sensor Node

Furthermore, we will demonstrate a moving objects detection system based on the proposed energy-driven nonvolatile sensor node. This system is depicted in Fig. 2. Each nonvolatile sensor node is equipped with a solar cell energy harvester with no batteries. The energy source can be the sun outdoors or light source indoors. Given an energy source, the sensor nodes continuously count the number. When a moving object (e.g., a person) comes in between the light and the sensor node, power to the sensor node is cut off. The nonvolatile sensor node will remember the current state and wait for the moving object passes by. After that, the power supply is recovered, and the sensor node will continue to count. The counting number and related information can be stored in the local nonvolatile memory or wirelessly transferred to the remote data center. An object recognition algorithm is used in the data center to analyze the object occurring time and other information. A graphic user interface (GUI) is provided to show the real-time detecting results.

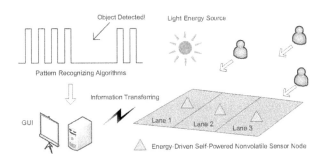

Figure 2: The Proposed Moving Objects Detection System

2. ON-SITE DEMONSTRATION

The on-site demonstration will contain two parts. The first one provides some stand alone energy driven sensor nodes for volunteers. Those sensor nodes will powered by the pressure, vibration or other mechanical energy harvesters. People can participate the activities and experience the new way in which nonvolatile sensor nodes work. The other interesting part shows the principle of energy driven technique in a moving objects detecting wireless network. It will accomplish the mission of counting people through the entrances. As is shown in Fig. 2, it consists of three sensor nodes representing three entrances from different directions, a light generator to simulate sunlight indoors, a data collection point and a GUI display.

We will call for volunteers in the exhibition hall, ask them to walk pass one of the three sensor nodes to block the light path from the light generator to the node. After a certain period, the collecting node will aggregate statistics from each node, calculate the number and the times that objects pass by the node and update the information on the GUI. A data collection point will work with a 2.4GHz 802.15.4 channel to acquire counting numbers from the sensor nodes. It can be considered as the gateway node with sufficient energy supply and strong processing capacity. We runs time synchronization and moving objects counting algorithm on it.

3. KEY TECHNIQUES

The most novel technique used in this demo is the nonvolatile processor based energy driven system. This system consists of the energy harvesting module (solar cell), the power management unit (PMU) and the nonvolatile processor (NVP), shown in Fig. 3. Only several square centimeters solar cell is needed to provide 6 V and more than 5 mW power supply under medium sun light which is sufficient for the processor. The PMU has functions of energy detection and voltage regulation. It measures the energy stored on the capacitor and generates activation signals to NVP as well as regulates voltage supply properly to the NVP.

The nonvolatile processor [2] is an emerging approach to nonvolatile computing. In our NVP, the registers are all replaced by the ferroelectric flip-flops. Its work mode can be changed between zero-leakage sleep mode and normal

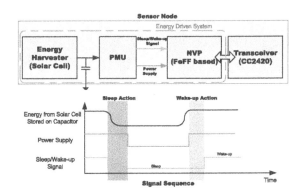

Figure 3: Architecture of Energy Driven Sensor Node and Its Controlling Signal Sequence

mode driven by intermittently available voltage supply. We designed a nonvolatile processor based on the hybrid ferroelectric CMOS process for the energy driven sensor node. We draw the transformations curves between the sleep and wake-up mode in Fig. 3. When the PMU detects a drop in the voltage level, it first generates the sleep signal and maintains the power supply via the capacitor until system state is stored in nonvolatile cells then cuts off the power. To wake up, the PMU detects power regaining, then provides power supply to the NVP until power is stable and after that generates the wake-up signal to restart the NVP. According to the measured results, the wake-up action consumes less than $100\,\mu s$ and the sleep action consumes around $50\,\mu s$ which reveals our system can work under a frequently interrupted power supply.

In the network level, a synchronization algorithm should be implemented among the collecting point and sensor nodes. After a certain period of time, the global time should be refreshed and synchronized with each node.

4. CONCLUSIONS

The energy driven nonvolatile sensor node provide an efficient way of eliminating power and lifetime constraint and the possibility of emergency detection based on energy interruption. Moreover it can continuously assemble information even in a poor power supply condition. We show above advantages in our moving object detection demo. Such NVP based systems offer tremendous potential at the interface of the cyber space and physical world.

5. ACKNOWLEDGEMENT

Thanks for many helpful suggestions from Prof. Xiaobo Sharon Hu. This work was supported by ROHM Co., NSFC under grant 60976032, ZX under contract 2010ZX03006-003-01 and 863 under 2009AA01Z130.

6. REFERENCES

[1] A. Kansal, J. Hsu, S. Zahedi, and M. Srivastava, "Power management in energy harvesting sensor networks," *ACM Transactions on Embedded Computing Systems (TECS)*, vol. 6, no. 4, p. 32, 2007.

[2] Y. Wang, Y. Liu, Y. Liu, D. Zhang, S. Li, B. Sai, M. Jiang, and H. Yang, "A compression-based area-efficient recovery architecture for nonvolatile processors," in *Proceedings of DATE*, 2012.

Demo Abstract: AudioDAQ: Turning the Mobile Phone's Headset Port into a Universal Data Acquisition Interface

Andrew Robinson
EECS Department
University of Michigan
Ann Arbor, MI 48109
androbin@umich.edu

Sonal Verma
EECS Department
University of Michigan
Ann Arbor, MI 48109
sonalv@umich.edu

Prabal Dutta
EECS Department
University of Michigan
Ann Arbor, MI 48109
prabal@umich.edu

ABSTRACT

Smartphone peripherals like the Square card reader, Red-Eye mini, and HiJack platform suggest a growing interest in using the headset port for more than just headsets. However, these peripherals only support sporadic activities in an efficient manner. Continuous sensing applications – like monitoring EKG signals – is possible but remains too inefficient for many realistic usage scenarios. We present AudioDAQ, a new sensor data acquisition platform. In contrast with prior work, AudioDAQ requires no hardware or software modifications on the phone, uses significantly less power, and allows continuous data capture over extended periods of time. The design is efficient because we draw all necessary power from the microphone bias voltage, and it is general because this voltage is present in every headset port. Data is modulated within the audible range, captured with the built-in voice recording app, and sent to a server for processing and storage. We show the viability of this approach by demonstrating an EKG monitor that can capture data continuously for hours.

Categories and Subject Descriptors

B.4.2 [**HARDWARE**]: Input/Output and Data Communications—*Input/Output Devices*; C.3 [**COMPUTER-COMMUNICATION NETWORKS**]: Special-Purpose and Application-Based Systems

General Terms

Design, Experimentation, Measurement, Performance

Keywords

Mobile phones, Energy harvesting, Phone peripherals, Audio communications, Participatory sensing

1. INTRODUCTION

Use of the mobile phone headset port as a peripheral interface is growing. A new class of devices including the HiJack platform [1] and RedEye mini [2] has recently emerged to exploit the ubiquitous nature of this port. However, many of these devices are only efficient for sporadic activities. Their power interfaces often harvest energy from waveforms continuously exported over the audio output channel(s) for

Peripheral Device	Run Power	Sample Power	Sample Time
AudioDAQ	66.7 mW	107 mW	32 hr
HiJack	205 mW	304 mW	11.5 hr
RedEye mini	451 mW	451 mW	7.5 hr

Table 1: Power draw breakdown of RedEye mini, HiJack, and AudioDAQ. For sensors requiring small amounts of power AudioDAQ allows for extended sampling periods.

power. Generating these waveforms often requires significant CPU time and prevents the phone from sleeping. As a result, the system as a whole consumes orders of magnitude greater power than delivered to the hardware peripheral itself, making the designs impractical for continuous or long-running applications.

We recognize that there exists a class of sensors that require a continuous, yet minuscule, amount of power to operate over extended intervals. This class includes biometric sensors such as EKG monitors and environmental sensors, such as electrochemical gas detectors and soil moisture probes. These sensors are well-matched for use in mobile phones, which provide rich auxiliary data in the form of location services, orientation detection, and context via annotation from the end-user.

In this demonstration, we present AudioDAQ, a new platform for continuous data acquisition using the headset port of a mobile phone. Our system differs from current peripheral interfaces by drawing all necessary power from the microphone bias voltage, and by making use of the built-in audio recording application, encoding all data in an analog signal within the audio passband. These differences are key in achieving much lower system power consumption, as shown in Table 1, and making our design more universal among smart and feature phones. The microphone bias voltage typically used to power amplifying circuitry found in electret microphones is provided for "free" by the phone, requiring no CPU time to generate. The built-in audio recording app makes use of optimized hardware audio encoding facilities. Both features were found in every phone we surveyed, suggesting that our design maybe universal.

The recorded data could include overlaid audio annotations, and the combined data maybe sent via e-mail or MMS to a cloud-based processor where the original signal is reconstructed and optional audio annotations are extracted and added to the data.

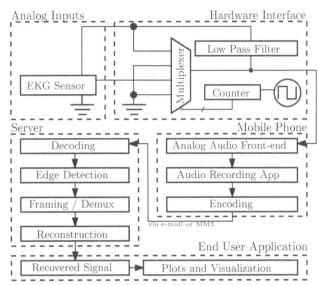

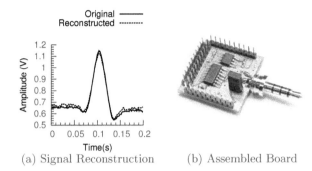

(a) Signal Reconstruction   (b) Assembled Board

Figure 1: System architecture. By using the built-in audio recording utility, and offloading the processing to cloud-based servers the load placed on the mobile phone is significantly diminished and sample time is extended.

Figure 2: (a) shows the overlay of the original signal, and the final output after feeding the signal through (b) AudioDAQ and reconstructing it on the server.

2. SYSTEM ARCHITECTURE

AudioDAQ is a low-power, continuous data acquisition platform for the mobile phone. It uses the headset port's microphone line to *both* power external sensors and acquire their data. Filters separate the power and data pathways from each other. A multiplexer circuit breaks up DC and low-frequency AC sensor signals to enable them to pass through the band-limited audio channel (with a typical passband of 20 Hz to 15-20 kHz). The multiplexed (or modulated) signal can be compressed efficiently (using a phone's voice memo application and native codecs) for subsequent processing offsite by remote servers. As seen in Figure 1, the architecture offloads the majority of the post processing to a remote server to allow for efficient data capture.

2.1 Acquiring Analog Sensor Data

The typical audio front-end can directly acquire signals in the 20 Hz to 20 kHz range with amplitudes between 1-25 mV. But, many signals have principal frequency components below 20 Hz, or consist entirely of a DC component, making them impossible to pass.

We use an analog multiplexer as a poor man's modulator. By switching at 1.5 kHz, a frequency within the passband of the audio system this allows the "modulated" signal to pass. Our system achieves a sample rate of 375 Hz.

We calibrate the signal by time-division multiplexing the microphone line between ground, the signal, and a reference voltage. By expressing the magnitude of the signal as a value between ground and the reference voltage, we can recover the original DC value. The simultaneous capture of multiple analog signals is possible via addition of channels to the multiplexer. Figure 2(a) shows the reconstructed signal overlaid with the original signal, scaled using the known reference voltage. This shows we can recover both AC and DC components of the signal.

By adding a momentary push-button disconnect switch between AudioDAQ and the phone we can temporarily en-

able the built-in microphone, allowing capture of voice annotations. AudioDAQ is distinctive enough from voice data that separation is easily done server-side.

2.2 Cloud Processing of Voice and Sensor Data

Cloud processing of the data frees us from the limited processing capabilities of a mobile platform, and makes it possible to use the built-in voice recording application. This gives us greater flexibility in the signal processing algorithms we can employ and allows AudioDAQ to work universally on phones where custom software is impossible for budgetary or technical reasons.

Data can be sent via e-mail or MMS message to a server, where the original signal is recovered, voice annotations are extracted, and graphs are automatically generated and sent back to the user via e-mail for analysis. The data may be stored on the server for later analysis and use.

3. DEMONSTRATION

In this demo, we show the full operation of the Audio-DAQ system. We capture a short 5-10s sample of EKG data from a user using the voice recording app on an iPhone attached to our system, shown in Figure 2(b), add a voice annotation at the end of the capture with the name of the participant, and then send this recording to our server for processing.

The data is reconstructed, voice data are extracted and processed using a voice recognition library, and finally a graph is constructed, containing the EKG waveform and the annotation data.

4. ACKNOWLEDGMENTS

This material is supported in part by NSF Awards #0964120 ("CNS-NeTS") and #1059372 ("CI-ADDO-NEW").

5. REFERENCES

[1] Y.-S. Kuo, S. Verma, T. Schmid, and P. Dutta. Hijacking power and bandwidth from the mobile phone's audio interface. In *DEV'10: Proceedings of the First Annual Symposium on Computing for Development*, Dec. 2010.

[2] ThinkFlood, Inc. RedEye Mini universal remote for iPhone, iPod Touch & iPad. http://thinkflood.com/products/redeye-mini/, Apr. 2011.

Demo Abstract: Scaling the Wireless AC Power Meter

Samuel DeBruin
EECS Department
University of Michigan
Ann Arbor, MI 48109
sdebruin@umich.edu

Jerome Grunnagle
EECS Department
University of Michigan
Ann Arbor, MI 48109
tgrunn@umich.edu

Prabal Dutta
EECS Department
University of Michigan
Ann Arbor, MI 48109
prabal@umich.edu

ABSTRACT

We explore the seemingly trivial problem of scaling the AC power meter to a cubic-inch form factor. This small volume, necessary for unobtrusive inline plug-load monitoring, requires aggressive electromechanical codesign and 3-D electronics packaging. However, the key scaling challenge across both size and efficiency lies in the power supply architecture and load power. Hence, contrary to conventional wisdom, power is not free, even if a device is attached to wall power. Since many existing power supplies exhibit high baseline power draw, this leads to poor efficiency and runs counter to the green goals of many applications. We claim there are two paths to scaling the plug-load meter to a space- and power-efficient design point without sacrificing measurement fidelity: (i) by duty cycling in some cases and (ii) by using an off-line switching regulator that is not capacitor-fed. To evaluate our claims, we design a modular power meter architecture, implement several design alternatives, and evaluate their size, efficiency, and cost. We show that an energy-efficient, cubic-inch-sized wireless power meter is viable. Our design is $10\times$ smaller, draws $3\times$ less standby power, and still offers equivalent measurement fidelity as the best previously reported results.

Categories and Subject Descriptors

B.m [**Hardware**]: Miscellaneous

General Terms

Design, Experimentation

Keywords

Energy Metering, IEEE 802.15.4, Sensor Networks

1. INTRODUCTION

We present PowerCube, an IEEE 802.15.4-compatible AC power meter designed to fit inside a cubic inch form factor. The size constraint, the largest difference between PowerCube and existing meters, comes from external factors. NEMA sockets have 1.5" spacing and typical surge protector strips have 1.1" spacing. With the cubic inch constraint, PowerCube is suitable for dense monitoring situations and studies of miscellaneous electrical loads.

Prior work has assumed that in AC metering applications, power comes for free [2]. However, this is only the case if size is not a constraint. When size is a significant constraint, then component sizing must be adjusted downward, forcing a comparable change in the ability of the power supply to either deliver power to the sensor or dissipate (waste) power. And, since the power dissipation grows quadratically with load current and linearly with surface area (quadratically with nominal component dimension), but volume grows cubicly with nominal component dimension, reducing load current has a super linear benefit on system size.

2. SYSTEM ARCHITECTURE

The PowerCube system can be broken down into three high level components - power supply, energy metering, and core control/radio. Figure 1 (a) shows the three power supplies evaluated in producing the system. PowerCube's six faces can be seen in Figure 1 (b). System components are tied together through two buses: a 12-pin data bus running "horizontally" between faces 1, 2, 3, and 4, and an 8-pin power bus running "vertically" between the base (face 0) and the power distribution face (face 5). This standard bus interface, along with the fact that each core component occupies its own face, allows for drop-in replacement of any of these components without redesigning the entire system.

In shrinking the wireless AC power meter, the inner volume of the cube is the major constrained resource. Each face has 0.75" x 0.75" of printed circuit board area (0.5" x 0.5" after inter-side connectors) but the volume is shared among all six faces. All high-volume components must occupy the interior space as the space between the PCB cube and the plastic enclose is less than 0.04". Additionally, The power prongs require much of the inner volume of the cube.

2.1 Power Supply

Shrinking the power supply is the major obstacle to fitting a power meter within a cubic inch. PowerCube rectifies 120V 60Hz AC with the Supertex SR-086 off-line inductorless switching regulator. This device uses a relatively low profile high-voltage transistor to interface with wall AC and an aluminum output capacitor to buffer energy. The output capacitor scales directly with load power but all other components remain constant. Along with its support components at max power (900mW output), the SR-086 occupies 0.063 in^3, 51% of the usable inner volume of the cube.

Prior work on power metering implemented the AC-DC power supply using the Supertex SR-10 capacitor coupled switched shunt regulator [1]. This design requires a high-

(a) Test Supplies   (b) PowerCube 6-Face Breakout   (c) PowerCube

Figure 1: The progression of PowerCube. En route to the final system was (a) an examination of the three power supplies to be tested, (b) a development setup providing debugging and interfacing opportunities, and (c) the fully-integrated system.

voltage input capacitor to interface with the wall. The capacitor functions as a voltage divider that must drop substantially all of the line voltage. Additionally, an aluminum output capacitor buffers energy as in the SR-086. Both of these components scale directly with load power, resulting in a power supply that dramatically increases with load. As seen in Figure 2 (a), the SR-10 would be limited to 26.7mW in order to fit inside the cubic inch.

A final option in low volume AC-DC power supplies is the LNK302. This regulator has a standard set of components, its volume does not scale with load power, but those components are so large as to make that option unusable for the cubic inch.

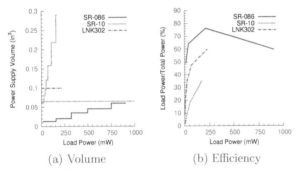

(a) Volume   (b) Efficiency

Figure 2: Volume and efficiency of the three power supplies studied. The horizontal line in (a) represents the maximum volume to fit inside the cube. SR-086 and SR-10 volumes increase with load current as the capacitors required get larger. The LNK302 has a standard set of components for all outputs, resulting in a fixed volume. The SR-10 and LNK302 have limited power output compared to the SR-086, but the key issue is power supply volume.

2.2 Energy Metering

Energy metering on PowerCube is done through the Analog Devices ADE7753 single phase multifunction energy metering IC. This compact package operates on the Serial Peripheral Interface (SPI) and can report active, reactive, and apparent power as well as rms voltage and current.

2.3 Core Control

Processing and wireless radio on PowerCube is accomplished through a combination of the MSP430F1611 microprocessor and CC2420 radio. This combination provides several benefits over other microcontroller and radio options. First, the MSP is a low-active-current device; ideal for a power constrained system. The radio, although much higher power than other system components, is still considered a low power device and can operate within the power confines of PowerCube.

Second, these devices are small. The usable surface area of each face is 0.5" x 0.5". The processor and radio collectively occupy face 4 - one on each side of the PCB. If either of the components were larger than roughly 0.35" on a side they, along with their support components, would not be usable in this size constrained design.

Finally, the CC2420 has both IPv6 and ZigBee network stacks, making it ideal for the multi-hop mesh network that PowerCube requires to operate.

3. DEMONSTRATION

This demo shows the feasibility of wireless AC power metering within a cubic inch form factor. Further, PowerCube accomplishes this metering without itself drawing much power.

We will show PowerCube monitoring load current and transmitting this information to an edge node. By using a commercial power line meter we will show not only that PowerCube's measurements are accurate but that the power overhead required to operate it is very low.

4. REFERENCES

[1] X. Jiang, S. Dawson-Haggerty, P. Dutta, and D. Culler. Design and implementation of a high-fidelity ac metering network. In *IPSN '09: Proceedings of the 2009 International Conference on Information Processing in Sensor Networks*, pages 253–264, Apr. 2009.

[2] T. Weng, B. Balaji, S. Dutta, R. Gupta, and Y. Agarwal. Managing plug-loads for demand response within buildings. In *BuildSys 2011: Proceedings of the 3rd ACM Workshop on Embedded Sensing Systems for Energy-Efficiency in Buildings*, Sept. 2011.

Demo Abstract:

RF Time-of-Flight Ranging on Commodity Software Radios

Benjamin P. Kempke
Computer Science and Engineering
University of Michigan
Ann Arbor, MI, 48109
bpkempke@eecs.umich.edu

Prabal Dutta
Computer Science and Engineering
University of Michigan
Ann Arbor, MI, 48109
prabal@eecs.umich.edu

ABSTRACT

Recent advances in RF ranging techniques have shown superior performance in difficult RF environments but either lack the practicality of a real-time implementation or lack flexibility through purpose-built hardware. We present SR2, a super-resolution ranging platform developed for the software radio environment. SR2 achieves low resource utilization and hardware complexity requirements through a coherent RF design, making SR2 realizable on commodity software radios.

Categories and Subject Descriptors

B.m [**Hardware**]: Miscellaneous

Keywords

FPGA, Software Radio, Super-Resolution, Time-of-Flight

1. INTRODUCTION

A plethora of papers assume that radio frequency (RF) time-of-flight (ToF) ranging is a basic primitive on which more sophisticated services, such as localization, can be built on. Unfortunately, a paucity of systems that support RF ToF makes evaluating these services in realistic situations nearly impossible. We present SR2, a system which enables compact realization of super-resolution ranging algorithms on commodity software radios. The open implementation of our design allows for easy adaptation as a research tool by those involved in super-resolution ranging research. SR2's simple implementation will also ease the realization of RF ranging functionality on existing low-power digital radio technologies.

2. DESIGN

Realized in the software radio's FPGA fabric, SR2 incorporates coherent RF techniques to provide fast and accurate characterizations of the observed RF channel impulse response between wireless nodes while keeping system complexity low. Our demo showcases our design along with a basic IFT-based [1] super-resolution ToF ranging protocol. Other super-resolution techniques can be easily tested on top of our existing interface.

Previous ranging systems either employ complex designs to compute super-resolution range estimates or ignore the multipath environment, leading to poor indoor performance. Table 1 shows the resource utilization of SR2 when implemented on a USRP1 software radio. Of particular note are the low memory requirements, low crystal accuracy, and no peripheral digital signal processor.

2.1 System Architecture

Figure 2 shows the system architecture of our coherent RF ranging design. The datapath is fully pipelined to process incoming RF baseband data at full speed, or one 12-bit I/Q sample per cycle. This pipelining allows range estimates to be calculated in near real-time. Stalls are forced during impulse response extraction - a short final step performed to extract Time of Arrival (ToA) estimates from the recorded data.

Baseband I/Q samples from the software radio front-end ADCs are first passed through a Costas loop, which provides the notion of coherency in our design. Coherency allows for the clock drift between wireless nodes to be accounted for, providing useful information for later portions of the datapath.

After the Costas loop, a BPSK demodulator is used to snoop the incoming data stream. All ranging information, protocol synchronization, and the ranging sequence itself are communicated using BPSK modulation over the RF channel.

Once the incoming range sequence is detected, a pipelined 256-point Radix-2^2 FFT core is used to convert the sampled range sequence into the frequency domain. Using frequency-domain techniques, the FFT data is time-shifted using the supplied timing error from the Costas loop. This process is repeated and the range sequence is averaged over time to produce a finalized representation of the refined range sequence.

After the range sequence refinement is complete, an estimate of the ToA is required in order to obtain an estimated range. ToA estimates are extracted from the calculated impulse response of the wireless environment. The impulse response is calculated through deconvolution of the refined range sequence with the expected range sequence. Using this calculated channel impulse response, the IFT-based super-resolution algorithm heuristically determines the time of arrival as the leading 6% height of the impulse response. Range is lastly determined through the calculation of the ToF of a range sequence exchange between nodes using the ToA estimates obtained.

Figure 1: Ranging demo consisting of SR2 implemented on two commodity USRP1 software radios. Range estimates are updated automatically between two autonomous nodes, then sent to a computer for display and visualization of the channel impulse response.

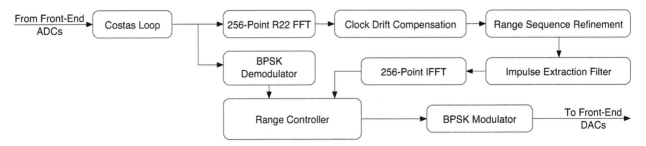

Figure 2: SR2 system architecture designed for software radio showing the data flow between system modules.

	SR2
Logic Elements	10,130
Memory	37kbit
DSP	None
Crystal Accuracy	15ppm
Range Accuracy	0.7m
Update Rate	>1000/sec possible
Bandwidth	64 MHz

Table 1: SR2 system implementation specifications on the USRP1 software radio platform.

Node 1	Idle	SYN	TXSEQ		RXSEQ		RXTOA/ TOACALC	TXTOA
Node 2	Listen		RXSEQ		TXSEQ/TOACALC		TXTOA	RXTOA

Figure 3: Ranging protocol flow. Exchange is initiated through transmission of a synchronization packet (SYN). The ranging sequence then immediately follows (TXSEQ), with the second node listening (RXSEQ). The nodes then trade roles with the first node listening. Lastly, ToA estimates are traded between nodes to come to a final ToF range estimate (RXTOA/TXTOA).

2.2 Ranging Protocol

Figure 3 shows the protocol used in performing ranging operations. Node A starts by sending a SYN packet to synchronize communications and request a ranging estimate to an addressed node. Immediately following, Node A sends a repeating ranging sequence for a pre-determined amount of time (denoted TXSEQ) while Node B listens (RXSEQ). The number of repetitions can be modified to increase SNR in demanding environments.

Node B follows by performing simultaneous transmission of the ranging sequence (TXSEQ) along with calculation of the recorded ToA (TOACALC) while Node A listens (RXSEQ). Now that the range sequence exchange is complete, Node B transmits its calculated ToA estimate to Node A (TXTOA and RXTOA) while it computes the recorded ToA from the last recorded range sequence. The ranging protocol is complete when Node A optionally transmits the calculated ToA estimate back to Node B if it is requested.

3. DEMO

This demo shows the feasibility of performing super-resolution RF ranging on commodity hardware. Operating on 5.8GHz, two USRP1 software radios will be loaded with the SR2 system. Range requests will be periodically requested between the nodes, and all ranging information will be transferred from one of the wireless nodes to a connected computer for data visualization.

The current range estimate, a histogram of recent range estimates, and a graph of the measured impulse response will be visualized on the attached computer. The range between the two software radios will be adjustable through direct movement of the free node. Dynamic changes in the environment such as body movement have a great impact on the observed shape of the impulse response. The live-update impulse response visualization provides an intuitive understanding of the difficulties faced in performing accurate range estimation in indoor environments.

4. REFERENCES

[1] T. Sathyan, D. Humphrey, and M. Hedley. Wasp: A system and algorithms for accurate radio localization using low-cost hardware. *IEEE Transactions on Systems, Man, and Cybernetics – Part C*, 41(2):211–222, Mar. 2011.

Personal Building Controls

Andrew Krioukov, David Culler
Computer Science Department
University of California, Berkeley
{krioukov, culler}@cs.berkeley.edu

ABSTRACT

Buildings are some of the largest energy consumers in the world and yet occupants are regularly dissatisfied with the interior environment in large part due to thermal discomfort [7]. Studies show that given personal control over their environment, occupants are comfortable in a much larger range of ambient temperatures [2]. We present a personalized control smartphone application designed with the dual goals of increasing occupant comfort and achieving building-wide energy savings.

The application allows occupants to directly control the lighting and heating/cooling in their vicinity. Using wireless localization combined with data from existing sensors in the building, we estimate room occupancy and use this to dynamically adjust ventilation and air conditioning to save energy in the building.

Categories and Subject Descriptors

H.4.3 [**Information Systems Applications**]: Communications Applications

1. INTRODUCTION

We present an experimental prototype of personal building controls built on top of a traditional commercial building lighting and HVAC control system combined with a wireless sensor net deployment of power meters and relays [8]. Modern commercial buildings are typically designed to minimize occupant control and interaction; windows are often inoperable and thermostats are centrally managed. The traditional view is that giving control to occupants is hard to implement, reduces energy efficiency and may lead to control problems. Yet occupants play a crucial role in building power management because ultimately they are the intended end users of energy. Occupants define the building operating requirements including lighting levels, ventilation, heating, cooling and plug loads. Using a control interface based on smartphones, we provide occupants with direct building control, give feedback on their personal contribution to building energy consumption and estimate room occupancy levels, providing both increased comfort and energy savings.

Our smartphone application combines energy consumption feedback, localization and actionable buttons that immediately affect energy use. Occupants use the interface

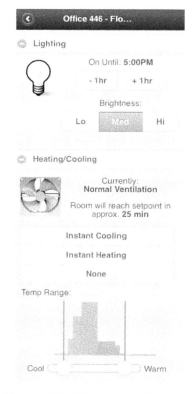

Figure 1: Personal building control smartphone app. Control settings move with the user. A backend process resolves conflicts and optimizes HVAC.

shown in Figure 1 to specify preferences for lighting and temperature range. Feedback is provided in the form of a scale based on a combination of metered plug load power from a power strip at the occupant's desk and preference settings. The feedback encourages occupants to specify wider temperature ranges and lower brightness settings. It also notifies users when they leave their desk for an extended time while continuing to consume energy from their desk power strip. This encourages users to turn off or sleep devices when leaving their desk. The application additionally has a remote off button to disconnect the power strip remotely if a monitor or other device was mistakenly left on.

Prior systems have focused on monitoring energy consumption [8, 6] and on providing online lighting controls [9]. In this work we combine energy feedback with actionable buttons that immediately change HVAC and lighting settings to reduce energy consumption. Additionally, we use localization to allow preferences to move with the users and to track room occupancy for energy efficiency.

2. DESIGN

Figure 2: Personal building control system design.

Our system is implemented in Sutardja Dai Hall at UC Berkeley. It consists of three major components shown in Figure 2: a smartphone application, building controls and existing building sensors and actuators. The smartphone application is show in Figure 1. It gives occupants an interface to specify a preferred temperature range using a relative scale from cool to warm. Occupants are bad at estimating precise room temperatures and studies show that comfortable temperature ranges vary, however, given personal control occupants are comfortable in a significantly wider range [2]. When given just the temperature range control we observed that occupants regularly pushed the sliders to 100% leading to inefficient continuous air conditioning. In response we added instant heating and cooling buttons to provide temporary blasts of air that can rapidly heat or cool a room without a long-term energy impact.

The app collects a list of WiFi access point signal strengths and sends this to the server for localization [10]. The estimated location is shown to the user. If the location is incorrect the user can manually click on a map to select the correct location. All corrections are used as additional training data. On the server, user locations are combined with per-floor power measurements and lighting states obtained from the building control system to estimate occupancy. Room ventilation rates are set to 15 CFM of fresh air per person based on estimated occupancy and as required by CA TITLE 24 [3] thus saving energy by allowing the supply fans to run slower when rooms are less occupied. Temperatures in rooms that appear to be unoccupied, with lights turned off and no known phone users in the vicinity, are allowed to float in a 10F range saving energy on air conditioning.

The server is also responsible for resolving conflicts among users. A number of policies are possible including using weighted voting, intersection, average, maximum or using a negotiation protocol. We are experimenting with all of these options. For temperature ranges we currently take the intersection of all users' preferences in a single control zone and fall back to using a narrow range around the average desired temperature if the intersection is empty. For lighting we take the maximum brightness.

Sensing and actuation are done by interfacing with the existing building control system augmented with a deployment of ACme [8] wireless power meters and relays. We communicate with all devices through sMAP [4] gateways that we develop. This allows the control code to use a uniform high-level protocol for accessing all devices. We use the BACnet [1] industrial control protocol to communicate with field panels controlling sensors and actuators throughout the building. BACnet allows discovery of the available sense and control points and reading/writing names, descriptions and values. A major challenge is mapping the BACnet control point names to physical locations. At the moment this is a labor intensive process requiring finding device locations in the building management system GUI.

For power metering we use a 6loWPAN/IPv6 mesh network of ACme devices measuring a power strip for each occupant. This is the same setup as used in [5] for a 450 node deployment studying plug-loads which were found to account for nearly 40% of energy use in that building. By notifying users if they leave significant loads turned on after leaving their desks and by allowing remote turn-off, we aim to reduce plug loads in addition to HVAC and lighting loads.

3. DEMONSTRATION

Our demo consists of two parts: (1) a remote dashboard of the system running in Berkeley showing the complete HVAC controls and (2) an on-site demo of a simulated office environment showing the lighting and plug-load components.

The remote component shows live updating time series plots of air handler power, room temperatures and power consumption in several unoccupied rooms in Sutardja Dai Hall. Attendees can click on a map to simulate visiting a location and use the phone application interface to remotely affect the real room temperature. A live fan power plot shows energy savings from choosing wider temperature ranges. A floor-level power meter shows energy savings from changing the lighting level or disabling power strips.

The on-site demonstration consists of several sets of lights and small appliances simulating cubicles spread out in the room. Attendees can download our demo android application or use one of our phones to run the app. Users specify lighting brightness preferences that affect the nearest "cubicle" as they move from around. Users are also shown their cubicle power consumption in real-time and given feedback suggesting remotely turning off devices when walking away from their cubicle with appliances left on.

4. REFERENCES

[1] ASHRAE. ANSI/ASHRAE standard 135-1995, BACnet, 1995.
[2] BRAGER, G., PALIAGA, G., AND DE DEAR, R. Operable windows, personal control and occupant comfort. In *ASHRAE* (2004).
[3] CA ENERGY COMMISSION. California's energy efficiency standards for residential and nonresidential buildings, 2008.
[4] DAWSON-HAGGERTY, S., JIANG, X., TOLLE, G., ORTIZ, J., AND CULLER, D. smap: a simple measurement and actuation profile for physical information. In *SenSys '10* (2010).
[5] DAWSON-HAGGERTY, S., LANZISERA, S., TANEJA, J., BROWN, R., AND CULLER, D. @scale: Insights from a large, long-lived appliance energy wsn. In *IPSN'12* (2012).
[6] HSU, J., MOHAN, P., JIANG, X., ORTIZ, J., SHANKAR, S., DAWSON-HAGGERTY, S., AND CULLER, D. Hbci: Human-building-computer interaction. In *BuildSys'10* (2010).
[7] HUIZENGA, C., ABBASZADEH, S., ZAGREUS, L., AND ARENS, E. Air quality and thermal comfort in office buildings. In *Healthy Buildings* (2006).
[8] JIANG, X., DAWSON-HAGGERTY, S., DUTTA, P., AND CULLER, D. Design and implementation of a high-fidelity ac metering network. In *IPSN'09* (2009).
[9] KRIOUKOV, A., DAWSON-HAGGERTY, S., LEE, L., REHMANE, O., AND CULLER, D. A living laboratory study in personalized automated lighting controls. In *BuildSys'11* (2011).
[10] KRISHNAKUMAR, A. AND KRISHNAN, P. The theory and practice of signal strength-based location estimation. In *CollaborateCom'05* (2005).

Demo Abstract: SEPTIMU – Continuous In-situ Human Wellness Monitoring and Feedback using Sensors Embedded in Earphones

Dezhi Hong[1], Ben Zhang[1], Qiang Li[2], Shahriar Nirjon[2]
Robert Dickerson[2], Guobin Shen[1], Xiaofan Jiang[1], John A. Stankovic[2]

[1]Microsoft Research Asia
No.5 Danling Street, Haidian District
Beijing, P.R.China, 100080

[2]University of Virginia
Department of CS, University of Virginia
Charlottesville, Virginia, USA, 22904-4740

{dzhong1989, nebgnahz, warren.q.li}@gmail.com, smn8z@virginia.edu
rfdickerson@gmail.com, {jacky.shen, fxjiang}@microsoft.com, stankovic@cs.virginia.edu

ABSTRACT

A mobile phone, as a pervasive device, has great potential in human wellness monitoring. In this demo, we first present the design and implementation of our hardware - SEPTIMU. SEPTIMU consists of a small baseboard and a pair of tiny sensor boards embedded inside conventional earphones. The baseboard provides power conversion and data communication through the normal audio jack interface. The embedded sensor board is $1\times1\text{cm}^2$ and integrates 3-axis accelerometer, gyroscope, thermometer, photodiode and microphone. Secondly, we evaluate SEPTIMU using a mobile application that continuously monitors body posture and provides feedback to the user.

Categories and Subject Descriptors

C.3 [SPECIAL-PURPOSE AND APPLICATION-BASED SYSTEMS]: Real-time and embedded systems

General Terms

Measurement, Performance, Design, Experimentation.

Keywords

Mobile Sensing, In-situ Monitoring, HiJack, Earphone.

1. INTRODUCTION

m-Health is gaining attention in both academia and industry in recent years as people become increasingly conscious of their everyday health conditions, and as mobile phones become much more capable than just simple messaging and gaming. The mobile phone is one of the few accessories that many people carry on a daily basis, and provides not only a computing platform, but also a networking interface and a range of sensors. While previous works [2, 3, 4] and commercial products (such as Sony Ericsson's MH907) have taken advantages of these on-device sensors for human-centric sensing applications, we augment the mobile phone with a suite of additional sensors embedded into both sides of the earphone. We utilize the conventional earphone jack for both power and communication to avoid using extra devices. This allows us to provide opportunistic and continuously in-situ human wellness monitoring.

SEPTIMU is a mobile phone accessory, comprised of a pair of sensor boards embedded into conventional earphones and communicates with the phone through the audio jack. We

choose to integrate sensors directly inside ear buds because earphones are perhaps the only piece of accessory that every mobile phone user has, and uses on a daily basis. And a set of sensors positioned near the ears can provide additional sensing modalities important for many wellness applications. For instance, the MEMS microphone placed inside the ear canal can act as a stethoscope to detect heartbeat, or placed on other parts of the body for diagnosing other symptoms. This brings convenience to the user and her doctor in remote locations.

In addition, with two sets of sensors, such as the IMU sensors, that are always positioned at fixed body positions (i.e., ears) SEPTIMU is able to provide more accurate motion detection and more subtle motion discrimination than single devices or ones placed elsewhere on body.

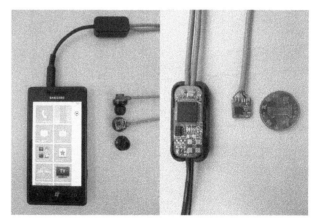

Figure 1. SEPTIMU hardware: the larger board is the baseboard ($3.4\times1.4\text{ cm}^2$), and the smaller board is the sensor board embedded in earphones ($1\times1\text{ cm}^2$).

2. HARDWARE DESIGN

Figure 1 shows SEPTIMU's sensor board and baseboard enclosed in a small box connected to mobile phone through the standard audio jack interface. The current version of SEPTIMU consists of two parts: two sensor boards and a baseboard. Each sensor board includes an IMU (InvenSense MPU6050, with 6-axis accelerometer and gyroscope), one thermometer (DS18B20), one photodiode (BH1750FVI), one MEMS analog microphone (ADMP401) and a LED. All of these sensors are placed onto a single double-sided board with a dimension of $1\times1\text{ cm}^2$, and integrate into a conventional earphone.

The baseboard design is based on HiJack [1], and contains a TI MSP430F1611 microprocessor and peripheral circuits for harvesting power directly from sound generated by the mobile phone. Similarly, the microprocessor transmits data to the mobile phone via the microphone ring on the audio jack as shown in Figure 2. In our design, the baseboard takes the position of the conventional line-controller.

Figure 2. Audio plug and pin. The pin connections are: (1) left earphone (tip), (2) right earphone (ring), (3) common/ground (ring), and (4) microphone (sleeve).

3. SYSTEM DESIGN

The firmware running on the baseband is based on TinyOS. The microprocessor collects data periodically from the two sensor boards through I^{2}C and one-wire bus; the majority of data come from the IMU set (with a full scale of ±2g/s for accelerometer and ±250° /s for gyroscope), which comprises 6-axis data with two bytes for each axis. The microprocessor sends data via the microphone ring on the audio jack to the mobile phone using Manchester coding. Data received from the audio jack interface is decoded inside the mobile phone by our driver at a low BER. We found that the average mobile phone at a sample rate of 44.1 kHz can transmit data reliably at a rate of more than 500 bytes/sec, which is enough to support our data communication requirements.

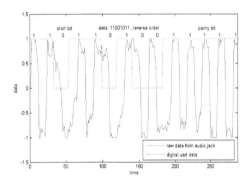

Figure 3. Raw data recovered from the audio jack (blue) and Manchester-decoded data (red).

4. CASE STUDY

We evaluate our system using a specific application to test its usability and accuracy. In this scenario, a user wears a pair of earphones integrated with SEPTIMU to monitor his posture. Combining the output of accelerometer and gyroscope from the user's head, we can determine how long the user remains in the same posture and decide whether he is lacking movement (see Figure 4a). The system can send a notification to the user and alert him to move in the case he has stayed too long in the same posture. At the same time, we are able to monitor the user's heartbeat with the microphone (shown in figure 4b). With this system, we see some opportunities and advantages provided by

the pair of SEPTIMU integrated into an average earphone. For example, the combined data from IMU, microphone, thermometer of continuous monitoring can be used to keep a health diary for users.

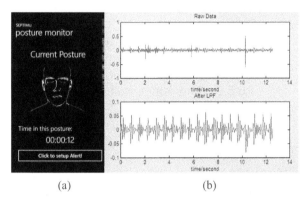

(a)   (b)

Figure 4. (a) Head posture monitoring application on Windows Phone; (b) Heartbeat detection with microphones in SEPTIMU.

5. FUTURE WORK

Current applications only utilize the IMU and microphone to some degree; we plan to develop applications using the other sensors on the board to provide better in-situ human wellness monitoring. In addition, we plan to explore more efficient ways for feedback.

6. DEMO SCRIPT

During the demo, a user will use SEPTIMU with her and exercise different motions as she desires, such as walking or remaining motionless. We will demonstrate that our system is able to detect how long a same posture lasts and gives feedback based on a model of healthy behaviors. We could also track the head movement and user may use it to ensure the correctness of a head exercise.

7. REFERENCES

[1] Y.S. Kuo, T. Schmid, and P. Dutta. 2010. Hijacking power and bandwidth from the mobile phone's audio interface. In *Proceedings of the 8th ACM Conference on Embedded Networked Sensor Systems* (SenSys '10). ACM, New York, NY, USA.

[2] S. Consolvo, D. W. McDonald, and et al. 2008. Activity sensing in the wild: a field trial of ubifit garden. In *Proceedings of the twenty-sixth annual SIGCHI conference on Human factors in computing systems* (CHI '08). ACM, New York, NY, USA.

[3] Q. Li, G. Zhou, and J. A. Stankovic. 2008. Accurate, fast fall detection using posture and context information. In *Proceedings of the 6th ACM conference on Embedded network sensor systems* (SenSys '08). ACM, New York, NY, USA

[4] M.Z. Poh, K. Kim, and et al. 2009. Heartphones: Sensor Earphones and Mobile Application for Non-obtrusive Health Monitoring, *Wearable Computers,. ISWC '09. International Symposium on* , vol., no., pp.153-154, 4-7 Sept. 2009

Strawman: Resolving Collisions in Bursty Low-Power Wireless Networks

Fredrik Österlind, Luca Mottola, Thiemo Voigt, Nicolas Tsiftes, Adam Dunkels
{fros,luca,thiemo,nvt,adam}@sics.se
Swedish Institute of Computer Science
Box 1263, SE-164 29 Kista, Sweden

ABSTRACT

Low-power wireless networks must leverage radio duty cycling to reduce energy consumption, but duty cycling drastically increases the risk of radio collisions, resulting in power-expensive retransmissions or data loss. We present Strawman, a contention resolution mechanism designed for low-power duty-cycled networks that experience traffic bursts. Strawman efficiently resolves network contention, mitigates the hidden terminal problem, and has zero overhead unless activated to resolve data collisions. Our testbed experiments show that Strawman instantaneously provides increased network capacity when needed, allocates the available bandwidth evenly among contenders, and increases energy efficiency in multi-hop collection networks compared to the traditionally used random backoff.

Categories and Subject Descriptors

C.2.2 [**Computer-Communication Networks**]: Network Protocols

Keywords

Low-power wireless, traffic bursts, sensor networks, duty cycling

1. INTRODUCTION

Low-power wireless networks employ radio duty cycling to reduce energy consumption. Duty cycling decreases the opportunities to receive data, since the radio is mostly turned off. As a result, the risk of data collisions increase, and is further aggravated in networks that experience traffic bursts. Event-driven networks, such as alarm applications [2, 17], remain quiescent for the majority of the time. When an event is detected, a surge of traffic must be handled by the network before it can return to quiescence. Such sudden bursts of traffic cause radio collisions and power-expensive retransmissions in the network, and motivate the use of complex traffic-adaptive duty-cycling mechanisms or statically over-provisioned networks.

We address the problem of data collisions in duty-cycled networks and present Strawman, a contention resolution mechanism

that copes with hidden terminals and is designed for receiver-initiated duty-cycled protocols. In Section 3 we illustrate the design of Strawman and how it instantaneously and dynamically provides increased network capacity when needed. Strawman is activated upon detecting data collisions. In absence of them, Strawman has zero runtime overhead. The Strawman approach to resolving collisions resembles the practice of drawing straws. Strawman uses radio transmissions to implement straws.

We implement Strawman on top of the Contiki operating system, targeting the TMote Sky [28] platform as described in Section 4. We leverage this implementation in Section 5, demonstrating that a Strawman-enabled MAC protocol is able to sustain a range of traffic loads, achieving a goodput increase of up to 77% compared to a scalable random backoff-based contention resolution mechanism. We achieve this result while evenly allocating the available bandwidth among the transmitters involved. Our testbed experiments further show that Strawman improves energy efficiency in multi-hop collection networks that experience bursts. We survey related work in Section 6, and end the paper in Section 7 with brief concluding remarks.

This work builds upon two previous papers that propose the basic Strawman protocol [25], and that theoretically study and derive Strawman's random distribution for generating packets of random lengths [12]. Compared to previous work, we improve Strawman along several dimensions and embed it within RI-MAC, a state-of-the-art, low-power MAC protocol rather than leveraging a simple proof-of-concept implementation. This allows us to test Strawman in a large-scale testbed where we verify Strawman's ability to cope with hidden terminals and a large number of contenders.

2. BACKGROUND

Radio communication is one of the most power-expensive activities in low-power networks. Radio duty-cycling mechanisms are employed to preserve power. Radio duty cycling, however, aggravates the risk of data collisions, especially in networks that experience traffic bursts.

2.1 Radio Duty Cycling

Modern low-power networks maintain communication with a radio duty cycle of only a few percent, where network nodes wake up regularly to receive transmissions from neighbors according to a pre-configured wake-up interval. Contention-based low-power MAC protocols belong to either of two classes: sender-initiated [6, 10, 27] or receiver-initiated [9, 35]. In sender-initiated protocols, the sender keeps track of past neighbor wake up times, and wakes up to start a data transmission just as it expects the receiver to wake up [10]. Sender-initiated protocols in lossy networks may cause congestion: the sender is unaware of whether an unsuccessful data

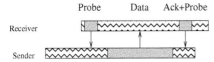

Figure 1: Receiver-initiated radio duty cycling. The sender wakes up and awaits a data probe. Upon receiving a probe, the data packet is sent. Both nodes turn off their radios after the acknowledgement.

transmission is due to link fluctuations, packet collisions, or bad wake up synchronization. The sender therefore repeatedly transmits the same data packet until it is acknowledged, or until it times out after a full wake-up interval.

Receiver-initiated duty-cycling protocols use data probes; nodes wake up periodically and probe for incoming data with a probe transmission. Neighbors that want to send data wake up just before they expect the data probe, and immediately transmit their data upon receiving such a probe, see Figure 1. The subsequent acknowledgement also serves as another data probe, enabling several data packets to be transmitted in a single wake-up. In contrast to sender-initiated protocols, receiver-initiated protocols do not repeatedly transmit radio packets if the data packet is lost. Therefore, compared to sender-initiated protocols, receiver-initiated protocols may offer lower congestion and higher throughput [9].

Duty-cycling mechanisms such as WiseMAC [10] and X-MAC [6] configure their wake-up intervals high enough to avoid collisions, but as low as possible not to waste energy on waking up when there is no data to be received. Another set of protocols additionally adapt their wake-up intervals throughout network operation to accommodate for varying traffic loads [1, 15].

2.2 Traffic Peaks

Traffic load variations are common in sensor networks. If all traffic flows in a network are static and known a priori, for instance by having fixed packet transmission schedules and time synchronization in a network, radio duty-cycling overhead can be minimized to a great extent [7]. Such networks are, however, uncommon. By contrast, many networks inherently induce traffic peaks. Consider an event-driven network, such as an alarm network, that lays dormant for an extended period of time until an event occurs. Upon detecting the event, several nodes simultaneously report it, causing a sudden burst of network traffic [17]. Other common reasons for temporarily increased network traffic include network code updates [21], and bulk downloads of sensor data [18].

Traffic peaks occur also in periodic data collection networks. The introduction of a new node causes neighbor discovery services to temporarily generate more network traffic [3]. Moreover, the network topology can change rapidly due to bursty links, generating further traffic [34]. Even in stable collection networks, a router that forwards data from other nodes will experience traffic peaks, due to randomness in data generation and forwarding times.

2.3 Collisions in Duty-Cycled Networks

Traffic peaks increase the risk of radio collisions in a duty-cycled network. Data collisions occur when multiple transmissions arrive at a receiver simultaneously, causing data loss and retransmissions. The risk of data collisions is aggravated in duty-cycled networks, since a receiver is awake less, and thus has fewer opportunities to receive data. Data collisions do not necessarily cause data loss; if one transmission is stronger than all others the receiver may still successfully decode it. This phenomenon is called capture effect [20]. Several protocols have exploited it, e.g., for fast flooding [22].

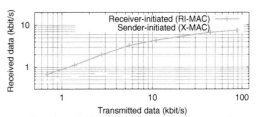

Figure 2: Receiver-initiated MAC protocols outperform sender-initiated in networks with hidden terminals and high traffic, since the sender-initiated network is flooded with colliding data packets.

Most low-power protocols are designed to cope with data collisions to some extent; typically using random backoff times before attempting to retransmit a packet to a busy receiver. However, in networks with bursty traffic, backoff mechanisms result in high latency and energy costs, since data packets may again collide at the receiver when they are retransmitted.

We perform a simple experiment that demonstrates how random backoff behaves in a congested network, using both a receiver-initiated and a sender-initiated protocol. The experiment is performed on the TWIST testbed [14], where a large set of neighbors send data to a single node, causing severe network congestion. Figure 2 shows that, as expected, the receiver-initiated network (RI-MAC) achieves a significantly higher receiver goodput than the sender-initiated network (X-MAC). This is due to packet floods in the sender-initiated network: when a lost data packet is not acknowledged by the receiver, the sender floods the network for a full wake-up interval (1 second), causing further data collisions. This experiment shows that receiver-initiated protocols have better performance than sender-initiated protocols in severely congested networks, and that random backoff does not fully avoid data collisions. Indeed, although the sender-initiated protocol should refrain from transmitting when it detects ongoing transmissions, data collisions still occur due to hidden terminals.

2.4 Hidden Terminals

The hidden terminal problem occurs when two or more nodes that are outside each others' communication ranges send data to the same receiver. Data transmissions may therefore collide at the receiver without the senders noticing; the nodes are hidden to each other. RTS/CTS schemes have long been used to mitigate the hidden terminal problem [36]. Data transmissions are preceded by a transmission request message (RTS). If the medium is available and the transmission is granted (CTS), any potentially interfering neighbor refrains from accessing the medium for the duration of the data transmission.

In the context of low-power wireless, however, traditional RTS/CTS protocols have been shown to induce a high overhead. Polastre et. al. show that an RTS/CTS mechanism can have an overhead of several hundred percent in low-power networks with small data payloads [27]. In receiver-initiated protocols, the problems of traditional RTS/CTS-based protocols are further aggravated: due to the implicit sender-synchronization by data probes, the RTS messages themselves collide at the receiver.

3. STRAWMAN

Strawman is a contention resolution mechanism designed for receiver-initiated radio duty-cycling protocols. Upon detecting data packet collisions, Strawman dynamically and instantaneously enables increased network capacity by quickly receiving data from several neighbors, and has otherwise zero overhead.

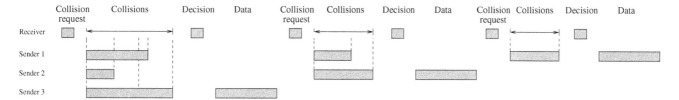

Figure 3: Strawman senders "draw straws" to gain channel access by simultaneously transmitting COLLISION packets with randomly picked lengths, resulting in a deliberate collision. The receiver does not have to correctly decode any of the COLLISION packets, but only needs to measure the duration of the collision. The sender with the longest COLLISION gains channel access and sends its packet. The process is repeated until all packets are sent.

3.1 All Transmit Simultaneously

We have designed Strawman for receiver-initiated MAC protocols, leveraging the implicit sender synchronization due to receiver-initiated operation. The receiver probes the channel for incoming data by transmitting a data probe packet. Next, neighboring devices with receiver-destined data transmit their DATA packets. In presence of multiple transmitters, the packets may collide at the receiver. Strawman intervenes at this stage *only if* a collision actually occurs. Note that the receiver samples the channel while waiting for a data packet, and regards channel activity without successfully receiving a packet as an indication of radio collisions.

Upon detecting a data collision, indicated by radio activity that exceeds the Clear Channel Assessment (CCA) threshold, the receiver sends a COLLISION REQUEST packet. The senders interpret this packet as the beginning of a Strawman *round*, and contend for the channel by sending a COLLISION packet of random length. The receiver estimates the length of the longest COLLISION packet by sampling the received signal strength. The receiver then broadcasts a DECISION packet containing the longest measured length, implicitly informing the corresponding transmitter that it is now granted access to the channel. While the selected transmitter transfers the DATA packet, the other contenders remain silent, as they also recognized *not* to be given access to the channel based on the information in the DECISION packet. The subsequent COLLISION REQUEST broadcasted by the receiver both initiates a new Strawman round and acknowledges the previously received data packet. In the case that several contenders have chosen the same random length and their DATA packets have collided, the receiver nevertheless sends another COLLISION REQUEST since it has detected the contenders' transmissions by sampling the channel. This process repeats until all contenders have successfully sent their DATA packets. Figure 3 depicts an example execution with Strawman that schedules and transfers three data packets.

Strawman's COLLISION and DECISION packets provide a functionality similar to RTS/CTS handshakes [36], but allow *multiple* transmitters to request access to the channel *simultaneously*.

3.2 Collisions of Random Length

The random lengths of COLLISION packets effectively determine which transmitter is granted access to the channel. In a sense, this resembles random back-off techniques, as it is still a random choice at the transmitter side that regulates channel access. However, in Strawman the contenders *actively* compete for the channel, using the COLLISION packet to inform the receiver on their random choice. Unlike random back-off techniques, this entails that the other contenders also know that they are *not* given access to the channel, based on the DECISION packet.

We use a truncated decreasing geometric distribution to draw the random lengths of COLLISION packets. Compared to the more common uniform distribution, a truncated geometric distribution provides higher variance within a bounded interval for random samples. In Strawman, this translates into better scalability [12].

We use a granularity of 7 bytes for the COLLISION packet length. 7 bytes correspond to a transmission time of $224\mu s$ at 250 kbits/s—the bandwidth of our target radios—enabling an accurate estimation of the COLLISION packet length, as we report in Section 5.1.

3.3 Multi-channel Operation

Strawman reduces contention by multi-channel operation; the receiver randomly selects which radio channel the senders should use. Like A-MAC [9], we allocate a pre-determined channel for the transmission of the initial data probe packets and then, for the DATA transfer and any subsequent Strawman rounds, all communication takes place on another radio channel. Particularly, the initial data probe contains an entry indicating the radio channel to use next. Upon receiving the data probe, every contender immediately switches to the indicated channel prior to sending the DATA packet. When the execution completes, all involved nodes return to the initial channel.

4. IMPLEMENTATION

We have implemented Strawman on Contiki, targeting the TMote Sky [28] platform equipped with 802.15.4-compliant CC2420 radios. As experimental and evaluation platform for Strawman, we implement our own version of RI-MAC [35], and extend it with multi-channel operation. Our implementation of RI-MAC uses wake-up schedule synchronization [10], and hop-by-hop acknowledgments.

We use this implementation of RI-MAC to evaluate Strawman's performance. For comparison, we build another version of RI-MAC with a random backoff-based contention resolution mechanism. In addition, we extend it with the geometric distribution proposed by SIFT [17] to increase contender scalability. We use a delay granularity of $320\mu s$—a minimum slot size enforced by the radio's turnaround time, also used by the original implementation of RI-MAC [35].

Length estimation. We implement the transmission of COLLISION packets as 802.15.4 frame transmissions. On every node, we preload a COLLISION packet in the radio's outgoing buffer, similarly to existing work [29, 24]. This improves the overall latency and allows for synchronized transmissions of COLLISION packets from multiple transmitters—the key to correctly determine the length of the longest COLLISION packet at the receiver.

We implement COLLISION packet length estimation by subsequent Clear Channel Assessment (CCA) checks at the receiver. We experimentally calibrate the number of CCA checks that are to return an indication of "busy channel" to determine a correct COLLISION length estimate. Unless otherwise specified, we always use the CC2420's default CCA threshold of -77 dBm.

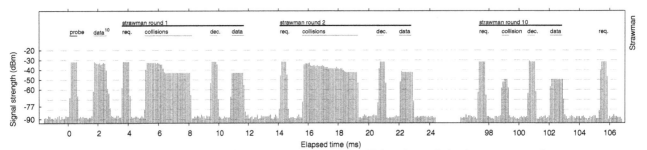

Figure 4: Signal strength profile of Strawman resolving collisions from 10 simultaneous contenders.

Alleviating channel noise. By relying on subsequent CCA checks to estimate packet lengths, we risk confusing channel noise with COLLISION transmissions. We leverage two simple techniques to alleviate the problem. First, as the transmissions of COLLISION packets from the contenders are synchronized, the receiver knows exactly when they occur, and starts sampling the channel immediately *before* this time. If the channel is busy, Strawman aborts its operation, as this condition indicates channel noise. Similarly, if a receiver estimates a longer COLLISION packet length than possible, it assumes channel noise and aborts its operation. If two consecutive Strawman rounds experience either of these conditions and also fail to receive DATA packets, the receiver returns to sleep and will operate on a different radio channel the next wake-up as described in Section 3.3.

Example run. Figure 4 shows a signal strength profile of a Strawman-enabled network operating on a single radio channel. These patterns correspond to a concrete execution of the processing intuitively described in Figure 3.

The setup in Figure 4 includes one receiver and ten contenders in the same collision domain. The individual Strawman rounds can be identified by the signal strength patterns. Starting from the leftmost side of the picture, a RI-MAC data probe is sent at time 0 ms, resulting in simultaneous data transmissions between 2 ms and 3 ms from all 10 contenders. These data packet transmissions collide at the receiver.

The collision causes the activation of Strawman, with the COLLISION REQUEST packet being sent out by the receiver at about 4 ms. In the first Strawman round, all 10 contenders transmit COLLISION packets, starting at about 5 ms. The signal strength profile of this phase indeed suggests that multiple COLLISION packets of different lengths collide. The receiver measures the length of the longest COLLISION packet, and sends out the DECISION packet at about 9.5 ms. The contender granted channel access transmits the data packet at 11 ms and drops out the following Strawman round, where the remaining contenders will repeat the same procedure.

At the rightmost side of the picture, only one contender is left. As a result, the COLLISION phase is shorter: with fewer contenders the probability to be granted channel access with a smaller COLLISION length increases. The 10th DATA packet is finally acknowledged at time 105 ms.

5. EVALUATION

We evaluate Strawman's performance along several dimensions. Our results reveal several key findings:

- Our technique for estimating the length of COLLISION packets, which determines which node is granted channel access, is accurate in a range of different situations, as illustrated in Section 5.1.
- Strawman has no overhead when data collisions do not occur,

and a limited energy cost when data collisions are resolved, as we illustrate in Section 5.2.

- A Strawman-enabled MAC protocol can sustain a range of different traffic loads, quickly reacting to changing conditions, and does so by evenly allocating the available bandwidth, as we show in Section 5.3 and 5.4.
- Strawman's performance is a result of its ability to cope with hidden terminals efficiently: we investigate the presence of hidden terminals in our experimental setup and how Strawman reacts to them in Section 5.5, comparing its performance against that of Black Burst [33].
- In a realistic scenario using standard tree routing protocols, Strawman makes the network much more robust to sudden traffic bursts and significantly reduces the corresponding energy overhead, as we show in Section 5.6.

Based on these results, we argue that Strawman is a welcome addition to receiver-initiated low-power MAC protocols. By not imposing any additional overhead in absence of collisions, it allows the MAC protocol to run without unnecessary performance penalties. Should collisions occur, Strawman quickly intervenes to resolve them efficiently.

5.1 Collision Length Estimation

Strawman relies on accurately estimating COLLISION lengths. A COLLISION length estimation determines who wins channel access via the subsequent DECISION transmission. If the COLLISION length is underestimated, multiple contenders may transmit DATA packets simultaneously, causing collisions. On the other hand, if it is overestimated, no contender will send its DATA. We now perform a set of micro-benchmarks to assess how effective our channel sampling technique is for estimating COLLISION lengths.

5.1.1 Collision Lengths

We study how the COLLISION length affects the accuracy of packet length estimation. We use two TMote Sky nodes configured as receiver and contender. The receiver periodically probes the channel for incoming data. The contender replies with a COLLISION packet of varying length. For every possible COLLISION length, we run at least 350 repetitions of the experiment. We furthermore use two different distances between the nodes: a *near-by* contender is placed 0.5 m. from the receiver, a *distant* contender is 10 m. from the receiver. We decrease the transmission power of the distant contender, so that it can barely communicate with the receiver. The receiver uses the CC2420's default CCA threshold of -77 dBm.

Results. Figure 5a shows the median error in estimating the COLLISION length, against the actual transmitted length. The error bars reflect the minimum and the 98th percentile of the estimated lengths. We observe that 98% of the estimations are within the

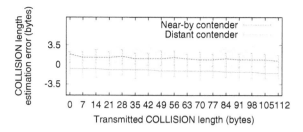

(a) The COLLISION length estimation error remains within the 7-byte granularity for both near-by and distant contenders.

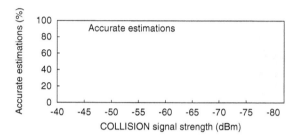

(b) The COLLISION length is accurately estimated when received with signal strength above the CCA threshold.

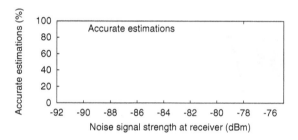

(c) The COLLISION length is accurately estimated when the external interference is below the CCA threshold.

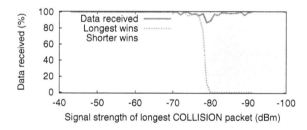

(d) The contender with the longest COLLISION packet wins channel access and sends data (up to -77dBm) unless its COLLISION is too weak to be detected, in which case the contender with the shorter COLLISION packet wins.

Figure 5: Micro-benchmarks: Strawman accurately estimates the lengths of COLLISION packets (a) of different lengths, (b) received with different signal strengths, (c) under external interference, and (d) under interference from an out-of-range contender.

7-byte level of granularity used in our implementation, indicated by the shaded area in the chart. This shows that in almost all cases a Strawman-enabled receiver accurately estimates the length of the COLLISION packet of a single contender, in absence of interference.

Figure 5a also illustrates the effect of distance, and therefore sig-

nal strength, on length estimation accuracy: packets from a distant contender are underestimated and packets from a near-by contender are overestimated. This phenomenon is an artifact of CC2420's CCA that is calculated from a moving average of the last 8 received signal strength values. Nevertheless, 98% of length estimations of both distant and near-by contenders' packets are still within the 7-byte level of granularity.

5.1.2 Collision Signal Strengths

We study how COLLISION packets' received signal strengths affect the accuracy of packet length estimation. We use the same experimental setup as above but also vary the receiver-contender distance to generate different signal strengths at the receiver. The receiver logs the signal strength of each received COLLISION packet along with the corresponding length estimate.

Results. Figure 5b shows the ratio of COLLISION length estimations inside the 7-byte level of granularity. In a real network, bad length estimations decrease network performance and cause data collisions. This experiment shows that bad length estimations are uncommon unless the COLLISION packet's signal strength is close to the CCA threshold.

5.1.3 Interference from External Noise

We study how external radio interference affects the accuracy of packet length estimation. We use two TMote Sky nodes: one receiver and one contender set 3 m. apart. In addition, to obtain repeatable experiments, we leverage the method by Boano et al. [5] to generate a constant and controllable interference, using a third TMote Sky node as interferer. We control the signal strength of external radio interference by moving the interferer closer to the receiver. We ensure that the single contender always receives the COLLISION REQUEST packet and sends the corresponding COLLISION. The receiver logs the noise level immediately before sending the COLLISION REQUEST packet as well as the COLLISION length estimation.

Results. As expected, Figure 5c shows that the correctness of our COLLISION length estimation starts falling outside the 7-byte granularity level only as the interference level approaches the CCA threshold. Under these conditions, the receiver is unable to discern the transmission of a COLLISION packet from noise. Similar situations, however, would break most traditional transmission schemes based on CCA checks. Indeed, the CCA check would always indicate the channel as busy. The transmission scheme would react first by deferring the transmission, and then ultimately dropping the packet upon expiration of a timeout or after a maximum number of CCA checks.

5.1.4 Interference from Out-of-range Contenders

A distant Strawman contender that receives a COLLISION REQUEST and sends back COLLISION packet may be unable to reach the receiver due to asymmetric or fluctuating radio links. In our final micro-benchmark, we study how such out-of-range contenders affect the outcome of Strawman rounds with multiple contenders.

We use three TMote Sky nodes: one receiver and two contenders. One contender is kept *near-by* the receiver at 0.5 m. whereas we vary the distance of the second contender from the receiver, from 0.5 to 20 m. We configure the output power so that the receiver cannot hear the moving contender at 20 m. distance. To obtain a controlled setting, we configure the two contenders to use fixed COLLISION lengths, rather than the previous random lengths. Particularly, the near-by contender always competes with the shortest possible COLLISION length (0 bytes payload), whereas the moving contender uses the longest possible (112 bytes payload). Therefore,

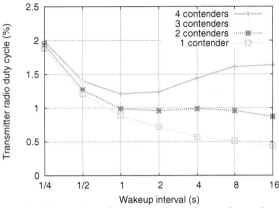

Figure 6: Contender radio duty cycle against wake-up interval. Strawman intervenes only when DATA collisions occur, and has no overhead otherwise. The x axis uses a logarithmic scale.

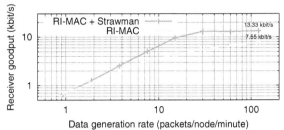

Figure 7: Goodput in RI-MAC using Strawman and random backoff. Strawman achieves up to 77% higher goodput than random backoff for high data rates.

the moving contender should always be the one granted access to the channel, as long as the receiver hears its COLLISION packet. To analyze this aspect, we log the signal strength of the COLLISION packet coming from the moving node.

Results. Figure 5d shows the total delivery ratio for DATA packets sent by either contender, against the signal strength of the COLLISION packet coming from the moving node. As long as the signal strength of the moving contender is sufficiently high to be perceived by the receiver, the moving contender is scheduled to transmit the DATA packet, corresponding to almost 100% data delivery from this node.

The situation progressively reverses as the COLLISION signal strength of the moving contender becomes weaker, until the receiver hears only the short COLLISION packet from the near-by fixed node. Under these conditions, only the near-by node is allowed to transmit the DATA packet. Nevertheless, the receiver almost always successfully receives a DATA packet from either of the two contenders.

5.2 Energy Cost of Resolving Collisions

Strawman makes networks robust against traffic bursts, but has an energy cost when used. If the network is constantly overloaded with traffic, queues of pending packet form that induce an energy cost in the network. We perform an experiment to demonstrate the relationship between network traffic, number of contenders, and the radio duty cycle.

Setting. We simulate a network with a single receiver and four contenders in Cooja, which allows us to have perfect control of the system execution. All contenders are hidden to each other but have a perfect and static link to the receiver. Every contender generates a DATA packet once every 4 seconds. We vary the nodes' wake-up intervals from four times per second to once every 32 seconds. By increasing the wake-up interval, we expect the risk of DATA collisions to increase.

Results. Figure 6 shows the average radio duty cycle for contenders against their configured wake-up interval. With short wake-up intervals, the collision risk is small. As the wake-up interval increases, collisions occur more often and Strawman intervenes to reschedule DATA packets. According to this chart, this generates a limited energy overhead in the configurations we tested. Strawman's cost of rescheduling colliding DATA packets is indeed the difference between the single and the multi-contender curves in Figure 6.

This experiment also demonstrates that Strawman networks are robust with regards to the configuration of the wake-up interval. Strawman's efficient contention resolution allows all packets destined to a given receiver to be delivered within the (few) wake-up intervals available. This is possible because Strawman quickly provides increased network capacity when needed, which in this case is precisely at the time of waking the receiver up.

5.3 Different Traffic Loads

We evaluate the performance of Strawman in sustaining a range of different traffic loads, especially in terms of the network capacity provided against different network demands. We also study the fairness properties of Strawman in allocating the available bandwidth among multiple contenders, and how the CCA threshold affects the performance we observe in this setting. We describe next the settings common to all experiments in this section.

Setting. We use TWIST [14], a testbed with 100 Tmote Sky sensor nodes that provides a particularly dense network: a single node transmission can be received by up to 65 other nodes. A dense network has a potentially large number of contenders, which is beneficial to study the performance of Strawman. We find that the TWIST topology results in a number of hidden terminals, an aspect that we investigate more deeply in Section 5.5. All nodes operate at maximum transmission power. We compare Strawman with our implementation of random backoff-based RI-MAC, as described in Section 4.

Our setup includes a single receiver node probing the channel for data once per second. All other nodes in the testbed act as contenders. The payload size of the DATA packets is 110 bytes: including the overhead of the network stack, this corresponds to a maximum sized 802.15.4 frame. We repeat the experiment using a wide range of data generation rates: from roughly one DATA packet per minute, up to 2 DATA packets per second. We expect the network to reach its maximum capacity within this interval. To measure the sink goodput, we log on the nodes all DATA packets transmitted and received. We exclude from the statistics duplicate DATA packets, which may occur in case of lost acknowledgements.

5.3.1 Goodput and Fairness

We start by measuring the receiver goodput against varying traffic loads, and by investigating the fairness properties of Strawman.

Results. Figure 7 shows the receiver goodput against varying traffic loads for both Strawman and random backoff, in logarithmic scale. Strawman is able to receive all generated DATA packets up until a data generation rate of one packet per node every 4 seconds. Random backoff, in contrast, loses packets already at lower data generation rates, resulting in reduced goodput. The maximum goodput achieved for Strawman is 13.33 kbit/s. For random backoff, the maximum goodput is 7.55 kbit/s. The experiment logs show that

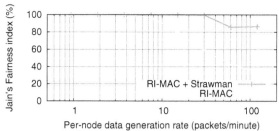

Figure 8: Fairness properties of Strawman and random backoff. Random backoff is driven by capture effect, and is thus unfair with regards to different contenders.

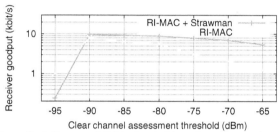

Figure 9: Influence of CCA threshold on Strawman and random backoff. In the best configuration, Strawman still performs better than random backoff.

Strawman successfully funnels over 15 DATA packets each wake-up, in comparison with random backoff's 8.6 packets.

We also investigate how Strawman divides the available bandwidth among contenders. To study this aspect, we use Jain's Index as a fairness measure calculated over the 30 most active contenders, as some nodes are in a grey-zone and do not participate in every round. Figure 8 shows the corresponding results in the same range of data generation rates of Figure 7 in logarithmic scale. The plot indicates that Strawman is generally more fair in scheduling contenders compared to random backoff. Indeed, the latter inherently relies on capture effect to decide which node, among multiple senders, ultimately delivers a packet. This entails that the choice is implicitly driven by the physical topology, and therefore likely to be biased towards near-by contenders. On the contrary, in Strawman the choice of which node is granted access to the channel is completely random.

5.3.2 Clear Channel Assessment Sensitivity

The detection of neighbors' ongoing transmissions is strongly influenced by the CCA threshold. In addition, it also affects the occurrence of hidden terminals, since contenders become more or less sensitive to hearing each other. Existing work postulate that, in principle, all hidden terminals conditions may be removed in a star network simply by increasing the sensitivity [39].

To investigate how Strawman is affected by the CCA threshold configuration, we repeat the experiments previously discussed using a fixed data generation rate: each node generates 15 DATA packets per minute, and we vary the CCA threshold across different repetitions.

Results. Figure 9 shows the goodput for different values of CCA threshold, ranging from -95 dBm to -65 dBm. Note that the y axis uses logarithmic scale. When the CCA threshold is set to low values, Strawman cannot distinguish COLLISION packets from background noise and does not schedule any DATA packets. The goodput performance consequently suffers. When the CCA threshold is set to a high value, Strawman cannot detect weak COLLISION trans-

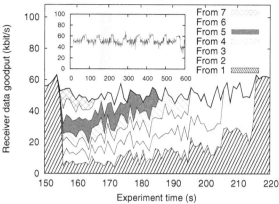

Figure 10: Saturated link: goodput over time. Every node quickly obtains its fair share of the medium while the total goodput remains high.

missions and ignores contenders far from the receiver. On the other hand, in such situations random backoff suffers even more, since the hidden terminal problem is severely aggravated, and random backoff cannot deal efficiently with it.

The best overall performance we obtain in these experiments corresponds to a CCA threshold of -90 dBm. With this configuration, Strawman still performs better than random backoff, yielding a goodput of 9.7 kbit/s against 7.3 kbit/s. However, we are not aware of real deployments using CCA threshold settings different from the default one. Indeed, it is very difficult, let apart tedious, to run a statistically significant set of experiments to determine the best CCA threshold in a given environment.

5.4 Reacting to Sudden Traffic Bursts

We now study how Strawman handles intense traffic surges in which multiple contenders attempt to transmit at full speed to a single receiver, and in particular how Strawman allocates the bandwidth among contenders when new bursts are introduced into the network. Ideally, we expect Strawman to provide each active contender with a fair share of the medium while maximizing the overall throughput.

Setting. We use a 1-hop network with 8 TMote Sky nodes running RI-MAC with Strawman, measuring the resulting goodput. Seven of the nodes are configured to *always* contend for permission to transmit data to the single receiver. In contrast to the experiments in Section 5.3, this network is both smaller and has reduced logging, resulting in higher total goodput. The number of active contenders during the experiment varies at intervals of 10 seconds. Each data packet has a payload of 100 bytes.

Results. Figure 10 shows an excerpt of the goodput measurements over time. In the beginning, only node #1 is active. After 155 seconds, all nodes (#1-#7) become active for 10 seconds. Node #7 is then deactivated at time 165 seconds, leaving 6 contenders active. The remaining contenders are then progressively deactivated, one every 10 seconds, until the system is back to a condition with only node #1 is active. The chart brings two fundamental insights:

1. Strawman *instantaneously* matches changed traffic conditions; when the number of contenders suddenly increases from 1 to 7, Strawman quickly reacts without a significant reduction in the total goodput.

2. As the number of contenders varies, Strawman *evenly* divides the available bandwidth among the contenders in the system;

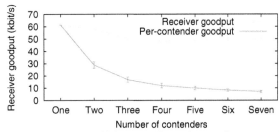

Figure 11: Saturated link: overall goodput performance. With Strawman, the receiver goodput remains high for up to 7 contenders, with no noticeable reduction already from the case with 3 contenders.

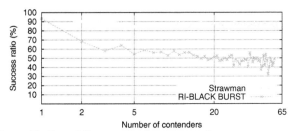

Figure 12: Data delivery using Strawman and RI-BLACK BURST. Strawman successfully mitigates hidden terminals up to 65 contenders. The x axis uses a logarithmic scale.

in the long run, this results in a fair allocation of bandwidth resources.

To provide a quantitative assessment on the overall goodput performance in this experiment, Figure 11 shows the average goodput depending on the number of active contenders. As expected, the total goodput is highest with only one contender: 61.3 kbit/s. At the opposite end of the spectrum, the total goodput with 7 active contenders is 50.1 kbit/s, yet there is no significant reduction already starting from the case with 3 active contenders. The chart therefore shows that Strawman successfully keeps the link almost saturated independently of the number of contenders.

5.5 Coping with Hidden Terminals

We aim at identifying the presence of hidden terminals in our setup, and their effect on Strawman's performance.

RI-BLACK BURST. To quantify the presence and effects of hidden terminals, we develop a variant of the Black Burst protocol proposed by Sobrinho et al. [33]. The Black Burst protocol, like Strawman, resolves contention by measuring the longest of several colliding transmissions. By contrast, Black Burst does not employ DECISION packets to inform the contenders who gains channel access, but instead relies on contenders' clear channel assessments: if the channel is clear, a contender concludes that its COLLISION packet was the longest and accesses the channel. The Black Burst protocol cannot cope with hidden terminals since it lacks the DE-CISION packet. We develop a receiver-initiated Black Burst variant that we call RI-BLACK BURST. The Black Burst protocol is designed for CSMA-based WiFi networks, and does not synchronize contenders with an initial COLLISION REQUEST transmission. To isolate the effects of hidden terminals, we therefore compare Strawman with RI-BLACK BURST.

Setting. We use the same TWIST testbed setup as in Section 5.3. In absence of hidden terminals, both Strawman and RI-BLACK BURST grant channel access to the same contenders. Indeed, as all contenders can hear each other, there will be only one of them that find the channel clear after transmitting of the COLLISION packet. However, in presence of hidden terminals, Strawman and RI-BLACK BURST behave differently. With RI-BLACK BURST multiple contenders that are hidden from each other may access the channel simultaneously. On the other hand, RI-BLACK BURST is slightly faster than Strawman, as it does not need to transmit the DECISION packet.

Results. Figure 12 shows the overall data delivery ratio of Strawman and RI-BLACK BURST against a varying number of contenders. We were unable to find more than 65 one-hop transmitters in our testbed. Based on these results, we conclude that hidden terminals do exist, but they affect the performance of RI-BLACK BURST only. Using Strawman, the overall data delivery remains high up

to 60 contenders: more than 85% of all Strawman rounds with 60 contenders successfully deliver the DATA packet. By contrast, RI-BLACK BURST delivers less than 60% of the DATA packets already with 3 contenders, and becomes drastically worse than Strawman as the number of contenders increases.

5.6 Multi-hop Data Collection

We assess the impact of Strawman in a realistic network scenario by setting up a data collection network over a multi-hop topology. In such a scenario, the network operation is subject to issues such as concurrent control and application traffic, inter-node wireless interference, and packet losses and retransmissions.

Setting. We use 82 nodes in the TWIST testbed, this time by configuring the CC2420 radio chip to use a lower transmission power mode to promote multi-hop topologies. The resulting network setup stretches across at least 4 hops.

To establish multi-hop routes, we use the Contiki Collect protocol, which establishes a tree-shaped routing topology from all nodes to a sink using a routing metric based on ETX. Contiki Collect and TinyOS CTP have been shown to achieve similar performance in low-power data collection [19]. To study how our network is affected by sudden traffic bursts, we also instrument the protocol with the ability to temporarily disable all route maintenance. By doing so, we ensure that multiple traffic bursts are forwarded over the same routes, thus factoring out the influence of route maintenance on our study. Nevertheless, the setup still includes data collisions, retransmissions, and acknowledgements.

Using this setup, we test three different traffic patterns, corresponding to different settings we study to isolate the effect of Strawman in absence or presence of traffic burst. We test every traffic pattern for at least 40 minutes:

No traffic (NT): the network generates no radio traffic. This profile serves to demonstrate Strawman's sensitivity to external noise and provides a baseline for the bursty traffic experiment.

Periodic traffic (PT): each node generates a DATA packet every 5 minutes, on average. This allows us to study how Strawman handles sporadic collisions, mostly due to hidden terminals.

Bursty traffic (BT): after making sure routes are stable, we disable route maintenance and instantaneously generate one DATA packet each on 8 randomly-selected nodes. This generates a sudden surge of traffic that yields intense collisions across multiple hops leading to the sink, which is the scenario we target.

Throughout the study, we compare Strawman against the random backoff-based version of RI-MAC. We draw our conclusions based on data delivery ratio at the sink and system-wide radio energy consumption.

	RI-MAC + Strawman	RI-MAC
NT radio duty cycle (%)	0.34	0.40
PT radio duty cycle (%)	3.94	4.40
BT radio on-time (sec)	*4.53*	*8.16*

Table 1: Strawman improves on RI-MAC's energy consumption both in absence and in presence of collisions.

Results. Regardless of the traffic pattern, the data delivery at the sink is always comparable using Strawman or random back-off. Specifically, all 8 packets included in a traffic burst are always delivered to the sink in either configuration.

Table 1 shows energy consumption figures under different traffic profiles. Already with no radio traffic (NT), Strawman slightly reduces the necessary radio duty cycle. We attribute this behavior to its ability to more quickly distinguish channel noise from actual transmissions. In particular, when RI-MAC mistakes channel noise for DATA and sends a COLLISION REQUEST packet, Strawman immediately expects a COLLISION packet in reply. If this does not happen, Strawman immediately turns the radio off. With random backoff, by contrast, RI-MAC must wait for the duration of the backoff window before turning off the radio again.

Under periodic traffic (PT), the Strawman-enabled network has a lower radio duty cycle than the backoff-based RI-MAC network. This improvement is due to Strawman's ability to immediately resolve collisions thus avoiding the need for later retransmissions.

To quantify the net energy overhead due to radio communication under bursty traffic (BT), we subtract the NT radio duty cycle discussed above from the total radio usage during each burst. We report the total radio on-time to funnel the packet burst to the sink on the bottom row of Table 1. Compared to the backoff-based RI-MAC, Strawman halves this figure in our setting. As a result, Strawman makes the network much more robust against sudden traffic bursts, by reducing the energy overhead of contention resolution when collisions occur.

6. RELATED WORK

Strawman builds on the body of work in contention resolution schemes, on protocols dealing with traffic bursts, as well as on recent findings about simultaneous wireless transmissions. In the following, we briefly survey the literature on these topics.

Contention resolution schemes. Common solutions to channel contention problems are random back-off schemes, even in traditional networks. Such techniques are also applied in the wireless domain, and specifically to sensor networks [17, 27, 38]. In this context, one of the main design choices is the random distribution to sample from. As examples, early solutions use uniform distributions [27], whereas Jamieson et al. propose a geometric distribution [17]. Strawman differentiates from these techniques in the use of *active* contenders, as opposed to the passive behavior of competing nodes when using random back-off. Nevertheless, the work on random distributions carried out in this context has inspired us to use a geometric distribution which provides advantages over uniform distributions [12].

Strawman's core mechanisms bear similarities with bit-dominance protocols. However, Strawman leverages dynamic priorities rather than static, as contenders in Strawman compete with different priorities every time. Solutions inspired by bit-dominance protocols exist also in the wireless domain [26, 30]. However, they require the underlying physical medium to be based on On-Off-Keying (OOK) modulation. By contrast, Strawman does not impose requirements

on the underlying modulation mechanism. The Black Burst [33] protocol by Sobrinho et al. and the HIPERLAN protocol [16] are similar to Strawman in that they measure packet lengths to resolve contention; the contender with the longest transmission wins channel access. Like Strawman, they are designed for wireless networks and do not rely on OOK modulation. Unlike Strawman, they do not cope with hidden terminals, and are not designed for duty-cycled low-power networks. We develop a receiver-initiated version of the Black Burst protocol and compare it with Strawman in Section 5.5, to quantify the performance effects of hidden terminals on receiver-initiated low-power protocols.

To avoid collisions due to hidden terminal problems, Request-To-Send/Clear-To-Send (RTS/CTS) protocols are typically used. However, they are shown to exhibit a considerable overhead when used for wireless transmissions [4, 27]. Alternative solutions also exist. For instance, ZigZag decoding [13] exploits the effects due to interference cancellation in 802.11 networks to enable decoding of colliding packets. Strawman uses a form of RTS/CTS mechanism to resolve collisions, yet this is based on multiple simultaneous transmissions, in a sense similarly to ZigZag decoding. We are not aware of other collision resolution mechanisms based on multiple simultaneous transmitters in sensor networks. Strawman leverages this technique to improve on the resulting latency and throughput.

Dealing with traffic bursts. Strawman operates at the MAC level. In this context, the predominant approach in sensor networks is CSMA, because of its simplicity and low overhead compared to TDMA [40]. To deal with traffic bursts, adaptive MAC protocols change their operation along different dimensions, e.g., by tuning the wake-up periods [1, 15], by using packet trains, and by alternating between CSMA and TDMA techniques [31]. Namboodiri and Keshavarzian designed Alert, a MAC protocol designed for traffic bursts in mostly idle networks [23]. Their goal is to minimize the delay of the first message. They reduce contention by a combination of time and frequency multiplexing. These MAC-level techniques are complementary to Strawman, as they operate at the protocol level rather than during the actual transmission of the individual packets, as Strawman does.

In a broader perspective, the existing literature includes several mechanisms for handling traffic bursts in sensor networks. These typically entail some form of cross-layer interaction, either by requiring information sharing between layers, or by affecting the performance of upper layers. As a result, these need to be aware of the underlying mechanisms to counteract their influence. Examples include ESRT that requires interaction between the application layer and the MAC layer [32], and the adaptive MAC layer by Woo and Culler [38], which uses random back-off, thus incurring performance penalties for the application layer. Differently, Strawman does not require application awareness or cross-layer interactions.

Simultaneous wireless transmissions. A few recent works exploit low-level radio effects [8, 9]. As examples, Demirbas et al. use radio collisions to implement Pollcast and Countcast, network primitives that enable voting among immediate neighbors [8]. Dutta et al. show that collisions of identical 802.15.4 packets do not necessarily lead to data corruption, and implement an anycast-like primitive called Backcast [9]. Lu and Whitehouse exploit the capture effect for rapid flooding of sensor networks [22]. The Glossy protocol relies on what the authors call *constructive interference*, i.e. the superposition of the same RF signals generated by multiple senders, to further improve flooding efficiency [11]. Whitehouse et al. present a mechanism for recovering partial information from semi-collided packets [37]. Unlike these approaches, Strawman does not attempt to extract information from the colliding packets, but we measure the duration of the longest transmission to infer the length of the longest packet. Once again, Strawman is therefore not bound to any specific radio modulation or encoding technique.

7. CONCLUSIONS

We present Strawman, a new contention resolution mechanism for low-power wireless networks. Strawman leverages synchronized packet collisions to implement efficient and fair contention resolution among hidden terminals.

Strawman is designed for low-power networks that experience traffic bursts, but is activated only upon detecting data collisions and has zero overhead unless needed. We have implemented and evaluated Strawman in a receiver-initiated protocol, where it replaces the traditional backoff-based mechanism. Our testbed experiments show that without Strawman, a small number of hidden terminals may drastically degrade performance during traffic bursts whereas Strawman enables high throughput even in the presence of a large number of hidden contenders. Lastly, we show that Strawman can reduce the radio duty cycles in data collection networks, both when the traffic is regular and when sudden traffic bursts occur.

8. ACKNOWLEDGEMENTS

This work was partially supported by VINNOVA, the Swedish Agency for Innovation Systems, by the Swedish Foundation for Strategic Research, by the EU Commission and by CONET, the Cooperating Objects Network of Excellence.

9. REFERENCES

[1] M. Anwander, G. Wagenknecht, T. Braun, and K. Dolfus. Beam: A burst-aware energy-efficient adaptive mac protocol for wireless sensor networks. In *International Conference on Networked Sensing Systems (INSS)*, 2010.

[2] A. Arora, P. Dutta, S. Bapat, V. Kulathumani, H. Zhang, V. Naik, V. Mittal, H. Cao, M. Demirbas, M. Gouda, Y. Choi, T. Herman, S. Kulkarni, U. Arumugam, M. Nesterenko, A. Vora, and M. Miyashita. A line in the sand: A wireless sensor network for target detection, classification, and tracking. *Computer Networks*, 46(5), Dec. 2004.

[3] G. Barrenetxea, F. Ingelrest, G. Schaefer, M. Vetterli, O. Couach, and M. Parlange. Sensorscope: Out-of-the-box environmental monitoring. In *ACM/IEEE IPSN*, 2008.

[4] V. Bharghavan, A. Demers, S. Schenker, and L. Zhang. MACAW: a Media Access Protocol for Wireless LANs. In *ACM SIGCOMM*, London, UK, 1994.

[5] C. A. Boano, Z. He, Y. Li, T. Voigt, M. Zuniga, and A. Willig. Controllable Radio Interference for Experimental and Testing Purposes in Wireless Sensor Networks. In *IEEE SenseApp*, Zurich, Switzerland, Oct. 2009.

[6] M. Buettner, G. V. Yee, E. Anderson, and R. Han. X-MAC: a short preamble MAC protocol for duty-cycled wireless sensor networks. In *ACM SenSys*, Boulder, Colorado, USA, 2006.

[7] N. Burri, P. von Rickenbach, and R. Wattenhofer. Dozer: ultra-low power data gathering in sensor networks. In *ACM/IEEE IPSN*, Cambridge, Massachusetts, USA, 2007.

[8] M. Demirbas, O. Soysal, and M. Hussain. Singlehop Collaborative Feedback Primitive for Wireless Sensor Networks. In *IEEE INFOCOM*, 2008.

[9] P. Dutta, S. Dawson-Haggerty, Y. Chen, C.-J. M. Liang, and A. Terzis. Design and Evaluation of a Versatile and Efficient

[10] A. El-Hoiydi, J.-D. Decotignie, C. C. Enz, and E. L. Roux. Poster Abstract: WiseMAC, an Ultra Low Power MAC Protocol for the WiseNET Wireless Sensor Network. In *ACM SenSys*, 2003.

[11] F. Ferrari, M. Zimmerling, L. Thiele, and O. Saukh. Efficient network flooding and time synchronization with Glossy. In *Proceedings of the International Conference on Information Processing in Sensor Networks (ACM/IEEE IPSN)*, Chicago, IL, USA, April 2011.

[12] E. Ghadimi, P. Soldati, F. Österlind, H. Zhang, and M. Johansson. Hidden terminal-aware contention resolution with an optimal distribution. In *The Eighth IEEE International Conference on Mobile Ad-hoc and Sensor Systems (MASS)*, 2011.

[13] S. Gollakota and D. Katabi. Zigzag decoding: combating hidden terminals in wireless networks. *SIGCOMM Comput. Commun. Rev.*, 38(4), 2008.

[14] V. Handziski, A. Köpke, A. Willig, and A. Wolisz. TWIST: a scalable and reconfigurable testbed for wireless indoor experiments with sensor networks. In *Proceedings of the 2nd international workshop on Multi-hop ad hoc networks: from theory to reality (REALMAN'06)*, 2006.

[15] P. Hurni and T. Braun. Maxmac: A maximally traffic-adaptive mac protocol for wireless sensor networks. In *Proceedings of the European Conference on Wireless Sensor Networks (EWSN)*, Coimbra, Portugal, Feb. 2010.

[16] P. Jacquet, P. Minet, P. Mühlethaler, and N. Rivierre. Priority and collision detection with active signaling - the channel access mechanism of hiperlan. *Wireless Personal Communications*, 1997.

[17] K. Jamieson, H. Balakrishnan, and Y. C. Tay. Sift: a MAC Protocol for Event-Driven Wireless Sensor Networks. In *Proceedings of the European Conference on Wireless Sensor Networks (EWSN)*, Zurich, Switzerland, Feb. 2006.

[18] S. Kim, R. Fonseca, P. Dutta, A. Tavakoli, D. Culler, P. Levis, S. Shenker, and I. Stoica. Flush: A reliable bulk transport protocol for multihop wireless networks. In *Proceedings of the International Conference on Embedded Networked Sensor Systems (ACM SenSys)*, Sydney, Australia, Nov. 2007.

[19] J. Ko, J. Eriksson, N. Tsiftes, S. Dawson-Haggerty, M. Durvy, J. Vasseur, A. Terzis, A. Dunkels, and D. Culler. Beyond Interoperability: Pushing the Performance of Sensornet IP Stacks. In *Proceedings of the International Conference on Embedded Networked Sensor Systems (ACM SenSys)*, Seattle, WA, USA, 2011.

[20] K. Leentvaar and J. Flint. The capture effect in FM receivers. *Communications, IEEE Transactions on*, 24(5):531–539, 1976.

[21] P. Levis, N. Patel, D. Culler, and S. Shenker. Trickle: A self-regulating algorithm for code propagation and maintenance in wireless sensor networks. In *Proceedings of the USENIX Symposium on Networked Systems Design & Implementation (NSDI)*, Mar. 2004.

[22] J. Lu and K. Whitehouse. Flash flooding: Exploiting the capture effect for rapid flooding in wireless sensor networks. In *IEEE INFOCOM*, Rio de Janeiro, Brazil, Apr. 2009.

[23] B. Namboodiri and A. Keshavarzian. Alert: An adaptive low-latency event-driven mac protocol for wireless sensor networks. In *ACM/IEEE IPSN*, St. Louis, USA, Apr. 2008.

[24] F. Österlind and A. Dunkels. Approaching the maximum 802.15.4 multi-hop throughput. In *HotEmnets*, June 2008.

[25] F. Österlind, N. Wirström, N. Tsiftes, N. Finne, T. Voigt, and A. Dunkels. StrawMAN: Making Sudden Traffic Surges Graceful in Low-Power Wireless Networks. In *Proceedings of the Workshop on Hot Topics in Embedded Networked Sensor Systems (HotEmnets)*, Killarney, Ireland, June 2010.

[26] N. Pereira, B. Andersson, and E. Tovar. WiDom: A dominance protocol for wireless medium access. *IEEE Transactions on Industrial Informatics*, 3(2):120, 2007.

[27] J. Polastre, J. Hill, and D. Culler. Versatile low power media access for wireless sensor networks. In *Proceedings of the International Conference on Embedded Networked Sensor Systems (ACM SenSys)*, Baltimore, MD, USA, 2004.

[28] J. Polastre, R. Szewczyk, and D. Culler. Telos: Enabling ultra-low power wireless research. In *Proceedings of the International Conference on Information Processing in Sensor Networks (ACM/IEEE IPSN)*, Los Angeles, CA, USA, Apr. 2005.

[29] B. Raman, K. Chebrolu, S. Bijwe, and V. Gabale. PIP: A Connection-Oriented, Multi-Hop, Multi-Channel TDMA-based MAC for High Throughput Bulk Transfer. In *Proceedings of the International Conference on Embedded Networked Sensor Systems (ACM SenSys)*, Zürich, Switzerland, 2010.

[30] M. Ringwald and K. Römer. BitMAC: A Deterministic, Collision-Free, and Robust MAC Protocol for Sensor Networks. In *Proceedings of the European Conference on Wireless Sensor Networks (EWSN)*, Istanbul, Turkey, Jan. 2005.

[31] M. Ringwald and K. Römer. Burstmac - an efficient mac protocol for correlated traffic bursts. In *International Conference on Networked Sensing Systems (INSS)*, 2009.

[32] Y. Sankarasubramaniam, O. Akan, and I. Akyildiz. ESRT : Event-to-Sink Reliable Transport in Wireless Sensor Networks. In *Proceedings of the 4th ACM international symposium on Mobile ad hoc networking and computing (MobiHOC 2003)*, 2003.

[33] J. L. S. Sobrinho and A. S. Krishnakumar. Real-Time Traffic over the IEEE 802.11 Medium Access Control Layer. In *Bell Labs Technical Journal*, 1996.

[34] K. Srinivasan, M. Kazandjieva, S. Agarwal, and P. Levis. The β-factor: measuring wireless link burstiness. In *Proceedings of the International Conference on Embedded Networked Sensor Systems (ACM SenSys)*, Raleigh, NC, USA, 2008.

[35] Y. Sun, O. Gurewitz, and D. Johnson. RI-MAC: A Receiver-Initiated Asynchronous Duty Cycle MAC Protocol for Dynamic Traffic Loads in Wireless Sensor Networks. In *Proceedings of the International Conference on Embedded Networked Sensor Systems (ACM SenSys)*, Raleigh, NC, USA, 2008.

[36] F. A. Tobagi and L. Kleinrock. Packet Switching in Radio Channels: Part II - The Hidden Terminal Problem in Carrier Sensing Multiple Access and Busy Tone Solution. In *IEEE Trans. on Commun.*, volume 23. IEEE, 1975.

[37] K. Whitehouse, A. Woo, F. Jiang, J. Polastre, and D. Culler. Exploiting The Capture Effect For Collision Detection And Recovery. In *Proceedings of the IEEE Workshop on Embedded Networked Sensor Systems (IEEE Emnets)*, Sydney, Australia, May 2005.

[38] A. Woo and D. Culler. A transmission control scheme for media access in sensor networks. In *Proceedings of the International Conference on Mobile Computing and Networking (ACM MobiCom)*, Rome, Italy, 2001.

[39] X. Yang and N. Vaidya. On physical carrier sensing in wireless ad hoc networks. In *IEEE INFOCOM*. IEEE, 2005.

[40] W. Ye, J. Heidemann, and D. Estrin. An Energy-Efficient MAC Protocol for Wireless Sensor Networks. In *Proceedings of the IEEE Conference on Computer Communications (INFOCOM)*, New York, NY, USA, June 2002.

pTunes: Runtime Parameter Adaptation for Low-power MAC Protocols

Marco Zimmerling*, Federico Ferrari*, Luca Mottola†, Thiemo Voigt†, Lothar Thiele*
*Computer Engineering and Networks Laboratory, ETH Zurich, Switzerland
†Swedish Institute of Computer Science (SICS), Kista, Sweden
{zimmerling, ferrari, thiele}@tik.ee.ethz.ch   {luca, thiemo}@sics.se

ABSTRACT

We present PTUNES, a framework for runtime adaptation of low-power MAC protocol parameters. The MAC operating parameters bear great influence on the system performance, yet their optimal choice is a function of the current network state. Based on application requirements expressed as network lifetime, end-to-end latency, and end-to-end reliability, PTUNES automatically determines optimized parameter values to adapt to link, topology, and traffic dynamics. To this end, we introduce a flexible modeling approach, separating protocol-dependent from protocol-independent aspects, which facilitates using PTUNES with different MAC protocols, and design an efficient system support that integrates smoothly with the application. To demonstrate its effectiveness, we apply PTUNES to X-MAC and LPP. In a 44-node testbed, PTUNES achieves up to three-fold lifetime gains over static MAC parameters optimized for peak traffic, the latter being current—and almost unavoidable—practice in real deployments. PTUNES promptly reacts to changes in traffic load and link quality, reducing packet loss by 80 % during periods of controlled wireless interference. Moreover, PTUNES helps the routing protocol recover quickly from critical network changes, reducing packet loss by 70 % in a scenario where multiple core routing nodes fail.

Categories and Subject Descriptors

C.2.2 [**Computer-Communication Networks**]: Network Protocols; C.2.1 [**Computer-Communication Networks**]: Network Architecture and Design—*wireless communication*

General Terms

Design, Experimentation, Performance

Keywords

Runtime adaptation, parameter optimization, MAC protocol, multi-objective, centralized, end-to-end, sensor network

1. INTRODUCTION

Media access control (MAC) protocols play a key role in determining the performance and reliability of low-power wireless networks, but very few of the many proposed solutions have been adopted in real deployments [23, 34].

Challenges. There exists a large conceptual gap between the high-level application requirements and the low-level MAC protocol operation [23]. In particular, it requires expert knowledge to find MAC operating parameters whose performance satisfies given application requirements.

In most deployments today, the choice of MAC parameters is based on experience and rules of thumb involving a coarse-grained analysis of expected network load and topology dynamics. This can yield a performance far off the application requirements [24]. Alternatively, system designers perform several field trials to identify suitable MAC parameters [8]. This time-consuming and deployment-specific practice, however, is hardly sustainable in the long term.

Even if the MAC parameters are appropriate at one time, they are likely to perform poorly when the network state changes. Wireless link quality varies significantly over time, leading to unpredictable packet loss [41]; harsh environmental conditions cause nodes to be temporarily disconnected or to fail [2]; and changes in the routing topology or the sensing activity result in traffic fluctuations. Statically configured MAC protocols cannot cope with these dynamics.

To perform efficiently, MAC protocols must adapt their operating parameters at runtime. One way to approach this problem is to embed adaptivity within the protocol operation [21]. This, however, hard-codes the adaptation decisions and thus limits their applicability. Instead, separating adaptivity from the protocol operation enables higher-layer services to dynamically adjust the operating parameters [32]. Although a few mechanisms utilize such control knobs, they focus either on a single metric—typically energy [9, 22, 28]—or consider only local metrics, such as per-hop latency [5, 31]. Real-world applications, however, often require to balance *multiple* conflicting needs such as reliability, energy, and latency, expressed on a *network-wide* scale [7, 36, 38].

Contributions and road-map. To tackle the issues above, we present PTUNES, a framework for runtime adaptation of low-power MAC protocol parameters. In PTUNES, users specify application requirements in terms of *network lifetime, end-to-end reliability,* and *end-to-end latency*—key performance metrics in real-world applications [7, 8, 36–38]. Using information about the current network state, PTUNES automatically determines optimized MAC parameters whose performance meets the requirements specification.

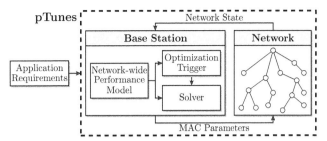

pTunes

Figure 1: The pTunes framework.

This paper makes the following contributions:

- We introduce the PTUNES framework, targeting data collection systems using tree-shaped routing topologies atop low-power MAC protocols. As shown in Fig. 1, the base station collects reports on the *network state*, such as topology and link quality information, required to evaluate the network-wide metrics we target. The *optimization trigger* decides when to carry out the parameter optimization, based on a periodic timer or a mechanism that uses the *network-wide performance model* to check if the *application requirements* are violated under the current network state. The *solver* determines a vector of *optimized MAC parameters*, which is disseminated in the network and installed on all nodes. Sec. 2 further characterizes the *multi-objective* parameter optimization problem in PTUNES.

- We design a well-structured modeling framework to solve the parameter optimization problem. Our layered modeling approach, described in Sec. 3, separates application-level, protocol-independent, and protocol-dependent quantities. This increases generality and flexibility, as it cleanly determines what needs to be changed to account for a different MAC protocol. We apply this modeling approach to two state-of-the-art protocols, X-MAC [5] and LPP [29], based on their implementations in Contiki. We leverage these models throughout the rest of the paper, ultimately demonstrating that they are both practical and accurate.

- We present the design and implementation of an efficient system support to meet the system-level challenges arising in PTUNES. These include, for instance, the timely collection of accurate network state with little energy overhead and minimum disruption for the application operation. As described in Sec. 4, unlike most approaches in the literature, we meet these requirements with a novel solution for collecting network state and disseminating new MAC parameters *independent* of other protocols running concurrently. Our approach utilizes fast and reliable Glossy network floods [16], allowing PTUNES to collect *consistent* network state snapshots, taken with microsecond accuracy at all nodes simultaneously, with very low energy cost.

After illustrating implementation details in Sec. 5, we evaluate PTUNES in Sec. 6 using experiments with X-MAC and LPP on a 44-node testbed. For instance, we find that adapting their parameters using PTUNES enables up to three-fold lifetime gains over static MAC parameters optimized for peak traffic, the latter being current practice in many real deployments [23]. PTUNES promptly reacts to changes in traffic load and link quality, meeting application-level requirements through an 80% reduction in packet loss during periods of controlled wireless interference. Moreover, we find that PTUNES helps the routing protocol recover from critical network changes, reducing the total number of parent switches and settling quickly on a stable, high-quality rout-

ing topology. This reduces packet loss by 70% in a scenario where multiple core routing nodes fail simultaneously.

We discuss design trade-offs of PTUNES in Sec. 7, review related work in Sec. 8, and conclude the paper in Sec. 9.

2. OPTIMIZATION PROBLEM

In PTUNES, we simultaneously consider three key performance metrics of real-world applications [7, 8, 36–38]: network lifetime T, end-to-end reliability R, and end-to-end latency L. The MAC parameter optimization problem thus becomes a *multi-objective optimization problem (MOP)*. This involves optimizing the objective functions $T(\mathbf{c})$, $R(\mathbf{c})$, and $L(\mathbf{c})$, where $\mathbf{c}$ is a vector of MAC parameters, or *MAC configuration* for short. There may exist not one unique optimal solution to this MOP, but rather a set of solutions that are optimal in the sense that no other solution is superior in *all* objectives. These are known as *Pareto-optimal* solutions and represent different optimal trade-offs among T, R, and L.

Given the many Pareto-optimal solutions, a natural question is which solution best serves the application demands. PTUNES needs to make this decision at runtime in an automated fashion, without involving the user (*e.g.*, to manually select a solution from a set of candidates). With this requirement in mind, we adopt from among the many MOP solving techniques an approach inspired by the epsilon-constraint method [20]. This method treats all but one objective as constraints, and thus provides a natural interface for specifying typical requirements of low-power wireless systems such as "batteries should last for at least 6 months." Using this approach, PTUNES solves the MOP by optimizing one objective subject to constraints on the remaining objectives

$$
\begin{array}{lll}
\text{Maximize/Minimize} & M_1(\mathbf{c}) & \\
\text{Subject to} & M_2(\mathbf{c}) \geq, \leq & C_1 \\
& M_3(\mathbf{c}) \geq, \leq & C_2
\end{array} \quad (1)
$$

where each M_i is one among $\{T, R, L\}$ and $\{C_1, C_2\}$ are *soft* requirements to be satisfied in the long run, corresponding to the best-effort operation of many data collection systems [18]. By varying $\{C_1, C_2\}$, all Pareto-optimal solutions can be generated. Based on concrete values for $\{C_1, C_2\}$ set by the user on some objectives, PTUNES translates the application requirements into a solution that optimizes the remaining objective. The resulting solution is Pareto-optimal while representing the trade-off provided by the user.

As an example, in long-term structural monitoring the major concern is typically system lifetime, but domain experts also require a certain reliability in delivering sensed data [7]. Based on (1), maximizing network lifetime subject to a minimum end-to-end reliability is specified as

$$
\begin{array}{lll}
\text{Maximize} & T(\mathbf{c}) & \\
\text{Subject to} & R(\mathbf{c}) \geq & R_{min}
\end{array} \quad (2)
$$

In addition, we may impose a constraint on end-to-end latency, $L(\mathbf{c}) \leq L_{max}$, if timely data delivery is relevant.

3. MODELING FRAMEWORK

To facilitate using PTUNES with different low-power MAC protocols, we break up the modeling into three distinct layers, as shown in the model frame in Fig. 2. The upper layer defines application-level metrics (R, L, T) as functions of link and node-specific metrics (R_l, L_l, T_n). The middle layer expresses these metrics in a protocol-independent manner,

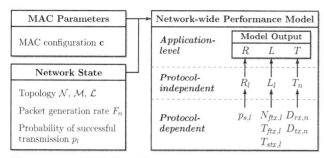

Figure 2: Modeling framework with inputs, output, and mapping between modeling layers. *Only the protocol-dependent layer must be changed to prepare the network-wide performance model for another MAC protocol.*

Term	Description
$\mathcal{N}$	Set of all nodes in the network excluding the sink
$\mathcal{M}$	Set of source nodes generating packets
$\mathcal{L}$	Set of all links forming the routing tree
F_n	Packet generation rate of node n
p_l	Probability of successful transmission over link l
$p_{s,l}$	Probability of successful unicast transm. over link l
$N_{ftx,l}$	No. of failed unicast transm. before success over link l
$T_{ftx,l}$	Time for a failed unicast transmission over link l
$T_{stx,l}$	Time for a successful unicast transmission over link l
$D_{rx,n}$	Fraction of time radio is in receive mode at node n
$D_{tx,n}$	Fraction of time radio is in transmit mode at node n

Table 1: Glossary of modeling terms used to denote network state and protocol-dependent quantities.

and provides the entry point for the modeling of a concrete MAC protocol by exposing six terms to the lower protocol-dependent layer. Binding these terms to concrete protocol-specific expressions is sufficient to adapt the network-wide performance model in PTUNES to a given MAC protocol.

Model inputs are the MAC parameters and the network state, comprising information about routing topology, traffic volumes, and link qualities. As a measure of the latter, we take the probability of successful transmission p_l over the link to the parent in the routing tree. To keep our models simple and practical, we assume the delivery of individual packets to be independent of their size, of the delivery of any other packet, and of the link direction they travel along. As illustrated in Sec. 4, our runtime evaluation of p_l captures the impact of channel contention on link quality, allowing us not to consider it explicitly in our models. Testbed experiments in Sec. 6.2 show that this approach results in highly accurate models for both X-MAC and LPP.

3.1 Application-level Metrics

In a typical data collection scenario with static nodes, a tree-shaped routing topology provides a unique path from every sensor node to a sink node. These paths are generally time-varying, as the routing protocol adapts them according to link quality estimates among other things [18, 33]. In the following, we use $\mathcal{N}$ to denote the set of *all nodes* in the network excluding the sink, and $\mathcal{M} \subseteq \mathcal{N}$ to denote the set of *source nodes* generating packets. We also indicate with $\mathcal{L}$ the set of *communication links* that form the current routing tree. The *path* $\mathcal{P}_n \subseteq \mathcal{L}$ originating at node $n \in \mathcal{M}$ includes all intermediate links that connect node n to the sink. Table 1 lists these and other modeling terms we use to denote network state and protocol-dependent quantities.

End-to-end reliability and latency. The reliability $R_{\mathcal{P}_n}$ of path $\mathcal{P}_n$ is the expected fraction of packets delivered from node $n \in \mathcal{M}$ to the sink along $\mathcal{P}_n$. Thus, $R_{\mathcal{P}_n}$ is the product of per-hop reliabilities R_l, $l \in \mathcal{P}_n$. We define the *end-to-end reliability* R as the average reliability of all paths $\mathcal{P}_n$.

$$R = \frac{1}{|\mathcal{M}|} \sum_{n \in \mathcal{M}} R_{\mathcal{P}_n} = \frac{1}{|\mathcal{M}|} \sum_{n \in \mathcal{M}} \left(\prod_{l \in \mathcal{P}_n} R_l \right) \quad (3)$$

Likewise, the latency $L_{\mathcal{P}_n}$ of path $\mathcal{P}_n$ is the expected time between the first transmission of a packet at node $n \in \mathcal{M}$ and its reception at the sink. Thus, $L_{\mathcal{P}_n}$ is the sum of per-hop latencies L_l, $l \in \mathcal{P}_n$. Similar to (3), we define the *end-to-end latency* L for *successfully delivered* packets as the average latency of all paths $\mathcal{P}_n$, and omit the formula.

We define R and L as averages of all source-sink paths since the global, long-term performance is of ultimate interest for most data collection systems [36–38]. Local, short-term deviations from the requirements are usually tolerated, provided they are compensated in the long run. In other scenarios (*e.g.*, industrial settings), it might be more appropriate to define R and L as the minimum reliability and the maximum latency among all source-sink paths, which would only require modifying the two definitions above.

Network lifetime. Similar to prior work [27], we define the *network lifetime* T as the expected shortest node lifetime T_n, $n \in \mathcal{N}$. We assume the sink has infinite energy supply.

$$T = \min_{n \in \mathcal{N}} (T_n) \quad (4)$$

This choice is motivated by the fact that a single node failure can lead to network partition and service interruption. It is also possible to express other notions of network lifetime in PTUNES, such as the time until some fraction of nodes fails, again requiring only to modify the definition in (4).

3.2 Protocol-independent Modeling

The section above expressed the application-level metrics R, L, and T as functions of per-hop reliability R_l, per-hop latency L_l, and node lifetime T_n (see Fig. 2). We now define the latter three in a protocol-independent manner, which increases flexibility and generality by isolating protocol-dependent quantities. We omit a few explicit expressions and refer to an extended report [42] where applicable.

Per-hop reliability and latency. Several factors influence these metrics: (*i*) the MAC operation when transmitting packets, (*ii*) packet queuing throughout the network stack due to insufficient bandwidth, and (*iii*) application-level buffering (*e.g.*, to perform in-network processing). The MAC parameters control (*i*) and may avoid the occurrence of (*ii*), provided a MAC configuration exists that provides sufficient bandwidth. Application-specific in-network functionality akin to (*iii*) is out of the scope of this work.

We present next expressions for per-hop reliability and latency due to the MAC operation, corresponding to (*i*). Additionally, PTUNES includes models to detect situations akin to (*ii*) [42]. In fact, as we show in Sec. 6.2, PTUNES automatically adjusts the MAC parameters to provide higher bandwidth against increased traffic, thus avoiding the occurrence of local packet queuing until the network capacity attainable in our experimental setting is fully exhausted.

We define the *per-hop reliability* R_l of link $l \in \mathcal{L}$, which connects node $n \in \mathcal{N}$ to its parent m in the routing tree, as the probability that n successfully transmits a packet to m.

$$R_l = 1 - (1 - p_{s,l})^{N+1} \quad (5)$$

Here, $p_{s,l}$ represents the MAC-dependent probability that a single unicast transmission over link l succeeds, and N is the maximum number of retransmissions per packet, modeling automatic repeat request (ARQ) mechanisms used by many low-power MAC protocols to improve reliability.

Furthermore, we define the *per-hop latency* L_l of link l as the time for node n to deliver a message to its parent m.

$$L_l = N_{ftx,l} \cdot T_{ftx,l} + T_{stx,l} \quad (6)$$

$T_{ftx,l}$ and $T_{stx,l}$ are the MAC-dependent times spent for each failed and the final successful transmission. The expected number of failed transmissions $N_{ftx,l}$ depends on $p_{s,l}$ and N, and the retransmission policy of the MAC protocol [42].

Node lifetime. Sensor nodes consume energy by communicating, sensing, processing, and storing data. Adapting the MAC parameters has no significant impact on the latter three, but affects energy expenditures on communication to a large extent, as the radio is typically the major energy consumer. Given a battery capacity Q, we define the *node lifetime* T_n of node $n \in \mathcal{N}$ as

$$T_n = Q/(D_{tx,n} \cdot I_{tx} + D_{rx,n} \cdot I_{rx} + D_{idle,n} \cdot I_{idle}) \quad (7)$$

where I_{tx}, I_{rx}, and I_i are the current draws of the radio in transmit, receive, and idle mode. T_n is thus the expected node lifetime based on the fractions of time in each mode $D_{tx,n}$, $D_{rx,n}$, and $D_{idle,n} = 1 - D_{tx,n} - D_{rx,n}$, which depend on the MAC protocol and the traffic volume at node n.

The *traffic volume* is the rate at which nodes send and receive packets. A node $n \in \mathcal{N}$ generates packets at rate F_n and receives packets from its children $\mathcal{C}_n \subseteq \mathcal{N}$ in the routing tree, if any. The rate of packet reception depends on each child's packet transmission rate $F_{tx,c}$ and the individual per-hop reliabilities R_{l_c} of links l_c, $c \in \mathcal{C}_n$, connecting each child c with n. Thus, node n transmits packets at rate

$$F_{tx,n} = (N_{rtx,l} + 1) \cdot \left(F_n + \sum_{c \in \mathcal{C}_n} F_{tx,c} \cdot R_{l_c} \right) \quad (8)$$

$N_{rtx,l}$ is the expected number of retransmissions per packet over link l, which is a function of N and the MAC-dependent probability that a retransmission occurs [42].

We demonstrate next the modeling of a concrete MAC protocol. This requires to find expressions for six protocol-specific terms, as shown in Fig. 2 and described in Table 1.

3.3 Protocol-specific Modeling

We use two state-of-the-art MAC protocols to exemplify the protocol-specific modeling. X-MAC [5] is representative of many sender-initiated MAC protocols based on low-power listening (LPL) [32] that proved viable in real-world deployments [23]. Recent work focuses on receiver-initiated MAC protocols such as low-power probing (LPP) [29]. In the following, we refer to implementations of X-MAC and LPP in Contiki 2.3, which we also use in our experiments in Sec. 6.

3.3.1 Sender-initiated: X-MAC

Fig. 3 shows a successful unicast transmission in X-MAC. Nodes wake up periodically for T_{on} to poll the channel $\langle 1 \rangle$, where T_{off} is the time between two channel polls. To send a packet, a node transmits a sequence of *strobes* $\langle 2 \rangle$, short

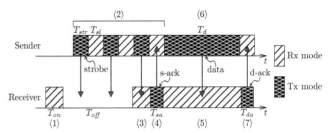

Figure 3: Unicast transmission in X-MAC.

packets containing the identifier of the receiver. Strobing continues for a period sufficient to make at least one strobe overlap with a receiver wake-up $\langle 3 \rangle$. The receiver replies with a *strobe acknowledgment (s-ack)* $\langle 4 \rangle$ and keeps the radio on awaiting the transmission of the *data packet* $\langle 5 \rangle$. The sender transmits the data packet upon receiving the s-ack $\langle 6 \rangle$ and waits for the *data acknowledgment (d-ack)* $\langle 7 \rangle$ from the receiver. Afterward, both nodes turn off their radios.

Failed s-ack, d-ack, and data packet transmissions are handled by timeouts. When a timeout occurs, the sender backs off for a random period and retries beginning with the strobing phase, for at most N times. Broadcasts proceed similarly to unicast transmissions, but the strobing phase lasts for $T_m = 2 \cdot T_{on} + T_{off}$ to make a strobe overlap with the wake-up of all neighboring nodes. Nodes receiving a broadcast strobe keep their radio on until they receive the data packet at the end of the sender's strobing phase.

Several variables are adjustable in the X-MAC implementation we consider. However, three specific parameters affect its performance to a major extent.

$$\mathbf{c} = [T_{on}, T_{off}, N] \quad (9)$$

We let PTUNES adapt these parameters at runtime, using the X-MAC-specific models presented next.

Per-hop reliability. We determine $p_{s,l}$ in (5), the probability that a single unicast from node n to its parent m succeeds. This is the case if m hears a strobe (with probability $p_{str,l}$), the s-ack reaches n, and m receives the data packet. Each of the latter two succeeds with probability p_l, collected at runtime as part of the network state (see Sec. 4).

$$p_{s,l} = p_{str,l} \cdot p_l^2 \quad (10)$$

The probability of receiving at least one strobe is

$$p_{str,l} = 1 - (1 - p_l)^{(T_{on} - T_{str})/T_{it}} \quad (11)$$

where $T_{it} = T_{str} + T_{sl}$ is the duration of a strobe iteration at the sender, which includes the length of a strobe transmission T_{str} and listening T_{sl} for an s-ack.

Per-hop latency. We determine $T_{ftx,l}$ and $T_{stx,l}$ in (6), the times spent for failed and successful transmissions. $T_{ftx,l}$ depends on whether node n receives an s-ack. If so, n stops strobing, sends the data packet, and times out after T_{out}. Otherwise, n sends strobes for T_m. In either case, node n backs off for T_b before retransmitting.

$$T_{ftx,l} = (N_{it}T_{it} + T_d + T_{out})p_{str,l} + T_m(1 - p_{str,l}) + T_b \quad (12)$$

Here, $N_{it} = (T_{on} + T_{off})/(2 \cdot T_{it})$ is the average number of strobe iterations before m possibly replies with an s-ack.

The time for a successful transmission $T_{stx,l}$ includes the time to wait for the s-ack and to send the data packet.

$$T_{stx,l} = N_{it} \cdot T_{it} + T_d \quad (13)$$

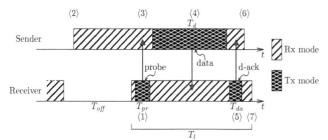

Figure 4: Unicast transmission in LPP.

Node lifetime. We determine $D_{tx,n}$ and $D_{rx,n}$ in (7), the fractions of time spent by the radio in transmit and receive mode. Both quantities depend on the rate F_{arx,l_c} at which node n attempts to receive a packet from child c over link l_c

$$F_{arx,l_c} = (N_{rtx,l_c} + 1) \cdot F_{tx,c} \cdot p_{str,l_c} \quad (14)$$

where $F_{tx,c}$ and p_{str,l_c} are given by (8) and (11).

We first consider $D_{tx,n}$. Node n transmits during packet receptions from child c (to send s-ack and d-ack) and during packet transmissions to its parent m (to send strobes and data packet). We define T_{rxt,l_c} and $T_{txt,l}$ as the average times spent by the radio in transmission mode during receptions over link l_c and transmissions over link l [42].

$$D_{tx,n} = F_{tx,n} \cdot T_{txt,l} + \sum_{c \in \mathcal{C}_n} F_{arx,l_c} \cdot T_{rxt,l_c} \quad (15)$$

Next we consider $D_{rx,n}$. Node n is in receive mode during packet transmissions to its parent m (to receive s-ack and d-ack) and packet receptions from child c (to receive strobe and data packet). Let $T_{txr,l}$ and T_{rxr,l_c} be the average times spent by the radio in reception mode during transmissions over link l and receptions over link l_c [42]. The fraction of time in receive mode for actual communication is

$$D_{rxc,n} = F_{tx,n} \cdot T_{txr,l} + \sum_{c \in \mathcal{C}_n} F_{arx,l_c} \cdot T_{rxr,l_c} \quad (16)$$

In addition, n is in receive mode for $F_{cc} = T_{on}/(T_{on} + T_{off})$ during channel checks, which leads to

$$D_{rx,n} = D_{rxc,n} + (1 - D_{rxc,n}) \cdot F_{cc} \quad (17)$$

3.3.2 Receiver-initiated: LPP

Fig. 4 shows a successful unicast transmission in LPP. Nodes periodically turn on their radio for T_l and transmit a short *probe* $\langle 1 \rangle$ containing their own identifier. To send a packet, a node turns on its radio $\langle 2 \rangle$ and listens for a probe from the intended receiver $\langle 3 \rangle$, for at most T_{on}. Then the sender transmits the data packet $\langle 4 \rangle$, waits for the d-ack from the receiver $\langle 5 \rangle$, and goes back to sleep $\langle 6 \rangle$. After sending the d-ack, the receiver keeps the radio on until a timeout signals the end of the active phase $\langle 7 \rangle$. Between two active phases nodes sleep for T_{off}. To send a broadcast, the sender keeps its radio on for $T_m = 2 \cdot T_l + T_{off}$ to receive a probe from every neighbor, immediately replying to each received probe with the data packet. We let PTUNES adapt the same set of LPP parameters **c** in (9) as for X-MAC (note that T_{on} has now a different meaning as explained above).

Per-hop reliability. A single LPP unicast from node n to its parent m succeeds if n receives a probe from m (with probability $p_{pr,l}$) and then successfully transmits the data packet (with probability p_l).

$$p_{s,l} = p_{pr,l} \cdot p_l \quad (18)$$

The probability that n receives a probe is given by

$$p_{pr,l} = 1 - (1 - p_l)^k \quad (19)$$

where $k = (T_{on} - T_{pr})/T$ is the number of possible probe receptions while node n listens for at most T_{on}. The term $T = T_l + T_{off} + T_{rm}/2$ denotes the LPP duty cycle period, which is the sum of radio on-time, radio off-time, and a small random quantity with uniform distribution $\{0, \ldots, T_{rm}\}$ to scatter probe transmissions.

Per-hop latency. We determine the time for a failed transmission. If node n receives a probe after waiting for $T_{pw,l}$, it sends the data packet and times out after T_{out}. Otherwise, n listens for T_{on}. Node n retransmits after backing off for T_b.

$$T_{ftr,l} = (T_{pw,l} + T_d + T_{out})p_{pr,l} + T_{on}(1 - p_{pr,l}) + T_b \quad (20)$$

On average, node n receives a probe from its parent m after

$$T_{pw,l} = T_{pr} + \sum_{i=1}^{\lfloor k \rfloor + 1} p_i \cdot T_i \quad (21)$$

where p_i is the probability that n receives the i-th probe, and T_i is the expected time to await the i-th probe [42].

The time for a successful transmission includes the time to wait for a probe and to send the data packet.

$$T_{str,l} = T_{pw,l} + T_d \quad (22)$$

Node lifetime. We determine the fractions of time in transmit and receive mode. Both depend on the rate F_{arx,l_c} at which node n receives packets from child c over link l_c

$$F_{arx,l_c} = (N_{rtx,l_c} + 1) \cdot F_{tx,c} \cdot p_{s,l_c} \quad (23)$$

where $F_{tx,c}$ and p_{s,l_c} are given by (8) and (18).

Node n transmits a probe every duty cycle period T and sends d-acks to child c with frequency F_{arx,l_c}. Further, n is in transmit mode for $T_{txt,l}$ to send packets to m [42].

$$D_{tx,n} = T_{pr}/T + T_{da} \sum_{c \in \mathcal{C}_n} F_{arx,l_c} + F_{tx,n} \cdot T_{txt,l} \quad (24)$$

Node n is in receive mode when the radio is turned on but does not transmit probes or d-acks. Additionally, node n is in receive mode for $T_{txr,l}$ during packet transmissions [42].

$$D_{rx,n} = (T_l - T_{pr})/T - T_{da} \sum_{c \in \mathcal{C}_n} F_{arx,l_c} + F_{tx,n} \cdot T_{txr,l} \quad (25)$$

4. SYSTEM SUPPORT

PTUNES must tackle several system-level challenges to obtain an efficient runtime operation. This section highlights these challenges and presents the system support we design to meet them. This includes a novel approach for collecting network state information and disseminating new MAC parameters, and the techniques and tools we use to solve the parameter optimization problem efficiently.

4.1 Challenges

Minimum disruption. PTUNES must reduce the amount of disruption perceived by the application, particularly with respect to application data traffic, to avoid influencing its behavior beyond the adaptation of MAC parameters. This is in itself a major challenge in low-power wireless networks [10].

Timeliness. Timely collection of accurate network state, computation of optimized MAC parameters, and their reliable and rapid dissemination are fundamental to PTUNES.

Only this way PTUNES can provide MAC operating parameters that do match the current network state. However, it is difficult to perform the above operations in a timely manner, especially when involving resource-constrained devices.

Consistency. PTUNES requires consistent snapshots of network state, possibly captured by all nodes at the same time. Otherwise, optimizing MAC parameters based on information different from the actual network conditions may even negatively affect the system performance. Coordinating distributed sensor nodes to achieve consistency is challenging, given their bandwidth and energy limitations.

Energy efficiency. PTUNES must meet all the previous challenges while introducing only a limited, possibly predictable, energy overhead at the sensor nodes. To be viable, the overhead of PTUNES must not outweigh the gains obtained from adapting the MAC parameters.

4.2 Collection and Dissemination

PTUNES uses Glossy network floods [16] to collect network state information and disseminate MAC parameters. In particular, PTUNES exploits Glossy's time synchronization service to schedule and execute both operations within short time frames, repeated every *collection period* T_c. Every frame starts with a Glossy flood initiated by the sink, which serves to time-synchronize the nodes and disseminate new MAC parameters. Following the initial flood by the sink, each of the other nodes initiates a flood in turn within exclusive slots, reporting network state for the subsequent trigger decision and parameter optimization.

The collection period T_c can range from a few tens of seconds to several minutes depending on network dynamics and application needs, and represents a trade-off between the energy overhead of PTUNES and its responsiveness to changes in the network: a shorter T_c permits more frequent parameter updates but increases the energy consumption of the nodes. The efficiency of Glossy allows us to limit the length of the periodic collection and dissemination frames, thus keeping the energy overhead to a minimum. For instance, we measure on a 44-node testbed an average duration of 5.2 ms for a single flood, and an average radio duty cycle of 0.35 % due to PTUNES collection and dissemination for $T_c = 1$ min, which reduces to about 0.07 % for $T_c = 5$ min. Given that state-of-the-art low-power MAC protocols exhibit duty cycles of 3–7 % in testbed settings comparable to ours [13, 18], the energy overhead of PTUNES is marginal.

An alternative to our approach may be to piggyback network state on application packets and to use a variant of Trickle [25] to disseminate MAC parameters. We employed this approach at an early stage of this work, but found it inadequate for our purposes. For instance, running Trickle concurrently with data collection increases contention, especially during parameter updates, which degrades application data yield [10]. Moreover, piggybacking on data packets induces a dependency on the rate and reliability of application traffic. In low-rate applications, it may take a very long time until network state from all nodes becomes available for optimization. Packets may also be generated at different times and experience varying end-to-end delays (*e.g.*, due to contention or routing loops), so the collected network state is likely to be out-of-date and inconsistent. Our approach avoids these problems by temporally decoupling collection and dissemination from application tasks, and by leveraging consistent network state snapshots taken with microsecond accuracy at all nodes independently of application traffic.

In particular, PTUNES collects three pieces of network state from each node: (*i*) the node id and the id of the routing parent, to allow PTUNES to learn about the current routing tree ($\mathcal{N}$, $\mathcal{M}$, $\mathcal{L}$); (*ii*) the number of packets generated per second F_n, allowing PTUNES to determine the traffic volumes; and (*iii*) the ratio $H_{s,l}/H_{t,l}$ of successful and total number of link-layer handshakes over link l to the routing parent. There are two handshakes in X-MAC, strobe/s-ack and data/d-ack; LPP features only the latter (see Figs. 3 and 4). To account for parent switches and link dynamics, a node maintains counters $H_{s,l}$ and $H_{t,l}$ in a way similar to an exponentially weighted moving average (EWMA). Based on their ratio received from each node and by taking the square root, PTUNES obtains estimates of the probability of successful transmission p_l of all links in the current routing tree. The collected information totals 6 bytes per node.

4.3 Optimization Tools

Applying the optimization problem in (1) to our X-MAC and LPP models in Sec. 3 leads to a mixed-integer nonlinear program (MINLP) with non-convex objective and constraint functions. To solve it efficiently, we use the ECL^{i}PS^e constraint programming system [1]. Its high-level programming paradigm allows for a succinct modeling of our optimization problem. We use modules to separate protocol-independent from protocol-dependent code; the latter amounts to about 100 lines for each X-MAC and LPP.

We use the branch-and-bound algorithm coupled with a complete search routine, both provided by the interval constraint (IC) solver of ECL^{i}PS^e. The running time of the optimization depends to a large extent on the size of the search space. To reduce it, we exploit the fact that MAC protocols are commonly implemented using hardware timers. The resolution of these timers determines the maximum required granularity of the MAC timing parameters. We therefore discretize the domains of T_{on} and T_{off} considered for adaptation, letting ECL^{i}PS^e determine values with millisecond granularity. Based on the literature and our own experience, we set the upper bounds of N and T_{off} to 10 retransmissions and 1 s; T_{on} is chosen such that a node listens long enough to overlap with exactly one receiver wake-up in LPP, and with at least one but not more than three strobe transmissions in X-MAC. For these settings and in the scenarios we tested, representative of a large fraction of deployed sensor networks, ECL^{i}PS^e finds optimized MAC parameters within a few tens of seconds on a standard laptop computer. Compared with our current approach, which leverages general-purpose algorithms and off-the-shelf implementations, dedicated solution techniques and implementations are likely to improve significantly on this figure.

5. IMPLEMENTATION DETAILS

On the sensor nodes, we use Contiki 2.3. We extended the existing X-MAC implementation with link-layer retransmissions and an interface to adjust the parameters in (9) at runtime. Since the existing LPP implementation suffered from performance problems that could bias our results, we re-implemented LPP within the Contiki stack and extended it in the same way as X-MAC. For data collection we use Contiki Collect, which maintains a tree-based routing topology using expected transmissions (ETX) as cost metric.

The PTUNES control application running on the base station is implemented in Java. It retrieves collected network state from the sink, starts the optimization process depending on the trigger decision, and transfers new MAC parameters back to the sink for dissemination.

An important decision for PTUNES is when to trigger the parameter optimization. In general, we want to optimize as often as possible to make the MAC parameters closely match the network state. At the same time, we want to minimize the energy overhead for collection and dissemination, and need to consider that running the solver takes time. Therefore, PTUNES provides three basic optimization triggers to decide when to start the solver. Nevertheless, PTUNES users can implement their own application-specific triggers using a set of basic interfaces we provide.

Among the triggers we provide, *TimedTrigger* optimizes periodically, where the period is typically a multiple of the collection period T_c. In this way, a TimedTrigger may launch the solver immediately after the collection of network state, and PTUNES floods the new MAC parameters at the next dissemination. Nevertheless, depending on application-specific requirements and performance goals, users may also combine a TimedTrigger with one of the following two triggers.

A *ConstraintTrigger* uses the model to estimate the current network performance based on the collected network state, and launches the solver only if any of the constraints in (1) is violated. A ConstraintTrigger may be implemented to tolerate short-term violations of a constraint, or a violation within some threshold around the constraint. Alternatively, a *NetworkStateTrigger* can infer directly from the network state if the MAC parameters should be updated. For example, a NetworkStateTrigger may fire if it detects a significant increase in traffic volume, thus starting the solver to find MAC parameters that provide higher bandwidth.

6. EXPERIMENTAL RESULTS

This section uses measurements from a 44-node testbed to study both the effectiveness of PTUNES and the interactions of MAC parameter adaptation with the routing protocol. Our experiments reveal the following key findings:

- Validation against measurements shows that our X-MAC and LPP models are highly accurate.
- PTUNES automatically determines MAC parameters that provide higher bandwidth when the traffic load increases. This avoids the occurrence of queuing until the network capacity attainable in our setting is fully exhausted.
- In the scenarios we tested, PTUNES achieves up to three-fold lifetime gains over static MAC parameters optimized for peak traffic volumes.
- In a scenario where the packet rates vary across nodes and fluctuate over time, PTUNES satisfies given end-to-end latency and reliability requirements at peak traffic while extending the network lifetime at relaxed traffic.
- During phases of controlled wireless interference, PTUNES reduces packet loss by 80 % compared to static MAC parameters optimized for the applied traffic without interference, satisfying given end-to-end reliability requirements.
- PTUNES helps the routing protocol recover from critical network changes, reducing the number of parent switches and settling quickly on a stable routing topology. This reduces packet loss by 70% in a scenario where multiple core routing nodes fail simultaneously.

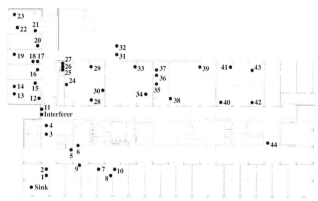

Figure 5: Testbed layout. *Nodes 31 and 32 are located outside on the rooftop; the interferer is only used in Sec. 6.6.*

6.1 Setting and Metrics

Testbed. Our testbed spans one floor in an ETH building [3, 14]. Fig. 5 shows the positions of the 44 Tmote Sky nodes distributed in several offices, passages, and storerooms; two nodes are located outside on the rooftop. The sink is connected to a laptop computer that acts as the base station. Paths between nodes and sink are between 1 to 5 hops in length. Nodes transmit at the highest power setting, using channel 26 to limit the interference with co-located WiFi.

Metrics. Our evaluation uses the metrics defined in Sec. 3.1. To measure network lifetime, we use Contiki's energy profiler to obtain the fractions of time the radio is in receive, transmit, and idle mode. Then, we compute *projected* node lifetimes using (7) and current draws from the CC2420 data sheet, assuming batteries constantly supply 2000 mAh at 3 V. When PTUNES is enabled, the measured network lifetime includes the energy overhead of PTUNES collection and dissemination, performed every $T_c = 1$ min in all experiments. We measure end-to-end reliability based on sequence numbers of data packets received at the sink. To measure end-to-end latency, we exploit Glossy's time synchronization service and timestamp data packets at the source.

Requirements. We consider typical requirements of real-world data collection applications: maximize network lifetime while providing a certain end-to-end reliability [7, 37]. We also enforce a constraint on end-to-end latency, accounting for applications that require timely delivery [8].

$$\begin{aligned} \text{Maximize} \quad & T(\mathbf{c}) \\ \text{Subject to} \quad & R(\mathbf{c}) \geq 95\,\% \ \text{ and } \ L(\mathbf{c}) \leq 1\,\text{s} \end{aligned} \qquad (26)$$

PTUNES solves (26) at runtime to determine optimized MAC parameters. If there exists no solution because either constraint in (26) is unsatisfiable (*e.g.*, due to extremely low link qualities), PTUNES maximizes R without constraints. This policy serves to exemplify the capabilities of PTUNES; other application-specific policies can be implemented within the PTUNES optimization triggers.

Methodology. We compare PTUNES with several static MAC configurations optimized for a variety of different workloads and application requirements, as listed in Table 2. We found these MAC configurations using PTUNES and extensive experiments on our testbed. Existing MAC adaptation approaches, on the other hand, consider only per-link and per-node metrics [5, 31] or focus solely on energy [9, 22, 28], rendering the comparison against PTUNES purposeless.

	Name	Configuration $[T_{on}, T_{off}, N]$	Performance Trade-Off (R, L, T)
X-MAC	S1	[16 ms, 100 ms, 8]	(high, low, low)
	S2	[11 ms, 250 ms, 5]	(medium, medium, medium)
	S3	[6 ms, 500 ms, 2]	(low, high, high)
	S4	[6 ms, 100 ms, 3]	optimized for IPI = 30 s
	S5	[11 ms, 350 ms, 2]	optimized for IPI = 300 s
	S6	[16 ms, 20 ms, 10]	(very high, very low, very low)
LPP	S7	[116 ms, 100 ms, 8]	(high, low, low)
	S8	[266 ms, 250 ms, 5]	(medium, medium, medium)
	S9	[516 ms, 500 ms, 2]	(low, high, high)

Table 2: Static MAC configurations optimized for different performance trade-offs and workloads.

6.2 Model Validation

Before evaluating PTUNES under traffic fluctuations, wireless interference, and node failures, we validate our models and assumptions from Sec. 3 on real nodes.

Scenario. We run experiments in which we let PTUNES periodically estimate the application-level metrics based on the collected network state, and compare the model estimation $e(M_i)$ against the actual measurement $m(M_i)$ by computing the absolute *model error* $\delta(M_i) = m(M_i) - e(M_i)$ for each metric $M_i \in \{R, L, T\}$. Using δ we assess the model accuracy depending on MAC configuration and network state.

To evaluate the dependency on the former, we use three static MAC configurations for each protocol (S1–S3 and S7–S9 in Table 2). We also perform one run with PTUNES enabled, using a TimedTrigger to adapt the MAC parameters every 10 min. To evaluate the dependency on network state, in each run we progressively decrease the inter-packet interval (IPI) at all nodes, from 300 s to 180, 60, 30, 20, 10, 5, and 2 s. In this way, we also validate our models against different probabilities of successful transmission p_l: a shorter IPI increases contention and thus lowers the link success rates. We conduct repeatable experiments by enforcing the same static routing topology across all runs.

Results. Table 3 lists average model errors in R, L, and T for X-MAC and LPP. We see that both models are highly accurate in all metrics. For example, with PTUNES enabled, our LPP models estimate R, L, and T with average absolute errors of 0.41 %, 0.08 s, and -0.73 days. Note that node dwell times, which are included in the measurements but ignored in the model of L, introduce only a negligible error since PTUNES aims at avoiding packet queuing, as explained next.

6.3 Impact on Bandwidth and Queuing

Based on the experiments above, we study also the impact of the MAC configuration on bandwidth and local packet queuing. To this end, we analyze queuing statistics collected from the nodes and the goodput measured at the sink (application packets carry 69 bytes of data).

Results. Fig. 6 plots total queue overflows and goodput for X-MAC as the IPI decreases. We can see from Fig. 6(a) that PTUNES avoids queue overflows up to IPI = 2 s, whereas S1–S3 fail to prevent overflows already at longer IPIs. The increasing traffic requires more and more bandwidth, leading to local packet queuing and ultimately to queue overflows when the bandwidth becomes insufficient. Unlike S1–S3, PTUNES tolerates such increasing bandwidth demands by automatically adjusting the MAC parameters to provide higher bandwidth. By doing so, PTUNES avoids the occurrence of queuing until even the MAC parameters providing

	X-MAC				LPP			
	S1	S2	S3	PTUNES	S7	S8	S9	PTUNES
$\delta(R)$ [%]	-0.68	-0.18	0.09	0.24	4.77	-0.22	0.49	0.41
$\delta(L)$ [s]	0.37	0.04	0.18	0.05	-0.12	0.07	0.04	0.08
$\delta(T)$ [d]	0.25	0.64	0.65	-0.50	0.37	-0.91	0.96	-0.73

Table 3: Average absolute errors of the network-wide performance model in testbed experiments, with pTunes and six static MAC configurations. *Our X-MAC and LPP models are highly accurate in all metrics.*

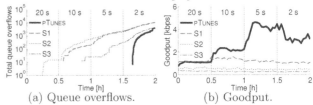

(a) Queue overflows.   (b) Goodput.

Figure 6: Queue overflows across all nodes and goodput at the sink with X-MAC as the traffic increases, using pTunes and three static MAC configurations. PTUNES *triples the goodput and avoids the occurrence of local packet queuing until the network capacity is fully exhausted.*

the highest bandwidth (S6 in Table 2), based on the settings and X-MAC implementation we use, are insufficient.

This is also confirmed by looking at the goodput, shown in Fig. 6(b). First, we note that PTUNES achieves a more than three-fold increase in goodput over S1–S3 at IPI = 5 s. When queuing occurs also with PTUNES at IPI = 2 s, goodput drops from 4.6 kbps to 3.1 kbps because increased contention leads to more transmission failures and queue overflows. This confirms that the network capacity is fully exhausted at this point. To keep satisfying the requirements in such situations, an application needs to employ higher-layer mechanisms, such as a rate-controlled transport layer that reduces the transmission rate in response to congestion [30].

6.4 Lifetime Gain

In real deployments, it is common practice to overprovision the MAC parameters based on the highest expected traffic load [23]. The goal is to provide sufficient bandwidth during periods of peak traffic, for example, when an important event causes nodes to temporarily generate more sensor data. However, because such traffic peaks are usually rare and short compared to the total system lifetime, overprovisioning results in a significant waste of resources [24]. We now analyze how PTUNES helps alleviate this problem.

Scenario. We conduct two experiments in which nodes gradually increase the IPI from 10 s to 20 s, 30 s, 60 s, 3 min, 5 min, and 20 min. In the first experiment, we use PTUNES exactly once at the very beginning to determine MAC parameters optimized for the initial IPI of 10 s, and then keep this overprovisioned MAC configuration until the end of the experiment. In the second experiment, we let PTUNES adapt the MAC parameters, using a TimedTrigger with a period of 10 min; PTUNES maximizes T subject to $R \geq 95\%$ and no constraint on L. We enforce the same static routing topology in both experiments to factor out effects related to routing topology changes, an aspect we consider in Secs. 6.5 and 6.7. We then compute the *lifetime gain* as the ratio between the measured network lifetime with and without PTUNES.

Results. Table 4 lists lifetime gains for X-MAC and LPP, *including* the energy overhead of PTUNES collection and dis-

Fraction of time at peak traffic (IPI = 10 s)	X-MAC Baseline IPI [min]				LPP Baseline IPI [min]			
	1	3	5	20	1	3	5	20
75%	1.05	1.17	1.24	1.43	1.14	1.27	1.35	1.57
50%	1.14	1.36	1.50	1.88	1.24	1.50	1.65	2.08
25%	1.21	1.55	1.75	2.33	1.33	1.72	1.95	2.60
0%	1.29	1.74	2.01	2.77	1.42	1.94	2.24	3.11

Table 4: Lifetime gains of pTunes over static MAC parameters optimized for peak traffic depending on baseline traffic and fraction of time at peak traffic. *pTunes achieves up to three-fold lifetime gains in settings with extremely rare traffic peaks and low baseline traffic.*

semination phases. We see that the lifetime gain achieved by pTunes increases as (*i*) the system spends less time at peak traffic (75–0 % from top to bottom), and (*ii*) the difference between the shortest, overprovisioned IPI of 10 s and the longest, baseline IPI increases (1–20 min from left to right). For instance, for a baseline traffic at IPI = 20 min and extremely rare traffic peaks at IPI = 10 s, the lifetime gain is close to 2.77 for X-MAC and close to 3.11 for LPP compared to static MAC parameters overprovisioned for peak traffic.

The above experimental results reveal that pTunes enables significant lifetime gains, not least due to its energy-efficient system support (see Sec. 4). The following sections examine how pTunes trades possible gains in network lifetime for satisfying end-to-end reliability and latency requirements under varying network conditions.

6.5 Adaptation to Traffic Fluctuations

Traffic fluctuations are characteristic of many sensor network applications, where the data rate often depends on time-varying external stimuli. The following experiments investigate the benefits pTunes brings to these applications.

Scenario. All nodes send packets with IPI = 5 min for 5 h. However, during two periods of 30 min each, two clusters of 10 and 5 spatially close nodes (14–23 and 40–44 in Fig. 5) send packets with IPI = 10 s, emulating the detection of an important event that deserves reporting more sensor data.

We run three experiments with X-MAC and dynamic routing using Contiki Collect. In the first two experiments, we use static MAC configurations S1 and S5: S1 provides high bandwidth when nodes send more packets, and S5 extends network lifetime at normal traffic (see Table 2). In the third experiment, we let pTunes adapt the MAC parameters according to (26). We couple a TimedTrigger with a NetworkStateTrigger as follows. When nodes transmit at low rate, the TimedTrigger starts the solver every 10 min. As soon as the NetworkStateTrigger detects the beginning of a traffic peak, it starts the solver immediately and adapts the period of the TimedTrigger to 5 min, setting it back to 10 min at the end of a peak. In this way, pTunes reacts promptly to traffic changes, and adapts more frequently during traffic peaks when nodes report important sensor data.

Results. Fig. 7 plots performance over time in the three experiments. We see that S5 approximately satisfies the reliability and latency requirements when nodes send at low rate, achieving also a high projected network lifetime. However, as soon as the two node clusters start transmitting at high rate, reliability drops significantly below 75 %. This is because S5 does not provide sufficient bandwidth, leading to high contention and ultimately to packet loss. Similarly, S5 violates the latency requirement during traffic peaks, making *L* exceed 2 s due to queuing and retransmission delays.

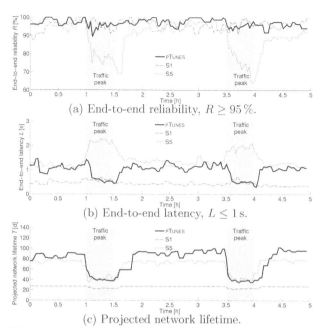

(a) End-to-end reliability, $R \geq 95\,\%$.

(b) End-to-end latency, $L \leq 1$ s.

(c) Projected network lifetime.

Figure 7: Performance of pTunes against two static MAC configurations as the traffic volume changes. *pTunes satisfies the end-to-end requirements at high traffic while extending network lifetime at low traffic. Static MAC parameters optimized for a specific traffic load fail to meet the application requirements as the traffic conditions change.*

S1, instead, provides sufficient bandwidth and satisfies the end-to-end requirements. However, network lifetime is always below 30 days: the higher bandwidth comes at a huge energy cost, paid also when a lower bandwidth would suffice.

By contrast, pTunes satisfies the end-to-end requirements under high and low rate. Moreover, when nodes transmit at low rate, the projected network lifetime increases up to 90 days. By adapting the MAC parameters, pTunes always provides a bandwidth sufficient to satisfy the end-to-end requirements without sacrificing lifetime unnecessarily: at the beginning of a traffic peak, pTunes reduces T_{off} from about 300 ms to 120 ms (and slightly adapts T_{on} and N), which explains why reliability stays up and latency is halved. Static MAC configurations lack this flexibility; they can only be optimized for a specific workload and thus fail to trade the performance metrics as the traffic conditions change.

6.6 Adaptation to Changes in Link Quality

Unpredictable changes in link quality are characteristic of low-power wireless [41]. Adapting the MAC parameters to these changes is important but non-trivial, as we show next.

Scenario. We use the technique by Boano et al. to generate controllable interference patterns [4], making the link quality fluctuate in a repeatable manner. To this end, we deploy an additional interferer node in a position where it affects the communication links of at least one fourth of the nodes in our testbed, as shown in Fig. 5. When active, the interferer transmits a modulated carrier on channel 26 for 1 ms at the highest power setting. Then, it sets the radio to idle mode for 10 ms before transmitting the next carrier.

All nodes generate packets with IPI = 30 s for 4 h. The interferer is active during two periods of 1 h each. In a first experiment, we use static MAC configuration S4, optimized for IPI = 30 s (see Table 2). We enable pTunes in a second

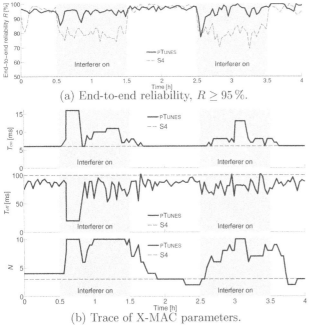

(a) End-to-end reliability, $R \geq 95\%$.

(b) Trace of X-MAC parameters.

Figure 8: End-to-end reliability and trace of X-MAC parameters as the link quality changes. PTUNES *reduces packet loss by 80% during periods of controlled wireless interference in comparison with static MAC parameters optimized for the applied traffic load without interference.*

experiment, using a TimedTrigger with a period of 1 min to adapt the MAC parameters according to (26). We deliberately enforce a static routing tree to separate effects related to link quality changes from those related to topology changes. We investigate the latter in detail in Sec. 6.7.

Results. Fig. 8 shows end-to-end reliability and the trace of X-MAC parameters. Looking at Fig. 8(a), we see that S4 and PTUNES satisfy the reliability requirement when the interferer is off. When the interferer is on, reliability starts to drop below 95%. However, as soon as PTUNES collects network state, it detects a decrease in link quality and adapts the X-MAC parameters accordingly. In particular, as shown in Fig. 8(b), PTUNES increases N from 3 or 4 to values between 6 and 10. T_{on} is also increased (from 6 ms to 10–16 ms) to further help satisfy the reliability requirement. Moreover, PTUNES decreases T_{off} (from 100 ms to 20–90 ms) to provide more bandwidth and combat increased channel contention, which is a consequence of numerous retransmission attempts over low-quality links. Indeed, these low-quality links make (26) temporarily unsatisfiable (while $T_{on} = 16$ ms in the first interference phase), triggering PTUNES to instead maximize R as explained in Sec. 6.1. As a result of these decisions, PTUNES achieves an average end-to-end reliability of 95.4% also in presence of interference.

S4, instead, fails to satisfy the reliability requirement when the interferer is active: reliability ranges between 70% and 80%, and never recovers while the interferer is on. In total, 2252 packets are lost with S4 during interference. PTUNES reduces this number to 418—a reduction of more than 80%.

6.7 Interaction with Routing

Several studies emphasize the significance of cross-layer interactions to the overall system performance [12]. We study this aspect between best-effort tree routing and parameter

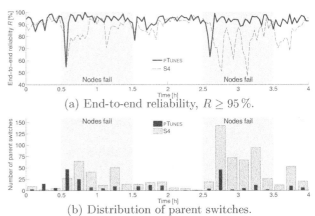

(a) End-to-end reliability, $R \geq 95\%$.

(b) Distribution of parent switches.

Figure 9: End-to-end reliability and distribution of parent switches when eight core routing nodes fail simultaneously. PTUNES *helps the routing protocol recover from node failures by settling quickly on a stable routing topology, thus reducing packet loss by 70% compared with static MAC parameters optimized for the applied traffic load.*

adaptation of an underlying low-power MAC protocol with PTUNES. To do so, during each of the following experiments, we temporarily remove multiple core routing nodes important for forwarding packets. In this way, we emulate node failures, which are common in deployed systems [2], and force the routing protocol to find new routes.

Scenario. We run two 4-hour experiments with Contiki Collect and X-MAC. After 30 min, we turn off eight nodes within the sink's neighborhood that forward most packets in the network (1–8 in Fig. 5). We turn them on again after 60 min, and repeat the on-off pattern after 1 h. Nodes generate packets with IPI = 30 s. In the first experiment, we use static MAC configuration S4, optimized for this traffic load (see Table 2). In the second experiment, we enable PTUNES and use a TimedTrigger to solve (26) every minute.

Results. Fig. 9(a) shows end-to-end reliability over time, accounting for packets from nodes that are currently turned on. During the first 30 min, both S4 and PTUNES satisfy the reliability requirement. However, when nodes are removed, reliability starts to drop below 70%. Many packets are indeed lost since children of removed nodes fail to transmit packets: the routing protocol needs to find new routes.

We see from Fig. 9(a) that end-to-end reliability recovers much faster when PTUNES is enabled. During the two periods when eight nodes are removed, S4 fails to deliver in total 2673 packets from the remaining 35 nodes. PTUNES reduces this number to 813—a reduction of 70%.

To further investigate this behavior, we plot in Fig. 9(b) the distribution of parent switches. PTUNES reduces the total number of parent switches compared to S4 (from 631 to 165), and shifts them to the beginning of the periods in which nodes are removed. At this point, PTUNES quickly realizes a significant drop in link quality, reported by nodes whose parent disappeared. PTUNES thus increases T_{on} and N to improve reliability, and decreases T_{off} to provide more bandwidth for retransmissions and route discovery.

As a result of increasing the maximum number of retransmissions per packet N, transmission attempts of nodes with a dead parent fail with a higher number of retries. This causes the corresponding ETX values to drop more severely than with S4 (which has a lower N), and so nodes switch much faster to a new parent. Moreover, the MAC parameters provided by PTUNES help deliver packets over the remaining links. Delivering more packets also enables the routing protocol to quickly detect route inconsistencies and eventually settle on a stable topology. As the topology stabilizes, PTUNES gradually relaxes the MAC parameters (reduce T_{on} and N, increase T_{off}) to extend network lifetime.

These results demonstrate that, by adapting the MAC parameters, PTUNES helps the routing protocol recover faster from critical network changes. Protocols like CTP [18] and Arbutus [33] also utilize feedback from unicast transmissions to compute the ETX. In addition, CTP uses data path validation to detect possible loops based on ETX values embedded in data packets [18]. Our findings with Contiki Collect, which uses similar techniques, suggest that these protocols could also benefit from PTUNES.

Additionally, the results demonstrate the advantage of decoupling network state collection from application packet routing, as we argue in Sec. 4.2. As long as the network remains connected, Glossy provides up-to-date network state to the base station with very high reliability [16]. Changes in the routing tree do no affect network flooding: information about faulty links is collected even when the routing protocol fails to deliver packets from nodes whose parent died, allowing PTUNES to react promptly and thus effectively.

7. DISCUSSION

Designing a MAC adaptation framework involves striking a balance between goals typically at odds with each other. We discuss in this section some of the trade-offs we make in PTUNES and the implications of our particular choices.

Feasibility *vs.* scalability. We adopt a centralized approach rather than a likely more scalable distributed solution; in return for this, PTUNES allows users to express their requirements in terms of network-wide metrics, which better reflect the way domain experts are used to state performance objectives compared to per-node or per-link metrics. In fact, distributing the tasks of collecting global state information, computing MAC parameters optimized for network-wide objectives, and coordinating the consistent installation of new parameters would hardly be feasible, if at all, on resource-constrained devices. Instead, PTUNES exploits the better resources of a central base station, which is already present in many sensor network deployments [34], and achieves simplicity of in-network functionality by moving most of its intelligence out of the nodes and into the base station.

Flexibility *vs.* optimality. We focus on existing MAC protocols rather than on the design or adaptation of cross-layer solutions (*e.g.*, coupling link and network layer) which may, in principle, achieve better performance; in return for this, PTUNES allows system designers to choose the MAC and routing protocol independently from existing code bases. In comparison, cross-layer solutions tend to enjoy little generality and flexibility, as they are often designed for very specific scenarios (*e.g.*, periodic, low-rate data collection [6]).

Robustness *vs.* optimality. We determine network-wide parameters rather than per-node parameters, which may better match the current role of a node in the routing tree (*e.g.*, with respect to traffic load); in return for this, the parameters PTUNES provides are much more robust to changes in the routing topology. It is not unlikely that, even in the most benign environment, slight variations in the link qual-

ities trigger drastic changes in the routing topology. For instance, Ceriotti et al. observe that nodes serving many children suddenly become leaves in the routing tree [7]. In such a case, per-node MAC parameters become inappropriate and must be quickly updated. Similar situations can happen frequently, even several times per minute [19], which would render per-node parameter adaptation impractical.

As a consequence of the design decisions above, PTUNES represents one particular point in a multi-dimensional design space. Corresponding to this point is a large fraction of deployed low-power wireless networks comprising tens of nodes, leveraging protocols such as X-MAC and LPP, and yet failing to meet the application requirements often due to communication issues ultimately related to inadequate MAC parameter choices and lack of adaptiveness [23,34]. PTUNES is directly and immediately applicable in these settings.

8. RELATED WORK

PTUNES uses a model to predict how changes in the MAC parameters affect the network-wide performance given the current network state. Based on iterative runtime optimization, it selects MAC parameters such that the predicted performance satisfies the application requirements. This approach is similar to the concept of model predictive control (MPC) [17], with the differences that PTUNES computes only the next step of the control law and uses no information about past control steps or measured system responses.

Several recent systems incorporate centralized control in their design, much like PTUNES does. For example, Koala implements a network-wide routing control plane, where the base station computes end-to-end paths used for packet forwarding [29]. RACNet uses centralized token passing to sequence data downloads [26]. In RCRT, the sink detects congestion and adapts the rates of individual sources [30]. PIP determines schedule and channel assignment for each flow centrally at the base station [35]. Like PTUNES, these systems exploit global knowledge and ample resources of the base station to achieve high performance and manageability.

Looking at the large body of prior work on adaptive low-power MAC protocols, we find solutions embedding adaptivity or separating adaptivity from the protocol operation.

In the former category, for instance, Woo and Culler propose an adaptive rate control mechanism, where nodes inject more packets if previous attempts were successful and fewer packets if they failed [39]. Van Dam and Langendoen introduce an adaptive listen period in T-MAC [11] to overcome the drawbacks of the fixed duty cycle of S-MAC [40]. El-Hoiydi and Decotignie adapt radio wake-ups in WiseMAC to shorten the LPL preamble [15]. More recently, Hurni and Braun propose MaxMAC, which schedules additional X-MAC wake-ups at medium traffic and switches to pure CSMA at high traffic [21]. Such hard-coded adaptivity mechanisms can be highly effective in specific scenarios, but lack general applicability and bear no direct connection to the high-level application demands. PTUNES is more general by adding parameter adaptation atop existing MAC protocols, thus leveraging available implementations, and by explicitly incorporating user-provided application requirements.

Polastre et al. instead separate adaptivity from the protocol operation and present a model of node lifetime for B-MAC [32]. Jurdak et al. use this model to dynamically recompute check interval and preamble length, showing substantial energy savings [22]. Buettner et al. demonstrate energy savings in X-MAC by adapting the wake-up interval to traffic load for one sender-receiver pair [5]. Meier et al. [28] and Challen et al. [9] extend network lifetime by adjusting the wake-up interval to traffic load in a static routing tree. Park et al. present numerical results that indicate the potential of adaptation policies for IEEE 802.15.4 MAC protocols, based on per-link and per-node metrics [31]. PTUNES builds on these foundations but extends them in several ways. First, PTUNES considers multiple network-wide metrics and adapts multiple MAC parameters. Second, our modeling is more realistic by accounting for packet loss and ARQ mechanisms, and more flexible by isolating protocol-dependent from protocol-independent functionality. Third, we evaluate PTUNES in real-world scenarios, including dynamic routing trees, wireless interference, and node failures.

9. CONCLUSIONS

PTUNES provides runtime parameter adaptation for low-power MAC protocols, automatically translating application-level requirements into MAC parameters that meet these requirements and achieve very good performance across a variety of scenarios, ranging from low traffic to high traffic, from good links to bad links, and wireless interference to node failures. PTUNES thus greatly aids in meeting the requirements of real-world sensor network applications by eliminating the need for time-consuming, and yet error-prone, manual MAC configuration when the network conditions change.

Acknowledgments. The authors thank Renato lo Cigno, Kay Römer, Olga Saukh, and the anonymous reviewers for their insightful comments. This work was supported by Nano-Tera, the National Competence Center in Research on Mobile Information and Communication Systems under SNSF grant number 5005-67322, the Swedish Foundation for Strategic Research, and the Cooperating Objects Network of Excellence under contract number EU-FP7-2007-2-224053.

10. REFERENCES

[1] K. R. Apt and M. G. Wallace. *Constraint Logic Programming using Eclipse*. Cambridge University Press, 2007.

[2] J. Beutel et al. PermaDAQ: A scientific instrument for precision sensing and data recovery under extreme conditions. In *ACM/IEEE IPSN*, 2009.

[3] J. Beutel et al. Poster abstract: The FlockLab testbed architecture. In *ACM SenSys*, 2009.

[4] C. A. Boano, T. Voigt, N. Tsiftes, L. Mottola, K. Römer, and M. Zuniga. Making sensornet MAC protocols robust against interference. In *EWSN*, 2010.

[5] M. Buettner, G. V. Yee, E. Anderson, and R. Han. X-MAC: A short preamble MAC protocol for duty-cycled wireless sensor networks. In *ACM SenSys*, 2006.

[6] N. Burri, P. von Rickenbach, and R. Wattenhofer. Dozer: Ultra-low power data gathering in sensor networks. In *ACM/IEEE IPSN*, 2007.

[7] M. Ceriotti et al. Monitoring heritage buildings with wireless sensor networks: The Torre Aquila deployment. In *ACM/IEEE IPSN*, 2009.

[8] M. Ceriotti et al. Is there light at the ends of the tunnel? Wireless sensor networks for adaptive lighting in road tunnels. In *ACM/IEEE IPSN*, 2011.

[9] G. W. Challen, J. Waterman, and M. Welsh. IDEA: Integrated distributed energy awareness for wireless sensor networks. In *ACM MobiSys*, 2010.

[10] J. Choi, M. Kazandjieva, M. Jain, and P. Levis. The case for a network protocol isolation layer. In *ACM SenSys*, 2009.

[11] T. Dam and K. Langendoen. An adaptive energy-efficient MAC protocol for wireless sensor networks. In *ACM SenSys*, 2003.

[12] S. R. Das, C. E. Perkins, and E. M. Royer. Performance comparison of two on-demand routing protocols for ad hoc networks. In *IEEE INFOCOM*, 2000.

[13] P. Dutta, S. Dawson-Haggerty, Y. Chen, C.-J. Liang, and A. Terzis. Design and evaluation of a versatile and efficient receiver-initiated link layer for low-power wireless. In *ACM SenSys*, 2010.

[14] M. Dyer et al. Deployment support network: A toolkit for the development of WSNs. In *EWSN*, 2007.

[15] A. El-Hoiydi and J.-D. Decotignie. WiseMAC: An ultra low power MAC protocol for multi-hop wireless sensor networks. In *ALGOSENSORS*, 2004.

[16] F. Ferrari, M. Zimmerling, L. Thiele, and O. Saukh. Efficient network flooding and time synchronization with Glossy. In *ACM/IEEE IPSN*, 2011.

[17] C. E. Garciá, D. M. Prett, and M. Morari. Model predictive control: Theory and practice—a survey. *Automatica*, 25(3), 1989.

[18] O. Gnawali, R. Fonseca, K. Jamieson, D. Moss, and P. Levis. Collection tree protocol. In *ACM SenSys*, 2009.

[19] O. Gnawali, L. Guibas, and P. Levis. A case for evaluating sensor network protocols concurrently. In *ACM WiNTECH*, 2010.

[20] Y. Y. Haimes, L. S. Lasdon, and D. A. Wismer. On a bicriterion formulation of the problems of integrated system identification and system optimization. *IEEE Trans. Syst., Man, Cybern.*, 1(3), 1971.

[21] P. Hurni and T. Braun. MaxMAC: A maximally traffic-adaptive MAC protocol for wireless sensor networks. In *EWSN*, 2010.

[22] R. Jurdak, P. Baldi, and C. V. Lopes. Adaptive low power listening for wireless sensor networks. *IEEE Trans. Mobile Comput.*, 6, 2007.

[23] R. Kuntz, A. Gallais, and T. Noel. Medium access control facing the reality of WSN deployments. *ACM SIGCOMM Comp. Comm. Rev.*, 39(3), 2009.

[24] K. Langendoen and A. Meier. Analyzing MAC protocols for low data-rate applications. *ACM Trans. on Sens. Netw.*, 7(2), 2010.

[25] P. Levis et al. Trickle: A self-regulating algorithm for code propagation and maintenance in wireless sensor networks. In *USENIX NSDI*, 2004.

[26] C.-J. M. Liang, J. Liu, L. Luo, A. Terzis, and F. Zhao. RACNet: A high-fidelity data center sensing network. In *ACM SenSys*, 2009.

[27] R. Madan and S. Lall. Distributed algorithms for maximum lifetime routing in wireless sensor networks. *IEEE Trans. Wireless Commun.*, 5(8), 2006.

[28] A. Meier, M. Woehrle, M. Zimmerling, and L. Thiele. ZeroCal: Automatic MAC protocol calibration. In *IEEE DCOSS*, 2010.

[29] R. Musaloiu-E., C.-J. M. Liang, and A. Terzis. Koala: Ultra-low power data retrieval in wireless sensor networks. In *ACM/IEEE IPSN*, 2008.

[30] J. Paek and R. Govindan. RCRT: Rate-controlled reliable transport for wireless sensor networks. In *ACM SenSys*, 2007.

[31] P. Park, C. Fischione, and K. Johansson. Adaptive IEEE 802.15.4 protocol for energy efficient, reliable and timely communications. In *ACM/IEEE IPSN*, 2010.

[32] J. Polastre, J. Hill, and D. Culler. Versatile low power media access for wireless sensor networks. In *ACM SenSys*, 2004.

[33] D. Puccinelli and M. Haenggi. Reliable data delivery in large-scale low-power sensor networks. *ACM Trans. on Sens. Netw.*, 6(4), 2010.

[34] B. Raman and K. Chebrolu. Censor networks: A critique of "sensor networks" from a systems perspective. *ACM SIGCOMM Comp. Comm. Rev.*, 38(3), 2008.

[35] B. Raman, K. Chebrolu, S. Bijwe, and V. Gabale. PIP: A connection-oriented, multi-hop, multi-channel TDMA-based MAC for high throughput bulk transfer. In *ACM SenSys*, 2010.

[36] R. Szewczyk, A. Mainwaring, J. Polastre, J. Anderson, and D. Culler. An analysis of a large scale habitat monitoring application. In *ACM SenSys*, 2004.

[37] G. Tolle et al. A macroscope in the redwoods. In *ACM SenSys*, 2005.

[38] G. Werner-Allen, K. Lorincz, J. Johnson, J. Lees, and M. Welsh. Fidelity and yield in a volcano monitoring sensor network. In *USENIX OSDI*, 2006.

[39] A. Woo and D. Culler. A transmission control scheme for media access in sensor networks. In *ACM MobiCom*, 2001.

[40] W. Ye, J. Heidemann, and D. Estrin. An energy-efficient MAC protocol for wireless sensor networks. In *IEEE INFOCOM*, 2002.

[41] J. Zhao and R. Govindan. Understanding packet delivery performance in dense wireless sensor networks. In *ACM SenSys*, 2003.

[42] M. Zimmerling, F. Ferrari, L. Mottola, T. Voigt, and L. Thiele. pTunes: Runtime parameter adaptation for low-power MAC protocols. Technical Report 325, ETH Zurich, 2012.

Low Power, Low Delay:
Opportunistic Routing meets Duty Cycling

Olaf Landsiedel[*][1], Euhanna Ghadimi[2], Simon Duquennoy[3], Mikael Johansson[2]
olafl@chalmers.se, euhanna@kth.se, simonduq@sics.se, mikaelj@kth.se

[1]Chalmers University of Technology, Sweden
[2]KTH Royal Institute of Technology, Sweden
[3]Swedish Institute of Computer Science (SICS), Sweden

ABSTRACT

Traditionally, routing in wireless sensor networks consists of two steps: First, the routing protocol selects a next hop, and, second, the MAC protocol waits for the intended destination to wake up and receive the data. This design makes it difficult to adapt to link dynamics and introduces delays while waiting for the next hop to wake up.

In this paper we introduce ORW, a practical opportunistic routing scheme for wireless sensor networks. In a duty-cycled setting, packets are addressed to sets of potential receivers and forwarded by the neighbor that wakes up first and successfully receives the packet. This reduces delay and energy consumption by utilizing all neighbors as potential forwarders. Furthermore, this increases resilience to wireless link dynamics by exploiting spatial diversity. Our results show that ORW reduces radio duty-cycles on average by 50% (up to 90% on individual nodes) and delays by 30% to 90% when compared to the state of the art.

Categories and Subject Descriptors

C.2.1 [**Network Architecture and Design**]: Wireless Communication; C.2.2 [**Network Protocols**]: Routing Protocols

General Terms

Algorithms, Design, Experimentation, Measurement

Keywords

Wireless Sensor Network, Energy Efficiency, Opportunistic Routing, Duty Cycle

---

[*]Work done while this author was at ACCESS Linnaeus Center, KTH Royal Institute of Technology, Sweden

1. INTRODUCTION

In Wireless Sensor Networks (WSNs), forwarding of packets to their intended destination commonly resembles a two-step process: First, the routing protocol determines the next hop utilizing a routing metric and link estimations. Second, the MAC protocol waits for the intended destination to wake up and to successfully receive the packet.

In this paper, we depart from this unicast design paradigm. Instead, we transmit packets opportunistically in duty-cycled sensor networks: A packet is forwarded by the first awoken neighbor that successfully receives it and offers routing progress towards the destination (see Fig. 1). As a result, we significantly improve energy efficiency, reduce end-to-end delay, and increase resilience to wireless link dynamics when compared to traditional unicast routing in WSNs.

1.1 Significance and Distinction

Low-power links in WSNs are highly dynamic [27, 28]. Link estimation [13, 32] enables routing protocols in WSNs [14,31] to limit forwarding to links of consistently high reliability, ensuring stable topologies. Our main departure from this work is that the opportunistic nature of our approach explicitly utilizes all neighbors, i.e, both stable and unstable links, for packet forwarding. As a result, we show significant improvements in terms of energy efficiency, delay, and resilience to link dynamics.

Originally, opportunistic routing [5,7,8,19] was developed to improve throughput in multi-hop, mesh networks. It benefits from the fact that in wireless mesh-networks radios are always-on and hence can overhear messages at practically no additional cost. In contrast, sensor networks are commonly duty-cycled to ensure long node and network lifetime, limiting the use of overhearing for opportunistic routing. Moreover, WSN applications demand for high energy efficiency and low delays instead of high throughput. The main distinction of this work over existing work on opportunistic routing is that it adapts the concept of opportunistic routing to WSNs tailoring it to the specific demands of sensor networks and applications.

1.2 Contribution

This paper has four contributions: First, it presents Opportunistic Routing in Wireless sensor networks (ORW). Specifically, it adapts the concept of opportunistic routing to the particular requirements and challenges in WSNs, e.g., by focusing on energy as a key metric and incorporating duty-

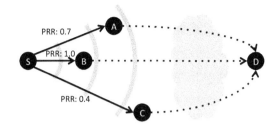

Figure 1: Opportunistic routing in ORW: The first awoken neighbor (A to C) that successfully receives a packet from S and provides routing progress, forwards it to the destination D. It utilizes all neighbors that provide routing progress independent of link quality.

cycled nodes. Second, it presents a novel anycast routing metric to build an anypath routing gradient and determine forwarder sets for opportunistic routing. Focusing on low-energy and low-delay routing, this metric estimates the delay in terms of wakeup periods required to deliver a packet to the sink. Third, we introduce a lightweight, coarse-grained link estimator that reduces probe traffic and state information. It reflects the reduced requirements of opportunistic routing in terms of timeliness and accuracy in link estimation. Fourth, it presents a practical realization of opportunistic routing and evaluates its benefits in both simulation and TinyOS-based testbed experiments. We show that ORW reduces radio duty cycles on average by 50% (up to 90% on individual nodes) and delays by 30 to 90% when compared to the state of the art. Additionally, we show an increased stability to link dynamics and churn.

The remainder of this paper is structured as follows: Section 2 provides the required background on opportunistic routing and introduces the basic concept of ORW. Next, we tailor opportunistic routing to the specific demands of WSNs and detail mechanisms for forwarder selection, our anycast routing metric, and link estimation (Section 3). We compare our design to the state of art in Section 4 and discuss related work in Section 5. Section 6 concludes.

2. ORW DESIGN OVERVIEW

In this section, we provide the required background on opportunistic routing in mesh networks and discuss why it cannot be directly utilized in wireless sensor networks. Next, we introduce the basic concept of our opportunistic routing scheme, show motivating examples, and outline its tailoring to the particular demands of wireless sensor networks.

2.1 Preliminaries

Opportunistic routing [5,7,8,19] improves network throughput in the context of multi-hop, mesh networks such as city-wide wireless networks. In contrast to traditional unicast routing, the underlying concept of opportunistic routing is to delay the forwarding decision until after the transmission. For example, in ExOR [5] each packet is addressed to set of potential forwarding nodes, prioritized by routing progress. Based on their priority, each node in the forwarder set is assigned a time slot for forwarding, which it only utilizes if it did not overhear the packet being forwarded in a previous time slot. Relying on such a consensus protocol or

other approaches [7], opportunistic routing avoids duplicate forwarding.

Overall, opportunistic routing leverages spatial diversity to ensure high routing progress and to limit the impact of link dynamics. This leads to a significant throughput improvement when compared to traditional routing schemes [5,7].

2.2 Opportunistic Routing in WSNs

Wireless sensor networks and their applications pose special requirements, such as low-power networking and resource constraints, that distinguish them from traditional multi-hop mesh networks. These limit the direct applicability of opportunistic routing in three key aspects: (1) reliability and energy efficiency vs. throughput, (2) duty cycling in sensor networks, and (3) complexity of unique forwarder selection.

Reliability, Energy Efficiency vs. Throughput: Opportunistic routing is designed to improve network throughput. However, WSN applications commonly demand reliable forwarding at high energy efficiency and not high throughput. In this paper, we show how opportunistic routing can be adapted to improve energy efficiency when compared to traditional WSN routing.

Duty Cycling in Sensor Networks: Sensor networks are commonly duty-cycled to ensure long node and network lifetime. Hence, nodes are in deep sleep states most of the time, with their radios turned off. Duty-cycling limits the number of nodes that concurrently overhear a packet (assuming no prior synchronization). As a result, it prevents the spatial reuse in the forwarding process, one of the key benefits of opportunistic routing. However, we show in this paper that opportunistic routing brings low latency to duty-cycled networks: Instead of waiting for a given forwarder to wake up, the anycast primitive allows a node to send to the first awoken parent.

Complexity of Unique Forwarder Selection: Commonly, opportunistic routing relies on a consensus protocol to determine a unique forwarder among the receiving nodes. For example, each packet in ExOR contains a list of potential forwarders and their priorities. Due to the small packet size in sensor networks such forwarder lists are not feasible. Similarly, assigning time slots to each potential forwarder poses implementation challenges. We introduce a lightweight algorithm for unique forwarder selection tailored to the resource constraints in WSNs.

In this paper we argue that the concept of opportunistic routing, i.e., delaying the decision of selecting a forwarder until the packet has been received, is well suited for the large node densities and high link dynamics in WSNs. However, many aspects of its realization need to be revisited and adapted to the specific requirements of WSNs.

2.3 Basic Idea of ORW

ORW targets duty-cycled protocol stacks. For simplicity we here illustrate the basic concept of ORW utilizing an asynchronous low-power-listening MAC, such as in X-MAC [6][1]. In low-power-listening a sender transmits a stream of

---

[1]The concepts in ORW are generic and apply also to both synchronous (phase-locked) and receiver-initiated schemes. For example, in a synchronous MAC, ORW transmits when the first neighbor that provides routing progress is scheduled to wakeup up.

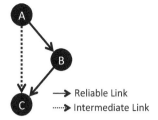
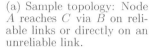

(a) Sample topology: Node A reaches C via B on reliable links or directly on an unreliable link.

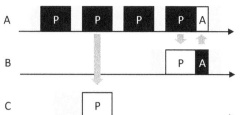

(b) Traditional unicast routing in WSNs: Although C might overhear some transmission from A, packets are addressed to B to ensure stable routing.

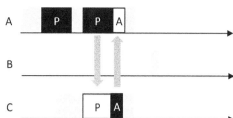

(c) Opportunistic Routing in ORW: The first node that wakes up, receives a packet, and provides sufficient routing progress acknowledges and forwards it.

Figure 2: Basic idea of ORW: Utilizing the first woken neighbor as forwarder, ORW reduces energy consumption and delay. This exploiting of spatial and temporal link diversity also increase resilience to link dynamics.

packets until the intended receiver wakes up and acknowledges it (see Fig. 2b). To integrate opportunistic routing into duty cycled environments, we depart from this traditional unicast forwarding scheme in one key aspect: The first node that (a) wakes up, (b) receives the packet, and (c) provides routing progress, acknowledges and forwards the packet, see Fig. 2c. For example, in Figure 2a node A can reach node C either directly via an unreliable link or via B. Commonly, traditional routing ignores the unreliable link $A \rightarrow C$ and relies on $A \rightarrow B \rightarrow C$ for forwarding. ORW extends this, by also including $A \rightarrow C$ into the routing process: If $A \rightarrow C$ is temporary available and C wakes up before B, ORW will utilize it for forwarding. This reduces the energy consumption and delay (see Fig. 2c).

Our design enables an efficient adaptation of opportunistic routing to the specific demands of wireless sensor networks: (1) In contrast to opportunistic routing in mesh networks, forwarder selection in ORW focuses on energy efficiency and delay instead of network throughput: It minimizes the number of probes until a packet is received by a potential forwarder. (2) It integrates well into duty-cycled environments and ensures that many potential forwarders can overhear a packet in a single wakeup period. Thereby, ORW exploits spatial and temporal link-diversity to improve resilience to wireless link dynamics. (3) The fact that only a small number of nodes receive a probe at a specific point in time simplifies the design of a coordination scheme to select a single forwarder. This limits overhead of control traffic.

3. DESIGN

After discussing the basic concept of ORW, we present its core mechanisms: We introduce (1) EDC, an anycast metric to determine forwarders, (2) a new, coarse grained link estimator that reflects the requirements of opportunistic routing, and (3) unique forwarder selection tailored to wireless sensor networks. We highlight the differences to traditional routing in WSNs and discuss key challenges such as stability and avoiding routing loops, duplicates, and asymmetric links.

3.1 Anycast Routing Metric

In ORW, a packet is forwarded by the first awoken neighbor that provides routing progress. As a result, the routing topology towards a destination is not a tree anymore

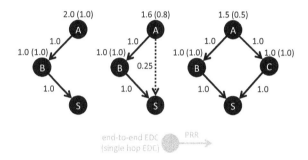

Figure 3: Example EDC for single and multi-path forwarding. EDC reduces delay and energy consumption by utilizing multiple, potentially unreliable links for forwarding. w is 0 in these examples. Please note that for a single path, EDC equals to ETX.

as in traditional unicast-based routing protocols. Instead, it assembles a Directed Acyclic Graph (DAG) with a single destination (Destination Oriented DAG, DODAG). In this DODAG, ORW allows each packet to traverse on a different route to the destination (anycast). Note that DODAGs are sometimes used instead of trees even in unicast-based routing protocols, such as RPL [31]. In this case, a single parent is selected before transmitting any packet.

3.1.1 Expected Duty Cycled Wakeups (EDC)

ORW introduces EDC (Expected Duty Cycled wakeups) as routing metric. EDC is an adaptation of ETX [9] to energy-efficient, anycast routing in duty-cycled WSNs. EDC describes the expected duration, i.e., number of wakeups, until a packet has reached its intended destination, possibly across multiple hops. It is based on the following observation: Multiple routing choices decrease the waiting time until one of the potential forwarders wakes up and successfully receives the packet.

We define EDC as the sum of the expected time to reach a potential forwarder (also called single-hop EDC), the time to travel from the next hop to the final destination, plus a small constant accounting for the cost of forwarding. First, we focus on the single-hop EDC. To transmit a packet to the next hop over a reliable link, it takes on average one time unit, i.e., one average wakeup period, if there is one

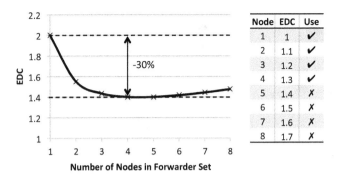

Figure 4: Optimal forwarder set: the node has an EDC of 1.4 and includes 4 neighbors with an EDC strictly lower than 1.4 in its forwarder set. PRR is 1 and w is 0 in this example. When compared to single path routing, it reduces the number of expected wakeup periods to reach the sink by 30%.

neighbor[2]. It takes half a unit of time when two neighbors offer routing progress. EDC takes both the number of possible next hops and the quality of their links into account. We therefore define the single-hop EDC as the inverse of the sum of the link quality of the neighbors, as exemplified in Fig. 3, where:

- In the left case, A has a single neighbor with a perfect link, its single hop EDC is $1/1 = 1$;
- In the right case, A has two neighbors both having perfect links, its single hop EDC is $1/(1+1) = 0.5$;
- In the middle case, A has two neighbors with link qualities 1 and 0.25. Its single hop EDC is $1/(1 + 0.25) = 0.8$.

We define the EDC_i of node i for a given subset S_i of neighbors with link quality p_{ij} and EDC_j $(j \in S_i)$:

$$EDC_i(S_i) = \frac{1}{\sum_{j \in S_i} p_{ij}} + \frac{\sum_{j \in S_i} p_{ij} EDC_j}{\sum_{j \in S_i} p_{ij}} + w \quad (1)$$

The first term is the aforementioned single hop EDC, it denotes how many units of time it requires on average to transmit a packet to one of the neighboring nodes in S_i. The second term describes the routing progress that the neighboring nodes in S_i offer, weighted by their link qualities p_{ij} (see Fig 3). The third term, w, adds a weight to reflect the cost of forwarding. Please note, for single path forwarding and a weight w of 0, EDC equals to ETX.

3.1.2   Forwarder Sets

We define the forwarder set F_i of a node i as the subset of its neighbor set that leads to the minimum EDC ($F_i \subseteq S_i$). Two key factors impact the forwarder set: (1) adding more neighboring nodes to the forwarder set reduces the time until one of the potential forwarders wakes up to receive. Hence, it decreases the single-hop EDC of the forwarding node and improves spatial diversity. However, (2) adding too many neighboring nodes to the forwarder set may decrease its average routing progress, as commonly not all neighbors provide good progress (see Eq. 1).

---

[2]For simplicity, we model both transmission success and the waking up of nodes to receive as Bernoulli processes.

The forwarder set F_i is computed by adding nodes sorted by their EDC – starting with the lowest EDC – to the forwarder set and determining the set with the minimum EDC (see example in Fig. 4). F_i defines the EDC_i of a node i and all neighboring nodes j that provide routing progress, i.e., $EDC_j < EDC_i - w$, are utilized as potential forwarders. As a node only selects nodes that provide strictly more progress than itself, the resulting topology forms a loop free graph, i.e., is a DODAG. Due to space limitations, we leave a deeper discussion and analytical performance analysis of EDC as energy-efficient routing-metric as future work.

Overall, our design departs from traditional opportunistic routing such as ExOR or MORE [7] in the following key aspect: Commonly, opportunistic routing notes a prioritized forwarder set in the packet header. In contrast, in ORW all nodes providing routing progress potentially forward the packet. This leads to two important benefits: (1) instead of long address lists in the packet header denoting a forwarder set, which is not feasible in resource constrained WSNs, a single value that describes the EDC of the sender is sufficient. (2) It allows ORW to utilize spurious neighbors and neighbors it did not yet discover for forwarding.

3.1.3   Cost of Forwarding: w

The weight w is a constant value and describes the cost of forwarding a packet over one hop (see Eq. 1). Increasing w increases the routing progress that a forwarding neighbor j of a node i is required to provide to be included in the forwarder set F_i. Thus, increasing w leads to a smaller forwarder set. This is reflected in three effects: (1) It limits forwarding to nodes that provide high routing progress, leading to fewer hops until a packet reaches its destination. (2) However, reducing the size of the forwarder set increases delay and energy consumption for packet delivery. (3) A too low choice of w increases the risk of temporary routing loops, as packets are forwarded by nodes that provide even minimal routing progress (see Section 4.2). Overall, w allows ORW to balance delay and energy with routing progress and stability.

In our evaluation we determine a range of values for w that ensure stable routing (see Sec. 4.2). From this we choose a default configuration that provides both high performance and high stability. We show that this default is independent from individual deployments and holds across all our evaluation scenarios.

3.1.4   Loop Avoidance and Detection

Although the routing topology of ORW converges to a DODAG. i.e, is loop free, a slow spreading of updates, such as new EDC values of neighboring nodes, can lead to temporary loops. This is common in routing protocols and we address it with three standard techniques: (1) when a parent node is downgraded to a child node, a node observes this and forwards its packets without dropping duplicates. Additionally, these packets are delayed for a couple of milliseconds to allow the topology to stabilize. (2) A TTL field in each packet avoids infinite loops. (3) The forwarding cost w (see Sec. 3.1.3) ensures a threshold between forwarding nodes to avoid oscillating packets.

3.2   Link Estimation and Discovery

Anycast routing in ORW utilizes a pool of forwarders, where each packet potentially travels on a different route.

Hence, when links to individual forwarders temporary fail or show reduced reliability, their impact on the overall quality of the forwarder set is limited. As a result, ORW does not require up-to-date estimates to each candidate forwarder, as traditional unicast routing.

Hence, we tailor link estimation and neighbor discovery in ORW to these specific demands. It mainly relies on overhearing: When a duty-cycled node in ORW wakes up to check for energy on the channel and subsequently receives a packet it (1) forwards it when providing routing progress, and (2) it updates its link quality estimate. For link estimation, a node maintains the link reception ratio from each neighbor. To this end, packets in ORW contain a header field that denotes the average rate at which a node is forwarding data. The link quality is obtained by dividing the rate of packets overheard from a neighbor by the forwarding rate of the same neighbor noted in the header field. As ORW operates with large forwarder sets and targets course grained link estimation, we argue that individual, asymmetric links have limited impact on the estimation and simplify link estimation by assuming $p_{ij} = p_{ji}$. Overall, this design departs from traditional link estimation used for unicast routing in WSNs in two key points: (1) stability, (2) limited use of probes.

Stability: While agility is a key design criteria for modern link estimators as they shall adapt quickly to changes in link quality, ORW may not even recognize when a link temporary fails, assuming it utilizes multiple links for forwarding. This is a design goal: as long as the aggregate of the neighbors performs stably, the dynamics of individual links will be masked. Aging slowly removes broken links from the forwarder set and neighbor table.

Limited Use of Probing: Traditional link estimation employs probing to determine the link qualities to neighboring nodes. In contrast, ORW commonly relies on overhearing during wakeups to update its neighbor table and link estimates. Probing is only utilized when not a single route is available. In our evaluation, we show that the routing topology in ORW converges quickly after boot-up and churn without the need for extensive probing. This reduces the overhead of control traffic in ORW.

To sum up, the bootstrap of a network using ORW is as follows: First, the nodes with no known parent probe their neighbors via a broadcast. The probing node i receives responses from a subset of its neighbors, depending on the link quality. For each received response from node j, node i adds the following entry to its neighbors table: (j, EDC_j, p_{ij}), where $p_{ij} = 1$. The link quality estimation, entirely based on overhearing, will refine the value of p_{ij} and may add new entries to the neighbor table, when overhearing a neighbor that didn't answer to the original probe. Node i won't use probing anymore, unless all its entries reach an estimated link quality of 0.

3.3 Unique Forwarder Selection

Once a packet has been received by one or more nodes in the forwarding set, the next step is to ensure that only a single one forwards it. In this section, we first show that in the majority of the cases a packet is only received by a single forwarder. Next, we introduce a lightweight coordination protocol to determine a unique forwarder in case the packet was received by multiple nodes.

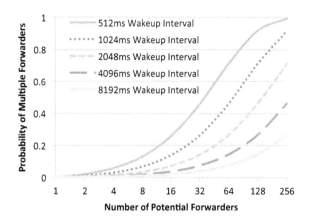

Figure 5: Probability that multiple forwarders receive the same packet for typical wakeup periods in ORW. For example, for 16 neighbors that provide routing progress, this probability is between 2% and 28% depending on the wakeup period.

3.3.1 Probability of Multiple Receivers

In ORW, a packet is forwarded by multiple nodes, if (1) multiple nodes are awake while the packet is transmitted and (2) more than one of these awake nodes successfully receives it and provides routing progress. This probability of multiple forwarders depends on two factors: the node density and the wakeup rate of each node. Both a high node density and a high wakeup rate increase the probability of a packet being received by multiple forwarders.

Figure 5 depicts the analytic probability of a packet being received by multiple forwarders for typical wakeup periods in ORW. For example, if 16 neighbors provide routing progress, the probability of multiple forwarders concurrently overhearing the same packet is between 2% and 28% for wakeup periods from 8192 to 512ms, respectively (assuming fully reliable links). The probability of multiple forwarders decreases with increasing wakeup intervals, a key benefit, as ORW targets low-power networking utilizing large wake-up intervals. Energy on the channel such as other data transmissions or noise, may extend the duration that a node is listening and hence may increase the risk of multiple receivers.

Overall, Figure 5 indicates that at our target wakeup rates a packet is received by only a small number of nodes, and commonly only by a single forwarder. This allows us to design a lightweight coordination protocol for ORW to determine a unique forwarder in case a packet was received by multiple nodes, which we introduce next.

3.3.2 Coordination Algorithm

The coordination protocol in ORW fulfills two tasks: (1) it determines the number of receivers of a packet, and (2) it ensures a unique forwarder in case of multiple receivers. It relies on three mechanisms:

Demand a Single Acknowledgment: Potentially, the sender receives multiple acknowledgments, one from each receiver[3]. In this case the sender retransmits the packet and both will (potentially) receive the packet again. Receiving

---

[3]The delay between a frame and its acknowledgement is bounded by the time for the receiver to take the forwarding decision, and an additional small random time we inject, to

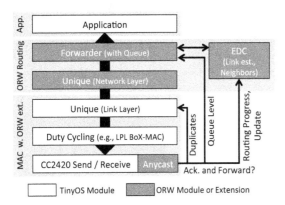

Figure 6: Cross-layer control flow in ORW: Before acknowledging and forwarding a packet, ORW checks whether (1) the node provides the requested routing progress, (2) has space in the queue, and (3) the packet is not a duplicate.

a link-layer duplicate, forwarders send a second acknowledgement only with 50% probability to reduce the number of duplicate acknowledgments. Furthermore, only the node that sent the final acknowledgment forwards the packet. The same mechanism is applied if acknowledgments collide, i.e., no acknowledgement is received (after a timeout) by the source.

Data Transmission Overhearing: When one nodes overhears another node forwarding the same packet while waiting for a clear channel, it cancels its own transmission.

Network-Layer Duplicate Detection: Network-layer duplicate detection serves as fall-back in case a packet slipped through the other mechanisms.

In corner case situations such as asymmetric or unstable links our practical design cannot guarantee a unique forwarder and packets may slip through. If they take different routes, this duplicate will only be detected at the sink. However, our evaluation shows that the lightweight mechanisms of ORW are sufficient to keep the duplicate rate at a level similar to traditional unicast routing such as CTP [14].

3.4 System Integration

ORW acts as replacement of the unicast forwarding logic of WSN routing protocols. As a case study we integrated ORW into CTP, the de-facto standard for collection protocol in TinyOS. In this section we discuss system integration, and the portability of our design.

ORW provides the same interfaces as CTP to the application, and uses its protocol headers, and in part its TinyOS modules such as the forwarder. Anycast routing in ORW relies on two headers: The EDC of a node and the required routing progress is stored as two 8-bit values in the 802.15.4 MAC header instead of the 16-bit destination address, which is not required for anycast routing. Thus, we allow EDC values from 0.0 to 25.5 at a granularity of 0.1. Overall, the integration into the 802.15.4 header allows a node to decide whether it provides the required routing progress after reading merely the header. Hence, it reduces energy consumption and ensures that 802.15.4 acknowledgments are triggered timely.

---

guarantee non-constant timing and make acknowledgement collision more unlikely.

Additionally, we extend the CTP routing header with one field: we add a weighted average of the transmission rate to facilitate link estimation (see Sec. 3.2). ORW places a small interface between routing and MAC layer (see Fig. 6): To decide whether to accept, i.e., acknowledge and forward, a packet, it determines whether (1) the node provides routing progress, (2) has space in its queue, and (3) the packet is not a duplicate (see Sec. 3.3.1). Hence, although ORW places functionality on both the routing layer and the MAC layer, its design is not bound to a specific routing protocol, MAC layer, or duty cycling scheme. ORW including link estimation requires slightly less RAM and ROM than CTP and its link estimator 4BitLE [13] which is mainly due to our simplified link estimator.

4. EVALUATION

In this section we evaluate ORW: we show (1) a simulation-based evaluation focusing on the EDC metric and its differences to ETX, and (2) use two large testbeds for a detailed, experimental comparison of ORW and CTP. We focus on four key metrics: radio duty-cycle, end-to-end delay, reliability and transmission counts.

4.1 Simulation: Anycast EDC

In our simulation-based evaluation, we explore the potential of anycast routing with EDC in terms of delay, and hops when compared to unicast ETX. Also, we explore the impact of network density on the performance of EDC-based routing and we evaluate the influence of the transmission cost w on EDC (see Sec. 3.1.1).

4.1.1 Simulation Setup

In our simulations, we solely focus on EDC and ETX as routing metrics and not individual protocol implementations. Thus, we compare two idealized protocols in this section: anycast routing with EDC and unicast routing with ETX.

We use randomly generated topologies ranging from 100 to 1000 nodes placed in a fixed area and employ the Friis transmission model for radio propagation in a custom simulator; results are averaged over 100 random topologies per data point. For each topology we determine the neighbor sets of all nodes and link qualities, i.e., PRR, between them. On top of this, we deploy our idealized protocols. Hence, in this simulation-based evaluation we deliberately exclude protocol mechanisms outside of the routing metric itself such as link estimation or neighbor discovery. Additionally, this allows us to avoid protocol artifacts such the slow spreading of route updates or packet collisions.

Overall, our goal is to evaluate the underlying performance of our routing metric EDC independent of a specific protocol implementation, before we compare EDC-based anycast routing in ORW to CTP in our testbed based evaluation (see Sec. 4.2).

4.1.2 Anycast EDC and Unicast ETX

Figure 7 shows that anycast routing with EDC benefits from an increased network density much more than unicast-based ETX. Compared to ETX, EDC reduces the average delay for packet delivery by factors of 1.3 and 6 for network sizes of 100 and 1000, respectively (see Fig. 7a). We later show that this leads to energy savings on a similar scale (see

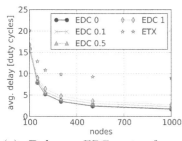
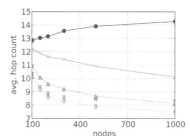
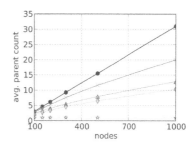

Nodes	Density
100	6.0
150	9.2
200	12.3
300	18.6
500	31.0
1000	62.0

(a) **Delay:** EDC outperforms ETX by a factor of 1.3 to 6, depending on network size and choice of w. For w of 0, EDC shows the lowest delay.

(b) **Hops:** For w of 1, EDC outperforms ETX in hops. For other configurations it trades lower delay for higher hop counts.

(c) **Parents:** Increasing network size and density allows EDC to utilize more parents for forwarding. Increasing w reduces their number.

(d) **Density:** average node densities.

Figure 7: Simulation-based evaluation: The results show that anycast routing with EDC benefits from increased density much more than unicast routing with ETX. Nodes are placed in an area of fixed size, leading to increased network density when the number of nodes increases.

Sec. 4.2). Commonly, EDC leads to hop counts larger than ETX (see Fig. 7b). However, for w of 1 it outperforms ETX.

Figures 7c and 7d show that with $w = 0$, EDC utilizes about half of the neighboring nodes as parents. This decreases to 15% of the neighbors for $w = 1$. Overall, EDC with $w = 0$ utilizes all forwarders that provide even the smallest routing progress. Hence, while minimizing delay, this increases the hop count when network density increases and as a result the number of parents increases, too. However, this aggressive forwarding, also makes this configuration of EDC sensible to link dynamics and potentially leads to routing loops, as we show in Section 4.2. In the experimental evaluation we next show that a configuration of w slightly above 0, such as 0.1, avoids these problems while utilizing many parents and providing low delay and high energy-efficiency.

4.2 Testbed Based Evaluation of ORW

In this section we evaluate ORW on real-world testbeds and compare its performance to CTP, the de-facto standard collection protocol in TinyOS. Please, note that the concepts in ORW are generic and independent of the chosen duty cycling scheme: They apply to both asynchronous and synchronous (phase-locked) MAC schemes as well as receiver-initiated ones (see Section 2.3). However, to ensure a fair comparison with CTP, we use BoX-MAC in this evaluation. It is the default MAC in both TinyOS and CTP; and resembles a combination of X-MAC and B-MAC [25]. We also show results for CTP with A-MAC [12], a state-of-the art synchronous, receiver initiated MAC. We do not compare to SCP-MAC [33], another synchronous MAC. Although it promises high energy efficiency, it is not available for current TinyOS releases, and recent work [30] indicates that its energy efficiency in multi-hop collection trees is well below BoX-MAC.

4.2.1 Testbeds and Metrics

We base our evaluation on two testbeds: Indriya [10] and Twist [16], with 120 and 96 nodes, respectively. For each we use two levels of transmission power, resulting in four evaluation scenarios (see Table 1). We use the following setup for both ORW and CTP: Every node generates a packet ran-

Test-bed	Size nodes, m^3	Sink id	Tx Power dBm	$\varnothing$ hops
Indriya	120,	1	0	5.6
	50 x 25 x 20	1	-10	9.1
Twist	96,	229	0	3.4
	30 x 13 x 17	229	-25	7.1

Table 1: We use four evaluation scenarios: two testbeds with two different power levels each. Each testbed contains about 100 nodes and the diameter ranges from 3 to 9 hops.

domly with an average interval of 4 minutes, and the network forwards it to the sink. Unless explicitly mentioned, we use wakeup interval of 2 seconds (with our settings, this leads to the optimal duty cycle in CTP, see Sec. 4.2.6). We use corner nodes 1 and 229 as sink nodes on Indriya and Twist, respectively.

We evaluate energy consumption through the average duty cycle in the network, i.e., the portion of time spent with the radio chip turned on. The average duty cycle is a good proxy for energy consumption because (1) the radio chip consumes far more power than the other hardware components involved in our experiments and (2) low-power radio chips in sensor motes have a comparable power draw when transmitting or listening. This metric provides us with results that are independent from environmental conditions, hold across different hardware platforms, and are therefore reproducible. For a fair comparison we also skip the first two minutes when measuring duty cycles, as CTP shows a high duty cycle in this time due to its initial link probing.

For each data point, experiments are executed for a minimum of 30 minutes and are repeated three times; Experiments are executed at random times of the day, but back-to-back to ensure fairness. We display average results and error bars show standard deviations. Overall, the results shown are based on more than 300 individual experiments, each between 30 minutes and 2 hours.

4.2.2 System Calibration: w

We start the testbed-based evaluation by calibrating the transmission cost w. Figure 8 shows that in all four sce-

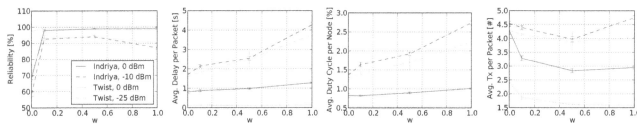

(a) **Reliability:** A w of 0 is prone to routing loops, causing packet loss.

(b) **Delay:** Increasing the transmission penalty w increases the delay.

(c) **Duty Cycle:** Increasing w increases the duty cycle.

(d) **Tx:** The transmission count decreases when increasing w.

Figure 8: **System Calibration**: a forwarding cost w of 0.1 is a good balance between energy efficiency, delay, and reliability.

narios, a low w leads to the best performance in terms of delay and duty cycle. A larger w reduces hop counts at the price of increased delay and duty cycle. However, reliability shows a sharp drop for w of 0. Our logs indicate that a w of 0 increases the risk of routing loops and duplicate packets, which increase packet drops and reduce reliability. Please note, that ORW limits us to evaluate w at a granularity of 0.1 (see Sec. 3.4).

Overall, all of our four evaluation scenarios show that a value of 0.1 for w provides a stable balance between reliability, delay, and duty cycle. As these scenarios cover a wide range of network densities and network diameters (see Table 1), we believe that a w of 0.1 is a good choice in general and use it as default in ORW.

4.2.3 Per Node Comparison of ORW to CTP

Next, we compare the performance of ORW and CTP in our four evaluation scenarios (see Table 1). Figure 9 and Table 2 show that ORW significantly improves duty cycles and delay. On average, ORW roughly doubles the energy efficiency, individual nodes show improvements up to 88%. The results show that ORW strongly benefits from network density: it shows the best results on the dense Twist deployment at a transmission power 0 dBm. Additionally, it improves delay by 30% to 90% depending on network density and achieves (re)transmission counts (unicast or anycast) that are similar, but slightly higher when compared to CTP.

In ORW, nodes in dense networks and the ones further away from the sink benefit the most from spatial diversity in anycast forwarding (see Fig. 10). We define spatial diversity as the number of different, i.e., unique, forwarders that are utilized per hop on the path from a node to the sink during the course of the experiment. As another benefit of anycast forwarding, ORW removes outliers both in terms of duty cycles and delay (see Fig. 9). This has two key advantages: (1) It reduces the time until the first node runs out of energy and hence, ensures that sensor coverage etc. can be maintained longer. (2) In terms of delay it allows us to switch to lower duty cycles in delay sensitive applications, what in turn reduces energy consumption even further.

4.2.4 Impact of Churn on ORW and CTP

We evaluate the impact of churn on both ORW and CTP. Each 15 minutes, we remove on average 10 nodes from the network. Throughout the course of two hours this reduces

the number of nodes from 120 to about 30 on the Indriya testbed.

Figure 11 depicts the impact of churn on the key metrics of reliability, transmissions, duty cycles, and delay. Both protocols show spikes of reduced reliability under churn. For increased churn these spikes grow strongly for CTP. Hence, ORW maintains connectivity much longer in the resulting sparse network. Additionally, it shows the benefits of anycast routing in ORW over unicast routing in CTP: churn has only minimal impact on the duty cycle, delay, or transmission of ORW, while these show sharp peaks in CTP.

4.2.5 Convergence of ORW

As ORW essentially operates without probing for link estimates (see Sec. 3.2), we discuss its convergence in this section. We track the evolution of the average EDC as well as number of neighbors and parents per node. Figure 12 shows that the routing metric EDC reaches an initial stable point within the first five minutes without the need for extensive beaconing or detailed link estimation. Over time it optimizes slightly.

Similarly, nodes in ORW continue to add new neighbors for routing. However, these lead to only minimal improvements, as we see only minimal changes to the duty cycle and delay over time (see Fig. 11). Overall, the results show that ORW stabilizes quickly without the need for expensive probing for link estimation and neighbor discovery. Additionally, Figure 11 shows that ORW maintains this stability even under churn.

4.2.6 Choice of Wakeup Interval

The previous experiments used a wakeup interval of 2 seconds, i.e., a node wakes up every two seconds to receive data from neighboring nodes. We used this interval to ensure a fair comparison, as it leads to the optimal duty cycle in CTP and its default BoX-MAC at an inter-packet interval of 4 min (see Fig. 13a).

In this section, we discuss the impact of the wakeup interval on duty cycle, delay, and reliability. Figures 13a and 13e show that ORW benefits much more than CTP from reduced wakeup intervals. The figures also depict the idle duty cycle, i.e., the energy that is consumed by just the wakeups of BoX-MAC without any data transfer. This baseline defines the lower bound for the duty cycle. For Indriya (see Fig. 13a) ORW stays closer to this line than CTP and in the dense Twist testbed (see Fig. 13e) ORW is marginally above

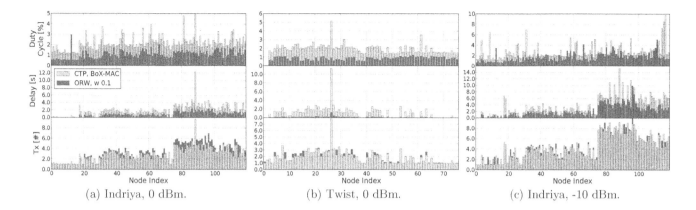

| (a) Indriya, 0 dBm. | (b) Twist, 0 dBm. | (c) Indriya, -10 dBm. |

Figure 9: **Per Node Comparison of ORW and CTP:** ORW improves duty cycles and delays while achieving slightly higher hop counts than CTP.

Testbed	Duty Cycle					Delay			Tx		
	Trace [%]		Improve [%]			Trace [s]		Impr. [%]	Trace [#]		Impr. [%]
	ORW	CTP	Avg.	Max.	Min.	ORW	CTP	Avg.	ORW	CTP	Avg.
Indriya, 0 dBm	1.1	2.2	50	79	-19	0.8	2.0	58	3.3	3.0	-11
Indriya, -10 dBm	1.6	2.8	41	88	-30	2.1	3.8	44	4.4	4.5	0
Twist, 0 dBm	0.8	2.0	57	82	0	0.1	1.2	91	1.8	2.0	10
Twist, -25 dBm	1.4	2.1	33	76	-39	1.8	2.4	29	4.1	3.8	-10

Table 2: **Testbed Experiments Summary:** ORW decreases average duty cycles up to 57% and delays up to 90%, while achieving similar, but slightly higher transmission count than CTP.

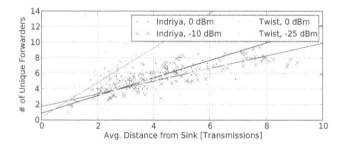

Figure 10: **Spatial Diversity (Number of Unique Forwarders):** nodes in dense networks and the ones further away from the sink exploit spatial diversity, i.e., using different forwarders, in anycast routing the most. We plot data points and their linear regression.

the baseline throughout all experiments. These results show that ORW efficiently exploits network density. Delay increases with increased wake-up intervals (see Fig. 13b and 13f). However, the increase for ORW is significantly lower than for CTP with BoX-MAC. Figures 13d and 13h show the resulting duty cycle for a given average delay. This underlines that ORW can operate at much lower duty cycles for a given average delay.

Both CTP and ORW show high reliability (see Fig. 13c and 13g). However, at high wakeup intervals reliability of CTP decreases due to queue overflows on individual nodes. In contrast, ORW avoids this by using multiple forwarders. The results for other inter-packet intervals, radio channels, and testbeds show similar performance gains of ORW over

CTP. As reference, the figures also depict results for CTP on A-MAC: However, it does not reach the performance of BoX-MAC for multihop routing with CTP. While we cannot conclude on the exact reasons, our traces indicate that its probes and loss of synchronization at low wakeup-rates increase duty cycles and delays.

4.3 Discussion and Limitations

After evaluating our anycast routing scheme in simulation and comparing it to the state of the art CTP collection protocol in testbeds, we reflect on the results and discuss limitations in this section.

4.3.1 Discussion

Our results show that ORW improves duty cycles and delays significantly while achieving similar reliability and transmission counts when compared to the state of the art. Our results show an average decrease in duty cycle by about 50%, individual nodes improve up to 90%. Similarly, it decreases delay by a 30% to 90% depending on network density.

Anycast forwarding allows ORW to forward a packet faster than traditional unicast routing. Overall, such a design works best at high network densities, as this gives the most choices for forwarding. As a result, ORW shows the best results for dense topologies, i.e., in both testbeds at high transmission power. Similarly, its optimal duty cycle is at lower wakeup rates when compared to CTP. Hence, our results show that ORW can operate at much lower wakeup rates without major impact on reliability or delay (see Fig. 13). At lower densities, ORW still outperforms CTP, but its benefits decrease (see Table 2). Similarly, at high wakeup rates, the delay and energy advantages of ORW decrease.

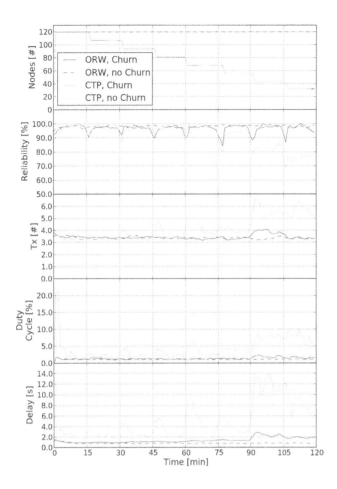

Figure 11: **Churn (Indriya, 0 dBm):** While both ORW and CTP achieve similar reliability under churn, CTP pays a higher price in terms of energy, delay, and transmissions.

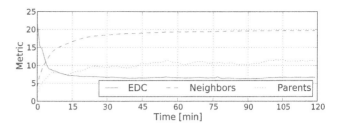

Figure 12: **Convergence of ORW (Indriya, 0 dBm):** Average per node values for EDC, neighbors in the routing table and parents selected in the forwarder set.

Additionally, its opportunistic nature allows ORW to take the state of wireless link into account and delay the decision of selecting a forwarder until the packet has been received. As a result, it reflects temporal and spatial diversity of wireless links (see Fig. 10) and increases the resilience of routing to link dynamics and churn (see Fig. 11).

4.3.2 Limitations

ORW targets applications with lifetime demands in the order of month or years, which are typical deployment scenarios in WSNs. Commonly, such applications rely on duty-cycled low-power networking with wake-up rates in the order of seconds. Our evaluation shows that ORW achieves the strongest improvement at such low wake-up rates when compared to CTP (see Fig. 13). At higher wakeup rates the baseline cost of the MAC layer accounts for the majority of the cost, and both CTP and ORW show similar performance in terms of energy and delay (see idle line in Fig. 13a and 13e). Additionally, ORW focuses on collection applications with low data rates. Thus, we believe that its design is not well suited for high throughput settings such as bulk transfers.

While ORW is agnostic to the underlying MAC scheme, it shows the strongest improvements for asynchronous MAC layers. For synchronous MAC layers, i.e., with phase lock-ing, we expect ORW to show similar improvements for delay but limited benefits in terms of energy. However, in dense deployments such as Twist (see Fig. 13e) the duty cycle in ORW closely approaches the idle base line of the MAC layer. This is also the cost of an ideal synchronous MAC, without considering its overhead in terms of time synchronization and guard times.

To ensure a fair comparison with CTP, our current implementation of ORW is tailored to collection applications with a single sink. Thus, we currently do not support mesh routing (or multiple sinks). However, the design of ORW is generic: When applications require it, this can be directly integrated by adding an extra header field that notes the intended destination next to the already existing requested routing progress (see Sec. 3.4).

5. RELATED WORK

In this section we discuss related work on opportunistic and adaptive routing in WSNs. Opportunistic routing itself is discussed in the preliminaries in Sec. 2.1.

GeRaF [34] pioneered the concept of anycast routing in duty-cycled wireless sensor networks. It utilizes geographic routing to determine routing progress of its neighboring nodes and a busy tone protocol to ensure a unique forwarder. CMAC [20] combines the concepts of GeRaF and ExOR: It includes prioritized forwarders, slotted acknowledgments and overhearing of acknowledgments to determine a unique forwarder as in ExOR. Relying solely on geographic routing, both do not address the key challenges for opportunistic routing in duty-cycled WSNs such as anycast routing metrics and wireless link dynamics.

The application of opportunistic routing in WSNs also received great attention from a more theoretical perspective [2,4,11,17,18,22,24,26,29]. Similar to our work, these mainly focus on energy and delay instead of throughput as core metrics; and include duty-cycled nodes. Their models and simulation results show that opportunistic routing can improve energy efficiency and delay when compared to traditional unicast routing. While they omit the practical challenges that this paper addresses, their results strongly motivated our work. Other approaches to opportunistic forwarding [3,21] are routing agnostic and do not include energy efficient routing metrics nor tailor link estimation to anycast routing.

Adaptive and low-power routing in WSNs proposes dynamic change of parents in routing. DSF [15] selects the next hop of a packet based on the sleep schedule of neighboring nodes and different metrics such delay, reliability, and

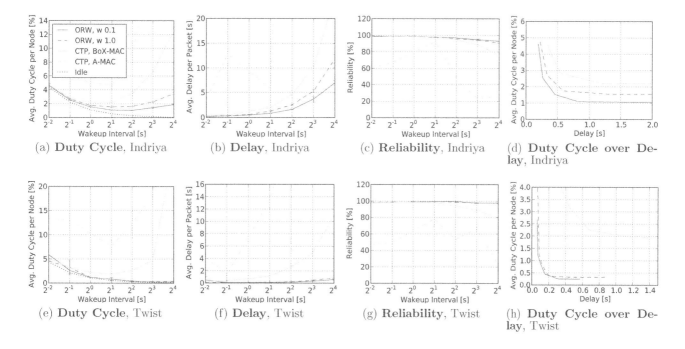

Figure 13: **Choice of Wakeup Intervals:** Performance of ORW and CTP on Indriya and Twist (with TX power of $0dBm$) for wakeup intervals between 0.25 and 16 seconds: ORW can operate at much lower wakeup intervals than CTP while achieving low delays and high reliability. Some data points for A-MAC are omitted due to inconsistent results.

energy consumption. Similar to ORW, DSF shows strong improvements over unicast routing in these metrics. However, it focuses on synchronized networks. Furthermore, it requires iterative message exchanges to stabilize the forwarding schedules of all nodes, leading to control traffic overhead in the presence of dynamic links.

The Backpressure Routing Protocol, BRP [23], forwards packets to the neighbor with the lowest queue level. This improves throughput when compared to traditional unicast routing, while increasing delay. However, BRP can only be applied when the overall system is saturated, i.e., nodes always have packets to forward. This is rare in WSN deployment scenarios as these commonly show low traffic rates. BRE [1] reduces hop counts by exploiting link dynamics: when a far ranging link of intermediate quality becomes temporary available, BRE uses it to short-cut in the routing tree. In duty-cycled environments, BRE shows two key limitations: (1) its short-cuts are only stable for a couple of milliseconds, making it difficult to exploit them in low traffic scenarios. (2) In BRE, nodes overhear data traffic to determine possible short-cuts. This is not practical when nodes are asleep most of the time.

6. CONCLUSIONS

This paper introduces opportunistic routing for Wireless Sensor Networks (ORW). It targets applications with low duty cycles. A packet in ORW is forwarded by the first awoken node that successfully receives it and offers routing progress. This provides two key benefits: By utilizing all neighbors as possible next hops, ORW reduces delay and energy consumption significantly when compared to unicast

routing. Additionally, it improves the resilience to link dynamics and churn.

Overall, ORW tailors the concept of opportunistic routing to the specific demands of WSNs. It integrates duty-cycled nodes and relies on energy and delay as key routing metrics. To enable opportunistic routing in WSNs, this paper introduces (1) a new anycast routing metric to reflect the multi-path nature of opportunistic routing, (2) mechanisms for selecting unique forwarders in duty-cycled opportunistic routing and (3) coarse-grained, long-term link estimation.

Our results show that ORW doubles energy efficiency in dense networks. It reduces duty cycles on average by 50% and delays by 30% to 90% while achieving reliability and transmission counts similar to the state of the art.

Acknowledgments

We would like to thank our shepherd, Chieh-Jan Mike Liang, and the anonymous reviewers for their feedback and insightful comments. We thank Adam Dunkels and Fredrik Österlind for providing feedback throughout this work and Philip Levis for motivating us to look into opportunistic routing. The first author gratefully thanks M. Hamad Alizai, Klaus Wehrle, et al. for the joint work on BRE [1], showing that highly adaptive approaches can be practical. This work was funded in part by SSF, the Swedish Foundation for Strategic Research, through the Promos project.

7. REFERENCES

[1] M. H. Alizai, O. Landsiedel, J. A. Bitsch Link, S. Götz, and K. Wehrle. Bursty Traffic Over Bursty Links. In *SenSys: Proc. of the ACM Int. Conference on Embedded Networked Sensor Systems*, 2009.

[2] F. Ashref, R. H. Kravets, and N. H. Vaidya. Exploiting Routing Redundancy using MAC Layer Anycast to Improve Delay in WSN. *SIGMOBILE Mob. Comput. Commun. Rev.*, 14, 2010.

[3] M. Autenrieth and H. Frey. PaderMAC: A Low-Power, Low-Latency MAC Layer with Opportunistic Forwarding Support for Wireless Sensor Networks. In *ADHOC-NOW'11: Proc. of the 10th Int. Conference on Ad-Hoc, Mobile, and Wireless Networks*, 2011.

[4] P. Basu and C.-K. Chau. Opportunistic Forwarding in Wireless Networks with Duty Cycling. In *CHANTS: Proc. of the ACM Workshop on Challenged Networks*, 2008.

[5] S. Biswas and R. Morris. ExOR: Opportunistic Multi-Hop Routing for Wireless Networks. In *SigComm: Proc. of the Conference on Applications, Technologies, Architectures, and Protocols for Computer Communications*, 2005.

[6] M. Buettner, G. V. Yee, E. Anderson, and R. Han. X-MAC: a Short Preamble MAC Protocol for Duty-Cycled Wireless Sensor Networks. In *SenSys: Proc. of the ACM Int. Conference on Embedded Networked Sensor Systems*, 2006.

[7] S. Chachulski, M. Jennings, S. Katti, and D. Katabi. Trading Structure for Randomness in Wireless Opportunistic Routing. In *SigComm: Proc. of the Conference on Applications, Technologies, Architectures, and Protocols for Computer Communications*, 2007.

[8] R. R. Choudhury and N. H. Vaidya. MAC-Layer Anycasting in Ad Hoc Networks. *SIGCOMM Comput. Commun. Rev.*, 34(1), 2004.

[9] D. S. J. De Couto, D. Aguayo, J. Bicket, and R. Morris. A High-Throughput Path Metric for Multi-Hop Wireless Routing. In *MobiCom: Proc. of the ACM Int. Conference on Mobile Computing and Networking*, 2003.

[10] M. Doddavenkatappa, M. C. Chan, and A. Ananda. Indriya: A Low-Cost, 3D Wireless Sensor Network Testbed. In *TridentCom: Proc. of the Int. ICST Conference on Testbeds and Research Infrastructures for the Development of Networks and Communities*, 2011.

[11] H. Dubois-Ferriè andre, M. Grossglauser, and M. Vetterli. Valuable Detours: Least-Cost Anypath Routing. *IEEE/ACM Trans. Netw.*, 19(2), 2011.

[12] P. Dutta, S. Dawson-Haggerty, Y. Chen, C.-J. M. Liang, and A. Terzis. Design and Evaluation of a Versatile and Efficient Receiver-Initiated Link Layer for Low-Power Wireless. In *SenSys: Proc. of the ACM Int. Conference on Embedded Networked Sensor Systems*, 2010.

[13] R. Fonseca, O. Gnawali, K. Jamieson, and P. Levis. Four Bit Wireless Link Estimation. In *HotNets: Proc. of the Workshop on Hot Topics in Networks*, 2007.

[14] O. Gnawali, R. Fonseca, K. Jamieson, D. Moss, and P. Levis. Collection Tree Protocol. In *SenSys: Proc. of the ACM Int. Conference on Embedded Networked Sensor Systems*, 2009.

[15] Y. Gu and T. He. Data Forwarding in Extremely Low Duty-Cycle Sensor Networks with Unreliable Communication Links. In *SenSys: Proc. of the ACM Int. Conference on Embedded Networked Sensor Systems*, 2007.

[16] V. Handziski, A. Köpke, A. Willig, and A. Wolisz. TWIST: a Scalable and Reconfigurable Testbed for Wireless Indoor Experiments with Sensor Networks. In *Proc. of the Int. Workshop on Multi-hop Ad Hoc Networks: from Theory to Reality*, 2006.

[17] J. Kim, X. Lin, and N. B. Shroff. Optimal Anycast Technique for Delay-Sensitive Energy-Constrained Asynchronous Sensor Networks. In *InfoCom: Proc. of the IEEE Int. Conference on Computer Communications*, 2009.

[18] J. Kim, X. Lin, N. B. Shroff, and P. Sinha. Minimizing Delay and Maximizing Lifetime for Wireless Sensor Networks with Anycast. *IEEE/ACM Trans. Netw.*, 18, 2010.

[19] P. Larsson. Selection Diversity Forwarding in a Multihop Packet Rradio Network with Fading Channel and Capture. *SIGMOBILE Mob. Comput. Commun. Rev.*, 5, 2001.

[20] S. Liu, K.-W. Fan, and P. Sinha. CMAC: An Energy-Efficient MAC Layer Protocol using Convergent Packet forwarding for Wireless Sensor Networks. *ACM Trans. Sen. Netw.*, 5, 2009.

[21] S. Liu, M. Sha, and L. Huang. ORAS: Opportunistic Routing with Asynchronous Sleep in Wireless Sensor Networks. In *ICFCC'10: Proc. of the 2nd Int. Conference on Future Computer and Communication*, 2010.

[22] X. Mao, X.-Y. Li, W.-Z. Song, P. Xu, and K. Moaveni-Nejad. Energy Efficient Opportunistic Routing in Wireless Networks. In *MSWiM: Proc. of the 12th ACM Int. Conference on Modeling, Analysis and Simulation of Wireless and Mobile Systems*, 2009.

[23] S. Moeller, A. Sridharan, B. Krishnamachari, and O. Gnawali. Routing without Routes: the Backpressure Collection Protocol. In *IPSN: Proc. of the ACM/IEEE Int. Conference on Information Processing in Sensor Networks*, 2010.

[24] B. Pavković, F. Theoleyre, and A. Duda. Multipath Opportunistic RPL Routing over IEEE 802.15.4. In *MSWiM: Proc. of the ACM Int. Conference on Modeling, Analysis and Simulation of Wireless and Mobile Systems*, 2011.

[25] J. Polastre, J. Hill, and D. Culler. Versatile Low Power Media Access for Wireless Sensor Networks. In *SenSys: Proc. of the ACM Int. Conference on Embedded Networked Sensor Systems*, 2004.

[26] G. Schaefer, F. Ingelrest, and M. Vetterli. Potentials of Opportunistic Routing in Energy-Constrained Wireless Sensor Networks. In *EWSN: Proc. of the European Conference on Wireless Sensor Networks*, 2009.

[27] K. Srinivasan, M. Jain, J. I. Choi, T. Azim, E. S. Kim, P. Levis, and B. Krishnamachari. The κ Factor: Inferring Protocol Performance using Inter-Link Reception Correlation. In *MobiCom: Proc. of the ACM Int. Conference on Mobile Computing and Networking*, 2010.

[28] K. Srinivasan, M. A. Kazandjieva, S. Agarwal, and P. Levis. The β Factor: Measuring Wireless Link Burstiness. In *SenSys: Proc. of the ACM Int. Conference on Embedded Networked Sensor Systems*, 2008.

[29] S. Unterschütz, C. Renner, and V. Turau. Opportunistic, Receiver-Initiated Data-Collection Protocol. In *EWSN: Proc. of the European Conference on Wireless Sensor Networks*, 2012.

[30] J. Vanhie-Van Gerwen, E. De Poorter, B. Latré, I. Moerman, and P. Demeester. Real-Life Performance of Protocol Combinations for Wireless Sensor Networks. In *Proc. of the IEEE Int. Conference on Sensor Networks, Ubiquitous, and Trustworthy Computing*, 2010.

[31] T. Winter (Ed.), P. Thubert (Ed.), and RPL Author Team. RPL: IPv6 Routing Protocol for Low power and Lossy Networks. Internet Draft draft-ietf-roll-rpl-19, work in progress.

[32] A. Woo, T. Tong, and D. Culler. Taming the Underlying Challenges of Reliable Multihop Routing in Sensor Networks. In *SenSys: Proc. of the ACM Int. Conference on Embedded Networked Sensor Systems*, 2003.

[33] W. Ye, F. Silva, and J. Heidemann. Ultra-Low Duty Cycle MAC with Scheduled Channel Polling. In *SenSys: Proc. of the ACM Int. Conference on Embedded Networked Sensor Systems*, 2006.

[34] M. Zorzi and R. R. Rao. Geographic Random Forwarding (GeRaF) for Ad Hoc and Sensor Networks: Multihop Performance. *IEEE Trans. on Mobile Computing*, 2, 2003.

Grafting Energy-Harvesting Leaves onto the Sensornet Tree

Lohit Yerva[†], Bradford Campbell[†], Apoorva Bansal[†], Thomas Schmid[‡], and Prabal Dutta[†]

[†]Computer Science & Engineering Division
University of Michigan
Ann Arbor, MI 48109
{lohity,bradjc,apoorvab,prabal}@eecs.umich.edu

[‡]Electrical and Computer Engineering Dept
University of Utah
Salt Lake City, UT 84112
thomas.schmid@utah.edu

ABSTRACT

We study the problem of augmenting battery-powered sensornet trees with energy-harvesting leaf nodes. Our results show that leaf nodes that are smaller in size than today's typical battery-powered sensors can harvest enough energy from ambient sources to acquire and transmit sensor readings every minute, even under poor lighting conditions. However, achieving this functionality, especially as leaf nodes scale in size, requires new platforms, protocols, and programming. Platforms must be designed around low-leakage operation, offer a richer power supply control interface for system software, and employ an unconventional energy storage hierarchy. Protocols must not only be low-power, but they must also become low-energy, which affects initial and ongoing synchronization, and periodic communications. Systems programming, and especially bootup and communications, must become low-latency, by eliminating conservative timeouts and startup dependencies, and embracing high-concurrency. Applying these principles, we show that robust, indoor, perpetual sensing is viable using off-the-shelf technology.

Categories and Subject Descriptors

B.m [**Hardware**]: Miscellaneous

Keywords

energy-harvesting sensor node, low power wireless networking

1. INTRODUCTION

For the past decade, academia and industry alike have labored to make battery-powered, multi-hop wireless sensornets a reality. Now, with multi-hop networking firmly ensconced in the standards bodies, many have concluded that periodic node maintenance represents *the* biggest impediment to continued technology deployment. Therefore, some have turned to energy-harvesting operation. However, the two prevailing approaches – EnOcean [4] and ZigBee Green Power [23] – adopt a star topology that requires leaf nodes to be within a single hop of an always-powered base station. This insidious constraint, we argue, regresses on a decade of advances in multi-hop mesh networking – and its diverse benefits – including better spatial reuse of spectrum, higher reliability due to path diversity, and longer lifetime due to reduced transmission power. Moreover, we argue that energy harvesting and mesh networking are not exclusive, and that they can coexist within a unified network architecture.

Today, industry is advocating a suite of new and emerging technologies – energy-harvesting transducers [13], thin-film batteries [1], micropower integrated circuits [9], and nanopower microcontrollers [12] – coupled with star network topologies, to address the pressing challenges of energy harvesting operation. In contrast, we show how existing technologies – solar cells, simple capacitors, switching regulators, field-effect transistors, and low-power microcontrollers and radios – can be combined in new ways, and coupled with simple protocols and good engineering, to achieve hassle-free, energy harvesting operation, without sacrificing the benefits of interoperating with battery-powered meshes.

This paper shows how the addition of a stable clock [11] and some minor software improvements to existing battery-powered mesh nodes (*branch* nodes in our terminology) prepares them to interact with energy-harvesting *leaf* nodes. And the leaf nodes themselves are nothing more than branch nodes whose batteries have been replaced with a small solar cell, a few capacitors, a pair of voltage monitors, and some transistors. Of course, such simple leaf nodes only work when the lights are on (even dimly), but night time operation would be possible from a source that could supply 3 V at 2.5 μW [15].

Although leaf nodes are constructed from widely-available electronic components, their integration requires some care. In particular, since leaf nodes operate from anemic power sources – as low as just few microwatts – their chief design constraint is *low-leakage, low-power* operation. Therefore, always-on switching regulators or even low-dropout linear regulators are often unsuitable due to their relatively high quiescent or ground currents. Our leaf design minimizes leakage and other losses by completely switching off and then cold booting the processor and radio during each activity cycle. We also eschew batteries due to their limited charge cycles

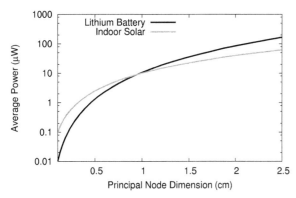

Figure 1: An energy-harvesting reality check. Shows how power harvested from indoor solar compares with power drawn from an internal battery. As a cubic sensor's length L falls below a centimeter, a solar cell of size L^2 can deliver higher average power than a Lithium battery of size L^3, over a seven year horizon. The key to continued sensor scaling lies in shifting the primary energy supply from battery to solar, and dealing with the implications of a dramatically reduced supply.

and high cost, and miniature (surface mount) supercapacitors due to their high impedance, and choose instead capacitors that offer very low impedance. Despite these many restrictions, leaf nodes are still able to interoperate with mesh networks at indoor irradiance levels of about 15 μW/cm^2, which is at the very low end of what we observe indoors.

While low-leakage hardware is the *sine qua non* of energy harvesting operation, several networking problems must also be solved to augment battery-powered mesh networks with energy-harvesting leaf nodes. These problems include initial synchronization, ongoing synchronization, and bidirectional communications (branch-to-leaf, leaf-to-branch). The chief challenge in solving these problems lies in achieving *low-energy* operation. While nodes with copious reserves can consume energy with few restrictions, and battery powered ones must merely operate at low *average* power, our energy-harvesting leaf nodes are constrained by the energy in their (tiny) capacitors. This translates to low-energy (i.e. roughly 1 mJ) budgets for synchronization and communications. Fortunately, low-energy neighbor discovery protocols exist [2], and low-energy communications is possible through networking and software optimizations. Most of these optimizations focus on achieving *low-latency* cold boot, radio startup, and radio RX/TX turnaround. No single optimization is sufficient, but all are required. Collectively, they enable a leaf to discover and communicate with a branch, and deliver data readings every minute, even under low-light, using a solar cell that is just a few square centimeters in surface area.

While the low-energy constraint may seem like an artificial one, the reality is that low-energy operation will become critical as nodes continue to scale in size. Since batteries and solar cells currently dominate node volume, they must shrink in order to enable future leaps in the minimization of sensor nodes. However, some may wonder whether energy-harvesting really makes sense or whether batteries will suffice, especially in the context of this continued scaling. Therefore, it is worth exploring the question, *at what scale is indoor photovoltaics the better primary power source?* One way to attack this question is to assume the entire volume (L^3) of a cubic sensor of length L is devoted to energy storage and that volume is occupied by a non-rechargeable Lithium primary cell whose energy density, ρ, is 653 mW-h/cm^3 and whose useful life, T, is bounded

to seven years (due to its shelf-life). The average power the battery could source is $P = \rho L^3/T$. A conservative estimate of the average solar irradiance on an indoor surface, H_d, is 10 μW/cm^2, and the average power is $P = H_d L^2$ [6]. Setting these two expressions equal to each other and solving for L gives 1 cm as the crossover point where solar (1 cm^2) beats batteries (1 cm^3) over a seven year horizon, as Figure 1 shows.

Of course, this analysis ignores several factors, such as the overhead of battery packaging, the low efficiency of solar conversion, and the unrealistic node volume dedicated to the battery. However, the general trend is clear: when nodes shrink to centimeter scales and beyond, energy-harvesting will play a critical role.

The goal of this research is to understand the design space of low-maintenance, high-density sensor networks. We do so by designing and studying an energy-harvesting, low-energy node using current technology. We show that using already available parts, we can build a working solar-powered node with ultra-low leakage currents (1.7 μA). Further, we show that this node works in very low indoor lighting conditions (15 μW/cm^2), and delivers data every minute, which is comparable to existing battery-powered nodes. We adapt existing protocols to meet the challenges of networking an extremely energy-limited node with battery-powered meshes. We demonstrate robust techniques for handling resynchronization when nodes suffer extended periods of power loss, thus solving the critical network bootstrap problem.

2. SYSTEM OVERVIEW

Figure 2 shows the overall system and network architecture, including wall-powered *trunk* nodes, battery-powered *branch* nodes, and energy-harvesting *leaf* nodes. Trunks and branches are roughly equal to basestations and mesh nodes, respectively, in contemporary architectures.

2.1 Leaf and Branch Platforms

Leaf nodes integrate a sensor node "core" like the Epic mote [3] with an energy-harvesting power supply and accurate time-keeping, as Figure 2(d) shows. We employ five basic design principles in leaf nodes to achieve high-efficiency operation. First, we minimize power transfer inefficiencies by operating near the solar cell's maximum power point. Second, we minimize power conversion inefficiencies by doing only one power conversion – from the solar cell buffer capacitor directly to the processor and radio supply voltage. Third, we minimize leakage by power cycling and cold booting the processor and radio. Fourth, we improve energy consumption efficiency by optimizing system software to minimize latencies. Fifth, we minimize communications costs by shifting most of the synchronization burden to more capable (but fewer in number) branch nodes, user hierarchical discovery, and employ temperature-compensated crystal oscillators (TCXOs) to further reduce that burden.

Branch nodes, shown in Figure 2(c), are very similar to leaf nodes. The key difference is that they replace the leaf node's power supply (including a solar panel, capacitors, transistors, voltage monitors, and regulator) with just a battery and regulator. The branch node also employs a real-time clock that is more stable and draws slightly more power than a leaf node's [11]. The greater clock stability allows branch nodes to limit communication guard times since the worst case drift is constrained by the *sum* of the magnitude of the two individual clocks. Branch nodes are otherwise identical to conventional sensor nodes like the Telos [16].

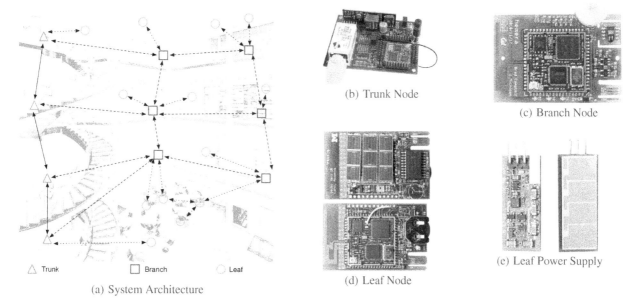

(b) Trunk Node

(c) Branch Node

(e) Leaf Power Supply

(d) Leaf Node

(a) System Architecture

△ Trunk   □ Branch   ○ Leaf

Figure 2: Integrating energy-harvesting leaf nodes with battery-powered mesh nodes. (a) The system architecture shows how different node classes interact with each other. Mains-powered "trunk" nodes provide connectivity between the external world (e.g. Internet) and the sensornet "tree." Trunk nodes communicate wirelessly with battery-powered "branch" nodes, and branch nodes mesh with other "branch" nodes, just like in today's sensornet mesh architectures. Leaf nodes may communicate with trunk, branch, or in some cases even other leaf nodes depending on a leaf's capabilities (but not explored in this paper, however). (b) A trunk node with an Ethernet and an 802.15.4 interface (using the Epic Core). (c) A battery-powered branch node with temperature, humidity, light, and motion sensors. (d) An energy-harvesting leaf node that can keep accurate time (using a coin cell). (e) Leaf node power supply details (the same electronics exist under the three solar cells on the leaf node).

2.2 Leaf-to-Branch Communications

Leaf nodes wake up on a fixed period, take a sensor reading, transmit a packet, and listen for inbound traffic. If a leaf does not have enough energy to perform these operations, it simply skips one (or more) activity cycles and simply resumes its activities when it has accrued enough energy. The key is that the nominal activity period is fixed and has low jitter and drift. Branch nodes learn of leaf node schedules using a low duty-cycle neighbor discovery protocol as described in section 4.2.1. Branch nodes subsequently track the nominal wakeup times of leaf nodes and listen briefly (i.e. 20 ms, searching over a variable-length guard time) for leaf transmissions, and to deliver any leaf-bound traffic.

3. LOW-POWER LEAF NODE DESIGN

This section presents the leaf node hardware and software. A leaf node integrates a processor and radio [3], real-time clock, and energy-harvesting power supply, as Figure 3 shows.

Epic Core mote [3] incorporates an MSP430F1611 microcontroller and CC2420 radio (802.15.4-compliant). The MSP430 offers very fast wakeup and low active current, allowing us to minimize both the startup and active energy.

Real-Time Clock. A real-time clock (RTC) provides a periodic time trigger to instigate leaf activity. Our leaf node uses the NXP PCF2127A RTC [14], a temperature-compensated crystal oscillator which runs at 32.768 kHz. This device offers excellent time-keeping stability (± 3 ppm), low current draw (0.65 μA) on backup battery, and flexible triggering options. Collectively, these features support efficient synchronization between leaf and branch nodes. The RTC also offers a battery-backed SRAM, which allows a node to maintain state across activity cycles without keeping the microcontroller powered on. The prototype's batteries can be replaced

with rechargeable super-capacitors to allow nearly infinite charge and discharge cycles at the cost of long term time keeping.

Power Supply. The energy-harvesting power supply (Figure 3(b)) integrates a solar panel, capacitors, overvoltage protection, various trip and enable triggers, a latching circuit, regulator, voltage sense circuits, and a rich interface to the power supply. We evaluate two different solar panels – an IXYS XOB17-4X3 (crystalline silicon) and a Sanyo AM-1437 (amorphous silicon) – for their response to different light sources. We chose (two 100 μF) tantalum capacitors as the primary energy buffer due to their high energy density and low DC Equivalent Series Resistance (ESR) compared to ceramic capacitors. Figure 5(b) shows how the voltage regulator efficiency is affected by two capacitor types (and their respective ESR ranges). The activity and overvoltage triggers use low-current voltage supervisors from Panasonic and Microchip, which draw only 0.25-0.5 μA, respectively. We use the MCP1640 boost converter with true load disconnect to provide a stable voltage and switch power to the Epic Core. Finally, a FET-gated sense path allows the microcontroller to measure the capacitor voltage.

3.1 Hardware Operation

The hardware goes through three distinct operating stages:

Charge. From a fully-discharged state, the solar cells begin to charge the buffer capacitors. Voltage supervisor U2, a Panasonic MS1382SEL rated to trip at 2.5 V, monitors the capacitor voltage. Since the solar cell maximum power point occupies a fairly narrow range of a few hundred millivolts, as Figures 4(a) and 4(b) show, we are able to use fixed voltage levels for the charge (and discharge) thresholds rather than needing or employing a costly maximum power point tracking (MPPT) scheme.

Startup. When the capacitors reach U2's trip voltage, U2's out-

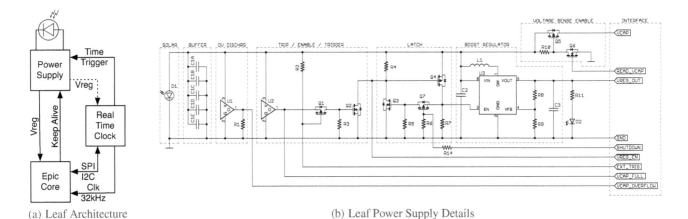

| (a) Leaf Architecture | (b) Leaf Power Supply Details |

Figure 3: (a) Energy-harvesting leaf nodes include a power-supply circuit, a processor/radio core (Epic Core), and a real-time clock (RTC). The power supply switches the core on and off in response to time triggers and capacitor voltages, and the core can choose to disconnect power. (b) The power supply stores indoor solar currents of just a few microamps and provides periodic burst of regulated voltage. The power supply exports several monitoring and control signals to allow applications to tailor their operation to the key power supply events.

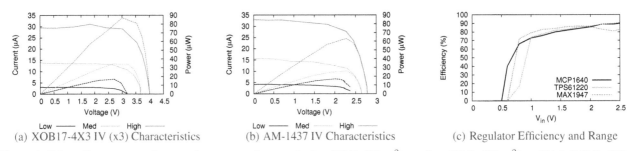

| (a) XOB17-4X3 IV (x3) Characteristics | (b) AM-1437 IV Characteristics | (c) Regulator Efficiency and Range |

Figure 4: Solar cell current vs voltage, and power vs voltage, under low (12.7 μW/cm^2), medium (53.8 μW/cm^2), and high (101.7 μW/cm^2) indoor lighting levels. Although solar cell output current varies by an order of magnitude, the maximum power point varies within a small range of approximately (a) 2.6 V to 3.0 V and (b) 2.1 V to 2.3 V, or about (10-15%). This lets us use fixed-threshold voltage trip switches for charge/discharge operation under typical indoor lighting conditions. (c) MCP1640 was choosen due to its efficiency over a large input voltage range, and because it has output disconnect and low leakage current.

put goes high, initiating the active phase. Assuming EXT_TRIG is low when this happens,[1] P-FET Q1's source goes high, turning Q1 on, and passing the U2's high output to Q2's gate, turning Q2 on. This drives Q4's gate low, turning it on, and causing regulator U3's VREG_EN to be driven high, initiating its startup. Instantly, the default *on* Q7 enables the bypass Q3. The bypass latch (Q4 keeps Q3 on, which keeps Q4 on) keeps the voltage regulator enabled even though U2 disables Q2, when the capacitor voltage eventually drops to 2.3 V (maximum U2's histeresis) as U3 goes into regulation. We use the MCP1640 boost regulator, which provides high conversion efficiency near our startup threshold voltage, and a slightly wider input voltage range as well for longer discharges, as Figure 4(c) shows. As U3 starts up and goes into regulation, it too discharges the buffer capacitor.

Active. After startup, the processor boots, configures the radio, takes sensor readings, and transmits/receives packets. Once done, the processor drives SHUTDOWN high, which disables the regulator and disconnects power to the Epic Core, saving unused energy. Figure 5(a) details the operation of the startup and active stages.

---

[1]This could be done efficiently by, for example: (i) connecting EXT_TRIG to the output of the RTC's periodic interrupt or (ii) connecting VCAP_FULL to an N-FET's gate, EXT_TRIG to an N-FET's drain, and GND to and N-FET's source. We use option (i) and preprogram the RTC during hardware bringup.

3.2 Software Operation and Optimization

Low-energy and low-power leaf nodes need efficient and optimized system software support, and tight hardware-software interaction. Low-power operation begins in the first few instructions the processor executes and continues through system startup, communication, and sleep/shutdown. We detail some of the software operations that a leaf node employs to maximize energy efficiency.

Shutdown. Mechanisms for software to quickly disconnect the processor and radio and shut down the regulator to conserve charge once the software completes its work.

Oscillator Fast Start. The hardware starts using an internal RC oscillator with a low Q, which allows fast startup but poor frequency tolerance. However, frequency error is not a significant problem as all timing-based operations (e.g. timeouts) are converted into either interrupt-driven or polling-driven operations, and all I/O operations are synchronous (i.e. the processor provides the clock). The software sets the clock speed to the maximum allowed, which minimizes startup latency.

Optimized Startup. The default TinyOS distribution requires 237 ms and consumes 2.174 mJ from power-on to Radio.sendDone(). Most of the time is spent waiting for the 32 kHz clock to start oscillating. Adding an external 32 kHz source reduces the boot time to 48 ms and 1.81 mJ. Much of the remaining startup costs are spent initializing memory. Setting the microcontroller clock speed to the maximum possible frequency ($\sim$8 MHz

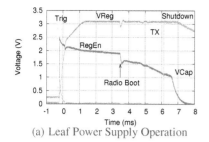

(a) Leaf Power Supply Operation

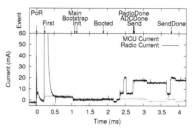

(c) Optimized TinyOS Cold Boot

Regulator	Ceramic	Tantalum
Startup	32%	57%
Overall	36%	86%

(b) Ceramic vs. Tantalum Efficiency

Figure 5: (a) Operation of the energy harvesting power system. The capacitor voltage is seen dropping from about 2.5 V to about 1 V. The boost regulator starts up and establishes a 3.0 V supply until the core requests shutdown after it finishes its radio transmission. *Radio Boot* refers to the execution of the first instruction, enable radio regulator. (b) Efficiency of tantalum vs ceramic capacitors as energy buffers for the boost voltage regulator. At startup and as the input voltage drops, capacitors struggle to provide the current needed by the regulator to maintain output power. Boost regulator *startup* refers to bringing output capacitors to the regulated voltage. The overall efficiency includes a 100 Ohm output load. (c) Stages of an optimized TinyOS cold-boot overlaid with the processor and radio current. Our design achieves cold-boot to packet transmission in less than 4 ms using all of the optimizations discussed. The net effect is a reduction in TinyOS cold boot by a factor of 69× in time and 14.6× in energy.

in the case of the MSP430F1611) before initializing memory reduces the cold-boot to 18.6 ms and 0.61 mJ. This figure can be further reduced to achieve a cold-boot time of 3.4 ms and 149 μJ by removing several layers of the TinyOS radio stack, parallelizing radio startup and memory initialization, and using the bare radio interface to transmit a packet as shown in Figure 5(c).

Concurrent Initializations. System software employs concurrency to minimize latency during system initialization (contrary to the far more typical serialized system initializations elsewhere). The radio initialization is started, for example, before the C runtime zeroes out data memory, and the two operations proceed in parallel. Similarly, the packet to be transmitted is pipelined into the radio's transmit FIFO. Branch nodes use similar radio stack optimizations to respond rapidly to a leaf's probe with pending data.

The result of these software optimizations is shown in Figure 5(c). This figure shows a detailed timeline of a cold-boot to packet transmission. The labels indicate stages of the boot process. They are, from left to right, PoR: Power-on-Reset; First: first instruction; Main: call of `main()`; Bootstrap: after call to `platform_bootstrap()`; Init: after call of `PlatformInit.init()`; Booted: first instruction of `Boot.booted()`; RadioDone: Radio initialization done; ADCdone: ADC initialization done; Send: start of packet; SendDone: Return from send, ready to shut off. The corresponding latencies are: PoR to First: 0.17 ms, First to Main: 0.87 ms, Main to Bootstrap: 0.5 μs, Bootstrap to Init: 58 μs, Init to Booted: 436 μs, Booted to RadioDone: 842 μs, RadioDone to AdcDone: 8.1 μs, AdcDone to Send: 9.1 μs, Send to SendDone: 1.04 ms.

4. EVALUATION

This section evaluates the viability of energy harvesting operation, characterizes typical indoor lighting conditions, demonstrates initial and ongoing synchronization, and shows that leaf and branch nodes can communicate successfully.

4.1 Energy Harvesting Operation

The first question we explore is the relationship between irradiance and leaf node activity.[2] For this experiment, two leaf nodes are equipped with one type of solar cell and two others are equipped with a different type of solar cell. The four leaf nodes are programmed to transmit a packet and then disconnect the processor and radio from the power supply. The nodes are exposed to varying irradiance levels from four different indoor light sources with different spectra. Our goal is to answer the question, *given a certain lighting level, how frequently can a leaf node transmit a packet?*

Figures 6(a) to 6(d) show the message interval vs irradiance for two different solar cells powering the same hardware under four different light sources across several decades of irradiance. Leaf nodes are configured to transmit a packet every time their capacitor voltage exceeds a threshold. The nodes are exposed to controlled light levels and have their packet transmissions logged. Nodes AM1 and AM2 use AM-1437 amorphous silicon solar cells while nodes Si1 and Si2 use *three* XOB17-4X3 crystalline silicon solar cells in series. Irradiance is measured using a custom sensor (based on the TAOS TSL230BR) calibrated with a professional meter.

Figure 6(a) shows that both amorphous and crystalline solar cells have similar conversion factors under fluorescent lighting conditions. Figures 6(b) and 6(c) show that crystalline solar cells exhibit better conversion in incandescent and halogen settings than amorphous solar cells by roughly an order of magnitude, as evidenced by the two distinct clusters that are visible. These results are to be expected since fluorescent lights have peaks in the 500 to 600 nm range which align with the spectral sensitivity of amorphous solar cells but tungsten-based lamps, like standard incandescent and halogen, emit much less energy in the 500 nm range than they do at longer wavelengths, like 700 nm. Figure 6(d) shows that both amorphous and crystalline solar cells perform more closely under LED lighting of 2500 K color temperature. Again, these results are to be expected since white LED lights have a peak near 450 nm from a blue GaN or InGaN monochromatic LED. The results show that baseline communications activity of leaf nodes is roughly linear with irradiance and that operation near fluorescent, incandescent, and LED indoor sources with irradiance levels below 20 μW/cm^2 is possible. The data also highlight the importance of considering the mix of light sources and matching them to the appropriate solar cells.

Figure 6(e) shows the average irradiance of four different offices (13 distinct locations) for a partly sunny ("good") and rainy ("bad") day. The data shows that even on a rainy day, average irradiance largely exceeds 100 μW/cm^2 during daylight hours, suggesting many indoor locations are viable for leaf nodes. Figure 6(f)

---

[2]Irradiance is a measure of radiation per unit area incident on a surface, and it is measured in μW/cm^2.

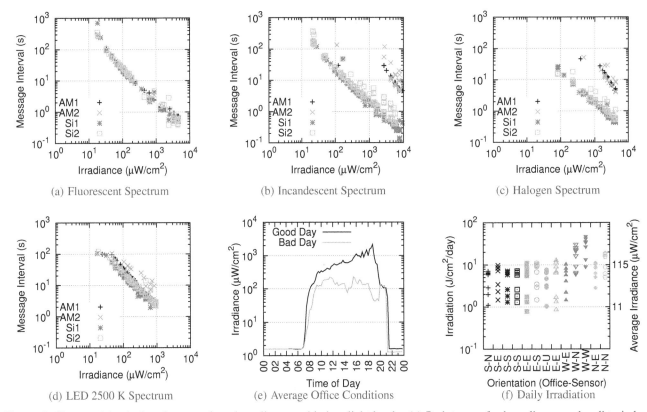

Figure 6: Characterizing leaf performance by solar cell type and indoor light levels. (a) Both types of solar cells respond well to indoor fluorescent lights. (b) Crystalline silicon solar cells (Si1 and Si2) respond well to incandescent but amorphous solar cells (AM1 and AM2) generate an order of magnitude fewer packets at the same irradiance. (c) Halogen lights also result in order-of-magnitude reduction in packet transmissions for amorphous solar cells compared to fluorescent lights. (d) LED lighting shows much more comparable performance between both the two types of solar cells and output in comparison with fluorescent lights. (e) shows the average irradiance of four typical offices over the course of a partly sunny day (good) and a rainy day (bad); even on a bad day, a leaf harvests enough energy for a packet transmission every few minutes. (f) shows daily irradiation across 13 sensors deployed in four offices over a one week period including sunny and rainy days. Thus, the IPV leaf design is viable.

shows that daily irradiation can vary by more than an order of magnitude for a single location.[3] Most locations receive 1-10 J/cm^2/day (or an average of 11-115 μW/cm^2), which is enough to ensure frequent leaf activity. Figure 7 shows the instantaneous, rather than average, irradiance of the underlying data over a one week period. The traces also show that during Friday and Saturday evenings, the North Office was illuminated, and during Wednesday evening, the West Office was illuminated. This suggest evening or nighttime human activity in those rooms. In all three cases of human activity, the light levels exceeded 100 μW/cm^2.

The U.S. Department of Labor's regulation on minimum office illumination [20] is 30 foot-candles, which corresponds to about 320 lux. The regulations are lower for indoor corridors and hallways at 5 foot-candles, or about 53 lux. From our own experiments using a commercial lux meter and a TAOS TSL230BR [19] light to frequency converter we find that 50 lux of a fluorescent light corresponds to 18.6 μW/cm^2, 100 lux to about 29.1 μW/cm^2, and 320 lux to 74.9 μW/cm^2.

These figures suggest that our leaf nodes, as built, are capable of operating at minimum office illumination levels and, in many cases, substantially below them. Furthermore, when high-fidelity

sensing is required – when people are present – typical light levels are far above the minimum levels needed for operation and nodes can easily report data every minute, without requiring supercapacitors or batteries. As processors and radios become more energy efficient, power supplies become more efficient, and real-time clocks draw lower power, cubic-cm scale pervasive sensors will become increasingly practical.

4.2 Initial Synchronization

We evaluate two techniques to synchronize leaf and branch nodes. The first approach employs an asymmetric, asynchronous neighbor discovery protocol that shifts much of the neighbor discovery burden onto branch nodes. The second approach employs a shared, external event from the node's common environment to synchronize nodes.

4.2.1 Asynchronous Neighbor Discovery

We use a variant of the Disco [2] neighbor discovery protocol in which nodes transmit beacons on eventually overlapping schedules. In our case, only leaf nodes transmit and only branch nodes listen. The listen and transmission schedules are chosen such that the worst case discovery latency is about 50 min and the discovery burden is small for both.

Leaf nodes transmit beacons during a 5 ms window ("slot") ev-

---

[3]Irradiation is accumulated irradiance per unit time, and it is measured in μJ/cm^2/day.

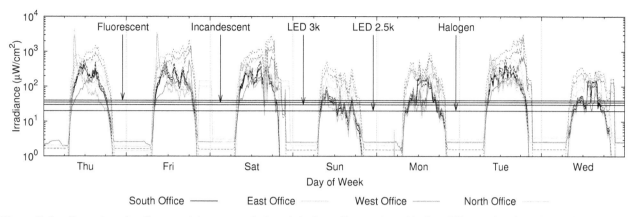

Figure 7: Irradiance (on a log-linear scale) over a typical week in four offices, oriented in four different directions. Each office is equipped with two to four typically wall-mounted sensors, each facing in different directions within the office, to capture different light environments. The horizontal lines correspond to the irradiance necessary for a leaf node to send a message every minute given the respective light source type. On most days, most leaf nodes have enough light to send a message once a minute, but on some days, some do not. This highlights the importance of node placement and solar cell sizing. It also illustrates the need to support a wide operating dynamic range.

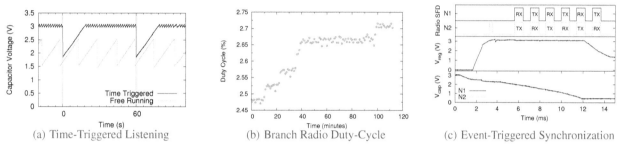

| (a) Time-Triggered Listening | (b) Branch Radio Duty-Cycle | (c) Event-Triggered Synchronization |

Figure 8: Achieving initial synchronization. Methods for achieving initial synchronization include both asynchronous neighbor discovery and synchronous event-triggered discovery. (a) A free-running leaf transmits a packet when it has sufficient energy. A triggered leaf transmits at a well-known interval. (b) Each point represents the duty cycle of each minute. Each step in the graph corresponds to the discovery of a leaf node. Even while synchronized with five leaf nodes, the branch node's duty cycle only slightly increases from 2.45% to 2.75%. (c) A trace of synchronous event-triggered discovery is shown. Leaf (N1) and branch (N2) nodes both respond to a sudden change in light level (triggered by a zero-power light detector circuit), choose a short backoff, and transmit packets back and forth until the leaf depletes the energy in its storage capacitor.

ery 60 s. This translates to a nominal duty cycle of 83 ppm (or 0.0083%). Figure 8(a) shows a free-running leaf transmits packets whenever it has sufficient energy but that a time-triggered leaf transmits packets at multiples of 60 s, allowing a branch node to both employ a compatible neighbor discovery schedule and predict future transmission times.

Branch nodes listen for beacons during a 5 ms window ("slot") every 245 ms (or 49 slots). This translates to a nominal duty cycle of 2.04% but inefficiencies and latencies in radio startup result in a higher duty cycle (2.5%), which translates to a roughly 1.5 mW power load due to discovery. The baseline discovery power is higher than ideal, but using newer radios that offer similar radio sensitivity at roughly 15% of the receive current, the baseline discovery power could be reduced to about 500 μW. Given the nominal duty cycles of 0.0083% and 2.04%, the worst case discovery latency is (5 ms)/(0.0083% × 2.04%), or about 50 min (2940 s) in the absence of communications failure, as Figure 8(b) shows.

4.2.2 Synchronous Event Triggered

To explore the viability of basic event-triggered synchronization, we design a simple, zero-power, light-activated trigger switch. It consists of a solar cell connected in parallel with a burden resis-

tor. The solar cell's negative terminal is connected to an N-channel FET's source (and leaf GND), and the positive terminal is connected to the FET's gate. The FET's drain is connected to the power supply's external trigger or an interrupt line. This forces the leaf node to cold boot, and the branch node to wake up from sleep, in response to a sudden change in lighting. The nodes then exchange packets.

Figure 8(c) shows the operation of two nodes, a leaf (N1) and a branch (N2), in response to an external trigger. The leaf node transmits first, and then the branch node responds. The two nodes transmit packets back and forth until the leaf depletes its energy. This illustrates that for sufficiently "sharp" triggers, like light, accoustics, or sudden movement, it is possible for both leaf and branch nodes to synchronize.

4.3 Ongoing Synchronization

Once a leaf and branch node have synchronized, they need to maintain ongoing synchronization to operate. In our design, the entire burden of maintaining synchronization rests with the branch node. The leaf node simply transmits synchronization beacons or data packets at every multiple of 60 s whenever it has enough energy to do so. The branch node is responsible for tracking the

Figure 9: Maintaining ongoing synchronization. Each vertical line represents a successful leaf to branch packet transmission. Around 20:00 hrs, the leaf stops transmitting due to a dark environment. When light returns at 4:45 hrs, the branch begins to receive the packets without requiring resynchronization.

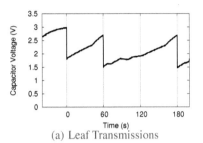
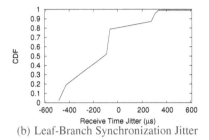
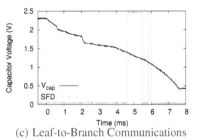

(a) Leaf Transmissions   (b) Leaf-Branch Synchronization Jitter   (c) Leaf-to-Branch Communications

Figure 10: Transmitting packets from leaf to branch nodes. (a) A leaf node transmits a packet when it has a sufficiently high capacitor voltage (at 0 s, 60 s, and 180 s) but the leaf node skips a transmission (at 120 s) if it does not have sufficient energy. (b) A branch node is able to track the leaf node's transmission times with very low error. The cumulative distribution of branch-leaf synchronization times over a 3.5 hr time window of minute-level transmissions shows less than ± 500 μs jitter. (c) A leaf node is able to successfully transmit a packet (first SFD pulse) and receive an acknowledgment (second SFD pulse) from a branch node before exhausting the limited energy in its capacitor. This demonstrates reliable transmission of data from leaf to branch nodes.

leaf node's transmission times and scheduling itself to be on during those times. Upon successful packet reception, a branch node can update its estimate of the leaf node's clock drift, if any. And, upon a missed transmission, the branch can adjust a guard window as needed.

In order to maintain a suitably low branch node duty-cycle, the maximum guard window size must be capped. When the clock drift requires a larger guard time, we use a local search pattern. In this search, the branch node iterates through the entire guard window by waking up for a different portion of the guard time in its periodic wakeups. For example, if the guard window is 100 ms, the branch would wake up for each 20 ms portion over a five minute period.

To evaluate the reliability of ongoing synchronization (and, by extension, data communications), a leaf node runs in a lit room. Initially synchronized, the nodes maintain synchronization for 6.6 hours. When the room becomes dark, the leaf ceases transmissions, except for a brief moment when it turns on for about two minutes. After seven hours, the leaf resumes transmissions, and the branch takes up to 4 minutes to find it again. The received packets are shown by vertical lines in Figure 9. The branch uses a fixed, 5 ms slot, but with clock stability's of ± 1 ppm for a branch and ± 2 ppm for a leaf, the guard times may need to be adjusted. In the worst case, $t_{guard} = (|\pm 1| + |\pm 2|) \times 3600 \times 8 = 86.4$ ms after eight hours, or a maximum of a five minute resynchronization delay due to the local search pattern.

4.4 Leaf to Branch Communications

Once a leaf and branch are synchronized, they may need to transfer data bidirectionally. Transmission from leaf to branch is relatively straightforward as a leaf simply wakes up at a multiple of 60 s and transmits. If the leaf does not have enough energy to transmit, as Figure 10(a) shows at time 120 s, it simply skips that transmission, but the branch still listens in anticipation.

Although communication data paths have been optimized for low-latency operation, some jitter still remains. To characterize this jitter, a leaf node is programmed to cold boot every 60 s and trans-

mit a packet to a branch nodes. The branch node records the reception time using a 32 kHz TCXO. Figure 10(b) shows the cumulative distribution of leaf-branch synchronization jitter. A ± 500 μs range captures the cold boot to packet transmission jitter. A branch node must account for this jitter with a 1 ms (or longer) guard time.

Finally, reliable communications requires that a leaf's transmissions be acknowledged. This is accomplished by transmitting a packet with an ACK request, which causes the branch to quickly transmit an ACK. Figure 10(c) illustrates this exchange. A leaf's packet transmission is seen as the first SFD pulse, from 4.8 to 5.4 ms, and ACK reception is the second SFD pulse. We use an 802.15.4 data packet for the ACK to allow the branch node to send additional data to the leaf, as discussed in [8]. Note that the leaf has sufficient energy to transmit its data packet and receive the data ACK packet.

4.5 Branch to Leaf Communications

Data transmission from branch to leaf nodes is more challenging than transmissions in the other direction. A leaf node's transmission serves to deliver data, optionally request an acknowledgment, and probe for pending inbound traffic. In a typical radio stack, a received packet is buffered in the radio until it is received fully and then dispatched to higher layers for processing. A response packet may then be generated, passed through the network stack, and transferred to the radio, and finally transmitted. Unfortunately, these latencies add up, as Figure 11(a) shows, where the default TinyOS network stack takes nearly 10 ms between a leaf's transmission (the first SFD pulse) and the branch's reply (the second SFD pulse), causing a leaf to deplete its capacitor.

To enable data transmission from branch to leaf, we modify the branch to pipeline payload reception with transmit FIFO loading. This allows the branch node to reply with a full packet with a 0.67 ms turnaround time, as Figure 11(b) shows. This optimization allows the leaf node to successfully receive the branch's transmission before depleting its energy reserves, as Figure 11(c) shows. In addition to ensuring that communications from branch to leaf is vi-

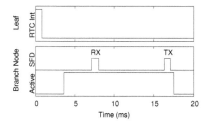

(a) RX/TX Non-Pipelined Branch Node

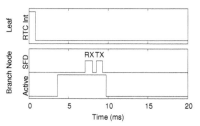

(b) RX/TX Pipelined Branch Node

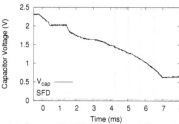

(c) Successful Bi-Directional Transfer

Figure 11: Transmitting packets from branch to leaf nodes. (a) Leaf and branch nodes wake up triggered by their respective real-time clocks (only the leaf's RTC init is shown). A leaf transmits a probe that is received by branch. The packet transmits data to the branch and also indicates that it is awake to receive a packet. The branch responds, but the long latency in serialized packet processing – receiving, dispatching, processing, and responding – results in the leaf exhausting its energy supply before receiving the branch's transmission, resulting in communications failure (the branch does not transmit first since the common case requires the leaf to transmit sensor data). (b) Low-latency optimizations to the packet processing datapaths in the branch dramatically reduce delays and allow a fast RX/TX turnaround. The key optimization is parallelizing and pipelining the various datapaths so that writing to the TX FIFO begins before the packet has been completely read out from the RX FIFO. (c) The capacitor voltage and radio activity (SFD) of a leaf communicating with a low-latency branch node shows that the communication completes before the leaf exhausts its energy supply.

able, this changes also lower the energy cost of communication for the branch node itself, cutting the radio active time in half – from about 14 ms to 7 ms.

5. RELATED WORK

The design and implementation of standards-based, near-nanopower, wireless sensornets raises challenges across the entire system. This work complements prior efforts in sensornet architectures, platforms, power systems, discovery protocols, and synchronization primitives, and is related to ongoing work in wireless sensing and computational RFIDs.

Architectures: The canonical patch sensornet is the Great Duck Island (GDI) deployment [18]. The battery-powered nodes generated a message every 5 minutes. In this work, we show that purely energy-harvesting indoor nodes can send a message about every minute during daylight hours. Tiered architectures, similar to our trunk, branch, and leaf partitioning were proposed by Gnawali et al. in Tenet [5]. Tenet describes an architecture of unconstrained masters (trunk) and battery-powered nodes (branch). We extend this architecture one level further, into energy harvesting leaves, and describe how these leaves can interoperate with the existing architectures.

EnHANTs: [6] The EnHANTS project explores the challenges for a new tier of energy-neutral, self-reliant nodes. Their research goals are very similar to ours: build and network indoor solar-based energy-harvesting sensor nodes with severe energy, size, and cost constraints. However, the approaches differ considerably. While we use currently available parts in a small and thin form factor designed for wall mounting, their tags are custom fabricated hardware in a flexible sticker design. Both methods face two main challenges: hardware design and network communication.

For hardware, EnHANTs use Ultra-Wide Band (UWB) impulse radios with low transmit energy per bit requirements (1 nJ vs 150 nJ for current 802.15.4 radios) at the cost of range (3 m at 25 kbps). They also use organic solar cells (as opposed to our more traditional amorphous and crystalline solar cells) for physical flexibility at the cost of power transfer efficiency. UWB impulse radios and organic solar cells are still in active research and have ground-breaking future prospects. However, we show that current 802.15.4 radios and commercial solar cells are sufficient to network of small, energy-harvesting sensor nodes. Our node designs achieve similar hardware goals – namely small volume and practical efficiency –

while using off-the-shelf components and offering a much lower overhead cost compared with custom silicon. Our sensor nodes can be deployed immediately for many reasonable indoor applications, and especially ones in which lighting is available when measurements are required.

For network communications, EnHANTs focuses on optimizing resource allocation – energy harvested, energy stored, and data communicated on local (per node) and global (network) scales [10]. This approach assumes that nodes are already time-slotted using some on some global time scale. More recent work focuses on synchronizing the tags to a beacon transmitting receiver (tag reader) [21]. The work does not address communication to other duty-cycled nodes nor does it address network communications with unreliable clocks or power intermittency. The work also sidesteps the issue of clocks – and especially accurate clocks – that may be too energy expensive to provide the necessary timebase, even though the work acknowledge the problem. Assuming a 40 hour work week, the cost of time-keeping requires a significant portion of the overall energy budget (40%):

P_{RTC}: 1.5 V * 1 μA = 1.5 μW
P_{leaf}: 3 V * 20 mA * 10 ms/60 s * (40/168) hrs/wk = 2.4 μW

In contrast, our work attacks the problem of energy-expensive clocks by letting nodes lose all sense of time by allowing for complete clock shutdown if energy reserves are depleted. This results in nodes churn, so robust and efficient network (re)synchronization is necessary as energy is harvested, stored, and depleted. To address this problem, hierarchical asynchronous neighbor discovery is a fundamental primitive in our system.

While EnHANTs seeks to push the boundary of low-power operation, we claim that practical energy harvesting sensor networks are viable today. We validate our claim by building and studying sensor platforms, protocols, and power systems using off-the-shelf components. We have shown that we can build energy harvesting sensor nodes that can measure, process, and transmit sensor data packets in a comparable fashion to current duty-cycled battery powered nodes. We have also shown that completely depleted and unsynchronized leaf nodes can recharge and join a network within a reasonable amount of time via asynchronous neighbor discovery. Our next challenge lies in making more robust leaf to branch discovery and ongoing communication protocols with large numbers of leaf and branch/trunk nodes. Eventually, we hope to enable leaf-to-leaf communications – a goal we share with the EnHANTs project.

Indoor Photo-Voltaic Systems TwinStar [22] is a mixed indoor-outdoor solar energy harvesting system that explores a capacitor-only energy storage design. The idea behind TwinStar is to use energy when it is available, and thus reduce energy leakage. The TwinStar platform uses two solar panels. A bootup panel triggers the DC/DC converter to solve the zero-energy bootup challenge, while a large solar panel ($\sim$36 cm^2) is used to charge the super capacitor. Our design is similar in that we use energy when it is available. However, our design is fully powered by a solar panel the size of TwinStar's bootup panel.

Raisigel et al. [17] describe an IEEE 802.15.4 compliant IPV platform. Raisigel's design uses a Schott solar panel with an active area of 8.5 cm^2, an Atmel AT86RF231 radio, and an Atmel ATMega644PV 8-bit microcontroller. The platform uses a manganese rechargeable lithium coin-cell battery and storage capacitors for peak currents. Using very shallow recharge cycles during nighttime sampling (minute intervals), they extended the life of the button cell battery beyond 10 years under nominal daytime lighting conditions. Raisigel's design focuses on ultra-low power sleep modes. Raisigel's battery/energy-harvesting hybrid sensors are fully capable sensors powered under indoor lighting conditions. Their design requires large batteries due to the shallow discharges necessitated by extending the life of the battery to 10 years. Their design is practical with batteries, however, our work explores the scenario in which complete energy loss is possible. This is a reasonable assumption for rooms with much less than 8 hours of light per day or 40 hours per week. For their design, this means that battery discharges will be far deeper and energy harvested needs far higher to replenish the battery, which affects battery aging adversely. With lower light levels, their nodes transition from energy-harvesting to battery-power. Therefore, their work demonstrates battery-powered nodes with longer life because of their hybrid approach. The work also does not consider protocol issues for duty-cycled nodes and instead assumes that an always-on receiver is available in range, thus sidestepping synchronization issues.

EnHANTs and Raisigel both explored the light intensity availabe via indoor solar. Our data also support their findings: if an office has a window, one can expect irradiance ranging from 10μW/cm^2 to 100μW/cm^2 [7].

EnOcean provides a commercial battery-less system with the STM300 and STM310 modules [4]. Both systems are powered by a solar panel of about 4.8 cm^2. The STM300 series provides a proprietary transceiver, while the STM310 is a transmitter only. The EnOcean system provides a proprietary solution for a leaf-to-trunk communications model, where the peer is an always-on node, and Raisigel's work describes an energy-harvesting platform without going into details of a system architecture. With this work, we delve deeper into the possibilities of system architectures in which leaf nodes communicate with battery-powered mesh nodes, as well as other energy-harvesting leaf nodes.

6. CONCLUSION

As the density of indoor wireless sensors increases, and their size decreases, battery-powered operation becomes increasingly less viable. Batteries have a finite lifetime, they incur replacement costs, and their average power delivery scales poorly compared with indoor photovoltaics. Hence, today many believe that energy-harvesting holds the key to long-term, cost-effective, and sustainable sensing. However, today's energy-harvesting sensors, like EnOcean and ZigBee Green Power, require that the nodes be within one hop of an always-powered base station or repeater. This regresses on a decade

of advances in multihop mesh networking – and its diverse benefits – including better spatial reuse of spectrum, more path diversity, greater deployment flexibility, and lower transmission power.

This paper shows that it is possible to augment battery-powered mesh networks with energy-harvesting leaf nodes. Thus, we create a new tier of sensor nodes that are free from the constraints of battery power, but still retain the many benefits of interoperating with contemporary wireless multihop mesh networks. Furthermore, these new energy harvesting leaf nodes can be built from standard components that have been around for years. We simply combine them in new ways to achieve low-leakage operation, optimize the system software for low-latency cold boot and communications, and employ low-energy protocols to achieve synchronization and maintain communications. Using newer, and lower power, technology would only improve performance, and using tiny batteries or supercapacitors would allow continuous operation, even in the absence of harvestable energy. This work paves the way for a new tier of perpetual computing systems, shows the viability of the architectural approach, and demonstrates interoperability with existing sensor network nodes.

Acknowledgments

This material is supported in part by a gift from Texas Instruments and by National Science Foundation Awards #0964120 ("CNS-NeTS") and #1111541 ("CNS-CSR"). Additional NSF support was provided under Grant #1019343 to the Computing Research Association for the CIFellows Project.

7. REFERENCES

[1] Cymbet Corporation. EnerChip CBC050-M8C: 50uah rechargeable solid state battery, Oct. 2011.

[2] P. Dutta and D. Culler. Practical asynchronous neighbor discovery and rendezvous for mobile sensing applications. In *SenSys '08: Proceedings of the 6th International Conference on Embedded Networked Sensor Systems*, pages 71–84, Nov. 2008.

[3] P. Dutta, J. Taneja, J. Jeong, X. Jiang, and D. Culler. A building block approach to sensornet systems. In *SenSys'08: Proceedings of the Sixth ACM Conference on Embedded Networked Sensor Systems*, nov 2008.

[4] EnOcean. STM310: General Purpose Sensor Transmitter Module, Apr. 2011.

[5] O. Gnawali, K. Jang, J. Paek, M. Vieira, R. Govindan, B. Greenstein, A. Joki, D. Estrin, and E. Kohler. The tenet architecture for tiered sensor networks. In *SenSys'06: Proceedings of the 4th international conference on Embedded networked sensor systems*, pages 153–166. ACM, 2006.

[6] M. Gorlatova, P. Kinget, I. Kymissis, D. Rubenstein, X. Wang, and G. Zussman. Energy harvesting active networked tags (EnHANTs) for ubiquitous object networking. *IEEE Wireless Communications*, 17(6):18–25, 2010.

[7] M. Gorlatova, A. Wallwater, and G. Zussman. Networking ultra low power energy harvesting devices: Measurements and algorithms. In *Proceeding of IEEE INFOCOM'11*, Apr. 2011.

[8] J. W. Hui and D. E. Culler. Ip is dead, long live ip for wireless sensor networks. In *SenSys '08: Proceedings of the 6th ACM conference on Embedded network sensor systems*, pages 15–28, New York, NY, USA, 2008. ACM.

[9] Linear Technology. LTC3108: Ultralow voltage step-up converter and power manager, Apr. 2010.

[10] A. B. M. Gorlatova and G. Zussman. Performance evaluation of resource allocation policies for energy harvesting devices. IEEE Symposium on Modeling and Optimization in Mobile, Ad Hoc, and Wireless Networks (WiOpt'11), 2011.

[11] Maxim Integrated Products. DS32kHz: 32.768khz temperature-compensated crystal oscillator. http:

//datasheets.maxim-ic.com/en/ds/DS32kHz.pdf,
Apr. 2010.

[12] Microchip Technology Inc. PIC16F1827: Flash mcu with nanowatt xlp, Oct. 2011.

[13] Micropelt GmbH. Micropelt Thermogenerator, Oct. 2011.

[14] NXP. PCF2127A: Integrated rtc, tcxo and quartz crystal, May 2010.

[15] Panasonic. ML621: Manganese lithium coin batteries, Oct. 2011.

[16] J. Polastre, R. Szewczyk, and D. Culler. Telos: Enabling Ultra-Low Power Wireless Research. In *Proceedings of the 4th International Conference on Information Processing in Sensor Networks (IPSN/SPOTS)*, 2005.

[17] H. Raisigel, G. Chabanis, I. Ressejac, and M. Trouillon. Autonomous wireless sensor node for building climate conditioning application. SENSORCOMM'10, Venice/Mestre, Italy, 2010. VDE Verlag.

[18] R. Szewczyk, A. Mainwaring, J. Polastre, and D. Culler. An analysis of a large scale habitat monitoring application. In *SenSys'04:*

Proceedings of the Second ACM Conference on Embedded Networked Sensor Systems, Nov. 2004.

[19] TAOS. Tsl230brd programmable light-to-frequency converters.

[20] US Dept. of Labor. Illumination regulations #1926.56 (standards - 29 cfr).

[21] Z. Wang, A. Tajer, and X. Wang. Communication of energy harvesting tags. IEEE Transactions on Communications.

[22] T. Zhu, Z. Zhong, Y. Gu, T. He, and Z.-L. Zhang. Leakage-aware energy synchronization for wireless sensor networks. In *Proceedings of the 7th international conference on Mobile systems, applications, and services*, MobiSys '09, pages 319–332, New York, NY, USA, 2009. ACM.

[23] ZigBee Alliance. New ZigBee green power feature set revealed, June 2009.

Improving RF-Based Device-Free Passive Localization In Cluttered Indoor Environments Through Probabilistic Classification Methods

Chenren Xu
WINLAB, Rutgers University
671 Route 1 South
North Brunswick, NJ 08902
lendlice@winlab.rutgers.edu

Bernhard Firner
WINLAB, Rutgers University
671 Route 1 South
North Brunswick, NJ 08902
bfirner@winlab.rutgers.edu

Yanyong Zhang
WINLAB, Rutgers University
671 Route 1 South
North Brunswick, NJ 08902
yyzhang@winlab.rutgers.edu

Richard Howard
WINLAB, Rutgers University
671 Route 1 South
North Brunswick, NJ 08902
reh@winlab.rutgers.edu

Jun Li
WINLAB, Rutgers University
671 Route 1 South
North Brunswick, NJ 08902
jonjunli@winlab.rutgers.edu

Xiaodong Lin
MSIS, Rutgers University
252 Janice H. Levin Hall
Piscataway, NJ 08854
lin@business.rutgers.edu

ABSTRACT

Radio frequency based device-free passive localization has been proposed as an alternative to indoor localization because it does not require subjects to wear a radio device. This technique observes how people disturb the pattern of radio waves in an indoor space and derives their positions accordingly. The well-known multipath effect makes this problem very challenging, because in a complex environment it is impractical to have enough knowledge to be able to accurately model the effects of a subject on the surrounding radio links. In addition, even minor changes in the environment over time change radio propagation sufficiently to invalidate the datasets needed by simple fingerprint-based methods. In this paper, we develop a fingerprinting-based method using probabilistic classification approaches based on discriminant analysis. We also devise ways to mitigate the error caused by multipath effect in data collection, further boosting the classification likelihood.

We validate our method in a one-bedroom apartment that has 8 transmitters, 8 receivers, and a total of 32 cells that can be occupied. We show that our method can correctly estimate the occupied cell with a likelihood of 97.2%. Further, we show that the accuracy remains high, even when we significantly reduce the training overhead, consider fewer radio devices, or conduct a test one month later after the training. We also show that our method can be used to track a person in motion and to localize multiple people with high accuracies. Finally, we deploy our method in a completely different commercial environment with two times the area achieving a cell estimation accuracy of 93.8% as an evidence of applicability to multiple environments.

Categories and Subject Descriptors

C.3 [**Special-Purpose and Application-Based Systems**]: Real-time and embedded systems; G.3 [**Probability and Statistics**]: Probabilistic algorithms

General Terms

Algorithm, Experimentation, Measurement

Keywords

Device-free Passive Localization, Discriminant Analysis, Multipath, RSS footprint

1. INTRODUCTION

There is growing interest in incorporating automatic "intelligence" in our homes and offices using a dense array of wireless radio/sensor nodes. Central to this intelligence is often the need to localize and track people in indoor environments. Many radio frequency (RF) based localization techniques have been proposed, such as those discussed in [1, 18, 5, 8, 12, 14, 24, 19, 6, 10, 4, 20, 9, 15]. Most of these techniques, however, require the subjects to carry wireless devices, and are referred to as device-based active localization. This requirement has several inherent disadvantages. First, tracking stops whenever the device is detached from the subject either accidentally or intentionally. Second, for applications such as elder care, we cannot assume the subjects will always agree or remember to carry the device.

Recognizing these limitations, the community has started the discussion on RF-based device-free passive (DfP) localization techniques [21]. Compared to its active localization counterpart, DfP offers a lower cost solution as it does not require the participation of the subject and uses low-power RF devices that may already be available in our home/office environment. In DfP localization, we capture the change of the RF signals caused by the subject and try to derive his/her location based upon this change.

Deriving a subject's location from the RSS change caused by the subject, however, is a challenging task, mainly due to the well-known "multi-path" effect [11] that is caused by the reflection and diffraction of the RF signal from subjects and objects in the environment. Let us look at a simple experiment to understand the

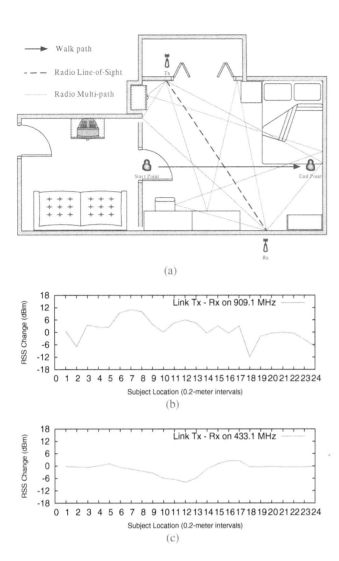

(a)

(b)

(c)

Figure 1: (a) shows the indoor environment in which the radio link has one LoS and four NLoS components; (b) and (c) show the fluctuation of RSS changes between Tx and Rx when the radios operate at 909.1 MHz and 433.1 MHz respectively.

effect is affected by many factors. Figure 1(c) shows a completely different behavior when the radio frequency is set to 433.1 MHz.

Many earlier DfP localization techniques either ignored multipath, or failed to treat multipath carefully enough. For example, radio tomography proposed in [17] tries to calculate a subject's location based upon the signal attenuation when the subject is blocking the LoS of the link. These schemes assume there is a direct relationship between a subject's location and the impact on radio signals. They will have good localization results either outdoor or in an empty room with little multipath. In a cluttered room, which is more common in real life than empty rooms, this assumption does not hold. In [21, 13], the authors acknowledge the importance of multipath, and propose a fingerprinting-based approach in which they first collect a radio map with the subject present in a few predetermined locations, and then map the test location to one of these trained locations based upon observed radio signals. While the fingerprinting approach is certainly a better fit for indoor DfP localization, the localization algorithm in [21, 13] adopts a point-based simplistic minimum Euclidean distance based matching algorithm, which is only practical when the training locations are sparse and the test location closely matches one of the training locations. As training points become denser, classification difficulty will grow significantly.

In this paper, we take on the challenge and strive to improve the performance of DfP localization. Considering the complexity of multipath, *we choose to adopt the fingerprinting approach, and try to achieve good results when we have dense training locations, and random test locations.* We believe these requirements are crucial to many smart home applications such as infant care or elder care. We achieve improved results with the following two optimizations. First, we apply discriminant analysis to the classification problem based on the assumption that the covariates follow a multivariate Gaussian distribution. We validate the assumption of Gaussian distribution through experimental data as well as theoretical approximations. Second, in collecting radio signal readings, we adopt various ways to mitigate the multipath effect so that signal variations within a short distance become smoother. This can increase the distance between classes and further lead to higher classification likelihood. Specifically, our study has the following contributions:

- We derive a sophisticated classification model to better describe the DfP localization problem.

- We improve the quality of data sets by mitigating the error caused by the multipath effect.

- We show that in a one-bedroom apartment of $5 \times 8\ m$ that consists of 32 cells (each being $0.75 \times 0.75\ m$ in size), with 8 transmitters and 8 receivers, we can estimate the occupied cell ID with an accuracy of 97.2%.

- We show that our approach can achieve cell estimation accuracies over 90% in degraded conditions, such as reducing the training overhead (taking 16 data samples per cell instead of 100 samples), reducing the computation overhead, using fewer radio devices (10 devices instead of 16), and conducting tests a month later after the training.

- We show that our approach can be used to track multiple people when they are standing still, walking, sitting, or even lying down. We can also localize multiple people that co-exist in the apartment.

- We also implement our approach in a much larger commercial office space, and report a cell estimation accuracy of 93.8% from 32 cubicle-size cells.

effect of the multipath problem. Figure 1(a) shows the topology of a one-bedroom apartment in which we conduct our experiments. We have one transmitter (Tx in the picture) and one receiver (Rx in the picture), and this radio link has one Line-of-Sight (LoS) component and four Non-Line-of-Sight (NLoS) (or, multipath) components. We only show four NLoS components for simplicity; in reality there are many more present. A person walks from the marked "Start Point" to the marked "End Point". During the movement, we record the received signal strength (RSS) at the receiver (operating at 909.1 MHz), and report the differences between these values and the RSS values when the subject is absent in Figure 1(b). Figure 1(b) shows that the person's effect on the RSS value is random and unpredictable – we observe RSS decreases at different levels, and sometimes we even observe an RSS increase. Figure 1(b) also shows that changes from motion relative to the LoS and NLoS components can be far larger when the subject is not on the LoS than when he is – the variation is as high as 10 db from location 17 to location 18 over a distance of less than 20 cm where the person is not crossing the LoS of the link. Finally, we note that the multipath

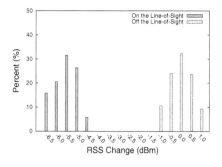

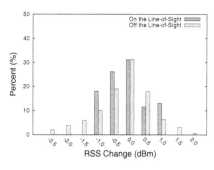

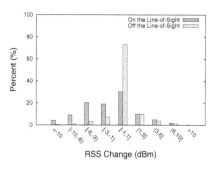

Figure 2: In an outdoor environment, when the radio devices are placed lower than the subject height, the subject causes distinctly different RSS changes for on-LoS cells and off-LoS cells.

Figure 3: In an outdoor environment, when the radio devices are placed higher than the subject height, the subject causes little effect on the radio signals regardless of his location.

Figure 4: In an indoor environment, when the radio devices are placed below the subject height, the subject's effect on the radio signal is unpredictable with respect to his location.

The rest of the paper is organized as follows. In Section 2, we highlight the challenges faced in indoor DfP localization. We model the system and present our localization algorithm in Section 3. In Section 4, we introduce our experimental setup and methodology. In Section 5, we implement our algorithm in a one-bedroom apartment and report detailed experimental results. We discuss the related studies in Section 6, and conclude the paper in Section 7.

2. CHALLENGES IN A CLUTTERED INDOOR ENVIRONMENT

In this section, through experimentation, we demonstrate the differences between RF-based outdoor and indoor localization, and highlight the challenges posed by indoor environments.

2.1 Outdoor Free Space Localization

We begin our experiments in an open outdoor environment. By setting up a transmitter and a receiver attached on tripods 4.5 meters away from each other in an empty parking lot, we only have a relatively small reflection from the ground. We partition the area into $0.75 \times 0.75 \, m$ cells and categorize the cells into two groups: those on the LoS, and those off the LoS. We first record the median of the RSS measurements when the subject is 9 meters away from either device, RSS_E, which represent the base RSS when the subject is absent. Then, we collect 10 continuous RSS readings from each cell while the subject remains stationary in that cell. For each cell, we calculate the RSS change caused by the subject.

We first place the radios such that their height from ground is less than a person's height. In this way, a person can block radio signals more pronouncedly. Figure 2 shows that in this setting, RSS changes in different cells caused by the person clearly fall into two disjoint sets. RSS changes in on-LoS cells are much larger than RSS changes in off-LoS cells. This observation suggests that we may perfectly determine whether the subject is on the LoS or not simply by setting an appropriate threshold for observed RSS changes, which agrees with the observations in earlier studies [3, 17].

Next, we repeat the same experiment, but place the radios above the height of the subject (radios were placed 2 meters above the ground, and the subject is 1.8 meters in height). In this case, the position of the subject has little effect on the RSS values, as shown in Figure 3. As a result, in the rest of the study, we place the radio devices vertically lower than the subject except when explicitly noted.

2.2 The Multipath Effect

Compared with straightforward localization in the outdoor space, localization in the indoor space is much harder because of the multipath problem. This is particularly true for environments of interest for most applications. Next we will support this statement using experimental observations.

In our indoor experiments, we attach the transmitters and receivers on the wall, 1.2 meters above the floor, which is below most adults and above most of the furniture so that the impact of a subject's presence on the radio signal is maximized. As explained earlier, in an indoor environment, the subject may have an unpredictable impact on the RSS. Figure 4 shows the histogram of RSS changes in different cells. We observe that, when a subject randomly blocks a LoS, *there is only a 50% probability of the signal being attenuated by 1 dB or more*. In other words, 50% of the time the signal will not attenuate or even increase. This observation clearly shows that *the assumption of "blocking LoS" means "attenuation" is misleading in cluttered environments*. On the other hand, the results show that if a subject does not block any LoS, there is a 15% probability that the RSS of a radio link will change more than 3 dB. This further shows the unpredictable nature of the multipath effect.

3. DEVICE-FREE PASSIVE LOCALIZATION THROUGH PROBABILISTIC CLASSIFICATION METHODS (PC-DFP)

As discussed earlier, indoor radio propagation is a very complex phenomenon such that the relationship between a subject's location and the resulting RSS of any radio links in the environment is hard to predict. Thus, statistical rather than deterministic methods are required to extract location information from the measured RF signals. In this section, we discuss in detail our probabilistic classification based device-free passive localization method, *PC-DfP* in short.

3.1 Overview of PC-DfP

We visualize a room as a grid of small square cells with unique addresses or ID numbers. By localizing a subject, we mean to estimate accurately the ID of the cell in which the subject is located. In our method, we assume there are L radio links in the environment, and there are K cells in a room. In the training phase, we first measure the RSS values for all L radio links when the room is empty (referred to as environmental RSS). Then for each cell k, we collect a set of RSS values with the subject present in this cell. The change between the environmental RSS and the RSS when the subject is in cell k, $[x_{k,1}, ..., x_{k,L}]$, gives the RSS change vector, $\mathbf{x_k}$, for cell k. $\mathbf{x_k}$ is referred to as the *footprint* for cell k. By the end of the training phase, we have obtained RSS footprints for every cell in the room. We build a K-class classifier based on the RSS footprints. Subsequently, in the testing phase, this classifier is used to classify the testing subject with an unknown label (i.e., cell ID).

3.2 Discriminant Analysis

In formulating our classification problem, we label a class k as the state with the subject in the k-th cell, with the associated RSS footprint $\mathbf{x_k}$. For each cell k, we collect the RSS footprint matrix X_k of dimension $\mathbb{R}^{n_k \times L}$, where n_k denotes the number of RSS footprints sampled in the training phase for the k-th cell. The class label is denoted as y_k. The goal of our analysis is to classify the subject with an unknown label into the correct cell ID based on the measured RSS vector.

A large number of classification techniques have been proposed in the literature, including density based approaches. Under the $0-1$ loss, the objective is to find the maximizer of the class posterior distribution $P(Y|X)$, where Y is the class label y_k and X is the RSS change vector $\mathbf{x_k}$. A simple application of the Bayes rule gives

$$P(Y = k | X = x) = \frac{f_k(x)\pi_k}{\sum_{j=1}^{K} f_j(x)\pi_j},$$

where $f_k(x)$ is the class-conditional density of X in class $Y = k$, and π_k is the prior probability of class k that sums to 1. Assuming f to be a multivariate Gaussian distribution, we have the classical discriminant analysis. In the remaining of this section, we present a few variations of this technique and describe the rationale for applying them to solve our localization problem.

3.2.1 Minimum Euclidean Distance (MED)

Suppose we have the mean vector $\mu_k \in \mathbb{R}^L$ of the RSS for each class k from the training data. We also have the testing RSS vector x and $\hat{y}$ associated with the unknown cell label to be estimated. The Euclidean distance between x and μ_k is defined as

$$d(x, \mu_k) = \sqrt{\sum_{i=1}^{l}(x_i - \mu_{k_i})^2},$$

where

$$\mu_k = \sum_{i \in class\ k} x_i / n_k.$$

Thus, we have the objective classifier function

$$\hat{y} = argmin_k d(x, \mu_k),$$

as studied in [13].

3.2.2 Linear Discriminant Analysis (LDA)

Linear discriminant analysis aims to find a linear combination of features which characterize or separate two or more classes of subjects [7]. We assume the density of each class k is multivariate Gaussian with mean μ_k and a common covariance matrix Σ:

$$f_k(x) = \frac{1}{(2\pi)^{\frac{L}{2}} |\Sigma|^{\frac{1}{2}}} exp\left[-\frac{1}{2}(x - \mu_k)^T \Sigma^{-1} (x - \mu_k)\right].$$

Applying Bayes rule, we have the objective function

$$\hat{y} = argmax_k f_k(x)\pi_k.$$

In the log-scale, we can write the discriminant function as

$$\delta_k(x) = x^T \Sigma^{-1} \mu_k - \frac{1}{2}\mu_k^T \Sigma^{-1} \mu_k + \log \pi_k,$$

and we find

$$\hat{y} = argmax_k \delta_k(x).$$

Maximization of the discriminant function results in the following parameter updates:

- $\hat{\pi}_k = n_k / n$;

- $\hat{\mu}_k = \sum_{i \in class\ k} x_i / n_k$;

- $\hat{\Sigma} = \sum_{k=1}^{K} \sum_{i \in class\ k} (x_i - \hat{\mu}_k)(x_i - \hat{\mu}_k)^T / (n - K)$;

In our experiment, the number of samples n_k is the same across the all the cells. Therefore the class probability $\pi_j = 1/K$ for all the classes.

3.2.3 Quadratic Discriminant Analysis (QDA)

In practice, it is rare that multiple classes share a common covariance matrix. Quadratic Discriminant Analysis (QDA) is a generalization of LDA that allows different covariance matrices. Such a generalization results in more flexible quadratic decision boundaries comparing to the linear decision boundaries from LDA. The resulting discriminant function is

$$\delta_k(x) = -\frac{1}{2}\log|\Sigma_k| - \frac{1}{2}(x - \mu_k)^T \Sigma_k^{-1}(x - \mu_k) + \log \pi_k.$$

The flexibility of QDA comes with the cost of estimating the different covariance matrices Σ_k. When the dimensionality of x is high, this amounts to a huge increase on the number of parameters to be estimated. Thus in practice, with limited sample size, the simpler LDA is preferable.

3.2.4 Dimension Reduction

In practice, parameter estimation can be challenging even for LDA when data dimension is high. One way to address this problem is through feature selection or dimension reduction. Herein we adopt the linear projection scheme so that the L dimensional vector x can be projected to a q dimensional space via $z = Wx$, where W is a $q \times L$ matrix and $q < L$. For a fixed q, the optimal W is computed by maximizing

$$J(W) = \frac{W^T S_B W}{W^T S_W W},$$

where the within class scatter matrix is

$$S_W = \sum_k (\mu_k - \bar{\mu})(\mu_k - \bar{\mu})^T,$$

and the between class scatter matrix is

$$S_B = \sum_k \sum_{i \in class\ k} (x_i - \mu_k)(x_i - \mu_k)^T.$$

Here $\bar{\mu}$ is the overall mean of x, and μ_k is the mean of the kth class. This leads to solving an eigenvalue problem whose solution is $W_l = S_B^{-1/2} v_l$, where v_l is the lth eigenvector of $S_B^{1/2} S_W^{-1} S_B^{1/2}$. The resulting z is a compact representation of x in a lower dimensional space by projecting the original data to the *first q principal discriminant components*. In this way, we can minimize the localization error, reduce the computational cost and prevent the potential over-fitting and singularity problem.

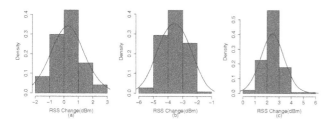

Figure 5: Three histograms for typical experimental RSS change measurements from an arbitrary link when a subject moves randomly within an arbitrary cell. The smooth curve is a log-normal density distribution.

3.3 Gaussian Approximation

In LDA and QDA, we assume that the conditional density given the class label is multivariate Gaussian. In this section, we first present experimental data to support this assumption, and then provide theoretical discussions on why our problem can be approximated by the Gaussian distribution.

Figures 5(a)-(c) show representative histograms for those links with RSS stable (a), attenuated (b) and increased (c). We observe that most of the links fit the log-normal distribution well enough to produce an acceptable fit. As a result, treating RSS values (in power) as Gaussian is a valid assumption. The fact that our results based upon this assumption achieve good classification accuracies (as high as 97% shown in Section 5) is a further support for this assumption.

Next, we explain why we expect that a Gaussian model approximation would work as a first approximation in our classification problem. First, we note that the problem we are addressing is not a typical problem discussed in the literature [11], where the statistics of the multi-path signals at the receiver are considered when either the transmitter or receiver are moved, like in active RF-based localization problems. In passive localization, all the path lengths remain fixed, but the presence of a subject introduces attenuation, scattering, or diffraction of a subset of the multi-path signals. Based upon the geometry of the experimentation room and some simple measurements, we can make analogies, though, to the more typical multipath problem.

In Figure 7(b), it is clear that the major fraction of the links between transmitters and receivers have a substantially clear LoS or at most are obstructed by one relatively transparent interior partition wall. Because of the dominance of the large planar and often perpendicular reflecting surfaces (floor, walls, ceiling), one would expect the multi-path signals to be dominated by LoS and a few, relatively strong components, as seen in [2], along with many components so much smaller than the LoS component that they are insignificant. Finally, we note that in moving around, even a subject that is completely out of the LoS can cause a change in RSS of 10-20 db. This is consistent with a situation in which there are only a small number of multipath components of a magnitude large enough that they could add up constructively and cancel the LoS component to within 10% in amplitude, resulting in a 20db change in energy.

Extending a simplified Rician model [11] to our model would result a dominant LoS signal and a limited number of important multipath signals whose energy was somewhat smaller in total. This would be the Rician limit where the statistics of the signal are approximately Gaussian, as we have seen. Our results show that this approximation is adequate for our environments.

(a)

(b)

Figure 6: (a) Wireless transmitter. (b) Wireless receiver with USB.

4. EXPERIMENTAL METHODOLOGY

In our experiments we will show that one or more subjects can be successfully localized in a home/office environment using our PC-DfP method. The system was deployed in two environments: a one bedroom apartment with home furniture and a commercial office space with cubicles and offices. Since most of the experiments were conducted in the first setting, we will focus on the first setting (i.e., the one-bedroom apartment) in the rest of the paper unless otherwise noted. The apartment pictures are shown in Figures 7(a). The apartment is below ground level with a floor area of $5 \times 8\ m$ and a height of $3\ m$. The floor is concrete, the walls are wallboard on wooden studs, and the ceiling is acoustic tile.

Our experimental setup consists of a host PC (Intel i7-640LM 2.13GHz, 3GB RAM) serving as the centralized system, and eight transmitters and eight receivers. Receivers are connected to the PC through a (wireless) USB hub. In our system, each transmitter broadcasts a 10-byte packet every 100 milliseconds. The receivers will forward received packets to the host PC for data collection and analysis. In Section 5, we show that we can reduce the number of radio devices while maintaining good localization results.

4.1 Hardware Description

The radio devices used in our experiments contain a Chipcon CC1100 radio transceiver and a 16-bit Silicon Laboratories C8051-F321 microprocessor powered by a 20 mm diameter lithium coin cell battery, the CR2032. The receivers have a USB connector for loss-free data collection but are otherwise identical to the transmitters. In our experiments, the radio operates in the unlicensed bands at 433.1 MHz or 909.1 MHz. Transmitters use MSK modulation, a 250kbps data rate, and a programmed output power of 0dBm. Each transmitter periodically broadcasts a 10-byte packet (8 bytes of sync and preamble and 2 bytes of payload consisting of transmitter's id and sequence number) ten times per second. When the receiver receives a packet, it measures the RSS values and wraps the transmitter id, receiver id, RSS, timestamp (on the receiver side) into a "data packet". This packet is sent to the centralized system over direct USB connection or through network hub for data analysis. The transmitter and receiver are shown in Figure 6.

(a)

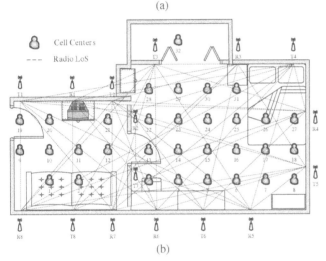

(b)

Figure 7: In (a), we show a rather cluttered one-bedroom deployment region. In (b), we show the experimental topology. The one-bedroom deployment region is partitioned into 32 cells. The center of each cell is marked in the picture. Eight transmitters and eight receivers are deployed. We only show the 64 LoS links here.

4.2 Experimental Setup

Transmitters and receivers are deployed alternatively one by one along the periphery of the wall depicted in Figure 7(b). Eight transmitters and eight receivers provide 64 independent radio links in total. We virtually partition the room into 32 cells, each roughly $0.75 \times 0.75\ m$ in size. We choose 0.75 m because it is the typical walking step size for adults.

Data Collection: Our method consist of the following two phases:

- Off-line training phase. In the training phase, we will con-

struct the radio map of the room by making 100 measurements in each cell (10 seconds) to determine the RSS footprint. We consider two training strategies. In the first case (*training case A*), the subject will stand at the center of each cell and spin around so that the resulting training data will focus on the cell center but involve different orientations. In the second case (*training case B*), the subject will walk randomly within the cell. Thus, the resulting training data treat all the voxels within that specific cell uniformly and includes all possible orientations.

- On-line testing phase. In the testing phase, the subject (who is different from the subject in the training phase in height and weight) will appear in a random location with a random orientation. In our experiments, we have 100 test locations in each cell, resulting in a total of 3200 test locations. Among the 100 test locations within each cell, 25 of them are the cell center, 25 of them are 0.13 m from the center, 25 of them are 0.25 m from the center, and the other 25 are 0.38 m from the center. For each test location, we take 10 RSS measurements and compute the median value for all the 64 radio links.

4.3 Deployment Cost

Unlike [17, 23], our localization algorithm does not require prior information about the locations of all the radio nodes. Transmitters and receivers can be deployed at random locations. This property enables that PC-DfP can be applied in an environment with no changes to the existing infrastructure. In our experiments, it takes 10 seconds to collect 100 training measurements. Even considering the extra overhead of moving and turning, 30 seconds are sufficient for each cell. **Usually we spend around 15 minutes training the whole deployed region**. Given 32 cells and 100 RSS training measurements for each cell in a 64 dimensional space, it takes 0.044 seconds to estimate the parameters of the classification algorithm, and takes only 0.007 second to estimate the subject location.

Overall, the runtime cost of our method is rather modest. In the results section, we discuss ways of further reducing this cost while maintaining high localization accuracies.

5. RESULTS

In this section, we first discuss performance metrics, and then present detailed experimental results.

5.1 Performance Metrics

The objective of a localization system is to maximize the likelihood of correctly estimating a subject's location and minimize the average distance between the estimated location and the actual location. For a specific test i, suppose a subject is actually located in cell y_i, and the estimated cell ID is $\hat{y}_i$ by *PC-DfP*. Further suppose we have N_{tst} tests. We thus define the following performance metrics:

- *Cell Estimation Accuracy* is defined as the ratio of successful cell estimations with respect to the total number of estimations, i.e., $\sum_{i=1}^{N_{tst}} I(y_i = \hat{y}_i)/N_{tst}$. In our system, we consider a test successful if the estimated cell is the same as the occupied cell. If the subject is located on the shared boundary between two adjacent cells, the test is considered successful if the estimated cell is either one of the two bordering cells.

- *Average localization error distance* is defined as the average distance between the actual point location of the subject and the estimated point location (i.e., the center of the estimated cell).

Table 1 summarizes the important parameters used in our experiments. To reiterate, our experiments were conducted in a one-bedroom apartment with the total area of $5 \times 8\ m$, which is divided into 32 cells (size of each cell being $0.75 \times 0.75\ m$). We have 8 transmitters and 8 receivers, resulting in 64 links in total. We note that this number can be made smaller with minimal impact on our localization results. We also note that we anticipate a reasonably large number of sensors/radio devices will be existing in a "smart" home environment. In the training phase, the first author stood in each of these 32 cells, and took 100 RSS measurements. The entire training was finished within 15 minutes by one person.

5.2 Comparing Three Discriminant Analysis Methods

We first compare the results of the three discriminant analysis methods, namely MED, LDA, and QDA. In this set of experiments, the radio frequency is set to 433.1 MHz, and we adopt the training case A. The results are summarized in Table 2.

We observe that LDA performs the best among the three. We expected LDA to outperform MED because it takes into consideration the property of radio propagation. The fact that QDA is the worst of all three, however, is somewhat counter intuitive. After some deliberation, we find out the reason is that QDA requires the estimation of separate covariance matrices for each class, which can lead to over-fitting, especially with a rather limited sample size. The same trend is demonstrated in Figure 8 through the CDF of error distances for the three methods. (We note that QDA does have a slightly shorter tail than LDA.)

In the rest of the performance section, we will thus focus our discussion on LDA.

5.3 Mitigating Multipath Effect

We have mentioned that the multipath effect has an adverse impact on indoor localization, and in this paper, we have devised approaches to mitigate its impact for improved localization results. Specifically, due to multipath, when a subject moves around, we will observe large and abrupt RF variations, even within a cell. Therefore, accurately estimating cell ID based upon the observed RF readings becomes a daunting task. To mitigate this impact, we take the following measures to smooth out the RF variations within a cell.

First, we operate our radios at the unlicensed frequency of 433.1 MHz instead of 909.1 MHz. Intuitively, the wavelength at 433.1 MHz is larger than that at 909.1 MHz, and thus the RF signal has a smoother variation when the subject is moving. We have conducted an experiment to demonstrate this idea. Figure 1(a) shows the experimental setup, and Figures 1(b) and Figures 1(c) shows the RF variation is much smaller at 433.1 MHz than at 909.1 MHz.

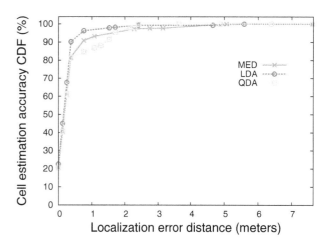

Figure 8: Comparing the CDF of error distances with different discriminant analysis algorithms (MED, LDA, and QDA) at 433.1 MHz.

Second, in the training phase, instead of standing still at a specific point within a cell and using the measurement at that point to represent the entire cell (as in training case A), we make random movements within that cell, take multiple measurements, and use them collectively for classification, as in training case B in Section 4. In this way, we sample the data for all the voxels with different orientations to average out the multipath effect within each cell.

Table 3 summarizes the LDA results with and without these two optimizations. We also varied the test location in these experiments. In general training case B gives better cell estimation accuracies than training case A. Within each training case, radio frequency of 433.1 MHz gives better results than 909.1 MHz with the node layout shown in Figure 7(b). *In summary, our cell estimation accuracy is as high as 97.2% with the average localization error distance of 0.36 meters.*

5.4 Reducing Training/Testing Overhead

Here we investigate methods for reducing the computing overhead for our algorithm. In this study, we formulate the localization problem as a classification problem that involves a training phase and a testing phase. Suppose we have N training data of L dimensions and K classes, where N is the number of measurements taken in each cell in the training phase, L is the number of radio links in the environment, and K is the number of the cells in the environment. In our default setting, we have $N = 100$, $L = 64$, and $K = 32$. For LDA, the algorithmic complexity is $O(KNL + K^3)$ in the training phase and $O(KL^2)$ in the testing phase. As K is fixed in our algorithm, we can try to use a smaller N and/or L to reduce the overhead.

First, we look at the possibility of having a smaller N, i.e., fewer

Parameter	Default value	Meaning
K	32	Number of cells
L	64	Number of radio links
N_{trn}	100	Number of training RSS vector per cell
N_{tst}	100	Number of testing RSS vector per cell

Table 1: System parameters.

Discriminant Analysis Method	Cell Estimation Accuracy (%)	Average Localization Error Distance (m)
MED	81.7	0.55
LDA	90.1	0.44
QDA	81.1	0.53

Table 2: Comparison of the three discriminant analysis methods: MED, LDA, and QDA in training case A.

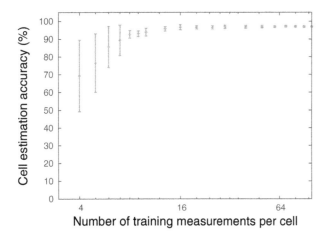

Figure 9: Cell estimation accuracy with 95% confidence interval error bar versus the number of training measurements.

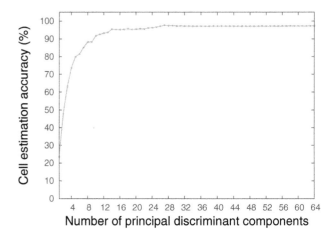

Figure 10: Cell estimation accuracy as a function of the number of most important principal discriminant components.

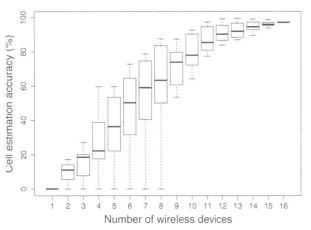

Figure 11: Boxplot of cell estimation accuracy versus the number of wireless devices that are used. For a given number, we show all the possible combinations.

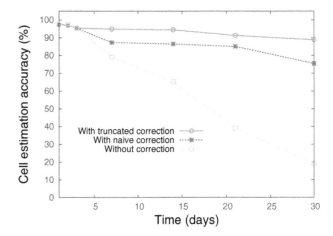

Figure 12: Cell estimation accuracies over one month after the training with different correction approaches.

training samples. Figure 9 shows the localization results with different training data sizes. We observe that we achieve a cell estimation accuracy of 90% by using 16 training measurements in each cell, and achieve a cell estimation accuracy as high as 90% by only using 8 training measurements in each cell. This will lead to a significant reduction of the training overhead.

Next, we look at the possibility of having a smaller L, i.e., smaller data dimensions. To do so, we adopt the optimization technique discussed in Section 3 to select the principal discriminant components for classification purpose. Figure 10 shows that we can achieve the same level of cell estimation accuracy when using only the first 28 principal discriminant components. Such a reduction

	433.1 MHz	909.1 MHz
Training case A	90.1%	82.9%
Training case B	97.2%	93.8%

Table 3: LDA cell estimation accuracies improve when the radios work on 433.1 MHz, and adopt the training case B.

on data dimension can lead to significant improvement on computation efficiency. If we are willing to relax the requirements for the cell estimation accuracy from 97% down to 90%, then choosing the 10 most principal discriminant components will be sufficient.

5.5 Localizing Subjects with Minimum Number of Radio Nodes

Next, we need to test whether our system can still function if we lose one or more radios. In the experiments, we use a subset of the radio nodes and derive the corresponding localization results, and investigate at what point the cell estimation accuracy will drop below a tolerable level. For example, if we would like to find out the results using 10 radio devices out of the default 16 (8 transmitters and 8 receivers), we would randomly remove 6 devices, and plot the localization results for all the possible combinations of transmitters and receivers.

These results are shown in Figure 11. We find that our algorithm can deliver a cell estimation accuracy of 90% when we remove 3 transmitters and 3 receivers in the process. Finally, we note that our system can achieve an even better accuracy (than having all

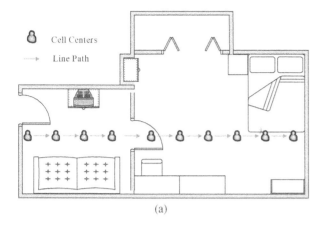 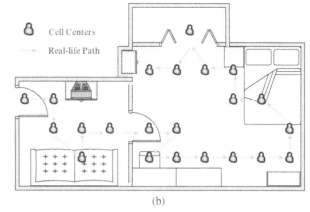

(a)   (b)

Figure 13: Two mobility paths: (a) a line path, and (b) a real-life path.

16 nodes), 99.4%, when three particular devices (i.e., T7, R4 and R6) are removed. Note that we do not reposition the remaining nodes to optimize the results, so this is an overestimate of the number of nodes needed for a given accuracy. Optimizing localization results by systematically removing radio devices (as well as the corresponding links) is a topic for further investigation.

5.6 Using the Same Training Set Over a Long Testing Period

All the results shown above have the testing phase done within three days after training the system. In reality, we are also interested in knowing how well our system will perform if the testing occurs much later in time, which could lead to performance degradation because of changes in the environment or drift in the radio. Different subjects or changes in the same subject could also affect the results.

All the above factors can change the relevance of the original RSS calibration and training. Thus, we need to find an effective correction technique to extend the accuracy of an original calibration over weeks or months. The basic idea is that before each experiment, be it training or testing, we always collect the environmental RSS vector RSS_E when the room is unoccupied. We refer to this vector as RSS_E^{trn} and RSS_E^{tst} for the training and testing phase respectively. This information provides the correction basis for the test data. We can determine when to collect RSS_E^{tst} based upon the subject's life style. For example, it can be collected at noon if he/she works regularly, or at midnight if he/she stays home most of the time.

Using the environmental RSS vector, we propose the following two correction approaches:

- Naive correction: For a simple correction of change over time, we first compute the pairwise difference between the RSS_E^{trn} and RSS_E^{tst}, and record the vector as RSS_E^{bias}. Then we add this bias vector to each RSS vector as the compensation and construct the new test data.

- Truncated correction: We compute RSS_E^{bias} as with naive correction and set an empirical threshold τ. Then we compare the ith entry $RSS_{E\ i}^{bias}$ with τ for $i \in 1, ..., L$. If $\mid RSS_{E\ i}^{bias} \mid \geq \tau$, then we eliminate that feature (link) from both training data and test data. Otherwise, we compensate the test data for that feature as in naive correction. The rationale behind this approach is that we want to eliminate those

links that have experienced a large variation due to environmental instabilities. Since our earlier results (Figure 11) show that our system is robust against missing a few links, we believe removing these links with large fluctuation will not significantly degrade the performance.

We summarize the results in Figure 12. In the case without correction, we do not subtract the environmental RSS from the training/test data. The results show that cell estimation accuracies drop significantly one week after training the system without any correction. With naive correction, we can achieve a cell estimation accuracy of 80% after one month, and truncated correction provides 90% cell estimation accuracy after one month, which is the best among all three.

5.7 Tracking a Moving Subject

Our approach can also be used to track a moving subject. In this set of experiments, the subject moves in the apartment, and we try to estimate which cells he passes during the movement. We choose the longest straight line path and a zigzag path as representatives to test PC-DfP's tracking performance. Specifically, the subject adopted the following two mobility patterns: (1) *line path*, in which the subject walked along a straight line at an average speed of about 3 meters per second (illustrated in Figure 13(a)), and (2) *real-life path*, in which the subject followed a path similar to the path taken in his real life, e.g., he might choose to walk to the bed and lie on the bed for a few seconds, and then walk to the couch and sit down on the couch for a few seconds (illustrated in Figure 13(b)). When the subject moved in the room, we continued to take measurements and estimated which cell he occupied.

We show the localization results in these two cases in Table 4. As expected, when the subject moves along a line path, he can be localized almost as well as when he is stationary, with an cell estimation accuracy of 99.1% and a localization accuracy of 0.3 m. The results for the real-life path are slightly worse (cell estimation accuracy being 91.1%) because there are more complicated movements including walking, lying down, getting up, and sitting. As a result, more uncertainties are introduced. In particular, the cell estimation accuracy is 86.1% when subject is moving and 98.6% when the subject stays still on bed, chair or sofa. We, however, would like to point out that the average localization error distance in this case, 0.37 m, is still rather good. We note that different paths will lead to varying accuracies as different cells have exhibited different classification accuracies.

In this study, we directly apply our approach to the mobile case without any modification. In our next step, we would like to investigate more sophisticated methods such as taking into consideration the trajectory information.

5.8 Localizing Multiple Subjects When Subject Count Is Known

Next, we extend our method to localizing multiple subjects that coexist in a room if we know the number of subjects. Here, we do not need to do any additional training, and the original training data is sufficient.

In our method, we plug the measured data into the classifier, and retrieve the class label which gives the maximum value from the discriminant functions to estimate the cell number. Similarly, to localize n subjects, we just simply pick n class labels which have the first n maximum values. For multiple subjects localization, we define the cell estimation accuracy as the ratio of the number of the occupied cells that are correctly estimated to the number of subjects. For instance, if there are three subjects and only two of their three cells are correctly estimated, then the cell estimation accuracy will be 66.7%.

We perform 32 independent tests, and show our results in table 5. As expected, the cell estimation accuracy decreases when the number of people increases because more people will cause a higher degree of uncertain interference with radio signals.

5.9 Deploying Our Method to a Larger Office Environment

We have shown that our localization method works well in a home environment where radio devices are installed on the walls. Next, we apply our method to a larger office environment to show that it can easily scale to a different setting. In our experiments, we deploy 13 transmitters and 9 receivers in the first author's office, which is $10 \times 15\ m$ in size. In such an environment, localizing subjects at a $0.75 \times 0.75\ m$ cell granularity is not needed; instead, a cubicle-size cell should be sufficient. Thus, we can still partition the deployed area into 32 cells, as shown in figures 14(a) and 14(b). This deployment has two main differences compared to our original deployment: heterogeneous cell sizes and random radio positions (i.e., not always on the walls). Using the same method, our cell estimation accuracy is 93.8% and the average localization error distance is 1.4 m. This degradation compared to the performance in the one-bedroom apartment can be explained as follows. Intuitively, a larger cell involves more voxels, which result in a large variance for each class. Therefore, for all the classes, there is a higher probability that each pair-wise class will have a larger intersection area, which leads to more classification error.

6. RELATED WORK

In this section, we discuss the related work in device-free passive localization (for stationary subjects) and tracking (for mobile subjects).

Device-free Passive (DfP) Localization: Several DfP approaches have been proposed in the literature. In [21, 13], DfP localization

Different Mobility Path	Cell Estimation Accuracy (%)	Average Localization Error Distance (m)
Line	99.1	0.3
Real-life	91.1	0.37

Table 4: Localization results with two different mobility paths.

(a)

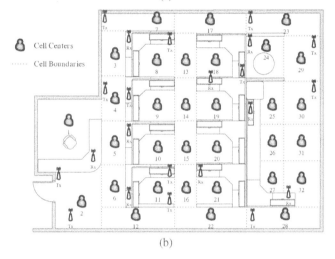

(b)

Figure 14: In (a), we show the first author's lab in which we deployed our system. In (b), we show the experimental topology. The office deployment region is partitioned into 32 cubicle-sized cells. Thirteen transmitters and nine receivers are deployed. We show the cell boundaries in this plot.

is done through fingerprint matching. A passive radio map is constructed during the training phase by recording RSS measurements with a subject standing at pre-determined locations. During the testing phase, the subject appears in one of these locations, and the system can match the observed RSS readings to the RSS readings from one of the trained locations based upon minimum Euclidean distance. Our method shares the same philosophy with [21, 13] in that multipath is so complex that we cannot understand the di-

Number of People	Cell Estimation Accuracy (%)	Average Localization Error Distance (m)
1	97.2	0.36
2	89.5	0.82
3	83.5	0.89

Table 5: Localization results with respect to number of people in the room when the number is known.

rect relationship between a subject's location and the radio signal changes. Instead, we have to train the system first. However, minimum Euclidean distance is shown not to be as efficient as LDA in classification in our study. Further, we have taken special care in the training phase to minimize the RF signal variation within short distances to mitigate the multipath effect. These measures are based upon our in-depth understanding of the radio propagation properties and can lead to much improved localization results.

Radio tomography imaging [17] is a technique to reconstruct the tomographic image for localizing device-free subjects. Here, the authors assume that the relationship between a subject' location and the radio signal variation can be mathematically modeled. In [17, 3], based upon the shadowing effect (RSS is attenuated when the LoS is blocked) caused by the subject, a linear attenuation model and a Sequential Monte Carlo model are proposed respectively. This technique is unlikely to fare well in a cluttered indoor environment because we observed that a person blocking the LoS can only attenuate the RSS with a 50% probability (Section 2).

Device-free Passive Tracking: Several techniques have been proposed to track a moving subject in a passive fashion. In [23, 24], a grid sensor array is deployed on the ceiling for the tracking purpose. An "influential" link is one whose RSS change exceeds a empirical threshold. The authors calculate a subject's location based upon the observation that these influential links tend to cluster around the subject. This work is extended in [22] with triangle sensor array deployment and training information. In VRTI [16], the authors leverage the RSS dynamics caused by the moving subject to generate a radio tomographic imaging for tracking.

Finally, we would like to point out not only fingerprint-based schemes (including ours) need a training phase, but other schemes such as radio tomography and grid sensor array also need a training phase to determine a suitable threshold value to detect if a subject is on the radio LoS.

7. CONCLUSION

In this paper, we present the design, implementation, and evaluation of a device-free passive localization method based on probabilistic classification. We compare three discriminant analysis techniques and find that linear discriminant analysis (LDA) yields much better localization results than minimum Euclidean distance (MED) and quadratic discriminant analysis (QDA). We also propose ways of mitigating the error caused by multipath effect for better localization results, and approaches for correcting training data to facilitate tests much later than the original training. We evaluate our method in a real home environment, rich in multipath. We show that our system can successfully localize a subject with 97% cell estimation accuracy within 0.36 m error distance. Through detailed experiments, we demonstrate that our method can achieve a basic accuracy of over 97%. More importantly, it can maintain an accuracy of over 90% with a substantial reduction in number of radio devices (from 16 down to 10), with far fewer training samples (from 100 to only 16 per cell), or the use of a training set taken a month before testing. In addition, the basic system, without modification, can also be used to track a moving subject or localize multiple subjects. Though originally tested in a small apartment, it performs well in a larger commercial office space.

8. ACKNOWLEDGMENTS

We sincerely thank the anonymous reviewers for their valuable feedback on this paper. We also thank Giovanni Vannucci, Richard Martin, Jinwei Wu and Robert Moore for their insightful comments and encouragement during the formative stages of this work.

9. REFERENCES

[1] P. Bahl and V. Padmanabhan. Radar: an in-building rf-based user location and tracking system. In *INFOCOM 2000. Nineteenth Annual Joint Conference of the IEEE Computer and Communications Societies. Proceedings. IEEE*, volume 2, pages 775 –784 vol.2, 2000.

[2] D. Cassioli, M. Win, and A. Molisch. A statistical model for the uwb indoor channel. In *Vehicular Technology Conference, 2001. VTC 2001 Spring. IEEE VTS 53rd*, volume 2, pages 1159 –1163 vol.2, 2001.

[3] X. Chen, A. Edelstein, Y. Li, M. Coates, M. Rabbat, and A. Men. Sequential monte carlo for simultaneous passive device-free tracking and sensor localization using received signal strength measurements. In *Proceedings of the 10th international conference on Information Processing in Sensor Networks (IPSN)*, pages 342 –353, april 2011.

[4] K. Chintalapudi, A. Padmanabha Iyer, and V. N. Padmanabhan. Indoor localization without the pain. In *Proceedings of the sixteenth annual international conference on Mobile computing and networking*, MobiCom '10, pages 173–184, New York, NY, USA, 2010. ACM.

[5] E. Elnahrawy, X. Li, and R. Martin. Using area-based presentations and metrics for localization systems in wireless lans. In *Local Computer Networks, 2004. 29th Annual IEEE International Conference on*, pages 650 – 657, Nov. 2004.

[6] E. Elnahrawy, R. P. Martin, W. hua Ju, P. Krishnan, and D. Madigan. Bayesian indoor positioning systems. In *In Infocom*, pages 1217–1227, 2005.

[7] T. Hastie, R. Tibshirani, and J. H. Friedman. *The Elements of Statistical Learning*. Springer, 2nd edition, July 2003.

[8] P. Krishnan, A. Krishnakumar, W.-H. Ju, C. Mallows, and S. Gamt. A system for lease: location estimation assisted by stationary emitters for indoor rf wireless networks. In *INFOCOM 2004. Twenty-third AnnualJoint Conference of the IEEE Computer and Communications Societies*, volume 2, pages 1001 – 1011 vol.2, Mar. 2004.

[9] L. Ni, Y. Liu, Y. C. Lau, and A. Patil. Landmarc: indoor location sensing using active rfid. In *Pervasive Computing and Communications, 2003. (PerCom 2003). Proceedings of the First IEEE International Conference on*, pages 407 – 415, march 2003.

[10] N. B. Priyantha, A. Chakraborty, and H. Balakrishnan. The cricket location-support system. In *Proceedings of the 6th annual international conference on Mobile computing and networking*, MobiCom '00, pages 32–43, New York, NY, USA, 2000. ACM.

[11] T. Rappaport. *Wireless Communications: Principles and Practice*. Prentice Hall PTR, Upper Saddle River, NJ, USA, 2nd edition, 2001.

[12] T. Roos, P. Myllymaki, and H. Tirri. A statistical modeling approach to location estimation. *Mobile Computing, IEEE Transactions on*, 1(1):59 – 69, Jan. 2002.

[13] M. Seifeldin and M. Youssef. A deterministic large-scale device-free passive localization system for wireless environments. In *Proceedings of the 3rd International Conference on PErvasive Technologies Related to Assistive Environments*, PETRA '10, pages 51:1–51:8, New York, NY, USA, 2010. ACM.

[14] A. Smailagic and D. Kogan. Location sensing and privacy in a context-aware computing environment. *Wireless Communications, IEEE*, 9(5):10 – 17, 2002.

[15] R. Want, A. Hopper, V. Falcão, and J. Gibbons. The active badge location system. *ACM Trans. Inf. Syst.*, 10:91–102, Jan. 1992.

[16] J. Wilson and N. Patwari. Through-wall tracking using variance-based radio tomography networks. *CoRR*, abs/0909.5417, 2009.

[17] J. Wilson and N. Patwari. Radio tomographic imaging with wireless networks. *Mobile Computing, IEEE Transactions on*, 9(5):621 –632, May 2010.

[18] K. Woyach, D. Puccinelli, and M. Haenggi. Sensorless sensing in wireless networks: Implementation and measurements. In *Modeling and Optimization in Mobile, Ad Hoc and Wireless Networks, 2006 4th International Symposium on*, pages 1 – 8, 2006.

[19] M. Youssef and A. Agrawala. Small-scale compensation for wlan location determination systems. In *Wireless Communications and Networking, 2003. WCNC 2003. 2003 IEEE*, volume 3, pages 1974 –1978 vol.3, 2003.

[20] M. Youssef and A. Agrawala. The horus wlan location determination system. In *Proceedings of the 3rd international conference on Mobile systems, applications, and services*, MobiSys '05, pages 205–218, New York, NY, USA, 2005. ACM.

[21] M. Youssef, M. Mah, and A. Agrawala. Challenges: device-free passive localization for wireless environments. In *Proceedings of the 13th annual ACM international conference on Mobile computing and networking*, MobiCom '07, pages 222–229, New York, NY, USA, 2007. ACM.

[22] D. Zhang, Y. Liu, and L. M. Ni. Rass: A real-time, accurate and scalable system for tracking transceiver-free objects. In *PerCom'11*, pages 197–204, 2011.

[23] D. Zhang, J. Ma, Q. Chen, and L. M. Ni. An rf-based system for tracking transceiver-free objects. In *Pervasive Computing and Communications, 2007. PerCom '07. Fifth Annual IEEE International Conference on*, pages 135 –144, march 2007.

[24] D. Zhang and L. M. Ni. Dynamic clustering for tracking multiple transceiver-free objects. In *Proceedings of the 2009 IEEE International Conference on Pervasive Computing and Communications*, pages 1–8, Washington, DC, USA, 2009. IEEE Computer Society.

Design and Evaluation of a Wireless Magnetic-based Proximity Detection Platform for Indoor Applications

Xiaofan Jiang, Chieh-Jan Mike Liang, Kaifei Chen, Ben Zhang, Jeff Hsu
Jie Liu, Bin Cao, and Feng Zhao
Microsoft Research Asia
Beijing, P.R. China, 100080
{fxjiang, liang.mike, v-kaiche, v-benzh, v-jehs, liuj, bincao, zhao}@microsoft.com

ABSTRACT

Many indoor sensing applications leverage knowledge of relative proximity among physical objects and humans, such as the notion of "within arm's reach". In this paper, we quantify this notion using "proximity zone", and propose a methodology that empirically and systematically compare the proximity zones created by various wireless technologies. We find that existing technologies such as 802.15.4, Bluetooth Low Energy (BLE), and RFID fall short on metrics such as boundary sharpness, robustness against interference, and obstacle penetration. We then present the design and evaluation of a wireless proximity detection platform based on magnetic induction - LiveSynergy. LiveSynergy provides sweet spot for indoor applications that require reliable and precise proximity detection. Finally, we present the design and evaluation of an end-to-end system, deployed inside a large food court to offer context-aware and personalized advertisements and diet suggestions at a per-counter granularity.

Categories and Subject Descriptors

B.0 [**Hardware**]: General; B.4 [**Hardware**]: Input/Output & Data Communication; H.4.m [**Information Systems Applications**]: Miscellaneous

General Terms

Design, Experimentation, Measurement

Keywords

Localization, Magneto-Inductive, Tracking, Virtual Zone

1. INTRODUCTION

Low-power wireless technologies are often used for both communication and proximity sensing. Many applications rely on short-range radio to restrict which receivers can receive their transmissions. This property is particularly useful in *person-scope* applications, where human wearable devices can discover and interact with other devices embedded in the environment without explicit human interventions.

To make these applications intuitive to human users, the discovered objects in the environment must be within the personal interaction sphere, i.e., "within arm's reach". For example, a computer may automatically wake up when a user sits in front of the desk. But, it should not react to people walking past the cubicle. A department store may tag a cloth rack to beacon the sizes and material information of clothes hanging on the rack. This information only needs to reach people who can see and touch these clothes. A home appliance (e.g., refrigerator or microwave) may change its user interface when a person stands in front of it. All these applications share the same architecture: wireless beacons are attached to stationary objects, and mobile nodes carried by human communicate with them when in their proximity. To make these applications robust, beacon nodes must create predictable and stable coverage zones for mobile nodes to discover. In fact, fuzzy zone boundaries introduce uncertainty to the user location, and can lower the user experience with false positives, such as in the case of targeted advertisement. Or, it can lower security such as in the case of building door access.

Many typical low power communication technologies, such as Bluetooth 4.0 (a.k.a. Bluetooth Low Energy or BLE) and ZigBee (with 802.15.4 as the physical layer) have difficulties maintaining robust communication zones. The 2.4 GHz band is prone to external interferences. Human bodies, Wi-Fi activities, and metal objects nearby can significantly alter the signal propagation patterns and the receiving noise floor. While many previous research studies these effects from the perspective of point-to-point communication link quality, such as bit-error rates and data goodput [8, 19], little has been done to quantify the impact on proximity sensing at the human interaction scale. For example, humans react to messages in the order of seconds. As long as a node can be discovered within a few seconds, there is no perceivable difference for the applications. On the other hand, human interactions are less tolerable to obstructions, such as human body or any object blocking the view, and the reach between senders and receivers.

One of the key challenges for characterizing and comparing across wireless proximity technologies is to define comparison metrics. Practically, one can sample the waveform propagation field with only discrete receivers. In this paper, we first propose a methodology to reconstruct spatial and temporal patterns from wireless receivers. Then, we apply a machine learning technique based on support vector machines (SVM) to infer parametric models from discrete samples. With model parameters defining the *white*, *grey*, and *black* zones, the comparison is resilient to temporary noise and disturbance.

Using this methodology, we empirically characterize and systematically compare the *proximity zones* across several technologies: BLE, 802.15.4, and 900 MHz RFID reader. Results show that none of them can produce robust proximity zones for person-scope applications. We then investigate an alternative wireless beacon based on magnetic-inductive (MI) coupling. Humans, furniture, and most construction materials do not affect magnetic propagation pattern. Thus, MI proximity zones are much more intuitive and practical for human interactions than those using existing technologies.

MI coupling components used to suffer from size, cost, and power inefficiency. However, recent development in the hardware, especially passive keyless entry (PKE) in the automotive industry, has made it feasible to integrate MI communication (MIC) onto mote-sized devices. To this end, we design and implement LiveSynergy, a MIC-capable platform with both MI transmitter and receiver. We evaluate the proximity zone generated by this new kind of wireless communication. The comparison to other alternatives shows significant advantages in zone consistency over time, boundary sharpness, and robustness to human obstruction. We also discuss our experience from deploying a LiveSynergy-enabled system in a cafeteria to deliver personalized nutrition and fitness information to diners at each food counter.

In summary, this paper makes the following contributions:

- We propose methodologies that empirically and systematically compare the proximity zones created by various wireless technologies.

- We design, implement, and evaluate a magnetic-induction based wireless proximity sensing platform - LiveSynergy.

- With real data traces, we show that MI solution exhibits significantly more robust zones than BLE, 802.15.4 and RFID alternatives.

- We share the experience from deploying LiveSynergy in an real-world application.

The rest of this paper is organized as follows: in Section 2, we survey related work in wireless proximity sensing. In Section 3, we give an empirical definition of proximity zones and how to compare them. After comparing the proximity zone for RF-based technologies in Section 4, we motivate and describe our design of LiveSynergy (Section 5). We evaluate LiveSynergy's proximity zone properties in Section 6 and demonstrate a real-world application deployment at cafeteria in Section 7.

2. RELATED WORK

Proximity detection can be achieved either directly by proximity sensing, or indirectly by inferring their absolute positions. Many proximity sensing are initiated by humans, for example, using RFID scanning [5], near field communication (NFC) touching, 1-D or 2-D barcode scanning, or optical sensing such as bokode [12]. These types of technologies require explicit actions from human, adding a level of inconvenience. Proximity sensing can also be initiated by the environment, typically through computer vision techniques using conventional cameras [2, 20] or Kinect-like depth cameras.

Indirect sensing technologies are hard to achieve proximity accuracy. Positioning services such as GPS are not feasible indoors as they require line-of-sight to satellites. Ultrasound-based localizations [16, 6] do not penetrate solid objects. Infrared-based systems, such as ActiveBadge [21], have difficulty localizing objects with fluorescent lighting or direct sunlight, and have an effective range on the order of meters, offering poor granularity for small spaces. Inertia sensors based approaches, such as double-integration of accelerometer data, are often inaccurate due to large DC/offset errors, and require frequent recalibration [3]. Wi-Fi fingerprinting typically requires a time-consuming training phase and costly recalibration [23, 1]. Wi-Fi also suffers from multi-path effect and Raleigh fading, leading to inaccurate location estimates [18]. Using pressure floor sensors for localization do not scale to large systems [13] and they do not work for lightweight objects such as those on the table.

These technology are either too fine grained, requiring explicit user actions for discovery, or too coarse grained to pinpoint objects or people within the vicinity of a few meters. As a result, current applications have to make compromises, such as requiring a person to actively swipe a security card when entering a building, or inaccurately localizing people based on association to the same Wi-Fi access point.

With increasing attention in this domain, several technologies have emerged as leading choices for proximity detection indoors. Bluetooth Low Energy (BLE) is a part of Bluetooth 4.0 specification, targeting directly at low energy application. While it suffers from the same interference problem as other technologies on the 2.4 GHz band, it has the unique advantage of being standard on newer mobile phones. Long-range RFID is another technology designed for locating objects. While it has the advantage of using passive tags, it is easily affected by obstructions, and often requires heavy post-processing for outlier reduction [22]. Devices based on 802.15.4 (PHY and MAC layers of the Zigbee specification) have also been used extensively, particularly in the sensornet community. In this paper, we evaluate these three technologies with respect to our application requirements.

LiveSynergy leverages dynamic magnetic fields for proximity sensing, which inductively couple the beacon and the receiver, alleviating much of the interference issues. The theory of operation for magnetic tracking has been explored initially by Raab et. al. [17], and has been commercialized for high-end motion tracking applications [15]. These commercial devices are typically expensive and not optimized for proximity detections at scale. In [9], Markham et. al. used magneto-induction for tracking underground beavers. Their system uses a relatively large antenna ($5m \times 1m$), which is not practical in indoor scenarios, but provided the inspiration for our work. We compare our platform against 802.15.4, BLE, and long-range RFID, and evaluate it under a real application deployment.

3. PROXIMITY ZONE

The desired length of "an arm's reach" is application dependent. For example, in the scenario of automatic computer-login, the desirable range of detection is perhaps the size of the cubicle or the immediate space in front of the monitor; in case of targeted advertising at the shopping mall, the desired detection range could be the two-meter space in front of a particular brand of merchandise. While the detection range is moderate in these applications, the *sharpness* and *consistency* of the detection boundary are of great importance, and directly impact the application performance and user experience. For example, in the first scenario, if the region of detection has a large "grey" area where detections happen sporadically and unpredictably, the computer may not identify the correct user in a timely manner.

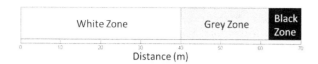

Figure 1: Example proximity zone from single dimensional dataset.

In this paper, we refer to this detection space as the **proximity zone**. Being able to accurately specify the "proximity zone" of an object or space, and reliably tell when someone enters and exits this zone are paramount for these applications. In the rest of this section, we first list a set of evaluation metrics for the proximity zones common to this class of person-scope applications. Based on these metrics, we propose an empirical definition of "proximity zone", which allows us to better evaluate and compare various technologies.

3.1 Evaluation Metrics

The following are the metrics for evaluating proximity zones:

- **Boundary sharpness**: The boundary of the proximity zone should be as binary as possible - either in or out. The region of sporadic detections, or the "grey" zone, should be minimal.

- **Boundary consistency**: Proximity detection should be consistent over time. This requires the technology to be robust against temporal interferences such as external noises and environmental variations.

- **Obstacle penetration**: Since both the beaconing node and the listening node can be mobile, e.g., being carried by humans, the radio technology should be robust against obstructions such as the human body. Specifically, the radio reception should not change significantly regardless locations on the body.

- **Additional metrics**: A number of additional properties also impact their real-world applicability, such as the *range* and the *geometric shape* of the zones, the *beaconing frequency* achievable by the transmitters, the *power consumption* of the devices, the *form-factor* of the mobile tag, and the *cost* of the overall system.

3.2 Empirical Definition

Since waveform propagation from beacons is a physical phenomenon, it is more useful to characterize the zones from the receiver's point of view. We propose an *empirical* definition for **proximity zones**, inferred over the packet reception ratio and the transmission distance. Unlike ranging, where RSSI or LQI is sometimes used to infer distance information, in the case of proximity detection, the event of successfully receiving a packet is the primary indicator of whether the receiver is within the proximity zone of a beacon [1].

While this definition relies on empirical data collected at the receiver, and is only a sampling of the space, it provides a practical metric for evaluation against real application requirements.

Conceptually, a **proximity region** consists of three adjacent zones: the *white zone*, the *grey zone*, and the *black zone*. It is also equivalently defined by two boundaries: the *white/grey boundary* and the *grey/black boundary*. Figure 1 shows the one-dimensional view of

[1] However, we do use RSSI in deciding the primary zone in the case of overlapping zones (c.f. Section 7)

a proximity zone based on measurement data along a single axis. With additional data, the same methodologies described below can work on two-dimensional and three-dimensional proximity zones. After empirically determining proximity zones, we can then evaluate the above metrics of boundary sharpness, consistency and so on.

The classification and evaluation procedure starts from collecting packet reception statistics at various distances from the transmitter. Then, these statistics allow us to classify and determine whether each location falls in the white, grey, or black zone. Finally, we apply a machine learning technique based on support vector machines (SVM) to infer the continuous coverage of the zones from these discrete samples.

3.2.1 Classification of Points

Assume a beacon broadcasts at a fixed frequency f, for a total of α packets from time t to time t'. Let:

$$P = \text{a point in space at a distance of } (p_x, p_y, p_z)$$
$$\text{from the beacon}$$
$$W = \text{detection window}$$
$$PRR_\tau = \text{packet reception rate measured between } \tau \text{ and } \tau + W$$
$$\text{where } \tau \in [t, t' - W]$$

We first define the indicator function $I(\tau)$ as:

$$I(\tau) = \begin{cases} 0, & \text{if } PRR_\tau \leqslant \epsilon \\ 1, & \text{if } PRR_\tau > \epsilon \end{cases}$$

where ϵ is the PRR threshold

Then,

$$Color(P, t, t') = \text{white},$$
$$\text{if } \prod_\tau I(\tau) = 1 : \forall \tau \in [t, t' - W]$$
$$Color(P, t, t') = \text{grey},$$
$$\text{if } \sum_\tau I(\tau) \geqslant 1 \text{ and } \prod_\tau I(\tau) = 0 : \forall \tau \in [t, t' - W]$$
$$Color(P, t, t') = \text{black},$$
$$\text{if } \sum_\tau I(\tau) = 0 : \forall \tau \in [t, t' - W]$$

Here P represents the location of the receiver node. W defines the sliding window size in computing all possible PRRs over the duration of the dataset at P. We collectively term these sliding-window PRR values as *WPRR*. $I(\tau)$ labels each sliding window into 1 if the corresponding PRR is above an application specific threshold ϵ, or 0 if otherwise. Using this indicator function, we can label P as "white" if all sliding windows are 1, "grey" if some but not all are 1, and "black" if all are 0. This definition allows us to label points around a beacon into $\{white, grey, black\}$, according to how likely beacons are detected by a receiver at that point over some period of time $[t, t']$.

We note that WPRR is fundamentally different from computing a single PRR over the entire dataset at P and then evaluating whether $PRR_p > \gamma$. Specifically, looking at a single PRR over the entire dataset does not consider the uniformity of successful packet receptions over time. Most applications can tolerate losing a few packets within a given time window, as long as the receiver hears at least one beacon in that time window.

Additionally, if ϵ is set to 0, it is equivalent to stating $I(\tau) = 1$ if the time between consecutive packet receptions is less than the detection window W, which is the minimum requirement for detection to happen. In the context of the sliding window, having $\epsilon = 0$ equates to having the inter-packet arrival time to be always smaller than the detection windows W. In this specific form, one could build a histogram of the inter-packet arrival times and see if any falls beyond the detection window W. However, to allow applications to specify the degree of likelihood of detection, we leave ϵ as a user definable parameter.

3.2.2 Classification of Zones

Given a set of points P and their colors, we can then find the boundaries that divide the proximity regions into three zones of *white*, *grey*, and *black* colors. There are multiple approaches to grouping points into zones. Due to the nondeterministic nature of the boundaries of the proximity zone, we take statistical learning approaches to find these boundaries. We could consider the boundary detection problem as a classification problem. We first define two boundaries.

- The *white/grey boundary* separates the white points $\{P \mid Color(P, t, t') = \text{white}\}$ from the grey points $\{P \mid Color(P, t, t') = \text{grey}\}$. We use notation $f_{w/g}$ as the classifier that $f_{w/g}(\mathbf{x}) > 0$ for any white point $\mathbf{x}$ and $f_{w/g}(\mathbf{x}') < 0$ for any grey point $\mathbf{x}'$. We use equation $f_{w/g}(\mathbf{x}) = 0$ to represents the decision boundary.

- The *grey/black boundary* separates the grey points $\{P \mid Color(P, t, t') = \text{grey}\}$ from the black points $\{P \mid Color(P, t, t') = \text{black}\}$. Similarly, we use notation $f_{g/b}$ as the classifier that $f_{g/b}(\mathbf{x}) > 0$ for any grey point $\mathbf{x}$ and $f_{g/b}(\mathbf{x}') < 0$ for any black point $\mathbf{x}'$. Equation $f_{g/b}(\mathbf{x}) = 0$ represents the decision boundary.

Based on the boundaries, we infer the three proximity zones as below.

- Grey zone: $\{\mathbf{x} \mid f_{w/g}(\mathbf{x}) > 0 \quad \text{and} \quad f_{g/b}(\mathbf{x}) < 0\}$. Between the white/grey boundary and grey/black boundary.

- White zone: $\{\mathbf{x} \mid f_{w/g}(\mathbf{x}) < 0\}$. Inside the white/grey boundary is the white zone.

- Black zone: $\{\mathbf{x} \mid f_{g/b}(\mathbf{x}) > 0\}$. Outside the grey/black boundary is the black zone.

We use support vector machines (SVM) as the classifier to find the boundaries of the zones in this paper. SVM seeks maximum-margin hyperplane to separate two classes. The objective of classical SVM is shown in Equation 1.

$$\mathbf{w} = \arg\min \ ||\mathbf{w}||^2$$
$$\text{s.t. } y_i(\mathbf{w}^T \mathbf{x}_i - b) \geq 1, \text{ for all } i \tag{1}$$

where $\mathbf{w}$ and b are the parameters to define the hyperplane to separate the two classes.

To accommodate application-specific requirements, we introduce two user-definable parameters in our classification model.

One parameter is the *error tolerance*, which indicates how clean the zones should be. There could be multiple boundary candidates sometimes. For example, we could choose one smooth boundary with some misclassified points. At the same time, we could also have a non-smooth boundary without any misclassified point. In terms of learning, it is a tradeoff between training loss and regularization. We could specify the cost parameter C for misclassified example to choose the best decision boundary for the specific scenario.

Another parameter is the *strictness* of a zone. We may expect the white zone, as well as the black zone, to contain no grey points. We should notice that although strictness is related to error tolerance, however, strictness is non-symmetry. For example, while we require no grey point be misclassified to white or black, we allow white or black points to be misclassified as grey. In terms of the classification problem, strictness could be controlled by the difference of costs for false positive and false negative. We could set the cost parameter (or the cost of false positive) C and the cost for false negative C' to be different. Formally, given C, we could define the strictness parameter γ to be $\gamma = 1 - \frac{C}{C'}$.

For our problem, we adapt the classical SVM model. By slacking on the hard constraints for error tolerance and adding the cost parameters, we formulate the problem as,

$$\mathbf{w} = \arg\min_f \Big\{ ||\mathbf{w}||^2 + C\big(\sum_{y_i=1}^{l} (1 - y_i f(\mathbf{x}_i))_+\big)$$
$$+ C'\big(\sum_{y_i=-1}^{l} (1 - y_i f(\mathbf{x}_i))_+\big) \Big\} \tag{2}$$

where $(z)_+ = \max(z, 0)$. Parameter C and C' are the costs for misclassification of false positive and false negative, respectively.

Since our zone boundary might not be linear, we apply the kernel trick in the SVM problem to obtain nonlinear boundaries. We use the RBF kernel as the kernel function. In this case, the decision boundary could be specified as $\{\mathbf{x} \mid f_{w/g} \equiv \langle \phi(\mathbf{x}), \mathbf{w} \rangle = 0\}$ for the classifier $f_{w/g}$, where $\phi(x)$ is the feature mapping function for the RBF kernel. Similarly, for the classifier $f_{g/b}$, the decision boundary is $\{\mathbf{x} \mid f_{g/b} \equiv \langle \phi(\mathbf{x}), \mathbf{w} \rangle = 0\}$. With the boundaries defined, we could compute the sizes of each zone for our evaluation purpose. Because the black zone is not closed, it can not be computed. In fact, the zone of the greatest interest is the grey zone. However, computing the area of grey zone is non-trivial since its boundaries might be irregular. Section 6.4 presents the heuristics we use to compute the area.

The SVM also provides information on how well boundaries fit the training data in terms of *loss*. Therefore, we could further capture the *fitness* of proximity zones by the classification accuracy.

In summary, user can specify the following input parameters to the classification model:

- **Error tolerance:** Corresponds to the cost parameter C in SVM, which specifies a trade-off between smoothness of the boundary and mis-classification.

- **Strictness γ:** Computes $C' = C \cdot \gamma + C$ to specify the application's tolerance to false positives (i.e., sporadic detections occurring outside the nominal zone range) and false negatives (i.e., missing detections inside the nominal zone range). For example, for applications that cannot tolerate any missing detection or false detections, γ can be set to 1 to coerce the model to include all grey points into the grey zone.

Together with the learning model in (2), we could obtain the boundaries, as well as the following metrics,

- **Size** of the white and grey zone, which can be computed numerically based on the boundaries.

- **Boundary sharpness**, defined as the area ratio of the white zone to the sum of white zone and grey zone, $\frac{size(white)}{size(white)+size(grey)}$.

- **Fitness** of proximity zones, which provides a measure of how well the zone boundaries fit the data, or a confidence measure of the proximity zone classification.

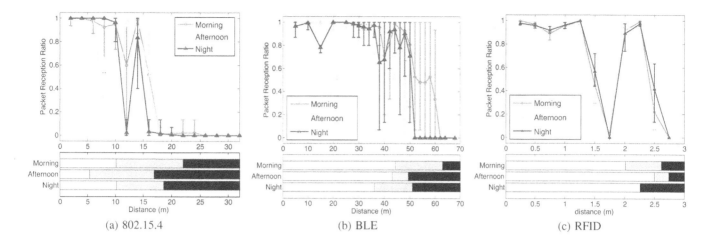

| | (a) 802.15.4 | (b) BLE | (c) RFID |

Figure 2: (*top*) the WPRR at different distances, and (*bottom*) zone boundaries, for the corresponding radio

4. EVALUATION OF EXISTING TECHNOLOGIES

Using the procedure for determining proximity zones in Section 3, we evaluate some of the common radios for beaconing: 802.15.4, Bluetooth Low Energy (BLE), and RFID.

4.1 Boundary Sharpness and Consistency

To characterize grey zones of each radio, we collected packet reception data at different positions from the transmitter as outlined below. We primarily focus on single dimensional data here since it can clearly illustrate our results. We defer the analysis of data from two dimensions to later sections.

Experiment methodology: The hardware setup consists of a pair of TI CC2540 BLE dev boards (transmitting on 2.4 GHz at 0 dBm), a pair of TelosB motes with 802.15.4-compliant TI CC24240 radio (transmitting on 2.4 GHz at 0 dBm), and a Impinj Speedway R1000 RFID reader (transmitting on 902 MHz at 8 dBm).

Experiments take place on a floor inside a typical office building, and the floor contains cubicles separated by semi-metallic walls and metallic over-head shelves. For each experiment, we position the receiver at various locations along a line from the beacon on a small hallway. The distance intervals are adaptive depending on the range of the technology. At each location, the packet reception data is collected over a period of 200 seconds. WPRR is then computed using a windows size of 3 seconds and an ϵ of 0. Using the algorithm described in Section 3, each point is then assigned a color from *[white, grey, black]*, and the white/grey and grey/black boundaries are computed for each experiment with a strictness parameter of 0.99.

Finally, to capture the time-variant nature of the radio due to environment changes, we repeated the experiments three times throughout the day: morning, afternoon, and night.

Results: Figure 2 shows the WPRR at each sampling location and zone boundaries for all three radio technologies at different times of the day.

From the PRR vs. distance figures on top of Figure 2, we observe that the average WPRR for 802.15.4 fluctuates significantly over a large distance between 5 and 20 meters, suggesting that the boundary is not sharp spatially. The confidence interval also varies with distances, suggesting that packet reception changes significantly over both space and time. In comparison, average WPRR for BLE is a little better than 802.15.4 spatially, leading to slightly

shorter grey zones. However, BLE has a relatively large confidence interval outside the white zone, signifying that the packet reception is not uniform over time. This suggests that BLE is more susceptible to bursty packet loss, in which case BLE requires a larger window, or human wait time, for the proximity detection to be reliable in the grey zone. However, inside the white zone, BLE has a smaller confidence interval than 802.15.4, possibly because BLE employs forward error correction rather than error detection. RFID, in comparison, has much smaller confidence intervals, which suggests that packet reception is consistent over time, and results in smaller grey zones. An interesting observation is the dip at around 1.75 m. Further experiments with different heights at the same distance reveal that this dip is isolated at that height, and is therefore an effect of the physical environment such as the multi-path effect. We summarize the boundary sharpnesses of all three in the table at the end of this subsection.

While we can see that RFID is more consistent than 802.15.4 and BLE over short periods of time from their respective WPRR confidence intervals, to better understand each radio's tolerance to environmental changes, we consider data across three different times of the day. From Figure 2, we can see that both 802.15.4 and BLE have large variances in WPRR curves and zone boundaries, while WPRR curves for RFID almost overlap. An explanation is that both 802.15.4 and BLE occupy the unlicensed 2.4 GHz band shared with many office equipments, such as Wi-Fi, whereas RFID operates on the fairly quiet 902 MHz band. We further quantify consistency in terms of the standard deviations across zone boundaries between the three trials:

$$RMS(\sigma(border_{white/grey}), \sigma(border_{grey/black}))$$

A smaller RMS value is preferable. We summarize consistencies in the table below.

	802.15.4	BLE	RFID
Boundary sharpness	0.32	0.70	0.77
Boundary consistency	0.12	0.13	0.13

4.2 Human Obstacle Penetration

Previous studies have shown that human body can significantly affect the packet reception of 802.15.4 [11]. This section extends the experiments to include BLE and RFID.

Experiment Methodology: The user carries the receiver in the right pants pocket, which is one of the most common locations to carry mobile devices. At each distance from the transmitter, we

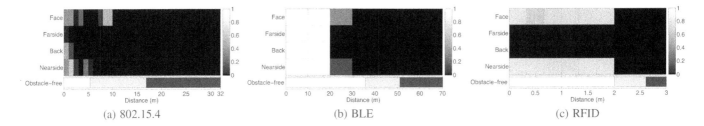

| | (a) 802.15.4 | (b) BLE | (c) RFID |

Figure 3: Packet reception ratio when the user, with the receiver in the right pants pocket, is in different body orientations

calculate PRR from 500 packets as the user changes the body orientation by 90° each round.

Results: In Figure 3, y-axis corresponds to different orientations of the user with respect to the beacon. "Face" means the user is facing the beacon at 0°; "farside" means the user is −90° with respect to the original orientation, standing between the receiver and the beacon; "back" means the user is at 180° with his back facing the beacon; and "nearside" sideways at 90°. x-axis is distance from the beacon, and color of the block represents PRR (white=1). Proximity zones from the same time period is added as a reference. This figure shows that human body has a significant impact on all three radio technologies. PRR for 802.15.4 is almost zero beyond one or two meters, regardless of orientation. BLE has PRR of 1 in the initial 20 meters, but drops sharply to zero for the rest 16 meters in the original white zone, also independent of orientation. PRR for RFID is zero for all distance at the "farside" and "back" orientations. The other two orientation are slightly better with 50% receptions. This result suggests that none of these three technologies are suitable for proximity detection of humans.

4.3 Additional Metrics

Signal propagation and geometry: Beaconing platforms based on 802.15.4 and BLE radios usually use omni-directional antennas, with typical transmission range of about 100 m. However, as previously shown, their signals attenuate with amoeba-like propagation patterns [10], which is not desirable for applications requiring a consistent boundary.

Off-the-shelf RFID readers are usually coupled with directional antennas, with a range in the neighborhood of meters. Compared to 802.15.4 and BLE, the radio propagation attenuates more evenly in different directions. RFID antennas usually have a radiation angle less than 180 degrees.

Form Factor and Costs: Form factor and costs play a huge role in realizing ubiquitous deployments. While RFID can produce a more consistent and smaller grey zone, 802.15.4 and BLE have advantages in both form factor and costs. Specifically, long-range RFID readers have a relatively large antenna due to the lower radio frequency, but the cost of long-range RFID readers range from hundreds to thousands of dollars, such as Impinj Speedway R1000.

5. LIVESYNERGY PLATFORM

Section 4 shows that existing beaconing technologies are not ideal for reliable and precise proximity detection. Fundamental problems such as external interferences motivate us to explore different beaconing hardware technology, rather than software tricks. In this section, we first discuss magnetic induction, then present a platform we developed for proximity detection - LiveSynergy.

5.1 Magnetic Induction Communication

Magnetic induction communication (MIC) has a different elec-

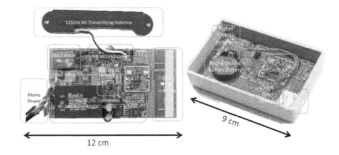

Figure 4: (*left*) Pulse, and (*right*) Link

tromagnetic radiation pattern and properties than most existing beaconing technologies.

First, MIC is near-field with a sharp signal drop off. Specifically, signals of far-field solutions such as Bluetooth attenuate at the square of distance from the transmitting antenna, or $1/r^2$, near-field signals attenuate at $1/r^3$. This implies that the transition zone of magnetic fields is relatively small, and results in a "sharper" boundary given a specific receiver sensitivity. Section 6 shows that LiveSynergy can produce a boundary in the sub-meter range.

Second, the physical environment has less impact on MIC signals. MIC is immune from radio frequency (RF) interference while most existing technologies mentioned in Section 4 operate on the crowded 2.4 GHz spectrum. In addition, the magnetic signal does not attenuate over non-metal obstacles, nor suffer from multi-path effect. As a result, MIC signal propagates and attenuates evenly in all directions and consistently over time.

5.2 Platform Design

Applying MIC to real-world proximity detection, we developed a platform called *LiveSynergy* with a transmitter – *Pulse*, and a receiver – *Link*. Specifically, spaces or physical objects can be instrumented with Pulses that beacon modulated magnetic fields to encode unique IDs. Links carried by humans read the signal strength of the magnetic field and demodulate the signal for the Pulse ID. Both Pulse and Link are equipped with 802.15.4 radios for data communication. In additional, similar to [7], Pulse is powered directly by AC, and has the ability to measure power and perform actuation, which is useful for some applications. The rest of this section discusses the hardware design choices of Pulse and Link in more detail.

5.2.1 Pulse Transmitter

Pulse (c.f. left of Figure 4) consists of four primary hardware components: microcontroller (MCU) and radio, magnetic transmitter tuned at 125kHz, energy metering, and a mechanical relay for actuation.

Magnetic Transmitter: Pulse generates the dynamic magnetic field in three stages. First, the MCU encodes the payload data and toggles its IO pins according to the bits. Then, a driver circuit amplifies the toggling pattern to provide sufficient power. Finally, the antenna transmits the signal as magnetic pulses in the air. The rest of the discussion focuses on each of these stages.

The magnetic transmitter software stack on MCU largely determines the data transmission rate and reliability through the choice of modulation scheme and maximum transmission unit (MTU). Preliminary results showed that simple duration-based on/off keying modulation does not achieve high reliability. We opted Manchester encoding, as the self-clocking nature reduces the chance of several types of data failure. In addition, preliminary results suggested an MTU larger than 16 bytes can significantly impact the PRR. Finally, the bit signal duration can impact the reliability or the transmission rate if the duration is too short or long respectively. In our system, a data rate of 2730 bps provides the sweet spot.

The I/O pin from the MCU, signaling at 3.3V, connects to the input of a buffer powered at 12VDC; the output of the buffer connects to the input of an inverter, also powered at 12VDC. The two ends of the MI antenna are connected to the outputs of both the buffer and the inverter. This design effectively doubles the voltage swing across the antenna. In addition, power-limiting resistors are put in series with the antenna to artificially decrease the range, if needed.

The antenna size and geometry partially determine the transmission range. In [9], a relatively large antenna ($5m \times 1m$) is used to obtain a range of 5m. However, such a large antenna is not practical in indoor scenarios. Pulse has a PCB mountable antenna specifically designed for PKE applications, with a dimension of $8cm \times 1.5cm$.

Microcontroller and Radio: To mitigate interference and noise issues that often exist in modern office buildings, and to ensure adequate RF range, we opted the sub-1 GHz band instead of the popular 2.4 GHz spectrum. Our radio stack conforms to 802.15.4c, a 779 Mhz PHY layer amendment to the 802.15.4 standard.

To simplify our RF design phase and ensure optimal RF performance, we use the SuRF core module from PeoplePower [14], which integrates TI CC430 and RF matching network (balun). CC430 is a SoC with MSP430 MCU (with 32 KB ROM and 4 KB RAM) and CC1101 low-power radio chipset. We designed a compact 1 dB monopole PCB antenna based on the TI reference design [4].

5.2.2   Link Receiver

Link (c.f. right of Figure 4) is a mobile device carried by humans to receive and decode the IDs from dynamic magnetic fields transmitted by Pulses. Link is battery-powered inside a $9.2cm \times 5.8cm \times 2.3cm$ enclosure. The three primary hardware components include MCU and radio, 3D magnetic coil, and wake up chip. Since Link and Pulse share the same MCU and radio, the discussion below focuses on the latter two.

The 3D receiver coil is tuned to 125 kHz, and sensitive in all three dimensions providing spatial freedom to the human carrying the Link. Since magnetic field is not significantly attenuated by non-ferrous materials, the signal reception is similar regardless of Link's location on the body. The outputs from the coil are small electrical signals in x, y, and z dimensions, and they are connected to a low-power wake up chip, AS3932. AS3932 reduces analog circuitry with an integrated programmable gain amplifier (PGA), offloads computation by digitizing the analog magnetic signals, and reduces MCU power consumption by firing a wakeup signal only when a magnetic field with valid preamble is decoded.

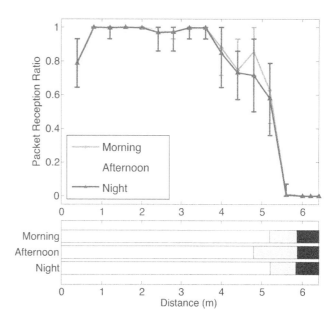

Figure 5: WPRR vs. distance for morning, afternoon, and night, and associated 1D proximity zones.

Upon being waken up by the AS3932 chip, the MCU uses its internal clock to periodically capture the value of the AS3932 output pins. After the software stack successfully verifies the 16-bit CRC, it delivers the payload data to the application.

Finally, we note that the magnetometer inside existing mobile phones use Hall elements and can theoretically detecting dynamic magnetic fields (in addition to static fields). Unfortunately, detailed inspection of popular magnetometer chips reveal that dynamic magnetic field is filtered out in hardware to reduce "noise" from the earth magnetic field. It is our hope that sensor manufacturers can lift this limit and enable MIC on future mobile phones.

6.   EVALUATION OF LIVESYNERGY

The evaluation methodology is similar to that used in Section 4. We place a pair of Pulse and Link to perform the test at three different times of the day. In each trial, the Pulse is fixed in position and transmits an ID using MI at 5Hz. We position the Link at different distances from the Pulse, with variable intervals to cover more points inside and near the grey region. For each distance, Pulse transmits 1,000 packets; the Link records successful receptions, together with timestamps and RSSI. In addition, for every position, we rotate Pulse with respect to the Link, at angles from $0°$ to $180°$ in $30°$ increments. While this is still a small subset of all the degrees of freedom between a pair of antennas, this at least enables us to create proximity zones in both 1D and 2D space.

6.1   Boundary Sharpness and Consistency

The top part of Figure 5 shows the WPRR vs. distance graph for MI in a single dimension, collected at three different times of the day. In comparison to 802.15.4 (Figure 2(a)) and BLE (Figure 2(b)), packet reception ratio of MI is significantly better – it is more uniform, as indicated by shorter confidence intervals; and it is more consistent over time, as indicated by the similar average WPRR readings across three trials. In comparison to RFID (Figure 2(c)), the variance of WPRR readings is about the same, but MI exhibits better signal decay characteristics than RFID. There are still some fluctuations in MI's WPRR curve since ferrous materials

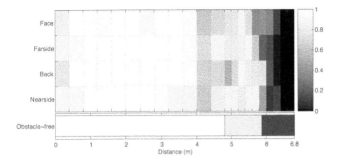

Figure 6: Body orientation vs. distance

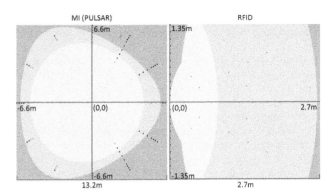

Figure 7: Proximity zones for MI and RFID in 2D space

in the environment do affect magnetic propagation, but much less severe than RFID. The bottom part of Figure 5 shows the proximity zone for MI, computed using our definition in Section 3. This figure shows that the zone boundary for MI is sharp in all three time periods of the day, with a boundary sharpness of 0.82, which is much better than 802.15.4, BLE, and RFID. From this result, we can conclude that LiveSynergy, using magnetic induction as the beaconing signal, is able to generate proximity zones with the most consistent and the sharpest boundaries among current technologies studied in this paper.

To better differentiate MI from RFID, we compare results in two dimensions, as described in more detail in Section 6.4.

6.2 Human Obstacle Penetration

Figure 6 shows the PRR vs. distance with the Link being carried in the right pant pocket at different orientations from the Pulse. This figure shows that human body has very little impact on the MI signal propagation. In contrast, 802.15.4, BLE, and RFID are easily affected by human bodies and other obstacles, as seen in Figure 3. This is because those technologies operate at much higher frequencies than MI, and also because MI is inductively coupled. This property makes MI ideal for applications where a mobile "tag" needs to be carried by a human. On the hand, MI signal is blocked by ferrous objects, which may be a problem for some applications, but desired for some others (e.g., applications using ferrous materials as natural zonal boundaries).

6.3 Additional Metrics

Geometry: From Figure 7, we can observe that the proximity zone of Pulse in two dimensions extends to all directions, covering all 360°. This same observation also applies to 3D.

Range: The maximum range (i.e., radius) is around 5m, but it can be artificially decreased by limiting the antenna output power. This range is desirable for a range of indoor applications as described in Section 1.

Beacon rate, power, size, and cost: We summarize these metrics in the table in Section 6.5.

6.4 Comparisons to RFID in 2D

Because long-range RFID exhibits the sharpest boundary among all previous technologies, as seen in Section 4, we compare MI with RFID in more detail here. Using packet reception data measured in the x-y plane, we were able to find the zone boundaries in 2D by applying our methodologies in Section 3. As Figure 7 shows, in two dimensions, the white/grey and grey/black boundaries are curves, and zones are represented as areas.

From the MI proximity zone on the left, we can see that the MI's white zone is relatively circular, centered at the MI transmitter, with a small grey zone surrounding it. In contrast, RFID has a much nar-

rower proximity zone with an angle less than 180°. This geometry is not as desirable for applications that require omni-directional coverage. The grey zone of RFID is also much bigger than that of MI. We used Monte Carlo method to estimate the areas of white and grey zones for both MI and RFID, and found that the boundary sharpness ratio for MI to be 0.70, and for RFID to be 0.25. This shows that MI has a much sharper boundary than RFID. Furthermore, the range of MI is about 5m omni-directionally where RFID is only about 1m in the right half plane. Combined with the advantages MI has over RFID in terms of consistency and body penetration, MI is the more viable proximity detection solution than RFID for many indoor applications.

6.5 Summary

Summary of evaluation results for LiveSynergy/MI:

Boundary sharpness	0.82
Consistency	0.03
Penetration	Excellent
Geometry	Omnidirectional
Range	5m
Max beacon rate	50Hz
Power	19.75mA
Tag form factor	9cm x 6cm x 2cm
Cost (tx, rx)	($50, $30)/pc @ 100 units

7. APPLICATION DEPLOYMENT

Results from Section 6 show that magnetic induction communication (MIC) is a viable solution for reliable and precise proximity detection. This section discusses a real-world deployment at a large cafeteria to provide personalized advertisements and diet suggestions. The discussion starts by giving the deployment overview, discussing the end-to-end system, and then presenting deployment results and experiences.

7.1 Deployment Overview

Providing personalized shopping experience has been a recurring application in the ubiquitous computing community. On one hand, shops can deliver targeted advertisements and coupons; on the other hand, shoppers can receive suggestions based on their shopping history and preferences. We highlight the potential of MIC communication in such applications by instrumenting the cafeteria inside a large company with Pulses, as seen in Figure 8. Diners carry Links, which are associated to their mobile phones running our mobile ap-

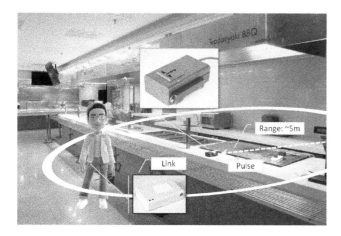

Figure 8: A Pulse is installed at the Teppanyaki counter, projecting a proximity zone of 5m radius. Links carried by diners in their pockets detect this zone as they enter.

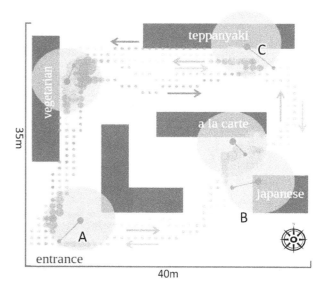

Figure 10: Movement trails from three customers in the cafeteria deployment.

plication. Food counters in the cafeteria are organized by types of food offered. The proximity readings are maintained at a back-end server, and used to deliver real-time targeted advertisements and coupons for the particular food counter that the customer is near. The entire user experience depends on performance of the LiveSynergy system in detecting diners, and how targeted advertisements and coupons are delivered.

Figure 10 shows Pulses at five different locations in the cafeteria: the entrance, the "Japanese" counter, the "A La Carte" counter, the "Teppanyaki" counter, and the "Vegetarian" counter. Pulses beacon twice per second, while Links report MIC beacons heard once every second. Aggregating beacon reports help lower the wireless network load, and help resolving cases where beacons from multiple Pulses are heard. Specifically, Link reports the Pulse ID with the highest signal strength in the current detection time window.

The back-end server performs a simple time-window threshold filtering on the location readings to differentiate between passing-by and staying. Using this data, the server can push context-aware information to the customer in a timely manner, through a native application running on the mobile phone.

7.2   System Architecture

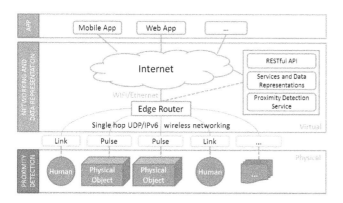

Figure 9: End-to-end LiveSynergy system architecture

Our system architecture (c.f. Figure 9) includes three main components: the LiveSynergy platform for detecting when humans enter and exit cafeteria counters; a networking and data representa-

tion layer enabling communication among counters, services in the cloud, and app clients; and an application layer consisting of a mobile application for providing feedback and visualization.

Networking: Our network needs to be *reliable* since interactions between humans and physical objects rely on reliable data exchange, and it should be *low latency* to support timely feedback to users. We designed our network to meet these requirements by using single-hop at the wireless sensor layer, reliable proxy gateway, and REST over IPv6. Nodes (Pulses and Links) directly connect to the edge router via single-hop, and communicate using UDP over IPv6. Applications, as well as multiple services hosted in the cloud, communicate with the edge router using HTTP over Ethernet.

Data Representation and Web Services: To enable interoperability between applications and services provide by our system, we designed a simple message format based on JSON, which is common in RESTful web services. Similar to XML, JSON is text-based, human-readable, self-describing, and language independent. However, compared to XML, JSON is light-weight with a smaller grammar and simpler data structure.

7.3   Deployment Results

Figure 10 shows the floor-map of the cafeteria, labeled with both the locations of each food counter, and the movement trails of the three diners in our study. Diners enter the cafeteria from the entrance at the lower left corner at different times. Each diner takes a different route and visits various food counters on the way. The trails are indicated by three different colors, and direction is indicated by arrows of the same color; purple-shaded circles represent proximity zones of Pulses (approximated to perfect circles in this figure), with radius equaling the mean of the actual ranges of Pulses. As our ground truth, we recorded a video as the customers walk around the cafeteria purchasing food. The video is timestamped so that we can correlate events in the footage to the actual proximity detection data we collected.

Figure 10 also overlays our deployment data over the floor-map. Circles of varying sizes indicate locations of detections, using data reported by Links as they intersect the proximity zones of Pulses. The size is proportional to the RSSI recorded by the Link, and red lines connecting green circles to the center of the purple circles

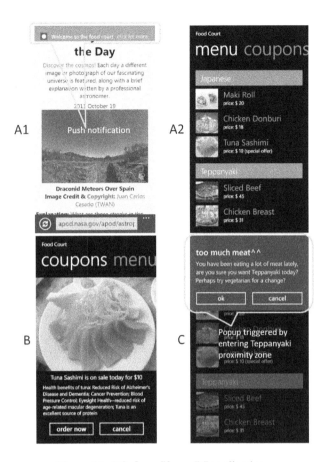

Figure 11: Windows Phone 7.5 application

indicate which Pulse that particular Link detects (i.e. being associated with). To avoid clustering the figure, we only draw red lines for the first detection after the "green" customer enters a new Pulse zone.

From this figure, one can observe a few key results. First, the boundaries of the Pulse proximity zones are sharp, with no false positives or negatives. The detections occur consecutively within each proximity zones projected by Pulses. There is a little delay between entering of a zone and the time of first detection, as seen by the slight offset between the edge of the purple circle and the first green circle. This delay is also observed at the exit of the zone. This is expected since Links run a simple window-based filtering before reporting the detection. This delay is well within the tolerance. Second, the detections are consistent for all three customers as they enter and exit the five zones, as evident from the detection locations for all three customers – the three different colors of detections circles all exist inside the same purple circles (+ the detection delay). Additionally, we observe that RSSI is indeed proportional to the distance between the Link and the Pulse. This allows the system to correctly resolve overlapping zones by "associating" to the closest proximity zone. For example, the "green" customer is first associated with the "Japanese counter", then switched (correctly) to the "A La Carte counter" in the overlapping area of both zones.

All three diners installed our native Windows Phone 7.5 application. Figure 11 shows "green" customer's screenshots as he walks past various food counters, as labeled by A, B, and C. First, after his Link detects the Pulse ID of the entrance and forward to the server, our web service sends a notification message to his mobile phone. Then, the phone displays a notification at the top of the

screen without interrupting the foreground application. Clicking the notification opens the main screen of our mobile application with the menu[2] and promotional items. At the "Japanese counter", the web service pushes counter-specific coupons (tuna sashimi). Then, at the meat-heavy "Teppanyaki counter", the diner receives a diet alert of excessive meat consumption based on his purchase history, with the advice of vegetarian dishes instead.

This simple mobile application demonstrates that the LiveSynergy proximity detection platform enables useful context-aware applications, without the need for heavy post-processing. We plan to build a personal energy footprint application and a cardless security entry system based on our LiveSynergy platform in the near future.

8. CONCLUSIONS

In this paper, we study the proximity zones established by wireless beacons in person-scale applications. We first propose a methodology based on sampling and classification techniques that enable us to compute zone boundaries and other metrics such as boundary sharpness, consistency, and body penetration. Using this methodology, we empirically evaluate three prominent technologies: 802.15.4, BLE, and 900MHz RFID, using data collected over a large period of time in both x and y dimensions. We show that 802.15.4 and BLE have large grey regions and are inconsistent over time. While RFID has sharp boundaries, it suffers heavily from attenuation by obstacles such as the human body. To overcome these shortcomings, we describe the design, implementation, and evaluation of a magnetic-induction based proximity sensing platform – LiveSynergy, which creates sharp and consistent boundaries that is not affected by human obstacles. These characteristics make MI significantly more robust than BLE, 802.15.4, and RFID alternative. Finally, through a real-world deployment, we demonstrate that LiveSynergy is able to successful support human interacting with a smart environment. As future work, we plan to explore the possibility of integrating MI into regular mobile devices and expanding its applications.

9. ACKNOWLEDGMENTS

We want to thank Caiquan Liu for his contributions in the early phase of the project, and Andrew Markham for his helpful feedback. And we would like to thank our shepherd, Anthony Rowe, and the anonymous reviewers for their feedback and insightful comments.

---

[2]Dish items in A2 are pre-populated and are not the actual menu. We plan to synchronize the menu with the cafeteria in the future.

10. REFERENCES

[1] P. Bahl and V. Padmanabhan. Radar: an in-building rf-based user location and tracking system. In *INFOCOM*, volume 2, pages 775 –784 vol.2, 2000.

[2] B. Brumitt, B. Meyers, J. Krumm, A. Kern, and S. A. Shafer. Easyliving: Technologies for intelligent environments. In *HUC*, 2000.

[3] I. Constandache, X. Bao, M. Azizyan, and R. R. Choudhury. Did you see bob?: human localization using mobile phones. In *Proceedings of the sixteenth annual international conference on Mobile computing and networking*, MobiCom '10, pages 149–160, New York, NY, USA, 2010. ACM.

[4] Fredrik Kervel. DN023: 868 MHz, 915 MHz and 955 MHz Inverted F Antenna. http://focus.ti.com/lit/an/swra228b/swra228b.pdf.

[5] D. H and D. Fox. Mapping and localization with rfid technology. In *International Conference on Robotics and Automation*, 2003.

[6] A. Harter, A. Hopper, P. Steggles, A. Ward, and P. Webster. The anatomy of a context-aware application. *Wireless Networks*, 8:187–197, 2002. 10.1023/A:1013767926256.

[7] X. Jiang, S. Dawson-Haggerty, P. Dutta, and D. Culler. Design and Implementation of a High-Fidelity AC Metering Network. In *Proc. IPSN/SPOTS*, 2009.

[8] C.-J. M. Liang, B. Priyantha, J. Liu, and A. Terzis. Surviving Wi-Fi Interference in Low Power ZigBee Networks. In *Proc. SenSys*, 2010.

[9] A. Markham, N. Trigoni, and S. Ellwood. Revealing the Hidden Lives of Underground Animals with Magneto-Inductive Tracking. In *Proc. SenSys*, 2010.

[10] Matthew M. Holland and Ryan G. Aures and Wendi B. Heinzelman. Experimental Investigation of Radio Performance in Wireless Sensor Networks. In *SECON*, 2006.

[11] E. Miluzzo, X. Zheng, K. Fodor, and A. T. Campbell. Radio characterization of 802.15.4 and its impact on the design of mobile sensor networks. In *EWSN*, 2008.

[12] A. Mohan, G. Woo, S. Hiura, Q. Smithwick, and R. Raskar. Bokode: imperceptible visual tags for camera based interaction from a distance. *ACM Transactions on Graphics*, 28, 2009.

[13] R. J. Orr and G. D. Abowd. The smart floor: a mechanism for natural user identification and tracking. In *CHI '00*, CHI EA '00, pages 275–276, New York, NY, USA, 2000. ACM.

[14] People Power. People Power | Helping Save the Green. http://www.peoplepowerco.com.

[15] Polhemus. Polhemus, Innovation in Motion. http://http://polhemus.com/.

[16] N. B. Priyantha, A. Chakraborty, and H. Balakrishnan. The cricket location-support system. In *MobiCom*, 2000.

[17] F. Raab, E. Blood, T. Steiner, and H. Jones. Magnetic position and orientation tracking system. In *IEEE Transactions on Aerospace and Electronic Systems*, 1979.

[18] B. Sklar. Rayleigh fading channels in mobile digital communication systems .i. characterization. *Communications Magazine, IEEE*, 35(7):90 –100, jul 1997.

[19] K. Srinivasan, M. A. Kazandjieva, S. Agarwal, and P. Levis. The b-factor: measuring wireless link burstiness. In *SenSys*, 2008.

[20] T. Teixeira, D. Jung, and A. Savvides. Tasking networked cctv cameras and mobile phones to identify and localize multiple people. In *Ubiquitous Computing/Handheld and Ubiquitous Computing*, pages 213–222, 2010.

[21] R. Want, A. Hopper, V. Falcão, and J. Gibbons. The active badge location system. *ACM Trans. Inf. Syst.*, 10:91–102, January 1992.

[22] E. Welbourne, K. Koscher, E. Soroush, M. Balazinska, and G. Borriello. Longitudinal study of a building-scale rfid ecosystem. In *MobiSys '09*, pages 69–82, New York, NY, USA, 2009. ACM.

[23] M. Youssef and A. Agrawala. The horus wlan location determination system. In *MobiSys*, 2005.

On Truth Discovery in Social Sensing: A Maximum Likelihood Estimation Approach

Dong Wang[1], Lance Kaplan[2], Hieu Le[1], Tarek Abdelzaher[1,3]

[1]Department of Computer Science, University of Illinois at Urbana Champaign, Urbana, IL 61801
[2]Networked Sensing and Fusion Branch, US Army Research Labs, Adelphi, MD 20783
[3]Department of Automatic Control, Lund University, Lund, Sweden (Sabbatical Affiliation)

ABSTRACT

This paper addresses the challenge of truth discovery from noisy social sensing data. The work is motivated by the emergence of social sensing as a data collection paradigm of growing interest, where humans perform sensory data collection tasks. A challenge in social sensing applications lies in the noisy nature of data. Unlike the case with well-calibrated and well-tested infrastructure sensors, humans are less reliable, and the likelihood that participants' measurements are correct is often unknown *a priori*. Given a set of human participants of unknown reliability together with their sensory measurements, this paper poses the question of whether one can use this information alone to determine, in an analytically founded manner, the probability that a given measurement is true. The paper focuses on binary measurements. While some previous work approached the answer in a heuristic manner, we offer the first *optimal solution* to the above truth discovery problem. Optimality, in the sense of maximum likelihood estimation, is attained by solving an expectation maximization problem that returns the best guess regarding the correctness of each measurement. The approach is shown to outperform the state of the art fact-finding heuristics, as well as simple baselines such as majority voting.

Categories and Subject Descriptors

H.4 [**Information Systems Applications**]: Miscellaneous

General Terms

Algorithm

Keywords

Social Sensing, Truth Discovery, Maximum Likelihood Estimation, Expectation Maximization

1. INTRODUCTION

This paper presents a maximum likelihood estimation approach to truth discovery from social sensing data. Social sensing has emerged as a new paradigm for collecting sensory measurements by means of "crowd-sourcing" sensory data collection tasks to a human population. The paradigm is made possible by the proliferation of a variety of sensors in the possession of common individuals, together with networking capabilities that enable data sharing. Examples includes cell-phone accelerometers, cameras, GPS devices, smart power meters, and interactive game consoles (e.g., Wii). Individuals who own such sensors can thus engage in data collection for some purpose of mutual interest. A classical example is geotagging campaigns, where participants report locations of conditions in their environment that need attention (e.g., litter in public parks).

A significant challenge in social sensing applications lies in ascertaining the correctness of collected data. Data collection is often open to a large population. Hence, the participants and their reliability are typically not known *a priori*. The term, participant (or source) *reliability* is used in this paper to denote the probability that the participant reports correct observations. Reliability may be impaired because of poor used sensor quality, lack of sensor calibration, lack of (human) attention to the task, or even intent to deceive. The question posed in this paper is whether or not we can determine, given only the measurements sent and without knowing the reliability of sources, which of the reported observations are true and which are not. In this paper, we concern ourselves with (arrays of) binary measurements only (e.g., reporting whether or not litter exists at each of multiple locations of interest). We develop a maximum likelihood estimator that assigns truth values to measurements without prior knowledge of source reliability. The algorithm makes inferences regarding both source reliability and measurement correctness by observing which observations coincide and which don't. It is shown to be very accurate in assessing measurement correctness as long as sources, on average, make multiple observations, and as long as some sources make the same observation.

Note that, a trivial way of accomplishing the truth discovery task is by "believing" only those observations that are reported by a sufficient number of sources. We call such a scheme, *voting*. The problem with voting schemes is that they do not attempt to infer source reliability and do not take that estimate into account. Hence, observations made by several unreliable sources may be believed over those made by a few reliable ones [19]. Instead, we cast the truth discovery problem as one of joint maximum likelihood estimation of both source reliability and observation correctness. We solve the problem using the Expectation Maximization (EM) algorithm.

Expectation Maximization (EM) is a general optimization technique for finding the maximum likelihood estimation of parameters in a statistic model where the data are "incomplete" [11]. It iterates between two main steps (namely, the E-step and the M-step) until the estimation converges (i.e., the likelihood function reaches the maximum). The paper shows that social sensing applications lend themselves nicely to an EM formulation. The optimal solution, in the sense of maximum likelihood estimation, directly leads to an accurate quantification of measurement correctness as well as participant reliability. Moreover, the solution is shown to be simple and easy to implement.

Prior literature attempted to solve a similar trust analysis problem in information networks using heuristics whose inspiration can be traced back to Google's PageRank [7]. PageRank iteratively ranks the credibility of sources on the Web, by iteratively considering the credibility of sources who link to them. Extensions of PageRank, known as fact-finders, iteratively compute the credibility of sources and claims. Specifically, they estimate the credibility of claims from the credibility of sources that make them, then estimate the credibility of sources based on the credibility of their claims. Several algorithms exist that feature modifications of the above basic heuristic scheme [6, 15, 22, 33, 34]. In contrast, ours is the first attempt to optimally solve the truth discovery problem in social sensing by casting it as one of expectation maximization.

We evaluate our algorithm in simulation, an emulated geotagging scenario as well as a real world social sensing application. Evaluation results show that the proposed maximum likelihood scheme outperforms the state-of-art heuristics as well as simple baselines (voting) in quantifying the probability of measurement correctness and participant reliability.

The rest of this paper is organized as follows: we review related work in Section 2. In Section 3, we present the truth discovery model for social sensing applications. The proposed maximum likelihood estimation approach is discussed in Section 4. Implementation and evaluation results are presented in Section 5. We discuss the limitations of current model and future work in Section 6. Finally, we conclude the paper in Section 7.

2. RELATED WORK

Social sensing has received significant attention due to the great increase in the number of mobile sensors owned by individuals (e.g., smart phones with GPS, camera, etc.) and the proliferation of Internet connectivity to upload and share sensed data (e.g., WiFi and 4G networks). A broad overview of social sensing applications is presented in [1]. Some early applications include CenWits [16], a participatory sensor network to rescue hikers in emergency situations, CarTel [18], a vehicular sensor network for traffic monitoring and mitigation, and BikeNet [14], a bikers sensor network for sharing cycling related data and mapping the cyclist experience. More recent work has focused on addressing the challenges of preserving privacy and building general models in sparse and multi-dimensional social sensing space [3,4]. Social sensing is often organized as "sensing campaigns" where participants are recruited to contribute their personal mea-

surements as part of a large-scale effort to collect data about a population or a geographical area. Examples include documenting the quality of roads [25], the level of pollution in a city [20], or reporting garbage cans on campus [24]. In addition, social sensing can also be triggered spontaneously without prior coordination (e.g., via Twitter and Youtube). Recent research attempts to understand the fundamental factors that affect the behavior of these emerging social sensing applications, such as analysis of characteristics of social networks [10], information propagation [17] and tipping points [32]. Our paper complements past work by addressing truth discovery in social sensing.

Previous efforts on truth discovery, from the machine learning and data mining communities, provided several interesting heuristics. The Bayesian Interpretation scheme [29] presented an approximation approach to truth estimation that is very sensitive to initial conditions of iterations. Hubs and Authorities [19] used a basic fact-finder where the belief in an assertion c is $B(c) = \sum_{s \in S_c} T(s)$ and the truthfulness of a source s is $T(s) = \sum_{c \in C_s} B(c)$, where S_c and C_s are the sources claiming a given assertion and the assertions claimed by a particular source, respectively. Pasternack et al. extended the fact-finder framework by incorporating prior knowledge into the analysis and proposed several extended algorithms: *Average.Log, Investment, and Pooled Investment* [22]. Yin et al. introduced *TruthFinder* as an unsupervised fact-finder for trust analysis on a providers-facts network [33]. Other fact-finders enhanced the basic framework by incorporating analysis on properties or dependencies within assertions or sources. Galland et al. [15] took the notion of hardness of facts into consideration by proposing their algorithms: *Cosine, 2-Estimates, 3-Estimates*. The source dependency detection problem was discussed and several solutions proposed [6, 12, 13]. Additionally, trust analysis was done both on a homogeneous network [5, 34] and a heterogeneous network [27]. Our proposed EM scheme is the first piece of work that finds a maximum likelihood estimator to directly and optimally quantify the accuracy of conclusions obtained from credibility analysis in social sensing. To achieve optimality, we intentionally start with a simplified application model, where the measured variables are binary, measurements are independent, and participants do not influence each other's reports (e.g., do not propagate each other's rumors). Subsequent work will address the above limitations.

There exists a good amount of literature in machine learning community to improve data quality and identify low quality labelers in a multi-labeler environment. Sheng et al. proposed a repeated labeling scheme to improve label quality by selectively acquiring multiple labels and empirically comparing several models that aggregate responses from multiple labelers [26]. Dekel et al. applied a classification technique to simulate aggregate labels and prune low-quality labelers in a crowd to improve the label quality of the training dataset [9]. However, all of the above approaches made explicit or implicit assumptions that are not appropriate in the social sensing context. For example, the work in [26] assumed labelers were known a priori and could be explicitly asked to label certain data points. The work in [9] assumed most of labelers were reliable and the simple aggregation of their labels would be enough to approximate the ground-truth. In contrast, participants in social sensing usually upload their measurements based on their own observations and the simple aggregation technique (e.g., majority voting) was shown to be inaccurate when the reliability of participant is not sufficient [22]. The maximum likelihood estimation approach studied in this paper addressed these challenges by intelligently casting the truth discovery problem in social sensing into an optimization problem that can be efficiently solved by the EM scheme.

Our work is related with a type of information filtering system called recommender systems, where the goal is usually to predict a user's rating or preference to an item using the model built from the characteristics of the item and the behavioral pattern of the user [2]. EM has been used in either collaborative recommender systems as a clustering module [21] to mine the usage pattern of users or in a content-based recommender systems as a weighting factor estimator [23] to infer the user context. However, in social sensing, the truth discovery problem targets a different goal: we aim to quantify how reliable a source is and identify whether a measured variable is true or not rather than predict how likely a user would choose one item compared to another. Moreover, users in recommender systems are commonly assumed to provide reasonably good data while the sources in social sensing are in general unreliable and the likelihood of the correctness of their measurements is unknown a priori. There appears no straightforward use of methods in the recommender systems regime for the target problem with unpredictably unreliable data.

3. THE PROBLEM FORMULATION OF SOCIAL SENSING

To formulate the truth discovery problem in social sensing in a manner amenable to rigorous optimization, we consider a social sensing application model where a group of M participants, $S_1, ..., S_M$, make individual observations about a set of N measured variables $C_1, ..., C_N$ in their environment. For example, a group of individuals interested in the appearance of their neighborhood might join a sensing campaign to report all locations of offensive graffiti. Alternatively, a group of drivers might join a campaign to report freeway locations in need of repair. Hence, each measured variable denotes the existence or lack thereof of an offending condition at a given location[1]. In this effort, we consider only binary variables and assume, without loss of generality, that their "normal" state is negative (e.g., no offending graffiti on walls, or no potholes on streets). Hence, participants report only when a positive value is encountered.

Each participant generally observes only a subset of all variables (e.g., the conditions at locations they have been to). Our goal is to determine which observations are correct and which are not. As mentioned in the introduction, we differ from a large volume of previous sensing literature in that we assume no prior knowledge of source reliability, as well as no prior knowledge of the correctness of individual observations.

Let S_i represent the ith participant and C_j represent the jth measured variable. S_iC_j denotes an observation reported by participant S_i claiming that C_j is true (e.g., that graffiti is found at a given location, or that a given street is in disrepair). Let $P(C_j^t)$ and $P(C_j^f)$ denote the probability that

---

[1]We assume that locations are discretized, and therefore finite. For example, they are given by street addresses or mile markers.

the actual variable C_j is indeed true and false, respectively. Different participants may make different numbers of observations. Let the probability that participant S_i makes an observation be s_i. Further, let the probability that participant S_i is right be t_i and the probability that it is wrong be $1 - t_i$. Note that, this probability depends on the participant's reliability, which is not known a priori. Formally, t_i is defined as the odds of a measured variable to be true given that participant S_i reports it:

$$t_i = P(C_j^t | S_iC_j) \tag{1}$$

Let us also define a_i as the (unknown) probability that participant S_i reports a measured variable to be true when it is indeed true, and b_i as the (unknown) probability that participant S_i reports a measured variable to be true when it is in reality false. Formally, a_i and b_i are defined as follows:

$$a_i = P(S_iC_j | C_j^t)$$
$$b_i = P(S_iC_j | C_j^f) \tag{2}$$

From the definition of t_i, a_i and b_i, we can determine their relationship using the Bayesian theorem:

$$a_i = P(S_iC_j | C_j^t) = \frac{P(S_iC_j, C_j^t)}{P(C_j^t)} = \frac{P(C_j^t | S_iC_j)P(S_iC_j)}{P(C_j^t)}$$
$$b_i = P(S_iC_j | C_j^f) = \frac{P(S_iC_j, C_j^f)}{P(C_j^f)} = \frac{P(C_j^f | S_iC_j)P(S_iC_j)}{P(C_j^f)} \tag{3}$$

The only input to our algorithm is the social sensing topology represented by a matrix SC, where $S_iC_j = 1$ when participant S_i reports that C_j is true, and $S_iC_j = 0$ otherwise. Let us call it the *observation matrix*.

The goal of the algorithm is to compute (i) the best estimate h_j on the correctness of each measured variable C_j and (ii) the best estimate e_i of the reliability of each participant S_i. Let us denote the sets of the estimates by vectors H and E, respectively. Our goal is to find the optimal H^* and E^* vectors in the sense of being most consistent with the observation matrix SC. Formally, this is given by:

$$< H^*, E^* > = \underset{<H,E>}{\operatorname{argmax}} \, p(SC | H, E) \tag{4}$$

We also compute the background bias d, which is the overall probability that a randomly chosen measured variable is true. For example, it may represent the probability that any street, in general, is in disrepair. It does not indicate, however, whether any particular claim about disrepair at a particular location is true or not. Hence, one can define the prior of a claim being true as $P(C_j^t) = d$. Note also that, the probability that a participant makes an observation (i.e., s_i) is proportional to the number of measured variables observed by the participant over the total number of measured variables observed by all participants, which can be easily computed from the observation matrix. Hence, one can define the prior $P(S_iC_j) = s_i$. Plugging these, together with t_i into the definition of a_i and b_i, we get the relationship between the terms we defined above:

$$a_i = \frac{t_i \times s_i}{d}$$
$$b_i = \frac{(1 - t_i) \times s_i}{1 - d} \tag{5}$$

4. EXPECTATION MAXIMIZATION

In this section, we solve the problem formulated in the previous section using the Expectation-Maximization (EM) algorithm. EM is a general algorithm for finding the maximum likelihood estimates of parameters in a statistic model, where the data are "incomplete" or the likelihood function involves latent variables [11]. Intuitively, what EM does is iteratively "completes" the data by "guessing" the values of hidden variables then re-estimates the parameters by using the guessed values as true values.

4.1 Background

Much like finding a Lyapunov function to prove stability, the main challenge in using the EM algorithm lies in the mathematical formulation of the problem in a way that is amenable to an EM solution. Given an observed data set X, one should judiciously choose the set of latent or missing values Z, and a vector of unknown parameters θ, then formulate a likelihood function $L(\theta; X, Z) = p(X, Z|\theta)$, such that the maximum likelihood estimate (MLE) of the unknown parameters θ is decided by:

$$L(\theta; X) = p(X|\theta) = \sum_Z p(X, Z|\theta) \qquad (6)$$

Once the formulation is complete, the EM algorithm finds the maximum likelihood estimate by iteratively performing the following steps:

- E-step: Compute the expected log likelihood function where the expectation is taken with respect to the computed conditional distribution of the latent variables given the current settings and observed data.

$$Q\left(\theta|\theta^{(t)}\right) = E_{Z|X,\theta^{(t)}}[\log L(\theta; X, Z)] \qquad (7)$$

- M-step: Find the parameters that maximize the Q function in the E-step to be used as the estimate of θ for the next iteration.

$$\theta^{(t+1)} = \underset{\theta}{\arg\max} \, Q\left(\theta|\theta^{(t)}\right) \qquad (8)$$

4.2 Mathematical Formulation

Our social sensing problem fits nicely into the Expectation Maximization (EM) model. First, we introduce a latent variable Z for each measured variable to indicate whether it is true or not. Specifically, we have a corresponding variable z_j for the jth measured variable C_j such that: $z_j = 1$ when C_j is true and $z_j = 0$ otherwise. We further denote the observation matrix SC as the observed data X, and take $\theta = (a_1, a_2, ...a_M; b_1, b_2, ...b_M; d)$ as the parameter of the model that we want to estimate. The goal is to get the maximum likelihood estimate of θ for the model containing observed data X and latent variables Z.

The likelihood function $L(\theta; X, Z)$ is given by:

$$L(\theta; X, Z) = p(X, Z|\theta)$$
$$= \prod_{j=1}^{N} \left\{ \prod_{i=1}^{M} a_i^{S_i C_j} (1 - a_i)^{(1 - S_i C_j)} \times d \times z_j \right.$$
$$\left. + \prod_{i=1}^{M} b_i^{S_i C_j} (1 - b_i)^{(1 - S_i C_j)} \times (1 - d) \times (1 - z_j) \right\} \qquad (9)$$

where, as we mentioned before, a_i and b_i are the conditional probabilities that participant S_i reports the measured variable C_j to be true given that C_j is true or false (i.e., defined in Equation (2)). $S_i C_j = 1$ when participant S_i reports that C_j is true, and $S_i C_j = 0$ otherwise. d is the background bias that a randomly chosen measured variable is true. Additionally, we assume participants and measured variables are independent respectively. The likelihood function above describes the likelihood to have current observation matrix X and hidden variable Z given the estimation parameter θ we defined.

4.3 Deriving the E-step and M-step

Given the above formulation, substitute the likelihood function defined in Equation (9) into the definition of Q function given by Equation (7) of Expectation Maximization. The Expectation step (E-step) becomes:

$$Q\left(\theta|\theta^{(t)}\right) = E_{Z|X,\theta^{(t)}}[\log L(\theta; X, Z)]$$
$$= \sum_{j=1}^{N} \left\{ p(z_j = 1|X_j, \theta^{(t)}) \right.$$
$$\times \left[\sum_{i=1}^{M} (S_i C_j \log a_i + (1 - S_i C_j) \log(1 - a_i) + \log d) \right]$$
$$+ p(z_j = 0|X_j, \theta^{(t)})$$
$$\left. \times \left[\sum_{i=1}^{M} (S_i C_j \log b_i + (1 - S_i C_j) \log(1 - b_i) + \log(1 - d)) \right] \right\} \qquad (10)$$

where X_j represents the jth column of the observed SC matrix (i.e., observations of the jth measured variable from all participants) and $p(z_j = 1|X_j, \theta^{(t)})$ is the conditional probability of the latent variable z_j to be true given the observation matrix related to the jth measured variable and current estimate of θ, which is given by:

$$Z(t, j) = p(z_j = 1|X_j, \theta^{(t)})$$
$$= \frac{p(z_j = 1; X_j, \theta^{(t)})}{p(X_j, \theta^{(t)})}$$
$$= \frac{p(X_j, \theta^{(t)}|z_j = 1)p(z_j = 1)}{p(X_j, \theta^{(t)}|z_j = 1)p(z_j = 1) + p(X_j, \theta^{(t)}|z_j = 0)p(z_j = 0)}$$
$$= \frac{A(t, j) \times d^{(t)}}{A(t, j) \times d^{(t)} + B(t, j) \times (1 - d^{(t)})} \qquad (11)$$

where $A(t, j)$ and $B(t, j)$ are defined as:

$$A(t, j) = p(X_j, \theta^{(t)}|z_j = 1)$$
$$= \prod_{i=1}^{M} a_i^{(t) S_i C_j} (1 - a_i^{(t)})^{(1 - S_i C_j)}$$
$$B(t, j) = p(X_j, \theta^{(t)}|z_j = 0)$$
$$= \prod_{i=1}^{M} b_i^{(t) S_i C_j} (1 - b_i^{(t)})^{(1 - S_i C_j)} \qquad (12)$$

$A(t, j)$ and $B(t, j)$ represent the conditional probability regarding observations about the jth measured variable and current estimation of the parameter θ given the jth measured variable is true or false respectively.

Next we simplify Equation (10) by noting that the conditional probability of $p(z_j = 1|X_j, \theta^{(t)})$ given by Equation (11) is only a function of t and j. Thus, we represent it by $Z(t, j)$. Similarly, $p(z_j = 0|X_j, \theta^{(t)})$ is simply:

$$p(z_j = 0|X_j, \theta^{(t)}) = 1 - p(z_j = 1|X_j, \theta^{(t)})$$

$$= \frac{B(t,j) \times (1 - d^{(t)})}{A(t,j) \times d^{(t)} + B(t,j) \times (1 - d^{(t)})}$$

$$= 1 - Z(t, j) \qquad (13)$$

Substituting from Equation (11) and (13) into Equation (10), we get:

$$Q\left(\theta|\theta^{(t)}\right)$$

$$= \sum_{j=1}^{N} \left\{ Z(t,j) \right.$$

$$\times \left[\sum_{i=1}^{M} (S_i C_j \log a_i + (1 - S_i C_j) \log(1 - a_i) + \log d) \right]$$

$$+ (1 - Z(t,j))$$

$$\left. \times \left[\sum_{i=1}^{M} (S_i C_j \log b_i + (1 - S_i C_j) \log(1 - b_i) + \log(1 - d)) \right] \right\}$$

$$\qquad (14)$$

The Maximization step (M-step) is given by Equation (8). We choose θ^* (i.e., $(a_1^*, a_2^*, ... a_M^*; b_1^*, b_2^*, ... b_M^*; d^*)$) that maximizes the $Q\left(\theta|\theta^{(t)}\right)$ function in each iteration to be the $\theta^{(t+1)}$ of the next iteration.

To get θ^* that maximizes $Q\left(\theta|\theta^{(t)}\right)$, we set the derivatives $\frac{\partial Q}{\partial a_i} = 0$, $\frac{\partial Q}{\partial b_i} = 0$, $\frac{\partial Q}{\partial d} = 0$ which yields:

$$\sum_{j=1}^{N} \left[Z(t,j)(S_i C_j \frac{1}{a_i^*} - (1 - S_i C_j) \frac{1}{1 - a_i^*}) \right] = 0$$

$$\sum_{j=1}^{N} \left[(1 - Z(t,j))(S_i C_j \frac{1}{b_i^*} - (1 - S_i C_j) \frac{1}{1 - b_i^*}) \right] = 0$$

$$\sum_{j=1}^{N} \left[Z(t,j)M \frac{1}{d^*} - (1 - Z(t,j))M \frac{1}{1 - d^*} \right] = 0 \qquad (15)$$

Let us define SJ_i as the set of measured variables the participant S_i actually observes in the observation matrix SC, and $\bar{SJ}_i$ as the set of measured variables participant S_i does not observe. Thus, Equation (15) can be rewritten as:

$$\sum_{j \in SJ_i} Z(t,j) \frac{1}{a_i^*} - \sum_{j \in \bar{SJ}_i} Z(t,j) \frac{1}{1 - a_i^*} = 0$$

$$\sum_{j \in SJ_i} (1 - Z(t,j)) \frac{1}{b_i^*} - \sum_{j \in \bar{SJ}_i} (1 - Z(t,j)) \frac{1}{1 - b_i^*} = 0$$

$$\sum_{j=1}^{N} \left[Z(t,j) \frac{1}{d^*} - (1 - Z(t,j)) \frac{1}{1 - d^*} \right] = 0 \qquad (16)$$

Solving the above equations, we can get expressions of the optimal a_i^*, b_i^* and d^*:

$$a_i^{(t+1)} = a_i^* = \frac{\sum_{j \in SJ_i} Z(t,j)}{\sum_{j=1}^{N} Z(t,j)}$$

$$b_i^{(t+1)} = b_i^* = \frac{K_i - \sum_{j \in SJ_i} Z(t,j)}{N - \sum_{j=1}^{N} Z(t,j)}$$

$$d_i^{(t+1)} = d_i^* = \frac{\sum_{j=1}^{N} Z(t,j)}{N}$$

$$\qquad (17)$$

where K_i is the number of measured variables observed by participant S_i and N is the total number of measured variables in the observation matrix. $Z(t,j)$ is defined in Equation (11).

Given the above, The E-step and M-step of EM optimization reduce to simply calculating Equation (11) and Equation (17) iteratively until they converge. The convergence analysis has been done for EM scheme and it is beyond the scope of this paper [31]. In practice, we can run the algorithm until the difference of estimation parameter between consecutive iterations becomes insignificant. Since the measured variable is binary, we can compute the optimal decision vector H^* from the converged value of $Z(t,j)$. Specially, h_j is true if $Z(t,j) \geq 0.5$ and false otherwise. At the same time, we can also compute the optimal estimation vector E^* of participant reliability from the converged values of $a_i^{(t)}$, $b_i^{(t)}$ and $d^{(t)}$ based on their relationship given by Equation (5). This completes the mathematical development. We summarize the resulting algorithm in the subsection below.

4.4 The Final Algorithm

In summary of the EM scheme derived above, the input is the observation matrix SC from social sensing data, and the output is the maximum likelihood estimation of participant reliability and measured variable correctness (i.e., E^* and H^* vector defined in Equation (4)). In particular, given the observation matrix SC, our algorithm begins by initializing the parameter θ^2. The algorithm then performs the E-steps and M-steps iteratively until θ converges. Specifically, we compute the conditional probability of a measured variable to be true (i.e., $Z(t,j)$) from Equation (11) and the estimation parameter (i.e., $\theta^{(t+1)}$) from Equation (17). After the estimated value of θ converges, we compute the optimal decision vector H^* (i.e., decide whether each measured variable C_j is true or not) based on the converged value of $Z(t,j)$ (i.e., Z_j^c). We can also compute the optimal estimation vector E^* (i.e., the estimated t_i of each participant) from the converged values of $\theta^{(t)}$ (i.e., a_i^c, b_i^c and d^c) based on Equation (5) as shown in the pseudocode of Algorithm 1.

One should note that a theoretical quantification of accuracy of maximum likelihood estimation (MLE) using the EM scheme is well-known in literature, and can be done using the Cramer-Rao lower bound (CRLB) on estimator variance [8]. In estimation theory, if the estimation variance of an unbiased estimator reaches the Cramer-Rao lower bound, the estimator provides the maximum likelihood estimation and the CRLB quantifies the minimum estimation variance. The estimator proposed in this paper is shown to operate

---

[2]In practice, if the a rough estimate of the average reliability of participants or the prior of measured variable correctness is known *a priori*, EM will converge faster

---

Algorithm 1 Expectation Maximization Algorithm

1: Initialize θ ($a_i = s_i, bi = 0.5 \times s_i$, d =Random number in $(0, 1)$)
2: **while** $\theta^{(t)}$ does not converge **do**
3:     **for** $j = 1 : N$ **do**
4:         compute $Z(t, j)$ based on Equation (11)
5:     **end for**
6:     $\theta^{(t+1)} = \theta^{(t)}$
7:     **for** $i = 1 : M$ **do**
8:         compute $a_i^{(t+1)}, b_i^{(t+1)}, d^{(t+1)}$ based on Equation (17)
9:         update $a_i^{(t)}, b_i^{(t)}, d^{(t)}$ with $a_i^{(t+1)}, b_i^{(t+1)}, d^{(t+1)}$ in $\theta^{(t+1)}$
10:    **end for**
11:    $t = t + 1$
12: **end while**
13: Let Z_j^c = converged value of $Z(t, j)$
14: Let a_i^c = converged value of $a_i^{(t)}$; b_i^c = converged value of $b_i^{(t)}$; d^c = converged value of $d^{(t)}$
15: **for** $j = 1 : N$ **do**
16:    **if** $Z_j^c \geq 0.5$ **then**
17:       h_j^* is true
18:    **else**
19:       h_j^* is false
20:    **end if**
21: **end for**
22: **for** $i = 1 : M$ **do**
23:    calculate e_i^* from a_i^c, b_i^c and d^c based on Equation (5)
24: **end for**
25: Return the computed optimal estimates of measured variables $C_j = h_j^*$ and source reliability e_i^*.

---

at this bound and hence reach the maximum likelihood estimation [30]. This observation makes it possible to quantify estimation accuracy, or confidence in results generated from our scheme, using the Cramer-Rao lower bound.

5. EVALUATION

In this section, we carry out experiments to evaluate the performance of the proposed EM scheme in terms of estimation accuracy of the probability that a participant is right or a measured variable is true compared to other state-of-art solutions. We begin by considering algorithm performance for different abstract observation matrices (SC), then apply it to both an emulated participatory sensing scenario and a real world social sensing application. We show that the new algorithm outperforms the state of the art.

5.1 A Simulation Study

We built a simulator in Matlab 7.10.0 that generates a random number of participants and measured variables. A random probability P_i is assigned to each participant S_i representing his/her reliability (i.e., the ground truth probability that they report correct observations). For each participant S_i, L_i observations are generated. Each observation has a probability t_i of being true (i.e., reporting a variable as true correctly) and a probability $1 - t_i$ of being false (reporting a variable as true when it is not). Remember that, as stated in our application model, participants do not report "lack of problems". Hence, they never report a variable to be false. We let t_i be uniformly distributed between 0.5 and 1 in our experiments[3]. For initialization, the initial values

---

[3]In principle, there is no incentive for a participant to lie

of participant reliability (i.e., t_i) in the evaluated schemes are set to the mean value of its definition range.

In recent work, a heuristic called *Bayesian Interpretation* was demonstrated to outperform all contenders from prior literature [29]. Bayesian Interpretation takes a linear approximation approach to convert the credibility ranks of fact-finders into a Bayesian probability that a participant reports correctly or the measured variable is true. In Bayesian Interpretation, the performance evaluation results were averaged over multiple observation matrices for a given participant reliability distribution. This is intended to approximate performance where highly connected sensing topologies are available (e.g., observations from successive time intervals involving the same set of sources and measured variables). In this paper, we consider more challenging conditions not investigated in [29], where only a *single observation matrix* is taken as the input into the algorithm. This is intended to understand the algorithm's performance in more realistic scenarios where the sensing topologies are sparsely connected. We compare EM to Bayesian Interpretation and three state-of-art fact-finder schemes from prior literature [19, 22, 33] that can function using only the inputs offered in our problem formulation. Results show a significant performance improvement of EM over all heuristics compared.

In the first experiment, we compare the estimation accuracy of EM and the baseline schemes by varying the number of participants in the system. The number of reported measured variables was fixed at 2000, of which 1000 variables were reported correctly and 1000 were misreported. To favor our competition, we "cheat" by giving the other algorithms the correct value of bias d (in this case, $d = 0.5$). The average number of observations per participant was set to 100. The number of participants was varied from 20 to 110. Reported results are averaged over 100 random participant reliability distributions. Results are shown in Figure 1. Observe that EM has the smallest estimation error on participant reliability and the least false positives among all schemes under comparison. For false negatives, EM performs similarly to other schemes when the number of participants is small and starts to gain improvements when the number of participants becomes large. Note also that the performance gain of EM becomes large when the number of participants is small, illustrating that EM is more useful when the observation matrix is sparse.

The second experiment compares EM with baseline schemes when the average number of observations per participant changes. As before, we fix the number of correctly and incorrectly reported variables to 1000 respectively. Again, we favor our competition by giving their algorithms the correct value of background bias d (here, $d = 0.5$). We also set the number of participants to 30. The average number of observations per participant is varied from 100 to 1000. Results are averaged over 100 experiments. The results are shown in Figure 2. Observe that EM outperforms all baselines in terms of both participant reliability estimation accuracy and false positives as the average number of observations per participant changes. For false negatives, EM has similar performance as other baselines when the average number of observations per participant is small and starts to gain advantage as the average number of observations per par-

---

more than 50% of the time, since negating their statements would then give a more accurate truth

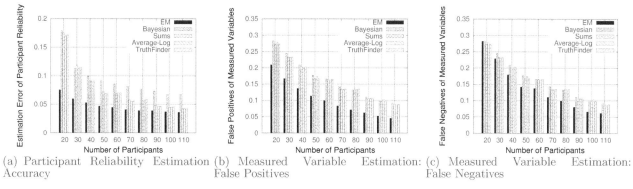

(a) Participant Reliability Estimation Accuracy

(b) Measured Variable Estimation: False Positives

(c) Measured Variable Estimation: False Negatives

Figure 1: Estimation Accuracy versus Number of Participants

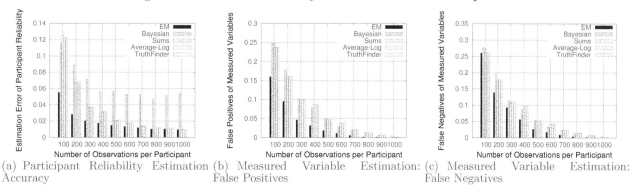

(a) Participant Reliability Estimation Accuracy

(b) Measured Variable Estimation: False Positives

(c) Measured Variable Estimation: False Negatives

Figure 2: Estimation Accuracy versus Average Number of Observations per Participant

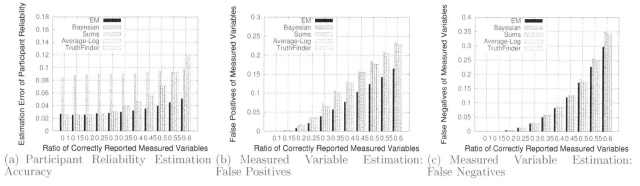

(a) Participant Reliability Estimation Accuracy

(b) Measured Variable Estimation: False Positives

(c) Measured Variable Estimation: False Negatives

Figure 3: Estimation Accuracy versus Ratio of Correctly Reported Measured Variables

ticipant becomes large. As before, the performance gain of EM is higher when the average number of observations per participant is low, verifying once more the high accuracy of EM for sparser observation matrices.

The third experiment examines the effect of changing the measured variable mix on the estimation accuracy of all schemes. We vary the ratio of the number of correctly reported variables to the total number of reported variables from 0.1 to 0.6, while fixing the total number of such variables to 2000. To favor the competition, the background bias d is given correctly to the other algorithms (i.e., $d = varying\ ratio$). The number of participants is fixed at 30 and the average number of observations per participant is set to 150. Results are averaged over 100 experiments. These results are shown in Figure 3. We observe that EM has almost the same performance as other fact-finder baselines when the fraction of correctly reported variables is relatively small. The reason is that the small amount of true mea-

sured variables are densely observed and most of them can be easily differentiated from the false ones by both EM and baseline fact-finders. However, as the number of variables (correctly) reported as true grows, EM is shown to have a better performance in both participant reliability and measured variable estimation. Throughout the first to the third experiments, we also observe that the Bayesian interpretation scheme predicts less accurately than other heuristics. This is because the estimated posterior probability of a participant to be reliable or a measured variable to be true in Bayesian interpretation is a linear transform of the participant's or the measured variable's credibility values. Those values obtained from a single or sparse observation matrix may not be very accurate and refined [29].

The fourth experiment evaluates the performance of EM and other schemes when the offset of the initial estimation on the background bias d varies. The offset is defined as the difference between initial estimation on d and its ground-

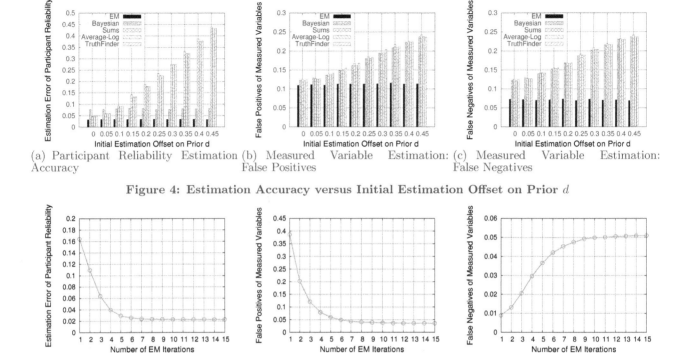

(a) Participant Reliability Estimation Accuracy   (b) Measured Variable Estimation: False Positives   (c) Measured Variable Estimation: False Negatives

Figure 4: Estimation Accuracy versus Initial Estimation Offset on Prior d

(a) Participant Reliability Estimation Accuracy   (b) Measured Variable Estimation: False Positives   (c) Measured Variable Estimation: False Negatives

Figure 5: Convergence Property of the EM Algorithm

truth. We fix the number of correctly and incorrectly reported variables to 1000 respectively (i.e., $d = 0.5$). We vary the absolute value of the initial estimate offset on d from 0 to 0.45. The reported results are averaged for both positive and negative offsets of the same absolute value. The number of participants is fixed at 50 and the average number of observations per participant is set to 150. Reported results are averaged over 100 experiments. Figure 4 shows the results. We observe that the performance of EM scheme is stable as the offset of initial estimate on d increases. On the contrary, the performance of other baselines degrades significantly when the initial estimate offset on d becomes large. This is because the EM scheme incorporates the d as part of its estimation parameter and provides the MLE on it. However, other baselines depend largely on the correct initial estimation on d (e.g., from the past history) to find out the right number of correctly reported measured variables. These results verify the robustness of the EM scheme when the accurate estimate on the prior d is not available to obtain.

The fifth experiment shows the convergence property of the EM iterative algorithm in terms of the estimation error on participant reliability, as well as the false positives and false negatives on measured variables. We fix the number of correctly and incorrectly reported variables to 1000 respectively and set the initial estimate offset on d to 0.3. The number of participants is fixed at 50 and the average number of observations per participant is set to 250. Reported results are averaged over 100 experiments. Figure 5 shows the results. We observe that both the estimation error on participant reliability and false positives/negatives on measured variable converge reasonably fast (e.g., less than 10 iterations) to stable values as the number of iterations of

EM algorithm increases. It verifies the efficiency of applying EM scheme to solve the maximum likelihood estimation problem formulated.

This concludes our general simulations. In the next subsection, we emulate the performance of a specific social sensing application.

5.2 A Geotagging Case Study

In this subsection, we applied the proposed EM scheme to a typical social sensing application: Geotagging locations of litter in a park or hiking area. In this application, litter may be found along the trails (usually proportionally to their popularity). Participants visiting the park geotag and report locations of litter. Their reports are not reliable however, erring both by missing some locations, as well as misrepresenting other objects as litter. The goal of the application is to find where litter is actually located in the park, while disregarding all false reports.

To evaluate the performance of different schemes, we define two metrics of interest: (i) *false negatives* defined as the ratio of litter locations missed by a scheme to the total number of litter locations in the park, and (ii) *false positives* defined as the ratio of the number of incorrectly labeled locations by a scheme, to the total number of locations in the park. We compared the proposed EM scheme to the Bayesian Interpretation scheme and to voting, where locations are simply ranked by the number of times people report them.

We created a simplified trail map of a park, represented by a binary tree as shown in Figure 6. The entrance of the park (e.g., where parking areas are usually located) is the root of the tree. Internal nodes of the tree represent forking of different trails. We assume trails are quantized into

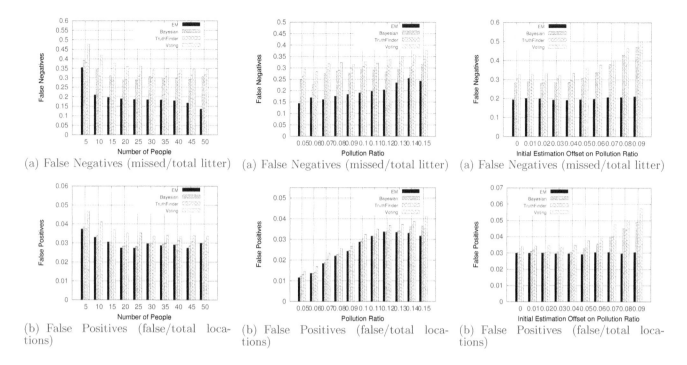

(a) False Negatives (missed/total litter) (a) False Negatives (missed/total litter) (a) False Negatives (missed/total litter)

(b) False Positives (false/total locations) (b) False Positives (false/total locations) (b) False Positives (false/total locations)

Figure 7: Litter Geotagging Accuracy versus Number of People Visiting the Park

Figure 8: Litter Geotagging Accuracy versus Pollution Ratio of the Park

Figure 9: Litter Geotagging Accuracy versus Initial Estimation Offset on Pollution Ratio of Park

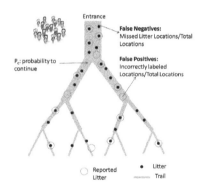

Figure 6: A Simplified Trail Map of Geotagging Application

discretely labeled locations (e.g., numbered distance markers). In our emulation, at each forking location along the trails, participants have a certain probability P_c to continue walking and $1 - P_c$ to stop and return. Participants who decide to continue have equal probability to select the left or right path. The majority of participants are assumed to be reliable (i.e., when they geotag and report litter at a location, it is more likely than not that the litter exists at that location).

In the first experiment, we study the effect of the number of people visiting the park on the estimation accuracy of different schemes. We choose a binary tree with a depth of 4 as the trail map of the park. Each segment of the trail (between two forking points) is quantized into 100 potential locations (leading to 1500 discrete locations in total on all trails). We define the pollution ratio of the park to be the ratio of the

number of littered locations to the total number of locations in the park. The pollution ratio is fixed at 0.1 for the first experiment. The probability that people continue to walk past a fork in the path is set to be 95% and the percent of reliable participants is set to be 80%. We vary the number of participants visiting the park from 5 to 50. The corresponding estimation results of different schemes are shown in Figure 7. Observe that both false negatives and false positives decrease as the number of participants increases for all schemes. This is intuitive: the chances of finding litter on different trails increase as the number of people visiting the park increases. Note that, the EM scheme outperforms others in terms of false negatives, which means EM can find more pieces of litter than other schemes under the same conditions. The improvement becomes significant (i.e., around 20%) when there is a sufficient number of people visiting the park. For the false positives, EM performs similarly to Bayesian Interpretation and Truth Finder scheme and better than voting. Generally, voting performs the worst in accuracy because it simply counts the number of reports complaining about each location but ignores the reliability of individuals who make them.

In the second experiment, we show the effect of park pollution ratio (i.e, how littered the park is) on the estimation accuracy of different schemes. The number of individuals visiting the park is set to be 40. We vary the pollution ratio of the park from 0.05 to 0.15. The estimation results of different schemes are shown in Figure 8. Observe that both the false negatives and false positives of all schemes increase as the pollution ratio increases. The reason is that: litter is more frequently found and reported at trails that are near the entrance point. The amount of unreported litter at trails that are far from entrance increases more rapidly compared to the total amount of litter as the pollution ratio increases. Note that, the EM scheme continues to find more actual litter compared to other baselines. The performance of false positives is similar to other schemes.

In the third experiment, we evaluate the effect of the initial estimation offset of the pollution ratio on the performance of different schemes. The pollution ratio is fixed at 0.1 and the number of individuals visiting the park is set to be 40. We vary the absolute value of initial estimation offset of the pollution ratio from 0 to 0.09. Results are averaged over both positive and negative offsets of the same absolute value. The estimation results of different schemes are shown in Figure 9. Observe that EM finds more actual litter locations and reports less falsely labeled locations than other baselines as the initial estimation offset of pollution ratio increases. Additionally, the performance of EM scheme is stable while the performance of other baselines drops substantially when the initial estimation offset of the pollution ratio becomes large.

The above evaluation demonstrates that the new EM scheme generally outperforms the current state of the art in inferring facts from social sensing data. This is because the state of the art heuristics infer the reliability of participants and correctness of facts based on the hypothesis that their relationship can be approximated *linearly* [22, 29, 33]. However, EM scheme makes its inference based on a maximum likelihood hypothesis that is most consistent with the observed sensing data, thus it provides an optimal solution.

5.3 A Real World Application

In this subsection, we evaluate the performance of the proposed EM scheme through a real-world social sensing application, based on Twitter. The objective was to see whether our scheme would distill from Twitter feeds important events that may be newsworthy and reported by media. Specifically, we followed the news coverage of Hurricane Irene and manually selected, as ground truth, 10 important events reported by media during that time. Independently from that collection, we also obtained more than 600,000 tweets originating from New York City during Hurricane Irene using the Twitter API (by specifying keywords as "hurricane", "Irene" and "flood", and the location to be New York). These tweets were collected from August 26 until September 2nd, roughly when Irene struck the east coast. Retweets were removed from the collected data to keep sources as independent as possible.

We then generated an observation matrix from these tweets by clustering them based on the Jaccard distance metric (a simple but commonly used distance metric for micro-blog data [28]). Each cluster was taken as a statement of claim about current conditions, hence representing a measured variable in our model. Sources contributing to the cluster were connected to that variable forming the observation matrix. In the formed observation matrix, participants are the twitter users who provided tweets during the observation period, measured variables are represented by the clusters of tweets and the element S_iC_j is set to 1 if the tweets of participant S_i belong to cluster C_j, or to 0 otherwise. The matrix was then fed to our EM scheme. We ran the scheme on the collected data and picked the top (i.e., most credible) tweet in each hour. We then checked if our 10 "ground truth" events were reported among the top tweets. Table 1 compares the ground truth events to the corresponding top

hourly tweets discovered by EM. The results show that indeed all events were reported correctly, demonstrating the value of our scheme in distilling key important information from large volumes of noisy data.

#	Media	Tweet found by EM
1	East Coast Braces For Hurricane Irene; Hurricane Irene is expected to follow a path up the East Coast	@JoshOchs A #hurricane here on the east coast
2	Hurricane Irene's effects begin being felt in NC, The storm, now a Category 2, still has the East Coast on edge.	Winds, rain pound North Carolina as Hurricane Irene closes in http://t.co/0gVOSZk
3	Hurricane Irene charged up the U.S. East Coast on Saturday toward New York, shutting down the city, and millions of Americans sought shelter from the huge storm.	Hurricane Irene rages up U.S. east coast http://t.co/u0XiXow
4	The Wall Street Journal has created a way for New Yorkers to interact with the location-based social media app Foursquare to find the nearest NYC hurricane evacuation center.	Mashable - Hurricane Irene: Find an NYC Evacuation Center on Foursquare ... http://t.co/XMtpH99
5	Following slamming into the East Coast and knocking out electricity to more than a million people, Hurricane Irene is now taking purpose on largest metropolitan areas in the Northeast.	2M lose power as Hurricane Irene moves north - Two million homes and businesses were without power ... http://t.co/fZWkEU3
6	Irene remains a Category 1, the lowest level of hurricane classification, as it churns toward New York over the next several hours, the U.S. National Hurricane Center said on Sunday.	Now its a level 1 hurricane. Let's hope it hits NY at Level 1
7	Blackouts reported, storm warnings issued as Irene nears Quebec, Atlantic Canada.	DTN Canada: Irene forecast to hit Atlantic Canada http://t.co/MjhmeJn
8	President Barack Obama declared New York a disaster area Wednesday, The New York Times reports, allowing the release of federal aid to the state's government and individuals.	Hurricane Irene: New York State Declared A Disaster Area By President Obama
9	Hurricane Irene's rampage up the East Coast has become the tenth billion-dollar weather event this year, breaking a record stretching back to 1980, climate experts said Wednesday.	Irene is 10th billion-dollar weather event of 2011.
10	WASHINGTON- On Sunday, September 4, the President will travel to Paterson, New Jersey, to view damage from Hurricane Irene.	White House: Obama to visit Paterson, NJ Sunday to view damage from Hurricane Irene

Table 1: Ground truth events and related tweets found by EM in Hurricane Irene

6. DISCUSSION AND FUTURE WORK

Participants (sources) are assumed to be independent from each other in the current EM scheme. However, sources can sometimes be dependent. That is, they copy observations from each other in real life (e.g., retweets of Twitter). Regarding possible solutions to this problem, one possibility is to remove duplicate observations from dependent sources and only keep the original ones. This can be achieved by applying copy detection schemes between sources [12, 13]. Another possible solution is to cluster dependent sources based on some *source-dependency* metric [6]. In other words, sources in the same cluster are closely related with each other but independent from sources in other clusters. Then we can apply the developed algorithm on top of the clustered sources.

Observations from different participants on a given measured variable are assumed to be *corroborating* in this paper.

This happens in social sensing applications where people do not report "lack of problems". For example, a group of participants involved in a geotagging application to find litter of a park will only report locations where they observe litter and ignore the locations they don't find litter. However, sources can also make conflicting observations in other types of applications. For example, comments from different reviewers in an on-line review system on the same product often contradict with each other. Fortunately, our current model can be flexibly extended to handle conflicting observations. The idea is to extend the estimation vector to incorporate the conflicting states of a measured variable and rebuild the likelihood function based on the extended estimation vector. The general outline of the EM derivation still holds.

The current EM scheme is mainly designed to run on static data sets, where the computation overhead stays reasonable even when the dataset scales up (e.g., the Irene dataset). However, such computation may become less efficient for streaming data because we need to re-run the algorithm on the whole dataset from scratch every time the dataset gets updated. Instead, it will be more technically sound that the algorithm only runs on the updated dataset and combines the results with previously computed ones in an optimal (or suboptimal) way. One possibility is to develop a scheme that can compute the estimated parameters of interest recursively over time using incoming measurements and a mathematical process model. The challenge here is that the relationship between the estimation from the updated dataset and the complete dataset may not be linear. Hence, linear regression might not be generally plausible. Rather, recursive estimation schemes, such as the Recursive Bayesian estimation, would be a better fit. The authors are currently working on accommodating the above extensions.

7. CONCLUSION

This paper described a maximum likelihood estimation approach to accurately discover the truth in social sensing applications. The approach can determine the correctness of reported observations given only the measurements sent without knowing the trustworthiness of participants. The optimal solution is obtained by solving an expectation maximization problem and can directly lead to an analytically founded quantification of the correctness of measurements as well as the reliability of participants. Evaluation results show that non-trivial estimation accuracy improvements can be achieved by the proposed maximum likelihood estimation approach compared to other state of the art solutions.

Acknowledgements

Research reported in this paper was sponsored by the Army Research Laboratory and was accomplished under Cooperative Agreement Number W911NF-09-2-0053. This work was partially supported by the LCCC and eLLIIT centers at Lund University, Sweden. The views and conclusions contained in this document are those of the authors and should not be interpreted as representing the official policies, either expressed or implied, of the Army Research Laboratory or the U.S. Government. The U.S. Government is authorized to reproduce and distribute reprints for Government purposes notwithstanding any copyright notation here on.

8. REFERENCES

[1] T. Abdelzaher et al. Mobiscopes for human spaces. *IEEE Pervasive Computing*, 6(2):20–29, 2007.

[2] G. Adomavicius and A. Tuzhilin. Toward the next generation of recommender systems: A survey of the state-of-the-art and possible extensions. *IEEE TRANSACTIONS ON KNOWLEDGE AND DATA ENGINEERING*, 17(6):734–749, 2005.

[3] H. Ahmadi, T. Abdelzaher, J. Han, N. Pham, and R. Ganti. The sparse regression cube: A reliable modeling technique for open cyber-physical systems. In *Proc. 2nd International Conference on Cyber-Physical Systems (ICCPS'11)*, 2011.

[4] H. Ahmadi, N. Pham, R. Ganti, T. Abdelzaher, S. Nath, and J. Han. Privacy-aware regression modeling of participatory sensing data. In *Proceedings of the 8th ACM Conference on Embedded Networked Sensor Systems*, SenSys '10, pages 99–112, New York, NY, USA, 2010. ACM.

[5] R. Balakrishnan. Source rank: Relevance and trust assessment for deep web sources based on inter-source agreement. In *20th World Wide Web Conference (WWW'11)*, 2011.

[6] L. Berti-Equille, A. D. Sarma, X. Dong, A. Marian, and D. Srivastava. Sailing the information ocean with awareness of currents: Discovery and application of source dependence. In *CIDR'09*, 2009.

[7] S. Brin and L. Page. The anatomy of a large-scale hypertextual web search engine. In *7th international conference on World Wide Web (WWW'07)*, pages 107–117, 1998.

[8] H. Cramer. *Mathematical Methods of Statistics*. Princeton Univ. Press., 1946.

[9] O. Dekel and O. Shamir. Vox populi: Collecting high-quality labels from a crowd. In *In Proceedings of the 22nd Annual Conference on Learning Theory*, 2009.

[10] S. A. Delre, W. Jager, and M. A. Janssen. Diffusion dynamics in small-world networks with heterogeneous consumers. *Comput. Math. Organ. Theory*, 13:185–202, June 2007.

[11] A. P. Dempster, N. M. Laird, and D. B. Rubin. Maximum likelihood from incomplete data via the em algorithm. *JOURNAL OF THE ROYAL STATISTICAL SOCIETY, SERIES B*, 39(1):1–38, 1977.

[12] X. Dong, L. Berti-Equille, Y. Hu, and D. Srivastava. Global detection of complex copying relationships between sources. *PVLDB*, 3(1):1358–1369, 2010.

[13] X. Dong, L. Berti-Equille, and D. Srivastava. Truth discovery and copying detection in a dynamic world. *VLDB*, 2(1):562–573, 2009.

[14] S. B. Eisenman et al. The bikenet mobile sensing system for cyclist experience mapping. In *SenSys'07*, November 2007.

[15] A. Galland, S. Abiteboul, A. Marian, and P. Senellart. Corroborating information from disagreeing views. In *WSDM*, pages 131–140, 2010.

[16] J.-H. Huang, S. Amjad, and S. Mishra. CenWits: a sensor-based loosely coupled search and rescue system using witnesses. In *SenSys'05*, pages 180–191, 2005.

[17] C. Hui, M. K. Goldberg, M. Magdon-Ismail, and

W. A. Wallace. Simulating the diffusion of information: An agent-based modeling approach. *IJATS*, pages 31–46, 2010.

[18] B. Hull et al. CarTel: a distributed mobile sensor computing system. In *SenSys'06*, pages 125–138, 2006.

[19] J. M. Kleinberg. Authoritative sources in a hyperlinked environment. *Journal of the ACM*, 46(5):604–632, 1999.

[20] M. Mun, S. Reddy, K. Shilton, N. Yau, J. Burke, D. Estrin, M. Hansen, E. Howard, R. West, and P. Boda. Peir, the personal environmental impact report, as a platform for participatory sensing systems research. In *Proceedings of the 7th international conference on Mobile systems, applications, and services*, MobiSys '09, pages 55–68, New York, NY, USA, 2009. ACM.

[21] N. Mustapha, M. Jalali, and M. Jalali. Expectation maximization clustering algorithm for user modeling in web usage mining systems. *European Journal of Scientific Research*, 32(4):467–476, 2009.

[22] J. Pasternack and D. Roth. Knowing what to believe (when you already know something). In *International Conference on Computational Linguistics (COLING)*, 2010.

[23] D. Pomerantz and G. Dudek. Context dependent movie recommendations using a hierarchical bayesian model. In *Proceedings of the 22nd Canadian Conference on Artificial Intelligence: Advances in Artificial Intelligence*, Canadian AI '09, pages 98–109, Berlin, Heidelberg, 2009. Springer-Verlag.

[24] S. Reddy, D. Estrin, and M. Srivastava. Recruitment framework for participatory sensing data collections. In *Proceedings of the 8th International Conference on Pervasive Computing*, pages 138–155. Springer Berlin Heidelberg, May 2010.

[25] S. Reddy, K. Shilton, G. Denisov, C. Cenizal, D. Estrin, and M. Srivastava. Biketastic: sensing and mapping for better biking. In *Proceedings of the 28th international conference on Human factors in computing systems*, CHI '10, pages 1817–1820, New York, NY, USA, 2010. ACM.

[26] V. S. Sheng, F. Provost, and P. G. Ipeirotis. Get another label? improving data quality and data mining using multiple, noisy labelers. In *Proceedings of the 14th ACM SIGKDD international conference on Knowledge discovery and data mining*, KDD '08, pages 614–622, New York, NY, USA, 2008. ACM.

[27] Y. Sun, Y. Yu, and J. Han. Ranking-based clustering of heterogeneous information networks with star network schema. In *15th SIGKDD international conference on Knowledge discovery and data mining (KDD'09)*, pages 797–806, 2009.

[28] P.-N. Tan, M. Steinbach, and V. Kumar. *Introduction to Data Mining*. 2005.

[29] D. Wang, T. Abdelzaher, H. Ahmadi, J. Pasternack, D. Roth, M. Gupta, J. Han, O. Fatemieh, and H. Le. On bayesian interpretation of fact-finding in information networks. In *14th International Conference on Information Fusion (Fusion 2011)*, 2011.

[30] D. Wang, T. Abdelzaher, L. Kaplan, and C. C. Aggarwal. On quantifying the accuracy of maximum likelihood estimation of participant reliability in social sensing. In *DMSN11: 8th International Workshop on Data Management for Sensor Networks*, August 2011.

[31] C. F. J. Wu. On the convergence properties of the EM algorithm. *The Annals of Statistics*, 11(1):95–103, 1983.

[32] J. Xie, S. Sreenivasan, G. Korniss, W. Zhang, C. Lim, and B. K. Szymanski. Social consensus through the influence of committed minorities. *CoRR*, abs/1102.3931, 2011.

[33] X. Yin, J. Han, and P. S. Yu. Truth discovery with multiple conflicting information providers on the web. *IEEE Trans. on Knowl. and Data Eng.*, 20:796–808, June 2008.

[34] X. Yin and W. Tan. Semi-supervised truth discovery. In *WWW*, New York, NY, USA, 2011. ACM.

SunCast: Fine-grained Prediction of Natural Sunlight Levels for Improved Daylight Harvesting

Jiakang Lu and Kamin Whitehouse
Department of Computer Science, University of Virginia
Charlottesville, VA, USA
{jklu,whitehouse}@cs.virginia.edu

ABSTRACT

Daylight harvesting is the use of natural sunlight to reduce the need for artificial lighting in buildings. The key challenge of daylight harvesting is to provide stable indoor lighting levels even though natural sunlight is not a stable light source. In this paper, we present a new technique called SunCast that improves lighting stability by predicting changes in future sunlight levels. The system has two parts: 1) it learns predictable sunlight patterns due to trees, nearby buildings, or other environmental factors, and 2) it controls the window transparency based on a quadratic optimization over predicted sunlight levels. To evaluate the system, we record daylight levels at 39 different windows for up to 12 weeks at a time, and apply our control algorithm on the data traces. Our results indicate that SunCast can reduce glare by 59% over a baseline approach with only a marginal increase in artificial lighting energy.

Categories and Subject Descriptors

C.3 [**Special-Purpose and Application-Based Systems**]: Real-time and Embedded Systems

General Terms

Design, Experimentation, Performance

Keywords

Fine-grained Prediction, Sunlight, Daylight Harvesting, Wireless Sensor Networks

1. INTRODUCTION

Artificial lighting is the single largest energy consumer in commercial buildings, accounting for 26% of their total energy usage [1]. *Daylight harvesting* is the approach of using natural sunlight inside a building in order to reduce the electricity demand of artificial lighting. This approach holds particular promise for commercial buildings because they are primarily occupied during daylight hours. The key challenge is to provide stable levels of illumination (typically 500 ± 250 lux) even though natural sunlight is not a stable light source. An office should have enough light to read and work but not so much that it causes glare and discomfort, despite the fact that sunlight levels can change from 100 lux to 1000 lux or more in a matter of minutes due to passing shadows from clouds, trees, and nearby buildings. An emerging approach is to use electrochromic glass, also called smart glass [2], or motorized window blinds [3] to automatically adjust the transparency of a window. When the natural light source is too bright, the window transparency is decreased. When it is too dim, the window transparency is increased and supplemental artificial lighting may be used. Daylight harvesting has been demonstrated to reduce lighting energy by up to 40% in offices that have significant amounts of daylight [4, 5]. In addition, natural light is more pleasant and comfortable than artificial light and has been shown to increase employee productivity [6].

Despite the potential benefits, current daylight harvesting installations have achieved limited effectiveness. A recent study shows that 50% of existing photo-controlled daylight harvesting systems are disabled by the users and the other 50% operate at 50% of their intended performance [7]. One reason is that natural lighting levels can change very quickly but window transparency can only be changed relatively slowly. Rapid changes to window transparency cause confusion and annoyance to building occupants [8], and some windowing systems also have a physical limit on the rate of transparency change [9]. Any difference between the maximum window change speed and the rate of change in natural daylight either introduces glare (people disable the system) or causes energy waste (poor performance).

In this paper, we address the problem of minimizing both glare and energy usage, given that window transparency is subject to a *maximum switching speed*: the maximum instantaneous rate at which the window transparency can be changed. A daylight harvesting system has two forms of lighting actuation that offer different points in the energy/speed trade off: window transparency changes slowly but consumes little or no energy, whereas electric lighting can change quickly but consumes significant energy. Importantly, electric lighting offers only one-directional actuation: it can increase illumination, but cannot reduce illumination. Therefore, bright sunlight can only be addressed by a reduction in window transparency but, being slow, this cannot prevent a temporary glare spike if natural lighting levels increase suddenly. To address this problem, a daylight harvesting system must *predict* glare before it happens so that it can reduce window transparency in advance, using electric lighting to compensate as necessary until the natural lighting levels increase. By predicting rapid increases in natural lighting, the system can provide constant lighting levels by converting temporary glare spikes into negative spikes that can be addressed through additional energy consumption. However, these daylight predictions must be fairly precise in terms of both the timing and magnitude of daylight changes: a rise in sunlight levels that is later or smaller than predicted will result in energy waste, whereas those that are earlier to larger than predicted will result in a glare spike. Thus, a key challenge of daylight harvesting is to adjust window transparency in anticipation of future changes in sunlight levels.

We present a new technique called *SunCast* that improves daylight harvesting performance by using fine-grained prediction of natural sunlight levels. SunCast is an on-line system that makes a new prediction and issues a new control command at every moment in time. It has two parts: a sunlight prediction algorithm and a control algorithm. To predict sunlight values, it first defines the *similarity* between sunlight values observed on previous days and those observed up until the current time on the current day. Then, it defines the distribution of future sunlight levels to be a weighted combination of historical sunlight levels at the same times of day, weighted by the previous days' similarity values. For example, by 10:00 AM one day, SunCast observes sunlight patterns typical of a sunny day. Of all historical data traces that exhibited similar patterns, some remained sunny while others became cloudy. Of those days that remained sunny, all days exhibited a trough from 11 to 11:30 AM due to a shadow from a nearby tree or building. SunCast combines all of these historical traces to produce a distribution of predicted sunlight values at every time in the future. Thus, instead of making an explicit model of a node's environment, SunCast uses a purely data-driven approach to create empirical distributions over both predictable and unpredictable features of sunlight time series. Weather predictions, day of year, or other explicit information about the environment can be integrated into SunCast by including it in the function used to match with historical traces.

In contrast to prior techniques that predict average sunlight levels over a time period, SunCast predicts the actual sunlight values for every minute in a future time window, which allows the daylight harvesting system to set a specific window transparency level for each minute. Furthermore, SunCast predicts a distribution of sunlight levels, instead of predicting just a point estimate. This allows the daylight harvesting system to calculate the expected glare and energy usage for any given transparency level at any point in time, weighted by the probability distribution over the predicted light values. These distributions allow the system to identify predictable sunlight patterns such as sunrise or shadows from trees and nearby buildings, and to distinguish these from unpredictable patterns such as cloud movement.

To control the window transparency, SunCast uses a form of predictive control. Given a set of sunlight predictions, it uses quadratic optimization to choose a complete sequence of future window transparencies to minimize expected glare and energy, subject to switching speed constraints. It issues the first transparency value in that sequence as a control signal to the window. Every minute, a new light value is ob-

served, the distributions and optimized values are updated, and a new control signal is issued. We evaluate this approach by deploying light sensors in 39 different locations for up to 12 weeks at a time, and applying the control algorithm on the data traces. Our results indicate that SunCast can reduce glare by 59% over a baseline approach with only a marginal energy penalty. We conclude that SunCast helps solar energy harvesting technologies exploit predictable, large-scale, short-duration fluctuations in solar energy levels to substantially reduce glare and improve the comfort levels produced by existing energy harvesting systems.

2. BACKGROUND AND RELATED WORK

Solar radiation accounts for most of the renewable energy on Earth, with total solar irradiance measuring roughly $1.3 \ kW/m^2$ [10]. Artificial lighting constitutes a large fraction of energy usage in commercial buildings, despite the fact that they are occupied primarily during daylight hours. The reasons for this energy usage are plentiful, and daylight harvesting cannot address all of these reasons. For example, lights are often left on at night for security reasons, and many buildings have a wide footprint so light from windows cannot reach the center of the building. However, daylight harvesting systems have gradually gained popularity in modern buildings and have been shown to have the potential for up to 40% energy savings [4, 11, 12]. Many new buildings are being designed with natural lighting in mind, and building codes in some countries as well as some LEED certification levels require all rooms to have natural lighting. The Lawrence Berkeley National Laboratory (LBNL) recently deployed a well-known daylight harvesting system in the new New York Times Headquarters Building [13] along with a field study that enhances the understanding of daylighting controls. Other daylight harvesting systems have been developed to minimize energy consumption, balance diverse user lighting preferences, and increases facilities managers' satisfaction [14]. In such systems, window shading technologies such as electrochromic windows [2] and motorized blinds [3] are widely used. However, the switching speed of electrochromic windows sometimes range from several minutes to up to two hours, depending on window size and outdoor temperature [9]. Even mechanical blinds have a maximum switching speed because rapid changes to the blind position have been shown to cause confusion to the user [8]. Furthermore, changing window transparency consumes energy. Limits on maximum switching speed can cause lighting errors and reduce user comfort, which ultimately leads to energy waste if users disable the system or configure it to be less aggressive in order to reduce glare [7].

The Illuminating Engineering Society of North America (IESNA) recommends 500 lux as the standard task illuminance for office workers performing regular tasks [15]. However, visual comfort depends on task requirements and individual user preferences. The upper limit on lighting depends on glare requirements, and is different for reading paper documents versus reading a back lit computer screen. The lower limit is usually discussed in terms of detectable vs. acceptable illuminance: 10-15% is generally within the undetectable range for most people assuming base levels of 500 lux [16], and up to 40% may be acceptable depending on how slowly the light is dimmed [17].

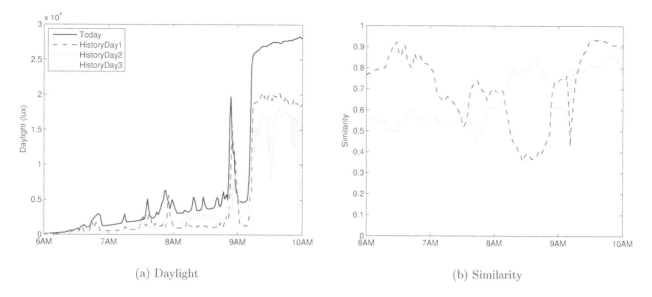

| (a) Daylight | (b) Similarity |

Figure 1: SunCast uses a *similarity metric* to identify historical data traces with patterns most similar to the current day. In this example, the most similar day changes over time.

Many sunlight prediction techniques have previously been developed, primarily in the context of solar energy harvesting with solar panels, and each techniques makes predictions based on different information and over a different period of time. Weather forecasts today are based on vast sensing infrastructure and advanced computer simulations [18, 19]. Sharma et al. explore the use of weather forecasts to improve energy harvesting prediction [20]. Forecasts can help predict cloudiness levels in the sky, but do not predict the effect of shadows and reflections at a particular location on the ground, which depends on the proximity to nearby buildings, the presence of leaves on trees, time of day, and seasonal changes in the azimuth of the sun. These factors affect solar energy levels as much haze, clouds, and precipitation. Today, websites provide hourly predictions of cloudiness levels, but even more fine-grained information is needed for control of window transparency. Classical time series analysis would suggest using auto-regression techniques [21], but any such model would change rapidly throughout the day and would depend on many external, unobserved variables.

Recently, several new approaches have been developed to predict the solar energy levels at a single point, most of which have focused on solar-powered sensing [22]. Some of these techniques choose a fixed sensor sampling rate based on long-term expected sunlight levels [23, 24, 25], while others make near-term predictions, e.g. 3-72 hours in advance [26, 27]. Other techniques use an EWMA over previous days [28, 29] or statistical correlations based on weather predictions [30, 31]. However, solar energy harvesting is very different from daylight harvesting because solar energy can be stored in a capacitor or battery, whereas sunlight cannot be stored. Therefore, fine-grained prediction is not as essential for solar energy harvesting: the storage unit acts as a buffer and delays the impact of sunlight changes, giving the system more time to adapt by, e.g. changing the sampling rate. Unless storage is extremely limited, therefore, solar-powered sensing applications can suffice with predictions of *average* sunlight levels. In contrast, daylight harvesting systems have no buffer to delay a glare spike, and must therefore use fine-grained prediction to accommodate rapid changes in sunlight levels.

Wireless sensor networks (WSNs) have previously been used for light sensing and actuation to achieve cost effectiveness, energy efficiency, and user comfort. For example, Singhvi et al. proposed and demonstrated a lighting control system with wireless sensors and a combination of incandescent desk lamps and wall lamps actuated by the X10 system [32]. In addition to office lighting applications, Park et al. designed and implemented Illuminator, an intelligent lighting control system for entertainment and media production [33]. High fidelity wireless light sensors were developed and implemented to form a sensor network for collecting stage lighting information [34]. The SunCast daylight harvesting system also senses and controls light values, but the goal different: to achieve stable task lighting despite unstable natural sunlight levels.

3. PREDICTING SUNLIGHT VALUES

SunCast uses a three-stage process to generate fine-grained, continuous distributions of predicted sunlight values. First, the system calculates the *similarity* between the real-time data stream and historical data traces (Section 3.1). Second, it uses a regression analysis to *map* the trends in the historical traces to more closely match patterns of the current day (Section 3.2). Third, the system combines the weighted historical traces to predict the *distribution* of sunlight in the near future (Section 3.3).

3.1 Finding Similar Days in History

SunCast calculates the similarity of the current sunlight levels with all historical data traces previously observed. Calculating the similarity has two steps. First, we calculate the squared error between the real-time data stream and the historical data stream, for a time window of n readings in the recent past. The current data stream in the sliding window between t_1 and t_n is defined as $DS = \{x_{t_1}, x_{t_2}, ..., x_{t_n}\}$, and

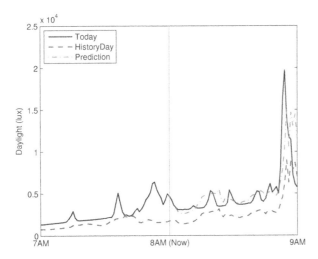

Figure 2: SunCast uses regression to improve the mapping between today (solid) and a historical day (dashed) to improve future the predictions based on that historical day (dashed-dot).

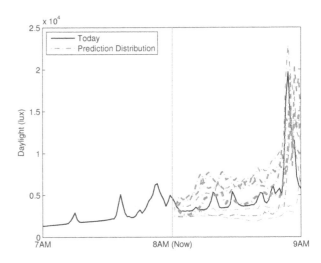

Figure 3: SunCast uses a weighted combination of historical data traces to create a distribution of predicted light values, depicted here by the weighted dashed lines.

the data stream of historical trace j is defined as $DS'_j = \{x'_{t_1,j}, x'_{t_2,j}, ..., x'_{t_n,j}\}$. The difference d between these two days is calculated as:

$$d(DS, DS'_j) = \sum_{i=1}^{n} (x_{t_i} - x'_{t_i,j})^2 \qquad (1)$$

Second, we define a relative ranking among all the h historical traces by normalizing the difference values. Thus, the *similarity* s_j of historical trace j among h history days is defined as:

$$s_j = 1 - \frac{d(DS, DS'_j)}{\sum_{k=1}^{h} d(DS, DS'_k)} \qquad (2)$$

These normalized values are used as *weights* to find the traces most similar to the current data, while still taking the entire historical data set into consideration.

Figure 1 illustrates the similarity metric for an example day with three historical traces using a 15-minute sliding window during the period from 6:00 AM to 10:00 AM. The example day has clear weather and 3 historical days that are hazy, partially cloudy, and sunny but becoming overcast, respectively. This particular sensor has direct sunlight around 8:50 AM, followed by a shadow due to a tree, and direct sunlight again around 9:10 AM. Early in the morning, History Day 3 is most similar, but once History Day 3 becomes overcast during the periods of direct sunlight, the hazy day becomes most similar. This example illustrates the benefits of a relative ordering rather than an absolute metric of similarity.

3.2 Mapping to Current Conditions

In the example above, the most similar historical trace was from a hazy day. This trace contained trends and patterns that are pertinent for predicting today's sunlight values, but the values are offset by a constant factor due to the level of haze. Similar effects are also produced by seasonal changes

in sunlight intensity or other factors, and SunCast uses linear regression analysis to map the patterns in a historical trace to the conditions of the current day. The regression is formulated as $Y = b_j + a_j X_j$, where Y is the current data stream $\{y_{t_1}, y_{t_2}, ..., y_{t_n}\}$ and X_j is the jth historical trace $\{x'_{t_1,j}, x'_{t_2,j}, ..., x'_{t_n,j}\}$. After solving for a_j and b_j, we use the linear regression model to predict the future sunlight values for today, based on the historical traces patterns: for a prediction length l, the predicted data based on history day j is

$$Y^*_j = b_j + a_j X^*_j \qquad (3)$$

where Y^*_j is the predicted data $\{y^*_{t_{n+1},j}, y^*_{t_{n+2},j}, ..., y^*_{t_{n+l},j}\}$ and X^*_j is the historical trace $\{x'_{t_{n+1},j}, x'_{t_{n+2},j}, ..., x'_{t_{n+l},j}\}$.

Figure 2 illustrates how this mapping process works. In the example, the current clock time is 8:00 AM and our system applies regression between the current data and a historical trace over the prior one-hour time window between 7:00 AM and 8:00 AM. Then, the model learned is applied to the next time one-hour time window between 8:00 AM and 9:00 AM to predict the future values today based on the historical trace. As the figure illustrates, the regression analysis preserves patterns in the historical trace while correcting for constant differences in the slope and bias between the two days.

3.3 Creating a Prediction Distribution

After applying regression analysis to all h historical traces, we apply the regression model to the future time window to produce h predictions of length l. These are combined into an h-by-l matrix. The similarity values can be multiplied against the prediction distribution to produce the *prediction distribution* $\hat{\mathbf{x}}$, as shown in Equation 4, where $\hat{x}_{t_{n+i},h} \in \hat{\mathbf{x}}$ is the weighted sunlight prediction for time $n + i$ based on historical day h.

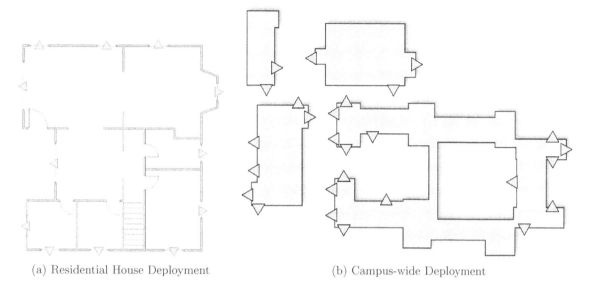

(a) Residential House Deployment

(b) Campus-wide Deployment

Figure 4: To evaluate SunCast, we deployed light sensors at 39 locations for up to 12 weeks at a time.

$$\hat{\mathbf{x}} = \begin{bmatrix} s_1 \\ s_2 \\ \vdots \\ s_h \end{bmatrix}^T \begin{bmatrix} x^*_{t_{n+1},1} & x^*_{t_{n+2},1} & \cdots & x^*_{t_{n+l},1} \\ x^*_{t_{n+1},2} & x^*_{t_{n+2},2} & \cdots & x^*_{t_{n+l},2} \\ \vdots & \vdots & \ddots & \vdots \\ x^*_{t_{n+1},h} & x^*_{t_{n+2},h} & \cdots & x^*_{t_{n+l},h} \end{bmatrix} \qquad (4)$$

Figure 3 illustrates an example of prediction distribution using the same example day above and ten historical traces. Each dashed-dotted line represents the expected sunlight based on the prediction of one historical trace, and the thickness of the line indicates the similarity between the current day and that history day. As the figure shows, SunCast produces a fairly wide distribution for the time between 8:00 AM and 8:50 AM, due to varying levels of haze that might be encountered. However, given that the data between 7:00 AM and 8:00 AM is fairly indicative of a clear day, the most heavily weighted predictions all have a peak in sunlight around 8:50 AM when direct sunlight first hits this node and before the shadow of a tree. Two predictions of a cloudy day (thin lines at the bottom) remain in the prediction distribution, but both have very low weights.

4. SETTING WINDOW TRANSPARENCY

In this section, we present a mathematical formulation of the daylight harvesting problem to illustrate how the SunCast prediction distributions can be used for on-line window control. We define window transparency wt to be the percentage of incoming daylight that penetrates the window: the window is fully closed at 0% transparency and fully open at 100%. The *setpoint* is the desirable lighting level for task illumination: too much harvested light will cause *glare*, while too little will increase *energy* consumption of artificial lighting. The window switching speed $wSpeed$ is the maximum percent change in window transparency allowed per minute. A daylight harvesting system does not need to predict far into the future because values in the far future do not affect current control parameters. We define

a maximum prediction window len to be

$$len = \frac{max(100\% - wt, wt - 0\%)}{wSpeed} \qquad (5)$$

This window size ensures that the system predicts far enough that it is always able to respond to predicted values; larger values of $wSpeed$ lead to smaller prediction windows. Then, the system finds a series of window transparency values that minimize the expected lighting error for the entire prediction window with k historical traces: $predDist_{k,len}$. The objective function is

$$minimize \sum_{j=1}^{k} \sum_{i=n+1}^{n+len} |wt_{t_i} \times \hat{x}_{t_i,j} - setpoint| \qquad (6)$$

subject to limits on both window transparency and switching speed

$$0\% \leqslant wt_{t_i} \leqslant 100\% \qquad (7)$$

$$|wt_{t_{i+1}} - wt_{t_i}| \leqslant wSpeed \qquad (8)$$

Once the optimization function is solved, the system updates the current window transparency to the first value from the solution derived: $wt^*_{t_{n+1}}$. All other transparency values from the solution are discarded, and were only calculated to ensure that target transparency values for the future could still be achieved given switching speed constraints. This entire process is repeated every time step when a new light reading is measured.

4.1 Balancing Prediction and Reaction

The algorithm described above is a pure prediction algorithm, which is ideal for preparing in advance for predictable rapid changes in sunlight, such as sunrise, sunset, or a shadow. However, during periods of stable sunlight, such as mid-day, predictions from historical traces will actually hinder performance because current conditions are a better predictor of future values than any historical trace. In such cases, better performance is achieved by a *reactive* algorithm that sets the window transparency based on the

(a) Light Sensor   (b) Open View

(c) Blocking Tree   (d) Blocking Building

Figure 5: The light sensors we deployed were subject to a wide range of environmental influencers that caused shadows and reflections throughout the day.

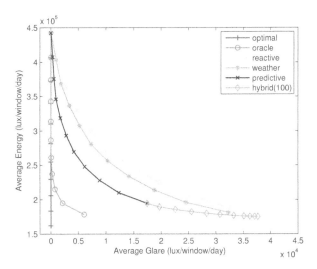

Figure 6: The two algorithms based on SunCast, *prediction* & *hybrid(100)*, offer a more desirable trade-off between glare and energy usage than the *reactive* scheme, and begin to approach the performance of *oracle* and *optimal* schemes.

current sunlight values, without making any predictions. In order to accommodate this condition, SunCast introduces a *hybrid* scheme that switches smoothly between prediction and reaction: it uses a purely reactive scheme on each historical trace j and, if the lighting error is below a threshold β, then all values in the row j of $\hat{\mathbf{x}}$ are replaced with the current light reading. The basic rationale is that if a historical trace is stable enough that pure reaction performs sufficiently well, then the trace is not providing any useful prediction information. In fact, it can even be harmful to performance because window transparency will be determined by small peaks and troughs from that day that are not likely to re-occur today. Therefore, the trace is only used if it indicates a rapid change in sunlight that cannot be accommodated to the switching speed limitations. The user can tune the balance between prediction and reaction by changing the parameter β.

4.2 Balancing Energy and Glare

Daylight harvesting systems must balance energy usage and glare when responding to predictions about future sunlight. Being too aggressive about energy conservation will introduce glare if there are rapid peaks in sunlight, but being too conservative will cause energy usage if sunlight levels are not as high as expected. In SunCast, we allow the user to customize the balance between energy and glare by introducing a new control variable called *daylight weight*, which tunes the maximum percentage of lighting that can be provided by natural daylight. If the daylight weight is 0%, then the system uses purely electric lighting without any concern about glare. If the daylight weight is 100%, then the system maximize the opportunity to harvest natural sunlight, but risks suffering from more glare. One alternative to this scheme is to define a different penalty function for glare or

energy usage, which would allow the system to achieve a more subtle trade off between energy and glare. However, such a scheme could no longer be formulated as a quadratic optimization, and we believe that users will find it easier to set a single linear knob rather than to create a customized penalty function.

5. EXPERIMENTAL SETUP

Daylight intensity and distribution are deeply dependent on geographic location, building orientation, sky conditions and nearby surroundings. Therefore, in order to evaluate SunCast in a realistic environment, we deployed two testbeds in different buildings: one in a residential house and another of deployment on university campus, as shown in Figures 4(a) and 4(b). The testbeds consist of 12 and 27 U012-12 Hobo data loggers designed by Onset, as shown in Figure 5(a). These nodes can monitor the environment with the built-in light, temperature, and humidity sensors. At each window, a node facing the outside measures the incoming daylight. Some nodes are deployed at windows with open views while others are located behind a blocking tree outside. Several examples of deployment are shown in Figure 5.

We collected the light sensor data from the testbed at a sampling rate of once per minute, and the duration of the sensor deployment lasted for 4 weeks at the house and 12 weeks on campus. During the deployment period, we observed a wide variety of weather patterns, including sunny, cloudy, rain, fog and snow storm. All the data were stored in the data loggers and are manually read out from the nodes every week. The system presented in this paper does not require communication among nodes, but these data loggers could be replaced with wireless sensors for convenience.

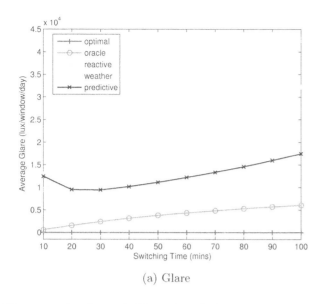

(a) Glare

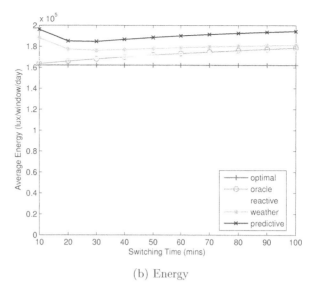

(b) Energy

Figure 7: As the switching time (minimum time to go from completely transparent to opaque) increases, the predictive scheme increasingly outperforms reactive in terms of glare and is a constant factor worse in terms of energy usage. For very short switching times, prediction does not help.

6. EVALUATION

In this section, we evaluate how SunCast predictions affect the performance of daylight harvesting. We evaluate the system on both campus and house testbeds. Due to space limitations, we present only the results of the campus testbed. The results from the residential testbed produced nearly identical trends.

6.1 Baseline and Optimal Algorithms

As a baseline for comparison, we use a purely *reactive* scheme that uses closed-loop feedback control to set the window transparency: it periodically measures the current daylight and sets window transparency to come as close to the target setpoint as possible, subject to the switching speed constraints.

We introduce another baseline scheme called *weather*, which uses the same optimization formulated in Section 4, except that it operates on the subset of history days that have the same cloudiness level as the current day. We classify the history days with the daily cloudiness levels based on the weather reports from local airports. This scheme provides insight on the impact of selecting history days on the system performance.

We upper bound the benefits of prediction using another scheme that we call *oracle*, which uses the same optimization formulated in Section 4, except that it operates on the actual future light values instead of predicted values. This scheme provides the best performance possible with the control algorithm used in our analysis, assuming perfect daylight prediction.

Finally, we upper bound daylight harvesting performance using an *optimal* algorithm that always uses the window transparency that minimizes both energy and glare. This scheme is not subject to switching speed constraints, and provides the theoretical upper bound on energy and glare for any control scheme. If daylight levels are high enough, it will produce no glare and no energy usage. Electric lighting

will only be used when daylight levels are below the target setpoint.

6.2 Evaluation Metrics

We evaluate the performance of the daylight harvesting system in terms of two evaluation metrics: energy and glare. *Energy* is defined as the amount of artificial lighting used by the scheme to maintain the setpoint at the window, measured in lux per window per day. We did not evaluate the energy in kilowatt hours, because that depends on the type of light bulb assumed. The values can easily be converted by assuming a particular type of light bulb. *Glare* is defined as the amount of the harvested light above the target setpoint, also measured in lux per daylight harvesting window per day.

6.3 Experimental Results

We evaluate our system against the baseline and optimal algorithms in a trace-based simulator that replays the empirical data traces from the campus testbed and executes the algorithm described in Section 4. The simulator allows the control scheme to adjust window transparency and measures both glare and electric lighting usage. In our experiments, we use 2,000 lux as the setpoint at the window, which is chosen to produce lighting levels in the interior spaces close to the industry standard of 500 lux. The control loops repeat every 1 minute, which is the sampling rate with which the light data was collected. We test a range of daylight weights from 0% to 100% for all the control schemes, and investigate the effect of balancing between prediction and reaction at the daylight weight of 100%. In the hybrid scheme, we set error thresholds varying from 0% to 100% of the setpoint at the window.

The experimental results of daylight harvesting are shown in Figure 6, where each line represents a different control scheme and the points on the line indicate the average energy and glare results as the daylight weight. All points on

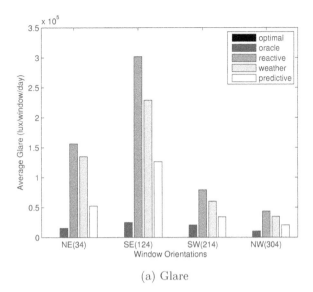

(a) Glare

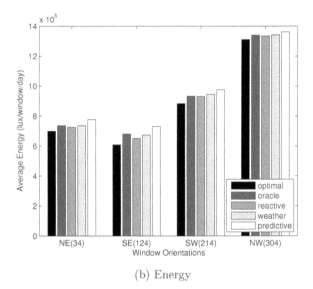

(b) Energy

Figure 8: The south-east facing windows suffer the most glare because the window is completely transparent right before sunrise. The predictive scheme reduces this glare substantially. Energy usage is dominated by dusk and dawn, and is therefore not sensitive to orientation.

the *hybrid(100)* line use 100% daylight weight, and instead the points represent the energy/glare performance for varying values of the β threshold that switches between reaction and prediction. If the daylight weight and the β threshold are integrated into a single user-controlled knob, the predictive and hybrid(100) schemes form a single curve that represents the range of SunCast performance. This curve provides the user with a much more desirable balance between glare and energy usage than the reactive scheme, and approximately halves the distance between *reactive* and *oracle* performance. For total glare levels of about 10,000 lux per day, the predictive scheme consumes about 20% less energy than the reactive scheme. Similarly, at artificial lighting levels of 200 kilolux per day, the predictive scheme produces more than 45% less glare than the reactive scheme. In contrast, the approach based on weather classification reduces only 3.7% energy and 18.6% glare over the reactive scheme.

7. ANALYSIS

In this section, we analyze the degree to which fine-grained prediction contributes to achieving stable task lighting under different scenarios. We also discuss the impact of window switching speeds, window orientations, and cloudiness levels on the performance of daylight harvesting.

7.1 Sensitivity to Switching Speed

To investigate the impact of switching speed on the system performance, we run the same control schemes with a range of switching times varying from 10 minutes to 100 minutes: these are the minimum times required to make a full transition from transparent to opaque. These values represent an estimated range of comfortable speed changes, as well as the physical limits of some electrochromic windows [9]. For a fair comparison, all of these experiments use 100% daylight weight. Figure 7 shows the energy and glare levels of all algorithms as the switching time is varied. Figure 7(b) shows that the predictive scheme always wastes

slightly more energy than the reactive scheme, for a given switching time, but Figure 7(a) shows that the predictive scheme outperforms reactive in terms of glare. Predictive performs best when the minimum switching time is long: at the switching time of 100 minutes, it achieves 59% less glare than the reactive scheme. As the minimum switching time gets smaller, prediction into the future is no longer beneficial and even hinders performance. At the same time, the *reactive* scheme approaches the *oracle* scheme, and at switching times of less than about 15 minutes, reactive begins to outperform predictive.

7.2 Sensitivity to Window Orientation

Figure 8 shows the results of energy and glare broken down by the direction that the sensors are facing on the campus testbed. These results indicate that windows facing the southeast have the highest level of glare. This is because the window is in the fully transparent state at dawn and is suddenly subject to bright, direct sunlight after sunrise. The predictive scheme anticipates the sunrise and reduces glare by over 50%. The northwest windows consumes the largest amount of energy because there the least direct sunlight from that direction. However, energy usage is dominated by dawn and dusk and therefore does not change substantially with window direction. This analysis does not illustrate the effects of predicting rapid changes due to trees, windows, or other predictable shadows, since these factors are different for each window and are averaged out over all windows facing each cardinal direction.

7.3 Sensitivity to Cloudiness Level

Figure 9 illustrates the system performance of the control schemes on the four example days that represent typical cloudiness levels: clear, partly cloudy, most cloudy, and overcast. The diagrams show detailed traces of: 1) sunlight levels during the day; 2) harvested daylight of control schemes; and 3) window transparency adjusted by control schemes. For all control schemes, the daylight weight is

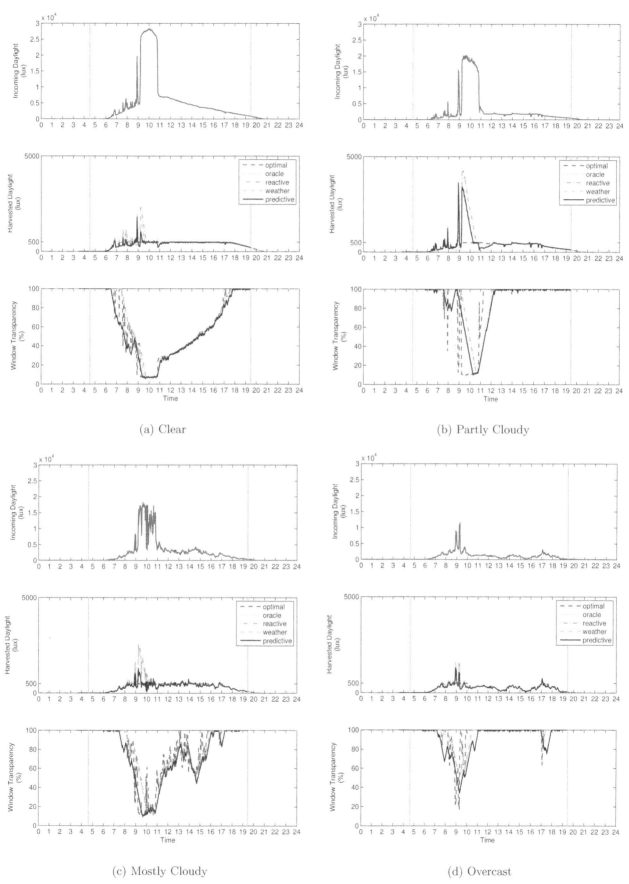

(a) Clear

(b) Partly Cloudy

(c) Mostly Cloudy

(d) Overcast

Figure 9: The predictive scheme based on SunCast is most advantageous over reactive on sunny and overcast days because the sunlight patterns are most predictable. On partially cloudy days, unpredictability causes both glare and energy waste.

100% and the window switching speed is 1%/min. The results show that the predictive scheme approaches the optimal window control on a clear or overcast day. This is because sunlight levels are relatively stable on a clear or overcast day, so sunlight patterns are more predictable. Cloudy days are less predictable. For example, the predictive scheme produces high glare between 9:00 AM and 10:00 AM on a partly cloudy day. This is caused by the sudden sunlight increase around 9:00 AM, which is not predicted by the historical traces: in the early morning, the sunlight levels resembled a cloudy day, but shortly after sunrise the levels approached that of a hazy day. As the sunlight variability becomes smaller, the predictive scheme has better performance on the mostly cloudy day.

7.4 Predictability Analysis

We analyze the times at which SunCast has the largest effect on *task lighting stability*: the variance of indoor lighting levels, as compared with the task lighting setpoint. Lower variance levels indicate that task lighting is more stable. For a fair comparison, all experiments use 100% daylight weight and the window switching speed of 1%/min.

Figure 10 illustrates the system performance of the control schemes on four example windows. Each window has a different predictable feature: morning light, a building shadow, a tree shadow, and blocked view. The diagrams show detailed traces of improvements in the task lighting stability due to both the predictive and the weather-based control schemes. The results show that prediction creates a large improvement in task lighting stability during predictable periods of lighting variability. At other times when the lighting values are not as predictable, the SunCast control algorithm achieves the same task lighting stability as a simple reactive scheme. This analysis demonstrates that the probability distributions created by SunCast help to accurately differentiate predictable and unpredictable patterns, allowing the system to exploit predictable patterns without paying a penalty during unpredictable periods.

8. LIMITATIONS AND FUTURE WORK

The results of this study demonstrate that a data-driven approach can effectively predict natural daylight levels in a way that can improve daylight harvesting effectiveness. However, Section 7.4 illustrates that this approach is limited to sunrise, sunset, trees, nearby buildings, and other relatively predictable environmental factors. Many rapid daylight changes such as those caused by passing clouds are still unpredictable. Our system is designed to revert to a reactive approach during unpredictable periods, as explained in Section 4.1, but in current work we are exploring ways to merge data traces from multiple light sensors deployed throughout a building or a group of buildings to predict cloud boundaries. This *group estimation* approach can also be used to help improve the distribution over future light levels, even for predictable changes. For example, an east-facing window may be best able to predict the intensity of the glare spike at a south-facing window, as the sun rounds the corner of a building. An important challenge of this approach is that it requires communication and coordination among a group of geographically distributed nodes. Therefore, the advantage in terms of daylight harvesting will need to be balanced with the communication and energy demands of the sensor devices.

In addition to daylight harvesting, SunCast can also be used for other applications that would benefit from sunlight prediction. We are currently developing new control algorithms for solar-powered sensing systems that employ photovoltaics to harvest solar energy for perpetually-powered sensing. These systems are typically coupled with rechargeable energy storage such as batteries or fuel cells that preclude the need for fine-grained sunlight prediction. However, storage capacity may be limited by cost, size, or weight. For example, a 9-cubic millimeter solar-powered sensing system recently developed uses a 12μAh battery [35]. Many existing approaches to solar-powered sensing choose a fixed sampling rate that minimizes the chance of fully depleting the energy supply, based on long-term predictions of solar energy levels. However, these approaches lose the ability to exploit the small peaks and troughs typical of natural daylight. For example, opportunities for energy harvesting are lost when sunlight levels rise suddenly but the battery is already fully charged. Similarly, data can be lost if the battery is depleted in order to harvest more energy, but sunlight levels unexpectedly drop.

9. CONCLUSIONS

In this paper, we present a new sunlight prediction framework called *SunCast* that produces a distribution of predicted sunlight values in the near future. SunCast is an improvement over existing sunlight prediction schemes in two ways: 1) continuous predictions over time enable exploitation of predicable, large, and short-duration peaks and troughs in sunlight levels, and 2) a distribution of predictions at each time point enables managing the risks and rewards, weighted by the probability that there will be too much or too little sunlight. We present a predictive control scheme based on quadratic optimization that performs daylight harvesting based on these predictions, and evaluate using data traces collected from 39 light sensors deployed in different windows. Our results demonstrate that SunCast can produce substantial performance improvements for daylight harvesting, reducing glare by 59% with only a marginal increase in electric lighting usage. The reduction in glare will improve the total energy savings from daylight harvesting systems because fewer people will disable the system due to unacceptable lighting comfort. The SunCast prediction and control algorithms can be incorporated into existing daylight harvesting algorithms simply by changing the control algorithm, adding storage for historical data traces, and configuring the parameters: *wSpeed*, daylight ratio, and β. In addition to daylight harvesting application explored in this paper, SunCast can be applied to other problems that would benefit from fine-grained, short-term sunlight prediction. Furthermore, the empirical data-driven techniques could possibly be extended to predict of any data stream that exhibits daily or periodic trends that results from a large number of factors, such as highway traffic patterns, city pollution levels, or office building occupancy.

Acknowledgements

Special thanks to our reviewers for helpful feedback, and to Tarek Abdelzaher for helping to clearly articulate the contributions of this paper. This work is based on work supported by the National Science Foundation under Grants No. 1038271 and 0845761.

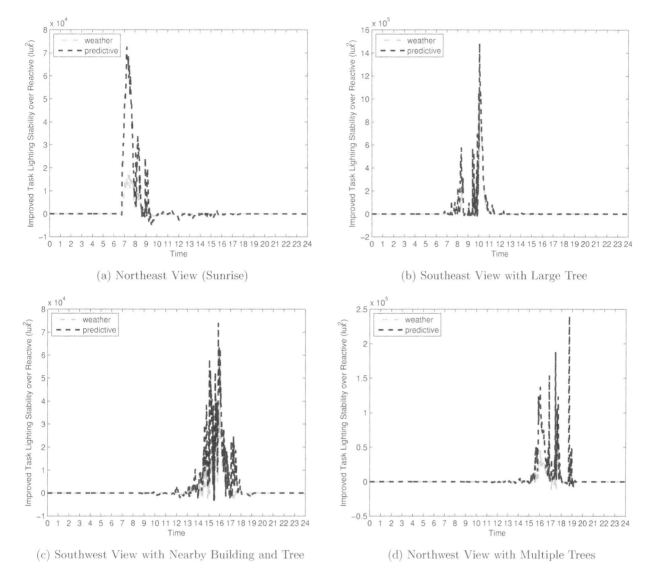

(a) Northeast View (Sunrise)

(b) Southeast View with Large Tree

(c) Southwest View with Nearby Building and Tree

(d) Northwest View with Multiple Trees

Figure 10: SunCast improves lighting stability over the reactive scheme at different times of day for each window, depending on the environmental factors that cause glare. During unpredictable periods, it performs no worse than reactive. The weather based scheme is much less effective at dawn.

10. REFERENCES

[1] U.S. Department of Energy. Energy Efficiency Trends in Residential and Commercial Buildings, 2008.

[2] National Renewable Energy Laboratory. Electrochromic Windows Basics. http://www.nrel.gov/buildings/electrochromic_basics.html.

[3] S. Selkowitz and E. Lee. *Integrating Automated Shading and Smart Glazings with Daylight Controls.* Lawrence Berkeley National Laboratory, 2004.

[4] J.D. Jennings, F.M. Rubinstein, D. DiBartolomeo, and S.L. Blanc. Comparison of Control Options in Private Offices in an Advanced Lighting Controls Testbed. *Journal-Illuminating Engineering Society*, 29(2):39–60, 2000.

[5] Y.J. Wen, J. Granderson, and A.M. Agogino. Towards Embedded Wireless-Networked Intelligent Daylighting Systems for Commercial Buildings. In *SUTC '06: Proceedings of IEEE International Conference on Sensor Networks, Ubiquitous, and Trustworthy Computing*, volume 1, pages 6–pp., 2006.

[6] M.G. Figueiro, M.S. Rea, A.C. Rea, and R.G. Stevens. Daylight and Productivity: A Field Study. In *ACEEE Summer Study 2002*.

[7] D. Rude. Why Do Daylight Harvesting Projects Succeed or Fail? *Construction Specifier*, 59(9):108, 2006.

[8] S. Stevens. Intelligent Façades: Occupant Control and Satisfaction. *International Journal of Sustainable Energy*, 21(2):147–160, 2001.

[9] E.S. Lee, S.E. Selkowitz, R.D. Clear, D.L. DiBartolomeo, J.H. Klems, L.L. Fernandes, G.J. Ward, V. Inkarojrit, and M. Yazdanian. Advancement of Electrochromic Windows. 2006.

[10] R.C. Willson and A.V. Mordvinov. Secular Total Solar

Irradiance Trend During Solar Cycles 21–23. *Geophys. Res. Lett*, 30(5):1199, 2003.

[11] D.H.W. Li and J.C. Lam. Evaluation of Lighting Performance in Office Buildings with Daylighting Controls. *Energy and Buildings*, 33(8):793–803, 2001.

[12] D.W.T. To, L.K. Sing, T.M. Chung, and C.S. Leung. Potential Energy Saving for a Side-lit Room Using Daylight-linked Fluorescent Lamp Installations. *Lighting Research & Technology*, 34(2):121, 2002.

[13] E.S. Lee, S.E. Selkowitz, G.D. Hughes, R.D. Clear, G. Ward, J. Mardaljevic, J. Lai, M.N. Inanici, and V. Inkarojrit. Daylighting the New York Times Headquarters Building. *Lawrence Berkeley National Laboratory, final report LBNL-57602*, 2005.

[14] J.A. Granderson. *Human-centered sensor-based Bayesian control: Increased energy efficiency and user satisfaction in commercial lighting*. PhD thesis, University of California, Berkeley, 2007.

[15] M.S. Rae. The IESNA Lighting Handbook–Reference and Application, Illuminating Society of North America, 2000.

[16] Y. Akashi and J. Neches. Detectability and Acceptability of Illuminance Reduction for Load Shedding. *Journal of the Illuminating Engineering Society of North America*, 33(1):3–13, 2004.

[17] G.R. Newsham, S. Mancini, and R.G. Marchand. Detection and Acceptance of Demand Responsive Lighting in Offices with and without Daylight. *Leukos*, 4(3):130–156, 2010.

[18] B. Plale, D. Gannon, J. Brotzge, K. Droegemeier, J. Kurose, D. McLaughlin, R. Wilhelmson, S. Graves, M. Ramamurthy, R.D. Clark, S. Yalda, D.A. Reed, E. Joseph, and V. Chandrasekar. CASA and LEAD: Adaptive Cyberinfrastructure for Real-time Multiscale Weather Forecasting. *Computer*, 39(11):56–64, 2006.

[19] T. Gneiting and A.E. Raftery. Weather Forecasting with Ensemble Methods. *Science*, 310(5746):248, 2005.

[20] N. Sharma, J. Gummeson, D. Irwin, and P. Shenoy. Cloudy Computing: Leveraging Weather Forecasts in Energy Harvesting Sensor Systems. In *SECON '10: Proceedings of the 7th Annual IEEE Communications Society Conference on Sensor Mesh and Ad Hoc Communications and Networks*, pages 1–9. IEEE, 2010.

[21] W. Ji, C. Chan, J. Loh, F. Choo, and LH Chen. Solar Radiation Prediction Using Statistical Approaches. In *ICICS '09: Proceedings of the 7th International Conference on Information, Communications and Signal Processing*, pages 1–5. IEEE, 2009.

[22] C. Bergonzini, D. Brunelli, and L. Benini. Algorithms for Harvested Energy Prediction in Batteryless Wireless Sensor Networks. In *IWASI '09: Proceedings of the 3rd International Workshop on Advances in Sensors and Interfaces*, pages 144–149. IEEE, 2009.

[23] D. Noh, L. Wang, Y. Yang, H. Le, and T. Abdelzaher. Minimum Variance Energy Allocation for a Solar-Powered Sensor System. In *DCOSS '09: Proceedings of the 5th IEEE International Conference*

on Distributed Computing in Sensor Systems, pages 44–57. Springer, 2009.

[24] K.W. Fan, Z. Zheng, and P. Sinha. Steady and Fair Rate Allocation for Rechargeable Sensors in Perpetual Sensor Networks. In *SenSys '08: Proceedings of the 6th ACM Conference on Embedded Network Sensor Systems*, pages 239–252. ACM, 2008.

[25] Lili Wang, Yong Yang, Dong Kun Noh, H.K. Le, Jie Liu, T.F. Abdelzaher, and M. Ward. AdaptSens: An Adaptive Data Collection and Storage Service for Solar-Powered Sensor Networks. In *RTSS '09: Proceedings of the 30th IEEE Real-Time Systems Symposium*, pages 303 –312, 2009.

[26] C. Moser, D. Brunelli, L. Thiele, and L. Benini. Real-time Scheduling for Energy Harvesting Sensor Nodes. *Real-Time Systems*, 37(3):233–260, 2007.

[27] C. Moser. *Power Management in Energy Harvesting Embedded Systems*. PhD thesis, ETH Zurich, 2009.

[28] A. Kansal, J. Hsu, S. Zahedi, and M.B. Srivastava. Power Management in Energy Harvesting Sensor Networks. *ACM Transactions on Embedded Computing Systems (TECS)*, 6(4):32–es, 2007.

[29] C.M. Vigorito, D. Ganesan, and A.G. Barto. Adaptive Control of Duty Cycling in Energy-harvesting Wireless Sensor Networks. In *SECON '07: Proceedings of the 4th Annual IEEE Communications Society Conference on Sensor, Mesh and Ad Hoc Communications and Networks*, pages 21–30. IEEE, 2007.

[30] H. Suehrcke and PG McCormick. A Performance Prediction Method for Solar Energy Systems. *Solar Energy*, 48(3):169–175, 1992.

[31] R. Iqdour and A. Zeroual. Prediction of daily global solar radiation using fuzzy systems. *International Journal of Sustainable Energy*, 26(1-4):19–29, 2007.

[32] V. Singhvi, A. Krause, C. Guestrin, J.H. Garrett Jr, and H.S. Matthews. Intelligent Light Control Using Sensor Networks. In *SenSys '05: Proceedings of the 3rd International Conference on Embedded Networked Sensor Systems*, pages 218–229. ACM, 2005.

[33] H. Park, J. Burke, and M.B. Srivastava. Design and Implementation of a Wireless Sensor Network for Intelligent Light Control. In *IPSN '07: Proceedings of the 6th International Conference on Information Processing in Sensor Networks*, pages 370–379. ACM, 2007.

[34] H. Park, J. Friedman, P. Gutierrez, V. Samanta, J. Burke, and M.B. Srivastava. Illumimote: Multimodal and High-Fidelity Light Sensor Module for Wireless Sensor Networks. *IEEE Sensors Journal*, 7(7):996–1003, 2007.

[35] G. Chen, M. Fojtik, D. Kim, D. Fick, J. Park, M. Seok, M.T. Chen, Z. Foo, D. Sylvester, and D. Blaauw. Millimeter-scale Nearly Perpetual Sensor System with Stacked Battery and Solar Cells. In *ISSCC '10: 2010 IEEE International Solid-State Circuits Conference Digest of Technical Papers*, pages 288–289. IEEE, 2010.

An Effective Coreset Compression Algorithm for Large Scale Sensor Networks

Dan Feldman
MIT
Computer Science and AI Lab
32 Vassar Street,
Cambridge, Massachusetts
dannyf@csail.mit.edu

Andrew Sugaya
MIT
Computer Science and AI Lab
32 Vassar Street,
Cambridge, Massachusetts
asugaya@csail.mit.edu

Daniela Rus
MIT
Computer Science and AI Lab
32 Vassar Street,
Cambridge, Massachusetts
rus@csail.mit.edu

ABSTRACT

The wide availability of networked sensors such as GPS and cameras is enabling the creation of sensor networks that generate huge amounts of data. For example, vehicular sensor networks where in-car GPS sensor probes are used to model and monitor traffic can generate on the order of gigabytes of data in real time. How can we compress streaming high-frequency data from distributed sensors? In this paper we construct *coresets* for streaming motion. The coreset of a data set is a small set which approximately represents the original data. Running queries or fitting models on the coreset will yield similar results when applied to the original data set.

We present an algorithm for computing a small coreset of a large sensor data set. Surprisingly, the size of the coreset is independent of the size of the original data set. Combining map-and-reduce techniques with our coreset yields a system capable of compressing in parallel a stream of $O(n)$ points using space and update time that is only $O(\log n)$. We provide experimental results and compare the algorithm to the popular Douglas-Peucker heuristic for compressing GPS data.

Categories and Subject Descriptors

H.3.1 [**INFORMATION STORAGE AND RETRIEVAL**]:

General Terms

Algorithms

Keywords

Linear Simplification, Streaming, Coresets, GPS, Douglas-Peucker

1. INTRODUCTION

Field-deployed sensor networks are collecting massive amounts of data in real time in applications ranging from environmental systems [17] to traffic [1] to city-scale observation systems [26]. In this paper we describe an algorithm that receives as input the data stream generated by a sensor network and produces as output a much smaller data set that approximates the original data with guaranteed bounds. The smaller data set can be used for faster, real-time processing. The results of computing on the smaller set are guaranteed to approximate the same computation on the original set within specified bounds.

We are motivated by traffic applications using vehicular sensor networks such as the network of 16,000 taxis in Singapore. Even in one hour, the GPS devices installed in the taxis in Singapore generate time-stamped GPS location triples (time, latitude, longitude) that require approximately 40MB. If we add acceleration, imaging, and status data, the amount of information is significantly larger. Yet we wish to collect and process this data in real time, in order to accurately predict city-scale congestion and traffic patterns. This data can also enable geo-location analysis, to identify the set of places visited by a particular device. But given a stream of GPS traces, how do we decide which points are critical for identifying the location of the vehicle in a human-readable way, such as "National University of Singapore" or "Starbucks"? One option is to pose a Google query for every data point. However, Google has a 2500 daily cap on queries, and running such a query for every GPS trace would be impractical.

By learning the critical points contained within the data and summarizing the data stream, we compress the original data and represent it using a much smaller set that ultimately enables much faster processing for a large set of applications.

If we store or send all the data from a given fielded sensor network, analyzing the data in real time is significantly harder. Most of the analysis tools today are based on data mining algorithms (e.g, MATLAB, Weka, SPSS, SPlus, R). They can only handle blocks of static data on the order of a few gigabytes, that fit in the internal memory (RAM). A small number of applications, for example IBM infosphere [7] and Apache Mahout [24]) support larger data sets for a few very specific model fitting heuristics, usually without quality guarantees. The user of such applications has to follow the constraints of the database and programming language used by the application. Spatiotemporal data mining ap-

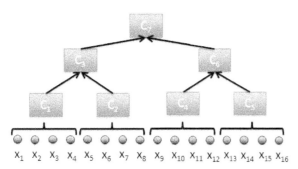

(a) *Tree for coreset construction*

Figure 1: (a) Tree construction for generating coresets in parallel or from data streams. Black arrows indicate "merge-and-reduce" operations. The (intermediate) coresets $C_1, \ldots, C_7$ are enumerated in the order in which they would be generated in the streaming case. In the parallel case, C_1, C_2, C_4 and C_5 would be constructed in parallel, followed by parallel construction of C_3 and C_6, finally resulting in C_7.

plications face storage-space problems as well as problems in efficiently accessing the motion data. For example, assuming that a GPS point takes 12 bytes and a GPS point is generated (i.e., sampled) every second for 24 hours a day, 10M cellular subscribers will generate a daily volume of over 9600 gigabytes.

Coresets.

We propose to use coresets as a way of approximating large data sets.

The existence and construction of coresets has been investigated for a number of problems in computational geometry (such as k-means and k-median) in many recent papers (cf. surveys in [13, 3]). Here we demonstrate how these techniques from computational geometry can be lifted to the realm of sensor networks. As a by-product of our analysis, we also provide a solution to the open question on the possibility of compressing GPS data.

More specifically, the input to the coreset algorithm described in this paper is a constant $\varepsilon > 0$ and a set P of n points in $\mathbb{R}^d$ (representing n signals from d sensors) that can be approximated by a k-spline or k segments. Our algorithm returns a coreset of $O(k)$ points (independent of n) such that that the Hausdorff Euclidean distance from P to any given query set of points is preserved up to an additive error of ε (Theorem 5.1 Corollary 5.2).

To our knowledge, this is the first type of compression that provides a guarantee on the approximation error for any query and not for a specific family of queries (k-points, k-lines, etc.).

Streaming and parallel computation.

One major advantage of coresets is that they can be constructed in parallel, as well as in a streaming setting where data points arrive one by one. For streaming data it is impossible to remember the entire data set due to memory constraints. The key insight is that coresets satisfy certain

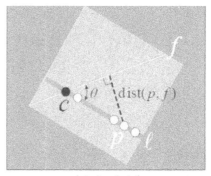

(a) $f \cap \ell \neq \emptyset$

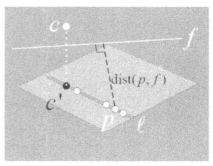

(b) $f \cap \ell = \emptyset$

Figure 2: (*left*) $\mathrm{dist}(p, f) = \sin\theta \cdot \mathrm{dist}(p, c)$, Hence, c, weighted by $\sin\theta$, replaces f for points on ℓ. (*right*) $\mathrm{dist}(p, f) = \sin\theta \cdot \mathrm{dist}(p, c)$, for any pair (ℓ, f) of lines in $\mathbb{R}^d$, where c is a point on the line that spans the shortest distance between ℓ and f, placed at distance $\mathrm{dist}(\ell, f)/\sin\theta$ from the point $c' \in \ell$, nearest to f, and θ is the angle between the (orientations of the) lines ℓ and f (a routine exercise in stereometry).

composition properties, described in Section 9 and Fig. 1(a). We use this insight to turn both existing heuristics (such as Douglas-Peucker) and our new coresets, from algorithms that assume that all data is in memory and on a single computer, into streaming algorithms that can also be run in parallel.

Experimental results and application.

We describe and analyze the coreset algorithm and evaluate it on several real data sets. We also show that coresets can be used to geo-locate vehicular networks efficiently. Using the GPS data streams from in-car networked devices (e.g. smart phones or customized sensor network probes), we demonstrate a sensor data processing application that generates a readable textual description (known as reverse geociting) for the node's current position using traffic landmarks retrieved from Google maps, e.g. "Elm street", "NUS", "Starbucks", etc.

This GPS-to-text service enables automatic logging and reporting. Databasing the output allows new types of text queries, searches, and data mining algorithms that were unsuitable for the original raw GPS points.

2. OUR TECHNIQUE

The most related technique to the coreset construction in this paper is the coreset for the k-line center by Agarwal et al. [4]. In the k-line center the input is a set of points P in $\mathbb{R}^d$ and the output is a set S^* of k-lines that minimizes the maximum distance $D(P, S^*)$ between every point in P to its closest line in S^*. Agarwal et al. proved that there is a (core)set $C \subseteq P$ of size $|C| = 2^{O(kd)}/\varepsilon^d$ such that $D(C, S) \geq (1 - \varepsilon)D(P, S)$ for every (query) set S of k-lines. An approximation to the k-line center of P can then be obtained by computing the k-line center of the small set C. However, they did not suggest an efficient construction for this coreset. This is essentially the same problem that we encounter in the simple construction of Section 4.3. Still, they provide an algorithm that takes time $O(n \log(n) \cdot |C|)$ and computes a $(1 + \varepsilon)$ approximation to the k-line center of P. The fact that a small coreset C exists was used only in the analysis.

Similarly to the inefficient construction of [4], our algorithm first projects P onto a few segments, and then scans the projected points from left to right. However, we were able to construct the coreset efficiently using bi-criteria approximation (Section 4.1). It is straightforward to plug our bi-criteria technique to the second part of the paper of Agarwal and obtain the first efficient ($O(n)$ time) construction of coresets for k-lines. In particular, this coreset yields an improved algorithm for computing a $(1 + \varepsilon)$ multiplicative approximation for the k-line center in only $O(n)$ time.

Unlike the case of our paper that deals with k-segments and k-splines, the Hausdorff distance between a point and a line is infinite; see Definition 2. Also, when k-lines queries are replaced by k-segments queries, there is no similar coreset C as described above; see [16]. Instead, we use a small additive error in the definition of our coreset (Definition 4.1). This also allows the coreset to approximate every query (and not just k-lines or k-segments queries).

Another difference between our coresets and coresets for k-lines (as in [4]) is that there is a lower bound of 2^k for coresets that provides a $(1 + \varepsilon)$ approximation for distances to any k-lines [16]. This bound is impractical for our applications, where usually $k > 100$. However, we were able to construct coresets of size *linear* in k for our problem, using the same relaxation of ε-additive error that was described above.

Our construction uses the fact that, after projecting a set of points on a line ℓ, every query line f can be replaced by a weighted point c; see Fig. 2. While this is trivial for lines on the plane (the case $d = 2$, Fig. 2(a)), it is less intuitive for the case $d \geq 3$ (Fig. 2(b)). We use the fact that when the angle between the two lines f and ℓ is $\theta = \varepsilon$, then the distance from every point $p \in \ell$ to f is similar to the (unweighted) distance to some fixed point $c \in \mathbb{R}^d$, up to a multiplicative factor of $O(\varepsilon)$.

One of the unique advantages of our coreset is its provable ability to handle streaming and parallel data. To this end, we had to use a different approach than those used by existing algorithms. For example, if P is a set of points on a single segment, existing algorithms will usually choose only the two endpoints of the segment (e.g. [2]). While this makes sense for static input, when new points are added to P, the distribution of the original points on the segment might be necessary for sub-dividing the segment, or merging it with a new one. Indeed, our algorithm adds such representatives to the output coreset, even if they are all lying on the same line.

Our contribution.

Our coreset is significantly different from previous compression techniques. (i) It guarantees both a threshold ε *and* a small coreset size that depends on ε; (ii) the construction is more involved, and based on global optimization, rather than on local relations between input points; and (iii) our coreset C is a set of points, not segments. In fact, the first step of our coreset construction computes a set of only $O(k/\varepsilon)$ segments that are provably close to P (See Lemma 4.2), but the final coreset C is a subset of P. This allows us to replace P with C while using existing algorithms that accept points as input, as in the database techniques above. For example, a road map can be used together with C in order to compute the final segments or trajectory that will approximate P. This problem of compressing the data in a way that will allow us to handle constraints such as road-maps was suggested as an open problem in [8].

To our knowledge, our coresets are the first that support the merge-and-reduce model with bounds on both error and space. In particular, we didn't find other parallel (distributed) computing algorithms for compressing trajectories with similar bounds.

Open problems addressed in this paper.

Abam et al. recently stated [2] that an obvious question is whether we can have a streaming algorithm that can approximate S using exactly k-segments (and not $\beta = 2k$ as in [2]). We answer this question in the affirmative by computing the optimal k-spline of our streaming coreset; see Section 8. In [2] it is also stated that the authors couldn't apply the merge-and-reduce technique on their coreset. They suggest the open problem of constructing such a coreset, which we answer in the affirmative in this paper.

Streaming heuristics such as Douglas-Peucker Heuristic (DPH), unlike [2], do not assume monotone/convex input, and provide bounds either on the running time or on the approximation error ε. Streaming simplification is considered a "challenging issue" and "important topic of future work" [8]. Our coreset provides the first bound on both the error and the update time/space simultaneously.

Abam et al. provided the first provable linear simplification streaming $\alpha = O(1)$-approximation algorithm, under the monotone/convex assumption, using $O(k^2)$ space. They suggested a second open problem for reducing this (sometimes impractical) size to $O(k)$, and the possibility of compression using the merge-and-reduce technique. Indeed, our coresets are of size $O(k)$ for every constant $\alpha = \varepsilon > 0$. They are suitable for the merge-and-reduce technique. In addition, our coresets yield the first algorithm that supports parallel (distributed) computing for line simplification. Other compressions that use the merge-and-reduce technique fail either in the merge or the reduce part of the method.

In [8] it was suggested to investigate the issues that arise when the uncertainty of the location technology (e.g. GPS) is combined with the ε-error due to the simplification. Indeed, the error of our coreset depends on ε, but also on the additional parameter k that corresponds to the optimal linear k-simplification of the input path. Unlike with existing heuristics that require the adjustment of the error parameter during the streaming, since our error depends on the current optimal solution, there is no need to adjust it.

3. K-SPLINE CENTER

Let P be a set of points in $\mathbb{R}^d$, where $d \geq 1$ is constant and every point $p \in P$ is of the form $p = (x_1, \cdots, x_{d-1}, t)$. The first coordinates $(x_1, \cdots, x_{d-1})$ represent outputs (real numbers) from $d-1$ sensors at time t. We denote the last coordinates of a point $p = (x_1, \cdots, x_{d-1}, x_d)$ by $p(t) := x_d$.

We call a set $S \subseteq \mathbb{R}^d$ a *k-spline* if it is the union of k segments $\overline{s_0 s_1}, \overline{s_1 s_2}, \ldots, \overline{s_{k-1} s_k}$ for some $s_0, \cdots, s_k \in \mathbb{R}^d$, where $s_0(t) < \cdots < s_k(t)$. The segment $\overline{s_{i-1} s_i}$ is called the *ith segment* of S, for $i \in \{1, \ldots, k\}$. See Fig. 3(a).

The *regression distance* $\mathrm{dist}_R(\{p\}, S)$ between a point $p \in \mathbb{R}^d$ and a k-spline S is the Euclidean distance between p and S along the last coordinate axis, i.e,

$$\mathrm{dist}_R(\{p\}, S) := \begin{cases} \|p - s\| & \text{if } \exists s \in S \text{ s.t. } p(t) = s(t) \\ \infty & \text{otherwise,} \end{cases}.$$

where $\|\cdot\|$ denotes the Euclidean norm. The regression distance between a set $P \subseteq \mathbb{R}^d$ and a k-spline S is the maximum regression distance between a point in P to S, i.e,

$$\mathrm{dist}_R(P, S) := \max_{p \in P} \mathrm{dist}_R(\{p\}, S).$$

A *k-spline center* $S^* = S^*(P, k)$ of P is a k-spline that minimizes the regression distance to P among all the possible k-splines in $\mathbb{R}^d$:

$$\min_S \mathrm{dist}_R(P, S) = \mathrm{dist}_R(P, S^*). \tag{1}$$

See Fig. 3(b).

The k-spline $\tilde{S} = \tilde{S}(P, k)$ is an *ε-rotation* of a k-spline center, if there is a k-spline center S^* of P such that, for every $i \in \{1, \cdots, k\}$, the ith segment of $\tilde{S}$ is a rotation of the ith segment of S^* by an angle ε around some point $s_i \in S_i$. See Fig. 3(c).

4. ε-CORESETS

4.1 Overview of construction

Let P be a set of points in $\mathbb{R}^d$ for some constant integer $d \geq 1$ and let $\varepsilon > 0$. In Section 4.3 we prove that a small ε-coreset C exists for P under the assumption that it can be approximated by an ε-rotation of its k-line center S^* for some integer $k \geq 1$. See Fig 4 for a sketch of the final coreset construction. See Fig 5 for example run on a real set of 5000 GPS points.

The set C is computed by first constructing a dense set T of $O(k/\varepsilon)$ segments around every one of the k segments in S^*. Then, we project every point of P onto its nearest segment in T. We prove that the resulting set C' (which contains n points) has a small Hausdorff distance to P. Since C' is contained in T, we can now scan the projected points on each segment t of T from left to right and select a representative point from every ε^2-fraction of t. The union of representatives is denoted by C''. Note that every point $p'' \in C''$ is a projection of some point $p \in P$ on T. Our output ε-coreset C is the union of points in P whose projection is in C''. We prove that for every such input set P, the resulting set C is a small ε-coreset with size independent of n.

The above construction is inefficient, since we assume that the optimal k-spline S^* was already computed. In Section 5 we will replace this assumption by a rough and fast approximation to S^*, called (α, β) or bi-criteria approximation.

4.2 Necessary assumptions

We define $\mathrm{dist}_H(A, B)$ as the Hausdorff Euclidean distance between a pair of sets $A, B \subseteq \mathbb{R}^d$:

$$\mathrm{dist}_H(A, B) :=$$
$$\max \left\{ \max_{p \in P} \min_{p' \in C} \|p - p'\|, \max_{p' \in C} \min_{p \in P} \|p' - p\| \right\}. \tag{2}$$

DEFINITION 4.1 (ε-CORESET). *An ε-coreset for P is a set $C \subseteq P$ such that*

$$\mathrm{dist}_H(P, C) \leq \varepsilon.$$

By scaling the points of P, we can see that in general an ε-coreset for P must contain all the points of P. Hence, we will add the assumption that P is not an arbitrary set of points, because it can be roughly approximated by its k-spline center for some $k \geq 1$.

Formally, let $S^* = S^*(P, k)$ denote a k-spline center of P. We assume that

$$\mathrm{dist}_R(P, S^*) \leq c \tag{3}$$

for some constant $c \in (0, \infty)$ (that is independent of n). Hence, it suffices to prove that

$$\mathrm{dist}_H(P, C) \leq \varepsilon \cdot \mathrm{dist}_R(P, S^*) \tag{4}$$

to conclude that C is an $c\varepsilon$-coreset. By applying the construction with ε/c instead of ε we obtain an ε-coreset.

Using assumption (3) we compute in the next section a set C (denoted by C') that satisfies (4). The resulting ε-coreset C' is still large (of size $n = |P|$), but is contained in only $O(k/\varepsilon)$ segments. Unfortunately, it is impossible to compute a *small* ε-coreset C', even if (3) holds for a small constant c. For example, if P is a set of points on a line, then $\mathrm{dist}_H(P, S^*(P, k)) = 0$ and we must have $C' = P$. Therefore, we replace $S^*(P, k)$ with its ε-rotation $\tilde{S} = \tilde{S}(P, k)$ in our assumption (3); see Section 3 for definition of $\tilde{S}$. Using the new assumption and the fact that C' is contained in a few segments we prove in Theorem 5.1 and Corollary 5.2 that we can always compute a small ε-coreset C for P in $O(n)$ time.

4.3 Inefficient Construction Algorithm

Let P be a sequence of n points in $\mathbb{R}^d$, $\varepsilon > 0$ and $k \geq 1$. In order to clarify the algorithm and its analysis, we first prove that a small ε-coreset C exists. For a point $p \in P$, and a segment S_i of a k-spline S, we say that S_i serves p if there is $s \in S_i$ such that $p(t) = s(t)$. That is, the last coordinates of s and p are identical. For a set $Y \subseteq \mathbb{R}^d$, we define $\mathrm{dist}(p, Y) = \min_{y \in Y} \|p - y\|$, and for a set $X \subseteq \mathbb{R}^d$ we define $\mathrm{dist}(X, Y) = \min_{x \in X} \mathrm{dist}(x, Y)$. For simplicity, we first describe the construction when P is a set of points on the plane (i.e., $d = 2$).

Step 1: Constructing C'.
Let $S^* = S^*(P, k)$ denote a k-spline center of P. Although we don't know how to compute S^*, such an optimum exists. Fix a segment S_i of S^*, and let P_i denote the points of P that are served by S_i. Let T_i denote an ε-grid of segments

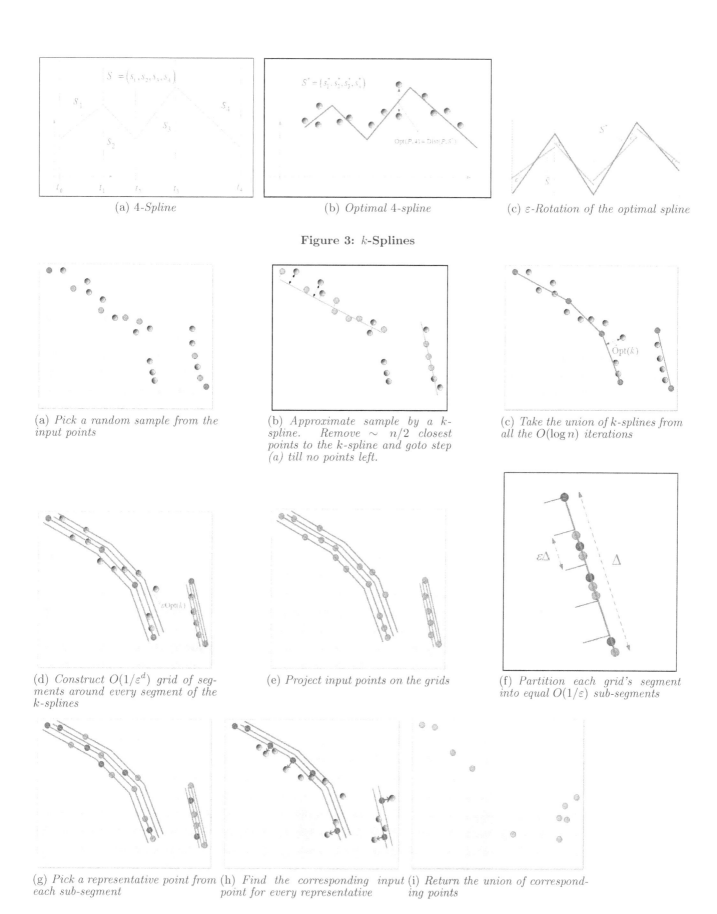

(a) 4-Spline   (b) Optimal 4-spline   (c) ε-Rotation of the optimal spline

Figure 3: k-Splines

(a) Pick a random sample from the input points

(b) Approximate sample by a k-spline. Remove $\sim n/2$ closest points to the k-spline and goto step (a) till no points left.

(c) Take the union of k-splines from all the $O(\log n)$ iterations

(d) Construct $O(1/\varepsilon^d)$ grid of segments around every segment of the k-splines

(e) Project input points on the grids

(f) Partition each grid's segment into equal $O(1/\varepsilon)$ sub-segments

(g) Pick a representative point from each sub-segment

(h) Find the corresponding input point for every representative

(i) Return the union of corresponding points

Figure 4: Algorithm for constructing ε-coreset that approximates every k-spline.

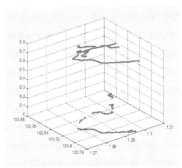

(a) *Input:* $n = 5000$ *points.*

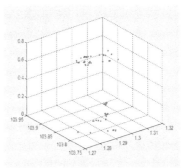

(b) *Pick a random sample of* $10k = 100$ *points.*

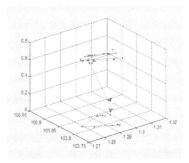

(c) *Compute optimal* $k = 10$ *spline for sample*

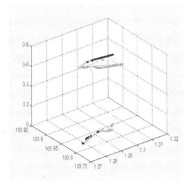

(d) *Compute distances from the* n *input points to the spline. Here, different colors mean different clusters.*

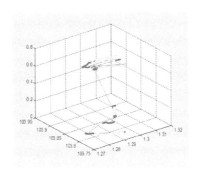

(e) *Remove closest* $n/2$ *points to spline.*

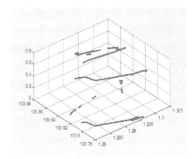

(f) *Repeat from step (b) on remaining* $n/2$ *points, until* $n < 10k$

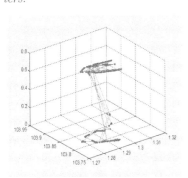

(g) *Take the union of 50 segments that were computed in Step (c) on all 5 iterations .*

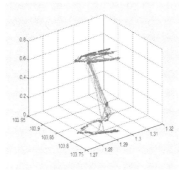

(h) *Extend to 80 segments that are parallel to the 50 segments*

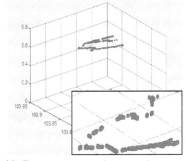

(i) *Project every point onto its nearest segment*

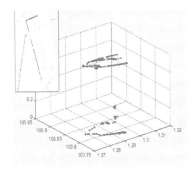

(j) *Pick 5 points from each segment*

(k) *Output corresponding input points*

Figure 5: Example coreset construction C **for** $n = 5000$ **input points, and any** $k = 10$ **spline, where** $|C| = 300.$

around S_i. More formally, T_i is the union of $\lceil 2/\varepsilon \rceil$ parallel segments, each of length $|S_i| + \text{dist}(P, S^*)$, such that the distance from a point $p \in P$ to its closest segment t in T_i is ε than its distance to S_i:

$$\text{dist}(p, T_i) \leq \varepsilon \text{dist}(p, S_i). \tag{5}$$

Let p' be the projection of $p \in P_i$ onto its closest segment in T_i. Let $C_i' = \{p' \mid p \in P\}$ be the union of these points, $T = \bigcup_{1 \leq i \leq k} T_i$ and $C' = \bigcup_{1 \leq i \leq k} C_i$

Step 2: Constructing C.

Let $t \subseteq T_i$ denote one of the segments of T_i that was constructed in Step 1, that contains at least one point from C', i.e., $C' \cap t \neq \emptyset$. Let p_L', p_R' denote the leftmost and rightmost points from C' on t, respectively. Partition the segment $\overline{p_L', p_R'} \subseteq t$, into $r = \lceil 10/\varepsilon \rceil$ equal sub-segments $t_1, \cdots, t_r$. For every such sub-segment t_j, $1 \leq j \leq r$ that contains at least one point from C', pick a single point $p_j' \in C' \cap t_j$. We call p_j' the *representative* of every $p' \in C' \cap t_j$. Let $C_t' = \{p_j' \mid 1 \leq j \leq r, t_j \cap C' \neq \emptyset\}$ be the union of these representatives on t. Let $C'' = \bigcup_t C_t'$ where the union is over all the segments of T. Recall that every point $p' \in C'' \subseteq C'$ is the projection of some $p \in P$ on t. Let $C = \{p \in P \mid p' \in C''\}$ be the final output set of the construction.

LEMMA 4.2. *Let P be a set of points in $\mathbb{R}^d$, $k \geq 1$ and $\varepsilon \in (0,1)$. There is a set C' that is contained in $O(k/\varepsilon)$ segments such that*

$$\text{dist}_H(P, C') \leq \varepsilon \text{dist}_R(P, S^*(P, k)).$$

PROOF. We use the construction in the beginning of this section and its notation. Let $C_i = C' \cap P_i$ for every i, $1 \leq i \leq k$. We have

$$\text{dist}_H(P, C') \leq \max_{1 \leq i \leq k} \text{dist}_H(P_i, C_i)$$

Put i, $1 \leq i \leq k$. Then

$$\text{dist}_H(P_i, C_i)$$
$$\leq \max \left\{ \max_{p \in P_i} \min_{q \in C_i} \|p - q\|, \max_{q \in C_i} \min_{p \in P} \|q - p\| \right\}$$
$$\leq \max \left\{ \max_{p \in P_i} \|p - p'\|, \max_{p' \in C_i} \|p' - p\| \right\}$$
$$\leq \max_{p \in P_i} \|p - p'\|.$$

Let $p \in P_i$. By (5),

$$\|p - p'\| = \text{dist}(p, T_i) \leq \varepsilon \text{dist}(p, S_i)$$
$$\leq \varepsilon \max_{p \in P_i} \text{dist}(p, S_i) \tag{6}$$
$$\leq \varepsilon \text{dist}_R(P_i, S_i) \leq \varepsilon \text{dist}_R(P, S^*).$$

Combining the last inequalities yields

$$\text{dist}_H(P, C') \leq \max_{1 \leq i \leq k} \text{dist}_H(P_i, C_i)$$
$$\leq \max_{1 \leq i \leq k} \max_{p \in P_i} \|p - p'\|$$
$$\leq \varepsilon \text{dist}_R(P, S^*).$$

Since $C' \subseteq T$, the last inequality proves the lemma. $\square$

LEMMA 4.3. *Let P be a set of points in $\mathbb{R}^d$, $k \geq 1$ and $\varepsilon > 0$. There is a set $C \subseteq P$ of size $|C| = O(k/\varepsilon^3)$ such that*

$$\text{dist}_H(P, C) \leq \varepsilon \text{dist}_R(P, \tilde{S}(P, k)).$$

PROOF. We use the construction and notation from the beginning of this section, and prove that

$$\text{dist}_H(P, C) \leq 10\varepsilon \text{dist}_R(P, \tilde{S}(P, k)) \tag{7}$$

By replacing ε with $\varepsilon/10$ in the construction, this would prove the lemma.

Using the triangle inequality,

$$\text{dist}_H(P, C) \leq$$
$$\text{dist}_H(P, C') + \text{dist}_H(C', C'') + \text{dist}_H(C'', C).$$

By (6) and the definition of S^*,

$$\text{dist}_H(P, C') + \text{dist}_H(C'', C) \leq 2 \max_{p \in P} \|p - p'\|$$
$$\leq 2\varepsilon \text{dist}_R(P, S^*)$$
$$\leq 2\varepsilon \text{dist}_R(P, \tilde{S}).$$

For every $p' \in C'$ let p'' denote its representative in C'' (as defined in the construction of C''). Hence,

$$\text{dist}_H(C', C'')$$
$$= \max \left\{ \max_{q' \in C'} \min_{q'' \in C''} \|q' - q''\|, \max_{q'' \in C''} \min_{q' \in C'} \|q'' - q\| \right\}$$
$$\leq \max_{p' \in C'} \|p' - p''\|.$$

Combining the last three inequalities yields

$$\text{dist}_H(P, C) \leq 2\varepsilon \text{dist}_R(P, \tilde{S}) + \max_{p' \in C'} \|p' - p''\|. \tag{8}$$

Next, we compute a bound for $\|p - p''\|$.

Let $p \in P$. Suppose that $p' \in C'$ is the projection of p on the segment $t \subseteq T_i$. Let P_L' and P_R' denote, respectively, the leftmost and rightmost point of $C' \cap t$. By construction,

$$\|p' - p''\| \leq \varepsilon^2 \|p_R' - p_L'\|. \tag{9}$$

We now bound $\|p_R' - p_L'\|$.

Recall that every segment of T_i, including t, is parallel to S_i. Let $\tilde{S}_i$ denote the corresponding ε-rotation of S_i in $\tilde{S}$. Let ℓ_i denote the line on the plane that contains $\tilde{S}_i$. Let ℓ denote the line that contains t. Let x denote the intersection point between ℓ and ℓ_i. The farthest point from x in $C' \cap t$ is either P_R' or P_L'. Hence,

$$\|p_R' - p_L'\| \leq \|P_L' - x\| + \|x - P_R'\|$$
$$\leq 2 \max \{\|P_L' - x\|, \|P_R' - x\|\} \tag{10}$$
$$\leq 2 \max_{q' \in C'} \|q' - x\|.$$

We denote by $\theta(\ell')$ the sinus of the angle between ℓ and a given line ℓ'. Hence, $\theta(\ell_i) = \sin(\varepsilon) \geq 2\varepsilon/\pi \geq \varepsilon/2$. Since $p' \in \ell$, we thus have

$$\text{dist}(p', \ell_i) = \sin(\theta(\ell_i)) \|p' - x\| \geq \frac{\varepsilon}{2} \|p' - x\|.$$

That is,

$$\|p' - x\| \leq 2 \text{dist}(p', \ell_i)/\varepsilon. \tag{11}$$

Since $\tilde{S}_i \subseteq \ell_i$, we have

$$\text{dist}(p', \ell_i) \leq \text{dist}(p', \tilde{S}_i) \leq \|p' - p\| + \text{dist}(p, \tilde{S}_i)$$
$$\leq \text{dist}_H(P, C') + \text{dist}_R(P, \tilde{S}).$$

By Lemma 4.2, $\text{dist}_H(P, C') \leq \varepsilon \text{dist}_R(P, S^*)$. By the assumption $\varepsilon < 1$ and the definition of S^*, the last inequality implies $\operatorname{dist}_H(P, C') \le \operatorname{dist}_R(P, \tilde{S})$. Combining the last inequalities with (11) yields

$$\begin{aligned}
\|p' - x\| &\le 2\operatorname{dist}(p', \ell_i)/\varepsilon \\
&\le \frac{2}{\varepsilon}\left(\operatorname{dist}_H(P, C') + \operatorname{dist}_R(P, \tilde{S})\right) \\
&\le \frac{4\operatorname{dist}_R(P, \tilde{S})}{\varepsilon}.
\end{aligned}$$

By plugging the last inequality in (9) and (10), we obtain

$$\begin{aligned}
\|p' - p''\| &\le \varepsilon^2 \|p'_R - p'_L\| \\
&\le 2\varepsilon^2 \max_{q' \in C'} \|q' - x\| \\
&\le 8\varepsilon\operatorname{dist}_R(P, \tilde{S}).
\end{aligned}$$

By (8), this proves (7) as

$$\begin{aligned}
\operatorname{dist}_H(P, C) &\le 2\varepsilon\operatorname{dist}_R(P, \tilde{S}) + \max_{p' \in C'} \|p' - p''\| \\
&\le 10\varepsilon\operatorname{dist}_R(P, \tilde{S}).
\end{aligned}$$

$\square$

5. EFFICIENT CONSTRUCTION

The above construction is inefficient since it assumes that we already computed a k-spline center S^* of P, which we don't know how to do in time near-linear in n. In Section 5, we prove that C can be constructed efficiently (in $O(n)$ time). The k-spline S^* can be replaced in our construction by a rough approximation S called bi-criteria approximation or (α, β)-approximation for S^*. The distance from P to S is larger by a multiplicative constant factor α than its distance to S^*. Still, we couldn't find any algorithm in literature that computes such a constant factor approximation for P in near-linear time. Hence, we add a relaxation that S can contain $\beta = O(k \log n)$ segments instead of k segments. We use random projections to obtain a simple algorithm that computes such an (α, β)-approximation S for the k-line center of P in $O(n)$ time as follows.

First, we pick a small uniform random sample Q of $O(k/\varepsilon)$ points from P. Next, we compute the k-spline center $S^*(Q, k)$ of the small set Q using an existing inefficient optimal algorithm for spline approximation, and remove from P the $|P|/2$ points that are closest to $S^*(Q, k)$. We then repeat this algorithm recursively until P is empty. The output of the algorithm is the union of the computed k-splines.

The algorithm runs using at most $O(\log n)$ iterations, and thus outputs $O(\log n)$ k-splines. This is straightforward from PAC-learning theory, and the technique is also popular for sensor networks applications [15]. The size of the final coreset is $O(\log n)$. In order to have a coreset of size independent of n, we compute a k-spline approximation S on our existing coresets, and repeat the construction with S instead of using the $O(\log n)$ splines from the bi-criteria approximation. De-randomization and straightforward generalization for other distance functions can be obtained using the framework of [13] with our observations.

THEOREM 5.1. *Let P be a set of n points in $\mathbb{R}^d$. Let $\varepsilon \in (0, 1)$ and $k \ge 1$. Then a set $C \subseteq P$ of size $|C| = O(k/\varepsilon^3)$ can be constructed in $O(n)$ time, such that*

$$\operatorname{dist}_H(P, C) \le \varepsilon\operatorname{dist}_R(P, \tilde{S}(P, k)).$$

COROLLARY 5.2. *Let P be a set of n points in $\mathbb{R}^d$. Let $\varepsilon \in (0, 1)$ be a constant and $k \ge 1$ be an integer. If $\operatorname{dist}_R(P, \tilde{S}(P, k)) \in O(1)$ then an ε-coreset C for P can be computed in $O(n)$ time. That is,*

$$\operatorname{dist}_H(P, C) \le \varepsilon.$$

PROOF. Since $\operatorname{dist}_R(P, \tilde{S}(P, k)) \le c$ for some constant $c = O(1)$, we can replace ε with ε/c in Theorem 5.1 to obtain

$$\operatorname{dist}_H(P, C) \le (\varepsilon/c)\operatorname{dist}_R(P, \tilde{S}(P, k)) \le \varepsilon.$$

$\square$

6. EXPERIMENT AND RESULTS

The data. We tested the practical compression ratio of our coreset construction by implementing it and running experiments using a public dataset of GPS traces [25]. This dataset contains mobility traces of taxi cabs in San Francisco, USA. It contains GPS coordinates of 500 taxis collected over 30 days in the San Francisco Bay Area.

The experiment. We applied the following procedure independently to every trace in the data set. The input set P was partitioned into two parts containing 10,000 traces each. We applied our coresets construction on each part to obtain two coresets of approximately 200 points. We then merged the two coresets and compressed the new set (of size 400) again, as shown in Fig 1(a). On the resulting coreset of 200 points, we then applied DPH with $k = 100$ (i.e, DPH approximates the coreset using 100 points, or 100-spline) to get a k-spline ($k = 100$) S_C which approximates the original set.

We then repeated the experiment, using DPH itself as the compression algorithm, as was done in [8]. That is, we partitioned the original 20k into two sets and applied DPH independently on every set using $k = 200$. We then applied DPH on the merged set of 400 points using $k = 200$. On the resulting set D of 200 points, we applied DPH using $k = 100$ to get a k-spline S_D.

The results. We computed the Hausdorff error between the original set P and the k-spline S_C that was obtained from our coreset. Similarly, we computed the error between P and the k-spline S_D that was constructed on the DPH-compressed set. The results for 20 such experiments on each taxi-cab are shown on Fig 6, where the y-axis is the error. Additional points would result in more merges that increase the comparison gap exponentially with the levels of the tree in Fig. 1(a).

The implementation. We implemented our algorithm in MATLAB [21]. We also used the official implementation of MATLAB for the DPH algorithm. DPH uses as input parameter the maximum allowed error ε instead of the number of desired segments k. We overcame this problem by applying binary search on the value of ε until DPH returned k lines.

For the bi-criteria approximation during the coreset construction, we used a random sample of 5 points, and connected them by a 5-spline S. We then removed half of the closest input points to S recursively as explained in Section 5 .We used 5 additional segments for the ε-grid around every segment of S. Sampling more input points and using a more involved algorithm for computing S, as in Section 5, will likely improve the result. We are in the process of testing this hypothesis. In addition, since we did not try to

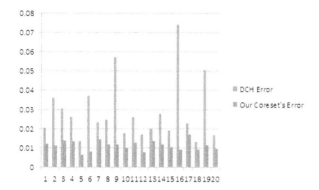

Figure 6: Comparison of experiments on traces of 500 taxi-cabs over a month. The y-axis is the Hausdorff distance from the original set to the k-spline approximation that was constructed on the compression. The x-axis is a sample of the first 20 taxi-cabs that had at least 20000 GPS traces.

configure the parameters of the construction to obtain better results, another direction of our current work is to tune the parameters.

7. DISCUSSION IN THE CONTEXT OF RELATED WORK

The challenge of compressing trajectories semantically (also known as "line simplification") has been tackled from various perspectives: geographic information systems [11], databases, [10], digital image analysis [20], computational geometry [5], and especially in the context of sensor networks [6]. The input to this problem is a sequence P of n points that describes coordinates of a path over time. The output is a set Q of k points (usually subset of P) that approximates P. More precisely, the k-spline S that is obtained by connecting every two consecutive points in Q via a segment should be close to P according to some distance function. The set Q is sometimes called a coreset [2] since it is a small set that approximates P. However, our definition of coreset for this problem is significantly different (see Definition 4.1) and more similar to its original definition in computational geometry [3].

Several books have been written about the line simplification problem [14]. Yet, it seems that every discipline improves the solution with respect to some parameters, but deteriorates others. Our coreset was inspired by several previous techniques, aiming to formalize the trade-offs and suggest a unified solution that enjoys the good benefits of all previous ones.

Simple heuristics.

The oldest heuristic [8] for line simplification is the Douglas-Peucker heuristic (DPH) [11]. DPH gets an input threshold $\varepsilon > 0$ and returns a set Q that represents a k-spline S as defined above. DPH guarantees that the Euclidean distance from every $p \in P$ to S is at most ε. This is also the attractiveness of DPH, compared to other lossy data compression techniques such as wavelets [9]. DPH is very simple, easy to implement, and has a very good running time in practice [8]. The guaranteed ε-error allows us to merge two compressed

sets Q_1 and Q_2 in the streaming model, while keeping the ε-error for $Q_1 \cup Q_2$.

We compared our experimental results to DPH not only because it is popular, but also because it "achieves near-optimal savings at a far superior performance" [8].

While DPH has a guaranteed ε-error, it suffers from serious space problems due to its local (ad-hoc, greedy) optimization technique. In particular, the size k of its output is unbounded, and might be arbitrarily larger than the smallest set $Q \subseteq P$ that obtained such an ε-error. While merging two sets preserves the error, it is not clear how to reduce the merged set again. The size of the compressed output will increase linearly with the input stream. Choosing a larger ε will result in too small or empty set Q for the first compressions. The worst case running time for the basic (and practical) implementation is $O(n^2)$. More modern versions of the DPH ([23]) appear to have similar pros and cons.

Approximation Algorithms.

Provable approximation algorithms from theoretical computer science and computational geometry seem to have opposite properties. They are based on much more involved global optimization algorithms with theoretical worst-case guarantees on the running time, error, and space. This is also their main disadvantage: the papers (at least in our context) usually do not contain experimental results (e.g. [2]), and it is not clear that an efficient implementation is possible due to problems such as numerical stability and hidden constants in the $O()$ notation. Few exceptions are recently available [12]. We run a popular heuristic (Douglas-Peucker) against itself, by simply running the heuristic once on P and once on C. Surprisingly, the running time improves and the approximation error is *reduced* on the representative set C as compared to the original P. This might be due to noise removal as a side effect of the coreset construction. In addition, since C is significantly smaller than P, we can apply the heuristic many more times, using different initial parameters, during a single competitive run on P. Overall, this technique combines provable guarantees with practical heuristics.

The optimal algorithm for simplifying $2d$-polygonal chain runs in $O(n^2)$ time for any Euclidean metrics and $O(n^{4/3+\delta})$ for L_1 and L_∞ metrics [5]. Sophisticated variations of DPH can be implemented in $O(n \log n)$ time [18] and even $O(n \log^* n)$ time [19]. Still, we couldn't find implementations for these algorithms, and DPH seems to have much more popularity and better running time in practice [8].

Abam, de Berg, Hachenberger and Zarei [2] recently suggested the provable construction of a coreset C for P under the streaming model. The set C is of size $O(k^2)$ and allows us to compute an $\alpha = O(1)$ ($\alpha > 2$) multiplicative-approximation to the optimal k-spline S of P using β-spline, where $\beta = 2k$. In our paper such an approximation is also used in the coreset construction and is called (α, β)-approximation; (see Section 4.1). The algorithms are non-trivial, interesting and followed by deep computational geometry proofs. However, this result holds *only if* S is xy-monotone or a convex linear function [2]. This assumption on S is unlikely to hold in many situations. The $O(k^2)$ space might also be infeasible for large values of k. While C can be computed in the streaming model, it cannot be computed in parallel.

Results that are similar or improve upon the results of

Abam et al. can be obtained using our coreset as follows. The first step of our construction projects P onto $O(k/\varepsilon)$ segments with a provable small ε-error. The maximum distance from a point on a segment to a monotone path will be obtained by either the leftmost or rightmost point on the segment. Hence, selecting these two points from P in each segment to the coreset C suffices to approximate every monotone function. Since there are $O(k/\varepsilon)$ segments, the resulting coreset will be of size $O(k)$. Similarly, our coreset approximates convex paths (using simple observation from [16]). Unlike the coreset of Abam et al., our coreset also supports the parallel computation model.

Database techniques.

Popular database servers, such as MySQL, support spatial queries (such as: nearest road or station to a given trajectory). Unlike the previous two approaches, here we are interested in a data structure for compressing P that will be used to answer general queries, rather than just to compute a line simplification S for P. Our coreset (Definition 4.1) is inspired by this approach and different from all previous coresets: it guarantees that every input point in P has an ε-close representative in the coreset C. Using the triangle inequality, the error for *every* query set is bounded by ε, regardless of the specific type of query (k-points, k-segments, etc.).

The lack of locality in trajectories makes their compression harder than other databases (that represent more static data such as house locations or ages). Indeed, there are small coresets for $(1 + \varepsilon)$ multiplicative approximation of P by k points for several distance functions [4], while there are lower bounds of 2^k for the size of such compression for k lines [16]. Unlike the case of points, covering P by k-lines is NP-hard [22] and bounding the complexity of the Voronoi diagram of k-lines is one of the main open problems in geometry.

Our coreset construction cannot be described as partitioning the space into simple shapes or cells and taking a single representative from each cell. The first step of our coreset construction *projects* the points onto *linear* objects, rather then compressing them. We prove that for a set of points projected onto the same segment, the distance to a given query segment or line can be represented as a distance to a point; see Fig 2. This observation allows us (in the second step) to partition *the segments* into cells and cluster the points on them, as in the database techniques.

8. APPLICATIONS

A small ε-coreset C for P can help us reduce the space and running time of many applications in the field of sensor networks.

Database queries.

Our coreset is a new type of compression that guarantees a small additive error for general types of queries, which makes it suitable for answering SQL or GIS spatial queries on the reduced coreset C as suggested in [10].

Suppose, for example, we require the nearest input point to a query curve that represents a road, or to a query point that represents a bus station. The property $\mathrm{dist}_H(P, C) \leq \varepsilon$ of the coreset guarantee that every point in P has a close representative point in C. After computing the coreset C

we can delete the original set P, and still be able to answer unbounded number of queries in $O(1)$ time using C. We give the following corollary.

COROLLARY 8.1. *Let P be a set of points. Suppose that C is an ε-coreset for P that was constructed using Theorem 5.1 for some constants $k \geq 1$ and $\varepsilon > 0$. Then, for every subset $Q \subset \mathbb{R}^d$, we have*

$$0 \leq \mathrm{dist}_H(P, Q) - \mathrm{dist}_H(C, Q) \leq \varepsilon.$$

Moreover, $\mathrm{dist}_H(C, Q)$ can be computed in $O(1)$ time, if this is the time it takes to compute the distance from a single point $p \in P$ to Q.

PROOF. Since $C \subseteq P$ by Theorem 5.1, we have $\mathrm{dist}_H(P, Q) - \mathrm{dist}_H(C, Q) \geq 0$. Since the Hausdorff distance is a metric, it satisfies symmetry and the triangle inequality. Hence,

$$\mathrm{dist}_H(P, Q) \leq \mathrm{dist}_H(P, C) + \mathrm{dist}_H(C, Q)$$
$$\leq \varepsilon + \mathrm{dist}_H(C, Q) = \mathrm{dist}_H(Q, C) + \varepsilon,$$

where in the second deviation we used Theorem 5.1. Therefore $\mathrm{dist}_H(P, Q) - \mathrm{dist}_H(C, Q) \leq \varepsilon$.

The time it takes to compute $\mathrm{dist}_H(C, Q)$ is $|C| \cdot t$ where t is the time it takes to compute $\mathrm{dist}_H(\{p\}, Q)$ for a single point $p \in C \subseteq P$. By Theorem 5.1, we have $|C| = O(k/\varepsilon^3) = O(1)$. For $t = 1$ we obtain $t \cdot |C| = O(1)$. $\square$

$(1 + \varepsilon)$ Approximations.

In a vehicular network application, we may have a series of GPS points representing a vehicle traveling between several destinations. Instead of using all n GPS points on its path to represent the path, we would like to create the k-spline center in order to compress the data. The k-spline center $S^*(P, k)$ of a set P of n points is a set of k connected segments that approximates P. The set $S^*(P, k)$ is also called the line simplification of P; See Section 3 for formal definitions. The time it takes to compute $S^*(P, k)$ is near-quadratic in n [5] and impractical [8]. Instead of trying to improve this kind of optimization algorithms, we can apply the (possibly inefficient) algorithm on the small coreset C to get its k-spline center $S^*(C, k)$ in $O(1)$ time. In particular, if $\mathrm{dist}_H(P, S^*(P, k)) \in O(1)$ then $S^*(C, k)$ is a $(1 + \varepsilon)$ multiplicative approximation for the k-spline center *of the original set P* as proved in the following corollary.

COROLLARY 8.2. *Let P be a set of n points, and $k \geq 1$ be a constant integer. Let $S^* = S^*(P, k)$ be the k-spline center of P. Let C be an ε-coreset of P for some constant $\varepsilon > 0$. Then a k-spline S' can be computed in $O(1)$ time such that:*

(i)

$$\mathrm{dist}_H(P, S') \leq \varepsilon + \mathrm{dist}_H(P, S^*).$$

(ii) If $\mathrm{dist}_H(P, S^*) \geq 1$ then

$$\mathrm{dist}_H(P, S') \leq (1 + \varepsilon)\mathrm{dist}_H(P, S^*).$$

PROOF. *(i)* The k-line center $S' = S^*(C, k)$ of C can be computed in $O(|C|^3) = O(1)$ time using the algorithm in [5]. By the triangle inequality and the definition of S',

$$\mathrm{dist}_H(P, S') \leq \mathrm{dist}_H(P, C) + \mathrm{dist}_H(C, S')$$
$$\leq \mathrm{dist}_H(P, C) + \mathrm{dist}_H(C, S^*)$$

Since C is an ε-coreset of P, we have $\mathrm{dist}_H(P, C) \leq \varepsilon$. Together with the previous inequality this proves Claim(i).

(ii) straightforward from (i). $\square$

9. STREAMING AND PARALLEL COMPUTATION

In this section we show that our (static, off-line) coreset scheme suffices to solve the corresponding problem in parallel and distributed computing, and in a streaming setting where data points arrive one by one and remembering the entire data set is futile due to memory constraints. We use a map-and-reduce technique (popular today as "Google's map-and-reduce"). The key insight is that coresets satisfy certain composition properties. Similar properties have previously been used by [13] for streaming and parallel construction of coresets for geometric clustering problems such as k-median and k-means. We extend these results for Hausdorff distances as follows.

OBSERVATION 9.1.

(i) Suppose that C_1 is an ε-coreset for P_1, and C_2 is a ε-coreset for P_2. Then $C_1 \cup C_2$ is an ε-coreset for $P_1 \cup P_2$.

(ii) Suppose C is an ε-coreset for P, and D is an ε-coreset for C. Then D is a 2ε-coreset for P.

PROOF.　(i) $\operatorname{dist}_H(C_1 \cup C_2, P_1 \cup P_2)$
$$\leq \max\{\operatorname{dist}_H(C_1, P_1), \operatorname{dist}_H(C_2, P_2)\}$$
$$\leq \max\{\varepsilon, \varepsilon\} = \varepsilon.$$

(ii) $\operatorname{dist}_H(D, P) \leq \operatorname{dist}_H(D, C) + \operatorname{dist}_H(C, P)$
$$\leq 2\varepsilon.$$

□

In the following, we review how to exploit these properties for streaming and parallel computation.

Streaming.

In the streaming setting, we wish to maintain a coreset over time, while keeping only a small subset of $O(\log n)$ coresets in memory (each of small size). The idea is to construct and save in memory a coreset for every block of consecutive points arriving in a stream.

When we have two coresets in memory, we can merge them (resulting in an ε-coreset via property (i)) and compress them by computing a single coreset from the merged coresets (via property (ii)) to avoid an increase in the coreset size.

Parallel computation.

Using the same ideas from the streaming model, a nonparallel coreset construction can be transformed into a parallel one. We partition the data into sets, and compute coresets for each set, independently, on different processors in a cluster (sensors, computer networks, cloud services, etc). We then (in parallel) merge (via property (i)) two coresets, and compute a single coreset for every pair of such coresets (via property (ii)). Continuing in this manner yields a process that takes $O(\log n)$ iterations of parallel computation. Fig. 1(a) illustrates this parallel construction.

GPU computation.

GPUs are installed today on most desktop computers and recently on smart phones (such as the Nexus One and iPhone). The GPU is essentially a set of dozens or hundreds of processors that are able to make parallel computations. However, the model of computation is very restrictive. In particular, non trivial linear algebra computations suffer from significant numerical problems. Our algorithm suggests a new paradigm to deal with such problems by computing the coreset on the GPU and using the CPU to compute the desired result on the coreset. As we explained in Section 5, most of the construction time of the coreset is spent on matrix multiplication (computing distances from points to segments) that can be computed on the GPU. Also, division operations (that usually cause the numerical problems) are applied by optimization algorithms only on the CPU.

10. CONCLUSION

In this paper we presented an algorithm for compressing the large data sets generated by sensor networks via coresets. Given a constant $\epsilon > 0$ and a set P of n points representing signals from sensors, our ϵ-coreset algorithm returns $O(k)$ points (independent of n) such that the Hausdorff Euclidean distance from P to any given query set of points is preserved up to an additive error of ϵ. Our compression algorithm departs from previous results by guaranteeing the approximation error for any query as compared to previous works that guarantee the solution quality only for subclasses of queries. Because our coreset algorithm is parallelizable, it can be used in off-line mode for historical data collected and databased, as well as in on-line mode for streamed data from sensors. To demonstrate the effectiveness of this coreset algorithm, we showed data from an experiment with GPS data collected from a vehicular network of taxis. We showed that the practical compression ratio of our coreset construction outperforms the Douglas-Peucker algorithm.

Our current results provide a theoretical step for enabling off-line and on-line computation on large-scale sensor networks. Much work remains to be done in order to provide practical solutions to in-network and off-line processing of large data sets. We are currently integrating our algorithms with sensor networks deployed in the field. This is a significant engineering challenge, which is important to undertake in order to close the loop from theory to practical applications. We are undertaking a more extensive experimental evaluation of this algorithm using data from a roving vehicular network of 15000 taxis, we are developing the georeferencing applications that take advantage of the potential benefits of our solution in this paper.

11. ACKNOWLEDGEMENT

Fig 1(a) was drawn by Andreas Krause and is taken from [**?**]. This research was supported in part by the Foxconn Company and the Future Urban Mobility project of the Singapore-MIT Alliance for Research and Technology (SMART) Center, with funding from Singapore's National Research Foundation. We are grateful for it.

12. REFERENCES

[1] Mobile millennium. Technical report.

[2] M.A. Abam, M. de Berg, P. Hachenberger, and A. Zarei. Streaming algorithms for line simplification. *Discrete and Computational Geometry*, 43(3):497–515, 2010.

[3] P. K. Agarwal, S. Har-Peled, and K. R. Varadarajan. Geometric approximations via coresets. *Combinatorial*

and *Computational Geometry - MSRI Publications*, 52:1–30, 2005.

[4] P. K. Agarwal, C. M. Procopiuc, and K. R. Varadarajan. Approximation algorithms for k-line center. In *Proc. 10th Ann. European Symp. on Algorithms (ESA)*, volume 2461 of *Lecture Notes in Computer Science*, pages 54–63. Springer, 2002.

[5] P.K. Agarwal and K.R. Varadarajan. Efficient algorithms for approximating polygonal chains. *Discrete & Computational Geometry*, 23(2):273–291, 2000.

[6] J. Aslam, Z. Butler, F. Constantin, V. Crespi, G. Cybenko, and D. Rus. Tracking a moving object with a binary sensor network. In *Proceedings of the 1st international conference on Embedded networked sensor systems*, pages 150–161. ACM, 2003.

[7] A. Biem, E. Bouillet, H. Feng, A. Ranganathan, A. Riabov, O. Verscheure, H. Koutsopoulos, and C. Moran. Ibm infosphere streams for scalable, real-time, intelligent transportation services. In *Proceedings of the 2010 international conference on Management of data*, pages 1093–1104. ACM, 2010.

[8] H. Cao, O. Wolfson, and G. Trajcevski. Spatio-temporal data reduction with deterministic error bounds. *The Very Large Databases (VLDB) Journal*, 15(3):211–228, 2006.

[9] K. Chakrabarti, M. Garofalakis, R. Rastogi, and K. Shim. Approximate query processing using wavelets. *The VLDB Journal*, 10(2):199–223, 2001.

[10] P. Cudre-Mauroux, E. Wu, and S. Madden. Trajstore: An adaptive storage system for very large trajectory data sets. In *Data Engineering (ICDE), 2010 IEEE 26th International Conference on*, pages 109–120. IEEE.

[11] D.H. Douglas and T.K. Peucker. Algorithms for the reduction of the number of points required to represent a digitized line or its caricature. *Cartographica: The International Journal for Geographic Information and Geovisualization*, 10(2):112–122, 1973.

[12] M. Feigin, D. Feldman, and Nir Sochen. From high definition image to low space optimization. In *Proc. 3rd Inter. Conf. on Scale Space and Variational Methods in Computer Vision (SSVM 2011)*, 2011.

[13] D. Feldman and M. Langberg. A unified framework for approximating and clustering data. In *Proc. 41th Ann. ACM Symp. on Theory of Computing (STOC)*, 2011.

[14] L. Forlizzi, R.H. Güting, E. Nardelli, and M. Schneider. *A data model and data structures for moving objects databases*, volume 29. ACM, 2000.

[15] S. Gandhi, S. Suri, and E. Welzl. Catching elephants with mice: sparse sampling for monitoring sensor networks. *ACM Transactions on Sensor Networks (TOSN)*, 6(1):1, 2009.

[16] S. Har-Peled. Coresets for discrete integration and clustering. *FSTTCS 2006: Foundations of Software Technology and Theoretical Computer Science*, pages 33–44, 2006.

[17] J.K. Hart and K. Martinez. Environmental sensor networks: A revolution in the earth system science? *Earth-Science Reviews*, 78(3-4):177–191, 2006.

[18] J. Hershberger and J. Snoeyink. An o (n log n) implementation of the douglas-peucker algorithm for line simplification. In *Proceedings of the tenth annual symposium on Computational geometry*, pages 383–384. ACM, 1994.

[19] J. Hershberger and J. Snoeyink. Cartographic line simplification and polygon csg formulé in o (n log* n) time. *Computational Geometry*, 11(3-4):175–185, 1998.

[20] J.D. Hobby. Polygonal approximations that minimize the number of inflections. In *Proceedings of the fourth annual ACM-SIAM Symposium on Discrete algorithms*, pages 93–102. Society for Industrial and Applied Mathematics, 1993.

[21] U. Matlab. The mathworks. *Inc., Natick, MA*, 1992, 1760.

[22] N. Meggido and A. Tamir. Finding least-distance lines. *SIAM J. on Algebric and Discrete Methods*, 4:207–211, 1983.

[23] N. Meratnia and R.A. By. Spatiotemporal compression techniques for moving point objects. *Advances in Database Technology-EDBT 2004*, pages 561–562, 2004.

[24] S. Owen, R. Anil, T. Dunning, and E. Friedman. Mahout in action. *Online*, pages 1–90, 2011.

[25] Michal Piorkowski, Natasa Sarafijanovic-Djukic, and Matthias Grossglauser. CRAWDAD data set epfl/mobility (v. 2009-02-24). Downloaded from http://crawdad.cs.dartmouth.edu/epfl/mobility, February 2009.

[26] S. Reddy, M. Mun, J. Burke, D. Estrin, M. Hansen, and M. Srivastava. Using mobile phones to determine transportation modes. *ACM Transactions on Sensor Networks (TOSN)*, 6(2):13, 2010.

mPuff: Automated Detection of Cigarette Smoking Puffs from Respiration Measurements

Amin Ahsan Ali, Syed Monowar Hossain, Karen Hovsepian, Md. Mahbubur Rahman,
Kurt Plarre, Santosh Kumar
Dept. of Computer Science, University of Memphis, TN 38152, USA
{aaali, smhssain, kshvspan, mmrahman, kplarre, skumar4}@memphis.edu

ABSTRACT

Smoking has been conclusively proved to be the leading cause of mortality that accounts for one in five deaths in the United States. Extensive research is conducted on developing effective smoking cessation programs. Most smoking cessation programs achieve low success rate because they are unable to intervene at the right moment. Identification of high-risk situations that may lead an abstinent smoker to relapse involve discovering the associations among various contexts that precede a smoking session or a smoking lapse. In the absence of an automated method, detection of smoking events still relies on subject self-report that is prone to failure to report and involves subject burden. Automated detection of smoking events in the natural environment can revolutionize smoking research and lead to effective intervention.

In this paper, we present *mPuff*, a novel system to automatically detect smoking puffs from respiration measurements, using which a model can be developed to automatically detect entire smoking episodes in the field. We introduce several new features from respiration that can help classify individual respiration cycles into smoking puffs or non-puffs. We then propose supervised and semi-supervised support vector models to detect smoking puffs. We train our models on data collected from 10 daily smokers and find that smoking puffs can be detected with an accuracy of 91% within a smoking session. We then consider respiration measurements during confounding events such as stress, speaking, and walking, and show that our model can still identify smoking puffs with an accuracy of 86.7%. The smoking detector presented here opens the opportunity to develop effective interventions that can be delivered on a mobile phone when and where smoking urges may occur, thereby improving the abysmal low rate of success in smoking cessation.

Categories and Subject Descriptors

J.4 [**Computer Applications**]: Social and Behavioral Sciences

General Terms

Design, Experimentation, Measurement, Human Factors

Keywords

Smoking Detection, Wearable Sensors, Respiration

1. INTRODUCTION

Since the first US Surgeon General's report in 1964 there has been overwhelming and conclusive evidence that use of tobacco, especially in the form of cigarette smoking, causes cancer in different organs throughout the body, leads to cardiovascular and respiratory diseases, and harms reproduction [3]. Smoking induced diseases account for nearly one of every five deaths in the United States [24]. Smokers die 13-14 years younger and cost $193 billion annually [1]. In addition, almost 60% of children are still exposed to secondhand smoking which is also a known human carcinogen. To reduce such harmful effects of smoking, there needs to be substantial progress in tobacco control, health education programs, and development of interventions to aid smoking cessation.

Given the adverse impact of smoking on human health, significant research is conducted on development of smoking interventions. Eight (out of 27) divisions at National Institutes of Health (NIH) award research grants for smoking cessation. Of these, National Cancer Institute (NCI) alone awards $100+ million annually in smoking research. Despite extensive efforts, smoking continues to be prevalent. Seventy percent of adult smokers want to quit completely, while 40% try to quit each year - but most quit efforts end in relapse [7]. Each day about 3,000 people become new daily smokers[5].

Most smoking cessation programs achieve low success rate (i.e., less than 10%) because they are unable to intervene at the right moment. Smokers who are trying to quit need to avoid high-risk situations and if they get into a high-risk situation, need an intervention to break their urge. Given the ubiquity of smart phones, such a smoking cessation assistant app can be developed for smart phones that intervenes if a quitter is found to be in a high-risk situation. The challenge, however, is to automatically identify when the quitter is in a high-risk situation. Considerable amount of research work is focused on identifying the factors (called

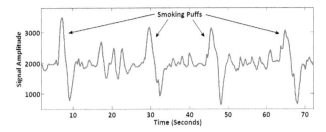

Figure 1: Respiration signals captured during a typical smoking episode.

antecedents) that lead to high-risk situations (and, eventually relapse) to design effective interventions [30, 11, 23] .

Identifying antecedents and precipitants of smoking lapse (i.e., an acute condition such as stress that causes a lapse) requires conducting scientific user studies in the natural environment so as to observe the psychological, social, and environmental factors that may be associated with smoking instances [19, 15, 18, 21, 27, 32, 31]. This is done by observing and recording the user's context when smoking occurs for daily smokers or when a smoking lapse occurs in those trying to quit [28]. These studies must have some mechanism of detecting when smoking occurs, so that physical, physiological, psychological, behavioral, social, and environmental contexts before, during, and after a smoking session can be identified. Most current studies on smoking behavior rely on various self-reporting techniques, where subjects are asked to self-report each smoking episode. These methods range from basic pen-paper methods and retrospective recalls, to electronic diary keeping and ecological momentary assessments(EMA) [29, 28, 20, 9]. These methods, in addition to imposing a burden on the study participants, have the limitation of introducing biases when recalling events, forgetting to report, among several others.

Technological methods to detect smoking episodes include carbon monoxide (CO) monitors such as piCO$^+$, CReSS Pocket[8], Micro$^+$[4], RespiTrace$^®$[13], and image processing [34]. As discussed in more detail in Section 2, each of these methods require manual intervention by subjects or an observer. To the best of our knowledge, there does not exist a method to automatically detect smoking events in real-time, in the natural environment, that is operator independent.

In this paper, we take the first step towards automatically detecting smoking in the natural environment by developing *mPuff*, a model to automatically detect smoking puffs from respiration measurements. mPuff uses respiration measurements collected from a respiration band that the user wears underneath their clothing. Detection of smoking puffs from respiration is feasible because they are associated with deep inhalation and deep exhalation (see Figure 1 for an example). It should be noted that a puff lasts only for one respiration cycle. Thus in order to detect puffs we need to find appropriate features that can help discriminate a smoking puff not only from usual respiration cycles, but also from those respiration cycles that may represent speaking, stress, or physical activity such as walking.

A smoking puff tends to lengthen the duration of a respiration cycle relative to its neighboring cycles. It also amplifies the degree of inhalation and exhalation (i.e., both

directions on *y*-axis) as compared to the usual level of peak and valley, as well as that compared to the neighboring cycles. We build on these insights to identify 12 new features in respiration measurements that together with 5 previously known features are used in mPuff to detect smoking puffs. A majority of these features are not person specific as they measure relative changes of some basic characteristics of the respiration cycles. For those features that depend on absolute values such as inspiration duration, we normalize it by computing the *z*-score of the feature values using the person-specific mean and standard deviation, thus accounting for the between-person differences. Therefore, mPuff self-calibrates to each person and does not need to be trained on a person prior to its usage.

In order to develop the mPuff model from the above mentioned features, we use support vector machine (SVM) that is trained over the respiration features. Given that various smoking researchers may need different sensitivities to false positive and false negative rate, the model we use can be customized for a target false positive or false negative rate. Given imperfection in automated models, the smoking research studies may continue collecting self-reports. These self reports, however, may not always be located before the start of a smoking session. They in some cases may be located during or after a smoking session. We propose a semi-supervised support vector model that improves the accuracy of detecting smoking puffs by making use of the self-report markings. Our model can potentially be used as a building block to develop a full-fledged smoking detector that can identify those smoking episodes that may not have received a self-report marking.

To train mPuff, we collected respiration data during smoking from 10 volunteer daily smokers. During the collection of labeled data, we carefully marked each puff in a smoking session. To ensure generalizability of our model, we also used data sets from major confounding events, e.g., physical activity, conversation, and stress, that may cause similar patterns in respiration as smoking puffs. All these data sets constitute the training and testing data sets of the supervised SVM. These data sets are supplemented by collection of respiration data from 4 volunteers (out of the original 10 volunteers) who wore the sensors for 7 continuous days in their natural environment and self-marked smoking episodes. Together with the labeled data, this data set is used for the training of the semi-supervised model. For additional generalizability of our models, we divided the data set into training and test set, where 10-fold cross-validation was conducted on the training set, but the test set was reserved purely for testing.

Results: We find that smoking puffs can be detected with an accuracy of 91% within a smoking session. When applying the model to confounding events, we obtain an accuracy of 84.5% for the supervised SVM model, which improves to 86.7% by using a semi-supervised model that is able to use a much larger data set from the field. We also find that the accuracy of the classifier increases by more than 10% by using the newly proposed features. We applied mPuff to our data set to observe patterns of smoking behavior. We find that the average duration of a smoking session is 6.62 minutes, a smoking session contains an average of 12 puffs, among several other interesting statistics.

Future Applications: Our model opens the opportunity for automated detection of smoking episodes in the natural environment. Since respiration measurements can be used to detect stress [25] as well, which has been found to be a leading predictor of smoking relapse, smoking research can potentially be revolutionized. It has been found that stress levels of abstinent smokers who relapsed rises hours before a lapse [30]. Now, it can be found out what happens in the minutes preceding a smoking lapse. Since several other contexts such as location, commuting, physical activity, and social interactions can also be detected on a smart phone, rich contextual analysis can be conducted to find true predictors of smoking lapses. Such analysis can then be used to design effective interventions which can be delivered on a mobile phone, when and where smoking urges may occur.

Organization of the paper: Section 3 describes the AutoSense sensor suite and the data sets we use for the development and evaluation of the mPuff puff detector. In section 4, we present the features used to train mPuff. We also describe the supervised and semi-supervised SVM models we use for puff and non-puff detection. Section 5 describes the performance of the classifiers and the effect of new features on improving the accuracy of classification. Section 6 describes the smoking topology statistics that we obtain by applying mPuff to our data sets. Section 7 presents some challenges in developing a model for detecting an entire smoking episode. It describes potential directions for research that leverage the patterns of conversation in the natural environment. We also propose a method for computing the confidence in detecting a smoking episode. Finally, section 8 concludes the paper.

2. RELATED WORKS

We discuss related works in two categories. We discuss technological methods to detect smoking and their shortcomings in Section 2.1. In Section 2.2, we discuss existing methods to analyze respiration measurements to make inferences of human states and point out why these methods are insufficient to detect smoking puffs from respiration.

2.1 Technological Methods to Detect Smoking

Technological methods to detect smoking episodes include carbon monoxide (CO) monitors such as piCO$^+$, CReSS Pocket [8], Micro$^+$ [4], RespiTrace$^®$ [13], and image processing [34]. piCO$^+$ and Micro$^+$ are handheld devices designed for use as motivational aid in smoking cessation programs. They display the amount of smoke inhalation and carbon monoxide levels in a single breath exhaled, measured through a mouthpiece attached to the devices. They also calculate and display the percentage of carboxyhaemoglobin in the blood, thereby providing visual motivation for the smoker to stop smoking. These device are, however, not intended to be used for automatically detecting smoking in an operator independent fashion.

CReSS Pocket/CReSS Micro [8] is a portable device that can be used to acquire the smoking behavioral information in the smoker's natural environment over weeks as they store the data on the device's memory. The subject is asked to insert a cigarette into a holder of CReSS and smoke through a mouthpiece attached to the device. The device then is able to compute several measures of smoking behavior including puffs per cigarette, puff volume, and puff duration and also the timestamps of cigarette insertion and removal. All this data can be downloaded later to a computer. Although CReSS has been used in some studies outside of the

laboratory settings, it has been mostly in studies by tobacco companies to establish brand differences [22, 17, 33] by observing the smoking pattern and the degree of tobacco intake. For example, it was observed that with light cigarettes, smokers take more frequent puffs in order to inhale the same amount of tobacco as in a heavy cigarette [17], negating the purpose of making lighter cigarettes. CReSS requires subject's compliance since each time they smoke, they need to smoke through CReSS. Furthermore, it may be embarrassing for the subjects to use it in the natural environment, since the device on their mouth will be visible to others in the vicinity.

Respitrace$^®$ is a newer device that uses a respiration sensor, such as RespiBand Plus, that measures the chest's expansion as the wearer breathes in and out. The timing of each puff is marked manually by an observer who presses a push button switch when the subject places the cigarette on lips. Authors in [13] make use of these measurements to analyze post-puff breathing patterns in smoking. The use of Respitrace$^®$ has been restricted to lab settings to study smoking patterns since it requires manual marking of each puff.

If the place of smoking is under the coverage of a video camera, then movement of hands and presence of cigarette in the mouth can be detected by image processing to automatically detect smoking [34]. Use of this method, however, requires installment of video cameras in all locations where a subject may smoke. Alternatively, the subject may be asked to have a portable video camera (e.g., on a smart phone) pointed to them before they smoke, which again requires the involvement of subject each time they smoke.

In summary, each of the above technological methods require subject compliance and hence are not suited for widespread usage in smoking research. Therefore, smoking researchers continue to rely on self-report method today. The prospect of having a method such as mPuff that enables the development of models that can automatically detect all smoking episodes in the field from an unobtrusively wearable respiration sensor measurement excites the entire smoking research community given its potential to revolutionize smoking research.

2.2 Analytical Methods to Infer Human States from Respiration

There have been several recent works on detecting various human states from respiration measurements. In [25], respiration measurements are processed to infer physiological and perceived stress. Various features such as inhalation duration, exhalation duration, minute ventilation, and respiration rate are computed from each minute of respiration measurements. Machine learning models are then trained over these features to infer whether the subject is stressed. In [26], features used in [25] are supplemented with some new features such as B-Duration, computed from 30 seconds of respiration measurements to detect if the subject is speaking, listening, or quiet. These states are then composed together in a Hidden Markov Model (HMM) to identify conversation episodes.

While some features identified in the above works can help in detecting smoking puffs, the features and models used in these and other works are not directly applicable to detecting puffs. First, robust statistics such as mean and median of various features are used in the detection of stress and conversation since there are several respiration cycles in 30 seconds or 1 minute. For smoking, each puff needs to be identified reliably. Second, there is a pattern of transitions among the speaking, listening, and quiet states that can be leveraged in an HMM to detect conversation episodes, such patterns are not observable in a smoking session. Third, the timing or number of respiration cycles between successive smoking puffs can vary widely among different subjects, and among different smoking session for the same subject, for instance, when smoking in a group or when smoking alone during work hours.

Fourth, the accuracy of detecting a smoking puff may need to be customizable for various use cases. A study on observing smoking behavior may want good accuracy for detecting an entire smoking session, whereas another study on abstinent smokers may want to detect individual puffs, at the cost of a higher false positive rate, since even a single puff can lead to a full relapse. The first puff in such scenarios constitutes the moment of lapse (also called first lapse) and is the main event which is used in the analysis for identifying antecedents and precipitants of smoking relapse. It is critical to be able to obtain the timing of the first lapse, and the entire subject data may need to be removed if the first lapse is not detected [28]. False positives may be acceptable, especially, if the analysis is to be done post-facto, where the goal is to be able to pinpoint the timing of relapse. Each puff may be presented to the subject to identify the one that may correspond to the actual first lapse. None of the above works present a way to customize the model to a given rate of false positive or false negative.

Fifth, none of the above works use a semi-supervised model to use the data collected from the field to improve the accuracy of the model. In a smoking research study, subjects are usually asked to mark each smoking episode in the field. These marks, however, may be before, during, or after the smoking episode. Some smoking episodes may have no marks at all. Hence, the marks provide a label for smoking episodes, but these labels are a noisy source. We develop a semi-supervised approach to make use of these noisy labels to improve the accuracy of our model. In summary, the requirements for the development of mPuff are more stringent than other works on detecting psychological and behavioral states from respiration measurements and hence require a new approach to model development.

3. DATA COLLECTION

In this section, we describe the AutoSense sensor suite we used to capture respiration measurements and the data collection procedure for collecting respiration measurements for developing, training, and testing the mPuff model.

3.1 The AutoSense Sensor Suite

We use the Autosense sensor suite [16] that includes a Respiratory Inductive Plethysmograph (RIP) band to measure relative lung volume and breathing rate. AutoSense also includes ECG, galvanic skin response and 3-axis accelerometer sensors, but only respiration measurements are used in this work. The sampling rate of RIP is 21.3 samples/sec. RIP uses a conductive thread that is sewn in a zigzag fashion to the elastic band. An alternating current source is applied to the resulting loop of wire, which, in turn, generates a magnetic field that opposes the current whose strength is proportional to the area enclosed by the wire according to

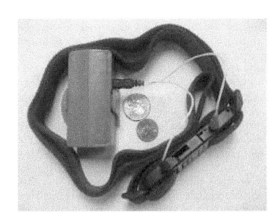

Figure 2: Respiratory Inductive Plethysmograph band (in blue color) is worn around the chest area and the wearable AutoSense sensor unit clips to the belt. A 3-axis Acceloerometer, ECG, and Galvanic Skin Response sensors are also included in the same sensor unit. Two coins (a quarter and a penny) are also shown in the picture to indicate the form factor.

Lenz's law. The ratio of the magnetic flux to the current is called self-inductance. Therefore, changes to the chest circumference can be measured by measuring the changes to the self inductance of the band. The inductance measurement purely depends on the geometry of the band and is not related to the tension in the band. As a result, the measurement is not prone to the trapping of the band and associated artifacts due to changes in tension. The sensors transmit data to an Android mobile phone in real-time over a low-power wireless link. We use the FieldStream mobile phone software available in [2]. Using the FieldStream software, we obtained the raw data files collected in the phone.

3.2 Data Collection for Model Development

To develop a model for smoking detection, we collected data from 10 volunteer participants over 13 individual smoking sessions. Each participant was a daily smoker. They wore the RIP sensor of the Autosense suite in their natural environment and were accompanied by an observer. The observer marked each puff the participant took by pressing a button on the mobile phone that also received the respiration measurements via wireless channel. The timing of the button press was saved. Marking the puff times on the same phone that received the measurements reduced the time lapse between the markings and sample timestamps. In order to get a more precise marking, the data from smoking session was visualized with the markings. The markings of puffs were then adjusted to match each puff, which is visually distinctive due to deep inhalation and exhalation associated with a puff.

Out of the 10 participants, 4 participants wore the sensor suite for 7 days in their natural environment during their awake hours. They were asked to self-report the each time they smoked a cigarette. We modified the interface of data collection software (FieldStream framework) on the phone to facilitate self reporting. Though the participants were asked to mark the smoking sessions as they light up a cigarette, we do not expect that the self reported times exactly corresponds to the beginning of the sessions; they can be anywhere (before, during, or after) in the vicinity of the smoking episode. Visual inspection confirmed this hypothesis. In total, we have 136 self-reports of smoking from these 4 participants.

3.3 Data Sets for Model Evaluation

We expect a smoking session to be confused with acute stress, conversation, and physical activity, since they all affect respiration measurements in a similar pattern as smoking. We call these events confounding events. In order to evaluate the model's performance on different confounding events, we use the data collected in our previous user studies [25, 26]. Both of these studies also made use of the AutoSense sensor suite. The first data set is from a study on 21 participants who were exposed to three real-life stressors (e.g. public speaking, mental arithmetic, and cold pressor tasks) in a lab setting [25]; successive stress periods were separated by rest periods. The second data set consists of conversation episodes from 12 participants. The start/end of each conversation episode as well as the start and end of speaking and listening periods in the conversation episode was marked. Total amount of data collected for this set is around 46 hours [26]. In both of these studies, the participants were suggested to behave naturally and not instructed in anyway that would confine their movement or posture. In addition to these two data sets, we also collected data from 5 participants that captured different levels of physical activities ranging from running and walking to sitting quietly. This data set consists of 1 hour worth of data.

4. PUFF IDENTIFICATION

In this section, we describe the development of the mPuff model that classifies each respiration cycle into *smoking puffs* and *non-puffs*. We first run a peak-valley detection algorithm to find the peaks and valleys in each respiration cycle. We use the peak-valley detection method proposed in [26]. Once peaks and valleys are located, features of interest can be computed to use in a classification algorithm. In Section 4.1, we describe the features we identify for use in puff detection. We then describe (in Section 4.2) the development of a supervised classifier that uses labeled data to detect smoking puffs. This model can be configured for prescribed target false positive or false negative rate. We next describe (in Section 4.3) a semi-supervised model that uses self-report labels obtained from field data to improve the accuracy of puff detection.

4.1 Features

Other works that use respiration measurements to infer human states such as [25, 26] make inferences on time windows that are 30 seconds or longer. Hence, these works are able to compute statistics over multiple respiration cycles making them robust to noise and outliers. In contrast, in this work, we need to make accurate decision at the level of an individual cycle since a smoking puff lasts only one respiration cycle. This makes the task of identifying appropriate features more challenging.

We identify 17 distinct features that are computed from the respiration signal. We identify 5 features from existing work and propose 12 new features. The new features are selected through visual inspection of data collected during smoking and other non-smoking episodes such as physical activity, stress and conversation. Computation of the

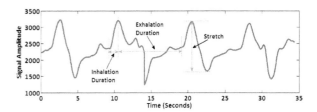

Figure 3: Illustration of three features extracted from respiration cycles.

features involves the identification of the respiration cycles, which are composed of an inhalation and an exhalation period. We now define all features in the following and illustrate three of them in Figure 3.

Existing Features. We first describe five features that have previously been proposed for identifying stress and conversation events from respiration [25, 26]. **Inhalation Duration** corresponds to the time elapsed from a valley of a respiration cycle, to the subsequent peak. The amplitude difference in signal values between these points is the maximum expansion of the chest during a respiration cycle (see Figure 3). **Exhalation Duration** corresponds to the time duration between a peak and the subsequent valley in a respiration cycle. **IE Ratio** is defined as the ratio of inhalation duration to the exhalation duration in a respiration cycle. **Respiration Duration** is the sum of inhalation and exhalation duration. **Stretch** is defined to be the difference between the maximum (legitimate) amplitude, and the minimum (legitimate) amplitude the signal attains within a respiration cycle (see Figure 3). These features have been shown to be effective in identification of stress and conversation from respiration [25, 26]. As we show in Section 5, using these features provides an accuracy of 73.55%, which improves to 86.7% once the new features described below are added.

New Features. Figure 4 shows the respiration patterns during smoking and three confounding events (stress, conversation and running). We observe that features such as stretch and expiration duration are distinct during a respiration cycle containing a puff as compared to respiration cycles in speaking, stress, or activity, and hence have discriminatory power. We further observe that the relative change in stretch and exhalation duration from one respiration cycle to the neighboring cycles are higher when there is a puff involved during smoking. On the other hand, we do not see such magnitude of change during running or conversation events. This is because it is quite unusual to take two consecutive puffs without taking any breaths in between. We define the first difference feature and ratio features in order to capture these information concerning relative change.

We also observe that during a puff, the respiration signals stretch in both upward (called *Upper Stretch*) and downward directions (called *Lower Stretch*), extending the peak amplitude and reducing the valley amplitude respectively, as compared to usual respiration cycles. This suggests that the measurement of relative change in the upper and lower stretch as compared to the running mean of the valley in

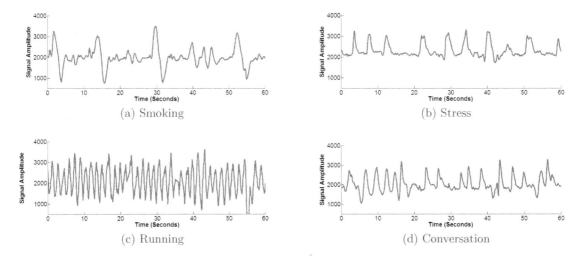

(a) Smoking	(b) Stress
(c) Running	(d) Conversation

Figure 4: The four figures above show the respiration signal during smoking and three confounding events. We observe that the stretch of a respiration cycle is higher during running and puffs, as compared to speaking and stress. We further observe that unlike during running events, during smoking sessions, the non-puff cycles around the puff do not have as high of a stretch. This simple visual inspection suggests the use of change in stretch relative to its neighboring cycles in discriminating puffs from conversation, stress, and running events. Similar observations can be made for other new features such as relative change in exhalation duration, and upper and lower stretch as described in Section 4.1.

respiration cycles, can further improve the accuracy of identifying smoking puffs. We now describe the 12 new features.

- **Forward and Backward First Differences** of a feature is derived by computing the first order differences of the feature values from their previous and next feature values respectively. We compute these first order differences for inhalation, exhalation and respiration durations and stretch and use them as features. Altogether, this procedure creates a total of eight new features.

- **Stretch Ratio** of a particular cycle c, is defined as the ratio of its stretch to the average stretch value in a window of five cycles, with the window centered on Cycle c. When computing the average, we exclude Cycle c. We use a window of five cycles because we never see successive puffs occurring in a window of five cycles, if the window is centered on a puff cycle.

- **Exhalation Ratio** of a particular cycle is similarly computed from the average exhalation duration in a window of five cycles.

- **Upper and Lower Stretch** values are the two features computed from the stretch of each cycle, by splitting it into two parts. The upper stretch magnitude is computed by taking the difference of peak amplitude and running mean value of the valley amplitudes of signal cycles ($ValleyMean$). Similarly, the lower stretch magnitude is computed by taking the absolute difference of minimum amplitude in a respiration cycle and $ValleyMean$. During the computation of the running mean, $ValleyMean$, any valley amplitude two standard deviations away from the current mean value is discarded in the computation.

In order to visualize the effectiveness of the features, we use the **Fisher's Linear Discriminant method**[10] to project the 17-dimensional data vectors to a single dimension using $y = \mathbf{w}^T x$. The idea is to adjust the components of $\mathbf{w}$ in such a way that the projection maximizes the class separation. The discriminant method maximizes the difference between the projected class means while minimizing the projected class scatter. This method can actually be used as a classifier, albeit a weak one, as much of the information inherent in the data gets lost in the projection. It, however, provides an easy way to visualize the separation of the classes and separation of the classes in the one dimension does hint to the fact that the features may be promising for classification in the higher dimensional space. Figure 5 shows the projected data points and it can be readily observed that there exists good enough separation of the puff and non-puff classes.

4.2 Classifier: Supervised Learning Model

The supervised classifier we use to detect individual puffs is learned using a supervised learning algorithm. The standard classification supervised learning framework is formulated as follows. Given an example set of input observations $X = \mathbf{x}_i \in \mathbb{R}^n | i = 1 \ldots N$, e.g., matrix of n RIP features by N inhalation cycles, with corresponding class labels $Y = y_i \in +1, -1 | i = 1 \ldots N$, e.g., puffs and not puffs, the training algorithm learns a classification function $f_\alpha(\mathbf{x})$, which estimates the class label $\hat{y}$ for a given unlabeled/novel input observation $\mathbf{x}$. The function f is parameterized by the parameter vector α.

Our puff from non-puff classification function is learned using the industry-standard Support Vector Machines (SVM) algorithm, which has been demonstrated to be highly competitive on a great number of problems and tasks, owing to its combination of high learning capacity, i.e., ability to learn highly complex classification functions, with a mathe-

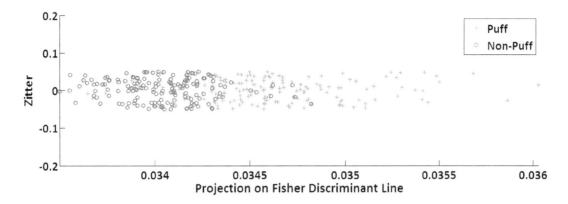

Figure 5: Projection of data on the Fisher's Linear Discriminant Line. The y-axis is used to spread the data points on the line for visual aid. The x-axis presents the value of the projection.

matically rigorous handling of the overfitting/training error trade-off via regularization in the space of kernel functions. Formally, the SVM classification function is defined, using the dual formulation, as

$$f_\alpha(\mathbf{x}) = \text{sign}\left(g_\alpha(\mathbf{x})\right).$$
$$g_\alpha(\mathbf{x}) = \sum_{i \in X_{\text{SV}}} \alpha_i K(\mathbf{x}_i, \mathbf{x}) + b. \qquad (1)$$

In the above formulation, α_i's and bias constant b are the parameters learned in the course of training, and the set X_{SV} contains the training observations, called support vectors, that define the boundary separating the two classes. The function $K(;)$ is the special kernel function that allows SVM to learn highly complex functions f, corresponding to a highly non-linear separation boundaries. This so-called kernel-trick makes it possible to implicitly transform all observations to a space of much higher dimensionality, called kernel feature space, where difficult problems are simplified. Formally, the kernel function $K(\mathbf{u}, \mathbf{v})$ corresponds to a dot product between the original vectors $\mathbf{u}$ and $\mathbf{v}$ in the kernel feature space, making the explicit transformation unnecessary. One powerful class of kernels is the Radial Basis Functions class: $K(\mathbf{u}, \mathbf{v}) = e^{\gamma \|\mathbf{u} - \mathbf{v}\|^2}$, leading to classification functions capable of classifying very complex datasets.

The training formulation is based on regularized empirical risk minimization, whereby the algorithm minimizes the error on the training observations, while minimizing the L2-norm of the function f, which works to minimize its complexity. The formal definition of the SVM primal learning problem is

$$\underset{\mathbf{w}, b}{\text{argmin}} \frac{1}{2}\|\mathbf{w}\|^2 + C \sum_i^N \max(1 - y_i(\mathbf{w}^T \mathbf{x}_i + b), 0), \qquad (2)$$

where the primal variables/parameters w and b represent the linear decision boundary. Note that minimizing the L2-norm of f is equivalent to maximizing The more useful formulation, however, is the Wolfe dual, which also specifies the implicit transformation of the problem into the kernel feature space.

$$\underset{\alpha}{\text{argmax}} \sum_i^N \alpha_i - \frac{1}{2} \sum_{i,j}^N \alpha_i \alpha_j y_i y_j K(\mathbf{x}_i, \mathbf{x}_j)$$
$$0 \le \alpha_i \le C, \qquad (3)$$
$$\sum_{i=1}^n \alpha_i y_i = 0.$$

The algorithm requires several user-defined parameters. The two main ones are: 1) the C constant, which directly penalizes the error on the train set, as per equation (2), by which it indirectly manages the trade-off between overfiting and training error, and 2) the choice of kernel function, along with any constants in it. We use the RBF kernel, and vary the γ hyper-parameter, in conjunction with the C constant, in order to attain the best performing function f. As per standard practice, we defined a set of candidate C's and a set of candidate γ's, and tried all combinations of values from these sets. For both C and γ, the candidate values ranged from 2^{-10} to 2^{10}, increasing in steps of $2^{0.5}$.

We follow the standard cross-validation approach to evaluate and fine-tune the learned model, with the number of cross-validation partitions equal to 10. We use the Area Under ROC Curve (AUC) metric to assess the performance of the model, which is a valid metric to use with cross-validation. The choice of AUC, as opposed to the accuracy (number of correctly classified observations), is preferred in our case because we have highly imbalanced class sizes. After performing cross-validation on the data set of puffs and non-puffs, we found the optimal C to be 4, and the optimal γ to be 5.65685. These values could then be used to train a single model for classifying puffs and non-puffs. In the next section, we present the performance characteristics of this fine-tuned model on the training set (evaluated via cross-validation), as well as on a separately withheld test set.

4.2.1 *Optimal classification threshold selection*

After we have fine-tuned the hyper-parameters C and RBF γ by finding the highest cross-validated AUC, we can introduce additional bias for one of the two classes in the problem, and fine-tune it either to improve accuracy (especially in cases of imbalanced class sizes) or to reflect our greater preference for minimizing the false positive rate or the false negative rate. We can modify the original formulation (1) by adding an additional bias constant λ to function $g_\alpha(\mathbf{x}) = \sum_{i \in X_{\mathrm{sv}}} \alpha_i K(\mathbf{x}_i, \mathbf{x}) + b + \lambda$. Intuitively, a positive λ pushes the separating boundary closer to the negative class, in which case it introduces bias for the positive class. Similarly, a negative λ biases against the positive class.

In our problem, we assumed equivalent preference for low false positive rate and low false negative rate. Therefore, we fine-tuned λ to maximize the accuracy. We found that this optimal λ is 0.103129, which gives preference to the positive class. This means that while the trained classifier is able to rank the cycles well, owing to high AUC, it is somewhat skewed in the direction of the positive class, making us misclassify some negative (non-puffs) observations, but achieving a higher recall rate. Figure 6 contains the ROC curve plots for the fine-tuned model on the training set (6(a)), as well as on the withheld test set (6(b)). The filled square and filled circle on each plot correspond to the default and optimal choices for the additional bias, λ. Note that the optimal choice in both cases leads to higher accuracy (ACC in the plot) by means of higher recall.

4.3 Using Unlabeled Data: Semi-Supervised Model

In this section, we describe a specific semi-supervised model that makes use of unlabeled data obtained from the field data collected from the four participants (see section 3.2). Semi-supervised learning has been shown to improve the classification accuracy when there is a scarcity of labeled data. We use the Semi-supervised Support Vector Machine (S3VM) model [35] that extends the basic supervised SVM to incorporate unlabeled data.

The basic intuition behind S3VMs is that if we have unlabeled data together with labeled data the decision boundary obtained by the learning algorithm should be such that it separates the labeled data with a maximal margin, while simultaneously maximizing its distance to unlabeled examples. The second part in the model formulation is motivated by the notion that the model should have as little ambiguity in classifying the unlabeled examples as possible, even if there's not assurance that these classifications are correct (given that there are no labels for them). This intuition is incorporated by modifying the objective function of the basic SVM, and is given by

$$\underset{\mathbf{w},\mathbf{b}}{\mathrm{argmin}} \frac{1}{2}\|\mathbf{w}\|^2 + C \sum_i^N \max(1 - y_i(\mathbf{w}^T\mathbf{x}_i + b), 0)$$
$$+ C^* \sum_j^M \max(1 - |\mathbf{w}^T\mathbf{z}_j + b|, 0),$$

where, $\{\mathbf{z}_j \in \mathbb{R}^n | j = 1 \ldots M\}$ is a set of unlabeled input data. We essentially add penalty in the objective function for the unlabeled data points that are too close to the decision boundary, specifically for which $-1 < |\mathbf{w}^T\mathbf{z}_j + b| < 1$, thereby, forcing the decision boundary to go through a low density area of the unlabeled instances. The S3VM experiments were conducted with the SVMlin toolbox [6].

The challenge in developing the semi-supervised learning model is to identify a feature that can connect the self-report to the smoking puffs, knowing that the self-report can be before, during, or after a smoking episode. The new feature we identify is the time distance of the respiration cycle in consideration to the closest self-report timestamp in the field data. As there should exist a marking before, during, or after every smoking session reported, the time distance from each cycle to the nearest self-report time should help the learning algorithm. Note that we do not have actual self-report time for the labeled data, but we can reasonably assume the existence of a hypothetical accurate self-report at the beginning of the carefully labeled smoking sessions (see section 3.2).

5. TRAINING & EVALUATION OF PUFF DETECTION MODELS

In this section, we present the performance of the classifiers for detecting smoking puffs. The training data set for the supervised classifier is comprised of the instances of puffs cycles and instances of non-puff cycles from the smoking sessions. The other sources of non-puff instances are data from the stress, conversation, and physical activity data sets. These data sets do not include any smoking events. Inclusion of these data sets are required in order to create a robust classifier that should generalize to the natural field environment better than a classifier that uses only the puff and non-puff cycles from the smoking session. Moreover, as stress, conversation and physical activity have been shown to be inferrable from respiration, they form the set of plausible confounding factors in smoking detection. In total, we have 161 puff instances and the same number of non-puff instances. The non-puff instances with equal proportion come from smoking sessions and the 3 confounding data sets.

The training data set for the semi-supervised model set includes the same labeled data set as described above and a large amount of unlabeled data taken from the field data sets obtained from 4 participants. However, not all data from the field data is included as it amounts to 28 hours worth of data. Such a large amount of data proved to be infeasible to run on the SVMlin tool. Experimenting with different amounts of data, we ended up including 10 times the amount of cycles in the labeled data. We ensured that data was included both from the neighborhood of self-report times (± 5 minutes) and far away of from any self reports, thereby ensuring that the unlabeled data included both puffs and non-puffs.

Training and Testing Performance: Tables 1 and 2 present the performance of the classifiers on labeled data set. Also for greater generalizability, we split our labeled data set into training and test sets — one subset contains 66% of the whole data set and other subset contains the remaining 34%. Table 1 shows the performance of the classifiers on whole data set with 10-fold cross validation. As mentioned above for supervised classification, we use Support Vector Machine (SVM). We then split the labeled dataset into training and testing sets. For this case, the classifier performance on the test data is presented in Table 2. Data used in the supervised classifier are carefully labeled. But, when we add the noisy labeled data set from the field, we use the S3VM classifier which is a semi-supervised support vector machine. For the first experiment, when we use all the labeled data, SVM provides 84.5% accuracy; S3VM is able to improve this accuracy to 86.7%. In the second experiment, when we apply these classifier models on the testing data set, we observe the performances of the classifiers are also similar

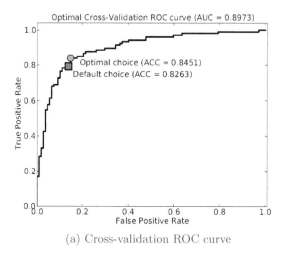

(a) Cross-validation ROC curve

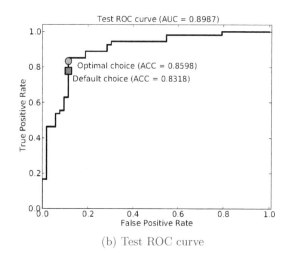

(b) Test ROC curve

Figure 6: ROC curves for the fine-tuned model, with $C, \gamma, \lambda = (4, 5.65685, 0.103129)$, plotted for, (a), the training set (via cross-validation) and, (b), the test set.

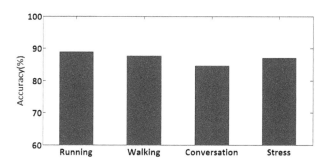

Figure 7: Accuracy of the classifier on the datasets for four confounding events.

to the training accuracies (as shown in Table 2). In both of these experiments, we get high precision, high recall or false positive rate, and high true positive rate. Moreover, if the training set consists of only the non-puffs taken from the smoking session the testing accuracy is 91.43% for the SVM classifier. This indicates that the classifier is quite efficient in detection of puffs and non-puffs in the absence of confounding factors.

Figure 7 presents the accuracy incurred when the puff detection model is run on the stress, conversation, and physical activity datasets. We note that that these datasets do not include any smoking sessions and therefore respiration cycles not correctly identified implies it was detected as a puff. We observe that conversation is the most confounding event for the puff detection model. One reason is that during speaking, we tend to take deep breaths at the beginning of the speech and that is sometimes detected as puffs. To remedy this problem, in the next section, we propose a technique that can be applied on the data in the field when the conversation and smoking detection models are both available on the phone.

Feature Analysis: The performance of the classifiers presented in the Tables 1 and 2 uses all the 17 features. Here, we present the effect of adding the 12 new features on the performance of the classifier. We partition the set of all the new features into 3 sets, namely, the set of first differences, the set of the stretch and exhalation duration ratio, and the set of Upper and Lower stretches. All the accuracy values reported are for the SVM classifier. The basic set of features comprising only the existing 5 features produces an accuracy of 73.55% on the whole labeled data set. From Table 3, we observe that among the three new sets of features, adding the first differences to the basic set improves the accuracy most, reaching up to 81.1% . With this set of features, adding the stretch and exhalation duration ratios increases the performance of the classifier most. With these 2 new sets of features, we obtain an accuracy of 82.7%.

Table 3: Effect of new features on the classification accuracy. The classification accuracy obtained using only the existing features is 73.55%. They constitute the basic set of features. Three different sets of features are introduced in this paper. Let S_1 = set of forward and backward first differences of basic features, S_2 = {Stretch ratio, Exhalation ratio} and S_3 = {Upper Stretch, Lower Stretch}. X denotes the inclusion of the set to the basic set of features.

S_1	S_2	S_3	Accuracy(%)
X			**81.1**
	X		76.33
		X	77.86
X	X		**82.7**
X		X	81.32
	X	X	75.79

6. SMOKING TOPOGRAPHY STATISTICS

Table 4 summarizes mean and standard deviation of various measures of interest, e.g., duration of smoking session, puff duration, inter-puff interval, and frequency of puffs per smoking session. These measurements are calculated from

Table 1: Performance of classifiers with 10-fold cross-validation.

Classifier	Performance Matrices			
	Accuracy(%)	Precision	TP rate	FP rate
SVM	84.5	0.85	0.84	0.15
S3VM	86.7	0.91	0.81	0.08

Table 2: Performance of classifiers on testing data when data is split into training and test sets.

Classifier	Performance Matrices			
	Accuracy(%)	Precision	TP rate	FP rate
SVM	85.98	0.88	0.83	0.11
S3VM	87.27	0.91	0.83	0.08

the data collected from the smoking sessions where puffs are marked carefully using a cell phone. As described in 3.2 there were 13 smoking session from 10 individuals in the data set.

Our observations are generally consistent with previous lab-based and field-based research on smoking topography and puff-analysis [17, 12, 14], thereby validating the use of respiration bands to collect respiration measurements of smoking in the field.

7. DISCUSSION

In this section, we consider two issues on detection of entire smoking episodes. We first discuss how the accuracy of detecting smoking episodes may be improved further by using insights from conversation patterns since conversation appears to be a frequent daily human activity that confounds detection of smoking. Next, we describe how the results of puff detection accuracy can be used with an extensive real-life data set to obtain confidence level in the detection of an entire smoking episode depending on the number of puffs contained in a smoking session.

Leveraging Patterns of Natural Conversations. Results on the confounding data sets indicate that during conversations, the puff detector may raise false positives. Upon running the conversation detector on smoking sessions, we find that the entire smoking session is detected as a long conversation. According to the findings in [26], most natural conversations are short, with an average duration of 3.8 minutes. Less than 20% of conversations are 6 minutes or longer. The average duration of a smoking session (M), on the other hand, is 6.62 minutes. We can use this difference in durations to eliminate a major source of false alarm in the detection of smoking events. One approach is to apply a conversation detector on the respiration measurements after applying the puff detector and then clear puff markings during those intervals that are detected as conversation, but have a duration less than $M - 2*SD$ minutes, where SD is the standard deviation of a smoking session duration. This approach will be useful only in those scenarios where the objective is to detect entire smoking episodes, and not single puffs (such as in a smoking cessation study). We plan to evaluate such approaches on data sets collected from real-life to evaluate its impact on both false positive rate and false negative rate.

Confidence in Detecting an Entire Smoking Episode. Since a smoking session usually consists of multiple puffs, the confidence in detecting a smoking session should increase with increasing number of puffs contained in it. We can compute the confidence of detecting of a smoking session using the following procedure. Let X be a binary random variable, where $X = 1$ indicates that a puff detected by the smoking detector is in a smoking session, and $X = 0$, otherwise. Also, in a sequence of output produced by the puff detector, when applied on a times series of respiration measurements, let $Y(i)$ denote the number of puffs detected in N respiration cycles preceding and including the ith cycle. A good choice for N is the average number of respiration cycles in a smoking session, which from our data set is equal to 72. Then, $\Pr[X = 1|Y(i) = y]$ is the probability of a the ith cycle which is detected to be a puff being in a smoking session, given that in the last N cycles y puffs were observed. We can use the Bayes' rule to obtain this probability. More specifically,

$$\Pr[X = 1|Y = y] = \frac{\Pr[Y = y|X = 1]\Pr[X = 1]}{\Sigma_{i\in\{0,1\}}\Pr[Y = y|X = i]\Pr[X = i]}$$

This enables the computation of $\Pr[X = 1|Y = y]$ if we have estimates for $\Pr[Y = y|X = i]$ and $\Pr[X = i]$, for $i \in \{0, 1\}$. These probabilities represent the behavior of the smoking detector on data set obtained from real-life of various subjects, if the subjects self-mark each smoking session in their mobile environment while wearing a respiration sensor. Any puff within the neighborhood of a smoking self-report can be used to estimate $\Pr[Y = y|X = 1]$ and puff instances that are not in the neighborhood of a self-report can be used to estimate $\Pr[Y = y|X = 0]$. $\Pr[X = i]$ can be estimated using the true positive rate and false positive rates of the puff detector. This approach can be applied to real-life data sets to obtain the corresponding confidence levels in detecting entire smoking episodes when using our smoking detector.

8. CONCLUSION

Extensive research in smoking literature is aimed towards the development of efficient smoking interventions. However, the absence of a real time smoking event detector hampers the development of interventions that work well. Consequently, the success rate of smoking cessation programs is abysmally low. As a first step towards building a reliable smoking episode detector, in this work we presented a model to automatically detect smoking puffs in the natu-

Table 4: Statistics of smoking topography obtained from the labeled data set (average value and standard deviation).

Statistic	Avg. $\pm$ St.Dev.
Duration of smoking session (minutes)	6.62 ± 1.66
Puff duration (seconds)	1.09 ± 0.53
Inter-puff interval (seconds)	28.38 ± 14.57
Number of puff per smoking session	12.38 ± 0.92

ral environment from respiration measurement. We achieve 86.7% accuracy on the detection of puffs even when there exists potential confounding events in the collected data. For the purpose of building the model, we identified 12 new respiration features that are found to be effective compared to the use of only the existing respiration features available in the literature. We also presented a semisupervised moded that improves the accuracy of the model when we provide unlabeled data with self reports that is also collected in the natural environment from participants who are daily smokers. Since other contextual factors such as stress, location, social activity can also be detected on a mobile phone, our work opens the opportunity for effective smoking research by allowing the collection of different contextual factors, that are potential predictors of smoking, in the natural environment of smokers.

9. ACKNOWLEDGMENTS

We thank Emre Ertin (at The Ohio State University), who designed the AutoSense sensors, Mustafa al'Absi (at University of Minnesota) for providing access to the lab stress data sets used in this work, and Saul Shiffman (at University of Pittsburgh) for many invaluable conversations on smoking research. This work was supported in part by NSF grant CNS-0910878 funded under the American Recovery and Reinvestment Act of 2009 (Public Law 111-5) and NIH Grant U01DA023812 from NIDA.

10. REFERENCES

[1] Smoking-attributable mortality, years of potential life lost, and productivity losses - United States, 2000 - 2004. *Morbidity and Mortality Weekly Report*, 57(45):1226–1228, 2008.

[2] Fieldstream. http://www.github.com/FieldStream/FieldStream, Accessed: October 2011.

[3] How tobacco smoke causes disease - the biology and behavioral basis for smoking-attributable disease - a report of the surgeon general. http://www.surgeongeneral.gov/library/tobaccosmoke/report/index.html, Accessed: October 2011.

[4] Smokerlyzer. http://www.bedfont.com/smokerlyzer, Accessed: October 2011.

[5] Substance abuse and mental health administration: Results from the 2009 national survey on drug use and health: National findings. http://www.oas.samhsa.gov/NSDUH/2k9NSDUH/tabs/Cover.pdf, Accessed: October 2011.

[6] Svmlin. http://vikas.sindhwani.org/svmlin.html, Accessed: October 2011.

[7] Treating tobacco use and dependence: 2008 update - clinical practice guideline. http://www.surgeongeneral.gov/tobacco/treating_tobacco_use08.pdf, Accessed: October 2011.

[8] CReSS. http://www.borgwaldt.de/cms/borgwaldt-kc/produkte/rauchmaschinen/geraete-zur-rauchtopographie/cress-pocket.html, Accessed: October 2011.

[9] H. Ashton, D. Watson, R. Marsh, and J. Sadler. Puffing frequency and nicotine intake in cigarette smokers. *The British Medical Journal*, pages 679–681, 1970.

[10] C. Bishop. *Pattern Recognition and Machine Learning*. Springer, 2006.

[11] H. Brendryen, P. Kraft, and H. Schaalma. Looking inside the black box: Using intervention mapping to describe the development of the automated smoking cessation intervention'happy ending'. *The Journal of Smoking Cessation*, 5(1):29–56, 2010.

[12] R. Bridges, J. Combs, J. Humble, J. Turbek, S. Rehm, and N. Haley. Puffing topography as a determinant of smoke exposure. *Pharmacology Biochemistry and Behavior*, 37(1):29–39, 1990.

[13] F. Charles, G. Krautter, and D. Mariner. Post-puff respiration measures on smokers of different tar yield cigarettes. *Inhalation toxicology*, 21(8):712–718, 2009.

[14] C. Collins, D. Epstein, C. Parzynski, D. Zimmerman, E. Moolchan, and S. Heishman. Puffing behavior during the smoking of a single cigarette in tobacco-dependent adolescents. *Nicotine & tobacco research*, 12(2):164–167, 2010.

[15] K. Doherty, T. Kinnunen, F. Militello, and A. Garvey. Urges to smoke during the first month of abstinence: relationship to relapse and predictors. *Psychopharmacology*, 119(2):171–178, 1995.

[16] E. Ertin, N. Stohs, S. Kumar, A. Raij, M. al'Absi, T. Kwon, S. Mitra, S. Shah, and J. W. Jeong. Autosense: Unobtrusively wearable sensor suite for inferencing of onset, causality, and consequences of stress in the field. In *ACM Conference on Embedded Networked Sensor Systems (SenSys)*, pages 274–287, 2011.

[17] D. Hammond, G. Fong, K. Cummings, and A. Hyland. Smoking topography, brand switching, and nicotine delivery: results from an in vivo study. *Cancer Epidemiology Biomarkers & Prevention*, 14(6):1370–1375, 2005.

[18] J. Hughes and D. Hatsukami. Signs and symptoms of tobacco withdrawal. *Archives of General Psychiatry*, 43(3):289, 1986.

[19] N. Hymowitz, M. Sexton, J. Ockene, and G. Grandits.

Baseline factors associated with smoking cessation and relapse. *Preventive Medicine*, 20(5):590–601, 1991.

[20] D. Kalman. The subjective effects of nicotine: methodological issues, a review of experimental studies, and recommendations for future research. *Nicotine & Tobacco Research*, 4(1):25–70, 2002.

[21] J. Killen and S. Fortmann. Craving is associated with smoking relapse: Findings from three prospective studies. *Experimental and Clinical Psychopharmacology*, 5(2):137, 1997.

[22] S. Kolonen, J. Tuomisto, P. Puusteinen, and M. Airaksinen. Puffing behavior during the smoking of a single cigarette in a naturalistic environment. *Pharmacology, biochemistry and behavior*, 41(4):701–706, 1992.

[23] K. Matheny and K. Weatherman. Predictors of smoking cessation and maintenance. *Journal of Clinical Psychology*, 54(2):223–235, 1998.

[24] A. Mokdad, J. Marks, D. Stroup, and J. Gerberding. Actual causes of death in the united states, 2000. *JAMA: the journal of the American Medical Association*, 291(10):1238, 2004.

[25] K. Plarre, A. Raij, S. M. Hossain, A. A. Ali, M. Nakajima, M. al'Absi, T. Kamarck, S. Kumar, M. Scott, D. Siewiorek, A. Smailagic, and L. E. Wittmers. Continuous inference of psychological stress from sensory measurements collected in the natural environment. In *ACM Information Processing in Sensor Networks (IPSN)*, pages 97–108, 2011.

[26] M. M. Rahman, A. A. Ali, K. Plarre, M. al'Absi, E. Ertin, and S. Kumar. mconverse: Inferring conversation episodes from respiratory measurements collected in the field. In *ACM Wireless Health*, 2011.

[27] S. Shiffman. Reflections on smoking relapse research. *Drug and alcohol review*, 25(1):15–20, 2006.

[28] S. Shiffman, J. Paty, M. Gnys, J. Kassel, and M. Hickcox. First lapses to smoking: Within-subjects analysis of real-time reports. *Journal of Consulting and Clinical Psychology*, 64(2):366–379, 1996.

[29] S. Shiffman, D. Scharf, W. Shadel, C. Gwaltney, Q. Dang, S. Paton, and D. Clark. Analyzing milestones in smoking cessation: illustration in a nicotine patch trial in adult smokers. *Journal of consulting and clinical psychology*, 74(2):276–285, 2006.

[30] S. Shiffman and A. Waters. Negative affect and smoking lapses: A prospective analysis. *Journal of Consulting and Clinical Psychology*, 72(2):192–201, 2004.

[31] M. Stitzer and J. Gross. Smoking relapse: the role of pharmacological and behavioral factors. *Progress in clinical and biological research*, 261:163–184, 1988.

[32] G. Swan, M. Ward, and L. Jack. Abstinence effects as predictors of 28-day relapse in smokers* 1. *Addictive Behaviors*, 21(4):481–490, 1996.

[33] J. Veilleux, J. Kassel, A. Heinz, A. Braun, M. Wardle, J. Greenstein, D. Evatt, and M. Conrad. Predictors and sequelae of smoking topography over the course of a single cigarette in adolescent light smokers. *Journal of Adolescent Health*, 48(2):176–181, 2011.

[34] P. Wu, J. Hsieh, J. Cheng, S. Cheng, and S. Tseng. Human smoking event detection using visual interaction clues. In *International Conference on Pattern Recognition*, pages 4344–4347. IEEE, 2010.

[35] X. Zhu and A. Goldberg. *Introduction to Semi-Supervised Learning*. Morgan & Claypool Publishers, 2009.

Accuracy-Aware Aquatic Diffusion Process Profiling Using Robotic Sensor Networks

Yu Wang*, Rui Tan*, Guoliang Xing*, Jianxun Wang†, and Xiaobo Tan†
*Department of Computer Science and Engineering, Michigan State University, USA
†Department of Electrical and Computer Engineering, Michigan State University, USA
{wangyu3, tanrui, glxing, wangji19, xbtan}@msu.edu

ABSTRACT

Water resources and aquatic ecosystems are facing increasing threats from climate change, improper waste disposal, and oil spill incidents. It is of great interest to deploy mobile sensors to detect and monitor certain diffusion processes (e.g., chemical pollutants) that are harmful to aquatic environments. In this paper, we propose an accuracy-aware diffusion process profiling approach using smart aquatic mobile sensors such as robotic fish. In our approach, the robotic sensors collaboratively profile the characteristics of a diffusion process including source location, discharged substance amount, and its evolution over time. In particular, the robotic sensors reposition themselves to progressively improve the profiling accuracy. We formulate a novel movement scheduling problem that aims to maximize the profiling accuracy subject to limited sensor mobility and energy budget. We develop an efficient *greedy* algorithm and a more complex near-optimal *radial* algorithm to solve the problem. We conduct extensive simulations based on real data traces of robotic fish movement and wireless communication. The results show that our approach can accurately profile dynamic diffusion processes under tight energy budgets. Moreover, a preliminary evaluation based on the implementation on TelosB motes validates the feasibility of deploying our movement scheduling algorithms on mote-class robotic sensor platforms.

Categories and Subject Descriptors

C.3 [**Special-purpose and Application-based Systems**]: Signal processing systems; C.4 [**Performance of Systems**]: Measurement techniques, modeling techniques; G.1.6 [**Numerical Analysis**]: Optimization—*Constrained optimization, gradient methods*

Keywords

Robotic sensor networks, diffusion process, movement scheduling

 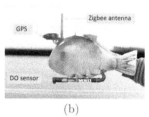

(a)   (b)

Figure 1: Prototypes of autonomous robotic fish developed by the Smart Microsystems Laboratory at Michigan State University [26].

1. INTRODUCTION

Water resources and aquatic ecosystems have been facing various physical, chemical, and biological threats from climate change, industrial pollution, and improper waste disposal. For instance, the last four decades witnessed more than a dozen major oil spills with each releasing more than 30 million gallons of oil [1]. Other harmful diffusion processes like chemical or radiation leaks could also have disastrous impact on public health and ecosystem sustainability. When such a crisis arises, an immediate requirement is to profile the characteristics of the diffusion process, including the location of source, the amount of discharged substance, and how rapidly it spreads in space and evolves over time.

Manual sampling, via boat/ship or with handhold devices, is still a common practice in the monitoring of aquatic diffusion processes. This approach is labor-intensive and difficult to adapt to the dynamic evolution of diffusion. An alternative is *in situ* sensing with fixed or buoyed/moored sensors [20]. However, since buoyed sensors cannot move around, it could take a prohibitively large number of them to capture spatially inhomogeneous information. The past couple of decades have seen significant progress in developing robotic technologies for aquatic sensing. Autonomous underwater vehicles (AUVs) [10] and sea gliders [9] are notable examples of such technologies. However, because of their high cost (over 50,000 U.S. dollars per unit [21]), weight (over 100 pounds), and size (1-2 meters long), it is difficult to deploy many AUVs or sea gliders for temporally and spatially resolved measurement of diffusion processes.

Recent advances in computing, communication, sensing, and actuation technologies have made it possible to create untethered *robotic fish* with onboard power, control, navigation, wireless communication, and sensing modules, which turn these robots into mobile sensing platforms in aquatic environments. Fig. 1(a) shows a prototype of robotic fish swimming in an inland lake. Fig. 1(b) shows the close-up of a robotic fish prototype, equipped with GPS, Zigbee antenna, and a dissolved oxygen (DO) sensor. Due to the low manufacturing cost, these platforms can be massively deployed to form a mobile sensor network that monitors harmful diffusion processes, providing significantly higher spatial and temporal sensing resolution than existing monitoring methods. Moreover, a school of robotic fish can coordinate their sensing and movements through wireless communication enabled by the onboard Zigbee radio, to adapt to the dynamics of evolving diffusion processes.

Despite the aforementioned advantages, low-cost mobile sensing platforms like robotic fish introduce several challenges for aquatic sensing. First, due to the constraints on size and energy, they are typically equipped with low-end sensors whose measurements are subject to significant biases and noises. They must efficiently collaborate in data processing to achieve satisfactory accuracy in diffusion profiling. Second, practical aquatic mobile platforms are only capable of relatively low-speed movements. Hence the movements of sensors must be efficiently scheduled to achieve real-time profiling of the diffusion processes that may evolve rapidly over time. Third, given the high power consumption of locomotion, the distance that mobile sensors move in a profiling process should be minimized to extend the network lifetime.

We make the following major contributions in this paper:

- We propose a novel accuracy-aware approach for aquatic diffusion profiling based on robotic sensor networks. Our approach leverages the mobility of robotic sensors to iteratively profile the spatiotemporally evolving diffusion process.
- We derive the analytical profiling accuracy of our approach based on the Cramér-Rao bound (CRB). Then we formulate a movement scheduling problem for aquatic diffusion profiling, in which the profiling accuracy is maximized under the constraints on sensor mobility and energy budgets. We develop gradient-ascent-based *greedy* and dynamic-programming-based *radial* movement scheduling algorithms to solve the problem.
- We implement the profiling and movement scheduling algorithms on TelosB motes and evaluate the system overhead. Moreover, we conduct extensive simulations based on real data traces of robotic fish movement and wireless communication for evaluation. The results show that our approach can accurately profile the dynamic diffusion process and adapt to its evolution.

The rest of this paper is organized as follows. Section 2 reviews related work. Section 3 introduces the preliminaries and Section 4 provides an overview of our approach. Section 5 derives the analytical profiling accuracy metric and Section 6 formulates the movement scheduling problem. Section 7 presents the two movement scheduling algorithms. Section 8 discusses several extensions. Section 9 presents evaluation results and Section 10 concludes this paper.

2. RELATED WORK

Most previous work on diffusion process monitoring is based on stationary sensor networks. Several different estimation techniques are adopted by these studies, which include *state-space filtering*, *statistical signal processing*, and

geometric trilateration. The state space approach [19, 31] uses discrete state-space equations to approximate the partial differential equations that govern the diffusion process, and then applies filtering algorithms such as Kalman filters [19, 31] to profile the diffusion process based on noisy measurements. In the statistical signal processing approach, several estimation techniques such as MLE [17, 29] and Bayesian parameter estimation [33] are applied to deal with noisy measurements. For instance, in [29], an MLE-based diffusion characterization algorithm is designed based on binary sensor measurements to reduce the communication cost. In [33], the parametric probability distribution of the diffusion profile parameters is passed among sensors and updated with sensor measurements by a Bayesian estimation algorithm. The passing route is determined according to various estimation performance metrics including CRB. In geometric trilateration approach [14, 4], the measurement of a sensor is mapped to the distance from the sensor to the diffusion source. The source location can then be estimated by trilateration among multiple sensors. Such an approach incurs low computational complexities, but suffers lower estimation accuracy compared with more advanced approaches such as MLE [4].

Recently, sensor mobility has been exploited to enhance the adaptability and sensing capability of sensor networks. For instance, heuristic movement scheduling algorithms are proposed in [24] to estimate the contours of a physical field. In [22], more complex path planning schemes are proposed for mobile sensors to reconstruct a spatial map of environmental phenomena that do not follow a particular physical model. Our previous works exploit reactive sensor mobility to improve the detection performance of a sensor network [25, 32]. Several studies are focused on using robots to improve the accuracy in profiling diffusion processes. As an extension to [17], the gradient of CRB is used to schedule the movement of a single sensor in [29]. Similarly, a robot motion control algorithm is proposed in [23] to maximize the determinant of the Fisher information matrix. However, as these diffusion profiling approaches [17, 23, 29] adopt complicated numerical optimization, they are only applicable to a small number (e.g., 3 in [23]) of powerful robots. In contrast, we focus on developing movement scheduling algorithms for moderate- or large-scale mobile networks that are composed of inexpensive robotic sensors.

3. PRELIMINARIES

In this section, we describe the preliminaries including the diffusion process and sensor models.

3.1 Diffusion Process Model

A diffusion process in a static aquatic environment, by which molecules spread from areas of higher concentration to areas of lower concentration, follows Fick's law [13]. In addition to the diffusion, the spread of the discharged substance is also affected by the advection of solvent, e.g., the movement of water caused by the wind. By denoting t as the time elapsed since the discharge of substance and c as the substance concentration, the diffusion-advection model can be described as

$$\frac{\partial c}{\partial t} = D_x \cdot \frac{\partial^2 c}{\partial x^2} + D_y \cdot \frac{\partial^2 c}{\partial y^2} + D_z \cdot \frac{\partial^2 c}{\partial z^2} - u_x \cdot \frac{\partial c}{\partial x} - u_y \cdot \frac{\partial c}{\partial y}, \quad (1)$$

where D is the diffusion coefficient, u is the advection speed, and the subscripts of D and u denote the directions (i.e., x-, y-, and z-axis). The diffusion coefficients characterize the speed of diffusion and depend on the species of solvent and discharge substance as well as other environment factors such as temperature. The advection speeds characterize the horizontal solvent movement caused by external forces such as wind and flow. The above Fickian diffusion-advection model has been widely adopted to study the spreading of gaseous substances [29] and buoyant fluid pollutants such as oil slick on the sea [16]. For many buoyant fluid pollutants, the two horizontal diffusion coefficients, i.e., D_x and D_y, are identical, while the vertical diffusion coefficient, i.e., D_z, is insignificant. For instance, in a field experiment [8], where diesel oil was discharged into the sea, the estimated D_x is $2,000 \, \text{cm}^2/\text{s}$ while D_z is only $10 \, \text{cm}^2/\text{s}$. Therefore, the vertical diffusion coefficient can be safely ignored and the diffusion can be well characterized by a 2-dimensional process. In this paper, our study is focused on buoyant fluid pollutants with the diffusion coefficients $D_x = D_y = D$.

Suppose a total of $A \, \text{cm}^3$ of substance is discharged at location (x_s, y_s) and $t = 0$. At time $t > 0$, the original diffusion source is drifted to (x_0, y_0) due to advection, where $x_0 = x_s + u_x t$ and $y_0 = y_s + u_y t$. Hereafter, by *source location* we refer to the source location that has *drifted* from the original position due to advection, unless otherwise specified. Denote $d(x, y)$ (abbreviated to d) as the distance from any location (x, y) to the source location, i.e., $d = \sqrt{(x - x_0)^2 + (y - y_0)^2}$. In the presence of advection, the diffusion is isotropic with respect to the drifted source location [6]. Therefore, the concentration at (x, y) can be denoted as $c(d, t)$. The initial condition for Eq. (1) is an impulse source, which can be represented by the Dirac delta function, i.e., $c(d, 0) = A \cdot \delta(d)$. Under this initial condition, the closed-form solution to Eq. (1) is given by [29]:

$$c(d, t) = \alpha \cdot \exp\left(-\beta \cdot d^2\right), \quad d \geq 0, t > 0, \qquad (2)$$

where $\alpha = \frac{A}{4\pi D t}$ and $\beta = \frac{1}{4D t}$. From Eq. (2), for a given time instant t, the concentration distribution is described by the Gaussian function that centers at the source location. As time elapses, the concentration distribution becomes flatter. In this paper, the *diffusion profile* is defined as $\Theta = \{x_0, y_0, \alpha, \beta\}$.

3.2 Sensor Model

Our approach leverages mobile nodes (e.g., robotic fish [26]) to collaboratively profile an aquatic diffusion process. The nodes form a cluster and a cluster head is selected to process the measurements from cluster members. The selection of cluster head will be discussed in Section 7.2. Moreover, we will extend our approach to address multiple clusters in Section 8.2. Many aquatic mobile platforms are battery-powered and hence have limited mobility and energy budget. For instance, the movement speed of the robotic fish designed in [26] was about 1.8 to 6 m/min. We assume that the mobile nodes are equipped with pollutant concentration sensors (e.g., the Cyclops-7 [28] series) that can measure the concentrations of crude oil, harmful algae, etc. Lastly, we assume that the sensors are equipped with low-power wireless interfaces (e.g., 802.15.14 ZigBee radios) and hence can communicate with each other when on water surface.

The measurements of most sensors are subject to biases and additive random noises from the sensor circuitry and

Table 1: Summary of Notation

Symbol	Definition
D	diffusion coefficient
A	total amount of discharged substance in cm^3
t	time from the discharge of substance
α, β	$\alpha = A(4\pi D t)^{-1}, \beta = (4D t)^{-1}$
(x_s, y_s)	coordinates of the original diffusion source
(x_0, y_0)	coordinates of the drifted diffusion source
(x_i+x_0, y_i+y_0)	coordinates of sensor i
d_i	distance from the drifted diffusion source
$c(d_i, t)$	concentration at sensor i and time t
Θ	diffusion process profile $\Theta = \{x_0, y_0, \alpha, \beta\}$
b_i, σ^2	sensor bias and noise variance
n_i	Gaussian noise, $n_i \sim \mathcal{N}(0, \sigma^2)$
z_i	sensor measurement, $z_i \sim \mathcal{N}(c(d_i, t) + b, \sigma^2)$
K	number of samples for computing a measurement
N	total number of sensors
$\mathbf{z}$	normalized observation, $\mathbf{z} = [\frac{z_1 - b_1}{\sigma}, \ldots, \frac{z_N - b_N}{\sigma}]^\text{T}$
ω	diffusion process profiling accuracy metric
v	sensor movement speed

* The symbols with subscript i refer to the notation of sensor i.

the environment. Specifically, the reading of sensor i, denoted by z_i, is given by $z_i = c(d_i, t) + b_i + n_i$, where d_i is the distance from sensor i to the diffusion source, b_i and n_i are the bias and random noise for sensor i, respectively. In the presence of constant-speed advection, the source and the sensors will drift with the same speed and therefore they are in the same inertial system. As a result, the concentration at the position of sensor i is given by $c(d_i, t)$. We assume that the noise experienced by sensor i follows the zero-mean normal distribution with variance ς^2, i.e., $n_i \sim \mathcal{N}(0, \varsigma^2)$. We assume that the noises, i.e., $\{n_i | \forall i\}$, are independent across sensors. The bias and noise variance for calm water environment are often given in the sensor specification provided by the manufacturer. They may also be measured in offline lab experiments. For instance, by placing a sensor in the pollutant-free fluid media, the bias and noise variance can be estimated by the sample mean and variance over a number of readings. When the water environment is wavy, the noise variance will increase. Therefore, to address wavy environment, the noise variance should be measured in offline lab experiments with various wavy levels. The above measurement model has been widely adopted for various chemical sensors [17, 29, 33].

In this paper, we adopt a temporal sampling scheme to mitigate the impact of noise. Specifically, when sensor i measures the concentration, it continuously takes K samples in a short time, and computes the average as its measurement. Therefore, the measurement z_i follows the normal distribution, i.e., $z_i \sim \mathcal{N}(c(d_i, t) + b_i, \sigma^2)$, where $\sigma^2 = \varsigma^2/K$.

Table 1 summarizes the notation used in this paper.

4. OVERVIEW OF APPROACH

In this section, we provide an overview of our approach. Our objective is to profile (i.e., estimate Θ) of an aquatic diffusion-advection process using a robotic sensor network. Our approach is designed to meet two key objectives. First, the noisy measurements of sensors are jointly processed to improve the accuracy in profiling the diffusion. Second, sensors can actively move based on current measurements to maximize the profiling accuracy subject to the energy consumption budget. With the estimated profile $\widetilde{\Theta}$, we can learn several important characteristics of the diffusion pro-

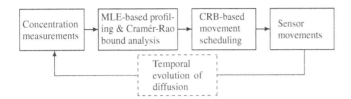

Figure 2: The iterative diffusion profiling process.

cess of interest.[1] First, we can compute the current concentration contour maps with Eq. (2). Second, we can estimate the elapsed time since the start of the diffusion and the total amount of discharged substance, with $\widetilde{t} = (4D\widetilde{\beta})^{-1}$ and $\widetilde{A} = \pi\widetilde{\alpha}\widetilde{\beta}^{-1}$. Third, we can estimate the original source location by $\widetilde{x}_s = \widetilde{x}_0 - u_x\widetilde{t}$ and $\widetilde{y}_s = \widetilde{y}_0 - u_y\widetilde{t}$. Moreover, we can predict the evolution of the diffusion in the future, which is often important for emergency management in the cases of harmful substance discharge.

We assume that the robotic sensors are initially distributed at randomly chosen positions in the deployment region that covers the diffusion source. For instance, the sensors can be dropped off from an unmanned aerial vehicle or placed by an aquatic vessel randomly. Note that random and sometimes uniform deployment of sensors around the source location is a good strategy when the characteristics of diffusion process have yet to be determined. This also avoids the massive locomotion energy required to spread sensors for a satisfactory profiling accuracy when the diffusion process evolves. We assume that all sensors know their positions (e.g., through GPS or an in-network localization service) and are time-synchronized. In Section 9.3.6, we will evaluate the impact of initial sensor deployment on the profiling accuracy and locomotion energy consumption of our approach.

After the initial deployment, sensors begin a diffusion profiling process consisting of multiple *profiling iterations*. The iterative profiling process is illustrated in Fig. 2. In a profiling iteration, sensors first simultaneously take concentration measurements and send them to the cluster head, using a possibly multi-hop wireless communication protocol. The cluster head then adopts the maximum likelihood estimation (MLE) to estimate Θ from the noisy measurements of all sensors. With the estimated diffusion profile, the cluster head schedules sensor movements such that the expected profiling accuracy in the next profiling iteration is maximized, subject to limited sensor mobility and energy budget. Finally, the movement schedule including moving orientations and distances is sent to sensors for directing their movements.

Our accuracy-aware diffusion profiling approach features the following novelties. First, it starts with little prior knowledge about the diffusion and progressively learns the profile of the diffusion with improved accuracy along the profiling iterations. As sensors resample the concentration in each iteration, such an iterative profiling strategy allows the network to adapt to the dynamics of the diffusion process while reducing energy consumption of robotic sensors. Moreover, although the profiling accuracy in each iteration is affected by errors in sensor localization and movement control, our approach only schedules short-distance movements for

sensors in each iteration and updates their positions in the next iteration, which avoids the accumulation of errors in sensor localization and movement control. Second, we analyze the CRB of the MLE-based diffusion profiling algorithm and propose a novel CRB-based profiling accuracy metric, which is used to direct the movement scheduling of robotic sensors. Third, we propose two novel movement scheduling algorithms, which include a gradient-ascent-based *greedy* algorithm and a dynamic-programming-based *radial* algorithm. The *greedy* algorithm only incurs linear complexity, while the *radial* algorithm can find the near-optimal movement schedule with a higher but still polynomial complexity.

5. PROFILING ALGORITHM AND ACCURACY ANALYSIS

In this section, we first present our MLE-based diffusion profiling algorithm, which estimates the diffusion profile Θ in each profiling iteration. We then analyze the theoretical profiling accuracy based on Cramér-Rao bound (CRB). The closed-form relationship between the profiling accuracy and the sensors' positions will guide the design of our accuracy-aware sensor movement scheduling algorithms.

5.1 MLE-based Diffusion Profiling Algorithm

MLE and Bayesian parameter estimation are two typical parameter estimation approaches [7]. The Bayesian estimation relies on prior probability distribution of the parameters, which is often unknown and difficult to model in practice. In this paper, we adopt MLE to estimate the profile of the diffusion process. Specifically, we assume that N aquatic sensors are deployed in the region of interest. In each profiling iteration, we first remove sensor biases and normalize the measurements to construct the observation vector $\mathbf{z}$, which is given by $\mathbf{z} = [\frac{z_1 - b_1}{\sigma}, \ldots, \frac{z_N - b_N}{\sigma}]^{\mathrm{T}}$. By denoting $\mathbf{H} = [\sigma^{-1}e^{-\beta d_1^2}, \ldots, \sigma^{-1}e^{-\beta d_N^2}]^{\mathrm{T}}$, $\mathbf{z}$ follows the N-dimensional normal distribution, i.e., $\mathbf{z} \sim \mathcal{N}(\alpha\mathbf{H}, \mathbf{I})$, where $\mathbf{I}$ is the $N \times N$ identity matrix. The log-likelihood of an observation $\mathbf{z}$ given Θ is given by [7]:

$$\mathcal{L}(\mathbf{z}|\Theta) = -(\mathbf{z} - \alpha\mathbf{H})^{\mathrm{T}}(\mathbf{z} - \alpha\mathbf{H}). \qquad (3)$$

MLE aims to maximize the log-likelihood given by Eq. (3). Formally, $\widetilde{\Theta}(\mathbf{z}) = \arg\max_{\Theta} \mathcal{L}(\mathbf{z}|\Theta)$. This unconstrained optimization problem can be solved by various numerical methods, e.g., Nelder-Mead's algorithm [18].

5.2 Cramér-Rao Bound for Diffusion Profiling

CRB provides a theoretical lower bound on the variance of parameter estimators [7], and has been widely adopted to guide the design of estimation algorithms [17, 33]. This section derives the CRB of profile Θ estimation. CRB is given by the inverse of the Fisher information matrix (FIM) [7]. For the diffusion profiling, the FIM is defined by $\mathbf{J} = -\mathbb{E}\left[\frac{\partial}{\partial\Theta}\left(\frac{\partial}{\partial\Theta}\mathcal{L}(\mathbf{z}|\Theta)\right)\right] = \alpha^2\frac{\partial\mathbf{H}^{\mathrm{T}}}{\partial\Theta}\frac{\partial\mathbf{H}}{\partial\Theta}$, where the expectation $\mathbb{E}[\cdot]$ is taken over all possible $\mathbf{z}$. The kth diagonal element of the inverse of $\mathbf{J}$ (denoted by $\mathbf{J}_{k,k}^{-1}$) provides the lower bound on the variance of the kth element of $\widetilde{\Theta}$ (denoted by $\widetilde{\Theta}_k$) [7]. Formally, $\mathrm{Var}(\widetilde{\Theta}_k) \geq \mathbf{J}_{k,k}^{-1}$. The number $\mathbf{J}_{k,k}^{-1}$ is the CRB corresponding to Θ_k, which is denoted as $\mathrm{CRB}(\Theta_k)$ in this paper. Although the CRB can be easily computed

---

[1]For the clarity of presentation, we denote $\widetilde{x}$ as the estimate of x.

via numerical methods, in order to guide the movements of sensors, we will derive the closed-form CRB.

Even though $\mathbf{J}$ is just a 4×4 matrix, deriving $\mathbf{J}^{-1}$ is challenging, because the N-dimensional joint distribution function in Eq. (3) leads to high inter-node dependence. To simplify the discussion, we set up a Cartesian coordinate system with the origin at the source location and let (x_i, y_i) denote the coordinates of sensor i. Note that the coordinates of the diffusion source and sensor i in the global coordinate system are (x_0, y_0) and $(x_0 + x_i, y_0 + y_i)$, respectively. We apply matrix calculus to derive the closed-form $\mathbf{J}$ and then derive $\mathbf{J}^{-1}$ by block matrix manipulations. Due to space limitation, the details of the derivations are omitted here and can be found in [30]. To facilitate the representation of CRB, we first define several notations, i.e., $\widehat{x}_i$, $\widehat{y}_i$, $\mathbf{L}_{X_1}$, $\mathbf{L}_{X_2}$, $\mathbf{L}_{Y_1}$, and $\mathbf{L}_{Y_2}$. First, $\widehat{x}_i$ is given by

$$\widehat{x}_i = \frac{\sum_{j=1}^{N} x_j (d_j^2 - d_i^2) e^{-2\beta d_j^2}}{\sqrt{\sum_{m=1}^{N} \sum_{n=1}^{N} (d_m^2 - d_n^2)^2 e^{-2\beta(d_m^2 + d_n^2)}}}. \quad (4)$$

By replacing x_j in Eq. (4) with y_j, we can define $\widehat{y}_i$ in a similar manner. Moreover, $\mathbf{L}_{X_1}$, $\mathbf{L}_{Y_1}$ are $1 \times N$ vectors, and $\mathbf{L}_{X_2}$, $\mathbf{L}_{Y_2}$ are $N \times 1$ vectors. The ith elements of them are

$$\mathbf{L}_{X_1}(i) = \sigma^{-1} e^{-\beta d_i^2}(x_i + \widehat{x}_i), \quad \mathbf{L}_{Y_1}(i) = \sigma^{-1} e^{-\beta d_i^2}(y_i + \widehat{y}_i),$$
$$\mathbf{L}_{X_2}(i) = \sigma^{-1} e^{-\beta d_i^2}(x_i - \widehat{x}_i), \quad \mathbf{L}_{Y_2}(i) = \sigma^{-1} e^{-\beta d_i^2}(y_i - \widehat{y}_i).$$

Based on the above notation, the CRBs for the estimates of x_0 and y_0 are given by

$$\text{CRB}(x_0) = \mathbf{J}_{1,1}^{-1} = \frac{(4\alpha^2\beta^2)^{-1}}{\mathbf{L}_{X_1}\mathbf{L}_{X_2} - \frac{(\mathbf{L}_{X_1}\mathbf{L}_{Y_2} + \mathbf{L}_{X_2}\mathbf{L}_{Y_1})^2}{4\mathbf{L}_{Y_1}\mathbf{L}_{Y_2}}}, \quad (5)$$

$$\text{CRB}(y_0) = \mathbf{J}_{2,2}^{-1} = \frac{(4\alpha^2\beta^2)^{-1}}{\mathbf{L}_{Y_1}\mathbf{L}_{Y_2} - \frac{(\mathbf{L}_{X_1}\mathbf{L}_{Y_2} + \mathbf{L}_{X_2}\mathbf{L}_{Y_1})^2}{4\mathbf{L}_{X_1}\mathbf{L}_{X_2}}}. \quad (6)$$

5.3 Profiling Accuracy Metric

In this section, we propose a novel diffusion profiling accuracy metric based on the CRBs derived in Section 5.2, which will be used to guide the movements of sensors in Section 6. Several previous works [23] adopt the determinant of the FIM as the accuracy metric, which jointly considers all the parameters. Such a metric requires the parameters to be properly normalized to avoid biases. However, normalizing the parameters with different physical meanings is highly problem-dependent. Moreover, as the closed-form determinant of the FIM is extremely complicated, the resulted sensor movement scheduling has to rely on the numerical methods with high computational complexities [23], which is not suitable for robotic sensors with limited resources. In this paper, we propose a new profiling accuracy metric, denoted by ω, which is defined according to the sum of reciprocals of $\text{CRB}(x_0)$ and $\text{CRB}(y_0)$. Formally,

$$\omega = \frac{\frac{1}{\text{CRB}(x_0)} + \frac{1}{\text{CRB}(y_0)}}{4\alpha^2\beta^2} = (1-\epsilon)\left(\mathbf{L}_{X_1}\mathbf{L}_{X_2} + \mathbf{L}_{Y_1}\mathbf{L}_{Y_2}\right), \quad (7)$$

where $\epsilon = \frac{(\mathbf{L}_{X_1}\mathbf{L}_{Y_2} + \mathbf{L}_{X_2}\mathbf{L}_{Y_1})^2}{4\mathbf{L}_{X_1}\mathbf{L}_{X_2}\mathbf{L}_{Y_1}\mathbf{L}_{Y_2}}$. By adopting reciprocals, the accuracy analysis can be greatly simplified. Note that as α and β are unknown but fixed in a particular profiling iteration, $4\alpha^2\beta^2$ in the denominator of Eq. (7) is a scaling factor.

Therefore, optimizing $\frac{1}{\text{CRB}(x_0)} + \frac{1}{\text{CRB}(y_0)}$ is equivalent to optimizing ω. As discussed in Section 5.1, we adopt the MLE to estimate Θ. The variance of the MLE result converges to CRB and hence a larger ω indicates more accurate estimation of x_0 and y_0. With the metric ω, the movements of sensors will be directed according to the accuracy of localizing the diffusion source. In the rest of this paper, the term *profiling accuracy* refers to the metric ω defined in Eq. (7). Note that our approach can also be applied to focus on the profiling accuracy of the elapsed time t and discharged substance amount A, by applying the same matrix manipulations to obtain $\text{CRB}(\alpha)$ and $\text{CRB}(\beta)$.

According to the derivations in Section 5.2, $\mathbf{L}_{X_1}$, $\mathbf{L}_{Y_1}$, $\mathbf{L}_{X_2}$ and $\mathbf{L}_{Y_2}$ depend on x_0, y_0, x_i and y_i. Therefore, ω is a function of the positions of the sensors and the diffusion source. As the location of the diffusion source, i.e., (x_0, y_0), is unknown to the network, it is impossible to compute the true profiling accuracy. In our approach, we compute ω based on the estimated location of the diffusion source, i.e., $(\widetilde{x}_0, \widetilde{y}_0)$, given by the MLE. As sensors are repositioned in each profiling iteration, the discrepancy between the true and estimated profiles is expected to be reduced along with the iterations. The profiling accuracy ω in Eq. (7) is still too complex for us to find efficient movement scheduling algorithms. Hence, we derive the approximation to Eq. (7). If sensors are randomly distributed around the diffusion source, ϵ is close to zero. By assuming a random sensor distribution and setting $\epsilon = 0$, the profiling accuracy can be approximated as:

$$\omega \approx \sum_{i=1}^{N} \omega_i, \quad \omega_i = \sigma^{-2} e^{-2\beta d_i^2}\left(d_i^2 - \min_{j \in [1,N], j \neq i} d_j^2\right), \quad (8)$$

where ω_i can be regarded as the *contribution* of sensor i to the overall profiling accuracy. As ω_i depends on d_i and the minimum distance to the source from other sensors, Eq. (8) highly reduces the inter-node dependence compared with Eq. (7). The accuracy of this approximation is validated by extensive numerical results, which are omitted here and available in [30]. In Section 9.3.5, we will evaluate the impact of sensor deployment on the profiling accuracy when the sensor deployment deviates from random distribution around the diffusion source.

6. DIFFUSION PROCESS PROFILING USING ROBOTIC SENSORS

In this section, we formally formulate the movement scheduling problem. Because of the limited mobility and energy budget of aquatic mobile sensors, the sensor movements must be efficiently scheduled in order to achieve the maximum profiling accuracy. As the power consumption of sensing, computation and radio transmission is significantly less than that of locomotion [26], in this paper we only consider the locomotion energy. Moreover, as the locomotion energy is approximately proportional to the moving distance [3], we will use moving distance to quantify the locomotion energy consumption. To simplify the motion control of sensors, we assume that a sensor moves straight in each profiling iteration and the moving distance is always multiple of l meters, where l is referred to as *step*. We note that this model is motivated by the locomotion and computation limitation typically seen for aquatic sensor platforms. First, the locomotion of robotic fish is typically driven by closed-loop motion control algorithms, resulting in constant course-correction during movement. Second, each profiling iteration has short time duration. As a result, the assumption of sensor's straight movement in an iteration does not introduce significant errors in the movement scheduling. As the estimation and movement are performed in an iterative manner, we will focus on the movement scheduling in one profiling iteration. Denote $m_i \in \mathbb{Z}^+$ and $\phi_i \in [0, 2\pi)$ as the number of steps and movement orientation of sensor i in a profiling iteration, respectively. Our objective is to maximize the expected profiling accuracy after sensor movements, subject to the constraints on total energy budget and sensor's individual energy budget. The movement scheduling problem for diffusion profiling is formally formulated as follows:

Movement Scheduling Problem. *Suppose that a total of M steps can be allocated to sensors and sensor i can move at most L_i meters in a profiling iteration. Find the allocation of steps and movement orientations for all N sensors, i.e., $\{m_i, \phi_i | i \in [1, N]\}$, such that the profiling accuracy ω (defined by Eq. (7)) after sensor movements is maximized, subject to:*

$$\sum_{i=1}^{N} m_i \leq M, \qquad (9)$$

$$m_i \cdot l \leq L_i, \quad \forall i. \qquad (10)$$

Eq. (9) upper-bounds the total locomotion energy in a profiling iteration. Eq. (10) can be used to constrain the energy consumption of individual sensors. For instance, L_i can be specified according to the sensor's residual energy. Moreover, L_i can also be specified to ensure the delay of a profiling iteration. If sensors move at a constant speed of v m/s and a profiling iteration is required to be completed within τ seconds to achieve the desired temporal resolution of profiling, L_i can be set to $L_i = v \cdot \tau$. As discussed in Section 4, the cluster head adopts MLE to estimate Θ, and then schedules the movements of sensors such that the expected ω in the next profiling iteration is maximized, subject to the constraints in Eqs. (9) and (10). An exhaustive search to the above problem would yield an exponential complexity with respect to N, which is $O((\frac{2\pi}{\phi_0} \cdot \frac{L_i}{l})^N)$ where ϕ_0 is the granularity in searching for the movement orientation. Such a complexity is prohibitively high as the problem needs to be solved in each profiling iteration by the cluster head. In the next section, we will propose an efficient *greedy* algorithm and a near-optimal *radial* algorithm that are feasible to mote-class robotic sensor platform.

7. SENSOR MOVEMENT SCHEDULING ALGORITHMS

In this section, we propose an efficient *greedy* movement scheduling algorithm based on gradient ascent and a near-optimal *radial* algorithm based on dynamic programming to solve the problem formulated in Section 6.

7.1 Greedy Movement Scheduling

Gradient ascent is a widely adopted approach to find a local maximum of a utility function. In this paper, we propose a *greedy* movement scheduling algorithm based on the gradient ascent approach. We first discuss how to determine the movement orientations for the sensors. Since the profiling accuracy ω given by Eq. (7) is a function of all sensors' positions, we can compute the gradient of ω with respect to

the position of sensor i (denoted by $\nabla_i \omega$), which is formally given by $\nabla_i \omega = \left[\frac{\partial \omega}{\partial x_i}, \frac{\partial \omega}{\partial y_i} \right]^T$. When all sensors except sensor i remain stationary, the metric ω will increase the fastest if sensor i moves in the orientation given by $\nabla_i \omega$. Therefore, in the greedy movement scheduling algorithm, we let $\phi_i = \angle(\nabla_i \omega)$. Note that sensors will move simultaneously when the movement schedule is executed. We now discuss how to allocate the movement steps. The magnitude of $\nabla_i \omega$, denoted by $\|\nabla_i \omega\|$, quantifies the steepness of the metric ω when sensor i moves in the orientation $\angle(\nabla_i \omega)$ while other sensors remain stationary. Therefore, in the *greedy* algorithm, we propose to proportionally allocate the movement steps according to sensor's gradient magnitude. Specifically, m_i is given by $m_i = \min \left\{ \left\lfloor \frac{\|\nabla_i \omega\|}{\sum_{i=1}^{N} \|\nabla_i \omega\|} \cdot M \right\rfloor, \left\lfloor \frac{L_i}{l} \right\rfloor \right\}$. Note that the $\left\lfloor \frac{L_i}{l} \right\rfloor$ in the *min* operator satisfies the constraint Eq. (10). This *greedy* algorithm has linear complexity, i.e., $O(N)$, which is preferable for the cluster head with limited computational resource.

7.2 Radial Movement Scheduling

In this section, we propose a new movement scheduling algorithm based on the approximations discussed in Section 5.3. In this algorithm, each sensor moves toward or away from the estimated source location along the straight line connecting the estimated source location and the sensor's current position. Hence, it is referred to as the *radial* algorithm. We first discuss how to determine sensors' movement orientations and then present a dynamic-programming-based algorithm for allocating movement steps.

From Eq. (8), the contribution of sensor i, ω_i, depends on the minimum distance between the cluster head and other sensors. Because of such inter-node dependence, it is difficult to derive the optimal distance for each sensor that maximizes the overall profiling accuracy ω. It can be shown that the problem involves non-linear and non-convex constrained optimization. Several stochastic search algorithms, such as simulated annealing, can find near-optimal solutions. However, these algorithms often have prohibitively high complexities. In our algorithm, we fix the sensor closest to the estimated source location and only schedule the movements of other sensors in each profiling iteration. As the sensor closest to the source receives the highest SNR, moving other sensors will likely yield more performance gain. Moreover, this sensor can serve as the cluster head that receives measurements from other sensors and computes the movement schedule. It is hence desirable to keep it stationary due to its higher energy consumption in computation and communication. We note that the sensor closest to the source may be different in each iteration after sensor movements, resulting in rotation of cluster head among sensors. By fixing the sensor closest to the source, the distance d_i that maximizes the expected ω_i, denoted by d_i^*, can be directly calculated by

$$d_i^* = \sqrt{\frac{1}{2\beta} + \min_{j \in [1, N]} d_j^2}, \quad \forall i \neq \arg\min_{j \in [1, N]} d_j. \qquad (11)$$

Note that as β is a time-dependent variable, d_i^* also changes with time and hence should be updated in each profiling iteration. Eq. (11) allows us to easily determine the movement orientation of sensor i. Specifically, if $d_i > d_i^*$, sensor i will move toward the estimated source location; Otherwise, sensor i will move in the opposite direction. Formally, by defining $\delta = \text{sgn}(d_i^* - d_i)$, we can express the movement orientation of sensor i as $\phi_i = \angle([\delta \cdot x_i, \delta \cdot y_i]^{\text{T}})$.

We now discuss how to allocate the movement steps. In the rest of this section, when we refer to sensor i, we assume sensor i is not the closest to the estimated source location. After sensor i moves m_i steps in the orientation of ϕ_i, its contribution to the overall profiling accuracy is given by

$$\omega_i(m_i) = \frac{(d_i + \delta \cdot m_i \cdot l)^2 - \min_{j \in [1,N]} d_j^2}{\sigma^2 \cdot e^{2\beta(d_i + \delta \cdot m_i \cdot l)^2}}, \quad (12)$$

where $\min_{j \in [1,N]} d_j^2$ in Eq. (12) is a constant for sensor i, and β can be predicted based on its current estimate to capture the temporal evolution of the diffusion, i.e., $\beta = (1/\tilde{\beta} + 4 \cdot D \cdot \tau)^{-1}$. Given the $radial$ movement orientations described earlier, the formulated problem is equivalent to maximizing $\sum_i \omega_i(m_i)$ subject to the constraints Eqs. (9) and (10), which can be solved by a dynamic programming algorithm as follows.

We number the sensors by $1, 2, \ldots, N-1$, excluding the sensor closest to the estimated source location. Let $\Omega(i, m)$ be the maximum ω when the first i sensors are allocated with m steps. Therefore, the dynamic programming recursion that computes $\Omega(i, m)$ can be expressed as:

$$\Omega(i, m) = \max_{0 \le m_i \le \lfloor L_i/l \rfloor} \{\Omega(i-1, m-m_i) + \omega_i(m_i)\}.$$

The initial condition of the above recursion is $\Omega(0, m) = 0$ for $m \in [0, M]$. According to the above equation, at the ith iteration of the recursion, the optimal value of $\Omega(i, m)$ is computed as the maximum value of $\lfloor L_i/l \rfloor$ cases which have been computed in previous iterations of the recursion. Specifically, for the case where sensor i moves m_i steps, the maximum profiling accuracy ω of the first i sensors allocated with m steps can be computed as $\Omega(i-1, m-m_i) + \omega_i(m_i)$, where $\Omega(i-1, m-m_i)$ is the maximum ω of the first $i-1$ sensors allocated with $m - m_i$ steps. The maximum overall profiling accuracy is given by $\omega^* = \max_{m \in [1,M]} \Omega(N-1, m)$.

We now describe how to construct the movement schedule using the above dynamic programming recursion. The movement schedule of sensor i is represented by a pair (i, m_i). For each $\Omega(i, m)$, we define a movement schedule $S(i, m)$ initialized to be an empty set. The set $S(i, m)$ is filled incrementally in each iteration when $\Omega(i, m)$ is computed. Specifically, in the ith iteration of the recursion, if $\Omega(i-1, m - m_x) + \omega_i(m_x)$ gives the maximum value among all cases, we add a movement schedule (i, m_x) to $S(i, m)$. Formally, $S(i, m) = S(i-1, m-m_x) \cup \{(i, m_x)\}$, where

$$m_x = \underset{0 \le m_i \le \lfloor v\tau/l \rfloor}{\arg\max} \{\Omega(i-1, m-m_i) + \omega_i(m_i)\}.$$

The complexity of the dynamic programming is $O\left((N-1)M^2\right)$, where N is the number of sensors and M is the number of allocatable movement steps in a profiling iteration.

8. DISCUSSIONS

8.1 Impact of Localization and Control Errors

The diffusion profiling process discussed in this paper suffers from localization and control errors introduced by GPS module and robotic fish movement. However, our iterative profiling algorithm can largely avoid the accumulation of such errors. First, to achieve desired temporal resolution of

profiling, as discussed in Section 6, we upper bound sensors' moving distances in a profiling iteration. Therefore, the cluster head only schedules short-distance movements for sensors in each iteration, hence avoiding the accumulated error in movement control. Moreover, the profiling algorithm avoids the accumulation of localization errors by having sensors update their positions in each profiling iteration. Therefore, the cluster head always leverages the latest sensors' positions that are corrupted only by the errors of current localization. As a result, our profiling algorithm is robust to the localization and control errors. In Section 9.3, we will evaluate the impact of such errors on profiling accuracy using real data traces of GPS and robotic fish movement.

8.2 Scalability of the Radial Algorithm

The complexity of the dynamic programming algorithm presented in Section 7.2 is $O\left((N-1)M^2\right)$. When the number of sensors increases, it is desirable to increase the number of allocatable movement steps. As the maximum moving distance of a sensor is limited by its energy budget, M is often a linear function of N, i.e., $M \sim O(N)$. As a result, the complexity will be $O(N^3)$. Such a complexity may lead to long computation delay at the cluster head, which jeopardizes the timeliness of the periodical profiling process. A basic idea to reduce the computation delay is to bound the number of sensors in each cluster. Although many clustering algorithms can achieve this objective [11], we adopt a simple clustering method, in which each node randomly assigns itself a cluster ID ranging from 1 to p, where p is the total number of clusters. When a diffusion process is profiled by multiple clusters, the dynamic programming procedures are executed separately in different clusters. To account for the interdependence among clusters, the overall estimated profile can be calculated as the average of results from all clusters. In Section 9.2, we will evaluate the trade-off between execution time and profiling accuracy of this algorithm.

9. PERFORMANCE EVALUATION

9.1 Evaluation Methodology

We evaluate our approach through a combination of real testbed experiments and trace-driven simulations. First, we implement the MLE, $greedy$ and $radial$ algorithms on TelosB motes and evaluate their overhead. The results provide insights into the feasibility of adopting advanced estimation and movement scheduling algorithms on mote-class robotic sensor platforms. Second, we validate the diffusion process model in Eq. (2) with real lab experiments of Rhodamine-B diffusion. Third, we evaluate the proposed profiling algorithm in extensive simulations based on real data traces. We collect three sets of traces, including GPS localization, robotic fish movement control, and on-water Zigbee wireless communication. We analyze the impact of several important factors on the profiling accuracy, including the temporal sampling scheme, the source location bias, the sensor density, and the network communication overhead. Our results show that our approach can accurately profile dynamic diffusion process with low communication overhead.

9.2 Overhead on Sensor Hardware

We have implemented the MLE and the two movement scheduling algorithms in TinyOS 2.1.1 on TelosB platform [15] equipped with an 8 MHz processor. We ported the C

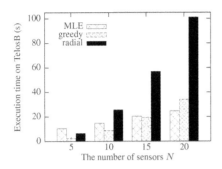

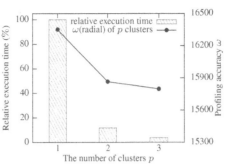

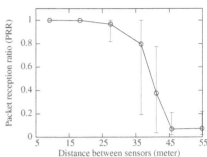

Figure 3: Execution time on Telos-B versus the number of sensors N.

Figure 4: Execution time and profiling accuracy versus the number of clusters p.

Figure 5: Packet reception ratio (PRR) (90% confidence) versus distance.

implementation of the Nelder-Mead algorithm [18] in GNU Scientific Library (GSL) [2] to TinyOS to solve the optimization problem in MLE (see Section 5.1). The porting is non-trivial because dynamic memory allocation and function pointer are extensively used in GSL while these features are not available in TinyOS. Our implementation of MLE requires 19 KB ROM and 1 KB RAM. When 10 sensors are to be scheduled, the two movement scheduling algorithms require 1 and 8.8 KB RAM, respectively. Fig. 3 plots the average execution time of the MLE, *greedy* and *radial* algorithms versus the number of sensors. We note that the complexity of MLE is $O(N)$. For both movement scheduling algorithms, the execution time linearly increases with N, which is consistent with our complexity analysis. The *radial* algorithm takes about 100 seconds to compute the movement schedule in a profiling iteration when $N = 20$. This overhead is reasonable compared with the movement delay of low-speed mobile sensors. The *greedy* algorithm is significantly faster, and hence provides an efficient solution when the timeliness is more important than profiling accuracy. For the *radial* algorithm, 30% execution time is spent on computing a look-up table consisting of each sensor i's contribution, i.e., $\omega_i(m_i)$ in Eq. (12), given all possible values of m_i. There are several ways to further reduce the computational overhead. First, our current implementation employs extensive floating-point computation. Our previous experience shows that fixed-point arithmetic is significantly more efficient on TelosB motes. Moreover, we can also adopt more powerful sensor platforms as cluster head in the network. For instance, the projected execution time on Imote2 [15] equipped with a 416 MHz processor is within 2 seconds for computing the movement schedule for 20 sensors.

Fig. 4 plots the execution time and the profiling accuracy of the scalable variant of *radial* approach, which is discussed in Section 8.2, versus the number of clusters, respectively. The left Y-axis is the ratio of execution time for p clusters with respect to the case of a single cluster. We can see that both the execution time and profiling accuracy decrease with the number of clusters. As discussed in Section 8.2, this is due to the fact that simply averaging results from all clusters does not fully account for the inter-cluster dependence in the accuracy of dynamic programming. Nevertheless, the *radial* algorithm of 2 and 3 clusters still outperforms the *greedy* algorithm of a single cluster in terms of the profiling accuracy.

9.3 Trace-Driven Simulations

9.3.1 Model Validation and Trace Collection

We collected four sets of data traces, which include chemical diffusion, GPS localization errors, robotic fish movement control, and on-water Zigbee wireless communication. First, we use the chemical diffusion traces to validate the diffusion process model in Eq. (2). To collect the traces, we discharge Rhodamine-B solution in saline water, and periodically capture diffusion process using a digital camera. We assume that the grayscale of a pixel in the captured image linearly increases with the concentration at the corresponding physical location [27]. Therefore, the evolution of diffusion process can be characterized by the expansion of a contour given a certain threshold of grayscale in the captured images. With the contour areas along the recorded shooting times, we can estimate D by linear regression. The detailed derivations are available in [30]. Fig. 6 plots the captured images with contours marked in white. Fig. 7 plots the contour areas observed in images and predicted by Eq. (2) versus t. We can see that the model in Eq. (2) well characterizes the diffusion of Rhodamine-B.

To evaluate the proposed profiling algorithms, we also collect traces of GPS localization errors, robotic fish movement control and on-water Zigbee wireless communication. First, the data traces of GPS error are collected using two Linx GPS modules [12] in outdoor open space. We extract the GPS error by comparing the distance measured by GPS modules with the groundtruth distance. The average GPS error is 2.29 meters. Second, the data traces of movement control are collected with a robotic fish developed in our lab [26] (see Fig. 1). The movement of robotic fish is driven by a servo motor that is controlled by continuous pulse-width modulation waves. By setting the fish tail beating amplitude and frequency to $23°$ and 0.9 Hz, the movement speed is 2.5 m/min. We then have the fish swim along a fixed direction in an experimental water tank, and derive the real speed by dividing the moving distance by elapsed time. Third, the data traces of Zigbee communication are collected with two IRIS motes[2] by measuring the packet reception rate (PRR) on the wavy water surface of Lake Lansing on a windy day. We note that the PRR in such wavy water environment is more dynamic than that in calm water environment, due

---

[2]The next generation of our robotic fish platform adopts the same RF230 radio chip equipped on IRIS.

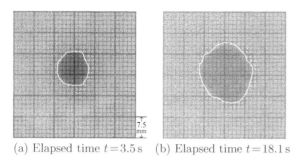

(a) Elapsed time $t=3.5$ s (b) Elapsed time $t=18.1$ s

Figure 6: Observations of the diffusion process of Rhodamine-B solution in saline water.

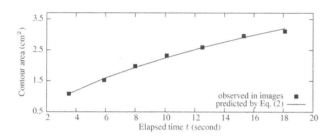

Figure 7: Observed and predicted contour area of diffusing Rhodamine-B in saline water versus elapsed time t.

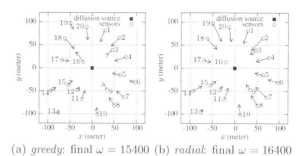

(a) *greedy*: final $\omega = 15400$ (b) *radial*: final $\omega = 16400$

Figure 8: Movement trajectories of 20 sensors in the first 15 profiling iterations.

to multipathing [5]. Specifically, we place the two motes about 12 centimeters above the water surface, and measure the PRR versus the distance between sensors. The results are plotted in Fig. 5. We note that the two IRIS motes achieve an average PRR of 0.8, when they are 37 meters apart. According to our experience, the communication range of IRIS on water surface decreases by about 50% compared to that on land.

9.3.2 Simulation Settings

We conduct extensive simulations based on collected data traces to evaluate the effectiveness of our approach. The simulation programs are written in Matlab. As discussed in Section 3.2, the effect of constant-speed advection is canceled because the sensors and source location are in the same inertial system. Therefore, we only simulate the diffusion process without advection. The diffusion source is at the origin of the coordinate system, i.e., $x_0 = y_0 = 0$. The sensors are randomly deployed in the square region of 200×200 m^2 centered at the origin. The reading of a sensor is set to be the sum of the concentration calculated from Eq. (2), the bias b_i, and a random number sampled from the normal distribution $\mathcal{N}(0, \varsigma^2)$. As discussed in Section 3.2, in each profiling iteration, a sensor samples K readings and outputs the average of them as the measurement. The amount of discharged substance is set to be $A = 0.7 \times 10^6$ cm^3 (i.e., 0.7 m^3) unless otherwise specified. The diffusion coefficient is set to be $D = 5,000$ cm^2/s. Note that the settings of A and D are comparable to the real field experiments reported in [8] where 2 to 5 m^3 of diesel oil were discharged into the sea and the estimated diffusion coefficient ranged from $2,000$ cm^2/s to $7,000$ cm^2/s. The noise standard deviation is set to be $\varsigma = 1$ cm^3/m^2, i.e., 1 cm^3 discharged substance per

unit area.[3] To easily compare various movement scheduling algorithms, we let the first profiling iteration always start at $t = 1800$ s, i.e., half an hour after the discharge. At $t = 1800$ s, the average received SNR is around $10/1$. The rationale of this setting is that moving sensors too early (i.e., at low SNRs) leads to little improvement on profiling accuracy, resulting in waste of energy. In practice, various approaches can be applied to initiate the profiling process, e.g., by comparing the average measurement to a threshold that ensures good SNRs. Other settings include $l = 0.5$ m, $\tau = 60$ s, $v = 2.5$ m/min and $K = 2$, unless otherwise specified.

We compare our approach with two additional baseline algorithms in the evaluation. The first baseline (referred to as *SNR-based*) schedules the movements based on the SNRs received by sensors. The SNR received by sensor i (denoted by SNR$_i$) is defined as $c(d_i, t)/\sigma$, where d_i and t can be computed from the estimated profile $\widetilde{\Theta}$. In the *SNR-based* scheduling algorithm, the sensors always move toward the estimated source location to increase the received SNRs. The movement steps are proportionally allocated according to sensors' SNRs. The rationale behind this heuristic is that the accuracy of MLE increases with SNR. The second baseline (referred to as *annealing*) is based on the simulated annealing algorithm. Specifically, for given movement orientations $\{\phi_i | \forall i\}$, it uses the brutal-force search to find the optimal step allocation under the constraints in Eqs. (9) and (10). It then employs a simulated annealing algorithm to search for the optimal movement orientations. However, it has exponential complexity with respect to the number of sensors.

9.3.3 Sensor Movement Trajectories

We first visually compare the sensor movement trajectories computed by the *greedy* and *radial* movement scheduling algorithms. A total of 20 sensors are deployed. Fig. 8 shows the movement trajectories of sensors in the first 15 profiling iterations. For a particular sensor, the circle denotes its initial position, the segments represent its movement trajectory of 15 profiling iterations, and the arrow indicates its

---

[3]As we adopt a 2-dimensional model to characterize the diffusion process, the physical unit of concentration is cm^3/m^2. As observed in the field experiments [8], diesel oil can penetrate down to several meters from the water surface. As a result, the equivalent ς that accounts for the depth dimension ranges from 0.1 cm^3/m^3 to 1 cm^3/m^3. Our setting is consistent with the noise standard derivation of the crude oil sensor Cyclops-7 [28], which is 0.1 cm^3/m^3.

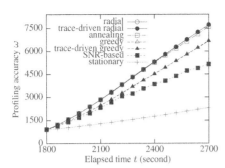 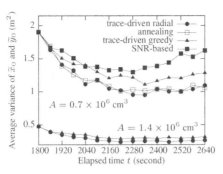 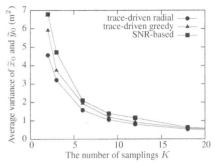

Figure 9: Profiling accuracy ω versus elapsed time t.

Figure 10: Average $\mathrm{Var}(\widetilde{x}_0)$ and $\mathrm{Var}(\widetilde{y}_0)$ versus elapsed time t.

Figure 11: Average $\mathrm{Var}(\widetilde{x}_0)$ and $\mathrm{Var}(\widetilde{y}_0)$ versus the number of samplings K.

movement orientation in the 15th iteration. The sensor with no segments remains stationary during all 15 profiling iterations. We can see that, with the *greedy* algorithm, several sensors (e.g., sensor 15, 16, and 17) have bent trajectories. This is because the movement orientation of each sensor is to maximize the gradient ascent of ω, hence not necessarily to be aligned along the iterations. In the *radial* algorithm, sensors' trajectories are more straight. This is because the movement orientation is along the direction determined by the current sensor position and the estimated source location that is close to the true source location. Moreover, we find that the *radial* algorithm outperforms the *greedy* algorithm in terms of profiling accuracy after the first 15 iterations. In the *greedy* algorithm, the orientation assignment and movement step allocation are based on the gradient derived from the current positions of sensors. Besides, the *greedy* algorithm does not account for the interdependence of sensors in providing the overall profiling accuracy. As a result, its solution may not lead to the maximum ω after the sensor movements and the temporal evolution of diffusion.

9.3.4 Profiling Accuracy

In the second set of simulations, we evaluate the accuracy in estimating the diffusion profile Θ. Total 10 sensors are deployed and our evaluation lasts for 15 profiling iterations. Fig. 9 plots the profiling accuracy ω (defined in Eq. (7)) based on the estimated diffusion profile $\widetilde{\Theta}$. The curve labeled with "stationary" is the result if all sensors always remain stationary. Nevertheless, we can see that the profiling accuracy improves over time because of the temporal evolution of the diffusion. In Fig. 9, the curves labeled with a prefix "trace-driven" are the simulation results based on the data traces of localization errors and robotic fish movement. Specifically, the position reading of a robotic sensor is corrupted by a localization error randomly selected from the GPS error traces. When a robotic sensor moves, its speed is set to be a real speed that is randomly selected from the data traces. We can see that, for both *greedy* and *radial*, the curves with and without simulated movement control and localization errors almost overlap with each other. As our iterative approach has no accumulated error, small movement control and localization errors have little impact on our approach. The *radial* algorithm outperforms the *greedy* and *SNR-based* algorithms by 16% and 50% in terms of ω at the 15th profiling iteration, respectively. And the accuracy performance of the *radial* algorithm is very close to the

annealing algorithm that can find the near-optimal solution. However, we note that in each iteration of the *annealing* algorithm, a new look-up table needs to be computed due to changed movement orientations. Hence its execution time highly depends on the number of iterations that can be very large. Therefore, the *annealing* algorithm is infeasible on mote-class platforms.

Fig. 10 plots the average of $\mathrm{Var}(\widetilde{x}_0)$ and $\mathrm{Var}(\widetilde{y}_0)$ in each profiling iteration under various settings of the discharged substance amount A. In order to evaluate the variances in each profiling iteration, the sensors perform many rounds of MLE, where each round yields a pair of $(\widetilde{x}_0, \widetilde{y}_0)$. The $\mathrm{Var}(\widetilde{x}_0)$ and $\mathrm{Var}(\widetilde{y}_0)$ are calculated from all rounds. From Fig. 10, we find that the variances may increase (for the *SNR-based* scheduling algorithm) or fluctuate (for other approaches) after several iterations. This is because the variances are time-dependent due to the involving of α and β in $\mathrm{CRB}(x_0)$ and $\mathrm{CRB}(y_0)$. Moreover, we can see that the variances decrease with A. As sensors receive higher SNRs in the case of higher A, our result consists with the intuition that the estimation error decreases with SNR. Compared with the *SNR-based* algorithm, the *radial* algorithm reduces the variance in estimating diffusion source location by 36% for $A = 0.7 \times 10^6$ cm^3. Compared with the *greedy* algorithm, the reductions are 12% and 18% for $A = 0.7 \times 10^6$ and 1.4×10^6 cm^3, respectively. We also evaluate the accuracy in estimating the substance amount A and elapsed time t. Both the *greedy* and *radial* algorithms can achieve a high accuracy. For instance, the relative error in estimating A for *radial* algorithm is within 1.4%. Due to space limitation, detailed evaluation results are omitted here and can be found in [30].

9.3.5 Impact of Sampling, Source Bias and Network Density

We characterize the profiling error after 15 iterations by the average of $\mathrm{Var}(\widetilde{x}_0)$ and $\mathrm{Var}(\widetilde{y}_0)$. Except for the evaluations on network density, a total of 10 sensors are deployed. In the temporal sampling scheme presented in Section 3.2, a sensor yields the average of K continuous samples as the measurement to reduce noise variance. Fig. 11 plots the profiling error versus K. We can see that the profiling error decreases with K. The relative reductions of profiling error by the *radial* algorithm with respect to the *greedy* and *SNR-based* algorithms are about 18% and 30%, respectively, when K ranges from 2 to 20.

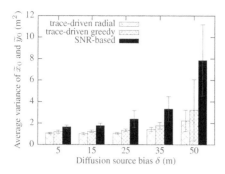
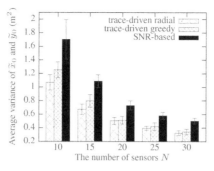
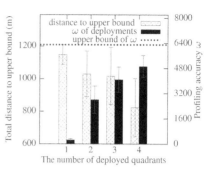

Figure 12: Average $\mathrm{Var}(\widetilde{x}_0)$ **and** $\mathrm{Var}(\widetilde{y}_0)$ **versus source location bias** δ.

Figure 13: Average $\mathrm{Var}(\widetilde{x}_0)$ **and** $\mathrm{Var}(\widetilde{y}_0)$ **versus the number of sensors** N.

Figure 14: Impact of initial deployment on the profiling accuracy.

The approximations discussed in Section 5.3 assume that the sensors are randomly deployed around the diffusion source. In this set of simulations, we evaluate the impact of source location bias on profiling accuracy. Specifically, the diffusion source appears at $(\delta, 0)$, where δ is referred to as the source location bias. Fig. 12 plots the profiling error versus δ. To jointly account for the impact of random sensor deployment, for each setting of δ, we deploy a number of networks and show the error bars. We find that the *radial* algorithm is robust to the source location bias. Moreover, we note that the *radial* algorithm is consistently better than other algorithms.

Fig. 13 plots the profiling error versus the number of sensors. When more sensors are deployed, the profiling error can be reduced. The *radial* algorithm is consistently better than the other algorithms. For all algorithms, the profiling error is reduced by about 40% when the number of sensors increases from 10 to 15. Moreover, the relative reduction of profiling error decreases with the number of sensors.

9.3.6 Impact of Sensor Deployment

In this section, we evaluate the impact of initial sensor deployment on the profiling accuracy and energy consumption in locomotion. We fix each d_i and randomly deploy sensors in one, two adjacent, three and four quadrants of the plane originated at the source location, resulting in four sensor deployments. We compute the upper bound of ω, in which sensors' angles with respect to the source location are exhaustively searched to maximize the profiling accuracy. Note that the sensor deployment with maximized profiling accuracy is still an open issue. Fig. 14 plots the upper bound of ω as well as the profiling accuracy of four sensor deployments. We can see that the profiling accuracy of the four-quadrant deployment is the closest to the upper bound. Fig. 14 also plots the minimum total distance that the sensors in a deployment have to move to achieve the upper bound ω. We can observe that if sensors are not deployed around the source location, spreading sensors first can significantly improve the profiling accuracy. However, if sensors have limited energy for locomotion, it is more beneficial to deploy sensors around the source to avoid energy-consuming spreading movements.

9.3.7 Communication Overhead

We conduct a set of trace-driven simulations to evaluate the communication overhead of our approach. Specif-ically, we choose the shortest distance path as the routing path from a sensor to the cluster head, where the distance metric of each hop is PRR^{-1}, i.e., the expected number of (re-)transmissions on the hop. When a node transmits packet to the next hop, the packet is delivered with a success probability equal to the PRR retrieved from the communication traces with the same distance between the sender and receiver. The node re-transmits the packet for 10 times before it is dropped until success. In the simulations, 30 sensors are randomly deployed. The packet to the cluster head includes sensor ID, current position and measurement, and the packet to the sensor includes moving orientation and distance. Our simulation results show that the number of packet (re-)transmissions in a profiling iteration has a mean of 158 and a standard deviation of 28. Even if all these transmissions happen sequentially, the delay will be within seconds, because transmitting a TinyOS packet only takes about 10 milliseconds. This result shows that our approach has low communication overhead under realistic settings.

10. CONCLUSION AND FUTURE WORK

In this paper we propose an accuracy-aware profiling approach for aquatic diffusion processes using robotic sensor networks. Our approach features an iterative profiling process where the sensors reposition themselves to progressively improve the profiling accuracy along the iterations. We develop two movement scheduling algorithms, including an efficient *greedy* algorithm and a near-optimal *radial* algorithm. We implement our algorithms on TelosB motes and evaluate their overhead. We also conduct extensive simulations based on real traces of chemical diffusion, GPS localization errors, robotic fish movement, and wireless communication. Our results show that our approach can accurately profile dynamic diffusion processes with low overhead.

The movement scheduling approach described in this paper is targeted at robotic sensors with limited sensing and motion capabilities in relatively calm water environment. We are developing the next generation of our robotic fish platforms that are capable of more complex sensing and motion control. In our future work, we will investigate distributed control algorithms that allow such robotic sensors to autonomously plan their motion paths, which reduce the overhead of cross-sensor coordination in collaborative sensing tasks. In addition, we will extend our approach to address wavy water environment by quantifying the impact of waves on sensor measurement and wireless link quality.

Acknowledgment

This research was supported in part by the U.S. National Science Foundation under grants ECCS-1029683 and CNS-0954039 (CAREER). We thank Ruogu Zhou for his contribution in traces collection and hardware design. We also thank the anonymous reviewers providing the valuable feedbacks.

11. REFERENCES

[1] http://www.infoplease.com/ipa/A0001451.html.

[2] GSL-GNU scientific library, 2011.

[3] D. Barrett, M. Triantafyllou, D. Yue, M. Grosenbaugh, and M. Wolfgang. Drag reduction in fish-like locomotion. *Journal of Fluid Mechanics*, 392(1):183–212, 1999.

[4] J. Chin, D. Yau, N. Rao, Y. Yang, C. Ma, and M. Shankar. Accurate localization of low-level radioactive source under noise and measurement errors. In *The 6th ACM conference on Embedded Networked Sensor Systems (SenSys)*, pages 183–196, 2008.

[5] P. Corke, T. Wark, R. Jurdak, W. Hu, P. Valencia, and D. Moore. Environmental wireless sensor networks. *Proceedings of the IEEE*, 98(11):1903–1917, 2010.

[6] J. Crank. *The mathematics of diffusion*. Oxford University Press, 1983.

[7] R. Duda, P. Hart, and D. Stork. *Pattern Classification*. Wiley, 2001.

[8] A. Elliott. Shear diffusion and the spread of oil in the surface layers of the north sea. *Ocean Dynamics*, 39(3):113–137, 1986.

[9] C. Eriksen, T. Osse, R. Light, T. Wen, T. Lehman, P. Sabin, J. Ballard, and A. Chiodi. Seaglider: A long-range autonomous underwater vehicle for oceanographic research. *IEEE Journal of Oceanic Engineering*, 26(4):424–436, 2001.

[10] Hydroid, LLC. REMUS: Autonomous technology for your world.

[11] V. Kumar. *Introduction to parallel computing*. Addison-Wesley Longman Publishing Co., Inc., 2002.

[12] Linx Technologies. Linx GPS receiver module data guide.

[13] N. March and M. Tosi. *Introduction to Liquid State Physics*. World Scientific Publishing, 2002.

[14] J. Matthes, L. Groll, and H. Keller. Source localization by spatially distributed electronic noses for advection and diffusion. *IEEE Transactions on Signal Processing*, 53(5):1711–1719, 2005.

[15] Memsic Corp. TelosB, IRIS, Imote2 datasheets.

[16] S. Murray. Turbulent diffusion of oil in the ocean. *Limnology and oceanography*, 17(5):651–660, 1972.

[17] A. Nehorai, B. Porat, and E. Paldi. Detection and localization of vapor-emitting sources. *IEEE Transactions on Signal Processing*, 43(1):243–253, 1995.

[18] J. Nelder and R. Mead. A simplex method for function minimization. *The Computer Journal*, 7(4):308, 1965.

[19] L. Rossi, B. Krishnamachari, and C. Kuo. Distributed parameter estimation for monitoring diffusion phenomena using physical models. In *The 1st annual IEEE communications society conference on Sensor, Mesh and Ad Hoc Communications and Networks (SECON)*, pages 460–469, 2004.

[20] S. Ruberg, R. Muzzi, S. Brandt, J. Lane, T. Miller, J. Gray, S. Constant, and E. Downing. A wireless internet-based observatory: The real-time coastal observation network (recon). In *OCEANS*, pages 1–6, 2007.

[21] D. Rudnick, R. Davis, C. Eriksen, D. Fratantoni, and M. Perry. Underwater gliders for ocean research. *Marine Technology Society Journal*, 38(2):73–84, 2004.

[22] A. Singh, R. Nowak, and P. Ramanathan. Active learning for adaptive mobile sensing networks. In *The 5th international conference on Information Processing in Sensor Networks (IPSN)*, pages 60–68, 2006.

[23] Z. Song, Y. Chen, J. Liang, and D. Uciński. Optimal mobile sensor motion planning under nonholonomic constraints for parameter estimation of distributed systems. *International Journal of Intelligent Systems Technologies and Applications*, 3:277–295, 2007.

[24] S. Srinivasan, K. Ramamritham, and P. Kulkarni. Ace in the hole: Adaptive contour estimation using collaborating mobile sensors. In *The 7th international conference on Information Processing in Sensor Networks (IPSN)*, pages 147–158, 2008.

[25] R. Tan, G. Xing, J. Wang, and H. So. Exploiting reactive mobility for collaborative target detection in wireless sensor networks. *IEEE Transactions on Mobile Computing*, 9(3):317–332, 2010.

[26] X. Tan. Autonomous robotic fish as mobile sensor platforms: Challenges and potential solutions. *Marine Technology Society Journal*, 45(4):31–40, 2011.

[27] E. Tsotsas and A. Mujumdar. Modern drying technology, vol. 2, experimental techniques, 2009.

[28] Turner Designs Inc. Cyclops-7 user's manual.

[29] S. Vijayakumaran, Y. Levinbook, and T. Wong. Maximum likelihood localization of a diffusive point source using binary observations. *IEEE Transactions on Signal Processing*, 55(2):665–676, 2007.

[30] Y. Wang, R. Tan, G. Xing, J. Wang, and X. Tan. Accuracy-aware aquatic diffusion process profiling using robotic sensor networks. Technical report, CSE Department, Michigan State University, 2011.

[31] J. Weimer, B. Sinopoli, and B. Krogh. Multiple source detection and localization in advection-diffusion processes using wireless sensor networks. In *The 30th Real-Time Systems Symposium (RTSS)*, pages 333–342, 2009.

[32] G. Xing, J. Wang, Z. Yuan, R. Tan, L. Sun, Q. Huang, X. Jia, and H. So. Mobile scheduling for spatiotemporal detection in wireless sensor networks. *IEEE Transactions on Parallel and Distributed Systems*, 21(12):1851–1866, 2010.

[33] T. Zhao and A. Nehorai. Distributed sequential bayesian estimation of a diffusive source in wireless sensor networks. *IEEE Transactions on Signal Processing*, 55(4):1511–1524, 2007.

Error-Resilient and Complexity-Constrained Distributed Coding for Large Scale Sensor Networks

Kumar Viswanatha, Sharadh Ramaswamy[*], Ankur Saxena[†] and Kenneth Rose[‡]
University of California - Santa Barbara
Santa Barbara, CA - 93106-9560, USA
{kumar,rsharadh,ankur,rose}@ece.ucsb.edu

ABSTRACT

There has been considerable interest in distributed source coding within the compression and sensor network research communities in recent years, primarily due to its potential contributions to low-power sensor networks. However, two major obstacles pose an existential threat on practical deployment of such techniques in real world sensor networks, namely, the exponential growth of decoding complexity with network size and coding rates, and the critical requirement for error-resilience given the severe channel conditions in many wireless sensor networks. Motivated by these challenges, this paper proposes a novel, unified approach for large scale, error-resilient distributed source coding, based on an optimally designed classifier-based decoding framework, where the design explicitly controls the decoding complexity. We also present a deterministic annealing (DA) based global optimization algorithm for the design due to the highly non-convex nature of the cost function, which further enhances the performance over basic greedy iterative descent technique. Simulation results on data, both synthetic and from real sensor networks, provide strong evidence that the approach opens the door to practical deployment of distributed coding in large sensor networks. It not only yields substantial gains in terms of overall distortion, compared to other state-of-the-art techniques, but also demonstrates how its decoder naturally scales to large networks while constraining the complexity, thereby enabling performance gains that increase with network size.

Categories and Subject Descriptors

E.4 [**Coding and information theory**]: Data compaction and compression, Error control codes; G.3 [**Probability and statistics**]: Probabilistic algorithms; I.4.2 [**Compression**]: Approximate methods

General Terms

Algorithms, Theory, Experimentation

Keywords

Distributed source-channel coding, Large scale sensor networks, Error resilient coding

1. INTRODUCTION AND MOTIVATION

Sensor networks have gained immense importance in recent years, both in the research community as well as in the industry, mainly due to their practicability in numerous applications. Sensors are typically low power devices and minimizing the number of transmissions is one of the primary objectives for a system designer. It is widely accepted that exploiting inter-sensor correlations to compress information is an important paradigm for such energy efficient sensor networks. The problem of encoding correlated sources in a network has conventionally been tackled in the literature from two different directions. The first approach is based on 'in-network compression' wherein the compression is performed at intermediate nodes along the route to the sink [8]. Such techniques tend to be typically wasteful in resources at all-but the last hop of the sensor network. The second approach involves 'distributed source coding' (DSC) wherein the correlations are exploited before transmission at each sensor [3].

The basic DSC setting involves multiple correlated sources (e.g., data collected by a number of spatially distributed sensors) which need to be transmitted from different locations to a central data collection unit/sink. The main objective of DSC is to exploit inter-source correlations despite the fact that each sensor source is encoded without access to other sources (see Fig. 1). The only information available before designing DSC is their joint statistics (e.g., a training dataset). Today the research in DSC can be categorized into two broad camps. First approach derives its principles from channel coding, wherein block encoding techniques are used to exploit correlation [1, 9, 18]. While these techniques are efficient in achieving good compression and error-resilience (using efficient forward error correcting codes), they suffer from significant delays and high encoding complexities, which make them unsuitable for several sensor network applications. The second approach is based on

[‡]This work was supported by the NSF under grants CCF-0728986, CCF-1016861 and CCF-1118075.
[*]S. Ramasway was with Mayachitra, Inc., USA, at the time of this work.
[†]A. Saxena is now with Samsung Telecommunications America, 1301 E. Lookout Dr., Richardson, TX, USA - 75082.

source coding and quantization techniques, which introduce practically zero delay into the system. Efficient design of such zero delay DSC for noiseless systems has been studied in several publications including [4, 5, 12, 14], and will be more relevant to us in this paper.

However, two major obstacles have deterred these approaches from gaining practical significance in real world sensor networks. Firstly, the decoder complexity grows exponentially with the number of sources making these conventional techniques (typically designed for 2 - 3 sources) infeasible for large sensor networks. Surprisingly, very few researchers have so far addressed this important issue, e.g. [6, 10, 19, 20]. However most of these approaches suffer from important drawbacks which will be explained in detail in section 3.

The second important reason for inefficiency of current DSC methods is the fact that sensor networks usually operate at highly adverse channel conditions and codes designed for a noise-less framework provide extremely poor error-resilience. The design of such error-resilient DSC is a very challenging problem, as the objectives of DSC and channel coding are counter-active in the sense that one tries to eliminate dependencies, while the other tries to correct errors using the dependencies. On the one hand, the system could be made compression centric and designed to exploit inter-source correlations analogous to the noiseless framework. However, this reduces the dependencies among the transmitted bits leading to poor error-resilience at the decoder and eventually poor reconstruction distortions. On the other extreme, the encoders could be designed to preserve all the correlations among the transmitted bits which could be exploited at the decoder to achieve good error resilience. However, such a design fails to exploit the gains due to distributed compression leading to poor over all rate-distortion performance.

Motivated by these practical challenges, in this paper we address the problem of error-resilient and zero-delay distributed compression for large scale sensor networks. In a recent work [16], a new decoding paradigm for large scale DSC was proposed in case of noiseless networks, wherein the received bits were first compressed (transformed) down to an allowable decoding rate and the decoding was performed in the compressed space. In this paper, we build upon the work in [16] and propose an optimal method to compress the received bits which naturally builds error resilience into the system leading to a unified error-resilient and complexity constrained mechanism for distributed coding in large scale sensor networks. Essentially, we map every received index to a cloud center based on a minimum distance criterion leading to a classification of indices into decoding spheres. The reconstructions are purely based on the sphere to which the received index belongs. These spheres (cloud centers), when designed optimally, lead to an error-correcting code which serves the dual purpose of a source-channel decoder. We use design principles from source-channel coding for individual sources, and propose a global optimization technique based on deterministic annealing [13] to address the intricate nature of the design problem. As we will present in section 4, our methodology overcomes all the drawbacks with the conventional approaches, presented in section 3, and provides significant improvements in reconstruction distortion over state of the art methods for both synthetic and real world sensor network datasets.

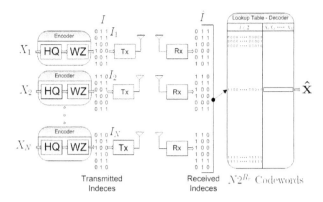

Figure 1: Basic DSC setup - Lookup table based decoder

The rest of the paper is organized as follows. In Sec. 2, we formulate the problem, introduce notation, and discuss the difficulties in the design of large-scale distributed source coding system. In Sec. 3, we review related work, and explain our proposed compression/classification based approach in Sec. 4. Sec. 5 describes the algorithm for system design with details about complexity in Sec. 6. Finally, results are presented in Sec. 7, followed by Conclusions in Sec. 9.

2. DESIGN FORMULATION

Before describing the problem setup, we state some of the assumptions made in this paper. Firstly, to keep the understanding simple, we only consider spatial correlations between sensors and neglect the temporal correlations. Temporal correlations can be easily incorporated using techniques similar to that in [15]. Secondly, in this paper we consider only channels with errors, noting that the methodology can be easily extended to incorporate erasures. We will briefly address this issue in section 8. Further, we assume that there exists a separate channel from every sensor to the central receiver, i.e., information is not routed in a multi-hop fashion. However, the method we propose is fairly general and is applicable to the multi-hop setting. Throughout this paper, we make the practical assumption that while the joint densities may not be known during the design, there will be access to a training sequence of source samples and channel errors during design. In practice this could either be gathered off-line before the deployment of the sensor network or could be collected during an initial phase after deployment.

We begin with the description of the conventional (zero delay) DSC setup. We refer to [6] for a detailed description. Consider a sensor network composed of N sensors (denoted by $s_1, s_2 \ldots, s_N$ respectively). The sensors communicate with a central receiver (denoted by S) at rates $(R_1, R_2 \ldots R_N)$ respectively over noisy channels as depicted in Fig. 1. At regular time intervals, each sensor observes some physical phenomenon (eg. temperature, pressure etc). These sensor observations are modeled as correlated random variables denoted by $(X_1, X_2 \ldots X_N)$. Sensor s_i encodes X_i using R_i bits and transmits it to the receiver. The central receiver attempts to jointly reconstruct $(X_1, X_2 \ldots X_N)$ using bits received from all the sensors. The objective is to design the encoders at each of the sensors and decoders (estimators) at the central receiver so that the overall distortion between the observations and the reconstructions is minimized.

Transmitted Bits (Gray Mapped)

Figure 2: Example of a typical encoder (irregular quantizer). In this example, $N_i = 16$ quantization regions and $R_i = 2$ bits.

Encoding at each sensor is composed of two stages. At sensor s_i, the first stage is a simple high rate quantizer (labeled as "HQ" in Fig. 1), $\mathcal{H}_i$, which discretizes the real space into a finite number of non-overlapping regions N_i. Specifically, $\mathcal{H}_i$ is a mapping which assigns one of the quantization indices to every point in the real space, i.e.,

$$\mathcal{H}_i : X_i \in \mathcal{R} \rightarrow \mathcal{Q}_i = \{1 \ldots N_i\} \quad (1)$$

Note, that the quantizers are *high rate* so as to exclude them from the joint encoder-decoder design. This is a practical engineering necessity, and the primary purpose of the high-rate quantizers is to discretize the sources. We refer to [14] for further details. The second stage of encoding, which we call a 'Wyner Ziv map'/WZ-map[1] (also called binning in some related work [20]), relabels the N_i quantization regions with a smaller number, 2^{R_i}, of transmission indices. Mathematically, the Wyner Ziv map at source i, denoted by $\mathcal{W}_i$, is the following function:

$$\mathcal{W}_i : \mathcal{Q}_i \rightarrow \mathcal{I}_i = \{1 \ldots 2^{R_i}\} \quad (2)$$

and the encoding operation can be expressed as a composite function:

$$I_i = \mathcal{E}_i(x_i) = \mathcal{W}_i\left(\mathcal{H}_i(x_i)\right) \; \forall i \quad (3)$$

A typical example of a WZ-map is shown in Fig. 2. Observe that the WZ-map performs lossy-compression. In fact, some regions which are far apart are mapped to the same transmission index, and this makes the encoding operation at each source equivalent to that of an irregular quantizer. Although this operation might seem counter intuitive at first, if designed optimally, it is precisely these modules which assist in exploiting inter-source correlations without inter-sensor communication. Essentially, the design would be such that, it enables the decoder to distinguish between the possible quantization regions for the transmitted index of the particular source using the indices transmitted from other sources. It is fairly well known in the source coding literature (see [12, 14, 20] and the references therein) that these WZ-maps, if properly designed, provide significant improvements in the over all rate-distortion performance compared to that achievable by regular quantizers operating at the same transmission rates (see also section 7.4). It is important to note that the WZ-maps must be designed jointly before the sensor network begins its operation using the source-channel statistics or a training sequence of observations. Efficient design of these mappings for noiseless networks has been studied in several prior publications such as [6, 14].

The encoder at sensor s_i transmits the binary representation of I_i, determined by a standard Gray mapping, to the remote receiver using a standard BPSK modulation scheme.

In this paper, we assume that the channels are independent additive white Gaussian noise and the receiver employs separate optimal detection. This makes the effective channel seen by each bit an independent Binary Symmetric Channel (BSC) whose cross-over probability depends on the variance of the noise. However, we note that the design principles presented in the paper are based on an available training set of source samples and channel errors and hence can be easily extended to more general modulation-demodulation schemes and channel error patterns. In particular, the method can be easily applied to the setting where bits are routed over multiple hops (in which case the channel errors are correlated), by collecting the corresponding training set of error samples and designing the system using the collected training sets. We denote the symbol obtained following optimal detection and inverse Gray mapping by $\hat{I}_i \in \mathcal{I}_i$ as shown in Fig. 1. We use the short-hand $I = (I_1, I_2 \ldots I_N)$ and $\hat{I} = (\hat{I}_1, \hat{I}_2 \ldots \hat{I}_N)$. Note that both I and $\hat{I}$ take values in $\mathcal{I} = \mathcal{I}_1 \times \mathcal{I}_2 \ldots \mathcal{I}_N$.

Observe that the total number of bits received at the decoder is $R_r = \sum_{i=1}^{N} R_i$, of which a subset could be erroneous. The decoder reconstructs each source based on the received index $\hat{I}$. Formally, the decoder for source i is a mapping from the set of received index tuples to the reconstruction space and is given by:

$$\mathcal{D}_i : \mathcal{I} \rightarrow \hat{X}_i \in \mathcal{R} \quad (4)$$

Usually the decoder is assumed to be a lookup table, which has the reconstruction values stored for each possible received index as shown in Fig. 1. For optimal decoding, the lookup table has a unique reconstruction stored for each possible received index tuple. Hence the total storage at the decoder grows as $\mathcal{O}(N \times 2^{R_r}) = \mathcal{O}(N \times 2^{\sum_{i=1}^{N} R_i})$, which is exponential in N. We call the total storage of the lookup table as the *decoder complexity*. In most prior work, DSC was performed for a few (typically 2 - 3) sources, with the implicit assumption of design scalability with network size. But this exponential growth in decoder complexity for optimal decoding with the number of sources and transmission rates makes it infeasible to use the conventional setup in practical settings even with moderately large number of sources. Just to illustrate, consider a sensor network with 20 sources communicating at $R_i = 2$ bits per source. The decoder receives 40 bits of information and has to store a unique reconstruction for every received bit combination. This would require a decoder storage of over $20 \times 2^{\sum_{i=1}^{20} 2} \approx 175$ TeraBytes... In the next section, we describe some of the related work which has been done to address this huge exponential storage at the decoder.

It is worthwhile to note that the encoding operation in the above scheme involves a simple quantization of the source samples followed by a direct look up of the transmission index. The total storage at each encoder includes its high rate quantization codebook (of size $|\mathcal{Q}_i|$) and the corresponding WZ-map (of size $|\mathcal{Q}_i| 2^{R_i}$). For typical values of $|\mathcal{Q}_i|$ and R_i, the encoder complexity is significantly small and hence can be easily implemented on a physical sensor mote. This inherent advantage makes such approaches to distributed coding more viable in low cost practical sensor networks than the channel coding based methods, such as [9, 18], which require complex Slepian-Wolf coders at each source. Hence, hereafter, our concern will be only towards addressing decoder complexity, assuming that the encoders can be easily implemented on a physical sensor mote.

---

[1]The term 'Wyner-Ziv map' is coined after Wyner and Ziv [17] who first solved the lossy version of the side information setup in information theory

3. RELATED WORK

One practical solution proposed in the past to handle the exponential growth in decoder complexity is to group the sources based on source statistics [6] and to perform DSC within each cluster. By restricting the number of sources within each group, the decoder complexity is maintained at affordable limits. Evidently, even in the noiseless scenario, such an approach does not exploit inter-cluster dependencies and hence would lead to sub-optimal estimates. Moreover, when there is channel noise, the resilience of the decoder to channel errors degrades significantly as it is forced to use only a subset of received bits to correct any error. Also in most prior work, source groups are designed only based on the source statistics, completely ignoring the channel conditions. Indeed, it is a much harder problem to come up with good source grouping mechanisms which are optimized for both source and channel statistics.

It is worthwhile to mention that an alternate approach, other than the lookup table has been proposed in the literature to practically implement the decoder [6, 19, 20]. In this approach, the decoder computes the reconstructions on the fly by estimating the posterior probabilities for quantization index q_i as $P(q_i|\hat{I})$, when a particular $\hat{I}$ is received. Such an approach requires us to store the high rate quantization codewords at the decoder, which grow only linearly in N. However, to compute the posterior probabilities $P(q_i|\hat{I})$, using Bayes rule, we have:

$$P(\tilde{q}_i|\hat{I}) = \gamma \sum_{Q:q_i=\tilde{q}_i} P(\hat{I}|I(Q))P(Q) \qquad (5)$$

where γ is a normalization constant, and $Q = (q_1, q_2 \ldots, q_N)$. The above marginalization requires an exponential number of operations to be performed at the decoder, let alone the exponential storage required to store the probabilities $P(q_1, \ldots q_N)$.

To limit the computational complexity, prior work such as [2, 6, 20] have proposed clustering the sources and linking the clusters using a limited complexity Bayesian network (or a factor graph), and thereby using message passing algorithms to find $P(\tilde{q}_i|\hat{I})$ with affordable complexities. These approaches provide significant improvement in distortion over simple source grouping methods at fixed transmission rates and channel SNRs as they exploit inter-cluster correlations efficiently. However, a major drawback of such techniques, which is usually overlooked, is that they require the storage of the Bayesian network/factor graph at the decoder. Though this storage grows linearly in N, it grows exponentially with the rate of the 'high rate quantizers'. To be more precise, if we choose $N_i = 2^{R_q} \forall i$, then the storage of the Bayesian network grows of the order of $\mathcal{O}(N2^{MR_q})$ where M is the maximum number of parents for any source node in the Bayesian network. Typically (see for example [12, 14, 6]), in source coding, R_q is chosen as $R+3$ or $R+4$ for the Wyner-Ziv maps to exploit the inter source correlations efficiently. This makes the Bayesian network based techniques less efficient as the gains in distortion obtained by introducing the Bayesian network are superseded by the excess storage required to store the Bayesian network. We will show in our results that the Bayesian network based methods under-perform even the source grouping techniques even for moderate values of N at a *fixed storage*. Hence, though it is counter-intuitive at first, it is indeed beneficial to group

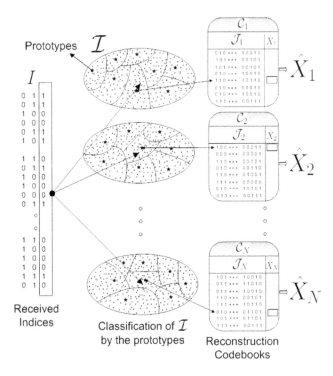

Figure 3: Prototype based bit-mapper approach to decoding

more sources within a cluster instead of connecting the clusters using a Bayesian network.

We note that, the storage required for transition probabilities in the Bayesian network can be significantly reduced if the joint densities of source distributions are parameterized (for example as multivariate Gaussian). However, such approximations are highly prone to estimation inaccuracies and could lead to sub-optimal designs for more general/real world source and channel statistics as has been observed in [20]. We next describe our proposed classification-based approach for decoding which overcomes these drawbacks and achieves a unified approach to error resilient and complexity constrained distributed compression.

4. THE CLASSIFICATION/COMPRESSION BASED APPROACH TO DECODING

Recall that the decoder receives $R_r = \sum_{i=1}^{N} R_i$ bits of information of which part could be erroneous. The look up table at the receiver cannot store a unique reconstruction for every possible received combination of bits. Hence, to decode source s_i, we first find an optimal classification scheme which groups the set of all possible received index tuples, $\mathcal{I}$, into K_i groups. We then assign a unique reconstruction for all received combinations which belong to the same group. Essentially, we decompose the monolithic decoder, which was a simple look-up table, into a compressor/classifier/bit-mapper followed by a look-up table of reconstructions. Note that the classification could possibly be different for decoding each source. This would bring down the total storage required for codebooks from $N2^{R_r}$ to $\sum_{i=1}^{N} K_i$, which can easily be controlled by varying the number of groups.

However, a generic bit mapper would require us to store the class information for every possible received index which entails a storage exponential in N, defeating the purpose of classification. Hence we impose the structure of a 'nearest neighbor classifier' or a 'vector quantizer' for the bit-mapper which enforces each received index tuple to be clustered to one of the cloud centers based on a minimum distance criterion as shown in Fig. 3. Such a modification to the bit-mapper, though leads to some loss in optimality, provides a two fold advantage. *On one hand, it dramatically reduces the storage overhead required to store the bit-mapper, as it requires us to store only the cloud centers. On the other hand, it builds error resilience into the system as it essentially implements an error correcting code at the decoder by assigning the same codeword to nearby received indices.* If the probability of channel error is not large, we would expect $\hat{I}$ to be sufficiently close to I and hence belong to the same decoding sphere (group) as I. If the prototypes, encoders and reconstruction codebooks are optimally designed for the given source-channel statistics/training sequences, such an approach would assist error correction leading to improved end-to-end reconstruction distortion.

These cloud centers are called 'prototypes' in the literature [13] and the structure is normally termed 'nearest prototype classifier'. Technically, these prototypes can be defined in any sub-space (for example $\mathcal{R}^N$) with an appropriate distance metric defined between the received index tuples to the prototypes. However, we require these prototypes to entail minimal excess storage, but at the same time provide enough diversity for achieving good error-resilience. Hence we enforce each prototype to belong to $\mathcal{I}$ and choose the corresponding distance metric to be the Hamming distance between the binary representations of the received indices and prototypes. Given a set of prototypes $\mathcal{J}_i = \{S_{i1} \ldots S_{iK_i}\}$, $S_{i,j} \in \mathcal{I}\ \forall i,j$, the bit-mapper can mathematically be written as:

$$\mathcal{B}_i(I) : \arg\min_{S \in \mathcal{J}_i} d_i(I, S) \qquad (6)$$

where $d_i(\cdot, \cdot)$ denotes the Hamming distance. We note that, the design methodology is applicable for prototypes chosen from any generic sub-space.

In the next stage of decoding, each prototype is associated with a unique reconstruction codeword. We denote this mapping by $\mathcal{C}_i(S_{i,j})$. Hence, if the received index is $\hat{I}$ and if the nearest prototype to $\hat{I}$ is $S_{i,j}$, then the estimate of source i is $\hat{x}_i = \mathcal{C}_i(S_{i,j})$, i.e., the composite decoder can be written as:

$$\hat{X}_i(\hat{I}) = \mathcal{D}_i(\hat{I}) = \mathcal{C}_i(\mathcal{B}_i(\hat{I})) \qquad (7)$$

5. ALGORITHM FOR SYSTEM DESIGN

As mentioned in section 2, we assume that a training set of source and channel samples is available during design. Hence, given a training set, $\mathcal{T} = \{(\mathbf{x}, \mathbf{n})\}$, of source and noise samples, our objective in this section is to find the encoders, prototypes and reconstruction codebooks which minimize the average distortion on the training set, which is measured as:

$$D_{avg} = \frac{1}{N|\mathcal{T}|} \sum_{(\mathbf{x}, \mathbf{n}) \in \mathcal{T}} ||\mathbf{x} - \hat{\mathbf{x}}||^2 \qquad (8)$$

Note that in the above equation, we have assumed the distor-

tion metric to be the mean squared error (MSE) and given equal weightings to all the sources similar to [6, 20]. However, the design methodology is applicable to any other general distortion measure.

We first note that the high rate quantizers are designed separately using a standard Lloyd-Max quantizer design technique to minimize the respective average squared error. The challenging part is to design the Wyner-Ziv maps jointly with the prototypes and the reconstruction codebooks to minimize D_{avg}. We note that readers who are not particularly interested in implementing the system, can conveniently skip the rest of this section.

Note that the design of such 'nearest prototype classifiers' or 'generalized vector quantizers' has been studied earlier in the context of source-channel coding for a single source and is known to be a very challenging problem [11]. The main challenge arises due to the fact that, unlike the standard quantizer design problem where the objective is to minimize the average quantization distortion, here the classifiers/quantizers are to be designed to minimize the distortion in the reconstruction space. One straight forward design approach is to employ a greedy-iterative descent technique which reduces D_{avg} in each iteration. Such an algorithm would initialize the Wyner-Ziv maps, the prototypes and the reconstruction codebooks *randomly* and then update the parameters iteratively, reducing D_{avg} in each step, until convergence. As the number of possible Wyner-Ziv maps and prototypes is finite, convergence is guaranteed to a local minimum for any initialization.

However, in (8), the prototypes are present inside a highly non-convex function which makes the greedy approach likely to get trapped in very poor local minima (even with multiple random initializations), thereby leading to sub-optimal designs. Finding a good initialization for such greedy iterative descent algorithms, even for problems much simpler in nature than the one at hand, is known to be a very difficult task. Hence in the following section, we propose a global optimization technique based on deterministic annealing (DA) which provides significant gains by avoiding poor local minima. Also note that the design approach we propose, optimizes all the system parameters for the given source *and* channel statistics. However the design approaches proposed in most prior work such as [6, 20] optimize the WZ-maps for the noiseless scenario (without the knowledge of the channel) and then design only the decoder codebooks for the given channel statistics. We particularly study the gains due to this optimal design later in section 7.

5.1 Deterministic Annealing Based Design

A formal derivation of the DA algorithm is based on principles borrowed from information theory and statistical physics. Here, during the design stage, we cast the problem in a probabilistic framework, where the standard deterministic bit-mapper is replaced by a random mapper which associates every training sample to all the prototypes in probability. The expected distortion is then minimized subject to an entropy constraint that controls the "randomness" of the solution. By gradually relaxing the entropy constraint we obtain an annealing process that seeks the minimum distortion solution. More detailed derivation and the principle underlying DA can be found in [13].

Specifically, for every element in the training set, the received index tuple, $\hat{I}$, is mapped to all the prototypes, $\mathcal{J}_i$, in probability. These probabilities are denoted by $P_i(j|k)$ $\forall i \in (1, \ldots, N)$, $j \in (1, \ldots, |\mathcal{J}_i|)$, $k \in (1, \ldots, |\mathcal{T}|)$, i.e., the received index tuple for training sample k is associated to prototype j in $\mathcal{J}_i$ with probability $P_i(j|k)$. Hence, the average distortion is:

$$D_{avg} = \frac{1}{N|\mathcal{T}|} \sum_{k=1}^{|\mathcal{T}|} \sum_{i=1}^{N} \sum_{j \in \mathcal{J}_i} P_i(j|k) \left(x_i(k) - \hat{x}_i(j)\right)^2 \quad (9)$$

where $x_i(k)$ is training sample k of X_i and $\hat{x}_i(j) = \mathcal{C}_i(S_{ij})$. Note that this includes the original hard cost function as a special case when probabilities are *hard*, i.e.,:

$$P_i(j|k) = \begin{cases} 1 & \text{if } \arg\min_{j'} d_i(S_{ij'}, \hat{I}(k)) = j \\ 0 & \text{else} \end{cases} \quad (10)$$

It is important to note that these mappings are made *soft* only during the design stage. Of course, our final objective is to design hard bit-mappers which minimize the average distortion.

Further, we impose the 'nearest prototype' structural constraint on the bit-mapper partitions by appropriately choosing a parametrization of the association probabilities. Similar methods have been used before in the context of design of tree-structured quantizers [13], generalized VQ design [11] and optimal classifier design [7]. It can be shown using the principle of entropy maximization that (refer to [13]), to impose a 'nearest prototype' structure, at each temperature, the association probabilities must be governed by the Gibbs distribution:

$$P_i(j|k) = \frac{e^{-\beta_i \left(d_i \left(\hat{I}(k), S_{ij}\right)\right)}}{\sum_j e^{-\beta_i \left(d_i \left(\hat{I}(k), S_{ij}\right)\right)}} \quad (11)$$

Observe that this parametrization converging to the 'nearest prototype classifier' as $\beta_i \to \infty$.

These mappings introduce randomness into the system measured by the Shannon entropy as:

$$H = \frac{1}{N|\mathcal{T}|} \sum_{k \in \mathcal{T}} \sum_{i=1}^{N} \sum_{j \in \mathcal{J}_i} P_i(j|k) \log P_i(j|k) \quad (12)$$

DA algorithm minimizes D_{avg} in (9), with a constraint on the entropy of the system, (12), where the level of randomness is controlled by a Lagrange parameter (usually called the temperature in the literature due to its roots in statistical physics), T as:

$$J = D_{avg} - TH \quad (13)$$

Initially, when T is set very high, our objective is to maximize H and hence all the β_i are very close to 0. This leads to a very fuzzy system where all the received indices are mapped to every prototype with equal probability. Then at each stage, the temperature is gradually lowered maintaining the Lagrangian cost at its minimum. β_i gradually raises as T reduces, thereby making the association distribution less fuzzy. Finally as $T \to 0$ all the $\beta_i \to \infty$ and we obtain hard mappings where every received index maps to the closest prototype. As $T \to 0$ our Lagrangian cost becomes equal to D_{avg} and our original objective is realized. At each temperature, we minimize J with respect to $\mathcal{W}_i$, $\mathcal{J}_i$, β_i and $\mathcal{Q}_i$ $\forall i$. This minimization is achieved using a standard gradient descent method with update rules given below.

5.1.1 Wyner-Ziv Map Update

At fixed T, the WZ-map update rules are given by:

$$\mathcal{W}_i^*(m) = \arg\min_{l \in \mathcal{I}_i} J(\mathcal{W}_i(m) = l) \quad (14)$$

$\forall i \in (1, \ldots, N), m \in \mathcal{Q}_i$ where $J(\mathcal{W}_i(m) = l)$ denotes the Lagrange cost obtained on the training set when $\mathcal{W}_i(m)$ is set to l with all the remaining parameters unchanged.

5.1.2 Prototype Update

Note that each prototype can take values in the set $\mathcal{I}$ and the size of the set $|\mathcal{I}| = 2^{\sum_{i=1}^{N} R_i}$, which grows exponential in N. Hence, for large sensor networks, it is infeasible to find the best prototype in each iteration from the set $\mathcal{I}$. Hence, in each step, we find an incrementally better prototype among the neighboring prototypes, which are at a Hamming distance of one. Mathematically, for fixed Wyner-Ziv maps and reconstruction codebooks, the update rule for prototypes is:

$$S_{ij}^* = \arg\min_{s \in N(S_{ij})} J(S_{ij} = s) \quad (15)$$

where $J(S_{ij} = s)$ is the Lagrange cost obtained by setting $S_{ij} = s$ with all the remaining parameters unchanged and $N(S_{ij})$ denotes all neighboring prototypes of S_{ij}.

5.1.3 β_i Update

As β_i are real values, we find the gradient of J with respect to β_i for fixed Wyner-Ziv maps, prototypes and reconstruction codebooks and employ a standard gradient descent operation to update β_i. The gradients of J with respect to β_i $\forall i$ is given by:

$$\frac{\delta J}{\delta \beta_i} = \frac{1}{N|\mathcal{T}|} \sum_{k,j} \left\{ (x_i(k) - \hat{x}_i(k))^2 + T\log(2P_i(j|k)) \right.$$
$$\left. P_i(j|k) \left(\sum_{j'} P_i(j'|k) d(\hat{I}(k), S_{ij'}) - d_i(\hat{I}(k), S_{ij}) \right) \right\} \quad (16)$$

Then the update rule for β_i is given by:

$$\beta_i^* = \beta_i - \triangle \frac{\delta J}{\delta \beta_i} \quad (17)$$

where $\triangle$ is the step size for descent.

5.1.4 Reconstruction Codebook Update

Note that, J is a convex function of the reconstruction values and hence the optimum codebook which minimizes J for any fixed encoders, prototypes and β_i is given by:

$$\hat{x}_i(j) = \mathcal{C}_i(j) = \frac{\sum_k P_i(j|k) x_i(k)}{\sum_k P_i(j|k)} \quad (18)$$

The complete steps for DA are shown as a flowchart in Algorithm 1[2]. T is initialized to a very high value and β_is are set very low. All the Wyner-Ziv maps and the reconstruction codebooks are initialized randomly. The prototypes are set to the median of the received indices so as to minimize the average Hamming distance. Temperature is gradually lowered using an exponential cooling schedule, $T^* = \alpha T$. In all our simulations, we used $\alpha = 0.98$. At each temperature, all the system parameters are optimized using Eqns. (14), (15), (17) and (18) till the system reaches equilibrium. This

---

[2]The simulation code is available at: http:www.scl.ece.ucsb.edu/html/database/Error_Resilient_DSC.

equilibrium is perturbed and used as an initialization for the next temperature. These iterations are continued till T approaches zero. In practice, the system is 'quenched', i.e, T is set to zero and the bit-mapper is made hard, once the entropy becomes sufficiently small. Note that the optimization steps at $T = 0$ are same as that for the greedy approach. However, instead of a random guess, the equilibrium at the previous temperature is now used as the initialization. We further note that under certain conditions on continuity of phase transitions in the process, DA achieves the global minimum [13], but its ability to track the global minimum as we lower the temperature depends on a sufficiently slow cooling schedule (i.e., α sufficiently close to 1). However in practice α is restricted based on the available design time. In our simulations, we observed that using $\alpha = 0.98$ achieves significantly better solutions compared to the greedy descent approach.

ALGORITHM 1. *DA Approach for System Design*

Inputs: N_i *(Number of high rate quantization indices),*
R_i *(Transmission rates),*
R_{d_i} *(Decoding rate, i.e.,* $|\mathcal{J}_i| = K_i = 2^{R_{d_i}}$ *),*
$\mathcal{T}$ *(Training set),* $T_{max} (\sim 1 - 10)$, $T_{min} (\sim 10^{-5} - 10^{-4})$,
$\beta_{min} (\sim 0.1 - 0.2)$, $H_{min} (\sim 0.1 - 0.2)$, $\alpha < 1$ *(Cooling Rate),*
$\triangle (\sim 0.1 - 0.2)$.
Outputs : $\mathcal{H}_i$ *(High rate quantizers),*
$\mathcal{W}_i$ *(WZ-maps),*
$\mathcal{J}_i$ *(Prototypes),*
and $\mathcal{C}_i$ *(Reconstruction codebooks)*

---

1. *Design the high rate quantizers individually using a standard Lloyd-Max algorithm.*

2. *Initialize:* $T = T_{max}$, $\beta_i = \beta_{min}$, *Initialize WZ-maps randomly, set* $S_{ij} = Median(\hat{I}(\mathbf{x})$, $\mathbf{x} \in \mathcal{T})$ $\forall i \in (1, \ldots, N), j \in (1, \ldots, \mathcal{J}_i)$.

3. *Compute:* $P_i(j|k)$ *using (11) and* $\mathcal{C}_i(j)$ *using (18).*

4. *Update:*
   - *WZ-maps using (14).*
   - *Prototypes using (15).*
   - β_i *using (17), and then compute* $P_i(j|k)$ *using (11).*
   - $\mathcal{C}_i(j)$ *using (18).*

5. *Convergence: Compute J and H using (13) and (12) respectively. Check for convergence of J. If not satisfied go to step (4)*

6. *Stopping: If* $T \leq T_{min}$ *or* $H \leq H_{min}$, *set* $P_i(j|k)$ *as (10) and perform last iteration for* $T = 0$. *Then STOP.*

7. *Cooling:*
   - $T^* \leftarrow \alpha T$.
   - *Perturb prototypes:* $S_{ij}^* \leftarrow s \in Neighborhood(S_{ij})$, *where s is chosen randomly.*
   - *Perturb* $\beta_i^* \leftarrow \beta_i + \delta$ *for small* $\delta > 0$ *generated randomly.*
   - *Go to (4)*

5.2 Note on Design Complexity

The design complexity for the proposed setup, either using the greedy approach or using DA grows as $\mathcal{O}(R_r^3 |\mathcal{T}|)$. The DA approach has a larger constant and requires more computations compared to greedy approach for a single initialization. However, as the greedy approach has to be run over multiple random initializations to achieve a good solution, the exact comparison of design complexities is difficult and depends on the actual source-channel distributions. A generally accepted and observed fact (see [13]) is that for a given design time, DA provides far better solutions compared to that achieved by greedy approaches over multiple random initializations for such complex non-convex optimization functions.

6. OPERATIONAL COMPLEXITY

In this section we compare the computational and storage complexities during operation of all the three approaches for large scale DSC described earlier. For comparison purposes, we assume that every source sends information at rate R and all the high rate quantizers operate at rate $R_q \geq R$. Also, we assume that the decoding rate is $R_{d_i} = R_d$ ($R_d \leq NR$) for all sources. For the source grouping approach, this means that the maximum number of sources in any cluster is R_d/R; for the Bayesian network approach, this implies that the maximum number of parent nodes for any source node is R_d/R and for the proposed approach, this implies that the number of prototypes for decoding any source is $|\mathcal{J}_i| = |K_i| = 2^{R_d} \forall i$.

6.1 Computational Complexity

Firstly, we note that the computational complexity during operation of all the three approaches is polynomial in N. It is easy to observe that the decoder in the source grouping method has literally no computations to make, i.e. the complexity is a constant, $\mathcal{O}(1)$. The decoder in the Bayesian network approach has to implement a message passing algorithm for every received combination of indices. This leads to a computational complexity which grows as $\mathcal{O}(N2^{R_q R_d/R})$. On the other hand, the proposed prototype based bit-mapper approach finds the closest prototype for every received index tuple, which requires $\mathcal{O}(2^{R_d} N \log N)$ bit comparisons. Note that, though the complexity grows slightly faster than N, it requires only bit comparisons, and will incur much lesser machine cycles than required for implementing each iteration in the Bayesian network approach. As all the three methods can be implemented in practice with affordable computational complexities, we hereafter assume they are 'equivalent' with respect to computations and focus only on their storage requirements.

6.2 Storage Complexity

Table I shows the order of growth in storage as a function of N, R, R_q and R_d for all the three approaches. Here, F denotes the bits required to store a real number or the floating point accuracy. In all our simulations, we use $F = 32$ bits.

Storage due to	Codebook	Module
Source grouping	$N2^{R_d}F$	$N\log_2(\frac{NR}{R_d})$
Bayesian network	$N2^{R_q}F$	$N2^{(R_qR_d/R)}F$ $+N\log_2(N)$
Prototype based bit-mapper	$N2^{R_d}F$	$N^2R2^{R_d}$

Table 1: Order of growth in storage complexities

The codebook storage in all the three settings are considerably easier to derive. For example in the prototype approach, there is a unique codeword associated with every prototype. There are 2^{R_d} prototypes for decoding each source and hence the total storage for the reconstruction codebooks is $N2^{R_d}F$. Similar arguments lead to the codebook storage for the other approaches as given in Table I.

For analysis of module storage, we first begin with the source grouping method. It requires us to store the group labels for each source. As there are at least NR/R_d groups, we need at least $N\log_2(\frac{NR}{R_d})$ bits to store the source groupings. For the Bayesian network approach, we require an order of $N\frac{R_d}{R}\log_2(N)$ bits to store the parent node information for each source. However, there is an additional storage required to store the transition probabilities which grows as $N2^{R_qR_d/R}F$. The prototype based bit-mapper approach requires us to store all the prototypes at the decoder. Each prototype requires NR bits to store and there are $N2^{R_d}$ such prototypes leading to a total storage of $N^2R2^{R_d}$.

A first look at Table I suggests that the prototype based bit-mapper approach entails a module storage which grows as N^2 in the number of sources and hence should entail a very high overhead due to module storage. However, for typical values of these parameters, (i.e., $N \sim 10-500$ sources, $R \sim 1-10$ bits, $R_q \sim (R+2)-(R+4)$ bits and $R_d/R \sim 2-4$) the storage overhead of the proposed approach is not very significant and the distortion gains obtained overhaul the minimal loss due to excess storage[3]. However, in these typical ranges, the Bayesian network approach entails a storage which is significantly higher than the other two methods and hence leads to higher distortions at a fixed storage. Note that, the values in Table I indicate the order of growth of storage complexity and hence are accurate only upto a constant. In all our simulations, we consider the exact storage required and not the values derived from Table I.

7. RESULTS

To test the performance of the proposed approach, we used 3 different datasets:

1) **Synthetic dataset:** A toy dataset consisting of 10 synthetic sources, randomly deployed on a square grid of dimensions 100 m × 100 m was generated according to a multivariate Gaussian distribution. All sources were assumed to have zero mean and unit variance. The correlation was assumed to fall exponentially with the distance. Specifically, we assumed $\rho = \rho_0^{d/d_o}$, $\rho_0 < 1$. For all our simulations with this dataset we set $d_o = 100$. The training set generated was of length 10000 samples. All results presented are on a test set, also of the same length, generated independently using the same distribution.

2) **Temperature sensor dataset :** The first real dataset we used was collected by the Intel Berkeley Research Lab, CA [4]. Data were collected from 54 sensors deployed in the Intel Berkeley Research Lab between February 28 and April 5, 2004. Each sensor measured temperature values once every 31 s [5]. We retained data from top 25 sensors that collected highest number of samples. Times when subset of these sensors failed to record data were dropped from the analysis. The data were normalized to zero mean and unit variance. Samples collected till March 18th, 2004 were used to train the system and the remaining were used as the test set.

3) **Rainfall dataset :** As a second real dataset, we used the rainfall dataset used in[8] [6]. This data-set consists of the daily rainfall precipitation for the Pacific northwest region over a period of 46 years. The measurement points formed a regular grid of 50km x 50km regions over the entire region under study. The first 30 years of data were used for training and the remaining to test the system. Note that the inter-source correlations in such 'large area' datasets are considerably lower. However, performance evaluation using such diverse real world datasets is important to validate the efficiency of the proposed setup.

We note that, all our results are in terms of the crossover probability of the effective BSC seen by each bit. We denote the cross over probability (error probability) by P_e, ie., $P(1|0) = P(0|1) = P_e$. Note that P_e is directly related to the channel SNR (CSNR) as $P_e = Q(\sqrt{CSNR})$. In all our simulations, we generated a training sequence of channel errors of the same size as the training set. The average distortion of the test set over 100 random (i.i.d.) channel realizations is used as the performance metric.

7.1 Complexity-Distortion Trade-off

Fig. 4 shows the total storage (complexity) versus the distortion trade-off for all the three datasets. For these simulations, the transmission rate was set to $R_i = 1$ bit. This allows us to compare the performances with the minimum distortion achievable using full complexity decoding. We will present results at higher transmission rates in section 7.4. The decoding rate was varied from 1 to 5 bits to obtain the distortion at different complexities. We plot the total storage, which includes both codebook and module storage, versus the distortion to obtain a trade-off curve. We show results obtained using all the three decoding methods - source grouping where the grouping is done using source optimized clustering approach described in [6], Bayesian network as described in [20] and the prototype based bit-mapper approach proposed in this paper. For fairness, we design the WZ-maps for the given channel statistics for all the approaches. However, note that, in most prior work the channel statistics were ignored while designing the WZ-maps [20]. We study the gains due to this optimal design in the following section. For comparison, we also include the performance obtained for designs using greedy-iterative descent approach (opti-

---

[3]Note that if $N >> 500$, then the optimal approach would be to group ~ 500 sources within each cluster and to perform decoding based on the proposed approach at affordable complexities within each cluster, instead of directly grouping at the allowed complexity

[4]Available at http://db.csail.mit.edu/labdata/labdata.html
[5]Note that the sensors also measured humidity, pressure and luminescence. However, we consider only the temperature readings here
[6]Available for download at http://www.jisao.washington.edu/data sets/widmann

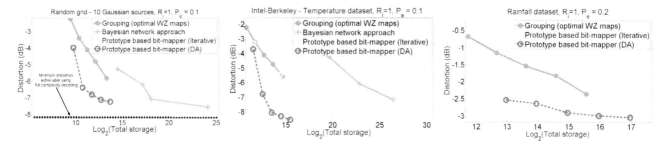

Figure 4: Total storage Versus Distortion for 3 different datasets. (a) Synthetic dataset, $R_i = 1 \forall i$ and $P_e = 0.1$ (b) Temperature sensor dataset, $R_i = 1$, $P_e = 0.1$ (c) Rainfall dataset, $R_i = 1$, $P_e = 0.2$

mized over upto 25 random initializations) along with that achieved using DA.

Fig. 4(a) shows the result obtained for the synthetic dataset using $\rho_0 = 0.9$ and $P_e = 0.1$. We see gains of over 2 dB in distortion compared to the source grouping technique at a fixed storage. Alternatively, the total storage can be reduced by $10X$ times while maintaining the same distortion. We also see that the performance of the prototype based bit-mapper approaches the optimal 'full complexity' decoder significantly faster than the source grouping method. However, observe that, though the Bayesian network based decoder gains substantially over source grouping approach in distortion at fixed decoding rates, the excess storage required to store the Bayesian network offsets these gains, leading to much higher storage at fixed distortions. Note that, in this case, the greedy approach also provides similar performance as DA, as the probability of getting trapped in local minima is low after 25 runs for smaller networks.

Figures 4(b) and 4(c) show the performance obtained for the temperature sensor dataset and the rainfall dataset at P_e of 0.1 and 0.2 respectively. As the temperature sensor dataset has considerably higher correlations, we see gains of over 2.5 dB in distortion at fixed storage over source grouping approach. Due to lower correlations in the rainfall dataset, we choose a higher P_e. Here, gains of about 1dB in distortion are obtained. In general, higher correlations assist the bit-mapper as it uses all the received bits to correct errors, unlike the grouping approach which is forced to use only the bits within each group. From 4(b), it also follows that the overhead required to store the Bayesian network aggravates at higher N and the performance degrades further, making the Bayesian network approach impractical for very large networks[7]. Also, for these datasets, observe that the performance of the greedy-iterative descent method is considerably poorer than that using DA. Hence, hereafter, we only show results for DA, noting that the greedy approach leads to poor designs for large networks.

In what follows, we compare the distortion performance of the prototype based bit-mapper and the source grouping approaches by varying the network and design parameters at a fixed decoding rate. As the total storage is not reflected in these plots, we do not consider the performance of the Bayesian network approach hereafter, noting that, the storage required to achieve good distortion performance is significantly higher.

---

[7]For the rainfall dataset, the storage required for the Bayesian network approach was significantly larger and hence we do not plot it along with the other curves

7.2 P_e Versus Distortion

In this section, we show the performance gains when P_e is varied. We restrict P_e to be in the range $0 - 0.2$ (i.e, CSNR > -1.5 dB). For all the simulations, we have chosen $R_i = 1$ and $R_d = 3$. Fig. 5(a) shows the distortion obtained as a function of P_e for the synthetic dataset. For the source grouping approach, we plot 2 curves. The first curve shows the performance when the WZ-maps are optimized jointly with the decoder for the given channel statistics. The second curve shows the performance when the WZ-maps are designed without the knowledge of channel statistics (instead designed to minimize reconstruction distortion at zero noise). However, after the design of the WZ-maps, the reconstruction codebooks are designed for the given channel statistics. Clearly, optimal design of the WZ-maps for the given channel provides about 0.5dB improvement in distortion. Further, major improvements of over 2 dB, is due to the error-resilience provided by the proposed decoder structure. We see similar behavior even for the two real world datasets in figures 5(b) and 5(c). The higher error-correction capability of the nearest prototype structure is further reflected as the gains improve when P_e increases (CSNR decreases). Again observe that the gains in case of the rainfall dataset are smaller due to lower correlations in the dataset.

7.3 Performance with Network Size

In this section we study how the gains vary with the size of the network. As random deployment makes it hard to compare, we consider a uniformly placed, linear grid of sensors between two fixed points. We increase the number of sensors from 6 to 90 while keeping the transmission and decoding rates fixed. We assume a correlation model which falls off exponentially with the distance and assume P_e to be 0.2 throughout. Fig. 6 compares the results obtained for the source grouping approach and the proposed bit-mapper approach. We see that the gains keep increasing with the network size. This is because, as the number of sources increase, the decoder receives several more correlated bits which are efficiently used by the proposed approach to correct errors. On the other hand, the inefficiency of the the source grouping method is directly evident as it uses only bits within each cluster.

7.4 Performance as a Function of Other Design Parameters

In the following, we show results only for the synthetic dataset described in the beginning of this section. We vary different design parameters and study the performance gains.

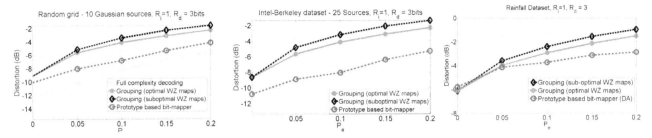

Figure 5: P_e versus Distortion for 3 different datasets. For all the plots, we have used $R_i = 1$ and $R_d = 3$ (a) Synthetic dataset (b) Temperature sensor dataset (c) Rainfall dataset

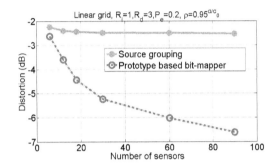

Figure 6: Variation of reconstruction distortion with the number of sources deployed on a linear grid placed uniformly along a length of 10 Kilometers. Correlation model is assumed to be $0.95^{dist(Km)}$, $R_i = 1$bit and $P_e = 0.2$

7.4.1 Correlation (ρ_o)

Fig. 7(a) shows the distortion as a function of ρ_o. The plot shows the results for the source grouping method, the proposed approach and the optimal full complexity design which uses all the received bits. 3 dB improvement of the proposed approach over the grouping method at very high correlations provides further evidence of improved error resilience.

7.4.2 Transmitted Bits (R_i)

In this section, we compare the performances when the transmission rates are increased. We consider 3 different transmission rates, $R_i = 1, 2$ and 4. However, we fix the decoding rate at 4 bits. We see that the gains increase radically to over 6dB, at higher transmission rates. This is primarily because of two reasons. Firstly, as R_i increases, the decoder has access to more correlated bits which can be used efficiently for correcting more errors. Secondly, the decoder for any source has the freedom of selectively giving importance only to a subset of bits sent from a different source. However, the source grouping approach does not exploit either of these advantages and hence suffers significantly more at higher transmission rates. However, the problem with operating at very high transmission rates is that the proposed design complexity grows as $(\sum_{i=1}^{N} R_i)^3$ and hence it requires sophisticated computing capabilities for efficient design.

7.4.3 Rate of Quantizers (R_q)

All results so far have focused on the decoder structure. One might be curious to know the importance of the encoder structure/WZ-maps. Figure 7(c) shows the decrease in dis-

tortion when the rates of $\mathcal{H}_i$ are increased from $R_q = 1$ to 4 bits, while keeping the transmission rate fixed at $R_i = 1$. Note that $R_q = 1$ is equivalent to having no WZ-maps (i.e., each encoder is a simple scalar quantizer). Results show over 2.5dB gains for the bit-mapper approach and about 1.5 dB improvement for the source grouping approach when R_q is increased from 1 to 4 bits. Such improvements (see also [20]) demonstrate the crucial role played by WZ-maps in exploiting inter-source correlations. Also note that the proposed structure for the decoder provides about 1dB improvement over source grouping method even when $R_q = 1$ (i.e., when there is no distributed encoding, for example see [2]). This result is particularly useful in practical sensor networks wherein the sensors employ standard scalar quantization.

8. DISCUSSION

8.1 Extension to Handle Erasures

It is critical to develop robust distributed source coding techniques for networks with bit/packet erasures - in fact, erasures are seen more often in low powered sensor networks than errors. In this section we briefly address this issue and describe how the proposed technique can be easily extended to handle erasures. In the erasure setting, it is assumed that a subset of the transmitted bits are lost due to sensor/channel failures and the decoder reconstructs all the sources based only on the received bits. The objective is to design the encoders (at each source) and decoders (for each bit erasure pattern) to minimize the average distortion at the decoder. In the most general setting, the decoder has an independent codebook for each possible erasure pattern and an estimate for each source is made by looking at the corresponding codebook when a subset of the bits are received. Quite evidently, for optimal decoding, the total number of codebooks grows exponentially with the number of sources and transmission rates, let alone the exponential growth in the number of estimates (codewords) within each codebook. It is easy to verify that the total storage at the decoder (the decoder complexity) for optimal decoding grows as $\mathcal{O}(3^{NR})$ if $R_i = R \forall i$.

In this paper, we describe one possible approach to extend the classifier based decoding paradigm to handle erasures. We note that there are several other possible methods to extend it and their performance comparisons will be performed as part of future work. Recall that, to build error resilience, the decoder mapped the received index tuple to one of the cloud centers based on a minimum distance cri-

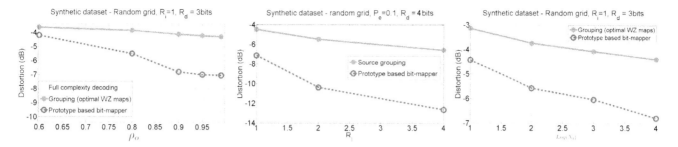

Figure 7: All the three plots are for the Synthetic dataset generated for a random grid of sensors (a) Performance gains with varying correlation coefficient (b) Performance gains as a function of R_i (c) Performance gains with the number of high rate quantization levels

terion leading to the classification of the index tuples into decoding spheres. The reconstructions were purely based on the sphere to which the received index belongs. In the current setting, however, a subset of the transmitted bits are not received at the decoder. The received index tuples are now mapped to one of the cloud centers only based on the bits that are received. The closest cloud center is chosen based on the Hamming distance between the received bits and the corresponding bits in the cloud centers. In other words, since the missing bits can be 0 or 1, we assume the corresponding value to be $1/2$ - a value that is equidistant from 0 and 1. Subsequently, the distance (now the absolute value of the difference) is computed between the cloud centers and the received index tuple, with every missing bit replaced by a $1/2$, and the source reconstruction is decided based on the nearest center. It is important to note that as a result of the prior $\{0,1,1/2\}$ subterfuge, the received index tuples are now mapped to one of the cloud centers only based on the bits that were actually received.

The proposed approach essentially mimics an erasure code at the decoder which attempts to recover the lost bits using the correlation across the sources. Observe that the method naturally provides better robustness to channel erasures as it uses all the *received* bits to correct erasures, unlike the source grouping method, which would have estimated the sources only using the received bits within corresponding subsets. The cloud centers and the reconstruction codebooks can be designed using an approach similar to that described in section 4 using a training sequence of source samples and erasure patterns to minimize the expected reconstruction distortion. Also note that, using the same principles, the proposed technique can be easily applied to networks which suffer from a combination of bit errors and erasures.

8.2 Handling Non-Stationary Statistics

In the proposed approach, the system parameters are designed using a training sequence of source and channel samples before deployment. Essentially, this design assumes that the source and channel statistics are stationary in time. This assumption is of course not always valid, and the purpose of this subsection is to briefly outline some options for adapting the proposed approach to non-stationary settings, so as to reap its benefits in such applications. One possible approach to handle time varying statistics is to design the system (collect raw training data) at regular intervals of time and to adapt the system parameters to the new statistics. This entails some additional overhead due to system training

and could lead to faster depletion of network resources if the statistics are highly non-stationary. An alternate approach approach is to store multiple sets of system parameters, designed for different statistics, and to use a particular set of parameters by estimating the current average statistic at the sink. The possible implications of these directions on practical deployment of sensor networks will be evaluated as part of our future work.

9. CONCLUSIONS

In this paper, we proposed a new coding approach to large scale distributed compression which is robust to channel errors/erasures. In the proposed approach, the set of possible received index tuples is first classified into groups and then a unique codeword is assigned for each group. This results in low complexity, practically realizable decoders that are scalable to large networks. The classification is achieved using a 'nearest prototype classifier' structure which assists in achieving good error-resilience. We also presented a deterministic annealing based global optimization algorithm for design, which enhances the performance by avoiding multiple poor local minima on the cost surface. Simulation results show that the proposed scheme achieves significant gains as compared to other state-of-the art techniques.

10. REFERENCES

[1] J. Bajcsy and P. Mitran. Coding for the Slepian-Wolf problem with turbo codes. *Proceedings of IEEE GLOBECOM*, 2:1400–1404, 2001.

[2] J. Barros and M. Tuechler. Scalable decoding on factor graphs - a practical solution for sensor networks. *IEEE Trans. on Communications*, 54(2):284–294, February 2006.

[3] R. Cristescu, B. Beferull-Lozano, and M. Vetterli. Networked slepian-wolf: Theory, algorithms and scaling laws. *IEEE Trans. on Information Theory*, 51(12):4057–4073, Dec 2005.

[4] M. Fleming, Q. Zhao, and M. Effros. Network vector quantization. *IEEE Trans. on Information Theory*, 50:1584–1604, Aug 2004.

[5] T. J. Flynn and R. M. Gray. Encoding of correlated observations. *IEEE Trans. on Information Theory*, 33(6):773–787, 1987.

[6] G. Maierbacher and J. Barros. Low-complexity coding and source-optimized clustering for large-scale sensor networks. *ACM Transactions on Sensor Networks*, 5(3), Jun 2009.

[7] D. Miller, A. Rao, K. Rose, and A. Gersho. A global optimization technique for statistical classifier design. *IEEE Trans. on Signal Processing*, 44(12):3108 –3122, dec 1996.

[8] S. Pattem, B. Krishnamachari, and R. Govindan. The impact of spatial correlation on routing with compression in wireless sensor networks. *IEEE Trans. on Sensor Networks*, 4(4), 2008.

[9] S. S. Pradhan and K. Ramchandran. Distributed source coding using syndromes (DISCUS): Design and construction. *IEEE Trans. on Information Theory*, 49:626–643, Mar 1999.

[10] S. Ramaswamy, K. Viswanatha, A. Saxena, and K. Rose. Towards large scale distributed coding. In *Proc. of IEEE ICASSP*, pages 1326 – 1329, Mar 2010.

[11] A. Rao, D. Miller, K. Rose, and A. Gersho. A deterministic annealing approach for parsimonious design of piecewise regression models. *IEEE Trans. on Pattern Analysis and Machine Intelligence (PAMI)*, 21:159–173, Feb 1999.

[12] D. Rebollo-Monedero, R. Zhang, and B. Girod. Design of optimal quantizers for distributed source coding. In *Proceedings of IEEE DCC*, pages 13–22, Mar 2003.

[13] K. Rose. Deterministic annealing for clustering, compression, classification, regression, and related optimization problems. *Proceedings of IEEE*, 86(11):2210–2239, Nov 1998.

[14] A. Saxena, J. Nayak, and K. Rose. Robust distributed source coder design by deterministic annealing. *IEEE Trans. on Signal Processing*, pages 859 – 868, Sep 2009.

[15] A. Saxena and K. Rose. Distributed predictive coding for spatio-temporally correlated sources. *IEEE Trans. on Signal Processing*, 57:4066–4075, Oct 2009.

[16] K. Viswanatha, S. Ramaswamy, A. Saxena, and K. Rose. A classifier based decoding approach for large scale distributed coding. In *Proc. of IEEE ICASSP*, pages 1513–1516, May 2011.

[17] A. D. Wyner and J. Ziv. The rate-distortion function for source coding with side information at the decoder. *IEEE Trans. on Information Theory*, 22:1–10, Jan 1976.

[18] Z. Xiong, A. Liveris, and S. Cheng. Distributed source coding for sensor networks. *IEEE Signal Processing Magazine*, 21(5):80–94, 2004.

[19] P. Yahampath. Joint source decoding in large scale sensor networks using markov random field models. In *IEEE ICASSP*, pages 2769 – 2772, Apr 2009.

[20] R. Yasaratna and P. Yahampath. Design of scalable decoders for sensor networks via bayesian network learning. *IEEE Trans. on Comm.*, pages 2868–2871, Oct 2009.

Fully Wireless Implementation of Distributed Beamforming on a Software-Defined Radio Platform

Muhammad M. Rahman   Henry E. Baidoo-Williams

Raghuraman Mudumbai[*]   Soura Dasgupta[†]

Electrical & Computer Engineering University of Iowa Iowa City USA

[mahboob-rahman,henry-baidoo-williams]@uiowa.edu,

[rmudumbai,dasgupta]@engineering.uiowa.edu

ABSTRACT

We describe the key ideas behind our implementation of distributed beamforming on a GNU-radio based software-defined radio platform. Distributed beamforming is a cooperative transmission scheme whereby a number of nodes in a wireless network organize themselves into a *virtual antenna array* and focus their transmission in the direction of the intended receiver, potentially achieving orders of magnitude improvements in energy efficiency. This technique has been extensively studied over the past decade and its practical feasibility has been demonstrated in multiple experimental prototypes. Our contributions in the work reported in this paper are three-fold: (a) the first ever all-wireless implementation of distributed beamforming without any secondary wired channels for clock distribution or channel feedback, (b) a novel digital baseband approach to synchronization of high frequency RF signals that requires no hardware modifications, and (c) an implementation of distributed beamforming on a standard, open platform that allows easy reuse and extension. We describe the design of our system in detail, present some initial results and discuss future directions for this work.

Categories and Subject Descriptors

C.2.1 [**Network architecture and design**]: Wireless communication

General Terms

Design, Experimentation

---

[*]This work was funded in part by a grant from the Roy J. Carver Charitable Trust.

[†]This work was funded in part by a grant from NSF CCF-0830747 and a grant from the Roy J. Carver Charitable Trust.

Keywords

Cooperative communication, software-defined radio, distributed beamforming

1. INTRODUCTION

In this paper, we describe the key ideas behind our recent all-digital implementation of distributed transmit beamforming on a GNU-radio [7] based software-defined radio (SDR) platform. Distributed beamforming refers to a cooperative transmission scheme whereby a number of nodes in a wireless network organize themselves into a *virtual antenna array* and cooperatively transmit a common message signal to a distant receiver. This technique is especially attractive for wireless sensor networks because it allows inexpensive nodes with simple omnidirectional antennas to collaboratively emulate a highly directional antenna and focus their transmission in the direction of the intended receiver. This potentially offers large increases in energy efficiency: an array of N nodes can achieve an N^2-fold increase in the power at a receiver compared to a single node transmitting individually; conversely each node in a N-node array can reduce its transmit power by a factor of $\frac{1}{N^2}$ and still achieve the same overall signal power at the receiver compared to a single transmitter.

It is important to note that this is not just a reduction in the *per node* transmitted power simply because there are more nodes transmitting; this is also an increase in the *energy efficiency* of the transmission: a N-node beamforming array can achieve the same received signal strength (RSS) at the receiver with as little as $\frac{1}{N}$ of the *total transmit power* required by a single node transmitting individually.

Physically this increased energy efficiency arises from the increased directivity of the transmissions; the signals from the individual transmitters combine constructively at the intended receiver and as a result a larger proportion of the transmitted power is concentrated in the direction of the intended receiver. This is illustrated in Fig. 1. This requires that the signals from the individual transmitters are all aligned in phase at the intended receiver. This in turn requires precise control of the phase of the RF signal from each transmitter.

The key challenge in realizing the large potential gains from beamforming is in precisely synchronizing the RF signals. Each transmitter in general obtains its RF carrier signal from its own local oscillator, and even when two oscillators are set to the same nominal frequency, because of manufacturing tolerances and temperature variations, they

Virtual antenna array

Figure 1: Energy efficient transmission using distributed beamforming.

would in general have a non-zero frequency offset with respect to each other. In addition all oscillators undergo random unpredictable phase drifts over time. Finally, unlike a traditional phased array, a virtual array made up of collaborating wireless sensor nodes does not have a regular and precisely known geometry; furthermore standard localization techniques such as GPS fall far short of the accuracy necessary to overcome this geometric uncertainty for the purposes of beamforming. Thus, distributed beamforming requires a highly sophisticated synchronization process that accounts for all of the above uncertainties.

The goals of our implementation are two-fold: (a) to provide a platform for prototyping and testing algorithms for distributed beamforming and other advanced virtual array techniques, and (b) to develop and publish an open-source implementation of the basic building blocks for RF carrier synchronization to stimulate further research into advanced networking algorithms based on distributed beamforming and application of this concept to practical wireless networks.

Note that there are other cooperative transmission schemes that unlike distributed beamforming, do *not* require precise phase alignment. This includes all relaying and multi-hopping schemes where different transmitters use orthogonal space/time/frequency channels so that their transmissions do not interfere with each other. In contrast, beamforming *depends* on transmitters interfering with each other in a carefully controlled way. Orthogonal cooperation schemes can provide diversity gains in fading channels, however, they cannot provide the energy efficiency gains achievable from beamforming.

The problem of synchronizing transmitters for distributed transmit beamforming has attracted a great deal of attention over the last decade; many techniques have been developed offering different sets of tradeoffs between simplicity, overheads associated with coordination messages between the transmitters, and overheads associated with channel feedback from the receiver.

The 1-bit feedback technique introduced in [17] offers one example of this tradeoff. This algorithm has attractive properties of robustness to noise, estimation errors, and other disturbances and it dynamically adapts to channel time-variations. The 1-bit algorithm also has the very desirable property of *scalability*: the implementation of the algorithm does not depend on the number of collaborating transmitters; nodes can join and leave the virtual array at any time

and the algorithm automatically adapts without any reconfiguration.

Finally the simplicity of this algorithm makes it possible to implement it on inexpensive hardware. For these reasons, we chose this 1-bit feedback algorithm as the starting point for our first implementation of distributed beamforming on the SDR platform.

1.1 Contributions

Our contributions in this paper are summarized as follows.

1. **Open-source implementation of distributed beamforming.** While distributed beamforming has been experimentally demonstrated before, our SDR implementation is noteworthy in several respects:

   - To the best of our knowledge, this is the first ever all-wireless implementation of distributed beamforming; previous experimental work in [19, 30, 31] all make use of reliable wired, secondary communication channels for channel feedback and/or to distribute a reference clock signal.
   - Our implementation does not require any RF hardware modifications and performs the necessary RF signal synchronization entirely in software.
   - Previous experimental work in [19, 30] are based on custom designed hardware and as such, they are not easily reusable and extendable. The only previous implementation of beamforming that used an open platform was [31], which however uses wired distribution of common oscillator signals to all nodes as noted above and therefore does not address the synchronization problem.

2. **Digital architecture for synchronization.** Our implementation of distributed beamforming is based on a novel signal processing architecture for digitally synchronizing high-frequency RF signals.

3. **Low complexity algorithms for synchronization.** We present low complexity digital techniques for several important synchronization sub-problems including an algorithm based on a modified version of the classical Costas feedback loop [3] for frequency locking, and a general method for using a reference signal at one frequency to synthesize a synchronized signal at a different frequency.

It is important to note that our goals with this implementation is to provide a proof-of-concept i.e. that cooperative MIMO techniques can be realized with modest overheads using simple digital processing techniques, and a starting point for more detailed investigations rather than a complete solution for practical wireless sensor networks. Thus many of our design choices were motivated by considerations of simplicity rather than efficiency or optimality. Developing and refining these ideas further for real-world applications is an important topic for future work.

Outline. The rest of the paper is organized as follows. Section 2 presents some background information including a survey of previous work related to cooperative transmission techniques for wireless sensor networks. We introduce our digital architecture for synchronization in Section 3. Section 4 introduces the setup for our implementation of distributed beamforming and describes several signal processing algorithms that serve as building blocks for the implementation.

We present experimental results from our implementation in Section 5 and conclude in Section 6.

2. BACKGROUND

We now present some background information and a brief survey of related work.

2.1 Cooperative transmission techniques

The large gains achievable through collaborative transmission schemes has been known to information theorists for many decades. Indeed the idea of cooperative beamforming is implicit in many early information theoretic works on multi-user channels [5]. The idea of distributed beamforming can also be further generalized to distributed MIMO [35], where nodes in a wireless network organize themselves into virtual arrays that use MIMO techniques such as spatial multiplexing and precoding to potentially achieve substantially better spatial reuse in addition to energy efficiency. In fact, it has been shown recently [22] that wireless networks using distributed MIMO can effectively overcome the famous capacity scaling limits of wireless networks due to Gupta and Kumar [8]. This literature has, however, largely ignored the synchronization requirements for achieving these cooperation gains.

More recently the concept of *user cooperation diversity* where nearby users in a cellular system use cooperation to achieve decreased outage probability in the uplink was first suggested in [29] and further developed using space-time coding theory [12]. As noted earlier, cooperative diversity techniques have less stringent synchronization requirements [13] as compared to beamforming, but do not deliver the energy efficiency gains achievable with beamforming.

2.2 Experimental implementations of cooperative transmission techniques

Following up on the recent interest in cooperative communication, there have been several experimental implementations to study the practical feasibility of these ideas. This body of experimental work is summarized in a recent survey article [2], and has focused largely on cooperative diversity techniques. A recent experimental study of the amplify-and-forward relaying scheme [20] on Rice University's WARP platform [27] suggested that large gains are achievable even with a simple Alamouti space-time code. A DSP-based testbed was used for a comparative study of cooperative relaying schemes in [34]. A general testbed for systematically studying different MAC and PHY cooperative schemes was reported in [11]. Implementations of cooperative relaying have also been developed [1, 36] for software-defined radio platforms very similar to the one used in our implementation.

Diversity schemes as pointed out earlier have substantially less stringent synchronization requirements than beamforming, which makes them easier to implement. However, there have also been several recent experimental studies of distributed beamforming [19, 30, 31]. All of the above implementations have been based on the 1-bit feedback algorithm.

Distributed beamforming is also at the heart of the Coordinated Multi-Point (CoMP) systems developed as part of the European EASY-C project [9, 10]; these make extensive use of various capabilities of cellular network infrastructure such as (a) uninterrupted availability of GPS signals, which are used to frequency-lock local oscillators and to supply symbol-level synchronization, (b) uplink channels with high bandwidths and low latencies to send detailed channel state feedback from the mobiles, and (c) a multi-gigabit backhaul network for Basestation coordination. In contrast, our work is aimed at the very different application setting of wireless sensor networks, where we cannot depend on the availability of such a sophisticated wired infrastructure.

2.3 Synchronization techniques for distributed beamforming

While early work on cooperative communication did not focus on the synchronization issues, this changed in the last decade, and a number of synchronization techniques for distributed beamforming have now been developed (see the survey article [16]), including full-feedback closed-loop [32], 1-bit closed-loop [17, 19, 18], master-slave open-loop [14], round-trip [4] and two-way [24] synchronization techniques. These techniques offer different sets of tradeoffs between simplicity, overheads associated with coordination messages between the transmitters, and overheads associated with feedback from the receiver.

In general, the overheads associated with the synchronization process has costs that must be weighed against the benefits available from beamforming. One of the important goals of our implementation is precisely to show that these overhead costs are modest even without expensive custom designed hardware. Specifically we used the inexpensive oscillators [21] that come standard with the Universal Software Radio Peripherals (USRP); these have frequency offsets on the order of ± 10 parts per million. In contrast, high quality ovenized oscillators with frequency tolerance of around 20 parts per *billion* are now available [25] for around 400 dollars. Highly stable chip-scale atomic clocks [33] are also now coming closer to commercial feasibility. As these high-quality oscillators become more widely used in commodity wireless hardware, the overheads associated with carrier synchronization will become correspondingly smaller and this will make cooperative techniques such as distributed beamforming even more attractive over an increasing range of frequencies.

2.3.1 The 1-bit feedback algorithm

The 1-bit feedback algorithm for beamforming was originally introduced in [17]; under this algorithm, in every time-slot, each transmitter independently makes a random phase perturbation in its transmissions to the receiver; the receiver monitors the received signal strength (RSS), and broadcasts exactly 1 bit of feedback to the transmitting nodes indicating whether the RSS in the preceding time-slot was greater than in previous time-slots. Using this 1 bit of feedback, the transmitters retain the favorable phase perturbations and discard the unfavorable ones.

Over time, it can be shown [18] that the transmitters converge to coherence *almost surely* under some mild conditions on the distribution of the phase perturbations. Furthermore the algorithm is extremely robust to noise, estimation errors, lost feedback signals and time-varying phases; these attractive properties make it possible to implement this algorithm on simple hardware, and indeed as noted earlier, distributed beamforming using variations of this basic algorithm has been demonstrated on multiple experimental prototypes [19, 30, 31] at various frequencies.

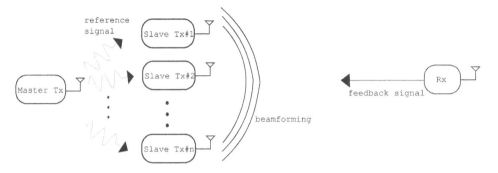

Figure 2: Experimental setup.

Nevertheless, this algorithm and its variants suffer from a number of shortcomings.

1. *Slow convergence rate.* While the convergence rate of the 1-bit algorithm, with appropriately chosen parameters, has good scaling properties for large arrays (convergence time increasing no faster than linearly with number of transmitters [18]), in absolute terms, it requires a large number of time-slots.

2. *Latency limitations.* The 1-bit algorithm neglects latency in the feedback channel; it assumes that the feedback signal is available instantaneously and simultaneously at all the transmitting nodes. In practice this may impose a high lower-bound on the time-slot duration which compounds the problem of slow convergence rate.

3. *Poor performance with frequency offsets.* Non-zero frequency offsets between transmitters manifest themselves as rapid time-variations in the phase. While variations of the 1-bit algorithm have been developed that can handle frequency offsets [30], these too require high feedback rates.

Recent work has shown that it is possible to overcome the above shortcomings of the 1-bit algorithm while retaining its attractive features by using richer feedback from the receiver [15]. In our experimental setup we have implemented the receiver feedback in a flexible way that allows for easy generalization to more advanced algorithms using multi-bit feedback.

The latency limitations mentioned above can be especially challenging for software-defined radio platform [28] that typically have multiple buffering stages in the data path, in addition to processing delays that depend on CPU loads and other uncontrollable factors. To get around this limitation, our current implementation uses a separate explicit mechanism for frequency locking the oscillators on the transmitters; this removes the frequency offsets and allows us to use the simple 1-bit algorithm for beamforming even with slow rates of feedback.

3. DIGITAL SYNCHRONIZATON OF HIGH-FREQUENCY RF SIGNALS

The key idea behind our implementation is that while the RF signals transmitted by the beamforming nodes are themselves not suitable for digital processing, the clock offsets between oscillators that are nominally set to the same frequency are typically quite small. For instance, even very cheap crystal oscillators [21] have worst-case frequency deviations on the order of ± 10 parts per million of the nominal center frequency. In our experimental setup, we used center frequencies around 900 MHz, and thus our clock offsets can be expected to be no greater than 9 kHz or so. In fact, our measurements with the oscillators on the USRP boards showed clock drifts that seldom exceeded 4 kHz. Furthermore, these offsets remained roughly constant over timescales on the order of hundreds of milliseconds.

Thus, as long as we are working with *relative offsets between two oscillators*, the frequencies are small enough and their time-variations slow enough that they can be tracked and compensated in software. This is the basic rationale behind our implementation.

Different protocols for distributed beamforming have been developed that solve the above problem in ways that represent different tradeoffs between in-network coordination, feedback from the receiver and so on. For instance, under beamforming schemes using a master-slave architecture [14], there is a designated master node that supplies the reference signal $c_0(t)$, whereas under round-trip synchronization schemes [23], the receiver itself implicitly provides the reference signal. The DSP-centric architecture developed in this paper is applicable to all of these schemes.

3.1 Two synchronization sub-problems

In this paper we focus specifically on our implementation of beamforming based on the 1-bit feedback algorithm; the setup is shown in Fig. 2. Our implementation divides the beamforming problem into two subproblems.

1. **Frequency locking the transmitters.** We use a master-slave architecture to frequency-lock the transmitters. A designated "Master" node broadcasts an unmodulated tone; this tone is used as a reference signal by the "Slave" nodes to digitally correct for frequency offsets.

2. **Beamforming using 1-bit feedback.** The frequency-locking process ensures that the Slave nodes have carrier signals that are frequency-locked to each other; they still have unknown but fixed relative phase offsets. The 1-bit feedback algorithm is used to estimate and correct for these phase offsets, so the Slave nodes' transmissions are aligned in phase at the Receiver.

The role of the Master node in our setup is simply to

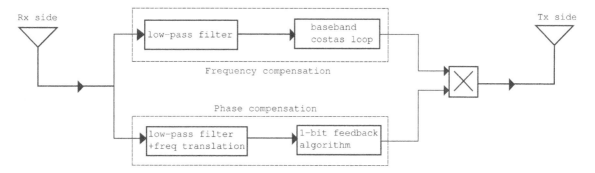

Figure 3: Signal processing at the Slave nodes.

transmit an unmodulated RF tone that the Slave nodes (digitally) lock on to. While we used a dedicated Master node in our setup for simplicity, it is straightforward to modify this setup to have the receiver itself transmit a reference tone, or to use an external reference such as the signal from a GPS satellite if it is available. Each of these alternatives have their advantages and disadvantages. Thus for instance, uninterrupted availability of a GPS synchronization signal may not be a good assumption for indoor networks or where cost and form-factor constraints preclude using dedicated GPS modules on each node. Similarly having the receiver send a reference carrier signal eliminates the need for a separate Master node, but the reference signal from a distant receiver is likely to be more noisy as compared to a signal from a Master node co-located with the Slaves.

In our setup, it is the Slave nodes that actually constitute the beamforming array, and in our implementation, most of the processing involved in synchronization and beamforming occurs at the Slave nodes. The beamforming implementation at the Slave nodes is shown in block-diagram form in Fig. 3; as indicated in the block diagram, we can think of the beamforming process at the Slave nodes as consisting of two parallel operations: frequency offset correction and phase offset correction corresponding respectively to the two steps of the synchronization process outlined above.

As noted earlier, the 1-bit feedback algorithm requires a high rate of feedback to effectively keep up with frequency offsets between transmitters. The above two-step procedure first eliminates the frequency offsets, so that the 1-bit algorithm can be effectively used with only a low rate of feedback from the distant receiver.

Before we describe our implementation of the two-step synchronization procedure, we first need to specify a suitable multiplexing scheme for the different concurrent transmissions in this setup.

3.2 Frequency division multiplexing scheme

One important thing to note about our setup is that there are three different RF signals being transmitted by various nodes in the network simultaneously: the reference tone from the Master node to the Slaves, the beamforming signal from the Slaves towards the Receiver, and the feedback signal from the Receiver to the Slaves. Specifically, we note that the Slave nodes receive both a reference tone from Master node and a feedback signal from the Receiver.

Thus we need to design a suitable multiplexing scheme to make sure these signals do not interfere with each other,

and can be extracted using relatively simple filtering operations implemented in software. In addition, we also need to ensure that *duplexing constraints* are satisfied i.e. a nodes' transmissions should not fall within the bandwidth of the same node's receiver, so there is sufficient amount of isolation between the transmit and receive hardware.

The frequency multiplexing scheme used in our experimental setup is illustrated in Fig. 4. The choice of the specific frequencies in this scheme reflects a balancing act between two conflicting objectives: on the one hand, we want to minimize the overall bandwidth of the signal received by the Slave node, so that the signal can be digitized with a relatively low sampling rate and therefore a small processing burden for the signal processing software. On the other hand, if we make the frequency separation between the reference signal from the master and the feedback signal from the receiver too small, then we will need sharp frequency-selective filters at the Slave nodes to separate the two signals, and this in turn increases the processing burden for the Slave nodes.

3.3 Simple baseband algorithm for frequency locking

We now describe the first step of the two-step synchronization process described in Section 3.1. The goal of the frequency offset correction process is to lock the RF signals transmitted by the Slave nodes to a common reference clock signal supplied by the Master node. This serves to compensate for the clock offsets between the oscillators at the Slave nodes.

Conceptually the frequency-locking problem can be formulated as follows. Given a reference signal $c_0(t) = \cos(2\pi f_1 t)$ from the Master node (i.e. a sinusoid at frequency f_1), and the pair of local oscillator signals $c_i(t) = \cos(2\pi(f_1 + \Delta f_i)t + \Delta\phi_i)$ and $s_i(t) = \sin(2\pi(f_1 + \Delta f_i)t + \Delta\phi_i)$ at Slave node i, we wish to digitally synthesize an RF signal $r_i(t) = \cos(2\pi f_2 t + \theta_i)$ at Slave i.

Note that the signals $r_i(t)$ at Slave i can have an arbitrary phase offset θ_i with each other, but must be locked to the same frequency f_2. The Slave nodes use the signals $r_i(t)$ for beamforming. As discussed in Section 3.2, because of the duplexing constraints on the Slave nodes, the beamforming frequency f_2 must be different from the frequency of the reference signal f_1. In our setup, we can see from Fig. 4 that $f_1 = 964$ MHz and $f_2 = 892$ MHz.

Our implementation achieves frequency locking by tracking the frequency *offset* between the reference signal from the

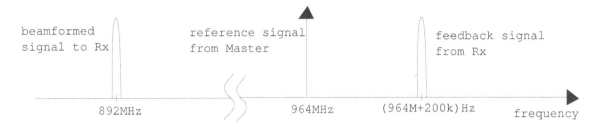

Figure 4: Frequency multiplexing scheme for beamforming experiment.

Master node and the Slave's local oscillator. In our setup, we used a modified baseband version of the classic Costas loop to achieve the frequency locking. This baseband loop is shown in Fig. 6 and it works as follows; the input to the baseband loop is the complex signal $\exp(j\phi(t))$ which represents the pair of signals $\cos\phi(t)$ and $\sin\phi(t)$, where for Slave node i, $\phi(t) = 2\pi\Delta f_i t + \Delta\phi_i$. These signals are obtained as the in-phase and quadrature components by downconverting the reference signal $c_0(t)$ using the local carrier signals $c_i(t)$) and $s_i(t)$ respectively as shown in Fig. 5.

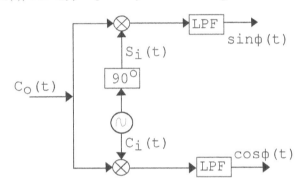

Figure 5: Oscillator offsets with reference signal.

The complex signal $\exp(j\hat{\phi}(t))$ is the output of a digital VCO with the frequency sensitivity K_1, and therefore we have by definition

$$\hat{\phi}(t) = K_1 \int_{-\infty}^{t} e(\tau)d\tau \qquad (1)$$

The "error signal" $e(t)$ is obtained from the difference of $\phi(t)$ and $\hat{\phi}(t)$ as shown in Fig. 6, and this relationship can be written as

$$e(t) = \cos\left(\phi(t) - \hat{\phi}(t)\right)\sin\left(\phi(t) - \hat{\phi}(t)\right)$$
$$= \frac{1}{2}\sin\left(2\left(\phi(t) - \hat{\phi}(t)\right)\right) \qquad (2)$$

Equation (2) is mathematically equivalent to the classic Costas loop [3], though our implementation shown in Fig. 6 is quite different from the traditional RF loop. Over time, the loop makes the "error signal" $e(t)$ very small, and therefore makes $\hat{\phi}(t)$ close to $\phi(t) \equiv 2\pi\Delta f_i t + \Delta\phi_i$. In other words this baseband loop at Slave i tracks the frequency offset Δf_i between the local oscillator signal of Slave i and the reference signal $c_0(t)$.

The Slave node i is now in a position to generate frequency-locked RF signals at frequency f_1 simply by upconverting

$\cos\hat{\phi}(t)$ and $\sin\hat{\phi}(t)$ using the in-phase and quadrature local oscillator signals $c_i(t)$ and $s_i(t)$ respectively. However, for beamforming, we want to generate frequency-locked carrier signals not at the same frequency f_1 as the reference signal $c_0(t)$, but rather at a *different frequency* f_2 as discussed earlier.

In order to accomplish this, we use the fact that PLL-frequency synthesizers [26] used to obtain RF signals at different frequencies can be well-modeled as frequency-multiplying devices. Thus if Slave i generates an RF carrier signal at frequency f_2 from the same underlying oscillator used to generate the signals $c_i(t)$ and $s_i(t)$ at frequency f_1, the resulting signals will have frequency offsets given by $\frac{f_2}{f_1}\Delta f_i$. In order to correct for these offsets, we need to use $\cos\hat{\phi}_2(t)$ and $\sin\hat{\phi}_2(t)$ obtained from the *scaled* offset estimate $\hat{\phi}_2(t)$ from the second VCO as shown in Fig. 6; this scaled estimate can be written as

$$\hat{\phi}_2(t) = K_2 \int_{-\infty}^{t} e(\tau)d\tau \equiv \frac{K_2}{K_1}\hat{\phi}(t) \qquad (3)$$

In the above, the VCO sensitivites K_1, K_2 must be chosen to satisfy $\frac{K_2}{K_1} = \frac{f_2}{f_1}$; this ratio is equal to $\frac{892}{964}$ in our setup as shown in Fig 4.

Note that this frequency-multiplication process may produce an unknown phase offset θ_i in the carrier signals at frequency f_2; however, this offset is constant and is easily compensated for by the 1-bit beamforming algorithm.

4. IMPLEMENTATION ON THE SOFTWARE-DEFINED RADIO PLATFORM

All the nodes used in this setup are based on the USRP RF and baseband boards [6] which is the most popular commercial SDR platform. We used the USRP-1 version of this platform, however our implementation is completely portable to the more recent versions.

The 1-bit feedback algorithm requires periodic feedback of 1 bit per time-slot from the receiver regarding the received signal strength (RSS) of the beamforming signal in the previous time-slot. In our implementation, the receiver simply sends a continuous wave signal proportional to the amplitude of the received signal. This signal is broadcast wirelessly to all the beamforming nodes. This feedback signal, of course, provides a lot more than 1 bit of feedback information, and indeed we designed our feedback channel in a flexible way to permit easy generalization of our implementation to more sophisticated algorithms [15] to take advantage of richer feedback information.

Each Slave node i receives this feedback signal with a delay because of latencies in the software-defined radio system; we

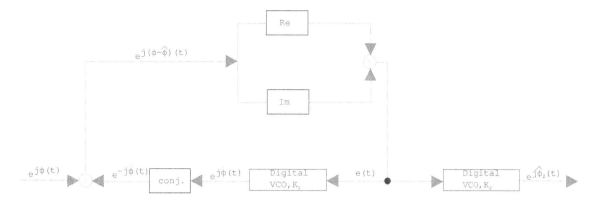

Figure 6: Modified baseband Costas loop for frequency-locking.

Parameter	Variable name	Value
Round-trip latency	r_t_latency	$\approx$30 ms
Averaging start time	avg_st_time	(r_t_latency+1)ms
Averaging end time	avg_end_time	(r_t_latency+21)ms
Beamforming time-slot end time	bf_t_slot_end	(r_t_latency+22)ms
Low-pass filter bandwidth	-	30kHz
Low-pass filter transition width	-	20kHz
Frequency correction factor of Costas loop	-	892/964
VCO sensitivity of Costas loop	-	100k rad/s/V
Baseband sampling rate	samp_rate	2 Msps
FPGA Decimation	-	32
FPGA Interpolation	-	64
Random phase perturbation distribution	-	uniform
Random phase perturbation angle	rand_pert	$\pm$15 degrees
Past RSS window size	past_rss_win	4

Table 1: Key parameters.

need to first estimate the round-trip (RT) latency between each Slave and the receiver in order to extract the 1-bit feedback required for the beamforming algorithm. We described our implementation of the frequency-locking process in Section 3.3 which forms the first synchronization subproblem outlined in Section 3.1. We now describe our implementation of the second subproblem i.e. the 1-bit beamforming algorithm. The beamforming algorithm on each Slave node consists of an initialization procedure that measures the round-trip latency in the feedback channel, followed by the actual implementation of the beamforming algorithm.

The latency measurement algorithm is based on the following simple idea. Initially when none of the beamforming nodes are transmitting, the signal level at the receiver consists of just background noise which is quite small and therefore the amplitude of the feedback signal is also correspondingly small. Then when one of the Slaves starts transmitting, it can estimate its RT latency simply by counting the number of samples it takes before it sees an increase in the amplitude of the feedback signal from the receiver. This, of course, requires that each Slave node be calibrated individually. In our setup, we do this by using special flags in the software that can be switched on and off in real-time to start and stop transmitting from each Slave node.

The pseudo-code for the initialization process and the beamforming algorithm are given in Algorithms 1 and 2 respectively. Key parameter values along with corresponding variable names referred to in the pseudo-code are in Table 1.

Algorithm 1 Round-trip latency measurement.

Initialization:
$initial\_flag \leftarrow true$
$samp\_count \leftarrow 0$
while $initial\_flag = true$ **do**
  Average every 1000 samples to get an $RSS\,estimate$
  Compare $RSS\,estimate$ with a pre-defined $threshold$
  if $RSS\,estimate \geq threshold$ **then**
    $initial\_flag \leftarrow false$
    //Round-trip latency in number of samples:
    $r\_t\_latency \leftarrow samp\_count$
    $avg\_st\_time \leftarrow r\_t\_latency + (1mS \times samp\_rate)$
    $avg\_end\_time \leftarrow r\_t\_latency + (21mS \times samp\_rate)$
    $bf\_t\_slot\_end \leftarrow r\_t\_latency + (22mS \times samp\_rate)$
    //Round-trip latency in milli-seconds:
    $r\_t\_latency \leftarrow (samp\_count/samp\_rate) \times 1000$
  end if
end while

---

5. RESULTS

We now show some experimental results from our implementation. Fig. 8 shows a photograph of the receiver node

Algorithm 2 1-bit feedback beamforming algorithm

Initialization:
$samp\_count \leftarrow 0$
$past\_rss\_win \leftarrow 0$
//cum_phase is the cumulative phase of a slave during a time-slot.
$cum\_phase \leftarrow 0$
while $initial\_flag = false$ **do**
  if $avg\_st\_time \leq samp\_count < avg\_end\_time$ **then**
    Average the received signal samples to obtain $current\_rss$, the estimate of RSS of current time-slot
  else if $samp\_count = avg\_end\_time$ **then**
    Compare $current\_rss$ with $past\_rss\_win$
    if $current\_rss > past\_rss\_win$ **then**
      $feedback\_bit \leftarrow true$
    else
      $feedback\_bit \leftarrow false$
    end if
    From $\pm rand\_pert$, generate random phase perturbation as c_rand_pert
    $cum\_phase \leftarrow cum\_phase + c\_rand\_pert$
    if $feedback\_bit = false$ **then**
      $cum\_phase \leftarrow cum\_phase - p\_rand\_pert$
    end if
    Shift the FIFO $past\_rss\_win$ by 1 to save $current\_rss$ in it
    Save c_rand_pert as p_rand_pert
  else if $samp\_count = bf\_t\_slot\_end$ **then**
    $samp\_count \leftarrow 0$
  end if
end while

in our experimental setup which is where the measurements reported in this section were recorded. In addition to the "Flex 900" RF daughterboard that the receiver node uses for receiving the beamforming signal and for transmitting the feedback signal, we also connected an additional "Basic Tx" daughterboard to the receiver node to enable us to view the received signal strength at the receiver on an external oscilloscope. This setup is illustrated in Fig. 7.

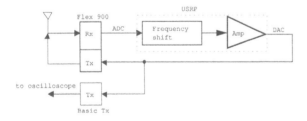

Figure 7: Measurement setup for beamforming experiment.

Figs. 9, 10 show screenshots from the oscilloscope of two runs of the beamforming experiment using two and three Slaves respectively. Specifically, Figs 9 and 10 show the amplitude of the received signal from the beamforming Slaves, with each Slave node transmitting individually at first, and then transmitting together while implementing the beamforming algorithm. Fig. 9 also has an interval (T6) where the Slaves are transmitting together incoherently (i.e. without running the beamforming algorithm).

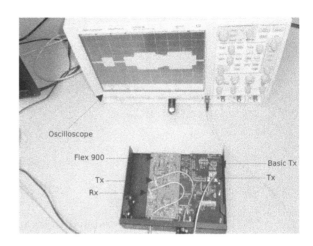

Figure 8: Photograph of measurement setup.

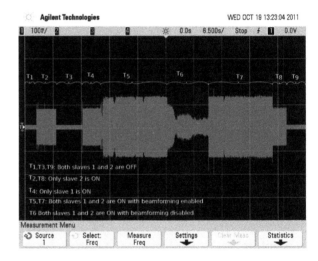

Figure 9: Received signal at the receiver with two transmitters.

It is also possible to dispense with the external oscilloscope completely and simply save samples of the received signal at the receiver node for offline processing and plotting; a typical result is shown in Fig. 11 which represents a run of the beamforming experiment with the same sequence of steps as Fig. 10.

The coherent gains from beamforming are apparent from the above plots. In other words, the amplitude of the received signal is seen to be close to the sum of their individual amplitudes. It can also be seen from Fig. 9 that the beamforming gains quickly deteriorate when the two Slaves are transmitting together but incoherently i.e. with the beamforming algorithm disabled.

While the transmitted signal in Figs. 9, 10, 11 is just an unmodulated sinusoidal tone, it is straightforward to adapt this setup to send a data signal. We illustrate this in Fig. 12 where the beamforming transmitters use a simple ON/OFF keying scheme to transmit a sequence of bits to the receiver. Specifically, Fig. 12 shows the envelope of two ON/OFF keyed received signals in two experimental runs: Experiment 1 with two beamforming transmitters and Experiment

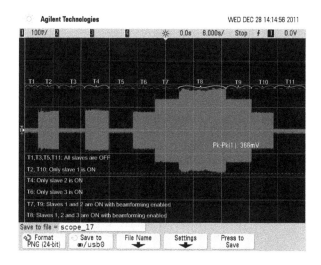

Figure 10: Received signal at the receiver with three transmitters.

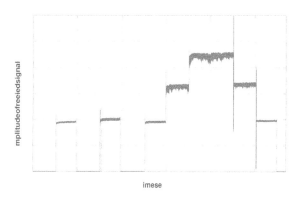

Figure 11: Received signal amplitude at the receiver with three transmitters.

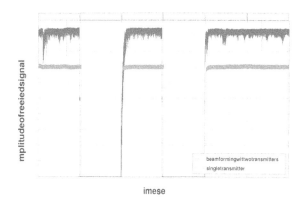

Figure 12: Data transmission using ON-OFF keying.

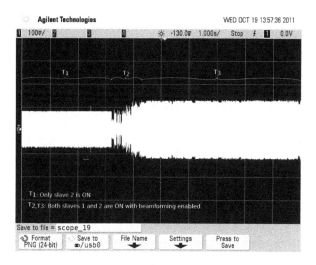

Figure 13: Transient of the beamforming process.

2 with a single transmitter. We calibrated the transmitted power in Experiment 2 such that the total transmitted power is the same in both experiments; specifically, in Experiment 1, the two beamforming nodes transmit with power P each, and the single transmitter in Experiment 2 transmits with power 2P. The stronger received signal in Experiment 1 shows the beamforming gain.

Finally, the plot in Fig. 13 shows the "transient" of the beamforming process; specifically it shows the amplitude of the received signal, with one Slave transmitting individually at first, then the second Slave being turned on with the beamforming algorithm activated on both nodes. It is seen that the convergence time of the beamforming algorithm is on the order of several hundred milliseconds, which represents around 15 timeslots.

6. CONCLUSIONS

We described our implementation of distributed beamforming on an open software-defined radio platform. This implementation is based on a novel signal processing architecture for the synchronization of high frequency RF sig-

nals entirely in software. Our results show that the synchronization requirements for beamforming can be satisfied with modest overheads on inexpensive commodity platforms without any hardware modifications and without any wired infrastructure. This opens up many interesting possibilities for future work in further developing open-source building blocks for bringing the large potential gains from virtual antenna arrays to real-world wireless networks. In addition, this poses a challenge of designing effective networking protocols to take advantage of cooperative communication schemes such as beamforming.

7. ACKNOWLEDGEMENT

The authors are grateful to Thomas Schmid for shepherding the final version of this paper and to the anonymous reviewers; we have added several additional details in response to their suggestions and we believe the paper is significantly improved as a result.

8. REFERENCES

[1] G. Bradford and J. Laneman. An experimental framework for the evaluation of cooperative diversity.

In *Conference on Information Sciences and Systems (CISS)*, pages 641 –645, March 2009.

[2] G. Bradford and J. Laneman. A survey of implementation efforts and experimental design for cooperative communications. In *IEEE International Conference on Acoustics Speech and Signal Processing (ICASSP)*, pages 5602–5605, March 2010.

[3] J. Costas. Synchronous communications. *Proceedings of the IRE*, 44(12):1713 –1718, dec. 1956.

[4] D.R. Brown III and H.V. Poor. Time-slotted round-trip carrier synchronization for distributed beamforming. *IEEE Trans. on Signal Processing*, 56(11):5630–5643, November 2008.

[5] A. El Gamal and T. Cover. Multiple user information theory. *Proceedings of the IEEE*, 68(12):1466 – 1483, dec. 1980.

[6] USRP products. http://www.ettus.com/products, 2011.

[7] Gnu radio. http://gnuradio.org/redmine/projects/gnuradio/wiki, 2011.

[8] P. Gupta and P. Kumar. The capacity of wireless networks. *IEEE Transactions on Information Theory*, 46(2):388 –404, mar 2000.

[9] R. Irmer, H. Droste, P. Marsch, M. Grieger, G. Fettweis, S. Brueck, H.-P. Mayer, L. Thiele, and V. Jungnickel. Coordinated multipoint: Concepts, performance, and field trial results. *Communications Magazine, IEEE*, 49(2):102–111, february 2011.

[10] V. Jungnickel, L. Thiele, T. Wirth, T. Haustein, S. Schiffermuller, A. Forck, S. Wahls, S. Jaeckel, S. Schubert, H. Gabler, C. Juchems, F. Luhn, R. Zavrtak, H. Droste, G. Kadel, W. Kreher, J. Mueller, W. Stoermer, and G. Wannemacher. Coordinated multipoint trials in the downlink. In *GLOBECOM Workshops, 2009 IEEE*, pages 1 –7, Dec, 2009 2009.

[11] T. Korakis, M. Knox, E. Erkip, and S. Panwar. Cooperative network implementation using open-source platforms. *IEEE Communications Magazine*, 47(2):134–141, Feb 2009.

[12] J. Laneman and G. Wornell. Distributed space-time-coded protocols for exploiting cooperative diversity in wireless networks. *IEEE Transactions on Information Theory*, 49(10):2415 – 2425, oct. 2003.

[13] J. Mietzner, J. Eick, and P. Hoeher. On distributed space-time coding techniques for cooperative wireless networks and their sensitivity to frequency offsets. In *Smart Antennas, 2004. ITG Workshop on*, pages 114 – 121, march 2004.

[14] R. Mudumbai, G. Barriac, and U. Madhow. On the feasibility of distributed beamforming in wireless networks. *IEEE Trans. on Wireless Communication*, 6(5):1754–1763, May 2007.

[15] R. Mudumbai, P. Bidigare, S. Pruessing, S. Dasgupta, M. Oyarzun, and D. Raeman. The unslotted feedback approach to distributed beamforming. In *to appear in Proc. International Conference on Acoustics, Speech, and Signal Processing (ICASSP)*, 2012.

[16] R. Mudumbai, D.R. Brown III, U. Madhow, and H.V. Poor. Distributed transmit beamforming: Challenges and recent progress. *IEEE Communications Magazine*, 47(2):102–110, February 2009.

[17] R. Mudumbai, J. Hespanha, U. Madhow, and G. Barriac. Scalable feedback control for distributed beamforming in sensor networks. In *IEEE International Symp. on Information Theory (ISIT)*, pages 137–141, Adelaide, Australia, September 2005.

[18] R. Mudumbai, J. Hespanha, U. Madhow, and G. Barriac. Distributed transmit beamforming using feedback control. *IEEE Trans. on Inform. Theory*, 56(1):411–426, January 2010.

[19] R. Mudumbai, B. Wild, U. Madhow, and K. Ramchandran. Distributed beamforming using 1 bit feedback: from concept to realization. In *44th Allerton Conf. on Comm., Control, and Computing*, pages 1020 – 1027, Monticello, IL, Sep. 2006.

[20] P. Murphy and A. Sabharwal. Design, implementation, and characterization of a cooperative communications system. *IEEE Transactions on Vehicular Technology*, 60(6):2534 –2544, July 2011.

[21] Datasheet for EC2620ETTS-64.000M oscillator. http://www.ecliptek.com/SpecSheetGenerator/specific.aspx?PartNumber=EC2620ETTS-64.000M, 2011.

[22] A. Ozgur, O. Leveque, and D. Tse. Hierarchical cooperation achieves optimal capacity scaling in ad hoc networks. *IEEE Transactions on Information Theory*, 53(10):3549–3572, Oct. 2007.

[23] I. Ozil and D.R. Brown III. Time-slotted round-trip carrier synchronization. In *Proceedings of the 41st Asilomar Conference on Signals, Systems, and Computers*, pages 1781 – 1785, Pacific Grove, CA, November 4-7, 2007.

[24] R. Preuss and D.R. Brown III. Two-way synchronization for coordinated multi-cell retrodirective downlink beamforming. *IEEE Trans. on Signal Processing*, November Accepted to appear in 2011.

[25] Rakon RFPO45 SMD oven controlled crystal oscillator datasheet. http://www.rakon.com/Products/Public_Documents/Specifications/RFPO45.pdf, 2009.

[26] B. Razavi. Challenges in the design of frequency synthesizers for wireless applications. In *Proc. IEEE Custom Integrated Circuits Conference*, pages 395–402, May 1997.

[27] Warp: Wireless open access research platform. http://warp.rice.edu/trac, 2011.

[28] T. Schmid, O. Sekkat, and M. B. Srivastava. An experimental study of network performance impact of increased latency in software defined radios. In *Proc. ACM international workshop on Wireless network testbeds, experimental evaluation and characterization*, WinTECH '07, pages 59–66, 2007.

[29] A. Sendonaris, E. Erkip, and B. Aazhang. Increasing uplink capacity via user cooperation diversity. In *Proc. 1998 IEEE International Symp. on Information Theory*, page 156, Cambridge, MA, August 1998.

[30] M. Seo, M. Rodwell, and U. Madhow. A feedback-based distributed phased array technique and its application to 60-ghz wireless sensor network. In *Microwave Symposium Digest, 2008 IEEE MTT-S International*, pages 683 –686, june 2008.

[31] S. Sigg and M. Beigl. Algorithms for closed-loop feedback based distributed adaptive beamforming in

wireless sensor networks. In *5th International Conference on Intelligent Sensors, Sensor Networks and Information Processing (ISSNIP)*, pages 25–30. IEEE, 2009.

[32] Y. Tu and G. Pottie. Coherent cooperative transmission from multiple adjacent antennas to a distant stationary antenna through AWGN channels. In *IEEE Vehicular Technology Conf. (VTC)*, volume 1, pages 130–134, Birmingham, AL, Spring 2002.

[33] D. Youngner, L. Lust, D. Carlson, S. Lu, L. Forner, H. Chanhvongsak, and T. Stark. A manufacturable chip-scale atomic clock. In *International Solid-State Sensors, Actuators and Microsystems Conference, TRANSDUCERS*, pages 39 –44, june 2007.

[34] P. Zetterberg, C. Mavrokefalidis, A. S. Lalos, and E. Matigakis. Experimental investigation of cooperative schemes on a real-time dsp-based testbed. *EURASIP J. Wireless Comm. and Networking*, 2009.

[35] H. Zhang and H. Dai. On the capacity of distributed mimo systems. In *Proc. Conference on Information Sciences and Systems*, 2004.

[36] J. Zhang, J. Jia, Q. Zhang, and E. Lo. Implementation and evaluation of cooperative communication schemes in software-defined radio testbed. In *Proc. IEEE INFOCOM*, pages 1–9, March 2010.

Magneto-Inductive NEtworked Rescue System (MINERS): Taking Sensor Networks Underground

Andrew Markham and Niki Trigoni
Institute for the Future of Computing, Department of Computer Science
University of Oxford
firstname.lastname@cs.ox.ac.uk

ABSTRACT

Wireless underground networks are an emerging technology which have application in a number of scenarios. For example, in a mining disaster, flooding or a collapse can isolate portions of underground tunnels, severing wired communication links and preventing radio communication. In this paper, we explore the use of low frequency magnetic fields for communication, and present a new hardware platform that features triaxial transmitter/receiver antenna loops. We point out that the fundamental problem of the magnetic channel is the limited bitrate at long ranges, due to the extreme path loss of 60 dB/decade. To this end, we present two complementary techniques to address this limitation. Firstly, we demonstrate *magnetic vector modulation*, a technique which modulates the three dimensional orientation of the magnetic vector. This increases the gross bitrate by a factor of over 2.5, without an increase in transmission power or bandwidth. Secondly, we show how in a multi-hop network latencies can be dramatically reduced by receiving multiple parallel streams of frequency multiplexed data in a many-to-one configuration. These techniques are demonstrated on a working hardware platform, which for flexible operation, features a software defined magnetic transceiver. Typical communication range is approximately 30 m through rock.

Categories and Subject Descriptors

C.2.1 [**Computer-Communication Networks**]: Network Architecture and Design

General Terms

Design, Experimentation, Measurement

Keywords

Search and Rescue, Magneto-Inductive, Magnetic, Mining, Triaxial, Network, Underground

1. INTRODUCTION

After a decade of intensive research in wireless sensor networks we are experiencing a flurry of sensing applications that rely on radio-based communication over the air. In stark contrast, sensor networks for underground environments are still in their infancy, and applications that could benefit from them are severely challenged. For example, in a mining disaster, a rockburst or collapse can isolate portions of underground tunnels, severing wired communication links and preventing radio communication. Miners who are trapped deep underground are unable to communicate with the surface.

In this paper, we introduce a communication layer based on low frequency magnetic communication. Operating in the near-field region, magnetic fields can penetrate rock, soil, fresh water and air with minimal attenuation. Due to the very low frequencies used (2500 Hz)wavelengths are in the order of kilometres and thus there is no multipath, another advantage over higher frequency radio.

However, unlike prior work [16] using a single loop antenna, to make the network operation invariant to node placement and orientation, each node is equipped with a *triaxial* loop antenna (which is used both as a transmitter and receiver). One of the challenges faced by magneto-inductive links is the inverse cube decay in signal strength with distance. In order to extend the communication range, nodes transmit over a narrow bandwidth, which helps to increase the SNR at the receiver but results in a low bitrate e.g. 32 bps. To improve the per-link bitrate, a novel technique, *magnetic vector modulation*, is introduced which modulates the transmitted signal over all three transmitter antennas, thus generating a magnetic vector whose amplitude and three-dimensional orientation can be controlled. The receiver, using its triaxial antenna, maps the detected magnetic vector to a signal constellation to decode symbols. We show that for the same transmitter power and bandwidth the effective bit rate can be increased by a factor of 2.58.

With regard to the network itself, the low bitrates of the magnetic channel result in large multihop latencies, especially if nodes have to contend for the medium. Although the transmitter bandwidth is small, a wider band receiver (e.g. 2kHz) can be used to simultaneously decode multiple frequency separated transmissions. As this is the opposite of one-to-many (broadcasting), we term this many-to-one approach *broadcatching*. We demonstrate that this technique can significantly reduce the latency of tree-based data collection, especially for aggregation queries. Used together in a network, these two techniques can reduce latency by over 4.5 times.

In summary this paper makes contributions in the following areas:

- We propose and have built magnetic transceiver nodes for underground sensor networks, that are able to transmit data through rock and soil at higher data rates than previously. We show how these nodes can fit in a hybrid sensor network architecture.

- We introduce *magnetic vector modulation*, a technique which modulates the spatial magnetic vector, more than doubling the effective bit rate, and also providing rotational invariance to node placement.

- We show how broadcatching can be used to reduce latency in the severely bandlimited magnetic channel.

- We demonstrate magnetic vector modulation and broadcatching on real hardware.

In Sec. 2, we discuss challenges and requirements the application scenario, underground mining. Sec. 3 presents our system design, motivating our new hardware platform and discussing the low bit rates of the magnetic channel. Sec 4 presents one solution to this problem by modulating the direction of the magnetic vector. Sec. 5 introduces a complementary solution which increases the overall network throughput. The benefits of the two solutions are evaluated on real hardware and in simulation in Sec. 6. The contributions of the work are contrasted with existing literature in Sec. 7 and we summarize the contributions in Sec. 8

2. MOTIVATING SCENARIO: MINING

As a motivating example, we consider communication in an underground mine.

2.1 Mine Operations and Disasters

There are two broad classes of mining operations, surface and underground. Typically an underground mine will have a central shaft following the dip of the ore body and usually about 10m below the ore body. From this will radiate access tunnels that are slightly angled from the horizontal to manage water drainage. There are larger tunnels, usually separated by a 30 m depth difference that are designed to transport ore using electric locomotives or conveyors. Mining is a hazardous occupation, with a fatality rate in 2007 of 21.4 per 100,000 fulltime workers in the United States [1]. Compared with the average rate for all private industry of 4.3 per 100,000, the fatality rate is nearly five times as large [1]. Within the mining sector, underground mining is significantly more dangerous than surface operations, with a fatality rate about twice as high [5]. Dangers include rockbursts which generally lead to a collapse of a tunnel, fire and explosion, a major risk in coal operations, and flooding. The rescue of 33 trapped Chilean miners in 2010 after 69 days underground brought the importance of underground safety and communication to the forefront of global awareness. However, communication was only made possible after sinking shafts. Along with the successful rescues, there have also been terrible tragedies. The Sago Mine disaster on January 2 2006 in Virginia, USA [9] is a particularly relevant example. An underground explosion in a coal mine trapped twelve miners behind a blast curtain. Although the way out was clear, they had no way of knowing as the mine telephone system had been destroyed during the blast and by the time rescuers reached them, all but one had died from carbon monoxide poisoning. This tragic example highlights how underground communication systems have to be improved and made robust to roof collapse and flooding.

In the event of a mining disaster a communication system could provide information such as: the number of miners still underground; their approximate location; concentrations of gases (methane, oxygen, carbon dioxide); flooding and whether miners can move freely or are trapped. In addition, a two-way communication link, even if operating over low baud rates, can be used to send messages to trapped miners, such as which access shaft they should move to to facilate rescue operations.

2.2 Mine Communication

Percussion: Trapped miners can communicate with rescue teams by banging on rock bolts with metal pipes and sledge-hammers. Rescue teams can use sensitive geophones to listen for rhythmic banging and try and localize the miners. This method is obviously exhausting for the trapped miners and cannot be used for effective communication to tell miners how best to escape.

Mine Telephone and Wired links: Modern mines are fully wired, often with ethernet or optical links. This allows for high speed data transmission and monitoring. However, in a collapse, flood or fire, wired links can be broken, preventing communication with other sections of the mine. In addition, wired links cannot be used directly to communicate with miners and require a bridge to wireless technologies.

Leaky Feeder: This is a "semi-wireless" approach where a coaxial cable with periodic breaks in the shield capacitively couples with a receiver device, enabling short range wireless communication. Amplified repeaters are placed every few hundred metres in order to boost the signal.

Wireless: Researchers have attempted to provide a communications infrastructure underground by using off-the-shelf technology such as Zigbee [4]. Due to the waveguide like nature of tunnels and sharp corners, high frequency radio waves suffer from severe multipath and heavy attenuation. Radio cannot be used to communicate through rock or soil in the event of a collapse, a fundamental drawback [18].

Through-the-earth: An alternative approach to transmitting information to miners is the use of low frequency magnetic fields, which are able to penetrate soil and rock strata largely unattenuated, so called through-the-earth (TTE) systems [20]. The most widely adopted system is the one-way PED (personal emergency device) system which consists of a very large loop antenna placed on the surface driven with over 1.5kW of power. This allows it to penetrate a few hundred metres of rock, depending on the conductivity. Its drawback is that it is only a one-way communication link and does not allow miners to send messages to the surface. The reason for this is that a device which is small enough to be carried by a miner is unable to generate a large enough magnetic field to be detected at the surface.

There is a clear need for a communication system which is able to maintain two-way connectivity in the event of a mining disaster. In the next section we propose a new node design and a hybrid network architecture that can meet these

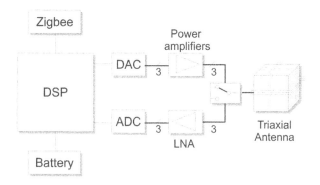

Figure 1: Block diagram of a magnetic transceiver node.

requirements. Note, however, that our proposed system is not applicable only to the mining scenario; it can be used in a wide range of scenarios that involve underground operations, such as geological studies, volcano monitoring, precision agriculture and animal monitoring.

3. SYSTEM DESIGN

The operational requirements as dictated by the application of miner rescue are:

- Information from trapped miners should be relayed to the surface with minimal latency

- The system should be able to maintain communication in the event of rockfall or failure of existing communication modalities

- The magnetic transceiver nodes should be small enough to be regularly deployed in an operational mine

- The nodes should not require precise placement or positioning

In this section, the design of our new node platform is presented and the design choices made at each level of the stack are highlighted. We then explain how our platform fits in a hybrid sensor network architecture that combines wired, radio and magnetic communication channels.

3.1 Node Design

The block diagram of a magnetic transceiver node is shown in Fig. 1. The digital signal processor (DSP) lies at the heart of the system and essentially acts as a software defined radio (SDR). The use of SDR allows for great flexibility in designing and evaluating different modulation schemes over the magnetic channel. Through analog-to-digital (ADC) and digital-to-analog (DAC) convertors the DSP modulates and receives data from the magnetic channel. The magnetic field is generated and detected by the triaxial antenna on the right hand side of the figure. The node is also equipped with a Zigbee (802.15.4) transceiver to allow for short range, high-data rate communication. We first discuss the design of the physical layer, namely how to generate a magnetic field, effects on the magnetic field due to the channel, and how to detect a magnetic field.

3.1.1 Generating a magnetic field

A current passing through a coil generates a magnetic field in the space around it. If the coil dimensions are small relative to the distance to the receiver, it can be approximated as a point dipole source, most conveniently expressed in spherical co-ordinates as

$$\vec{B} = \frac{\mu_0 \mu_r N I A}{4\pi r^3}(2\cos(\theta)\hat{r} + \sin(\theta)\hat{\theta}) \quad (1)$$

where $\mu_0 = 4\pi 10^{-7}$ H/m is the permeability of free space, μ_r is the relative permeability of the medium, N is the number of turns, I is the current flowing through the coil, A is the cross sectional area, θ is the azimuthal angle, $\hat{\theta}$ is the unit normal vector in the azimuthal direction, $\hat{r}$ is the unit radial vector and r the distance between the source and the sensor [8]. There are a number of important factors to note about this equation which guide the design process.

Rolloff: The magnitude of the magnetic field decays with increasing range as an inverse cube ($\propto r^{-3}$), rather than following an inverse square law as is typical for electromagnetic radiation in free space. This results in a 60 dB/decade attenuation in signal strength with range. This rolloff significantly reduces the range that can be practically obtained. For example, to double the range of a given transmitter, the magnetic moment has to be increased eightfold. Hence to span a given distance, it is more power efficient to use many smaller hops, rather than one single large hop. This factor suggests the use of distributed multi-hop networks [15].

Coupling: Soil, air, water and most rocks have a relative permeability μ_r very close to 1. This means that magnetic fields are not attenuated differently by these media and hence can be used for communication through rock. However, ferrous materials such as iron, steel and nickel have much higher permeabilities, ranging between 100 and 600, depending on composition. Rather than preventing communication, induced eddy currents in the conductor can actually be used to increase transmission range, with the metal object acting as a passive re-radiator [20].

3.1.2 Magnetic Channel

With respect to the magnetic channel, there are two effects to consider, namely frequency dependent absorption (skin effect) and background noise. These factors dictate the operational frequency that the magnetic transceiver node adopts.

Skin effect: The conductivity of rock and other objects has a frequency dependent effect on the magnetic field. This is because a time-varying field induces a current in the rock, which acts to cancel the magnetic field. Thus, even though the media can have a permeability close to 1, over long distances the skin effect starts to dominate the channel. The skin depth, the distance at which a signal is attenuated to $1/e = 0.368$, is given as

$$\delta = \sqrt{\frac{2}{\omega \mu_0 \sigma}}, \quad (2)$$

where ω is the frequency and σ is the conductivity of the media, measured in mho/m [7]. For a typical overburden conductivity of 0.01 mho/m, the skin depth at 5 kHz is 71m and at 1 MHz is only 5 m [7]. After four skin depths, the signal is attenuated by over 20 dB. Eq. 2 demonstrates that the use of higher carrier frequencies comes at the cost of significantly increased attenuation.

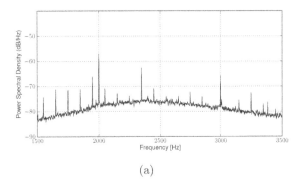 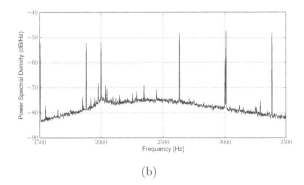

(a)   (b)

Figure 2: Power spectral density of background noise. (a) shows the PSD as captured by the x-axis sensor. (b) shows the PSD as captured by the z-axis sensor.

Background noise: The magnetic channel is dominated by low frequency noise, caused by a variety of natural and man-made factors, such as lightning, mains noise and earth resonance. Noise can be approximated as roughly following a $1/f$ distribution, with strong narrowband interferers.

The power spectral density (PSD) of background noise in the range of 1500-3000 Hz is shown in Fig. 2 for the x and z channels. The mains harmonics can be seen as strong peaks, as high as 30dB above the noise floor, in the PSD plot. Note also that the harmonics are different for the x and z channels as the noise sources are directional. To avoid the strong interference, channels can be centred halfway between adjacent harmonics.

Together, these competing constraints dictate operation around the very low frequency (VLF) frequency band (3 kHz to 30 kHz). At these low frequencies, the wavelengths are typically much larger than the distance between nodes, ranging from 100 km to 3 km respectively. Operation is thus in the reactive (quasi-static) near field. The field is non-propagating and hence there can be no multipath or fading.

3.1.3 Detecting a Magnetic Field

There are a number of sensors which can be used to detect magnetic fields, such as solid state magnetometers, SQUIDS and search coils. All of these are based on changes in measurable characteristics, such as resistance or voltage which are created in response to an incident magnetic field. For simplicity, the same transmitting coil is used as a receiving loop. The voltage produced by a multi-turn coil is

$$V = \mu_0 N A 2\pi f B \cos\theta, \qquad (3)$$

where N is the number of turns, A the cross-sectional area f the carrier frequency, $\vec{B}$ the magnetic field vector and θ is the angle between the magnetic field and sensor.

Angular dependence: The $\cos\theta$ term in Eq. 3 (essentially the dot product between the magnetic field vector and the unit normal to the antenna aperture) has a very significant effect on reducing the robustness of the communication channel. As $\theta \to \frac{\pi}{2}$, the term $\cos\theta \to 0$. Essentially, when source and sensor are mutually perpendicular, the sensor cuts no lines of flux and hence communication is impossible.

If magnetic nodes are equipped with single loops, as in [16], deployments have to be carefully made such that nodes line up along a common axis. This is not robust enough for many applications, in particular mining, and thus a solution

using three mutually orthogonal receiver coils is used. With this configuration, as the axes of the antenna are at right angles to each other, as one antenna's signal is minimized, another is maximized. Thus, the total received voltage is never zero. Note that there is still an amplitude dependence due to the impact of the radial component of the magnetic field being twice as high as the tangential component in Eq. 1. However, if the transmitter is also equipped with tri-axial antennas, and the signal to be transmitted is whitened such that no one antenna is favored, then the received power at various orientations is constant. Note that a triaxial coil arrangement permits operation with arbitrarily positioned and oriented nodes in 3-D space, but if only a planar (2-D) layout is required, nodes can be equipped with biaxial orthogonal coils.

3.1.4 Summary of Design Choices

Motivated by the directional nature of uniaxial magnetic loops, each transceiver node is equipped with three orthogonal antennas, making the system rotationally invariant. However, due to the narrow channel bandwidth, the achievable bit rates are very low, e.g. 32 bps. By adopting the triaxial antenna configuration, both on transmitter and receiver, we demonstrate in Sec. 4 that by modulating the orientation of the magnetic vector, more information can be encoded on the channel per unit of energy. This increases the effective bit rate.

3.2 Network Design

In this section, we consider how a network comprised of magnetic transceivers would operate, under the constraints highlighted in Sec. 3.1. This is shown graphically in Fig. 3. Each transceiver is equipped with wired and wireless (RF) links which are used in normal mining operations, transferring information from workers and sensors about position and conditions. Sensors can either be wired or wireless and data is forwarded to each magnetic transceiver node which then relays the information over a wired or wireless link to another magnetic transceiver, until it reaches the surface. Control messages can also be relayed from the surface to actuate various underground machinery. A hybrid wired/wireless approach is used as the limited bitrate of the magnetic channel is not adequate for normal operations. Miners are equipped with small Zigbee based transceivers, with various sensors such as accelerometers. These emit pe-

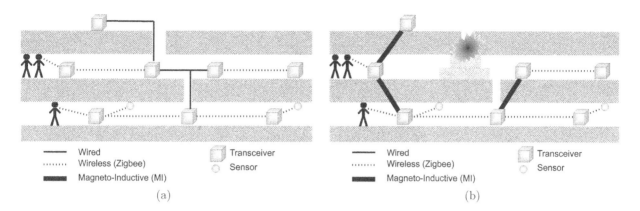

Figure 3: Network overview. (a) Shows normal operation. The mine-wide sensing system communicates through a combination of wired and wireless links, transferring information from sensors and people to the surface. (b) Shows operation in a disaster scenario. The network re-organizes and uses low frequency magneto-inductive communication to bridge the destroyed links, penetrating rock. Thus the positions of the trapped miners can be relayed to the surface.

riodic, uniquely coded radio beacons which are detected by the magnetic transceivers when they are within range or via multi-hop data gathering.

In the event of a disaster, which can break wired communication and prevent wireless communication, the system falls over to low-bandwidth magneto-inductive communication, which is able to penetrate rock and soil, maintaining network connectivity. The magnetic transceiver nodes are equipped with backup batteries to enable operation to continue even if power fails. The magnetic transceiver nodes can also be equipped with sensors themselves to directly measure parameters such as carbon monoxide concentration or temperature. They can also query wireless sensor devices and hence act as a gateway between the surface and underground. Thus, this system aims to augment existing wireless technology by providing a robust backup path.

The low bitrate magnetic channel has significant implications for network operation, in particular the latency of query responses. To this end, we present two complementary techniques to dramatically speed up data dissemination through a magnetic network: 1) magnetic vector modulation, a technique at the physical layer discussed in Sec. 4), and 2) broadcatching, a technique at the medium access control layer discussed in Sec. 5.

4. MAGNETIC VECTOR MODULATION

The use of tri-axial sensors to measure vector fields is commonplace, e.g. tri-axial accelerometers. What is less well known is that tri-axial *transmitters* (comprising three mutually orthogonal loops) can be used to generate magnetic vector fields. By controlling the phases and amplitudes of the currents in each transmitting coil, the three dimensional vector field at a receiver can be oriented in any arbitrary direction. In this way, more information can be encoded using the same available bandwidth and the same total transmitter power.

A simple demonstration of the principles behind magnetic vector modulation is shown in Fig. 4. At each time step, a separate coil is energized. The magnetic fields detected by the sensors at the three different locations A, B and C

vary in magnitude and polarity depending on which coil is energized. Thus it can be seen that by changing the three-dimensional current phasing of the source, the magnetic field vector detected at the receiver also changes. This provides the basis for the communication system.

Transmitter Chain: In scalar BPSK, a constant frequency carrier is multiplied by a lower frequency bipolar data message, with values of +1 and -1. Scalar BPSK results in a maximum theoretical spectral efficiency of 1 bit/s/Hz. There are many possible ways to convert BPSK to a vector based representation. For simplicity, we allow a single coil to be energized per symbol (either with positive or negative phase) and the other two coils are left open. This gives a total of $M = 6$ possible symbol values. These are shown in Table 1, along with the corresponding baseband currents in each coil.

To send a data message, the transmitter first sends a carrier tone, followed by a multichannel preamble. This allows the receiver to learn the channel transfer function. Following this, the incoming serial binary data stream is mapped to a base-6 representation. The symbol mapping dictates which coils are energized at a particular time and their respective phasing. The baseband signals are then modulated with the higher frequency carrier wave and after amplification, applied to the transmitter coils. To reduces the overall bandwidth of the signal it is passed through a root raised cosine pulse shaping filter.

Table 1: Coil energizations

Symbol	i_x	i_y	i_z
0	+1	0	0
1	0	+1	0
2	0	0	+1
3	-1	0	0
4	0	-1	0
5	0	0	-1

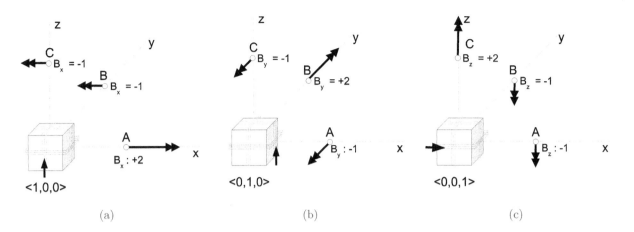

(a)   (b)   (c)

Figure 4: The basic method of communication: a triaxial source of magnetic field, shown as a cube at the origin, generates magnetic fields. The resultant magnetic fields at three different sensors placed on the x-axis (A), the y-axis (B) and the z-axis (C) are shown. (a) The X coil in the transmitter is energized. Note the field at A is twice as large and opposite in sign to the fields at B and C. (b) The Y coil in the transmitter is energized. (c) The Z coil in the transmitter is energized.

Receiver chain: The receiver chain is shown in Fig. 5. Like a conventional receiver, the weak signals are first amplified by a low noise amplifier followed by automatic gain control to maintain an acceptable dynamic range. The three channels are downconverted using a complex carrier to form in-phase (real) and quadrature (imaginary) components.

Similar to a normal single channel receiver, the first block in the chain is carrier phase/frequency tracking to adjust the local oscillator's generated frequency in order to maintain phase synchronicity. This is performed using a Costas Locked Loop which synthesizes a single carrier, not three separate ones. This is because there is frequency or phase shift between the three channels. The error signal applied to the feedback loop is derived from all three input channels, giving more weight to those with better signal-to-noise ratios. The next stage in the receiver chain is to perform timing recovery. This is like a normal receiver except that the vector amplitude (i.e. the RMS amplitude of the three channels) of the incoming signal is used to control the data sampler, which determines at which point a symbol sample should be taken to maximize the energy.

The following stage in the process is the block used to estimate the channel transfer function, **H**. This is a 3×3 matrix that contains coefficients which represent the coupling between the transmitter and receiver antennas. Note that although there are six symbols, only three vector coefficients need to be stored as the remaining three are simply opposite in sign and lie in an antipodal position within the constellation. The transmitter sends a known preamble character on each of the three channels in sequence. The receiver averages the 3-D magnetic vector it receives over the duration of each preamble character. Each of these is used to populate a column of **H**. Note that the magnetic vector is purely real, as no phase shift can occur due to multipath. As shown in Fig. 4, the **H** matrix will have different values depending on the relative separation and orientation between the transmitter and receiver.

To decode the incoming data, the receiver chooses the symbol that minimizes the Euclidean distance between the

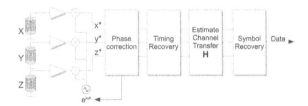

Figure 5: System diagram showing the receiver communication chain.

received 3-D vector and the known **H**. The 6-ary symbols are then unmapped to recover the serial data stream. This is explained with reference to an example constellation shown in Fig. 6. The constellation is established using **H** determined during the initial channel estimation phase. The preamble symbols are averaged to form a cluster, where the centroid of the cluster is the respective column vector in **H**. To decode a symbol, the 3-D Euclidean distance between the received vector signal measured from all three channels, marked with an 'x' in the figure, is determined to every point in the symbol constellation. A hard decision is made based on which point of the constellation the symbol is closest to, returning in this case, the symbol 0.

To compare against the scalar BPSK case, note that the power consumed is identical, as only one coil is energized at each point in time. Also, note that the bandwidth occupied is identical. However, instead of sending $M = 2$ possible symbol values, in the vector case $M = 6$ symbol values have been sent. Thus, the gross bitrate has been increased by a factor $\frac{\log_2(6)}{\log_2(2)} = 2.58$.

Note that compared to the scalar BPSK case, an extra two preamble characters have to be sent. Assume that the length of each preamble character is P symbols, and that scalar BPSK also sends a preamble byte to synchronize the

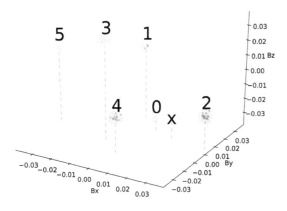

Figure 6: Example constellation showing how the incoming symbol, marked by 'x' is decoded. It is closest within the three-dimensional magnetic field strength to symbol 0.

receiver, then the time taken to send D bits of data is

$$t_{scalar} = t_s(P + D), \qquad (4)$$

where t_s is the symbol time. For the vector case, the total time taken to send D bits of data is

$$t_{vector} = t_s(3P + \frac{D}{\log_2(6)}). \qquad (5)$$

For a preamble character length of $P = 8$ bits, magnetic vector modulation is more efficient if the data is longer than $D = 32$ bits or 4 bytes. Thus, it can be seen that the additional overhead of determining the channel transfer function is negligible for the magnetic vector modulation case.

Note that any modulation schemes can be extended using these extra orthogonal dimensions. For example, a transmitter can use quadrature modulation by using a complex carrier. The drawback of the magnetic vector approach is that the transmitter and receiver chains needs to be triplicated, which can increase cost and complexity. However, the advantages such as rotational invariance and increased bit rate far outweigh the additional hardware and software requirements.

5. BROADCATCHING

The small transmitter bandwidth of the transmitter in Sec. 3 was highlighted as a potential drawback of the magnetic channel. Magnetic vector modulation (Sec. 4) was presented as one solution to this problem that does not consume additional energy or bandwidth. The small transmitter bandwidth has the effect of limiting the maximum achievable bit rate. For example, within a bandwidth of 32 Hz, the bit rate, even when using magnetic vector modulation is approximately 80 bps. Although the transmitter bandwidth is very small (32 Hz), the receiver is able to capture signals over a wider range, e.g. 2000Hz. Furthermore, due to the low operating frequencies and the software defined demodulator, it is computationally simple and feasible to simultaneously decode multiple, frequency separated, data streams. This is similar to orthogonal frequency division multiple access (OFDMA) which is used in multichannel

WiFi [21]. We term this many-to-one concept *broadcatching*, as it is the reverse of broadcasting, which is one-to-many. Broadcatching has some significant implications for the low data rate, high latency magnetic network.

Contention free: The first implication of broadcatching is that through frequency division, contention can be eliminated entirely (static channel allocation through graph coloring [6]) or greatly reduced (random channel allocation). This is important as the high latencies of the magnetic channel will be exacerbated if nodes have to contend for access to the medium. Interference will also be eliminated, which again is important both in terms of latency and energy consumption, as failed packets have to be retransmitted and hence waste energy and bandwidth. In the prototype system, if channels are spaced every 50 Hz, 40 distinct frequency channels can be packed into a 2 kHz bandwidth. Given the low probability of collision, nodes can randomly hop to a new channel for each transmission. Although this introduces contention, the probability of interference is very low. Also note that the receiver does not need to be aware of the channel hopping sequence and it can be completely random. In terms of implementation, the number of channel decoders does not need to be equal to the number of input channels, only to the number of children. Channel decoders only need to be executed when a valid signal is received. Thus, channel decoders can be dynamically mapped to particular frequency bands. Channels with low SNR, such as those with strong mains harmonics can be avoided.

Network Algorithms: The second major difference is in operation of standard network algorithms, such as tree collect and query propagation. In a mine rescue scenario, aggregation queries such as sum, max, average etc., can be used to determine the number of people underground, the maximum methane concentration, the minimum oxygen concentration and so forth. It is important for a rescue that such information can be gathered rapidly.

To execute an aggregation query, data originates at the leaves of the query tree and percolates upwards. Once each parent has obtained all the data from its children, it combines its own sensor value with the query function, ready to send to its parent. In conventional wireless sensor networks, this means that each child must send its data in a time-slotted fashion to its parent, in order to prevent collisions at the receiver. Hence, the time taken for each node to gather the data to execute the query is related to the number of children it has. In general, if each parent has B children, and the depth of the tree is D, then the total time taken to execute the aggregation query using conventional time slots is proportional to DB. This implies that to minimize the time taken to execute the query, the breadth B and the depth D of the tree should be equal. In addition, trees should be balanced such that each node has an approximately equal number of children in order to minimize the maximum breadth.

In the broadcatching tree, the children can all send their data during the same time slot. Thus, the number of children that a node has does not alter the data gathering time. Thus, the total time taken to collect information from such a tree is proportional to D units of time, where D is the depth of the tree. This is an important result, as the execution time is *independent* on the number of nodes in the network and only related to the tree depth. It also suggests that trees should be broad rather than deep and that bal-

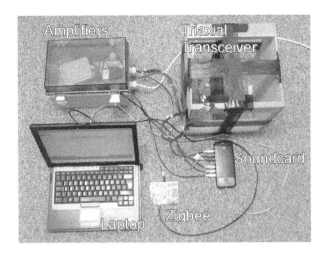

Figure 7: The proof-of-concept transceiver.

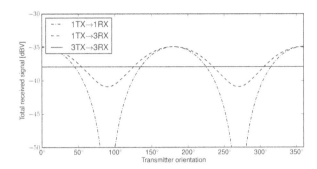

Figure 8: Impact on total received power with different combinations of receiver and transmitter antennas, as the transmitter is rotated.

ancing the number of children per node is not important, subject to channel availability. It is also more energy efficient to use a broadcatching tree, as nodes do not need to stay awake to gather data over multiple time periods.

Broadcatching can also be used in decentralized algorithms which require state information to be gathered from all their one hop neighbours [6]. If nodes are divided into two groups, such that no nodes which share a link are in the same group, then nodes can establish a two stage cycle, alternating between transmitting and receiving. At the end of the cycle, all nodes will have complete state information from all their neighbours.

6. EXPERIMENTAL RESULTS

In order to demonstrate the principles of magnetic vector modulation, a small testbed was constructed. The key concept was to take advantage of software defined radio (SDR) principles to allow for maximum flexibility in testing different symbol rates, carrier frequencies and modulation schemes.

6.1 Hardware implementation

Magnetic Transceiver Node: A magnetic transceiver node is shown in Fig. 7. In the implementation, a laptop is used as a DSP, due to the low computational requirements and to enable rapid prototyping. The magnetic transceiver is interfaced through a 4 channel USB external soundcard (MAYA44-USB). The transmitted signals are amplified using conventional Class-B audio amplifiers. The antenna loops are equipped with series capacitors to enable them to resonate at the carrier frequency. The received signal for each loop is amplified using an LT1028 precision low power instrumentation amplifier, operating in transimpedance configuration (current feedback) to allow for a wide bandwidth to be obtained. The low noise amplifiers are placed inside a shielded metal box to minimize interference and noise. A Zigbee interface is also provided via USB. A C++ program was written to generate and decode the magnetic vector modulation signals. With the current implementation, the system is able to broadcatch up to 15 magnetic vector modulation streams simultaneously. The same coils were used for both transmitting and receiving, and each consisted of

80 turns of 0.5 mm diameter enamelled copper wire wound over a wooden cube with sides 30 cm. In the following experiments, the effective magnetic moment of each loop is 7.2 Am^2.

Miner unit: The miner unit is a miniature Atmel ATZB-A2 Zigbit module, which contains an 8 bit Atmega1281V microcontroller and a Zigbee transceiver. It has also been equipped with a low power triaxial accelerometer, LIS302DL, and an LED which simulates a miner's cap lamp and which flashes when an evacuation message is received. To reduce bandwidth, the dynamic RMS acceleration is averaged over a 60 second moving average window. This data is periodically beaconed, along with the node's ID.

6.2 Magnetic link

Rotational invariance: The primary motivation for the adoption of triaxial transceivers in Sec. 3.1.3 was the fact that the relative orientation of the transmitter-receiver pair was irrelevant. This is shown in Fig. 8. Note how with a single antenna on both the transmitter and receiver, there are strong nulls at 90° and 270°, preventing communication. If the receiver is equipped with a vector antenna, then regardless of the orientation, a signal can be obtained. There is still an amplitude variation, due to the factor 2 in the radial component of Eq. 1. If vector antennas are used on both transmitter and receiver, the signal received is constant, regardless of relative orientation, as shown by the solid line in Fig. 8. This approach makes deployment of a magneto-inductive wireless network simple, as devices do not need to be placed in a line or plane.

Vector modulation: An example of a magnetic vector modulated signal is shown in Fig. 9 for a transmitter/receiver separation of 5 m. In Fig. 9(a), it can be seen that only one transmitter antenna is active at a time. The received signal in Fig. 9(b) shows how each received channel is a linear combination of the transmitter channels and varies in amplitude according to the active antenna. Note how when the X-axis on the transmitter is energized, the strongest signal actually appears in the Y-axis of the receiver. These values alter as the transmitter-receiver orientation and location is changed. The frame begins with a carrier tone, which enables the receiver to phase-lock to the transmitters relative phase and frequency. This is followed by a preamble on each channel in turn. The receiver uses this to compensate for the inherent 180° phase ambiguity presented by the use of BPSK.

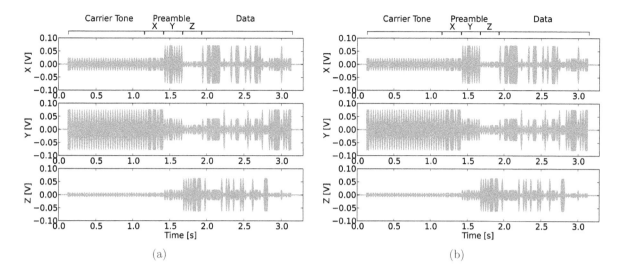

(a)   (b)

Figure 9: Triaxial transmitter and receiver waveforms. (a) shows the signal transmitted with a bitrate of 32 bps and a carrier frequency of 2 kHz. Note how only one channel is active at each point in time and how the raised cosine filter smooths the envelope. (b) shows the received signal. Note how the signal received is a linear combination of the transmitted signal, with amplitude dependent on the active transmitter axis.

During this multichannel preamble, the receiver estimates the channel transfer function, which it uses to construct the constellation for symbol decoding. Finally, the data itself is sent.

Range and Link Characterization

In terms of maximum communication range, in an environment free from mains interference, the maximum achievable communication range was 35 m. Mains interference has the effect of raising the noise floor and in an office environment the maximum achievable communication range was 23 m. The variation in symbol error rate with distance is shown in Fig. 10, with both simulated and measured results in an office environment. Note the steepness of the error rate curve, due to the 60dB/decade rolloff. A greater range would be possible using an optimized low noise amplifier and matched loop antenna.

6.3 Network Results

Broadcatching: Two transmitters were configured to send 8 byte messages to a single receiver in broadcatch mode. The spectrogram of the received broadcatch messages are shown in Fig. 11. The two input streams are frequency separated, with one having a carrier frequency of 2025 Hz and the other 2075 Hz. These streams were successfully decoded, in parallel, thus demonstrating the merits of broadcatching. The 2025 Hz signal has been magnetic vector modulated (i.e. alternating on all three transmitting axes), whereas the 2075 Hz signal has been sent using a single axis transmitter using conventional BPSK. Note that they occupy identical bandwidths and although the message length is the same, the time taken for magnetic vector modulation is shorter.

6.4 Combination

The relative contribution of magnetic vector modulation is demonstrated, as these techniques are complementary and can either be used singly or together. As an example, the latency of conventional time-slotted network access is compared against the proposed broadcatching approach for

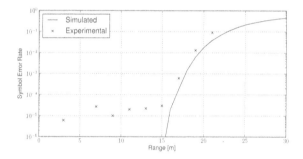

Figure 10: Variation in symbol error rate with distance.

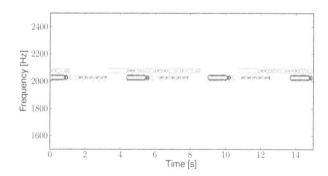

Figure 11: Spectrogram of the signal captured on the x-axis coil showing broadcatching two transmitters sending an 8 byte message on 2025 Hz and 2075 Hz. The bottom packet has been magnetic vector modulated and is hence quicker to send.

a subtree with two children relaying data to a single parent, shown in Fig. 12 for various message lengths. In this experiment, two nodes were configured to send their data to a receiver. If both A and B occupy the same channel, they cannot send their data at the same time as it will collide at the receiver. This is shown as the solid line on the graph. If the broadcatching approach is used, A and B can transmit in the same time slot, effectively halving the latency, as reflected in the dash/dot line. It is interesting to note that in this two child example, magnetic vector modulation with two separate time slots can achieve lower latencies for larger messages than just using broadcatching alone. However, if three or more children are present, using broadcatching and the scalar transmission will always result in a lower latency. The largest performance gains are demonstrated using a combination of broadcatching and magnetic vector modulation, shown as the thick dotted line. For this two child example, the speedup relative to single channel, single axis communication is from 53 s to 11 s, an improvement of over 4.5 times for a 100 byte message.

7. RELATED WORK

The use of multi-hop magneto-inductive networks was first introduced in [15], with the specific application of undersea communication. Underground sensor networks using a magneto-inductive communication channel were proposed in [2]. The use of magneto-inductive networks in a district heating system was presented in [14]. The use of a distributed magneto-inductive waveguide was suggested in [3], as a solution to the high path loss of the magnetic channel. Passive resonating coils are placed between the transmitter and receiver and act as a waveguide, reducing overall attenuation [16]. Magneto-inductive networks have also been proposed for monitoring leaks in pipelines [17]. The use of magneto-induction to localize animals underground was shown in [12], and more recently in [13], demonstrating a tracking accuracy of 0.45 m in 3-D. To date, the work in this area has considered the case of equipping each node with a *single* coil, which makes network operation highly dependent on network deployment. In the extreme case, if two coils are mutually perpendicular to each other, communication is impossible, as the receiver coil will not cut any magnetic flux lines. This is a serious drawback. However, through the use of three antennas, both on the transmitter and receiver, the presented system is omnidirectional and rotationally invariant. To the best of our knowledge, until now, no practical demonstration of low frequency communication in an underground sensor network using magneto-induction has been demonstrated.

It is important to note the distinction between conventional MIMO and magnetic vector modulation. MIMO relies on the fact that signals radiating from spatial distinct antennas travel over different path lengths through the diversity provided by a rich multipath environment, leading to delay spread [10]. In magnetic vector modulation, operation is within the near field and hence the channel response is purely real and as multipath does not occur. In addition, MIMO can be arbitrarily scaled according to the number of transmitter/receivers, subject to there being a rich scattering environment. Due to the extremely long wavelengths of the magnetic channel, it is not possible to arbitrarily scale it as closely spaced receiver loops will receive virtually identical signals.

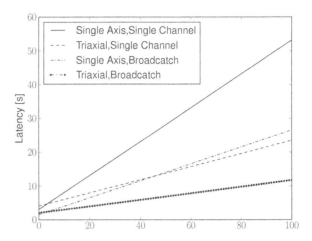

Figure 12: Latency for a node with two children, showing the relative merits of broadcatching and magnetic vector modulation with varying message lengths.

Multichannel trees have recently been suggested as a technique to improve data gathering performance and reduce network load [19]. This approach creates disjoint trees which are rooted at the same node but occupy distinct frequency bands. This is different to our work in that each receiver listens to a single input frequency. A recent work has considered the use two conventional radio receivers operating in different frequency bands [11], but has not considered the impact of this to reduce network latency.

8. CONCLUSIONS AND FUTURE WORK

In this work, we have considered a simple 6-ary method to modulate the magnetic vector. However, it is possible, through control of the relative amplitude and phase of currents in the three orthogonal coils to create arbitrary signal constellations, to increase bit rates or maximum communication range. Furthermore, using feedback from the receiver, the transmitter can alter the distribution of points in its constellation to avoid strong directional interference and optimize signal detection. A cognitive magnetic network could dynamically adapt to changing operational requirements or environmental conditions. Such a network is conceptually possible with our current software-defined prototype transceivers, and we suggest this as a future area of research.

In summary, in the event of a mining disaster, rapid and robust communication is essential in order to save lives. Through the use of magnetic vector transceivers, the system is made invariant to relative transceiver orientation and location, greatly simplifying deployment and making it robust to variations in position due to collapse or disturbance. The fundamental problem of the low frequency magnetic channel is the limited bitrate, mainly as a result of the extreme path loss of 60dB/decade. We introduced magnetic vector modulation which exploits the triaxial antenna arrangement to improve the bit rate by over 250%. When considering the network as a whole, further gains are made through the use of broadcatching, leading to over a four-fold decrease in system latency. Such techniques make the adoption of magnetic transceiver nodes a reality. The unique characteristics of the magnetic channel are applicable to a number of different applications, such as indoor, underground or underwater networks where conventional RF is attenuated or subject to severe multipath.

9. ACKNOWLEDGMENTS

The authors would like to thank their shepherd Mani Srivastava and the anonymous reviewers for their helpful comments. This work was supported by the Oxford Martin School and EPSRC SUAAVE EP/F064217/1.

10. REFERENCES

[1] Census of fatal occupational injuries. Technical report, Burea of Labour and Statistics, USA, 2007.

[2] I. F. Akyildiz and E. P. Stuntebeck. Wireless underground sensor networks: Research challenges. *Ad Hoc Networks*, 4(6), 2006.

[3] I. F. Akyildiz, Z. Sun, and M. C. Vuran. Signal propagation techniques for wireless underground communication networks. *Physical Communication*, 2(3), 2009.

[4] A. Chehri, H. Mouftah, P. Fortier, and H. Aniss. Experimental Testing of IEEE801.15.4/ZigBee Sensor Networks in Confined Area. In *Communication Networks and Services Research Conference (CNSR)*, 2010.

[5] J. N. de la Vergne. *Hard Rock Miner's Handbook*. McIntosh Engineering Limited, 2003.

[6] A. Farinelli, A. Rogers, A. Petcu, and N. R. Jennings. Decentralised coordination of low-power embedded devices using the max-sum algorithm. In *AAMAS '08*, 2008.

[7] A. Farstad and R. Kehrman. Electromagnetic Location Systems for Metal/Non Metal Mines. *BuMines OFR*, 1979.

[8] R. Feynman. *The Feynman lectures on physics*. Addison Wesley Longman, 1970.

[9] R. A. Gates. Sago Mine Report ID No. 46-08791. Technical report, United States Department of Labor, 2007.

[10] D. Gesbert, M. Shafi, D. shan Shiu, P. Smith, and A. Naguib. From theory to practice: an overview of MIMO space-time coded wireless systems. *Selected Areas in Communications, IEEE Journal on*, 21(3):281 – 302, April 2003.

[11] B. Kusy, C. Richter, W. Hu, M. Afanasyev, R. Jurdak, M. Brunig, D. Abbott, C. Huynh, and D. Ostry. Radio diversity for reliable communication in WSNs. In *Information Processing in Sensor Networks (IPSN)*, 2011.

[12] A. Markham, N. Trigoni, S. A. Ellwood, and D. W. Macdonald. Revealing the hidden lives of underground animals using magneto-inductive tracking. In *Proceedings of the 8th ACM Conference on Embedded Networked Sensor Systems*, 2010.

[13] A. Markham, N. Trigoni, D. Macdonald, and S. Ellwood. Underground localization in 3-D using magneto-inductive tracking. *Sensors Journal, IEEE*, PP(99):1, 2011.

[14] S. Meybodi, J. Nielsen, J. Bendtsen, and M. Dohler. Magneto-inductive underground communications in a district heating system. In *Communications (ICC), 2011 IEEE International Conference on*, pages 1 –5, June 2011.

[15] J. J. Sojdehei, P. N. Wrathall, and D. F. Dinn. Magneto-inductive (MI) communications. In *Oceans 2001, MTS/IEEE Conference, Honolulu, USA*, 2001.

[16] Z. Sun and I. Akyildiz. Magnetic induction communications for wireless underground sensor networks. *Antennas and Propagation, IEEE Transactions on*, 58(7):2426–2435, 2010.

[17] Z. Sun, P. Wang, M. C. Vuran, M. A. Al-Rodhaan, A. M. Al-Dhelaan, and I. F. Akyildiz. MISE-PIPE: Magnetic induction-based wireless sensor networks for underground pipeline monitoring. *Ad Hoc Netw.*, 9:218–227, May 2011.

[18] M. C. Vuran and A. R. Silva. Communication Through Soil in Wireless Underground Sensor Networks:Theory and Practice. In *Sensor Networks*. Springer Berlin Heidelberg, 2009.

[19] Y. Wu, J. Stankovic, T. He, and S. Lin. Realistic and efficient multi-channel communications in wireless sensor networks. In *INFOCOM 2008. The 27th Conference on Computer Communications. IEEE*, pages 1193 –1201, April 2008.

[20] S. Yarkan, S. Guzelgoz, H. Arslan, and R. Murphy. Underground mine communications: A survey. *Communications Surveys Tutorials, IEEE*, 11(3):125 –142, 2009.

[21] H. Yin and S. Alamouti. OFDMA: A Broadband Wireless Access Technology. In *Sarnoff Symposium, 2006 IEEE*, pages 1 –4, March 2006.

Sensing Through the Continent: Towards Monitoring Migratory Birds Using Cellular Sensor Networks

David Anthony †, William P. Bennett, Jr.†, Mehmet C. Vuran †, Matthew B. Dwyer †,
Sebastian Elbaum †, Anne Lacy ‡, Mike Engels ‡, Walter Wehtje §

†Department of Computer Science and Engineering
University of Nebraska - Lincoln, Lincoln, NE
{danthony,wbennett,mcvuran,dwyer,elbaum}@cse.unl.edu

‡International Crane Foundation, Baraboo, WI
{anne, engels}@savingcranes.org

§The Crane Trust, Wood River, NE
wwehtje@cranetrust.org

ABSTRACT

This paper presents CraneTracker, a novel sensor platform for monitoring migratory birds. The platform is designed to monitor Whooping Cranes, an endangered species that conducts an annual migration of 4,000 km between southern Texas and north-central Canada. CraneTracker includes a rich set of sensors, a multi-modal radio, and power control circuitry for sustainable, continental-scale information delivery during migration. The need for large-scale connectivity motivates the use of cellular technology in low-cost sensor platforms augmented by a low-power transceiver for ad-hoc connectivity. This platform leads to a new class of cellular sensor networks (CSNs) for time-critical and mobile sensing applications. The CraneTracker is evaluated via field tests on Wild Turkeys, Siberian Cranes, and an on-going alpha deployment with wild Sandhill Cranes. Experimental evaluations demonstrate the potential of energy-harvesting CSNs for wildlife monitoring in large geographical areas, and reveal important insights into the movements and behaviors of migratory animals. In addition to benefiting ecological research, the developed platform is expected to extend the application domain of sensor networks and enable future research applications.

Categories and Subject Descriptors

C.2.1 [**Computer-Communication Networks**]: Wireless communication

General Terms

Experimentation

Keywords

Wireless sensor networks, cellular, tracking

1. INTRODUCTION

The Whooping Crane (*Grus americana*) is one of the most endangered bird species native to North America. As of spring 2011, there are only 575 birds in existence, with no more than 279 individuals in the Aransas-Wood Buffalo Population (AWBP). The AWBP is the only wild migratory population and the source of the nearly 300 birds that are in captivity or have been released in efforts to re-establish the species in Wisconsin, Florida and Louisiana [9]. These birds conduct an annual migration of 4,000 km (∼2,500 miles) between southern Texas and north-central Canada, during which they travel as much as 950 km/day (∼600 miles/day). Tracking and monitoring the cranes during migration reveals potential causes of mortality, and the impact of changing habitat on bird behaviors. This knowledge is of prime importance to conservation efforts.

Migratory bird tracking has many system, hardware, and software design challenges. The tracking devices must be lightweight and compact so that bird behaviors are not impacted. The extremely high mobility during migration creates severe challenges in maintaining communication links with the birds. Moreover, it is very difficult to recapture a bird once the device is attached. Hence, a tracker must operate reliably under unpredictable environmental conditions during the deployment. The weight and mission duration requirements also impose significant challenges to energy management. Furthermore, due to the lack of existing quantitative measurements on crane behavior, detailed field measurements are needed to establish a baseline for comparison in later experiments. Finally, the endangered status of Whooping Cranes necessitates extensive evaluations of the system on other "proxy" animals prior to deployment on the target species.

Wireless sensor networks (WSNs) have been playing an increasing role in wildlife monitoring [11, 14, 17, 19, 20]. Their light weight, low cost, and communication capabilities are a desirable combination for scientists seeking to analyze animal behavior. However, existing solutions have focused on tracking animals in much smaller geographic areas than the cranes' habitat. The data is not considered time-sensitive, and there is no restriction on the upper bound of the communication delay. In contrast, ecologists studying cranes require the data within 24 hours so that field observations can be made, and causes of death determined. Furthermore, the cranes' migratory paths are unpredictable, which makes it

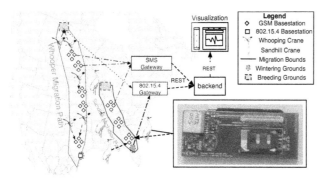

Figure 1: System Overview

impractical to rely on short range, pre-deployed infrastructure. Currently, satellite based trackers are used to provide a high degree of connectivity without relying on fixed terrestrial infrastructure, but have communication delays that exceed 48 hours [31]. These solutions are impractical for many types of wildlife studies which require latencies of less than one day. Finally, existing studies have been characterized by either limited durations and/or frequent maintenance. These limitations prevent existing solutions from being re-used for monitoring birds during migratory periods.

In this paper, we present a multi-modal platform, CraneTracker, for monitoring Whooping Cranes and our experiences from field experiments on wild turkeys and cranes. An overview of the system architecture is shown in Fig. 1, where the migration path of the cranes is highlighted over North America. This figure shows the need for communications connectivity at an extremely large scale. This motivates the use of cellular technology in low-cost sensor applications, where the existing coverage of cellular networks is exploited. In addition, with a second low-power radio, small-scale deployments of ad-hoc networks can still be used to improve communication coverage in key areas, e.g., well-known nesting, breeding, and wintering grounds, and in cases where the ecologists need to acquire information from the field.

Developing software for this new sensing paradigm is complicated by the fault tolerance needed in these systems [6]. The system must cope with defective behavior caused by faulty or physically damaged components. To this end, extensive validation and testing is conducted to eliminate potential faults before the system is deployed. Moreover, the platform must be capable of handling periods of low energy reserves, where the system capabilities are restricted. This is addressed through an energy-aware software and hardware architecture. Finally, a complete monitoring system is developed that incorporates storage and visualization components.

The rest of the paper is organized as follows: First, we present related work in Section 2. Our requirements and the associated challenges for monitoring cranes are described in Section 3. The details of the CraneTracker platform are described in Section 4. The performance of the system is evaluated in Section 5 through component evaluations and field experiments on "proxy" species: wild turkeys, captive Siberian Cranes, and wild Sandhill Cranes. Finally, the paper is concluded in Section 6.

2. RELATED WORK

Whooping Cranes have been the focus of many conservation efforts since the 1930s [9]. However, prior efforts have relied on tracking devices that provide a very limited set of data and require intensive labor. On the other hand, WSNs

have successfully been used in wildlife tracking experiments involving other species [11, 14, 17–20]. However, these solutions are limited in terms of mobility, study duration, and communication delays. In this section, we summarize these prior efforts.

2.1 Whooping Crane Tracking

Initial Whooping Crane tracking attempts relied on people maintaining visual contact with the birds. Colored leg bands were placed on the birds to differentiate between them [15]. Ground based spotters would then monitor areas where the birds were known to travel, and keep a record of when and where a bird was seen. The reliance on visual contact meant that birds could not be observed for large portions of their migration.

The lightweight leg bands were eventually augmented by short-range VHF transmitters [16]. Teams of ecologists were then able to follow the birds by using radio direction finding equipment. While this method was an improvement over visual observations, it was still limited in terms of communication range and the effort required to follow a bird.

State-of-the-art tracking methods use GPS receivers and send their findings over satellite communication links. These devices eliminate the need for field researchers to be in close proximity to the cranes. These devices still have several undesirable traits. First, the devices use a 15 cm long antenna that affects the birds' behavior and is a potential failure point. Second, the costs of purchasing and operating the devices are very high. This high cost limits the number that are deployed in the wild. Finally, the quality of the data collected by the devices suffers from the device's limited energy reserves and high latency in reporting the collected data.

2.2 Wildlife Monitoring with Wireless Sensor Networks

Existing wildlife monitoring studies using WSNs can be characterized into two groups based on the network architecture: infrastructure-based and ad-hoc. Data from many of these experiments is stored in a common repository [3].

The first class relies on a carefully deployed infrastructure of nodes to collect information about animals and/or their environment. For example, the burrows of sea birds have been monitored using hierarchically deployed nodes placed in and around burrows [28]. Similarly, WSNs have been used to track and localize badgers using both RFID tags and magneto-induction [11, 19]. These badger tracking experiments utilize fixed infrastructure. Fixed communication and sensing devices are deployed over the badgers' habitat to retrieve the data. These approaches are unsuitable for tracking migratory birds for two reasons. First, it is infeasible to deploy infrastructure over all of the birds' habitat. Second, these approaches do not have an upper bound on the tolerated communication delays, i.e. 24 hours.

As the mobility of the animal increases, infrastructure based solutions become infeasible. Instead, ad-hoc solutions have been employed, where nodes deployed on animals have a higher complexity. ZebraNet utilized GPS receivers and high powered transmitters attached to zebras via collars [14,18]. The high population density of the zebras allows for multi-hop radio communication in a relatively limited area. In contrast, cranes travel in isolated family groups of two or three, which makes it impractical to solely rely on multi-hop communications. Devices such as UvA [4] and the $CTT-1000$ [1] are capable of using cellular communications or short range radios to track migratory birds. However, these devices do not include both technologies.

The use of GSM modems has been considered for monitoring seals [17, 20]. Similar to the previous work, no strict bounds are considered on when the data is to be delivered. Recently, smartphones with on-board sensors have been utilized for large-scale tracking applications [27]. However, these solutions are heavy and consume too much power to operate unattended for years.

We employ a hybrid architecture for monitoring cranes that relies on global infrastructure (cellular networks) during migration, and short range, ad-hoc networks in breeding and nesting grounds.

2.3 Reliability

In our previous work, we have examined the use of simulation and aspect-oriented programming in testing an older version of the platform [6]. This prior work examined the difficulties in testing systems that are deployed for extended periods in difficult to reproduce environmental conditions. Aspect-oriented programming techniques were adapted to TinyOS for run-time monitoring in simulations. We utilized this technology in this work on a newer platform that has greater capabilities, complexity, and fault-tolerance when compared to the prior system.

Accordingly, a low-cost sensor platform is developed that augments existing sensor network solutions with a cellular modem. To the best of our knowledge, this is the first study that aims to monitor migratory animals in such large areas with a device capable of exploiting both infrastructure and ad-hoc based networking, with a combination of GPS and compass based sensors.

3. BACKGROUND

Tracking and monitoring Whooping Cranes during migration is essential for conservation efforts since the majority of mortalities occur during this period. Moreover, continuous monitoring of cranes is important to reveal the impacts of changing habitat on bird behaviors. Characterizing crane behaviors can lead to accurate estimations of a bird's energy needs. These estimates can reveal relationships between habitat usage and population. In this section, we present the requirements and the challenges encountered for monitoring cranes.

3.1 Requirements

Working with ecologists with experience in maintaining the crane population, we developed goals and requirements for a new tracker. The key requirements are briefly listed. A detailed description and rationale for them will then be presented.

- Weight: < 120 grams

- GPS: 2 samples per day

- Location Accuracy: < 10m desired, < 25m acceptable

- Compass: 0.5Hz sampling rate

- Communication Latency: < 24 hours

Migration tracking: During migration, the birds are highly mobile and highly unpredictable in terms of their paths and nightly roost sites. Timely location information can be used to locate the cranes' roosts during migration and can create insights into how the birds choose these intermediate stops. Knowledge of a bird's location can also

be used to determine whether or not it has perished, and whether to use field personnel to ascertain a cause of death.

To support this research, at least one location must be provided by the GPS during the day, and one during the night. It is desirable, but not necessary, for the GPS location to be accurate with 10 meters of the true position so detailed habitat monitoring can be conducted. GPS measurements that are within 25 meters of the true position are desired for tracking the birds during migration and determining mobility patterns. Such insights into the birds' travel habits are of great importance to ecologists because they can help measure the effects of habitat changes and other human development on the birds' behavior and migration patterns. Gaining knowledge into the real world performance of the GPS solution will enable more efficient power management and data sampling algorithms.

Reduced latency: Many open research questions regarding the cranes, such as when and how they die during migration, require timely data to be sent during migrations. If information on a crane's location and behavior is delayed, it may be impossible to locate the crane in the wild to conduct field observations, or if necessary, recover the corpse. Existing, state of the art, satellite based solutions frequently have communication delays exceeding 48 hours [31]. The requirements for this project specify an ideal delay requirement of less than 24 hours during migration.

Bird movement characterization: Collecting information on how the cranes move is another important step in ensuring their survival. Their flight behavior is not well quantified, because the existing data comes from qualitative and opportunistic visual observations. While on the ground, information about their movements such as foraging, roosting, and preening help characterize their energy usage and can lead to the development of time-energy budgets for the cranes. A greater understanding of their behavior is important because it may expose changes in the birds' behavior caused by climate or habitat change. Movement data can be used to determine whether or not a bird is alive. If the bird is dead, then field personnel can retrieve the corpse for further study. To collect behavioral data, the compass must be sampled faster than 0.5Hz. The studies presented in this paper sampled the compass at 1Hz for 10 seconds, with 4 hours in between sampling periods.

Long-term operation: Gathering statistically valid movement and behavior data from migratory birds requires multi-year operation, during which an individual can be observed for several migration cycles. To prevent any impact on the behavior, it is not desirable to re-capture a crane after a tracker has been mounted. Consequently, the harnesses are designed to eventually wear out and detach from the birds within several years. During the time a tracker is on a bird, it is expected to function properly without outside intervention.

Flexible operation: Multi-year and continuous monitoring of the same bird can reveal important insights into behavior over its lifetime. There are very few prior studies of this type, which leads to a lack of baseline data. Thus, at this point, the best data collection policy for ecologists is to get all the raw data in order to establish a baseline for future experiments. Further complicating data collection is the wide variety of environmental conditions the trackers will encounter. This makes it hard to *optimize* system operation since input space is largely unknown. The tracker should be flexible, so that its operation can be revised based on experimental results. This allows for more advanced filtering and data collection schemes to be implemented in the future.

Backpack Mounting: State-of-the-art Whooping Crane tracking systems use a leg-band design. There are several drawbacks with such a design. First, the added weight can unbalance the bird, and add drag, which makes it more difficult to fly. More importantly, there has been anecdotal evidence that a leg-band can adversely affect copulation which is unacceptable for conservation efforts. Instead, a backpack mounting design is employed, which is evaluated with Siberian and Sandhill Cranes.

3.2 Challenges

Monitoring migratory birds during migration faces several challenges, some of which are common to wildlife monitoring platforms (e.g., weight limits) and some of which are more specific to cranes (e.g., extreme mobility during migration). In the following, we summarize these challenges.

Weight and Size Restrictions: Using guidelines developed for other birds, a device and all supporting equipment must weigh less than 2% of a crane's bodyweight [30]. An average crane weighs 6kg. The equipment used to attach the device to the cranes weighs approximately 10 grams, so the device itself must weigh less than 110 grams.

These requirements are very restrictive when compared to many efforts. For example, the collars used to track zebras in ZebraNet [14] weigh over 1.1kg. A tracking experiment with badgers faced weight requirements similar to cranes [19] (105g), but the mission duration was much shorter (3 months) and the trackers used a lower power sensor. For cranes, ecologists have recommended that the tracker be no larger than 19.5cm long, 2.5cm tall, and 6.5cm wide. This allows the tracker to be attached to the bird as a backpack without affecting the bird. The weight and size restrictions place a significant restriction on the type of battery to be included and makes energy harvesting a necessity for the system.

Mobility: Whooping Cranes travel as much as 950 km per day, and can move 4,000 km over the course of migration. Along with their rapid movement, the birds travel as family groups instead of in large flocks. Hence, it is extremely difficult to predict flight paths, stopover points, and flight durations during migration. This unpredictability makes maintaining communication links with the birds a major challenge. Placing ad-hoc infrastructure along migration flyways is a near impossibility. On the other hand, cranes use the same region for breeding and wintering for years. These locations are ideal spots for ad-hoc communication.

Unattended Operation: The required mission duration is 5 to 7 years, which is significantly longer than existing tracking efforts [19, 20], which run for weeks or months. Since trackers cannot be accessed once harnessed to a wild bird, the system should be self-sustainable in terms of energy resources during this time. In addition, the software should operate without any errors despite the device being exposed to many unknown conditions. This makes it extremely desirable for the device to have a runtime that lasts for multiple migration periods. Moreover, the software must be able to cope with low voltage conditions or physical damage.

Unknown Behaviors: The lack of quantitative measurements on crane behavior makes the design of a sensing scheme highly challenging. Lacking solid baseline data makes it difficult to develop effective sensing or communication routines to record the relevant aspects of crane behavior. Developing software that can handle these conditions is

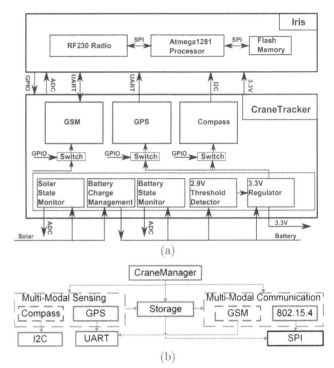

Figure 2: CraneTracker (a) hardware and (b) software architectures.

a difficult task because not all possible environmental conditions can be recreated in a controlled environment. The long term nature of wildlife tracking means that some software faults may manifest very slowly and be difficult to expose prior to deployment.

Endangered Status: Whooping Cranes are a federally endangered species. Hence, any potential new technology to study them is highly scrutinized. The platforms developed for studying Whooping Cranes must first be tested on other "proxy" species before being accepted by the U. S. Fish and Wildlife Services. Once the platform has been accepted, it can be used for monitoring the AWBP Whooping Cranes.

4. CRANE TRACKER

To address the challenges discussed in Section 3.2, and achieve the requirements listed in Section 3.1, a crane monitoring system is developed. The system consists of two major components: (1) The CraneTracker that is attached to the cranes and monitors their movement throughout the continent and (2) the back-end components that are used to store, analyze, and visualize the collected data. Next, we describe in detail the CraneTracker platform, system development, and evaluation tools. A more detailed description of these components is available in [7].

4.1 Overview

CraneTracker consists of a family of integrated hardware software components, which are illustrated in Figs. 2(a) and 2(b), respectively. The hardware architecture consists of an Iris mote and a custom sensor board with a rich set of sensors, modem, and power control circuitry. The software architecture was built on top of TinyOS and includes sensor and communication drivers, and storage, power, and overall system management. This system overcomes the challenges enumerated in Section 3 through:

- Weight and Size Restrictions: careful selection and

integration of hardware components into the custom board (Sections 4.2 and 4.3), and a custom built enclosure (Section 4.6).

- Mobility: integrated multi-modal communications which includes an Iris mote with an 802.15.4 compatible transceiver and a GSM modem, and support to handle holes in coverage through temporary data storage (Sections 4.2 and 4.5).

- Unattended operation: integrated energy harvesting through a solar panel, and power control sub-system to maximize data capture and battery recharge opportunities (Sections 4.4 and 4.5)

- Unknown behaviors: integrated multi-sensing capabilities with GPS, GSM, 3D acceleration, magnetometer, and temperature sensors delivering data to the scientists on the fly (Sections 4.3 and 4.5)

- Endangered status: incremental deployments on turkeys, Siberian Cranes, and Sandhill Cranes (Sections 5.2, 5.3 and 5.4).

4.2 Multi-Modal Communication

As discussed in Section 2, short-range multi-hop communication schemes are insufficient for maintaining connectivity in a highly mobile sensor network. On the other hand, well-known breeding and wintering grounds provide an opportunity for establishing ad-hoc communication with the cranes. Additionally, ecologists seek time critical information while in the field. This unique requirement calls for a multi-modal communication scheme.

For a long-range communication solution, two alternatives exist: satellite and cellular communication. Satellite technology was avoided because of the drawbacks listed in Section 2.1. Cellular communication is desirable because the necessary infrastructure is already deployed throughout the migration path. The experiments also reveal that this infrastructure enables the trackers to communicate *in flight*. Moreover, the operating cost is significantly lower than that of satellite systems.

Two main technologies exist when choosing the cellular device: CDMA and GSM. GSM technology is used for this project because its widespread international adoption will enable future experiments in a wide variety of locations. A GE865 cellular module from Telit is used for the GSM functionality [29]. This module has several appealing features for this project. First, it only weighs 3.5g. Second, it uses UART lines to interface to a microcontroller. This interface is very common in microcontrollers, and is simple to implement. Third, it supports domestic and international GSM bands, which means it can be deployed to many places in the world. Lastly, it is controlled through standard AT commands [5], which allows future versions of the platform to use alternative modules and technologies.

The GSM module requires careful power supply design. While the rest of the platform components operate at 3.3V, the GSM has a normal operating voltage of 3.4V to 4.2V [29]. According to the datasheet, the module consumes an average of 240mA during a voice call, and up to 420mA if the GPRS functionality is used. Testing on the CraneTracker showed the module used an average of 64mA while sending a text message. The current consumption of the GSM while associating with the cellular tower and sending repeated SMS messages is shown in Fig. 3. Although not shown in Fig. 3,

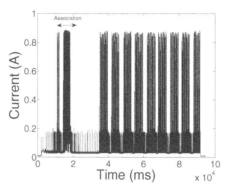

Figure 3: GSM current while sending SMS

under certain circumstances, the peak power demand of the GSM can reach 2A.

To communicate between the Iris mote and the GSM module, a GSM driver is developed for TinyOS [2]. Using standard AT commands, a subset of the commands needed to establish communication with the cellular network and send an SMS is implemented. Additional information, such as the cellular tower used for the connection, is fetched through the interface as well. By tracking which cellular towers the system associates with, the GSM module also provides coarse grain localization.

Despite its extensive coverage, cellular infrastructure is focused on covering human population needs. Given the remote areas the cranes travel to, cellular coverage can occasionally be missing. Occasional holes in coverage during migration can be compensated for with a storage mechanism as will be explained in Section 4.5. However, in breeding and wintering locations, cranes generally use the same locations over several years. If cellular coverage is lacking at this particular location, long-term storage may not be sufficient to store all of the recorded information. Since the locations of breeding and wintering grounds are well known, it is feasible to deploy short-range base stations at these locations. Thus, the CraneTracker utilizes the 802.15.4 compatible radio located on the Iris mote. The radio utilizes single-hop communications with the default protocols implemented by Memsic [21] in MoteWorks. This radio will be used in future experiments once the mobility patterns and family dynamics of the cranes are better explored. The resulting network architecture is shown in Fig. 1, where the two modes of communication are illustrated.

4.3 Multi-modal Sensing

Sensing components were selected to provide information about the bird, the environment, and the system. The sensing requirements specify position information, movement information, ambient solar power, temperature, and battery voltage.

The GPS sensor is a PA6B module manufactured by GlobalTop Technologies [12]. The selection of this receiver is based on multiple factors including power consumption, chip weight, antenna weight, size, channels, sensitivity, position accuracy, durability and time-to-first-fix (TTFF). The selected GPS module has a quick TTFF (34s cold start), low energy consumption (43mA), and small size (16mm x 16mm x 6mm) [12]. In addition to these characteristics, the module features an integrated patch antenna, which makes it compact and easy to integrate into the tracker. The GPS interfaces to the host microcontroller through UART lines. The NMEA 0183 protocol is used to communicate information such as the location, altitude, speed, and course over ground of the bird. This data is then used to track where the bird has traveled, where it is heading, and whether or not the bird is still alive.

To characterize the bird movements and behaviors an HM-C6343 solid-state compass, which includes a three dimensional accelerometer and magnetometer, and temperature sensor in a single package, is selected [13]. The solid-state compass provides a yaw accuracy of 2° and pitch and roll accuracy of $\pm1^o$ between 0°-15° and a $\pm2^o$ accuracy between 15°-60°. The compass communicates this information over the I2C interface. The default TinyOS I2C implementation was replaced with an interrupt-driven component to correct timing problems between the compass and microcontroller. To provide baseline data of crane movements, our strategy has been to obtain raw data from the cranes for this work.

Environmental data is collected through the temperature sensor in the compass and through the solar panel. To infer the intensity of ambient light through the solar panel, the voltage and current are recorded from the panel. In addition to bird-specific and environmental data, information about the system performance is also desired. To this end, the solar panel and battery are monitored as a part of the power control component which is described next.

4.4 Energy Harvesting and Power Control

To maximize the lifetime of the device, a flexible solar panel from PowerFilm [26] is used to recharge a lithium polymer battery. The solar panel specification states it is capable of providing 50mA at 4.8V. A lithium polymer battery is used because its high energy density minimizes the weight of the device, while allowing it to run for extended periods when solar energy is not available. The use of a lithium polymer battery complicates the power supply of the system, as it must be recharged using specific routines to maximize the battery lifetime and to avoid damaging the battery. Over- and under-discharging the battery must also be avoided, as this will also damage the battery.

An overview of the circuit that implements these operations is shown in Fig. 2(a). The power provided by the solar panel is used as the input to a charge management circuit [24]. The voltage and current supplied by the solar panel is monitored and logged by the mote as well. The output from the charge management circuit is used to charge the battery. The battery voltage and discharge current are also monitored by the microcontroller to profile the energy consumption of the device and enable power-aware operation. The battery state is monitored by a dedicated IC [25], which enables a 3.3V linear regulator [22] when the battery is sufficiently charged. This linear regulator is used to power the components which are unable to cope with the 4.2V that the battery can potentially supply. The power to the individual components is controlled by an IC switch, which provides a low-complexity method of disabling the devices [23].

The separation of software from system control enables the system to recover from unforeseen software errors. The usefulness of this approach is empirically supported through the deployments, where the system is able to recover from an unknown error state, as will be discussed in Section 5.4.

4.5 Data Management

The 512 kB of flash memory on the Iris is used to store information before being transmitted to a base station. Data is organized into sensor records, as shown in Fig. 4(a). The records stored in flash are divided into compass and GPS records that are prefixed with a common header. The stored

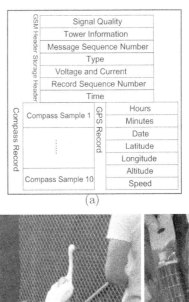

(b)   (c)

Figure 4: (a) Packet format (b) CraneTracker enclosure designs (b) and (c).

data is organized into a FIFO circular queue that can hold up to 16, 912 records. In the event that the queue fills without data being transmitted, the oldest data in the system is overwritten first. This behavior is motivated by the expected communication patterns. The data collected during migration periods is of greater interest than the data that is collected during wintering and roosting periods. However, the wintering and roosting periods will probably experience the longest periods of communication silence, due to the lack of cellular coverage and difficulties in placing short range base stations near the birds. Thus, during these times, the buffer may fill with less interesting data, that will be overwritten as part of the FIFO process.

When the data is transmitted, a second header is prepended to the data that contains information for detecting dropped packets and logging information on the cellular connectivity. The data is transmitted according to the FIFO protocol, where the oldest data is transmitted first. This greatly simplifies the implementation of the storage mechanism. However, in some cases, this behavior can be undesirable, as during migration it is more interesting to see the recent locations of the birds. Investigating trade-offs in storage and data retrieval policies, e.g. LIFO, is left as a future work once sufficient data about tracker behavior is collected.

As illustrated in Fig. 2(b), at the highest level of the system, a software manager is implemented that schedules when sensors and communication devices are used. The manager is power-aware and monitors the battery voltage before activating a component. Consequently, the system avoids wasting power by using components that will not be able to operate effectively. This improves the chances that future tasks will have enough power to run.

4.6 Enclosure Design

To fulfill the durability and environmental protection requirements, several harness and enclosure designs were evaluated.

Based on the feedback from ecologists, a backpack approach is used. This allows the tracker to be mounted near a bird's center of gravity, and minimize the effect on copulation. In addition, a backpack design has potential benefits to system design since exposure to the sun and movement monitoring accuracy increases when compared to a leg band. Three designs were used in field tests including a hard plastic enclosure, a pouch, and flexible plastic tubing.

The turkey tests used hard plastic enclosures, with the solar panel attached to the outside. These are too bulky for the cranes. The second design is used in short-term field experiments with captive cranes (Fig. 4(b)), where the tracker is retrieved within a day. The pouches were made from heat-sealable Oxford cloth that is waterproof and easy to prepare.

The final enclosure design is inspired by an outdated VHF transmitter package, which operated for three years on a crane, that used heatshrink tubing. A transparent heat shrink is used to enclose all components and still allow for solar recharging. A high strength plastic welder is used to bond the ends of the tubing. These enclosures are tested by submerging them in water, freezing, physical stress, and exposure to weather. A functioning mote is kept inside the enclosure during the tests to make sure it is unharmed. This plastic tubing approach is extremely durable, and passes all of these tests. The final unit is shown in Fig. 4(b) and Fig. 4(c) on a Sandhill Crane and is used in on-going alpha experiments that will be explained in Section 5.4.

4.7 Fault Detection and Tolerance

To maximize the chance of a mission's success, the system must be fault tolerant. Additionally, the system software should undergo thorough testing and verification. In our previous work, we presented work on testing the system software on an earlier platform [6]. We utilized these techniques in the current design. Next, we will present the new fault-tolerant features of the updated platform.

The first area of fault tolerance is in the communication scheme. The combination of GSM and short-range radio enables the tracker to continuing operating when one method is damaged or unable to communicate. Second, the GPS and compass can redundantly sense some of the information about the cranes, such as whether they are alive or dead. Finally, the hardware provides fault tolerance for the software. In cases where a software fault leaves the system in a high energy consumption state, the hardware is capable of removing power and rebooting the system after too much energy has been consumed.

5. EVALUATION AND DISCUSSION

The CraneTracker has been extensively evaluated via component evaluations, controlled system experiments and ongoing field experiments. Through component evaluations, the individual hardware components are characterized and the associated software components are validated. Controlled system experiments provide insight to the operation of the whole system and allows us to tailor the operation parameters.

Due to the endangered status of Whooping Cranes, the platform has been tested on "proxy" species that share similar habitat or similar characteristics with the Whooping Cranes. Preliminary platforms were evaluated on Wild Tur-

keys (*Meleagris gallopavo*), which share habitat with the cranes and provide a convenient method of testing many aspects of the platform because of their abundant population and low mobility. These experiments also allowed us to evaluate the latency of the cellular interface in the wild. Once successful, system evaluations have been conducted with captive Siberian Cranes (*Grus leucogeranus*), a close cousin of Whooping Cranes. These experiments were conducted at the International Crane Foundation (ICF), in Baraboo, Wisconsin, where the captive cranes are held in pens. The backpack design, ad-hoc communication, and the compass monitoring capabilities are tested on these cranes with short-term experiments. The final experiments consist of alpha deployments with wild Sandhill Cranes (*Grus canadensis*) - another abundant cousin of Whooping Cranes - where the system is fully tested in a realistic environment. At the time of this writing, five trackers have been placed on wild Sandhill Cranes. Two of the birds have completed migrations from Wisconsin to Indiana and Florida.

5.1 Preliminary Evaluations

Characterization of performance at the component level was performed to validate the system design. In Fig. 5(a), a high level view of the system's power consumption is shown. The details of this analysis are not discussed due to space limitations. As can be observed, power consumption profile of CraneTracker is fundamentally different than traditional WSNs, where the energy consumption for sensors is generally neglected. In contrast, the compass on the CraneTracker uses approximately the same amount of power as the microcontroller, and the GPS uses significantly more. Furthermore, the GSM consumes by far the most power. The power usage of the different components calls for energy-aware management of all the parts of the system.

Initial system-wide evaluations were performed by driving approximately 160km through an area commonly used by the Whooping Cranes during their migration. These experiments provide insights into the communication delays of the system and the accuracy of the measured results. The communication delay over the duration of the experiment is found to be only 6.07 minutes ($\sigma = 1.53$ min). As shown in Section 5.4, this latency is optimistic since well covered highways are used, but shows significant improvements compared to the 48 hour satellite tracker delays.

The experiment also reveals the localization accuracy of GSM. Over the course of 160 km, 18 base stations were seen and each base station provided an estimate of the mote's location. Using the GPS sensor as a baseline, it is observed that the error has a relatively large variance, where 50% of the error is less than 4 km and the maximum error is bounded by 14 km, which is useful for coarse localization in case of GPS failures. The satisfactory results with controlled experiments motivated the evaluation of the system on animals as explained next.

5.2 Field Experiments with Wild Turkeys

Field observations reveal that 2/3 of the Whooping Cranes' migration is spent foraging and roosting in habitat very similar to wild turkeys'. To evaluate the tracking accuracy, communication performance, power consumption, and recharge performance in a limited area, field experiments were performed with wild turkeys. These initial experiments demonstrated the viability of cellular-based sensing for remote and time critical wild bird monitoring.

In the experiments, two sets of data are used: (1) *Turkey tracker:* A tracker is attached to the back of a captured

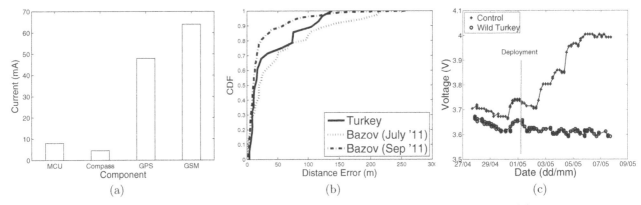

Figure 5: (a) Power consumption of platform components, (b) CDF of GPS error, (c) Battery voltage of control and turkey tracker.

hen and the hen is released for monitoring for a week. (2) *Control:* A stationary control mote is placed in the open within 1 km of the hen's habitat. This mote consists of the same hardware and software as attached to the captured turkey.

The collected data includes 480 SMS messages, 105 GPS, and 9,170 compass-related data over a period of 10 days. The system provides 100% reliability, where the turkey tracker sent SMS messages every 4 hours except for 9 cases, where the missing SMS was received in the following communication window, i.e., with a 4-hour delay.

System Evaluation: In Fig. 5(b) the CDF of the GPS location error for the experimental evaluations is shown. For the turkey experiment, the accuracy is evaluated by placing a tracker at a known position, and comparing the reported location to the known location. A large portion of this error is caused by operating mode of the GPS. In this trial, the GPS was turned off immediately after it acquired a fix in order to save power. This is insufficient time for the error in the GPS receiver to converge to its lower bound. This truncation contributes to the GPS error, along with the non-ideal environmental conditions.

The position of the wild turkey was acquired every 4 hours during the 10 day release, where the turkey was successfully monitored in a 2km x 1km area using the cellular communication capabilities of the tracker. The location data is divided into sets based on the time of day (night, early morning, morning, early afternoon, and afternoon) as illustrated in Fig. 6. The roosting location of the turkey can be clearly observed by the congregated fixes during night, early morning, and afternoon (see zoomed-in graph). It is observed that most of the movement occurred during early morning and afternoon when the bird was feeding with the bird moving as far as 1 km over a 4 hour period.

In Fig. 5(c), the recharge performance is depicted, where the deployment time is indicated by a vertical line. The control mote clearly outperforms the turkey tracker because it was placed directly under the sun. Although self-sustaining, the turkey tracker results in a lower recharge rate due to the woodland habitat, where the turkey spends most of its time. Moreover, Fig. 6 yields evidence that the wild turkey was in woodland coverage during mid-day, when the sun exposure is at its peak. Both data sets provide insight into how the CraneTracker will perform during a crane migration. The control set represents conditions similar to flight, when cranes are known to migrate up to 8.8 hours a day. This allows the device with sufficient time to recharge un-

der direct sunlight. In contrast, the turkey data provides a lower bound on the energy regeneration performance on the ground.

Ecological Observations: Even though it was not our primary goal, the turkey tracker data also provides important insight into turkey behavior. Turkeys spend up to 95% of the day feeding and are able to move at a rate of 200 m/hr during feeding periods [10]. The collected data supports these conjectures. The locations during the night and afternoon correspond to the hen's brooding and nesting area. The other GPS positions are probable feeding areas, in which the turkey is found in the rest of the day. GPS positions from one day are also connected in Fig. 6, where observed movements of up to 1 km over a 4 hour period fall closely into the 200 m/hr observations [10]. The close agreement of the collected data with the observed behaviors of wild turkeys provide an additional validation to the platform operation.

5.3 Captive Siberian Crane Experiments

To evaluate the performance on a real crane in a semi-controlled environment, the CraneTracker was tested in July 2011 with three captive Siberian Cranes: A. Wright, Bazov, and Hagrid, held in separate pens of 10m x 10m. A soft water-resistant pouch was used to harness the instruments to the captured Siberian Cranes as shown in Fig. 4(b) for a day. During the experiments, GPS and GSM communication capabilities as well as compass accuracy were tested. The ecologists also observed the impacts of backpack harness technique on the cranes.

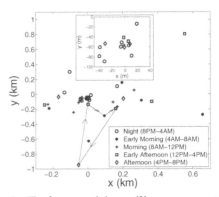

Figure 6: Turkey positions (lines connect consecutive fixes for one day).

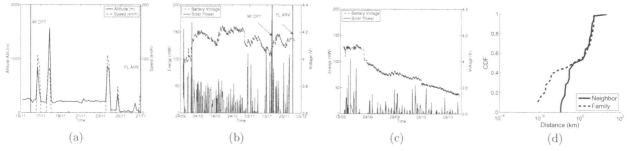

| (a) | (b) | (c) | (d) |

Figure 7: (a) SH-Chick altitude and speed. Solar power and battery voltage for (b) SH-Chick and (c) JB-Female. (d) Distance between SH-Chick and family and neighbors.

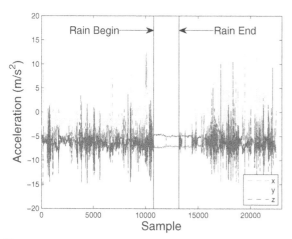

Figure 8: Three-axis acceleration readings from a Siberian Crane.

System Evaluation: With A. Wright and Bazov, the tracker was programmed with a 4 hour duty cycle. During each cycle an attempt was made to acquire a GPS fix and the compass was sampled. After the sensors were sampled, an attempt was made to send the data using the GSM. A. Wright incapacitated the device immediately after deployment by hitting a fence.

With Bazov, over 27 hours, a GPS fix ratio of 97% was achieved out of 135 attempts. Fig. 5(b) shows the CDF of the GPS error for Bazov, assuming that the bird was located in the center of the pen. The results show that 58% of the errors are less than 25m. To improve the accuracy, the GPS sampling scheme is updated so that at every attempt, 10 GPS fixes are acquired before firing a success event. With this update, the experiments were repeated in September 2011 with Bazov in the same pen. As shown in Fig. 5(b), this update improves the accuracy of GPS so that 81% of the errors are less than 25m. In this experiment, a large portion of the errors are due to the bird moving around the cage, and not staying in the center ($\pm$7m). These movements contribute to the errors in the figure. The remainder of the errors are due to environmental factors, and the GPS not operating for an extended time period to minimize the energy consumption. The distribution of errors satisfied the ecologists working on the project, and the quality of data met their needs.

To evaluate the compass accuracy on a crane, Hagrid was monitored by a closed-circuit camera system and compass readings were collected at a high rate of 10Hz for 30 sec every 3 minutes using the Iris mote's radio. Data from the compass was collected over 4 hours and 21,882 records were

received. A part of the results is shown in Fig. 8, where the three dimensions of acceleration are shown before, during, and after a heavy rain. During the rain, the crane was observed to stand still, which can be observed on the marked area of the graph. Moreover, during the experiment, the researcher logging data was able to determine movements without actually seeing the bird. The movements were confirmed by another researcher observing the crane through a video camera. Such strong correlation between accelerometer readings and crane behaviors motivate the utility of the compass for developing and validating energetics models for cranes [8] and further study on the collected compass data is left for future work.

Lessons Learned: During the experiments at the site, heading, pitch, and roll were inconsistent even though component tests were successful in other locations. This erroneous behavior was confirmed with all compass units available as well as an alternate inertial measurement unit and a smartphone. Unfortunately, the compound sits on a dense magnetic field due to a moraine that affects sensitive magnetic electronic readings. This behavior highlights the significant fluctuations sensors may experience during a long migration that encompasses several states.

5.4 Wild Sandhill Crane Deployments

The wildlife experiments with CraneTracker have been conducted with alpha deployments on five Sandhill Cranes. The cranes are captured in the wild by trained professionals and released to the wild after necessary measurements are taken and the trackers are attached. Five cranes from three families have participated in the experiments. The cranes are designated JB-Male and JB-Female; SH-Female and SH-Chick; and BB-Female. The two letter prefix identifies the crane's family, and the suffix is the crane's gender. Relevant information about the trackers is summarized in Table 1. The trackers will be left on the cranes for a year to observe their migration.

The software follows a schedule such that the system wakes up, collects a GPS fix, gathers 10 compass samples over 10 seconds, and then attempts to communicate with both the 802.15.4 radio and the GSM, and sleeps for 4 hours 5 minutes. The GPS fix is recorded after acquiring 10 valid fixes, which is found to improve the location accuracy as discussed in Section 5.3. To prevent excessive energy consumption, the GPS is turned off if a fix was not acquired within 5 minutes. The 4-hour 5 minute sampling interval and 10-second compass sampling duration was recommended by the ecologists. The sampling interval was selected so that the sampling times shift in time and in long-term, information from each time of day is collected.

System Evaluation: Fig. 10 shows the migration

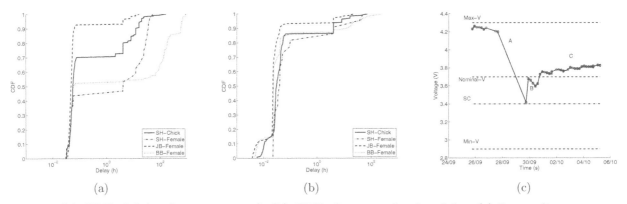

(a)   (b)   (c)

Figure 9: (a) CDF of delay (comm.+queue), (b) CDF of communication delay, (c) Low-voltage recovery.

Table 1: Experiment Summary

Name	Exp. Duration (days)	# SMS	# Fixes	Distance Traveled (km)	Comments
JB-Male	13	0	0	-	Failed to recharge
JB-Female	41	2,795	208	20	Unknown
SH-Female	29	525	468	4.3	Fell off
SH-Chick	66	1,890	330	1,725	Operational
BB-Female	121	2,213	468	603	Operational

paths taken by SH-Chick and BB-Female during the fall of 2011. SH-Chick completed the migration to the southern habitat in Florida, while BB-Female chose to halt the migration in Indiana. This figure demonstrates the unpredictability of the cranes, and the extreme geographic distances the devices operate over.

Experimental results from the birds confirm the viability of using the cellular network for monitoring during migra-

tion. During the migration, SH-Chick recorded 330 total GPS locations. Of these 330 locations, the bird's velocity indicated that in 12 of them it was flying. During these flying periods, SH-Chick communicated 10 times. These results show that the tracker is capable of maintaining a high degree of connectivity during all phases of the bird's life cycle.

Fig. 7(a) shows the altitude and speed of SH-Chick over the course of the migration. Naturally, there is a strong correlation between the speed and altitude of the bird, as the cranes are capable of flying much faster than walking. This figure also illustrates the difficulty in monitoring the cranes. They are capable of achieving high speeds while in the air, and flight periods comprise a surprisingly small portion of the actual migration process.

In Fig. 7(b) and Fig. 7(c), the battery voltage and the solar power collected by the monitoring circuit is shown for JB-Female and SH-Chick. These figures show that there is a close correlation between the monitored solar power and the battery recharge rate and solar power levels higher than 20mW leads to a recharge. Below this power level, the recharge circuitry is unable to utilize the power to recharge the battery. Accordingly, the readings can be used for adaptive operations, where the battery levels are predicted based on solar power.

The differences in recharging behavior between different birds is due to their location. In the breeding grounds, where the cranes spend most of their time, the birds are often in vegetation. This vegetation can obscure the solar panel. It can be observed that JB-Female has a lower recharge rate but the battery levels are above the critical threshold of 3.65V. As shown in Fig. 7(b), during migration (16/11-28/11), the device is capable of recharging the battery in a matter of days.

The power control circuit prevents the battery from draining below a minimum energy level, in order to prevent damage to the battery. This results in a sustainable albeit potentially *intermittent* operation. The collected information will provide insight into suitable sampling ranges and adaptive operation to reach a *continuous* sustainable operation.

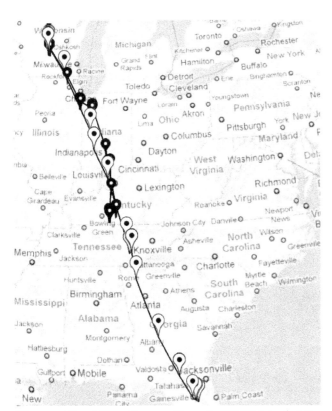

Figure 10: Migration paths of SH-Chick (white marker) and BB-Female (black marker)

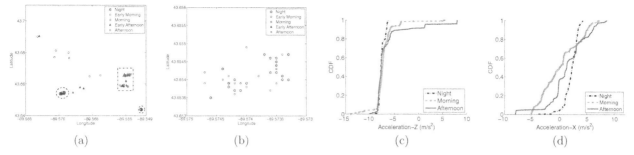

Figure 11: (a) GPS locations of JB-Female over 24 days, overall fixes (b)and zoomed circle cluster, Acceleration for SH-Chick for (c) z-axis and (d) x-axis.

The distance between the SH-Chick and SH-Female, and SH-Chick and JB-Male, is shown in Fig. 7(d). The close proximity of the chick and its mother raises the possibility of creating ad-hoc networks with short range radios in the future. Such networks could enable better data collection and experimentation through improved sensor coordination between family members. Moreover, these networks could improve the data delivery reliability, and possibly improve the lifetime of the motes.

The delay performance of the tracker is shown in Fig. 9(a), where the CDF of the delay is shown for JB-Female, SH-Chick, SH-Female, and BB-Female. The delay is defined as the time between a sensor sample is taken and it is received by the backend. Fig. 9(a) demonstrates that for JB-Female and SH-Chick, more than 98% of the delay is less than 24 hours. For BB-Female and SH-Female, the 24-hour quantiles are 55% and 72%. Most of the delay above 24-hours is due to the FIFO queue used in the system for the initial deployments. A long missed communication window leads to queue build up, which affects the delay even if the tracker can communicate afterwards. In Fig. 9(b), the delay due to *only* missed communication windows are shown. This corresponds to the delay if a LIFO queue were to be used in the system. It can be observed that for all the birds, more than 94% of the delay is less than 24 hours, which justify the use of GSM communication technology to meet the requirements of ecologists and motivate our future work for more efficient queueing models.

Lessons Learned: In two occasions, JB-Male and SH-Female, the system failed. The first tracker was harnessed to JB-Male in July-August 2011 and transmitted information for 13 days, during which all GSM packets were received within 8.3 hours. However, the GPS was unable to acquire a valid fix, and the battery voltage steadily decreased without showing any signs of recharging. While it was impossible to recover the device from the crane, it is likely that the solar panel became detached and slid over the GPS antenna. Based on the JB-Male experiment results, the mechanical design and the enclosure were improved to prevent movement and the second set of experiments were performed in Sept. 2011 with four additional cranes.

In the case of SH-Female, the tracker exhibits irregular behavior. The battery voltage for the bird is shown in Fig. 9(c). The results show that the system was stuck in an unknown error state, and recovered from this state after battery depletion. At time A in Fig. 9(c), the battery voltage was at full capacity and at time B, the tracker sent a message with a minimum allowed voltage and a system reset notification. Then, the system returned back to a steady state, after a small amount of recharge time. This behavior validates the effectiveness of the power control circuit but re-

sults in an intermittent communication with the backend. It is postulated that the failure was due to the GPS component since no valid fixes have been received since the failure. The GSM header still provides coarse location information so it was decided to leave the tracker on the crane and further observe the harness impacts and the system behavior. However, field observations soon after revealed the tracking device was no longer attached. The results highlight the increased connectivity provided by the GSM interface in the wild while revealing practical problems that the tracker will endure during operation.

Ecological Observations: The 4-hour sampling interval and the staggered operation provides insight into the daily movements of cranes. In Figs. 11(a) and 11(b), the locations of JB-Female are shown for different times of day over 24 days. It can be observed that all the night and most of afternoon data correspond to two distinct roosting locations as indicated by circles. The roosting locations in this area have generally been known by the ecologists but the collected information revealed individual information about where each specific crane roosted and the dynamics of roosting locations. The breeding territory of the couple is also indicated by a rectangle, within which most of the morning and early afternoon data reside. This territory is used for daily activities such as feeding, and preening.

In Figs. 11(c)-11(d), the acceleration in the z- and x-axes for the SH-chick is shown, which reveals important insights on the small-scale movements. The absolute value of acceleration is heavily influenced by the gravitational force, especially in z-axis, and provides an information about the bird posture. It can be observed in Fig. 11(c) that during night, when the bird stays still, the sample variance is the lowest and the mean is close to $9.8 m/s^2$. The morning and afternoon data exhibit higher variance and the higher acceleration values suggest flying ($\sim 0 m/s^2$) and takeoff (positive values).

The acceleration in the x-axis shown in Fig. 11(d) has a similar trend in terms of the CDF shape. The steeper slope of the CDF during the night corresponds to limited movements compared to the morning and evening. The majority of the values during night are slightly higher than 0, which indicates the bird was standing still (see Fig. 4(b) for bird posture, x-axis points towards the tail). As shown in Fig. 11(a), during morning and evening, cranes generally do not fly and stay in their territory and roosting site, respectively. Consequently, x-axis acceleration can be used to reveal posture since the walking speed effects are negligible compared to gravity. The negative values suggest that the bird's head was leaning to the ground, which is a typical posture during feeding. Similar trends have been observed for the other cranes.

6. CONCLUSIONS AND FUTURE WORK

We have presented our work on developing and evaluating a tracking platform for Whooping Cranes, which present unique challenges in their mobility and extremely low population size. The developed cellular sensor network platform seeks to provide more detailed data on these birds' behavior. CraneTracker's design aims to provide multi-modal sensing and multi-modal communication capabilities that allow reliable and time-critical monitoring on a continental scale. Field experiments illustrate the low-delay in communication, which motivates the use of a GSM modem as a second communication device. Finally, the extreme rareness of the birds necessitates an extended testing plan on more abundant species.

In the future, we will investigate the potential of the 802.15.4 radio in our device. Given the close proximity of the family members during the migration, the short range radio can create multihop networks. These networks may allow for more efficient energy management, and the use of one of the family members to act as a gateway to the cellular network. Furthermore, the radio can be used in the nesting and wintering grounds, where the cellular service is not prevalent.

In the near future, the platform will be deployed on extended missions with captive-reared Whooping Cranes. These trials will provide the opportunity to evaluate the performance of the sensors and communication mechanisms under conditions more comparable to those that the AWBP experiences. Given successful field tests, the devices can then be deployed to the Whooping Crane population. The collected data from the Whooping Cranes will be used to identify and protect critical habitat areas for this iconic bird species.

7. ACKNOWLEDGMENTS

This work was supported, in part, by the National Science Foundation under CAREER Award CNS-0953900 and Award CNS-0720654; and by the National Aeronautics and Space Administration under grant number NNX08AV20A.

8. REFERENCES

[1] CTT-1000. http://celltracktech.com/, Feb. 2012.
[2] Cyber-Physical Networking Laboratory. http://cpn.unl.edu, Feb. 2012.
[3] Movebank. http://www.movebank.org, Feb. 2012.
[4] UvA Bird Tracking System. http://www.uva-bits.nl, Feb. 2012.
[5] 3GPP. *AT command set for User Equipment (UE)*, 10.6.0 ed., Dec. 2011.
[6] ANTHONY, D., AND ET AL. Simulating and Testing Mobile Wireless Sensor Networks. In *Proc. ACM MSWIM '10* (Bodrum, Turkey, Oct. 2010), pp. 49–58.
[7] ANTHONY, D., AND ET AL. CraneTracker100 Platform Description. Tech. rep., University of Nebraska - Lincoln, Feb. 2012. http://cpn.unl.edu/?q=node/768.
[8] BARTELT, P. E., AND ET AL. Modeling amphibian energetics, habitat suitability, and movements of western toads, Anaxyrus (=Bufo) boreas, across present and future landscapes. *Ecological Modelling 221* (2010), 2675–2686.
[9] CANADIAN WILDLIFE SERVICE AND U.S. FISH AND WILDLIFE SERVICE. International recovery plan for the whooping crane. Tech. rep., Albuquerque, New Mexico, 2007.
[10] DICKSON, J. G. *The Wild Turkey: Biology and Management.* National Wild Turkey Federation (U.S.), United States. Forest Service, 1992.
[11] DYO, V., AND ET AL. Evolution and sustainability of a wildlife monitoring sensor network. In *Proc. ACM SenSys '10* (Zurich, Switzerland, Nov. 2010), pp. 127–140.
[12] GLOBALTOP TECHNOLOGY. *PA6B Datasheet.*
[13] HONEYWELL. *HMC6343 3-Axis Compass with Algorithms.*
[14] JUANG, P., AND ET AL. Energy-Efficient Computing for Wildlife Tracking: Design Tradeoffs and Early Experiences with ZebraNet. *SIGPLAN Not. 37* (Oct. 2002), 96–107.
[15] KUYT, E. Banding of juvenile Whooping Cranes and discovery of the summer habitat used by nonbreeders. In *Proc. 1978 Crane Workshop* (Rockport, Texas, Dec. 1979), pp. 109–111.
[16] KUYT, E. Aerial radio-tracking of Whooping Cranes migrating between Wood Buffalo National Park and Aransas National Wildlife Refuge, 1981-1984. Tech. rep., Canadian Wildlife Service, 1992.
[17] LINDGREN, A., AND ET AL. Seal-2-Seal: A delay-tolerant protocol for contact logging in wildlife monitoring sensor networks. In *Proc. of IEEE MASS '08* (Atlanta, Georgia, Sep. 2008), pp. 321–327.
[18] LIU, T., AND ET AL. Implementing software on resource-constrained mobile sensors: experiences with Impala and ZebraNet. In *Proc. of ACM MobiSys '04* (Boston, MA, 2004), pp. 256–269.
[19] MARKHAM, A., AND ET AL. Revealing the hidden lives of underground animals using magneto-inductive tracking. In *Proc. of ACM SenSys '10* (Zurich, Switzerland, Nov. 2010), pp. 281–294.
[20] MCCONNELL, B., AND ET AL. Phoning Home- A New GSM Mobile Phone Telemetry System To Collect-Mark Recapture Data. *Marine Mammal Science 20* (2004), 274–283.
[21] MEMSIC CORPORATION. *Memsic Inc.* http://www.memsic.com/, Feb. 2012.
[22] MICREL, INC. *MIC5301 Datasheet.*
[23] MICREL, INC. *MIC94060 Datasheet.*
[24] MICROCHIP TECHNOLOGY, INC. *MCP73831 Datasheet.*
[25] MICROCHIP TECHNOLOGY, INC. *TC54 Datasheet.*
[26] POWERFILM, INC. *MPT4.8-75 Datasheet.*
[27] PRIYANTHA, B., AND ET AL. LittleRock: Enabling Energy-Efficient Continuous Sensing on Mobile Phones. *IEEE Pervasive Computing 10* (2011), 12 –15.
[28] SZEWCZYK, R., AND ET AL. An Analysis of a Large Scale Habitat Monitoring Application. In *Proc. ACM SenSys '04* (Baltimore, MD, Nov. 2004), pp. 214–226.
[29] TELIT WIRELESS SOLUTIONS. *GE865.*
[30] USGS. Methods for Attaching Radio Transmitters to Passerines and Associated Impacts to their Behavior. http://www.npwrc.usgs.gov/resource/wildlife/telemtry/passerin.htm, Feb. 2012.
[31] WEHTJE, W. Aransas Wood Buffalo Population Radio-Marked Whooping Crane Fall 2010 Migration Report. April 2011.

Author Index

www.ingramcontent.com/pod-product-compliance
Lightning Source LLC
Chambersburg PA
CBHW080151060326
40689CB00018B/3934